NIXON

An Oliver Stone Film

NIXON

An Oliver Stone Film

EDITED BY ERIC HAMBURG

INCLUDES THE ORIGINAL SCREENPLAY BY STEPHEN J. RIVELE, CHRISTOPHER WILKINSON, AND OLIVER STONE

HYPERION
NEW YORK

"*Nixon's Policies Didn't End Communism*" copyright © 1994 by Michael Mandelbaum. *Appeared originally in New York* Newsday, *Monday, April 25, 1995.*

"*Nixon's Tapes: The 18 1/2-Minute Gap*" copyright © 1994 by Harper's Magazine. *Appeared originally in Harper's Magazine. Distributed by Los Angeles* Times *Syndicate.*

"*Mission Impossible*" copyright © 1974 by Eugenio Martinez. Appeared originally in Harper's Magazine.

All photos by Sidney Baldwin. Copyright © 1995 Track 2 Productions, Inc.

Library of Congress Cataloging-In-Publication Data
Nixon : an Oliver Stone film / edited by Eric Hamburg.
   —1st ed.
      p.   cm.
   "Includes the original screenplay by Stephen J. Rivele,
Christopher Wilkinson, and Oliver Stone. Also includes interview
with Oliver Stone, essays by John Dean, Howard Hunt, Daniel Schorr
and others, Watergate documents, transcripts, photos, and complete
annotation and bibliography"—Added t.p.
   ISBN 0-7868-8157-7
   1. Nixon (Motion picture) 2. Nixon, Richard M. (Richard Milhous),
1913–1994. I. Stone, Oliver. II. Hamburg, Eric.
PN1997.N5234044   1995
791.43′72—dc20   95-31302
                                                 CIP

BOOK DESIGN BY DEBORAH KERNER

FIRST EDITION

10 9 8 7 6 5 4 3 2 1

It is not the critic who counts; not the man who points out how the strong man stumbles, or where the doer of deeds could have done them better. The credit belongs to the man who is actually in the arena, whose face is marred by dust and sweat and blood; who strives valiantly; who errs, and comes short again and again; because there is not effort without error and shortcoming; but who does actually strive to do the deeds; who knows the great enthusiasms, the great devotions; who spends himself in a worthy cause, who at the best knows in the end the triumphs of high achievement and who at the worst, if he fails, at least fails while daring greatly, so that his place shall never be with those cold and timid souls who know neither victory nor defeat.

—THEODORE ROOSEVELT,
as quoted by Richard Nixon

Contents

PART 3
WATERGATE DOCUMENTS AND TAPES
319

Contents: Watergate Documents and Tapes   *322*

Foreword

ROBERT SCHEER

Richard Milhous Nixon may not have been the greatest leader of this century, but he certainly was the most tormented. As a statesman, he was unquestionably in the front rank, helping to shape global politics like few others. But as a politician, he was a tortured soul unable to gracefully accept even certain success, tormented by the slightest risk of failure.

Nixon was always a larger-than-life presence, but one filled with enormous insecurities and contradictions, the closest this country has come to a truly tragic Shakespearean figure on the order of King Lear. From young adulthood, when he launched a fiery red-baiting campaign for a seat in Congress, to the disgrace of Watergate, he would never stop pushing and twisting towards some obsessive goal. Even during twenty years of forced retirement, he continued to stride boldly across the world stage, offering mostly welcomed advice to respectful heads of state. Yet, he still bristled and felt compelled to strike back in response to the most trivial slight by the media. He remained a dark enigma to the end, smoothly successful at influencing the politics of the world while fumbling in personal relations and inept at ordering his emotions.

These contradictions were obvious, indeed jarring, to most who encountered him. That was my experience when I interviewed him for the L.A. *Times* at the tail end of his most amazing life. Despite an enormous wealth of knowledge and achievements that he was poised once again to impart to a journalist, he telegraphed a personal insecurity that was truly sad. I instantly felt sorry for the Nixon I met, which was no small feat, given that I am one of those whose taxes were audited in response to one of his typically mean-spirited commands.

But it was difficult not to be sympathetic. Nixon seemed painfully awkward, even insecure. We did a box-step as he welcomed me into his Manhattan office, and I wondered if he was one of those who felt that a proper distance from others would prevent catching the common cold. He was friendly enough, speaking about his daughter, whom I knew, and mentioning surfing in California, which neither of us really cared about.

Clearly, the preliminary chitchat was not his thing, and so we soon settled into an intense discussion, for almost three hours, about what ails the world. Suddenly, Richard M. Nixon was brilliant and in every way self-assured.

That was 1984, ten years after he was hounded out of office, but boy, could he hold forth. Pick a spot anywhere on the map, from Beirut to Kansas City, and he knew the players, the issues, and the likely result.

Even before that visit, I had developed a soft spot for the man, thinking him attacked more for quirks of personality than for errors of policy. Indeed, the occasion of our visit was an article I had written for *The Los Angeles Times* suggesting that a revisionist view of the Nixon Presidency was overdue.

He wrote, thanking me for the article—which he termed "very objective," despite the harsh quotes from critics—and agreed to my request for an interview. I had wanted to talk with him because, even as an ex-President, he had re-emerged as a force for sanity and peace in the midst of a degenerating Cold War.

Nixon had written a book called *The Real Peace,* which defended his policy of détente with the Soviet Union and urged caution on the Reagan Administration, which was developing the potentially destabilizing nuclear-shield notion of "Star Wars." Nixon knew that there was no such thing as winnable nuclear war.

You have to recall the nuclear-war-fighting climate of the early 1980s to understand why I wanted to cheer when he told me, speaking of nuclear warheads, "When you have 10,000 of these damn things, there is no defense." Not everyone, President Reagan included, seemed to grasp that.

At the time, Nixon looked good not only to me but to George McGovern, his Democratic opponent in the 1972 campaign, who had as much right to hold a grudge as anyone. But McGovern was always a fair and serious person, and as he told me then: "In dealing with the two major communist powers, Nixon probably had a better record than any President since World War II." Nixon, added McGovern, "Put us on the course to practical working relationships with both the Russians and Chinese."

Because of the back-channel negotiations, Henry Kissinger is often given the credit for the historic opening of China. But the record is quite clear that the courageous proposal to acknowledge that the true government of China was in Beijing and not Taipei was Nixon's. He advanced this course in an article in *Foreign Policy* magazine in 1967, before he had ever met the man who would end up as his top gun on foreign policy.

Little noticed for all the reporting on the voluminous documents released from the Nixon archives, which overwhelmingly stress indications of personal instability and highlight profanity, is the fact that they prove that Nixon and not Kissinger ran foreign policy. It was Nixon who decided to be the first U.S. President to visit Jerusalem, and it was Nixon who first treated Arab leaders as more than caricatures.

Nixon was a true visionary along the lines of Woodrow Wilson. But instead of projecting a messianic role for this country, Nixon understood the "limits of power" of the United States in the emerging multi-polar world; he detailed this notion in his "Nixon Doctrine" speech.

Still, he made his mistakes. Some, like extending the Vietnam War to Cambodia, extracted a horrible human price. But it was neither Nixon nor the Republicans who started that war, and it was Nixon who ended it.

Watergate revealed a mentality all too willing to sabotage the spirit of democracy, but no more so than Lyndon Johnson's persistent lying about Vietnam or Ronald Reagan's stonewalling on Iran-Contra. Every modern President has used the claim of national security to stay in office, democracy be damned.

Nixon was subjected to a double standard, being judged much more harshly because he was, by virtue of personality, the anti-Teflon President, with every bit of the normal dirty grease of government sticking to the media perception of his essential soul.

Face it: Reporters, including many Republican ones, never liked Nixon. He was inaccessible, quirky, devious, and in most of his mannerisms light years away from the breezy style and the prevalent, if not always genuine, bonhomie of our world.

Nixon had his deadly failings, and we in the media made much of them. He had no personal moral compass, and in the end all of politics and the Presidency was mere fuel to feed the drive of his insatiable ambition and to stave off his fatal foreboding of impending disaster. Throughout much of his life he never gave the slightest evidence of ethical restraint or just a common sense of decency. The evil Nixon was real and is well documented.

Which only makes the success of Nixon the successful statesman so much more inexplicable. He pursued détente, arms control, and most important made the historic opening to the country that we used to demonize as "Red China." History will acknowledge that it was the master red-baiter, the man who ordered break-ins of offices looking for security risks, who also broke the back of the Cold War. We may owe our lives to it.

On the other hand, we may also owe the survival of our democratic government to the fact that Nixon was hounded out of office. The "dirty tricks" which marked his presidency genuinely threatened the very foundations of the separation of powers and of constitutional government.

How, then, to reconcile the twin Nixons? Certainly not by simply obliterating one in favor of the other. That has been done ad nauseum by his friends and enemies, and it doesn't work. Instead, one has to concede that profound forces both for good and evil continuously wrestled inside this man's head for the possession of his soul.

Coming to understand that complex battle, which to some degree resides in all of us, is what the movie *Nixon* is all about. After being on the set for a few days, I knew it would succeed like nothing else that had attempted to comprehend this compelling if infuriating personality. I knew it because of the performance of Anthony Hopkins cast as Nixon. No one could have more perfectly captured the anguish, pettiness, and yet stunning authority and grandeur of vision of Richard Milhous Nixon. He was deeply flawed, even detestable, but he intrigues us because he always had the potential to be so much more. He did rise grandly to the important occasion, as in his dealings with China. But he also stumbled badly, out of control, crashing to the floor. At the end of his Presidency, this once all-powerful figure was a helpless, profane drunk, ineptly threatening one and all. What a waste. Never has this country's politics tossed up for our examination a more complex tragic figure or a more compelling subject for a movie biography.

ROBERT SCHEER is a contributing editor to *The Los Angeles Times*. He is the author of *With Enough Shovels: Reagan, Bush and Nuclear War* and *Thinking Tuna Fish, Talking Death*.

Introduction

ERIC HAMBURG

It has been reported that as Richard Nixon was preparing to leave the White House, Henry Kissinger said to him, "History will treat you kindly." Nixon responded, "That depends on who writes the history."

The history of the Nixon Presidency has been written many times, by many authors—not least by Richard Nixon himself. It is perhaps too much to expect one film to encompass all of these varying points of view. Our intention in *Nixon* has been to create a fair and balanced portrait of Richard Nixon—not the final word on Nixon, but our interpretation of the man.

In preparing to make the film, we did extensive research in the literature on Richard Nixon. We consulted many sources, with many different points of view. We met and talked with many who had worked with Nixon, including Elliot Richardson, John Dean, Alexander Butterfield, Len Garment, Ron Ziegler, Stephen Hess, John Sears, Alexander Haig, Paul Nitze, Howard Hunt, and Rolando Martinez. We also talked with those who had covered Nixon, and those who had opposed him, such as Frank Mankiewicz, Robert McNamara, John Kerry, Lee Hamilton, and Daniel Schorr. Needless to say, many differing views on Nixon were expressed. Some of them are in this book.

Richard Nixon is a figure who evokes strong responses, both positive and negative. Even a year after his death, he continues to influence the political debate in the United States. Political candidates from Bob Dole to Pete Wilson vie to be considered the heir to Nixon's political legacy in the Republican Party. Columns continue to be written about Nixon, and cartoons continue to be drawn. New books reconsider Nixon's legacy and his contributions, both positive and negative. The controversy continues.

It is our hope that this film, and this book, will serve to educate, to inform, and to provoke new interest in Richard Nixon and his influence on America and the world. The film should not be taken as the last word on Richard Nixon by any means. Rather, I hope that it will spur the curiosity of its viewers to read more about Nixon, to explore recent American history, to educate themselves further, and to draw their own conclusions.

Nixon's legacy is indeed complex. His achievements were great, as were his failings. His accomplishments in foreign policy were considerable—opening up a relationship with China, bringing a period of détente with the Soviet Union, working toward peace in the Middle East. At the same time, he continued the war in Vietnam for four years as President, ultimately bringing it to an ambiguous conclusion. And his abuses of power cannot be denied. Two decades later, Watergate might be seen as the mother of all political scandals, and the beginning of a cynical view of politicians and government that has continued to this day. Richard Nixon is surely responsible for much of the cynicism that has followed in his wake.

But Nixon's story can also be seen as a tribute in a sense to the flawed but nevertheless vital institutions of American democracy—a free press and a government that is ultimately accountable to its people. One can only wonder what Nixon might have done had he functioned in a totalitarian society like the Soviet Union. Would he have tolerated criticism by the press or by his political opponents? Would he have arrested his "enemies" and put them in jail, or worse? Would he have become another Stalin, perhaps? Surely he would not have left office voluntarily, if not for the threat of impeachment and possible legal proceedings. Under another, less democratic system of government, Richard Nixon might have been President for life—from 1969 to his death in 1994. If so, what would our country look like today?

Nixon is a tragic figure of Shakespearean proportions—an immensely intelligent and gifted man, but one who carried within him the seeds of his own destruction. Visiting Nixon's boyhood home at the Nixon library in Yorba Linda, one cannot help but be struck by the humbleness of his origins. Nixon, as he himself put it, came from "dirt"—from poverty and a background lacking in every advantage. But he worked and fought his way to the top by sheer determination and force of will, only to be brought down by the very characteristics that put him there. Nixon himself recognized this in his farewell speech when he said, "Others may hate you. But they don't win unless you hate them—and then you destroy yourself."

Nixon destroyed himself. His resignation brought to a close a period unprecedented in American history. But his resignation, and his subsequent pardon by President Ford, also closed the door on many questions about Nixon and his Presidency that have yet to be answered. We can't answer all of those questions in a film. But we can raise the questions, and hope that others will investigate further and help to provide some answers.

For example, it has been reported in the press that our film implicates Richard Nixon in the Kennedy assassination. This is not true. But what we are trying to do is to raise some questions about the Watergate tapes that have not yet been answered.

In the famous "smoking gun" tape of June 23, 1972, Nixon instructed

H.R. Haldeman to talk to the CIA and have them tell the FBI to stay out of the Watergate case for national security reasons. The disclosure of this tape led directly to Nixon's resignation.

What Nixon actually said on the tape was, "We protected (Richard) Helms from one hell of a lot of things . . . (Howard) Hunt will uncover a lot of things. You open that scab, there's a hell of a lot of things . . . tell them we just feel it would be very detrimental to have this thing go any further. This involves these Cubans, Hunt, and a lot of hanky-panky that we have nothing to do with ourselves . . . When you get the CIA people in, say, "Look, the problem is that this will open up the whole Bay of Pigs thing again. So they should call the FBI in and for the good of the country don't go any further into this case. Period . . . Tell them that if it gets out, it's going to make the CIA look bad, it's going to make Hunt look bad, and it's likely to blow the whole Bay of Pigs thing, which we think would be very unfortunate for the CIA."

In his memoir, *The Ends of Power,* Haldeman reported that he relayed this message to Richard Helms, then head of the CIA. Haldeman writes, "Turmoil in the room, Helms gripping the arms of his chair, leaning forward and shouting, 'The Bay of Pigs had nothing to do with this. I have no concern about the Bay of Pigs." Haldeman writes, "I was absolutely shocked by Helms' violent reaction. Again I wondered, what was such dynamite in the Bay of Pigs story?"

This was a good question, since the Bay of Pigs fiasco took place under President Kennedy, not Nixon, and JFK took full responsibility for it. What, then, was Nixon referring to? Haldeman answered the question in his book.

He wrote, "It seems that in all of those Nixon references to the Bay of Pigs, he was actually referring to the Kennedy assassination. . . . After Kennedy was killed, the CIA launched a fantastic cover-up. . . . In a chilling parallel to their cover-up at Watergate, the CIA literally erased any connection between Kennedy's assassination and the CIA. . . . And when Nixon said, "It's likely to blow the whole Bay of Pigs," he might have been reminding Helms, not so gently, of the cover-up of the CIA assassination attempts on the hero of the Bay of Pigs, Fidel Castro—a CIA operation that may have triggered the Kennedy tragedy and which Helms wanted desperately to hide."

These are not Oliver Stone's words—they are H.R. Haldeman's. They are in Haldeman's own book, *The Ends of Power*. Some have claimed that Haldeman later disavowed parts of this book, claiming they were written by his co-author, Joseph DiMona. But in an afterword to the paperback edition of the book, which he wrote to answer the controversy about it, Haldeman described Joe DiMona as a "collaborator," and said, "the writing style is essentially DiMona's. The opinions and conclusions are essentially mine." Neither Bob nor Jo Haldeman disavowed the earlier book in their introduction and final notes to the recent *Haldeman Diaries*. Furthermore, DiMona has stated that Haldeman read and approved every word of *The Ends of Power*. And it is implausible to think that a "control freak" like Bob Haldeman would have allowed a book to be published in his name without knowing and approving of its contents.

Bob Haldeman is gone now, as is Richard Nixon. So we are left only with Haldeman's account in his book. But no one has come up with a better explanation, or a more plausible explanation, of what Nixon meant when he said, "It's likely to blow the whole Bay of Pigs thing."

Perhaps this helps account for what may have been contained in the famous 18 1/2-minute gap on the Watergate tapes. Perhaps it reminds us that we still do not have all the answers about Nixon and Watergate, 20 years later. Nor do we have all the answers about the Kennedy assassination.

In a recent column in the *New York Times,* Caryn James wrote, "Presenting history on screen is not a simple issue or a new one. . . . History is the interpretation of those facts, and even ostensibly "objective" versions have some implicit point of view. . . . What is really at issue is not the use of fiction to tell history, but the use of fiction to challenge history's accepted views. . . . Movies are unfairly expected to provide a phantom 'truth' that doesn't exist."

In *Nixon,* we are not trying to rewrite history, or even to write it. We are placing an interpretation on history. But ours is not the only possible interpretation by any means. In this book, we have documented the facts we have presented in the film. Each scene is fully annotated, with references to the sources we have relied on in creating it. Where we have imagined or conjectured—as in scenes of private conversations between Mr. and Mrs. Nixon—we have so indicated. We have also included a comprehensive bibliography that readers can consult for further information. We have included documents that shed new light on Nixon and Watergate. And we have included essays that express some of the many points of view on Richard Nixon.

I hope this film, and this book, will help inspire a new generation of students—who were not even born when Richard Nixon resigned—to read, to study, and to learn more about this crucial chapter in American history. I hope it will inspire those who did live through these events to take a new look at some old history. And I hope it will make us think—about what kind of leaders we want to elect, and what kind of country we want to be.

Interview with Oliver Stone

Michael Singer

Q: Why did you choose Richard Nixon as the subject for your newest film? Why now?

A: Why now? Why not? It's a year after his death, and Nixon remains one of the most compelling, frustrating, infuriating, and fascinating figures of 20th-century American history. In fact, Nixon is, in the truest sense of the word, a man of the century: He lived through the promise of the California pioneers, the Depression, World War II, the Cold War, Vietnam, the war at home during those years, the end of the Cold War, and Communism. It's almost as if he embodies everything that's right and wrong about America in general and American politicians in particular. There's no question that he was brilliant, but he used it for less than noble ends. His potential was limitless, but ultimately was limited by powers that even he couldn't control. To some degree, *Nixon* is about the *illusion* of power.

More than that, Richard Nixon is a giant of a tragic figure in the classical Greek or Shakespearean tradition. Humble origins, rising to the top, then crashing down in a heap of hubris. Nixon himself said that he had been to the highest peaks and the lowest valleys. That's great drama.

Q: How have your personal feelings about Nixon changed through the years, or even since you began your research for the film?

A: My feelings about Nixon veer back and forth even in the course of a shooting day. It's hard not to admire his incredible tenaciousness, his pure, wild need to keep getting up off the mat after 15-round knockdowns. It's also hard not to loathe him for McCarthyism, Alger Hiss, Helen Gahagan Douglas, the Checkers speech, Cambodia, Laos, the "Silent Majority," and the final deception. Researching for the film, there are times I admire him more than I ever expected to, or vice versa. In the end, though, it's tough not to feel some compassion for a guy who just never thought he was good enough to join the establishment, even when he emblemized that very entity.

Q: YOUR POLITICAL VIEWS ARE HIGHLY MISUNDERSTOOD, USUALLY CATEGORIZED AS LEFTIST RADICAL. CAN YOU ELUCIDATE WHERE YOU STAND?

A: No, because categories are boring and dangerous, and you can't elucidate what's constantly in flux. The world doesn't sit still, and neither can we. I will agree that my political views are indeed highly misunderstood because they're not simplistic. I never follow one Party line. We have a responsibility to think individually about individual issues, not apply belief systems across the board.

Q: PLEASE DISCUSS YOUR CHOICE OF ANTHONY HOPKINS—A WELSH ACTOR—TO PORTRAY ONE OF THE MOST "AMERICAN" OF PRESIDENTS.

A: Typecasting actors according to their nationality is to insult their abilities as professionals. And there are few actors in the world as professional as Anthony Hopkins. For over 30 years, he's demonstrated his chameleonlike talents over and over again in movies, theater, and television. Tony can morph without the assistance of special effects, and he does it from the inside out. Some of Tony's previous roles have shown a melancholy, lonely quality that was perfect for Nixon. He also has the right look to play the man. But aside from everything, he's just a great actor who can, I believe, play anything he sets his mind to.

Q: WHY DID YOU DECIDE TO ESCHEW HEAVY MAKEUP FOR HOPKINS?

A: Because I didn't want the audience to sit there and say, "Wow, what a fantastic makeup job! He looks *exactly* like Nixon!," instead of concentrating on the character and story. We decided to go for intimation rather than imitation, both physically and vocally. We wanted to *suggest* Nixon rather than a nightclub impressionist's act, which would only distract the audience. In fact, we did experiment with Nixonian prosthetics—the jowls and prominent nose—but you always risk the Madame Tussaud pitfall. Nobody wanted the movie to look like a moving wax museum. Tony is a strong enough actor so you don't need those cosmetic effects.

Q: PLEASE DISCUSS THE GENESIS OF THE PROJECT.

A: I had two consecutive projects about strong but fatally flawed political leaders—*Noriega* and *Evita*—which for one reason or another I decided not to proceed with. I was interested in doing a character study of a powerful leader against a large historical backdrop, and Eric Hamburg—who had come to me from Representative Lee Hamilton's office in Washington, where he helped draft the JFK Records Act of 1992—suggested Richard Nixon. He asked Steve Rivele and Chris Wilkinson to submit a treatment. The idea appealed to me, and we hired these brilliant screenwriters, with whom I wrote the script. We also had help with research and consultation from Robert Scheer, a political columnist for the L.A. *Times*, and his son Christopher, a fine young writer. Their ideas helped shape the script into its final form. Additional consultation was provided by historian John Newman, who wrote *JFK and Vietnam.*

Q: You took a big hit from the media in the aftermath of *JFK*. Now, with *Nixon*, certain publications have already attacked you for "speculative" history based on obsolete drafts of the script. How much of the film is based on identifiable historical record, and how much of it is indeed conjecture or dramatic license?

A: Let's make one thing perfectly clear. Every historically based film in the history of the medium has utilized dramatic license and speculation, including documentaries. Even Flaherty's *Nanook of the North* fictionalized, to some degree, the life of its subject. That's the nature of art. A painting is the artist's rendering of the reality that he perceives, which he transforms into something more personal. Much of the script can—and will—be annotated with historical sources. Of course there's license and speculation, but they are based on reasonable assumptions, which we've discussed with highly reliable technical advisers who lived through the history we're recounting in the film.

Q: Talk about life after *Natural Born Killers*, cinematically speaking. With that film, you pushed the envelope about as far as it could go. What's your visual approach to *Nixon*?

A: Different from anything we've done previously, including *JFK* and *NBK*. Falling back on what we've done before would be uninteresting to me, [cinematographer] Bob Richardson, and everyone else on the crew. It's exciting to experiment and reinvent. We're using the anamorphic format, which allows for dynamic compositions and interesting spatial use of the screen. The story, characters, and physical backgrounds of *Nixon* are visually inspirational.

Q: This is the first time you've tackled such a prominent public figure as the subject of a film. How else does *Nixon* differ from your previous work?

A: Although many of my other films have portrayed real people—Richard Boyle in *Salvador,* Ron Kovic in *Born on the Fourth of July,* Jim Morrison in *The Doors,* Jim Garrison in *JFK,* and Le Ly Hayslip in *Heaven and Earth*—none, not even Morrison, have been so world famous and instantly recognizable as Richard Nixon. It's a challenge to portray a character that everyone on earth has their own preconceptions about. Also, despite its epic scope, much of *Nixon* is like chamber drama, intimate interior scenes both in political and personal circles of Nixon's life. We're shooting a lot more interiors than we usually do, and it's important to prevent the film from becoming static and talky.

Q: Please talk about Alexander Butterfield's contributions to the film as technical adviser.

A: Alex is an invaluable on-set resource for any number of details, large and small, about life in the White House during the Nixon Administration. You can read a thousand books about Nixon and his circle, but none of them are worth the direct reactions from Alex during filming. As deputy assistant to the President, Alex saw Nixon and his people every day, and was brilliantly observant. He keeps us honest and on our toes, because if something's wrong, he'll be the first to tell us what it is.

Q: You've assembled a huge ensemble cast, à la *JFK.* Please discuss your casting choices beyond Hopkins.

A: What can I say? We're lucky to have about 30 of the best actors available, totally professional and incredibly dedicated. The remarkable thing about our cast is even though it's filled with "big names," not one of them has ever allowed themselves to become stereotyped in their careers. Some of them are major stars, but all of them are great character actors. We decided to use actors of note, because when you have so many important characters, it's important for the audience to identify who they are, which they can do because they're already familiar with the performers who are playing them.

NIXON

An Oliver Stone Film

PART I
ESSAYS

Oliver Stone's Look at Nixon's Footprints

JOHN DEAN

Lives of great men oft' remind us,
We can make our lives sublime,
And departing, leave behind us,
Footprints on the sands of time.

This verse from Longfellow's *Psalm of Life,* written in the hand of Richard Nixon's Grandmother Milhous and accompanied by a picture of Abraham Lincoln, hung in the boyhood room of the future President. Today that small room is part of a shrine to the 37th President of the United States: the humble birthplace, the gleaming Presidential library, and more recently the grave site of Richard Nixon. Sir Anthony Hopkins rose from similar modest beginnings to a knighthood bestowed upon one of England's most accomplished actors, and he understood Richard Nixon a bit better after visiting that room in Yorba Linda, California.

"I suppose an actor shouldn't get caught up in that kind of emotion," he told me. "But I just got all choked up, what with this little house where Mr. Nixon heard the train whistles, and dreamed of his future." His Lordship, dressed in attire indistinguishable from the homeless on the streets of Santa Monica where we were meeting, was removing his Army fatigue jacket. Oliver Stone urged us to join him at his large conference table, where a carryout Thai lunch was being served.

"I didn't think they would recognize me," Tony Hopkins continued. "But this woman, who I guess is the curator, she spotted me. She said, 'I understand you are playing Mr. Nixon.' I told her, yes, I was. She said, 'Well, I certainly hope you're not going to do a hatchet job on the President.' Oh, no, no, no, I assured her." Then, turning those searching *Silence of the Lambs* blue eyes on me, he asked, "I'm not doing a hatchet job, am I?"

I assured him, as I saw it, he was not. While Oliver Stone's *Nixon* is not in the ilk of the puff stuff and everyone-else-is-wrong that fills the Nixon Library, it is in no way an anti-Nixon polemic. After a few weeks of exposure to the project it was clear to me that Oliver Stone was trying to understand Richard Nixon, a man he sees in Shakespearean dimension, so he hired the greatest Shakespearean actor alive to play the role. The trip that morning from Santa Monica to Yorba Linda and back was a small part of a massive undertaking by Stone, his staff, and all of the actors in the film to understand the characters and the story they would collectively bring to the screen. Their attention to detail is staggering. They would rebuild the relevant rooms of the Nixon White House on a sound stage, accurate down to recreating the pictures on the walls. They even made Anthony Hopkins's blue eyes brown.

It was because of my relationship with Richard Nixon that I was invited to lunch. Weeks earlier a mutual acquaintance asked if I would meet with Oliver Stone. The initial buzz on *Nixon* had it filled with conspiracies of which I knew nothing. Before I would share my knowledge, I wanted to find out much more. Frankly, I was dubious. I had been shown a bootleg script that suggested Oliver Stone was buying into a part of the latest conspiracy theory that claims what we know about the Watergate break-ins is wrong.

Watergate and Richard Nixon are not subjects I enjoy visiting. But well before Oliver Stone had started his project, I had been forced back to these events. Using tabloid-style journalism, faded memories, leading questions, and ignoring facts to the contrary, a couple of information polluters and sleaze suckers had waded into the muck and mire of Watergate to produce a new revisionist account of the events. When I discovered fragments of this baseless revisionism in Oliver Stone's script, I doubted I wanted anything to do with the project. My doubts, however, were proven to be totally misplaced. When Oliver Stone learned the true facts (which he personally checked by talking with the persons involved), he pulled the phony material from his film. Thus, there was no question in my mind about the sincerity and legitimacy of his effort to base the film on hard information. Indeed, this film falls nowhere near the George Danby *(Bangor Daily News)* cartoon that made its way to the *New York Times:* a banner reads "A SCENE FROM OLIVER STONE'S UPCOMING FILM ON NIXON" and the drawing shows a sinister-looking Richard Nixon standing behind a curtain at Ford's Theater, April 14, 1865, with a gun drawn, and the silhouette of Abraham Lincoln over Nixon's shoulder. *Nixon* does not offer newly concocted conspiracies involving Richard Nixon. As the annotated script in this book demonstrates, Stone and his co-writers have documentation for it all, including very reasonable and anything-but-baseless speculation.

Not only Oliver Stone and Anthony Hopkins expressed concern that their depiction of history be accurate. I visited with a number of the actors. None of them have any interest in this film as an exercise in historical deconstruction. Rather they want to capture the essence of the persons they are portraying. To do so they have read biographical material, studied taped conversations from the Nixon White House, watched news clips and footage from the period, and talked to people familiar with that person, and in some instances actually talked with the person they would portray. For example, David Hyde Pierce, who is playing my role, read my books, studied my testimony, and visited with me at some length. Then he reached his own conclusions.

A few years ago in a speech before the National Press Club, Oliver Stone explained his thinking about history when answering his critics on the film *JFK.* At the outset of that speech he noted there was no "accepted, settled, respected, carefully thought-out and researched body of history about the assassination of John F. Kennedy." It was the fact that this traumatic national event was one of "the most undocumented, unresearched, unagreed-upon" periods of American history that enticed Stone to make a movie that would provoke thinking, debate, research, and digging anew into the event. Indeed, *JFK* created the needed momentum to open sealed government files related to the assassination.

Unlike the Kennedy tragedy, Watergate and Nixon's abuses of power are well documented; they have been heavily investigated and researched, and the central events are almost uniformly agreed upon. As this fact became evident, the movie gravitated toward that mass of hard material as its foundation. Where solid source material is available, I can attest to the fact that Oliver Stone follows it.

Unfortunately, much primary source material relating to the Nixon presidency remains unavailable because Richard Nixon, with the concurrence of many of his former aides, kept it buried for two decades. The most glaring example is Nixon's secret tapes of his recorded conversations, some four thousand hours. In addition to the tapes, however, countless papers and documents have been removed from the public files at the National Archives. Like *JFK, Nixon* can create a new momentum to force the release of this buried material. Hopefully it will foment public interest in making this long hidden information public.

Oliver Stone wants to be more than a catalyst, however. He would like public documents that are available more easily attainable and usable by students, academics, the media, and anyone interested in studying and understanding the period and the former President. Thus, he is trying to use this movie as a vehicle to bring forward such material in a highly usable form such as a CD-ROM, which is an ideal medium for the thousands upon thousands of pages of sworn testimony and documents from the Senate Watergate Committee and the criminal trial transcripts that document this history. These sources contain hard evidence of what happened and why. Indeed, the criminal trials are the culmination of massive investigative and Grand Jury work by the Watergate Special Prosecutor's Office, where they made their cases "beyond a reasonable doubt." At present, this material is only available at a few university libraries (on difficult-to-use microfilm) or at the National Archives in Washington, D.C. As the annotations of the original script and bibliography suggest, a vast body of information is already available; it is the primary source material that is not. Oliver Stone's efforts to get this primary source material in the hands of everyone, when accomplished, will make it much more difficult for the phony revisionists and Nixon apologists to push their false history. I applaud Oliver Stone's efforts, as I know others will.

While the movie *Nixon* cannot recreate times past for those of us who lived it, it does give true glimpses of those times to others because the compressed scenes, the carefully considered conjecture, and the dramatizations are all reasonable and fair, if not largely accurate in a broader view of history. Certainly there are scenes with dramatic license. For example, the script has me meeting Howard Hunt on a bridge in Washington. As the annotated script notes, it never happened. Oliver made a good case to me why he did not want to change the scene when I told him "some revisionist will claim, there are Dean and Hunt secretly meeting, when it never happened."

"It could have happened in Nixon's mind and that is what I'm looking at," he countered.

"True," I conceded.

"Well, there you go. If you think it is too much dramatic license you can obviously say so publicly. Fair enough?"

While I would rather the scene be dropped, from Nixon's point of view—and Oliver's—the scene with Hunt is not unreasonable dramatic license. In fact, after closely examining the script, I found nothing that really was unreasonable or unfair, although I am sure I am not the only person who will be less than happy with the scenes involving himself. This film, however, is not a documentary. Oliver Stone is a dramatist who works on the big screen with bold and broad strokes. For this film he is standing solidly on history and only reaching in a few instances. The totality of it all is a fascinating character study. This is not a film with which to agree or disagree, for it is a portrait. Clearly, you may like or dislike it.

Nixon is cinematic biography that forces you to think. And thought, I sense, is precisely what Oliver wants his art to provoke. He is sending his audience off to reexamine Richard Nixon. For example, *Nixon* ends with the President's emotional farewell to the White House staff. Until this movie I had never realized this emotionalism was part of Nixon's character. I assumed the farewell speech was merely a terrible and passing moment at the lowest point of the man's public life. The movie shows otherwise, which caused me to investigate. In doing so I discovered a document I not seen before, a hand-

written eulogy by a 17-year-old Richard Nixon, a freshman at Whittier College, describing the events leading up to the death of his younger brother.
His essay, in many regards, parallels his farewell address. It begins,

> *We have a picture in our home which money could not buy. It is not a*
> *picture for which great art collectors would offer thousands of dollars.*
> *There is nothing outstanding about its frame or coloring. It is only*
> *about five inches tall and two inches wide. It is probably unnoticed by*
> *those who come to visit us, for they all have seen pictures of small boys*
> *and probably could not be interested in this one.*

The eulogy goes on to describe Nixon's memories of his younger brother,
who would die as depicted in the film. The film's choice of this event as one
of several defining moments in Richard Nixon's life is documented by his own
words, when the young Nixon wrote,

> *There is a growing tendency among college students to let their child-*
> *hood beliefs be forgotten. Especially we find this true when we speak*
> *of the divine creator and his plans for us. I thought that I would also*
> *become that way, but I find that is almost impossible for me to do so.*
> *Two days before my brother's death, he called my mother into the*
> *room. He put his arms around her and said that he wanted to pray be-*
> *fore he went to sleep. Then, with closed eyes, he repeated that age-old*
> *child's prayer which ends with those simple yet beautiful words: "If I*
> *should die before I awake, I pray Thee, Lord, my soul to take."*
>
> *There is a grave out now in the hills, but, like the picture, it con-*
> *tains only the bodily image of my brother.*
>
> *And so when I am tired and worried, and am almost ready to quit*
> *trying to live as I should, I look up and see the picture of a little boy*
> *with sparkling eyes, and curly hair; I remember the childlike prayer; I*
> *pray that it may prove true for me as it did for my brother Arthur.*

I hope Richard Nixon's prayer was answered. He experienced his own
hell during life, and pulled many others into it. As Oliver Stone with his cast
and crew have shown, Richard Nixon's Presidency, his life, and character
are worthy of study, for they are poignantly and uniquely instructive. Footprints worth looking at closely, as *Nixon* has done.

Nixon's Secrets

DANIEL SCHORR

I wish I could say I heard the wings of history flapping when first I met Richard Milhous Nixon in September 1947. I was a correspondent in the Netherlands and he was one of 19 members of a House committee touring Europe to investigate prospects for the Marshall Plan. Either he was very reticent or I was very insensitive, but he made no impression on me at all.

Nixon made a greater impression when I next saw him as Vice President in the summer of 1959, briefing reporters in Warsaw after his "kitchen debate" with Premier Nikita Khrushchev in Moscow. Exhilarated by what he clearly considered a political coup, he talked expansively about East-West relations and Khrushchev's coming visit to the United States. Still I had no foreboding that this politician, operating in the shadow of President Eisenhower, handing out to Polish crowds ballpoint pens with his name on them and obviously preparing to run for President in 1960, would, eight years later, be elected President and come to cast a shadow over America and, incidentally, over my life.

Indeed, it may have been the White House that brought out the darkest side of Nixon, freeing him from the restraints of being number 2 and giving him vast powers to vent his paranoia. He seemed always to savor crisis more than success and, having written about his *Six Crises* before becoming President, he seemed bent on creating more. I shall always remember, assigned to his reelection headquarters on election night, 1972, being struck by the grim face Nixon showed to the tumultuous crowds cheering his landslide victory. Next day, as we later learned, he took no time out for celebration, but instead demanded letters of resignation from most of his top officials and began planning a reorganization to make the government a more effective weapon against his enemies.

"Enemies"! That was the word Nixon introduced to the political lexicon. We had known of opponents, rivals, and adversaries. But "enemies" seemed to denote some form of warfare against an implacable foe. No wonder Nixon tended to confuse his political aims with national security!

Let me stipulate here that I bear no grudge against the memory of Nixon, although he clearly, as we eventually discovered, long nourished a grudge against me. In March 1971, he accused me to reporters of "a lie" because of my CBS report about misgivings in the Administration on the proposed antiballistic missile system. I figured as number 17 on his "top 20" Enemies List. On his Oval Office tape he referred to me as "that son of a bitch, Schorr." Speech writer Patrick Buchanan's idea of an uproarious joke was a tongue-in-cheek memo proposing that the President meet with me and other "sympathetic" journalists like Jack Anderson and John Chancellor.

In August 1971, irritated by my criticism of a speech promising federal aid to Catholic parochial schools that he was in no position to deliver in the face of Supreme Court decisions, Nixon had FBI Director J. Edgar Hoover launch an investigation of me. When that became publicly known, the White House made the deadpan claim that I had been under consideration for a Presidential appointment. Eventually that cover-up was exploded and the unwarranted FBI probe figured in the Senate Watergate investigation and the House impeachment inquiry. In the Articles of Impeachment, it became an item under Article II, "Abuse of Power."

Yet, I gained a certain respect for Nixon's 20-year effort at rehabilitation—his campaign for ex-President. And, not long before his death, I met him at a think-tank dinner at which he discoursed about a trip to the former Soviet Union. Not sure he would remember me, I reintroduced myself.

"Sure, I remember you," he said, smilingly. "Damn near hired you once."

It is with no sense of vindictiveness that I examine what made this talented and tormented politician go off the rails. I conclude that his paranoia, whatever its origin, led him to imagine conspiracies that he came to believe and which served as premises for action. The line between deception and self-deception seemed often blurred, leading his subordinates to act on premises that sometimes mystified them. My research leads me to conclude that Nixon nourished at least four grand delusions.

1. The Bay of Pigs "Secret"

President Nixon often spoke to aides about some deeply hidden scandal connected with the 1961 Bay of Pigs invasion of Cuba—an assassination or something on that order. It was supposed to involve the CIA and President Kennedy. Nixon talked of "nailing" Kennedy on the Bay of Pigs, and he kept demanding that his aides produce for him the "full secret file" he was sure the CIA was hiding.

Although no such file was produced for him, Nixon felt sure enough of his ground to use the Bay of Pigs as a form of pressure on the CIA to take responsibility for the Watergate break-in, intending thus to abort the FBI investigation. On June 23, 1973—on the lethal "smoking gun" tape—Nixon instructed Chief of Staff H. R. Haldeman to remind CIA Director Richard

Helms that "we have protected him against a helluva lot of things" and that the Watergate investigation threatened to "blow the whole Bay of Pigs thing, which we think would be very unfortunate for the CIA and the country." A mystified Haldeman went into John Ehrlichman's office, saying, "Guess what? It's Bay of Pigs time again!" But Haldeman carried out his assignment, repeating to Helms what he had been told to say, only to have Helms explode, "The Bay of Pigs has nothing to do with this! I have no concern about the Bay of Pigs!"

To this day Helms vows that he has no idea what dark secret Nixon was alluding to. But, whatever it was, it led Nixon into trying to enlist the CIA in an attempted obstruction of justice that became his final undoing.

2. The Diem Assassination "Plot"

It is a matter of record that the Kennedy Administration supported the coup that resulted in the ouster and death of South Vietnamese President Ngo Dien Diem on November 1, 1963. But Nixon spoke as though he knew President Kennedy to have been personally responsible for the assassination, and repeatedly Nixon issued orders to dig up the proof. He ordered Secretary of State Henry Kissinger to get him the "files on the murder of Diem," and he demanded of John Ehrlichman "the full Diem story" on his desk before the end of the week.

When the information was not forthcoming, Nixon gave the assignment to White House plumbers G. Gordon Liddy and Howard Hunt. When they couldn't find the damning files, Hunt forged a message suggesting Kennedy approval for the Diem assassination and tried, unsuccessfully, to peddle the forgery to *Life* magazine.

Despite the lack of evidence, President Nixon, at a news conference on September 16, 1971, went public with the assertion that "the way we got into Vietnam was through overthrowing Diem and the complicity in the murder of Diem."

3. The "Bugged" Campaign Plane

It was an article of faith for Nixon that all the dirty tricks, surveillance, and wiretaps he sponsored were simply getting back at Democrats who had done the same things. As his favorite example he often said that in 1968 the FBI had bugged his campaign plane on orders from President Lyndon Johnson. The FBI had, in fact, wiretapped a Nixon supporter, Mrs. Anna Chennault, who served as a contact with the Saigon government. But there had been no eavesdropping on Nixon or his campaign plane. Nevertheless, Nixon told Haldeman he thought the "Johnson bugging process" could be "cranked up" to get the former President to use his influence with congressional Democrats to call off the Watergate investigation.

The message was conveyed to the LBJ ranch and Johnson countered with the threat that "if the Nixon people are going to play with this," he would release something about Nixon. That something was deleted from Haldeman's published diary as a national security secret. However, the secret was revealed in the book, *Hoover's FBI,* by Cartha D. (Deke) DeLoach, who was number 3 in the FBI and liaison with the White House in both the Johnson and Nixon Administrations. Not only did the FBI wiretap Anna Chennault but the National Security Agency intercepted and decoded cablegrams from the South Vietnamese Embassy to Saigon, urging that President Thieu hold off on peace negotiations to get a better deal from Nixon after the election.

What the FBI did not do, DeLoach says, is bug the Nixon campaign plane. For one thing, DeLoach told me, it would have been unfeasible to get a bug on a plane guarded by the Secret Service. But, soon after the election, says DeLoach, Director J. Edgar Hoover, currying favor with the new President-elect, visited him and told him his campaign plane had been bugged on President Johnson's orders. It was a myth that Nixon believed, probably until his dying day.

4. The Hughes–O'Brien Threat

If you look for the phobia that most probably led to the Watergate break-in, you will find it in Nixon's fear that Democratic National Chairman Lawrence O'Brien, a former consultant to the eccentric industrialist, Howard Hughes, knew something about Nixon's dealings with Hughes that would be sprung at some critical moment in the campaign. There had been the 1956 Hughes loan to Nixon's brother, Donald, and Donald's continuing relationship with the Hughes empire. More dangerous, there had been the illegal Hughes "campaign contribution" of $100,000 in $100 bills after the 1968 campaign, held by the President's friend, Bebe Rebozo, in a safe deposit box in Key Biscayne, Florida.

Nixon talked often to his aides about "going after" O'Brien without specifying why. But in May 1972 as plans were being made for Gordon Liddy's "political intelligence project," word sifted down that O'Brien was to be a principal target. Campaign aide Jeb Magruder says the word he got from Charles Colson in the White House was to go after O'Brien for the "information regarding the Florida dealings"—presumably an elliptical reference to the Rebozo cache of Hughes money. It finally dawned on Liddy, as he wrote in his book, that the reason for the break-in to Democratic headquarters and the effort to tap O'Brien's phone was "to find out what O'Brien had of a derogatory nature about us, not for us to get something on him."

And, irony of ironies, the O'Brien "threat" that lured Nixon into Watergate was a phantom. O'Brien, who died in 1990, said he never knew about the Hughes money. "If I had known, you wouldn't have to break into my office to get it. I would have told the whole world."

All those demons and dragons—the Kennedys, the FBI, the CIA, and who knows what else?—haunted Nixon's fevered dreams and beckoned him to the abuse of power that would destroy him. President Johnson had already opened a Vietnam credibility gap, but Nixon, in pursuit of his "enemies," shattered, perhaps forever, the assumption of regularity in the White House. That may be the ultimate legacy of the driven man who almost drove constitutional government off the rails.

The Nixon Perplex

E. Howard Hunt

"The villany you teach me I will execute,
and it shall go hard . . ."
—The Merchant of Venice

The long sweep of recorded history has its defining moments, more often than not eponymized by figures noble and ignoble from the legendary past. Moses, Christ, Alexander, Socrates, Caesar, Columbus, Washington, Victoria, Lincoln, Roosevelt, Kennedy, and—Nixon.

Historians debate and quarrel; revisionism has become a modern cottage industry; debunking is a varlet's tribute to the great.

"Paint me as I am," said Cromwell—"Less than truth my soul abhors." And Churchill, an illustrious successor, thought truth so precious as to require a bodyguard of lies. In June 1972, a bodyguard of otherwise honorable men began shielding Nixonian Truth with lies. And that was the beginning of Watergate and the fall of Richard Nixon.

I was one of those liars, and subterfuge cost me everything I held dear, except my life. I lied to protect the Presidency—until it became clear that the President was frantically trying to preserve himself, not his high office.

Equally clear was Nixon's contempt for those he sacrificed to lighten his sinking boat—intimate friends, longtime supporters, and advisers—until all were gone and he sank alone, rejected and unregretted.

But in reality the genesis of Watergate is to be found in our Vietnam War. The Nixon White House was deeply disturbed and baffled by mass antiwar demonstrations, spreading campus unrest and destruction, the Kent State killings, and publication of the Pentagon Papers. Their cumulative effect produced in the White House a bunker mentality: Us against Them.

A year after retiring from CIA, I was hired as a part-time White House consultant by Presidential Assistant Charles Colson, who charged me with researching the origins of the Vietnam War. And from a small office in the Old Executive Office Building I began work with enthusiasm. After all, I admired Richard Nixon as a leader and a man who had survived, persevered, and triumphed. I wanted to help this extraordinary exemplar of the

American success story in any way I could: no task too great, none too small.

While Nixon was still a Congressman, my wife Dorothy and I encountered him and Pat in a Washington restaurant. I expressed admiration for his pursuit of Alger Hiss, and was not to speak with him again until the White House Christmas party in 1971. By then, Colson had involved me in other missions, and when I told the President I was working for Colson he said, "Oh, yes, I know about that," a response I interpreted as meaning that Nixon was aware of my sub rosa activities and they had his blessing.

Earlier, through Colson, I had met G. Gordon Liddy, with whom I struck up an immediate friendship. An ex-FBI agent, Liddy was a low-level White House staffer with easily discernible ambitions to better his station in life. We shared basement office space in OEOB Room 16, later to become notorious as the haunt of the Plumbers, and in which the Special Investigations Unit was formed. We traveled together on catchall jobs until Liddy informed me that he was to become Counsel for the Finance Committee to Re-Elect the President (CREEP), and would be moving to Committee offices across Pennsylvania Avenue. Liddy attributed his designation to Attorney General John Mitchell.

In addition to overt work for the Committee, Liddy told me, he was to form a political action unit to counter Democratic dirty tricks with those of our own. A half-million dollar budget was only the beginning. Could he count on me? Yes, he could. In CIA I'd been harassing the Soviet Union for years. Now I was to have the opportunity of working against domestic enemies. The prospect was not only golden, it was legitimized by the Attorney General, the strong right arm of the President from whom he withheld no secrets.

In late winter of 1972, Liddy and I began drawing up plans for protecting the Republican Nominating Convention in San Diego from any repetition of the violence that had disrupted the Chicago Democratic Convention four years before. In addition, plans were made to harass the Democratic Convention scheduled for Miami that summer.

Included in our planning were several Miami Cuban Americans I had known during the Bay of Pigs operation. Initially they were used as a team to search the Beverly Hills office of Daniel Ellsberg's psychiatrist, the White House mantra being that either Ellsberg was insane, an agent of the KGB, or both. However, no Ellsberg file was discovered, so convention planning resumed while Liddy sought budget approval from John Mitchell. Eventually a scaled-down operational budget was authorized and we examined the future Democratic Convention site for vulnerabilities.

In May, Liddy told me of current information that the Democratic National Committee (DNC) was receiving illegal contributions from the North

Vietnamese. Miami contacts relayed a companion rumor that Fidel Castro was clandestinely funding the Democrats. If either illegality could be proved and publicized, Democratic hopes to elect Senator McGovern would be destroyed; Nixon would be reelected, and Congress could well become Republican. Somewhere, we theorized, Democratic National Committee books would reflect foreign contributions, and those books were most likely kept in the files of Democratic National Chairman Larry O'Brien—in the Watergate office building.

On the night of May 28, DNC offices were entered, and two rolls of photos taken by the entry team. James McCord bugged O'Brien's office and tapped his telephone. The developed film showed the contents of O'Brien's desk drawers, but no account books or lists of Democratic contributors. Worse, McCord reported poor results from his electronic intercepts, and presently Liddy informed me that he had been ordered to make another attempt to photograph the files. During the entry McCord was to replace his microphone. No one involved was pleased, but the team reassembled for a reprise the night of June 16.

Despite alarming indications that the building guard was alerted, Liddy forced the issue and the five men who entered DNC offices were arrested.

Immediate legal efforts to free them failed, but Liddy repeated promises from his superiors of money for legal fees and family maintenance. Within a few days of the fiasco my name became known, and Liddy told me I was to leave Washington and join my wife and children in Europe, a suggestion I declined. Instead, I retained the first of several attorneys, who told me I was to be arraigned and indicted. At first, through Liddy, large amounts of cash were received to pay legal fees for all seven of us, but each delivery was less than what was needed and promised, and disillusionment set in. McCord was the first to sense that our sponsors were not going to provide payments or pardons—especially after the November election, when Nixon easily defeated McGovern. (Subsequently, McCord made a separate peace with the government and received a light prison sentence. He was the most prescient of us all.)

By then the Miamians were reduced to near beggary, and I played every conceivable card to persuade our White House sponsors to provide promised funds to meet our legal and living expenses. By many, unfamiliar with the clandestine tradition of major intelligence agencies, my overtures were interpreted as blackmail, but I regarded them as reasonable reminders of obligations offered but unmet. In any event, the funding trickle ended and our abandonment was complete.

The December death of my wife Dorothy in a Chicago plane crash devastated me. I had four motherless children to care for, and felt I could not endure the rigors or expense of trial. Although I continued to hope that Nixon would intervene and quash the proceedings in his own interest, I arranged to enter a guilty plea. The Miami men did likewise, and after we were all jailed in Washington I told Liddy that my attorney recommended I cooperate with the Grand Jury. He turned, walked away, and we have never spoken since.

Gradually, Nixon's intimates were snagged by the prosecution's net: Haldeman, Ehrlichman, Mitchell, and Dean. From prison I watched the ballooning spectacle, incredulous that this could be happening to the office of the most powerful man on earth. Prospects for our release and rehabilitation were nonexistent, though I continued to lie to the Grand Jury, prosecutors, and Sam Ervin's Senate investigating committee. For I believed that only by protecting the Presidency could I hope for reduction of my 35-year sentence. Then, after nearly a year in prison, I was released on appeal. My children had scattered, effectively dissolving a once happy family.

Alone in my house, I began writing the Watergate story in my autobiography, *Undercover: Memoirs of an American Secret Agent*. But even before publication in the fall of 1974, Ehrlichman's attorney questioned me in court concerning errors in the text, some deliberate misstatements, others inadvertent mistakes that I had to concede. My publisher was furious as book sales diminished, and we parted on unpleasant terms.

In the spring of 1974, I had read transcripts of Nixon's Oval Office tapes and realized that the President I had so long admired and for whom I had sacrificed so much was indifferent to our fate. For me that was a turning point, and I resolved to testify truthfully, and did so from then on.

After my appeal was denied I returned to prison for the balance of my horrific sentence, though glad that during freedom I had been able to reconcile with all my children.

Paroled finally, in 1977, I remarried and fathered two children by my wife, Laura. Now and then I reflect on what my involvement in Watergate cost me: the disruption of my family; legal fees of nearly $800,000; the fall of the Cubans who trusted me; publishers' resistance to current books after a long, successful writing career; the permanent labels of "Watergater" and "burglar"; and 33 months in prison.

Collaterally, my name, published photographs, and CIA background attracted the unwelcome attention of assassination buffs who fantasized that a Watergate conspirator could have conspired to murder John Fitzgerald Kennedy.

Nixon left the Presidency in disgrace, but miraculously reinvented himself. Still, when I think of him I think also of our WWII officer's training: that a leader takes care of his followers before seeing to himself, a code Nixon may have forgotten, but disastrously ignored. Long before his death Nixon admitted responsibility for Watergate, but took none of the blame. Cold comfort for those who lost so much in a vain effort to protect him from himself.

One example of the surreal atmosphere that suffused the White House even as Nixon was fighting impeachment: his attorney telephoned, asking if I would come to the White House to help prepare the President's defense. The invitation was so incredible that it took a few moments to comprehend what was being asked of me. Finally, I managed to decline civilly, though outrage and profanity were on the tip of my tongue.

And, as Richard Nixon lay on his deathbed I uncharitably recalled Shelley's words on George III: "An old, mad, blind, despised and dying king."

Without expiation in life, Nixon gained a measure of redemption in death. But his legacy of misfeasance is found in diminished respect for the Presidency and suspicion of government itself: an imprint as enduring as it is unforgivable.

Classical Greek dramatists focused on hubris, the tragic flaw in a man's character that inevitably brought him from high to low estate. Nixon's flaw was overweening pride, obsession with self-preservation at the expense of the Republic's governance.

The tragedy of Richard Nixon is not his alone; he forced it on his country and his countrymen. Our 37th President will be remembered—but not in ways he would have wished.

Nixon's Policies
Didn't End Communism

MICHAEL MANDELBAUM

Foreign policy was Richard Nixon's passion, and foreign policy was the source of both his considerable successes and his devastating failures as President.

He entered office in 1969 proclaiming a transition from "an era of confrontation to an era of negotiation." He launched three sets of negotiation that made the world more stable and the United States more secure. They led to policies that lasted decades beyond his term of office.

One set of negotiations was with the Soviet Union. Nixon's policy of détente never became the broad and enduring engagement with America's chief adversary that he initially sought. But it did give rise to several agreements on nuclear arms. While the agreements stopped a potentially costly competition in missile defenses, they had little overall impact on the Soviet-U.S. military balance.

Rather, their chief significance was political: They demonstrated a recognition of the need to keep the superpower rivalry from erupting into a catastrophic war. Moreover, the two decades of arms control talks produced a cadre of Soviet officials with whom the West could talk seriously. Some contributed to the revolution in Soviet foreign policy in the late 1980s under Mikhail Gorbachev.

The second set of talks was with the People's Republic of China. He saw that the increasingly acrimonious Sino-Soviet conflict of the late 1960s presented a diplomatic opportunity for Washington. His dramatic trip to Beijing in February 1972 shifted the balance of power in East Asia. By bringing the United States into alignment with China he offset the damage done to U.S. power and prestige in the region by the Communist victory in Vietnam.

The third crucial negotiations involved Israel and its Arab neighbors. At the end of their two-week war of October 1973, the U.S. position in the region was perilous. The warring armies were poised to resume fighting. This could have drawn the United States into direct conflict with the Soviet Union: During the war a veiled Soviet threat to send forces to the Mideast had triggered a decision to put U.S. military forces worldwide on a heightened state of alert. The Arab oil producers had reduced their output to punish Washington for its support of Israel, sending the price of petroleum skyrocketing and provoking fears of economic collapse in the West.

The skillful diplomacy of Nixon's Secretary of State, Henry Kissinger, separated the Arab and Israeli armies. This had the effect of ensuring that the fighting would not resume, pacifying the most important Arab oil producer, Saudi Arabia, and establishing a pattern of U.S. mediation in Arab-Israeli negotiations that continues to the present day.

These three negotiations, and the policies they inaugurated, so quickly became permanent features of the diplomacy of the second half of the Cold War that it is easy to presume they were obvious initiatives that any President would have taken. This is not so. All three required geopolitical imagination and diplomatic finesse, qualities Nixon possessed in abundance.

But his failures also stemmed from foreign policy. The clearest of them was in Vietnam. When he became President, two not necessarily compatible goals were plausible for the United States: ending the conflict quickly, to minimize the costs to the country; and winning it—that is, preserving an independent, non-Communist South Vietnam. Nixon achieved neither. The war dragged on until mid-1975, when Communist forces defeated the pro-American governments of Vietnam, Cambodia, and Laos.

Because he had withdrawn U.S. ground combat personnel by the end of 1972, Nixon did not pay an electoral price for the failure of his policy; he overwhelmingly defeated his Democrat George McGovern. But the war was at the root of his disgrace and downfall in the Watergate scandal. It created the poisonous, polarized domestic political climate in which Nixon's subordinates committed crimes against his political opponents. The President himself directed the ultimately unsuccessful effort to conceal them.

As the cover-up of the burglary of the Democratic National Committee headquarters in the Watergate office building unraveled, Nixon attempted to protect himself by invoking extraordinary Presidential powers. He claimed executive privilege to avoid turning incriminating tape recordings he himself had made over to federal prosecuters.

In wartime, Presidents have exercised extraordinary, extraconstitutional powers: Lincoln in the Civil War, for example, and Franklin Roosevelt during World War II. At the outset of the Cold War, when the American fear of the Soviet Union was at its height, the country might have accepted a similarly expansive definition of the powers of the office. By the 1970s it would no longer do so. The sense of danger had eased—in part, ironically, because of détente.

There is a final irony to Nixon's political career. He adopted a distinctive approach to foreign policy, based on the assumption that the conflict with the Soviet Union was both permanent and manageable. This meant that it could be put on a businesslike basis, free from the crusading spirit that had so often marked American foreign policy.

His two immediate elected successors reverted to the previous pattern. Jimmy Carter and Ronald Reagan were crusaders—for human rights in the first case, for the overthrow of the "evil empire" of the Soviet Union in the second. In office, neither was as deft or successful as Nixon at foreign policy. But in the long run they were right and he was wrong: The Soviet empire did collapse, in no small part because of the political power of the idea of individual rights and liberties, an idea that Nixon had relegated to the periphery of his foreign policy.

The 37th President's true political heir was George Bush. Of all his successors, Bush was the one whose definition of the office, with its emphasis on international rather than domestic concerns, and whose approach to the conduct of foreign policy, featuring power politics and high-level diplomacy, most closely corresponded to Nixon's. And it was Bush who presided over U.S. policy when Communism collapsed in Europe, thereby ending the world in which Nixon had operated with such skill.

Nixon in the Jungle

JIM HOUGAN

It is one of the most mysterious incidents in the Vietnam War, and I can't get it out of my mind.

It was the spring of 1964, and the former Vice President of the United States, who was also the *next President* of the United States, Richard M. Nixon, was standing in a jungle clearing northwest of Saigon, negotiating with a man who, to all appearances, was a Vietcong lieutenant. Wearing battle fatigues "with no identification," Nixon was flanked by military bodyguards whose mission was deemed so secret that, when they returned to Saigon, their clothing was burned.[1]

At the time, Nixon had been out of public office (though not out of politics) for more than three years. After losing the Presidential election in 1960 and the California gubernatorial race in 1962, he'd gone into private practice as an attorney with the Mudge, Rose law firm, subsiding into what amounted to an enforced retirement from the world's stage. It's all the more surprising, then, to find this political castoff on a secret mission in the Orient—only a few months after the Kennedy and Diem assassinations.

Not that Nixon was a stranger to intrigue. On the contrary, his political career might easily be graphed as a parabola of Cold War conspiracies. As a Red-baiting congressman in the forties, he'd made the most of a lovely "photo opportunity" by uncovering stolen State Department secrets—in a Maryland pumpkin field. In the fifties, while Vice President, he'd run a stable of spooks—actually *run* them—in an off-the-books operation to destroy the Greek shipping tycoon, Aristotle Onassis.[2] In that operation, Nixon acted as a case officer to Robert Maheu (himself a linkman between the CIA and the Mafia)[3] and a former *Washington Post* reporter named John Gerrity.

---

[1]"Secret Nixon Vietnam Trip Reported," *New York Times,* Feb. 17, 1985.
[2]Jim Hougan, *Spooks* (New York: Morrow, 1978), pp. 286–306. Onassis was targeted because of an agreement he'd reached with the Saudi government, monopolizing the shipment of Arabian oil.
[3]Hougan, *Spooks,* pp. 286–300, and Donald L. Bartlett and James B. Steele, *Empire* (New York: Norton, 1979), pp. 282–285.

Gerrity later recalled that "Nixon more or less invented the *Mission Impossible* speech, and he gave it to us right there, in the White House. You know the spiel, the one that begins, 'Your assignment, gentlemen, should you choose to accept it. . . .'"[4] Years afterward, when the Eisenhower Administration was drawing to a close, Nixon served as the de facto focal point officer for the Administration's plans to overthrow Fidel Castro. In that role, he was in regular contact with the CIA and with some of the darker precincts of the Pentagon.

It's fair to say, then, that Richard M. Nixon knew what he was doing when it came to covert operations—but *what* was he doing in the jungle in 1964?

The story surfaced, briefly, some 20 years later, when the *New York Times* reported that Nixon, "while on a private trip to Vietnam in 1964, met secretly with the Vietcong and ransomed five American prisoners of war for bars of gold. . . ."[5] In reporting this, the *Times* relied on an account that had appeared in the catalog of a Massachusetts autograph dealer. The dealer was selling a handwritten note that Nixon had given to one of his bodyguards. The note read, "To Hollis Kimmons with appreciation for his protection for my helicopter ride in Vietnam, from Richard Nixon."

The value of the note was increased by the circumstances that generated it, circumstances that Sergeant Kimmons described in the catalog:

> *When Nixon arrived at Ton Son Nhut Airport in Saigon, Sergeant Kimmons was assigned to security detail and was accompanying Nixon on all excursions away from the 145th Aviation Battalion where Nixon was staying. On the second day, Nixon dressed in Army fatigues with no identification and climbed aboard a helicopter with Sergeant Kimmons and a crew of four.[6]*
>
> *They proceeded to Phuoc Binh, a village northwest of Saigon, where they met with Father Wa, a go-between that arranged the exchange of the gold for U.S. prisoners. The following day, Nixon and his party departed for An Loc, a village south of Phuoc Binh, where in a clearing somewhere in this area Nixon met with a Vietcong lieutenant who established a price for the return of five U.S. prisoners.*
>
> *A location for the exchange was arranged and the crew departed for Saigon. Later the same day, the crew, this time without Nixon because of the extreme danger, departed for Phumi Kriek, a village across*

---

[4]Hougan's interview with Gerrity.
[5]"Secret Nixon Vietnam Trip Reported," p. 3.
[6]Fatigues typically have the owner's last name sewn on a plaquet on the breast.

the border in Cambodia. A box loaded with gold bars so heavy it took
three men to lift it on the helicopter accompanied the crew.

    At the exchange point, five U.S. servicemen were rustled out of the
jungle accompanied by several armed soldiers. The box of gold was un-
loaded and checked by the Vietcong lieutenant and the exchange was
made without incident. The crew and rescued prisoners immediately de-
parted for Saigon, and they were sent to the hospital upon their arrival.

    Sergeant Kimmons's mission was secret, and there were no written
orders for his duty during this period. His clothes were destroyed as well
as the film in his camera, and he signed an agreement not to reveal this
incident for 20 years. Nixon's note to him was hurriedly written at the
conclusion of his assignment to guard Nixon on the following day.[7]

That Nixon traveled to Vietnam in 1964 is a matter of fact. He departed
the United States in late March on a round-the-world trip that took him, first,
to Beirut, and then to Karachi, Calcutta, Kuala Lumpur, Bangkok, and
Saigon. There, he dined with the American Ambassador, Henry Cabot Lodge,
who had been his running mate in the 1960 Presidential race. In the days that
followed, Nixon helicoptered into the countryside,[8] and then continued on
to Hong Kong, Manila, Taiwan, and Tokyo before returning home.[9] Nixon
later wrote that the purpose of the trip was to meet with Mudge, Rose clients
and foreign leaders. Contemporary reports make it obvious, however, that
the real purpose of the trip was to drum up international support for what
was about to become America's massive intervention in Vietnam.[10]

    There is nothing in the *Times*'s account to suggest that the exchange of
gold on April 3 was in any way relevant to the impending escalation of the
war, but the possibility is an intriguing one. The *Times*'s article is anything
but conclusive. On the contrary, it simply parrots the cover story that
Sergeant Kimmons had been given, while at the same time neglecting to identify the mission's middleman, the so-called Father Wa.

    According to the Pentagon, which kept meticulous records of American
prisoners of war, the POW release that Sergeant Kimmons described could
not have occurred. The few Americans in captivity in 1964 were all ac-
counted for in 1965—and most of them were still in cages. (Even so, we

---

[7]The *Times* article quotes from a catalog printed by Templeton, Massachusetts, autograph
dealer Paul C. Richards.
[8]*New York Times,* Apr. 3, 1964, p. 5.
[9]*RN: The Memoirs of Richard M. Nixon* (New York: Touchstone, 1990), pp. 256–258, and
articles in the following editions of the *New York Times,* covering his trip: March 23–28, 1964;
March 30–31, 1964; April 2–10, 1964; and April 16, 1964.
[10]*Ibid.*

needn't rely on the Pentagon to give the lie to Nixon's cover story. Whatever else may be said about Richard Nixon, he was a consummate politician and, if he'd risked his life to rescue American prisoners of war, we'd have heard about it—if not in 1964, then most definitely in 1968.)

As for the identity of Father Wa, Sergeant Kimmons (and the *Times*) fell victim to phonetics. Far more than an anonymous interpreter, the Rev. Nguyen Loc Hoa was a legendary figure in Vietnam. A bespectacled Catholic priest whose black cassock was usually cinched with a web ammo belt and a pair of holstered .45s, he was *the* symbol of militant anti-Communism in the south.[11] Twenty years before, he'd fought a successful guerrilla war against the Japanese in China. Soon afterward, and as a colonel in the Chinese Nationalist Army, he'd battled Mao Tse Tung's Communist insurgency. Driven from China, he and two thousand followers lived for a while in Cambodia before moving to a mangrove swamp in the Mekong Delta—where they set up a village and went to war against the Vietcong.

Father Hoa's story was told in an article that appeared in *The Saturday Evening Post*, a few months after President Kennedy took office. Entitled "The Report the President Wanted Published," the piece was published under peculiar circumstances. Authored by "An American Officer" whose identity could not be made public "for professional reasons,"[12] the article was in fact written by Gen. Edward Lansdale, an Air Force–CIA officer whose counterinsurgency theories and practice had inspired at least two books *(The Ugly American* and *The Quiet American).*[13] According to Lansdale, President Kennedy personally telephoned him to ask that he arrange for publication of what, until then, had been a secret report.

The article, and a follow-up piece that came out a year later, were blatant propaganda.[14] In sentimentalizing Father Hoa's ferocious anti-Communism while demonizing the Vietcong, the articles did much to prepare the American public for the larger war to come.

Whatever Kennedy's motives may have been in pushing Lansdale to publish his secret report, Nixon's visit to the jungle is even more mysterious. Why should a former Vice President of the United States, accompanied by a legendary guerrilla fighter with excellent ties to the CIA, dress up in battle fatigues and adopt a cover story to facilitate a journey into the Vietnamese bush? The answer, obviously, is to make a very secret deal. But if, as we've

---

[11]Cecil Currey, *Edward Lansdale: The Unquiet American* (Boston: Houghton Mifflin, 1988), p. 220.
[12]An American Officer, "The Report the President Wanted Published," *Saturday Evening Post,* May 20, 1961, p. 31.
[13]Currey, *Edward Lansdale,* p. 225.
[14]Don Schanche, "Father Hoa's Little War," *Saturday Evening Post,* Feb. 17, 1962.

discovered, Nixon was engaged in something other than ransoming prisoners, what was he buying with so much gold—and who *were* those guys that came out of the jungle near Phumi Kriek?

Recently declassified reports of the top-secret Military Assistance Command/Studies and Observations Group (MACSOG) raise the possibility that Nixon's mission may have had to do with OPLAN 34-A. This was a covert operation to undermine the North Vietnamese by inserting "specially trained" Vietnamese commandos behind enemy lines.[15] The operation was run by the CIA from 1961 to 1963, and by the Pentagon from 1964 to 1967. We're told that the activity was paid for with money the CIA had received from the U.S. Navy and then laundered offshore.[16]

Since Nixon's mission had nothing to do with prisoners of war, it seems likely indeed that the Americans who dashed from the jungle at Phumi Kriek were CIA operatives or paramilitaries. This likelihood, coupled with the large amount of untraceable gold, suggests a mission of surpassing sensitivity—which, in turn, suggests OPLAN 34-A.

But what makes the incident at Phumi Kriek seem important, however, is not just the secrecy that surrounded it, or even the large amount of gold that was involved. It is, instead, the presence of Richard Nixon. Why *him?* What could such an *outré* politician have possibly brought to a covert operation in Vietnam?

The answer, of course, is nothing—except his face. Which is to say, *the unmistakable face of American political authority*. With Richard Milhous Nixon present at the negotiations, and with the fabled Father Hoa as his interpreter, the supposed "Vietcong lieutenant" (himself, perhaps, a MACSOG operative) would never have questioned the legitimacy of the mission on which he was being sent. He would have known that, no matter how improbable, the mission was sanctioned by the highest echelons of the American government.

But what can that mission have been?

With Nixon, Hoa, and Kimmons dead, one can only speculate. But it's worth noting that exactly four months after the meeting at Phumi Kriek, OPLAN 34-A commando raids were carried out against the North Vietnamese in the Gulf of Tonkin. Two days later, an American destroyer, the *Maddox,* was attacked in the Gulf by North Vietnamese patrol boats—which led, almost instantly, to American air raids on North Vietnam and the passage of the Tonkin Gulf Resolution, escalating America's involvement in the war.

---

[15]"Once Commandos for U.S., Vietnamese Are Now Barred," *New York Times,* Apr. 14, 1995, p. 1.
[16]*Ibid.*

In his recent mea culpa,[17] former Secretary of Defense Robert S. McNamara writes that the attack on the *Maddox* was "so irrational" that "some believed the 34-A operations had played a role in triggering North Vietnam's actions." Though McNamara does not say so, his implication is clear: OPLAN 34-A operatives deliberately provoked the North Vietnamese and, in so doing, transformed "a small, out-of-the-way conflict into a full-bore war."[18]

If that is what happened, it's understandable that OPLAN 34-A operations should be so secret that their very existence was omitted from the Pentagon Papers.[19] What's less clear is whether or not Richard M. Nixon was directly involved in funding those operations, operations that, in effect, jump-started the Vietnam War.

---

[17]Robert S. McNamara, *In Retrospect: The Tragedy and Lessons of Vietnam* (New York: Times Books, 1995), p. 133.

[18]"Once Commandos for the U.S. . . . ," p. 1.

[19]This, according to Sedwick Tourison, a Defense Intelligence Agency (DIA) analyst, who called OPLAN 34-A operations *"the* secret" of the Vietnam War ("Once Commandos for the U.S. . . . ," p. 1).

The CIA, Assassination, and Nixon

Stephen J. Rivele

The CIA was born in the chaotic landscape of the post–World War II era, but it had its roots deep in that war. Its predecessor, the wartime Office of Strategic Services, or OSS, was America's first full-time intelligence agency. Created as an aggressive front-line elite, the OSS laid down many of the precedents the CIA would follow upon its creation. Among these was the OSS's fervor for clandestine operations, which, though not specifically included in the CIA's charter,[1] became bound up with the new agency's identity. Another was a penchant for enlisting figures from the criminal underworld, especially drug dealers, as agents. A third was a willingness to use political assassination as an operational tool. A few examples taken from the history of the OSS will illustrate these points.

On December 24, 1942, French Admiral Jean Darlan, the pro-Nazi High Commissioner of North Africa, was shot and killed in his office in Algiers. While it has never been clear who was behind the murder, an OSS officer was in touch with the plotters and was believed to have supplied the weapon.[2] Later in the war, the OSS gave strategic support to leaders of the vicious Corsican Mafia in the South of France, who dealt in drug smuggling, sabotage, and the retaliatory killing of pro-German agents.[3] Finally, OSS scientists and operations officers conducted an ultrasecret search for a truth drug that could be used to unmask and manipulate spies and double agents.[4] It is possible that one of these truth drug experiments was responsible for the death of Dr. Jean Tatlock, a San Francisco psychiatrist and member of the Communist Party, who was the mistress of

---

[1] United States Senate, *Alleged Assassination Plots Involving Foreign Leaders: An Interim Report of the Select Committee to Study Government Operations with Respect to Intelligence Activities* (Washington D.C.: USG, 1975), p. 9.

[2] R. Harris Smith, *OSS* (Berkeley: University of California Press, 1972), pp. 60–64.

[3] Code-named Jedburgh, this operation marked the beginning of a 30-year collusion between American intelligence and Corsican drug traffickers, many of whom were used as operatives in southern France, Southeast Asia, Africa, and Latin America.

[4] Peter Dale Scott, *Deep Politics and the Death of JFK* (Berkeley: University of California Press, 1993), pp. 164–173.

Dr. J. Robert Oppenheimer, director of the wartime atomic bomb project.[5]

On its founding in 1947, the CIA inherited many of the OSS's personnel, and absorbed its wartime philosophy and operational methods. The difference, of course, was that, unlike the OSS, the CIA was involved in a *cold* war in which there were few clearly defined front lines, and in which the enemy, while invariably labeled as Communist, could be armed or unarmed, of any nationality, and of a wide range of political views. The CIA's assassination activity began in earnest in the late 1950s under the Eisenhower-Nixon Administration, when two figures emerged on the world scene who appeared to threaten vital American interests: Patrice Lumumba of the Belgian Congo and Fidel Castro of Cuba.

Lumumba was a charismatic pan-Africanist visionary who made the fatal mistake of accepting aid from the Soviet Union for his desperately poor infant nation. A plot to murder him either with toxins manufactured by the CIA's Technical Services Division or a long-range rifle shot was devised and approved at the highest levels of the U.S. Government.[6] To carry out the plot, the Agency recruited two European criminals who were code-named QJ/WIN and WI/ROGUE.

The identities of these men have been among the CIA's most closely guarded secrets, and they are being revealed here for the first time. Recently released top-secret CIA documents indicate that QJ/WIN was a Luxembourg-based smuggler named Jose Mankel, and WI/ROGUE was a Soviet-born Paris bank robber named David Dzitzichvili (also spelled Tzitzichvili; alias David Dato).[7]

In late 1960, the CIA sent both of these criminals to the Congo to assassinate Lumumba. Whether either man was actually involved in Lumumba's kidnapping and murder in January 1961 remains in dispute. What is clear is that the Lumumba plot led directly to the institutionalization of political murder within the CIA.

---

[5]Dr. Tatlock, who was suspected of leaking Manhattan Project secrets to the Soviet consulate in San Francisco, was the subject of intense surveillance by the FBI, Army Intelligence, and OSS officers at the time of her death. Though Tatlock's death was officially ruled a suicide, an examination of the autopsy records indicates she may have been murdered. The OSS officer in charge of the truth drug program, George White, reports in his diary that he was in San Francisco with experimental drugs at the time of her death. The admitted killer of at least one suspected double agent, White later participated in unwitting CIA-sponsored drug experiments on American citizens, which led to the death of CIA scientist Dr. Frank Olson (John Marks, *The Search for the Manchurian Candidate* [New York: Times Books, 1978], pp. 80–86). White also participated in CIA plots to assassinate Fidel Castro. At the time of Tatlock's death, White was being supervised by Army Intelligence officer Col. Boris Pash. Pash would later join the CIA's clandestine services, and would be described by CIA agent and Watergate burglar E. Howard Hunt as the Agency's chief assassin.
[6]United States Senate, *Alleged Assassination Plots Involving Foreign Leaders,* pp. 13–70.
[7]I am indebted to Mark Allen for his permission to publish this information.

Shortly after Lumumba's death, Deputy CIA Director Richard Bissell charged a subordinate, former OSS agent William Harvey, with creating an "Executive Action" capability within the Agency (Executive Action was the CIA euphemism for assassination). The result was the ZR/RIFLE program, to which QJ/WIN was assigned as the primary "asset." WIN was tasked with spotting and recruiting criminals for ZR/RIFLE, and was consulted on the program's first major operation, the assassination of Cuban Premier Fidel Castro.

The idea of killing Castro had first been broached within the CIA in late 1959, after Vice President Richard Nixon concluded that Castro was not a democratic revolutionary, but a Communist. Between 1960 and 1965 there were at least eight attempts to murder the Cuban leader, the first few of which took place during the Eisenhower Administration.[8] In July and August 1960, the CIA attempted to eliminate Castro by an "accident," and then by poisoning. When these efforts failed, the Agency placed a contract on the Cuban premier's life with the American Mafia.[9]

The CIA-Mafia murder plots are among the Agency's most complex and least understood operations. It has been known since the mid-1970s that the Agency used a Howard Hughes associate, Robert Maheu, to recruit prominent members of the Mob, including Chicago's Sam Giancana and Florida's Santos Trafficante, both of whom had lost substantial gambling revenues in Havana as a result of Castro's revolution.[10] The Mafia's intermediary was Las Vegas gangster Johnny Roselli, who, like his organized crime colleagues, profited by his CIA connection to secure legitimacy and a measure of protection from Justice Department prosecution.[11]

Authorization for the initial CIA-Mafia assassination plot appears to have come from the White House,[12] which included the murder of Castro in

---

[8]In 1975, Castro gave an American senator a list of 24 attempts on his life in which, he alleged, the CIA had been involved. See United States Senate, *Alleged Assassination Plots Involving Foreign Leaders,* p. 71n.

[9]United States Senate, *Alleged Assassination Plots Involving Foreign Leaders,* pp. 71–179.

[10]Giancana and Trafficante, together with New Orleans Mob boss Carlos Marcello, were cited by the House Assassinations Committee as those most likely to have been behind the assassination of President John F. Kennedy. Marcello was overheard on FBI surveillance predicting the murder of Kennedy; Trafficante confided to an FBI informant that Kennedy was to be killed; and Giancana's brother has recently written that Giancana was directly involved in the assassination.

[11]Roselli was also an intimate of FBI Director J. Edgar Hoover. There is evidence that Roselli and other mobsters such as Meyer Lansky and Carlos Marcello were blackmailing Hoover by means of information in their possession that Hoover was a homosexual. (See Anthony Summers, *Official and Confidential: The Secret Life of J. Edgar Hoover* [New York: Putnam's, 1993], pp. 80–88, 91–95, 240–258, 377–378.) This may explain why Hoover insisted for most of his career that organized crime did not exist, and may help to explain some of the inconsistencies, omissions, and errors in the FBI's investigation of the JFK assassination.

[12]United States Senate, *Alleged Assassination Plots Involving Foreign Leaders,* pp. 109–116.

its plans for the invasion of Cuba at the Bay of Pigs. The White House official who most closely supervised the invasion plans was Vice President Nixon, who served as the "action officer" for the operation.[13] It is likely that Nixon was counting on the invasion, originally planned for the fall of 1960, to act as an October surprise and tip the balance in his seesaw election battle with John F. Kennedy. However, the invasion was postponed until the spring of 1961, and Nixon was defeated by Kennedy.

In this way, President Kennedy inherited the Bay of Pigs invasion plan and its accompanying CIA-Mafia murder plot.[14] Reluctantly, he agreed to go forward with both. Yet when the invasion failed, humiliating his three-month-old administration, Kennedy decided to pursue the assassination track, and, indeed, pressed it more aggressively than had his predecessors.[15] In April 1962, Richard Helms replaced Bissell as Deputy Director of the CIA, and, though he had carefully distanced himself from the Bay of Pigs operation, he now undertook the Castro murder project in earnest. He ordered Harvey to reactivate the Mafia connection, and, in May, Roselli dispatched a team of three agents to Cuba to shoot or poison Castro. When this failed, another three-man team was recruited in September, but they met with no more success.[16]

Despite this, Helms plunged on, creating Task Force W to explore even more exotic and bizarre ways to eliminate the Cuban leader. In early 1963, the CIA's Technical Services Division hatched a plot to plant exploding seashells in lagoons where Castro was known to go scuba diving. Another scheme was to make a gift to Castro of a diving suit impregnated with tuberculosis bacillus.[17] There were also plans to slip LSD to the Cuban leader while he was on the radio, and to inject him with a chemical that would cause his beard to fall out.[18] While nothing came of these sophomoric intrigues,

---

[13]E. Howard Hunt, *Undercover: Memoirs of an American Secret Agent* (New York: Berkeley, 1974), p. 131. The Bay of Pigs operation involved future Watergate burglars E. Howard Hunt, Frank Sturgis, Bernard Barker, Virgilio Gonzales, and Eugenio Martinez. Evidence has recently surfaced that James McCord may also have been involved in the Bay of Pigs planning. It is highly probable that Richard Nixon, as the project's action officer and a member of the Special Group that oversaw the invasion, knew of, and approved, the Castro assassination plot. (See Claudia Furiati, *ZR/RIFLE* [Melbourne, Australia: Ocean, 1994], p. 14.)

[14]In contrast to long-standing reports, evidence has recently come forward from Judith Exner, a Kennedy intimate, that the President knew of the CIA-Mafia murder plots as early as November 1960, and, more surprisingly, that his brother Robert Kennedy also knew of them during this period. As Attorney General, Robert Kennedy publicly and vociferously denounced the CIA-Mafia collusion, but this may have been done in an attempt to conceal the fact that he knew the Agency was protecting the very gangsters he was trying so energetically to prosecute.

[15]Recently, Exner has reported that she served as a go-between, carrying cash from Giancana and Trafficante to Kennedy for his election campaign, and, after his inauguration, carrying cash from President Kennedy to the mobsters for the Castro murder plot.

[16]United States Senate, *Alleged Assassination Plots Involving Foreign Leaders,* pp. 83–84.

[17]*Ibid.*, pp. 85–86.

[18]Jim Hougan, *Spooks* (New York: Morrow, 1978), pp. 332–333.

they were followed by the most serious plot of all, code-named AM/LASH.

AM/LASH was Rudolfo Cubela, a disaffected Cuban official who had offered his services to the CIA in 1961.[19] In September 1963, a CIA official met with Cubela to discuss the murder of Castro. Cubela agreed to participate on condition he obtain assurances that President Kennedy concurred in the plan. This presented the CIA with a problem, since the operation's supervisors had informed neither the White House nor Kennedy-appointed CIA Director John McCone of the AM/LASH plot. The likely reason was, at that very time, the Kennedy Administration was making secret overtures to Castro in an attempt to normalize relations with Cuba.

Accordingly, the CIA dispatched a senior official, Desmond Fitzgerald, to meet with Cubela and pose as the personal representative of Robert Kennedy.[20] Fitzgerald told Cubela he was a U.S. Senator and close friend of the Attorney General, and that the President had sanctioned the plan.[21] Thus assured, Cubela asked the CIA to furnish him with assassination devices. Technical Services provided a rifle with a telescopic sight, and a pen gun that fired a poisoned syringe. The weapons were delivered to Cubela in Paris on November 22, 1963, the very day President Kennedy was assassinated in Dallas.

Though the CIA's attempts to murder Castro, including AM/LASH, continued into the Johnson Administration, they by no means exhausted the Agency's Executive Action capability. In a plot that began under the Eisenhower-Nixon Administration, Dominican dictator Raphael Trujillo was assassinated in May 1961 by dissidents in the employ of the CIA. While the Agency has denied direct involvement in the murder, it is clear CIA officers encouraged and armed the plotters.[22] On November 2, 1963, South Vietnamese President Ngo Dinh Diem and his brother Ngo Dinh Nhu were murdered during a military coup. The generals who led the coup were being advised by Lt. Col. Lucien Conein, a senior CIA officer, who later admitted he knew of the assassination plan in advance.[23] Conein, who supervised Daniel Ellsberg in Vietnam, was also a close associate of the Corsican heroin traffickers[24] in Southeast Asia who regularly used CIA airplanes to transport opium base to Saigon for transshipment to Marseille.[25]

In 1972 Conein was recruited by the Nixon White House Plumbers unit

---

[19]United States Senate, *Alleged Assassination Plots Involving Foreign Leaders*, pp. 86–90.

[20]*Ibid.*, pp. 174–175: "Helms decided 'it was not necessary for Fitzgerald to seek approval from Robert Kennedy to speak in his name' " (p. 174).

[21]Anthony Summers, *Conspiracy* (New York: McGraw-Hill, 1980), pp. 349–352.

[22]United States Senate, *Alleged Assassination Plots Involving Foreign Leaders*, pp. 191–215.

[23]*Ibid.*, pp. 217–223.

[24]Alfred W. McCoy, *The Politics of Heroin* (New York: Lawrence Hill, 1991), pp. 249–250.

[25]Henrik Kruger, *The Great Heroin Coup* (Boston: South End, 1980), pp. 132–136.

to organize an assassination squad that was to disrupt the international drug trade.[26] To that end, it has been reported, some 150 leading drug traffickers were targeted, and over a million dollars in funding was to be made available.[27] While it remains unclear how far this planning proceeded, there is evidence that the CIA's collusion in the government's scheme to murder narcotics traffickers may not have been altruistic.[28] Several traffickers who were killed during this period were replaced by individuals who were assets of the CIA, including a number of Bay of Pigs veterans.[29]

This was not the Nixon Administration's only flirtation with political murder, however. In the fall of 1970, Executive Action surfaced again in the form of Track 2, though in this case the target was not drug traffickers, but the government of Chile. Following the election of Salvador Allende as President, Nixon authorized CIA Director Helms to use $10 million and any means necessary to destabilize the new leftist Chilean regime.[30]

One obstacle in the CIA's way was Chilean Army commander Gen. René Schneider, who had sworn to defend the constitutional process that brought Allende to power. On October 22, 1970, General Schneider was shot to death in his car by several assailants. His murderers had been in contact with the CIA station in Santiago, which had supplied them with submachine guns.[31] Within a year of Schneider's murder, Salvador Allende himself was shot and killed during the coup that overthrew his government.[32]

In the years since the creation of the CIA, a good deal of circumstantial and incomplete evidence has emerged regarding the Agency's involvement in the assassinations of political leaders. However, the secrecy that surrounds the Executive Action program remains nearly as tight today as it was in the heyday of QJ/WIN, ZR/RIFLE, and AM/LASH. Even the U.S. Senate was unable to determine whether the Agency had been directly responsible for the deaths of any foreign leaders.

It is difficult to resist the conclusion that this secrecy continues in order to conceal the wrongdoing of CIA officials and operatives, living and dead.

---

[26]Hougan, *Spooks,* pp. 143–148.

[27]Ibid., pp. 145–146.

[28]In 1990, the author interviewed a former CIA asset who claimed to have participated in this operation. He stated that he had personally killed "more than ten" foreign narcotics traffickers for the Agency. The author was able only to partially corroborate this claim.

[29]Peter Dale Scott and Jonathan Marshall, *Cocaine Politics* (Berkeley: University of California Press, 1991), pp. 33–34.

[30]Tom Wicker, *One of Us: Richard Nixon and the American Dream* (New York: Random House, 1991), pp. 667–669.

[31]United States Senate, *Alleged Assassination Plots Involving Foreign Leaders,* pp. 243–246.

[32]The author has interviewed a former CIA operative who claimed to have been assigned to kill Allende with a high-powered rifle. He stated that he had been flown to a U.S. Navy aircraft carrier off the Chilean coast and was preparing to fly to Santiago when the coup occurred, and the operation was cancelled.

One of the great ironies of our time is that the opening of the secret files of the Soviet KGB and Eastern European security services has not been matched by an equal openness on the part of our own government. If we are ever fully to understand the history of our nation in the postwar world, a frank accounting must be made of its clandestine history, and especially of the darkest and most lethal of its aspects: the use of political murder as a tool of foreign policy.

Nixon's Tapes:
The 18 1/2-Minute Gap

ALEXANDER BUTTERFIELD

It's always been hard for me to "just say no." Yet, when first asked to contribute to this book on Richard Nixon—"anything at all," I was told—I did exactly that. I declined. And why? Well, it was a matter of circumstance. I was, and still am, under contract with Little, Brown to do a book of my own, not about Nixon per se, but about me and my humorous and not-so-humorous experiences while one of three persons most closely involved with Nixon during his first Presidential term—Bob Haldeman, now deceased, and Steve Bull being the other two. (Henry Kissinger, John Ehrlichman, and Rose Mary Woods, in that order, rounded out the true Nixon inner sanctum.)

But here I am digressing, precisely Little, Brown's fear when they suggested I cool it a bit and pass this opportunity by. Why take a chance, they asked politely, of giving away here and now to Oliver Stone some anecdotal gems that might lend pizzazz to your own book later on? Their point was well taken, even though my literary effort will not come to fruition until mid-1997 as the nation prepares to whoop it up yet again (and perhaps for the last time) in celebration of Watergate's silver anniversary.

My suitors, however, were surprisingly persistent. Eric Hamburg, one of Stone's bright young men, knew of an article I'd written for *Harper's Magazine* back in August 1994, some five months prior to my signing with Little, Brown. He contacted *Harper's* and later the Los Angeles Times Syndicate, which held the reproduction rights to my *Harper's* contribution, and, within the span of a day and a half, cut a deal. But the tiny article he gained access to, that you're about to read, requires an explanation because it wasn't written to stand alone. It's about the mysterious 18 1/2-minute gap in a Nixon White House tape, and, as published, serves as the concluding portion of a three-part piece entitled "Nixon's Last Trump." Ideas for the story and three-part format were those of Jack Hitt, one of the magazine's contributing editors. As the author of Part I, subtitled "End Game," Hitt gives the reader an interesting bit of background on the notorious "gap" and makes clear the fact that it was not due to a long lull in conversation. It was due, instead, to a manipulated erasure. What Hitt did not say, however, and what many readers may not know or recall, is that (1) according to a panel of experts, the erasing process was applied as many as five times, so was probably purposeful; (2) the erased dialogue was not just any old conversation on any old day, but was part of the private June 20, 1972, conversation between the President of the United States and his executive assistant, Bob Haldeman, during their first White House meeting after word came of the Watergate break-in; and (3) the burglars had been caught in the act by the Washington, D.C., police, apprehended and identified as having some kind of tie to or association with the Committee to Re-Elect the President (or "CREEP," as it was affectionately referred to in those days). It goes without saying, therefore, that at this particular time—when the missing conversation took place—the name of the game was to keep the President and the White House out of the picture.

Naturally, there's been much conjecture over the years about the missing 18 1/2 minutes of dialogue. What was said in that meeting which at all costs had to be erased? No one alive knows the answer. So Jack Hitt decided to have a little fun. He invited several of us to guess.

The separate written submissions of Oliver Stone; E. Howard Hunt, one of the ringleaders of the Watergate break-in and an ex-CIA operative; and James Rosen, a student of the Watergate saga who is writing a book about John Mitchell, constitute Part II of the larger text. It is appropriately subtitled "Three Imaginary Dialogues."

And my response to Hitt, probably because of his awareness of my close day-to-day working relationship with Nixon, and my insights relative to the Nixon and Haldeman personalities, was published as Part III. Here, then, courtesy of *Harper's Magazine* and the Los Angeles Times Syndicate, is that article.

A Coda

To understand what the 18 1/2-minute silence really means, one must know that two men, both doppelgängers of the same dark persona, ran the presidency: Richard Nixon and his top aide, Bob Haldeman. History has accustomed us to think of "Haldeman and Ehrlichman." But John Ehrlichman was much like other senior staffers. He saw Nixon at scheduled meetings. Only Bob Haldeman saw the President nearly every hour of every day. He was in and out, conferring, reporting, debating, even arguing with the President. Then, on a typical evening, long after Haldeman had left the office for home, the two talked on the phone. No one had greater access to Nixon. No one knew better the Mephistophelian art of summoning his dark side. No one had greater control.

I remember an afternoon meeting with the President and Haldeman at which I mentioned Transportation Secretary John Volpe's request that the President attend a Transportation Department function. Nixon seemed favorably disposed when suddenly Haldeman leaned forward and slammed a fist down hard on the President's desk.

"Fuck Volpe!" he shouted. "Fuck the son of a bitch! He hasn't done a goddamn thing for us! Nothing! Fuck him!"

The President backed off immediately. "Uh, well, yeah, I guess you're right, Bob. I don't want to go to the goddamn thing anyway. Fuck'm."

No one else would have dared speak to the President that way or to be the least bit irreverent, but these two were partners. They were both tough, each in his own way. What one knew, the other knew. Without question, they, together, were responsible for the infamous erasure.

So what was in that 18 1/2-minute gap? To me it's not a mystery. But to accept what I believe was there, one must be aware of three facts that have never been well understood, despite 20-plus years of press coverage.

First, Richard Nixon never came close to explaining his role in Watergate. He admitted only that he had made mistakes—"errors in judgment," he called them—the intimation being that he shouldn't have allowed the weighty affairs of state to be his preoccupation, that by doing so he tended to keep a less than watchful eye on his zealous, albeit well-intentioned, aides. That was the Nixon line. The objective, of course, was to foist the blame for Watergate onto his staffers. Let's get serious here: aides to presidents do not run around participating in shenanigans willy-nilly. Having been a regular visitor to the Eisenhower White House, having worked closely with Lyndon Johnson and his aides as White House liaison officer for the Secretary of Defense, and having sat 20 feet from Richard Nixon for four years to oversee the smooth running of his official day, I do, in fact, have a fairly good feel for Presidential staffs and how they operate. And it is my opinion that the Nixon staff was the most tightly run and procedure oriented of this century. Nixon was a detail man, the director of all activity. Had these burglars been true "rogue" adventurers or "loose cannons," operating without Haldeman's or Nixon's knowledge, all implicated parties would have been lined up and publicly "executed"—forced to resign—immediately upon the President's return to Washington. But the dogs did not bark.

Second, the Committee to Re-Elect the President (CREEP) was a *creation* of the White House. It was staffed by people from the Nixon Administration, all carefully screened by Haldeman. Key slots went to White House staff members who were transferred over only for the period of the campaign. In short, it was not an independent organization. It was totally controlled by the White House, which is to say, in this case, by the President and Haldeman together.

Third, as news of the break-in dribbled into the White House offices Saturday morning, June 17, 1972, and throughout the following week, most of us just assumed *we* had done it, that it was a White House-directed caper approved by Haldeman and the President. There were no discussions of the break-in at the water cooler, of course, nor were there snickers or guffaws. But there were knowing smiles and glances, the wink or two of an eye . . . and silence. That in itself was a confirming clue.

Now to the gap.

The principal reason for the erasure was to deny the investigators evidence of the President's advance knowledge and approval of the Watergate break-in. I do believe, however, that true to his word, the President did *not* know about the June 17 break-in, only about the *initial* penetration carried out by the same cast of characters (on the third try in two days) three weeks earlier, on May 28. He *had* to have known about that. It simply could not have happened otherwise. But when word came back to Haldeman later that one of the planted bugs was faulty, he (Haldeman) might have felt that because the President had approved the initial installation of the electronic listening devices only weeks before, it would not be necessary to inform him about sending Jeb Magruder's team back in to make repairs.

Nixon, understanding there would be no general awareness of the May 28 event and that all publicity would be directed toward the June 17 break-in, would express his pleasure that Haldeman's "understandable oversight" had given him the opportunity to "truthfully" deny any knowledge.

And there were other incriminating matters discussed during the span of the erasure. Because bugging is a federal offense, the FBI had just the day before assumed control of the investigation from the Washington, D.C., police. Haldeman would have reported this turn of events and explained this was both good news and bad—good in that the FBI would be easy to control; bad in that they would be quick to jump on the $2,400 found in the burglars' possession and trace the sequentially numbered $100 bills to a Mexican bank and from there to the coffers of CREEP's Finance Committee.

Finally, Haldeman would have reviewed what he called "White House vulnerabilities"—the personnel links between the White House and CREEP, which the White House would have to deny or play down. In this context, although Howard Hunt and Gordon Liddy were not yet in custody, he would have reminded the President of Hunt's current status as a consultant assigned to the White House office of Charles Colson, and of Gordon Liddy's position as counsel to the Campaign Finance Committee. The Hunt problem, Haldeman would explain, could be handled easily by cleaning out his office and backdating his "White House release" to March or April. But what about

Liddy? And another problem was the connection of Haldeman's staff assistant Gordon Strachan to Jeb Magruder, the deputy director of CREEP, who in turn worked for CREEP director John Mitchell, who, on all matters big and small, reported directly to Haldeman and the President.

This, I feel certain, is the essence of what Richard Nixon and Bob Haldeman talked about on the morning of June 20; and in that meeting the cover-up was born. They, in my view, were the true Watergate co-conspirators, and the silences that passed between them in the Oval Office and elsewhere spoke volumes. I can think of no more fitting monument to these two men than the quiet hiss of the 18 1/2-minute gap.

The Love Song of Richard M. Nixon

FRANK MANKIEWICZ

No! I am not Prince Hamlet, nor was meant to be;
Am an attendant lord, one that will do
To swell a progress, start a scene or two,
Advise the prince; no doubt, an easy tool,
Deferential, glad to be of use,
Politic, cautious, and meticulous;
Full of high sentence, but a bit obtuse;
At times, indeed, almost ridiculous—
Almost, at times, the Fool.
—FROM *"The Love Song of J. Alfred Prufrock,"*
   BY T.S. ELIOT

Alas, Richard Nixon was often "full of high sentence," as when he re-ferred, from time to time, to "my historic journey for peace to China," or when he discussed a rather muddled version of the policy of containment during a speech in Hawaii, and then referred to it as "the Nixon Doctrine" by the time he had reached Guam a few hours later. He was "at times, in-deed, almost ridiculous," as when he would stride on the beach at San Clemente in dress black oxfords with black socks, and he was certainly "al-most, at times, the Fool," as when, in the wake of the American invasion of Cambodia and an unparalleled student uprising on campuses across the na-tion, he walked among protesting students on the Mall at 5 o'clock one morn-ing, as they were preparing for a mass dawn vigil, and asked some students what university they attended. When they replied they were from Syracuse, Nixon replied, eagerly, "Ah yes, the Orangemen," referring to the school's athletic teams' nickname. The students snickered (like The Eternal Foot-man?). It is possible Nixon may have thought of himself at that moment as Henry V with his troops before Agincourt—"a little touch of Harry in the night"—but it came out as pure Prufrock. He might as well have worn the bottoms of his trousers rolled.

It should also be noted that the most likely possibility for a Republican Presidential resurgence next year—Sen. Robert Dole—once brought down the house at a classic Washington banquet by pointing to a picture of then former Presidents Ford, Carter, and Nixon, standing solemnly at the funeral of some foreign leader, and observed, "look at them—See-No-Evil, Hear-No-Evil—and Evil!"

And yet, scorned, belittled, and made a figure of fun—hated and fiercely attacked in politics, in campaigns, and in office, he nevertheless was twice elected President of the United States, served two terms in the House of Representatives and part of a term in the Senate, and certainly did no harm to the victorious campaigns and Administrations of Dwight Eisenhower, whom he served as Vice President. It is no exaggeration, indeed, to say Richard Nixon was the dominant American political figure of the second half of the 20th century.

Indeed, less than 20 years after a crisis in which his Administration emerged as the most corrupt in our history, with Cabinet and sub-Cabinet members off to jail along with much of his staff, in which his government dissolved in a welter of perjury, obstruction of justice, deceit, illegal contributions, and other offenses, and in which Nixon himself was demonstrably observed to have cheated on his income taxes, lied to his staff and the American public, connived and conspired to obstruct justice in a variety of ways, revealed consistent anti-Semitism in his recorded speech, and appeared as petty, vengeful, and contemptuous of the Constitution—he still exerted enough influence after his death to persuade, almost without exception, high officials, editorialists, and even Presidents that public favor lay with embarrassingly fulsome eulogies at and surrounding his funeral.

How could this be so? How could this small-town boy from southern California, without the slightest mastery of history or of the English language, reach a point where he could even talk about his own "historic journey for peace," while bringing about the opening of relations between the world's two great powers after decades of hostility?

How could he sweep to reelection even as the scandal of Watergate was unfolding and emerging into public view? How could he survive having twice selected as his running mate a cheap political hack who took illegal payoffs in his White House office?

Largely, one thinks, because Nixon understood, better than any other mid-century politician, the play of politics and media. He understood the mystery of power and particularly the mystery (much of which has since been stripped away, largely as a consequence of his actions) of power in the White House.

Criticism of a sitting President—indeed, criticism of the personal actions of *any* politician—was then largely unknown and highly condemned among the members of the Washington press corps. Today, in mid-1995, to be sure, no action by a President—or even a candidate for President, or even any sitting elected official—will be taken at face value by the Washington press corps. If a President or a candidate was, for example, to propose a balanced budget by a given year, or to propose or oppose a cut in veterans' benefits or old-age pensions or a vigorous foreign policy in Africa—it would be analyzed in terms of its impact on the vote of a particular segment of the electorate. Thus, "in a bid for the valued senior citizens' vote . . ." a President might seek an extension of the cost-of-living allowance in Social Security, but the action would never be evaluated in terms of its impact on the lives of the elderly or the bankrolls of the taxpayers. Foreign policy with respect to Africa or the Caribbean is evaluated in terms of the reaction of the Congressional Black Caucus, and even "old" and "new" Republicans are judged, not on the basis of their moderate or conservative views on issues, but whether they reflect an electorate oriented toward Wall Street or Main Street.

But in Nixon's time, exactly the reverse was true. Indeed, historians may very well trace a shift in America media attitudes toward holders of political office—from unquestioning to totally skeptical—to the time and actions of the Nixon Administration, specifically its corruption with respect to Watergate and its deceit with respect to Vietnam.

In Nixon's prime operative years—from 1946 to 1974—the Washington press rolled over or sat up, depending on the urging of a President and his minions. So Richard Nixon understood that the "bold" moves of a President elected as a conservative Republican, to open up relations with what we then called "Red China," to espouse and secure the passage of a widespread program of affirmative action in the field of race relations, or to propose a revised welfare program that embodied the most liberal ideas of family support, would "play well" with the national press corps, and to hell with the ideology. Thus, the fierce and unscrupulous "anti-Communist" Nixon of the 1940s (and the landmark negative campaign against Helen Gahagan Douglas in 1950) gave way to Nixon the moderate Eisenhower (Vice President) in the 1950s to Nixon the surprising liberal in domestic policy (under the tutelage of Daniel Patrick Moynihan) in the 1960s. In that climate of acceptance of Presidents at face value, it could seriously be debated whether there was indeed, after Nixon's reemergence with the election of 1968 from the defeats of 1960 and 1962, a "new Nixon." In fact, the "new" moderate Nixon was no different from the "old" right-wing Nixon, but the times had changed and the manipulative Nixon, who had been there all along, found new buttons to push and new gushes of response from the press corps in Washington, who increasingly set the national agenda and rewarded those on whom it bestowed the mantle of statesmanship.

This lasted almost through the Watergate scandal. In the campaign of

1972 and through the first six months of Nixon's second term, the national press was extremely reluctant to accept the evidence that *Washington Post* reporters Bob Woodward and Carl Bernstein had been turning up almost daily for a year. It was hard enough for a Washington press corps accustomed to immediate endorsement of Presidents to accept the argument that *this President* was sitting at the heart of a vast criminal conspiracy to withhold evidence, obstruct justice, suborn perjury, postdate and even forge documents, and generally act in contravention—or worse, deliberate flouting—of the Constitution. It was even more difficult to credit this story when the charges were largely coming from the man who was opposing Nixon for the Presidency, and still more difficult for all but one newspaper in the country to begin a news story with the words, "The *Washington Post* revealed today . . ."

Nixon was a superb politician and a masterful analyst and manipulator of the media, but hubris brought him down, and with him vanished for future Presidents all but a trace of that trust and confidence that may prove to be the indispensable commodity in American politics. Today, the oil seems to have leaked out of the political machine, as though metal were rubbing against metal at every junction and joint, and the mechanic who caused this damage turns out to be Richard Nixon. But the machine really hummed there for a while.

Richard Nixon: Man and Monument

STANLEY I. KUTLER

Ronald Reagan dispatched the living ex-Presidents, Richard Nixon, Gerald Ford, and Jimmy Carter, to represent the United States at Anwar Sadat's funeral. As they left, Sen. Robert Dole cracked, "There they go: See-No-Evil, Speak-No-Evil, and Evil." It was not difficult to figure out the order he had in mind. *Forrest Gump,* one of the most widely viewed movies of all time, evoked gales of laughter in its references to Nixon and Watergate. In Woody Allen's movie *Sleeper,* some 21st-century anthropologists view mysterious videotapes from the 1970s. They have no idea who the subject is until Allen's character points out it was a President Nixon, and added, "I know whenever he used to leave the White House, the Secret Service would count the silverware." Alas! Nixon has left us with the unforgettable image of "Tricky Dick," a somewhat comic figure.

Comic or not, Richard Nixon is fated to carry the additional, terrible burden of disgrace. Yet nothing is more certain than death, taxes, and historical revisionism. Undoubtedly, at some point in the future, historians will attempt to rescue Nixon from the Watergate morass; indeed, already some have attempted to characterize him variously as the designer of the Cold War victory, the statesman of peace, and yes, even as the greatest domestic President of the 20th century. But Watergate is his spot that will not out—10, 20, 100 years from now, he will be remembered as the first American President to resign because of his violation of his constitutional oath of office.

To control the past is to control the future, George Orwell once wrote. Few figures in contemporary American public life understood that better than Richard Nixon. He admittedly taped his Presidential conversations to provide future "protection" and "insurance" against any attempts by "people close to me" to "turn against me." When he told a relieved nation on August 8, 1974, that he would resign, he promptly added we would see more of him in the future.

Thus began Richard Nixon's final campaign—his campaign for the verdict of history. For nearly two decades, he was the foremost Revisionist Historian of his Presidency. He labored mightily, writing books, making carefully timed public appearances and statements, and providing well-staged dinners for journalists, particularly younger ones. His efforts peaked with the opening in July 1990 of the Richard Nixon "Library and Birthplace" in Yorba Linda, California.

According to law, the National Archives maintains custody and control of Presidential documents, a situation intolerable for Nixon. When the Supreme Court upheld the validity of the law, Justice John Paul Stevens referred to the former President as an "unreliable custodian" of his papers. Unlike all Presidents since Herbert Hoover, some of whom also built their libraries with private funds (contrary to Nixon's assertion that he was the only one to do so) and then turned them over to the administration of National Archives, Nixon had no intention of letting outsiders interfere with his control over the history of his presidency.

For the past half century, presidents have sought carefully to preserve historical memories in their own image and writ. We have numerous presidential museums, all clearly designed to celebrate the man. Inevitably, they exaggerate. But Richard Nixon, who always sought to celebrate his uniqueness and "firsts," gave us a museum unsurpassed for perverting history. It gives us a wartless Nixon. It is a shrine for the faithful and the unknowing.

Nixon planned and executed this museum to safeguard his historical standing. In one sense, it does. Nixon was largely incapable of accommodation, compromise, and conciliation in the political arena. He rarely understood that today's adversary might be tomorrow's ally. The running narrative on the museum's walls puts it well: "He was not by nature a 'compromiser' . . . but rather a leader who believed [in giving] people a stark choice." "Fight," "battle," "crises," "enemies" are favorite metaphors of Nixon's endless memoirs. The museum's exhibits and explanations faithfully reflect that spirit.

After paying the admission fee and admiring the plaque denoting prominent contributors and patrons (a story in itself), visitors are steered toward a movie theater to view a film, *Never Give Up: Richard Nixon in the Arena.* Technically, it is superb; predictably, it lacks subtlety and shading altogether. Nixon is depicted in his own image: the fighter, the battler, the man who engages in the arena, the man of comebacks. The film almost dodges the most important fact of Nixon's Presidency: He quit.

The exhibits center on the highlights of Nixon's public career. We see the young Navy war veteran who returned home to win his maiden political campaign in 1946. In the accompanying film, the narrator claims that Nixon "risked everything" to make the race. Some risk. Nixon then was unemployed and local businessmen bankrolled the campaign.

Nixon's two terms as a member of the House of Representatives are best remembered for his role on the House Committee on Un-American Activities, and particularly for the Alger Hiss-Whittaker Chambers confrontation. An exhibit at Yorba Linda contains a replica of the Woodstock typewriter that Hiss used to type purloined documents, a microphone, and a pumpkin (like the one Chambers used to hide microfilm). In familiar fashion the affair is interpreted as the event that made Nixon a hero to millions and earned him the enduring enmity of the "liberal establishment." Nothing is said here of well-documented accounts that question Nixon's commitment to pursuing the case and reveal how the reluctant Congressman had to be pressured by committee aides to continue.

The exhibit entitled "Re-shaping the Vice Presidency" not surprisingly omits Dwight Eisenhower's devastating remark that if given a week, he might think of something significant that Nixon did as Vice President. The exhibit opens with a videotape of the "Checkers" speech from the 1952 campaign, a talk that heralded the familiar Nixon technique of deflecting attack by smearing others. Hence the tag "Tricky Dick." Better yet, the tape plays Nixon's introduction of Pat, his good Irish wife, who wore Republican cloth coats and who was "born on St. Patrick's Day." She was not. A little lie perhaps, but a harbinger of bigger ones to come.

Following mention of Nixon's narrow defeat in 1960, with the usual dark hints that the Democrats had stolen the election in Illinois—never mind that a Nixon victory there would still not have ensured his victory—we come to an exhibit labeled the "Wilderness Years." Nixon loved to identify with "great men," apparently believing that such comparisons enhanced himself. The "Wilderness Years" recalls Winston Churchill's period of isolation and powerlessness before World War II. Churchill was then an outsider, largely removed from public attention. A more appropriate analogy could have been borrowed from Nixon's great friend Mao Zedong, who executed the "Long March" of retreat to establish a new base for conducting guerrilla forays and for eventually gaining power. Nixon was hardly in the wilderness at this time. He ran for governor of California, traveled the length of the land supporting Republican candidates, and shrewdly managed to keep strong ties to both camps in the bloody civil war that rent his party in those years. By 1968, Nixon was "the one"—the only survivor.

The rooms portraying the Presidential years offer a replica of the Lincoln Sitting Room, some mementoes portraying glimpses of family life, gifts from foreign leaders, and an exhibit designed to show that Nixon wrote his own speeches. In the real Nixon Archives in Washington, we find numerous Nixon memoranda instructing his staff to inform reporters that Nixon was the first President since Woodrow Wilson to write his own speeches—followed by memoranda to his speechwriters requesting particular speeches.

The Presidential exhibits contain relatively little on domestic policies, which Nixon frankly admitted bored him. But he shamelessly portrayed himself as a leader on environmental issues, taking credit for the Environmental Protection Act which, though passed at the outset of his Administration, had been wending its way through Congress for several years. Numerous memoranda in the National Archives by Nixon and his aides in the first term contemptuously dismissed the environmental issue. Ignored here, of course, is Nixon's veto of the Clean Water Act.

Foreign affairs, Nixon always claimed, was his forte. The museum offers us a lengthy view of the Vietnam War with a familiar thesis. Nixon inherited it, fought the enemy to a standstill, and steadfastly sought "peace with honor." After 20 years and conclusive evidence to the contrary, the museum insists that the Cambodian "incursion" in 1970 destroyed Communist "sanctuaries." The Paris Peace Accords of 1973 are highlighted here, but historically offer a dubious claim to "peace with honor"; in fact, these accords provided only a "decent interval" between our withdrawal of support for South Vietnam and the eventual takeover by the North. Who lost Vietnam? According to Nixon, it was Congress, of course—as if it were ours to lose in the first place.

A large room gives us a taste of the monumental with life-size statues of various world leaders. Like Nixon, presumably, we walk among giants. We see those who had significant contact with President Nixon: Mao, Golda Meir, Anwar Sadat, Leonid Brezhnev. But there is less here than meets the eye. Why include the towering figures from another generation, who had only marginal dealings with Nixon?

Nixon dealt with Konrad Adenauer only as Eisenhower's messenger boy in the 1950s. Is Charles de Gaulle included because he supposedly called Nixon a "serious man"? Churchill because he, too, spent time in political purgatory? Churchill left office late in 1954, when Nixon had been Vice President for only a year, a year noted for Churchill's declining powers and influence. Nikita Khrushchev is depicted, probably because of the famous "kitchen debate" in Moscow in 1959. Nixon publicist William Safire in 1959 persuaded his fellow media flacks that Nixon calmly demolished his adversary. But Milton Eisenhower offered quite a different report to his brother (the President), noting Nixon's nervousness, his concessions to Khrushchev, and his excessive drinking.

And why include Yoshida Shigeru (standing alone, unlike the others who are grouped), the great postwar Japanese Prime Minister who led his nation on the road to recovery and respectability? This borders on the absurd. Dean Acheson, Douglas MacArthur, and John Foster Dulles were Yoshida's peers and fellow players in diplomatic activities, not Richard Nixon. Yoshida, too, left office during Nixon's first full year as Vice President, after having met Nixon during a largely ceremonial visit. That visit was notable for two things: Nixon denounced the antiwar clause of the Japanese Constitution and offered support for Yoshida's bitterest party enemies, including former war criminals.

Hard on the heels of all this celebration comes Nixon's attempt to whitewash the most fateful and symbolic episode of his Presidency—Watergate. Truly, it is his nemesis, but in his museum exhibits he was as determined as ever to drive a stake through its heart.

The film that museum visitors view at the start of the tour casually dismisses Watergate in about one minute. That tragic, even pathetic, scene of Nixon leaving the White House grounds on a helicopter is transformed into a triumphal exit. Hollywood never did it better. In the film, Nixon departs from the White House and then we hear that such great men as Gandhi and Lenin did their best writing in exile before returning as great leaders. Comeback, comeback, comeback—to what? To respectability, honor, esteem—and even the love of his grandchildren, who dutifully sing for him while garbed in identical gingham dresses. Republican Congressmen eagerly flock to meet the Great Man, years after his disgrace, and admiringly look up to him on the Capitol steps. But we do not hear the voice of the Iowa Republican Congressman who rejected any suggestion that Nixon campaign for him because "folks out there remember."

By the time we reach the Watergate room ("the second largest exhibit" in the museum, according to the publicity), one feels numbed by the great achievements of the 37th President. We are ripe for a large whiff of Nixon A, a gas for inducing historical amnesia.

The Watergate exhibit offers familiar refrains, ones that take us back to the workings of the White House spin doctors between 1972 and 1974. Incredibly, Press Secretary Ron Ziegler's immediate characterization of the break-in as a "third-rate burglary" offers the leitmotif. Never mind that Ziegler once had to declare his previous Watergate statements "inoperative." The narrative then follows the theses established in 1972 and reiterated by Nixon in every public utterance on Watergate. First, campaign manager John Mitchell was distracted by the drunkenness and mental instability of his wife, Martha, and as a result failed to control unruly subordinates. Second, Nixon's longtime media enemies relentlessly and unfairly imposed the Watergate story on the nation, denying the President an opportunity to extricate himself. Finally, his ancient blood enemies in Congress—Democrats and liberals—used the occasion to force Nixon from the White House and thereby reverse the "mandate of 1972." The Democratic assault—never mind that it was bipartisan—is depicted as nothing less than a coup, as if no constitutional procedures were followed. Never mind that Republican National Committee Chairman George Bush hand-delivered a letter to Nixon on August 5, urging that "resignation is best for this country, best for this President."

Obstruction of justice—the first impeachment count against Nixon and one eventually supported by nearly every Republican member of the Committee on the Judiciary—never really happened in the Nixon version of events. The "smoking gun" tape of June 23 included an exchange between Nixon and his chief aide, H. R. Haldeman, in which the President agreed to have the CIA throttle the FBI's investigation of the Watergate burglary, an investigation that eventually would lead to the involvement of Nixon's closest aides and friends. At one time, the museum offered the tape for public listening—in a carefully edited form, of course.

Tourists, particularly younger and foreign ones, listened to the tape, but when asked what it means, confessed confusion and ignorance. Understandably so. The exchange between Nixon and Haldeman is one between knowing conspirators, in which the conversation is disjointed and often unclear to the uninformed. Without some broader context, without supporting documents, their conversation has little meaning.

The explanatory material underlines the sheer audacity of it all. First, we are told that within days of the apparently meaningless conversation with Haldeman, Nixon reversed himself and ordered the Acting FBI Director actively to pursue the case. We also learn that eventually CIA Director Richard Helms heroically withdrew his cooperation—but no mention is made of Nixon's firing of Helms in November 1972 for just such defiance.

Thus Nixon had it both ways: He "openly" presented the most important evidence against him, but then concluded that these few moments of conversation mark the only evidence of his obstruction of justice. The long rejoinder is that other taped conversations demonstrate his deep, active complicity in the cover-up, including his failure to object to the payment of "hush money" to the burglars. The short one is that it is like being a little bit pregnant. The best answer, finally, is that the Grand Jury included Richard Nixon as an unindicted co-conspirator—another "first" in the history of the Presidency.

Nixon's greatest regret about the tapes, it seems, is that he offered transcripts with "expletive deleted." His words would earn him a PG-13 Hollywood film rating, he insisted. (A few years ago, however, he insisted that the greatest lesson of Watergate was "to burn all the tapes.") Perhaps the museum ought to give the public his March 22 conversation. "I don't give a shit what happens," Nixon defiantly told his aides. "I want you all to stonewall it, let them plead the Fifth Amendment, cover-up or anything else, if it'll save the plan." Imagine! Nixon believed that a mere four-letter *word* is the obscenity.

Most striking is the failure to mention Gerald Ford's pardon of Nixon in September 1974. Nixon accepted that pardon, noting Watergate was "the burden I shall bear for every day." By our legal standards, Nixon thus acknowledged his guilt. The pardon that Ford delivered in the name of the American people also conveyed "forgiveness," a notion that Nixon's publicists eagerly claimed he eventually earned. But they wanted us also to forget.

In classic Uriah Heep fashion, Nixon always portrayed himself as the victim of some imagined liberal establishment, of professional Nixon haters "on the left." "History will treat me fairly," he said. "Historians probably won't[,] because most historians are on the left." Nixon might have been reminded that "leftist historians" led the effort to upgrade Herbert Hoover's reputation.

Nixon's museum perpetuates his patterns of lies and subsequent cover-ups. "[L]et us begin by committing ourselves to the truth, to see it like it is and tell it like it is, to find the truth, to speak the truth and to live the truth. That's what we will do," Richard Nixon told fellow Republicans when they nominated him for the Presidency in 1968. But lies engulfed him, estranged him from his natural political allies, and eventually snapped the fragile bond of trust between leaders and led that binds government and the people. Nixon's lies brought him to the dock and cost him his presidency. "I have impeached myself," Nixon confessed in 1977—a rare moment, indeed.

How shall we remember Richard Nixon? Perhaps it is best to remember what leading conservatives thought of his Presidency. The absence of truth "was the crux of Nixon's failure," Barry Goldwater once remarked, noting that Nixon had lied to his friends, his political supporters, the nation, the world, and even his daughters. Columnist and longtime Nixon admirer James Kilpatrick despairingly wrote in 1974, "My President is a liar. I wish he were a crook instead." Nixon's lies and deceit eventually corroded his political support in the nation and resulted in his resignation. His lies are the heart of his history. Fittingly, Nixon enshrined that legacy in his own memorial.

Richard Nixon: The Loner

John Sears

It may well take another 100 years before historians can properly evaluate Richard Nixon's contribution to, or responsibility for, the world that will now unfold in the post–Cold War era. For Nixon, more than any modern political leader, the passage of time is necessary to separate his actions from what we knew of him as a person, and therefore come to some reckoning of his worth.

To say he was an extremely complicated person is an understatement. He had interviewed me when I applied for a job at his law firm in New York, and although he had run for President, spent considerable time in the presence of the world leaders of the day, and served for eight years as Vice President, I couldn't help but notice that *he* was the one who was nervous. Later, after I had joined his law firm, he asked me to work for him. I have never known why, and I certainly don't remember anything I did that might have impressed him, so it remains a mystery to me.

It was an amazing experience to work for him. One of his favorite ploys was to launch into some ill-reasoned diatribe about a person or policy, at the end of which he would lean forward and loudly say, "Don't you think?" The listener was simply being tested on whether he had the guts to disagree, but I was impressed over the years that the vast majority of the better people simply agreed.

You couldn't give him advice in front of anyone; it was too embarrassing. In my particular case (I was over 25 years younger than he), giving him advice in private usually led to a dressing down, but I knew he was simply "keeping me in my place." When I got this treatment, I actually felt good, since it meant he would do as I suggested. But he treated everyone differently, so I don't know that anybody else had the same experience.

Once in the White House, when I had been called to his office, he abruptly turned to Haldeman and asked him if arrangements had been made for him to attend a baseball game. "Yes," Haldeman quickly replied, "next Thursday, the Senators and the Red Sox." "No, no, no, Bob," Nixon said, "It's the people listening on the radio we're after. We'll never carry Massachusetts; wait until the Angels or the White Sox are in town."

I remember him saying to me in the mid-1960s that the Republican Party—which was of interest to pundits at that time only in terms of whether the Party would survive—wasn't describable as liberal or conservative.

"There are two groups of people in the Republican Party," he said. "One group can't do anything for anyone else because it would violate their principles; the other will do anything for anyone as long as they don't have to *see* any of them. I find both attitudes ridiculous."

I never bothered asking Nixon why he stayed in a Party, the two wings of which he thought were equally ridiculous. It would have been a foolish question, since the Democrats were the Party of the elites, the "experts," the intelligentsia, who could tell you in a moment what was best for the poor, even though the people making this determination weren't poor, could claim the Soviets were rational people, even though experience taught they were not, and promised that government could solve all problems if people would simply obey those who were smarter than they.

Nixon was the supreme loner in a country of loners. We don't think of ourselves in that way, but how else could you describe a country whose people came to America to get *away* from the dominant cultures of the world, distrust government and put their trust in individual freedom, and uniformly bring up their children to believe they have to "make it on their own"? The American family has always been much more of a launching pad than a sanctuary of peace and unquestioned support. Especially among the poor, whose means of supplying security are severely limited, there has always been a fragility about the American family that does not exist in other cultures.

Richard Nixon grew up in such a household. People who knew his father described him as "mean"; his mother was "strong," and a paragon of virtue in Nixon's eyes, but I never heard anyone who knew her speak of her as kind. Sickness, death, and poverty were the things Nixon learned about as a child. There was no happiness.

Nixon's mother taught him he could escape. One can almost hear her telling him, "keep your head down," "work hard," "don't waste time," "don't let your emotions get the best of you," advice hundreds of millions of Americans have heard from loving parents who wanted their children to succeed.

Loners don't trust elites or experts, and they certainly don't trust them to make decisions for them. By the late 1960s, America had witnessed two revolts of loners: one from the right wing in 1964 that challenged the ability of government to restrict individual freedom for the common good, and another from the left that challenged the authority of the experts to wage war in Vietnam for the "national interest," an authority which is basic to the legitimacy of government. And there was Nixon, alone in the political middle, where there were few votes, feeling that neither challenge was completely justified.

When you are poor, and you go to college, and on to law school, you necessarily bump up against people for whom school, and the need to do well at it, doesn't have the same all-or-nothing consequences they do for you. They are more self-assured, less dogged, and seem to be able to roll with the punches much better than you can. Most of them don't do as well in school, but they get the same degree, and usually start out in life ahead of you because their fathers know somebody, or their uncle gives them a job, or they simply seem more at ease when they have a job interview.

They make you feel self-conscious, remind you of all the things you never had, and you can easily feel there is something corrupt about a system that promises success if you *do* better than the rest but leaves you without as good a job when you beat them. You resent these people, especially if you've been brought up to believe that hard work and application of your God-given talents constitute the only moral route to success. And this is especially true when you are a little clumsy, not very good looking, and inept in social settings.

But even resentment is a feeling, and Nixon was brought up to ignore his feelings. The trouble was, he couldn't do it. So what was necessary was an elaborate scheme. Nixon had to create a person so unlike the person he really was that no one would ever suspect that underneath it all was a very sensitive, vulnerable human being.

It was by "toughness" that Nixon would lick his lack of style, his insecurities; he would show them he could beat them at their own game just by being "tougher." In the land of the "tough," kindness often looks like weakness, honesty often looks stupid, and to trust anyone else is an extreme foolishness.

The Cold War, which people will now soon forget, pitted the United States against a foe that believed in exactly the same kind of "toughness." To the doctrinaire Communist, kindness, honesty, and trust were not virtues but inventions of capitalistic society aimed at keeping the worker in permanent enslavement. Utility, geared toward the advancement of the state, was the only criterion; there was no such thing as objective right and wrong.

No two countries, with the power over the destiny of the entire world, had ever faced each other so starkly as did the United States and the Soviet

Union. It was a miracle that two such powers, so devoid of experience in world affairs, so paranoid about each other, so divergent in political thought as to what was best for the world, could face each other down for 45 years without destroying it.

Richard Nixon's public life encompassed all of the Cold War. First elected to Congress in 1946, by his death in 1994 he had lived to see the Soviet Union dismembered and reduced in power. He is the only elective politician whose influence and opinions on the conduct of the Cold War were consistently present during this entire period.

He seemed to like the Communist leaders he dealt with. I can remember his speaking fondly of Khrushchev on many occasions, and there seemed no doubt that he and Brezhnev achieved a personal relationship superior to that of any previous American President and Soviet leader at that time. Why was he perhaps more comfortable with the enemy than he was at home? Probably because they were loners too, uncomfortable with the sophisticated circles of the world that had little use for crude, hard-drinking Soviets or poor-boy American Presidents.

He developed a strong attachment for the Chinese leaders, but here again, these were men who fought the Japanese in the 1930s, made the "Long March" with Mao, overthrew the Chiang Kai-shek government, and refused to become the vassals of a Communist world run from Moscow. Loners as much as any group of Chinese could be. He expressed admiration for Marshal Tito, ruling a divided country successfully while gaining significant independence from the Soviet Union and economic concessions from the West. Tito was obviously a man who played a lonely game.

As Watergate unfolded, the sentiment abroad was one of astonishment at the prospect that the United States might seriously consider impeaching a man who was in the process of easing the tensions between the world's two major combatants. But they didn't understand America; in America, we cannot excuse illegal conduct on the basis that others did it and got away with it; we cannot fail to punish if the government abuses its power. We are a land of loners and our only protection is the law. Not even a President could violate the rights of an individual, or else winning the Cold War meant nothing.

And so Nixon was yanked unceremoniously from the pinnacle of power to appease the system of laws that safeguards our freedom. I cannot argue with this result, but looking back on it, his ouster failed to renew our confidence in the system and the media has never recovered any balance of optimism to counter its all-pervading pessimism. Ever more critical eyes shine upon our leaders, and the country drifts, not knowing whom to trust or what to do next.

Did I want him to escape at the time? Yes. Did I think he would? No. Once he became the major subject of the investigation, I knew he could never admit anything, never beg for mercy, never try to explain what really happened—he had to be *tough*.

We respect—even admire—toughness in America, and so, the only man in American history who was forced to resign the Presidency had recovered much of his influence by the time he died. The Cold War was not over, so succeeding Presidents, the press, and the general public eagerly sought out our greatest Cold Warrior's views.

I don't pretend to know what forces combine to bring the right man forward during critical times, I only know it has happened before. Only Lincoln had the patience to see the country through the Civil War, only Roosevelt had the arrogance to confront the Depression and lead the country to victory in World War II. Only Nixon had the toughness to move the Cold War from permanent stalemate toward victory for our side. None of them seem to have had happy personal lives, all were determined in their pursuit of power, each paid a heavy penalty in the way he left the Presidency.

But we assume we would have liked the other two and we find it difficult to like Nixon. I have been asked many times over the years whether I liked him, and after I thought about it, I realized it wasn't a proper question. I sometimes admired his independence, respected his mind, applauded what he was trying to do, marvelled at his work ethic—but *liked* him? I *wanted* to like him, but he wouldn't permit it.

You see, if you let people *like* you, you'll like them back and then your feelings will start governing your life and you won't see things as they are and you'll get "soft" and you won't get to be President and you can't deal with the Soviets. Or, at least that's sort of how Nixon thought about it.

Nixon—the poor boy with no natural ability for politics, no social presence, no background in foreign policy, no connections, no nothing—toughened up, got where he wanted to go, and changed the world. It's an *American* story.

For those who wonder whether the balance sheet on Nixon doesn't leave the country in the negative, I would submit that if the world survives for a million years, perhaps its finest hour may be that in the last half of the 20th century, when the power to blow up the world rested in the hands of a few men in two very unsophisticated and suspicious countries, we didn't do it, and one American, Richard Nixon, moved the Cold War away from permanent confrontation toward victory. How can any wrong that he did compare with that?

But perhaps the better question is whether it was worth it for Richard Nixon—in terms of the sacrifices, the punishments, the shame, the insecurity, the lies, the loneliness. I doubt it. But we don't ask that question here, in the land of the individual. It's none of our business.

The Year of the Beast

CHRISTOPHER WILKINSON

Imagine spending a year with Richard Nixon. At close quarters, hunkering down with the Old Trickster. Looking into his soul. Fingering his black heart. Sharing his dreams, his fears, his dark, dark secrets.

At first it seemed impossible to fix him: Nixon is nothing if not slippery. Just when we thought we were at the center, he mutated into something else. Equally enigmatic. Equally venal.

Equally fascinating.

So we read and talked. And read and talked. And read. And talked. We visited the Nixon Library in Yorba Linda, California. American strip malls, American golf courses, American cheese.

Nixon country.

The library is a kind of Nixon theme park. There is an exact replica of the Lincoln Sitting Room—during the last days of Watergate, Nixon spent his free time there, ripped on Scotch and antidepressants, listening to "Victory at Sea" at top volume. There is a room with life-size statues of the world leaders Nixon stood toe-to-toe with. You can belly up to Mao and Chou, Nikita and Leonid, Winston and Golda. If felonies are your game, you can listen to Nixon commit one in a carefully selected excerpt from the "smoking gun" tape.

Why, the damn "Checkers" speech is on a continuous loop: Young Dick Nixon, upper lip sweating, pleading into the camera in a full-court grovel. And poor Pat, sitting behind him in the cardboard living room set, campaign smile plastered on, embarrassed beyond words, as he detailed the family finances. This towering monument to smarm and deception marks the first time Nixon did what he would do countless times as President: lie to us on television.

In the history of American liars, Richard Nixon is Babe-frigging-Ruth. He told white lies and he told whoppers. He lied for power, to incinerate his enemies. He lied to save his skin and he lied when he didn't have to. He was at his most imaginative and devious when he was lying about having ever lied in the first place. He was the master of massive denial, spewing out streams of homilies, wrapping himself in truth, justice, and the American way. And millions believed him.

Nixon lied to destroy his political opponents. From his first congressional campaign against the long-winded liberal Jerry Voorhis, to his last run at the Big Derby against the long-winded liberal George McGovern, his rivals underestimated him. Being in a campaign with Richard Nixon had all the niceties of a knife fight in a back alley. With his catch phrases and cheap shots, he pioneered techniques that are now business as usual in American politics: Fuck the issues; win baby, just win.

Nixon turned lying into an art form. Professionally. And personally: During Watergate, he let Julie make 150 speeches defending him when he knew he was guilty. *His own daughter.*

Oh, I could go on.

But that would be wrong.

The more we got to know Nixon, the more it struck us how *odd* he was. He was a man who referred to himself in the third person and called his wife "Buddy." He was physically awkward, socially graceless, and sexually repressed. Other than Bebe Rebozo, he had no real friends. When he needed to relax, he would just sit silently with Rebozo. For hours. Bob Haldeman was with him for nearly twenty years and *never shook his hand.*

This was a strange man, an extremely strange and mysterious man.

I cannot remember the precise moment when we started to empathize with Nixon. To begin to understand the tragedy of his life. To appreciate the true dimensions of his character.

Nixon came from nothing—the wrong schools, the wrong clothes, the wrong parents—and, by dint of hard work and self-sacrifice, rose to the heights. In many ways he is the American Dream incarnate, the self-made man who tortured himself to be a Somebody. And he never gave up. He came off the canvas again and again, rehabilitating himself, reinventing himself. Admittedly, the notion of Nixon the Indestructible is often trotted out to evoke sympathy for him.

But it's true.

There are other poignant and peculiar details that reached us, that slowly eroded our contempt. The emotionally distant mother who rarely touched him. The brutish father who directed fits of blind rage at him. The lonely, clumsy boy who was sure that no matter what he did, he would never be good enough.

And the dead brothers. First his beloved little Arthur. Then Harold, outgoing, attractive, a boy Richard idolized. A boy whose lingering death allowed the family to afford Richard's tuition to law school.

The guilt.

When Nixon fell in love with Pat, he drove her on dates with other boys to prove himself to her. He wore her down with a barrage of flowers and letters. He would do whatever it took to win her and he never let up until she was his.

Classic Nixon.

The only clean campaign he ever ran was 1960. Kennedy (like Harold) was everything Nixon was not—handsome, charming, articulate, witty. Nixon could have used any number of smear tactics against him: the religion, the Mob connections, the women. But he didn't. He respected Jack Kennedy more than any opponent he had ever faced. So, for the only time in his political life, Nixon played it straight.

And Kennedy stole the election from him.

The fact that he didn't completely come apart during the crushing pressure of the final days of Watergate is a testament to his bullheaded resolve. To his perverse brand of courage. Everyone was against him. The country wanted his head on a pike and he wouldn't give it to them. A lesser man might have run screaming and drooling down Pennsylvania Avenue. Or had a stroke. Or committed suicide. But not Nixon. He wouldn't give them the satisfaction.

As President, he did more to desegregate the schools than any of his predecessors. He created the first and most effective Environmental Protection Agency. He has few (if any) Presidential peers in foreign policy: the spectacular opening of China, achieving détente with the Russians. Accomplishments that Nixon, the quintessential Commie hunter, was uniquely suited for. If a liberal Democratic President had tried it, he would have been crucified.

And Nixon would have brought the nails.

Nixon stretched our idea of what greatness is. He is a huge character who embraces the entire American landscape from its loftiest ambitions to its most malignant schemes. To understand Nixon is to understand what we have been. To understand Nixon's destiny is to understand what has happened to us. To understand Nixon's life is to understand the history of our times.

But how to find a way in? How to explain the morass of ironies and contradictions? How to dramatize rather than simply document?

It started with a discussion of Nixon's defeat in 1962.

After "The Last Press Conference" he was finished. He should have disappeared, but he didn't. In order for Nixon to have become President in 1968, Jack Kennedy had to die, Lyndon Johnson had to be forced into retirement, Dr. King had to die, Bobby Kennedy had to die, Hubert Humphrey had to be eviscerated in Chicago. It almost seemed that Nixon was being helped, helped by something dark, something sinister, something frightening. Some *thing*.

And we called it The Beast.

The Beast became a metaphor for the darkest organic forces in American Cold War politics: the anti-Communist crusade, secret intelligence, the defense industry, organized crime, big business. People and entities with apparently divergent agendas. But at certain moments in history, their interests converged.

And people died.

We conjured up a most chilling truth about The Beast. Not that it exists—but that *it does not know* it exists.

We imagined The Beast as a headless monster lurching through postwar American history, instinctively seeking figureheads to wear its public face, creating them when need be, destroying them when they no longer serve its purposes.

We had this primeval image of thousands of robed acolytes arranged according to rank, attending on the body of The Beast. Like a Breughel painting.

And in the highest place of all, Richard Nixon.

Why did Watergate overwhelm Nixon? Why was the most skillful political operator of the 20th century unable to mount a coherent defense to the continuing revelations? Was the truth behind Watergate that Nixon had created a kind of karmic critical mass of enemies that were finally able to destroy him under a common banner?

Perhaps.

Or had Nixon violated the cardinal rule of American politics: Don't piss off The Beast. Nixon's Administration was dismantled when he was well on his way to arguably becoming the most effective *centrist* President in American history: SALT I, China, the schools, the EPA.

Watergate was great television. It was served up in living color for public consumption: the idiot burglars, the fearless prosecutors, the crusty-but-benign senator, the incorruptible judge. And Tricky Dick, the arch villain, who, along with the nest of vipers who worked for him, tried to cover it all up.

But it is also possible that what Nixon was really covering up had nothing to do with Watergate itself. It had to do with the *implications* of Watergate. Implications that perhaps only Nixon truly understood.

It is reasonable to assume that whatever was on the 18 1/2-minute gap was substantively different from any of the other *blatantly incriminating* material Nixon exposed. It was the first "Monday morning" conversation he had about Watergate with Haldeman and it was erased. Probably by Nixon himself. *Deliberate, multiple erasures.*

It is reasonable to assume that whatever was on that tape was absolute dynamite.

The Beast also became a metaphor for the dark side of Nixon himself. The monster within that relentlessly drove him. To claw his way to the top. To lie. To cover up. The thing that protected him from *them:* the press, the liberals, the Ivy League eggheads and highbrows who condemned him and made him a figure of fun. Well, no one is laughing now.

The Beast within organized his fantasies and numbed his self-loathing. It guarded his feeble sense of self-respect and fueled his paranoia. Because deep inside, Nixon believed he was unworthy. Despicable. Dirty. And that is the hideous reality he was always covering up.

And perhaps that is the reason he didn't just burn the tapes. In some warped way he wanted us to see him. All of him. He wanted us to see the deceit, the trickery, the vile scheming.

And he wanted us to love him for it.

Very late in our Year of the Beast, we realized a banal truth: Richard Nixon was a man who simply did not have the self-confidence to lead a normal life.

Mission Impossible

Eugenio Martinez

We Cubans have never stopped fighting for the liberation of our country. I have personally carried out over 350 missions to Cuba for the CIA. Some of the people I infiltrated there were caught and tortured, and some of them talked.

My mother and father were not allowed to leave Cuba. It would have been easy for me to get them out. That was my specialty. But my bosses in the Company—the CIA—said I might get caught and tortured, and if I talked I might jeopardize other operations. So my mother and father died in Cuba. That is how orders go. I follow the orders.

I can't help seeing the whole Watergate affair as a repetition of the Bay of Pigs. The invasion was a fiasco for the United States and a tragedy for the Cubans. All of the agencies of the U.S. Government were involved, and they carried out their plans in so ill a manner that everyone landed in the hands of Castro—like a present.

Eduardo was a name that all of us who had participated in the Bay of Pigs knew well. He had been the maximum representative of the Kennedy Administration to our people in Miami. He occupied a special place in our hearts because of a letter he had written to his chief Cuban aide and my life-long friend, Bernard Barker. He had identified himself in his letter with the pain of the Cubans, and he blamed the Kennedy Administration for not supporting us on the beaches of the Bay of Pigs.

So when Barker told me that Eduardo was coming to town and that he wanted to meet me, that was like a hope for me. He had chosen to meet us at the Bay of Pigs monument, where we commemorate our dead, on April 16, 1971, the tenth anniversary of the invasion. I always go to the monument on that day, but that year I had another purpose—to meet Eduardo, the famous Eduardo, in person.

He was different from all the other men I had met in the Company. He looked more like a politician than a man who was fighting for freedom. He was there with his pipe, relaxing in front of the memorial, and Barker introduced me. I then learned his name for the first time—Howard Hunt.

There was something strange about this man. His tan, you know, is not the tan of a man who is in the sun. His motions are very meticulous—the way he smokes his pipe, the way he looks at you and smiles. He knows how to make you happy—he's very warm, but at the same time you can sense that he does not go all into you or you all into him.

We went to a Cuban restaurant for lunch and right away Eduardo told us that he had retired from the CIA in 1971 and was working for Mullen and Company.[1] I knew just what he was saying. I was also officially retired from the Company. Two years before, my case officer had gathered all the men in my Company unit and handed us envelopes with retirement announcements inside. But mine was a blank paper. Afterward he explained to me that I would stop making my boat missions to Cuba but I would continue my work with the Company. He said I should become an American citizen and soon I would be given a new assignment. Not even Barker knew that I was still working with the Company. But I was quite certain that day that Eduardo knew.

We talked about the liberation of Cuba, and he assured us that "the whole thing is not over." Then he started inquiring: "What is Manolo doing?" Manolo was the leader of the Bay of Pigs operation. "What is Roman doing?" Roman was the other leader. He said he wanted to meet with the old people. It was a good sign. We did not think he had come to Miami for nothing.

Generally I talk to my CIA case officer at least twice a week and maybe on the phone another two times. I told him right away that Eduardo was back in town, and that I had had lunch with him. Any time anyone from the CIA was in town my CO always asked me what he was doing. But he didn't ask me anything about Eduardo, which was strange.

That was in April. In the middle of July, Eduardo wrote to Barker to tell him he was in the White House as a counselor to the President. He sent a number of memos to us on White House stationery, and that was very impressive, you know. So I went back to my CO and said to him, "Hey, Eduardo is still in contact with us, and now he is a counselor of the President."

A few days later my CO told me that the Company had no information on Eduardo except that he was not working in the White House. Well, imagine! I knew Eduardo was in the White House. What it meant to me was that Eduardo was above them and either they weren't supposed to know what he was doing or they didn't want me to talk about him anymore. Knowing how

---

[1]The Robert Mullen Co., a public-relations firm and reported CIA front in Washington, D.C.

these people act, I knew I had to be careful. So I said, well, let me keep my mouth shut.

Not long after this, Eduardo told Barker there was a job, a national security job dealing with a traitor of this country who had given papers to the Russian Embassy. He said they were forming a group with the CIA, the FBI, and all the agencies, and that it was to be directed from within the White House, with jurisdiction to operate where all the others did not fit. Barker said Eduardo needed two more individuals and he had thought of me. Would I like my name submitted for clearance? I said yes.

To me this was a great honor. I believed it was the result of my sacrifice for the previous ten years, for my work with the Company. In that time I had carried out hundreds of missions for the U.S. Government. All of them had been covert, and most were very dangerous. Three or four days later, Barker told me my name had been cleared and several weeks after that came the first assignment. "Get clothes for two or three days and be ready tomorrow," he said. "We're leaving for the operation."

Barker didn't tell me where we were going and I did not ask. I was an operative. I couldn't afford to be aware of any more sensitive information than was critical for the success of my missions. There would be times when I would take men wearing hoods to Cuba. They might have been my friends. But I did not want to know. Too many of my friends have been caught and tortured and forced to talk. In this kind of work you learn to lose your curiosity.

So it was not until I got to the airport in Miami that I discovered we were going to Los Angeles. There were three of us on the mission. The third man, Felipe de Diego, was a real-estate partner of ours. He is an old Company man and a Bay of Pigs veteran whom we knew we could trust.

In all my years in this country I had never been out of the Miami area before that day. I had always been on twenty-four-hour call. I kind of expected my CO to ask where I was going, but he simply said it was fine for me to take a few days off, that there wasn't much to do at the time. I sort of thought he did not want to know what I was doing.

We stayed at the Beverly Hills Hotel and met in Eduardo's room for our only briefing. As we walked in I noticed the equipment—devices to modify the voice, wigs and fake glasses, false identification. Eduardo told us all these things belonged to the Company. Barker recognized the name on Hunt's false identification—Edward J. Hamilton—as the same cover name Eduardo had used during the Bay of Pigs.

The briefing was not like anything I was used to in the Company. Ordinarily, before an operation, you have a briefing and then you train for the operation. You try to find a place that looks similar and you train in disguise and with the code you are going to use. You try out the plan many times so that later you have the elasticity to abort the operation if the conditions are not ideal.

Eduardo's briefing was not like this. There wasn't a written plan, not even any mention of what to do if something went wrong. There was just the man talking about the thing. We were to get into an office to take photographs of psychiatric records of a traitor. I was to be the photographer. The next day we went to Sears and bought some little hats and uniforms for Barker and Felipe. They were supposed to dress up as delivery men and deliver the photographic equipment inside the office. Later that night we would break in and complete the mission.

They looked kind of queerish when they put on the clothes, the Peter Lorre-type glasses, and the funny Dita Beard wigs. But that was not my responsibility, so I waited in the car while they went to the office of Dr. Fielding to deliver the package. Just before leaving Barker had whispered to me: "Hey, remember this name—Ellsberg." Eduardo had told him the name, and he told me because he was worried he would forget it. The name meant nothing to me.

Barker and Felipe were supposed to put the bag inside the office, unlatch the back door, and come out. After the cleaning lady left, we were to go back in. Now, it happened that we had to wait for hours and hours because no one had figured out when the cleaning woman would leave. Finally, I believe, a gentleman came in a car and picked her up.

So at last we went to open the door—and what happened? The door was locked. Barker went around to see if the other door was open, and after a long wait he still did not show up. We didn't know what to do. There had been another man in the briefing the night before in Eduardo's room who hadn't said anything. Later, I learned it was probably Gordon Liddy, but at the time I only knew him as George. Just at that moment, he came up to us and said, "Okay, you people go ahead and force one of the windows and go in."

Eduardo had given us a small crowbar and a glass cutter. I tried to cut the glass, but it wouldn't cut. It was bad, bad. It would not cut anything! So then I taped the window and I hit it with this very small crowbar, and I put my hand in and unlocked the window.

According to the police, we were using gloves and didn't leave any fingerprints. But I'm afraid that I did because I didn't wear my gloves when I put the tape on the window—you know, sometimes it's hard to use gloves. I went all through the offices with my bare hands but I used my handkerchief to wipe off the prints.

Inside the doctor's office we covered the windows and took out the equipment. Really, it was a joke. They had given us a rope to bail out from the second floor if anyone surprised us; it was so small, it couldn't have supported any of us.

This was nothing new. It's what the Company did in the Bay of Pigs when they gave us old ships, old planes, old weapons. They explained that if you were caught in one of those operations with commercial weapons that you could buy anywhere, you could be said to be on your own. They teach you that they are going to disavow you. The Company teaches you to accept those things as the efficient way to work. And we were grateful. Otherwise we wouldn't have had any help at all. In this operation it seemed obvious—they didn't want it to be traced back to the White House. Eduardo told us that if we were caught, we should say we were addicts looking for drugs.

I had just set up the photographic equipment when we heard a noise. We were afraid. Then we heard Barker's familiar knock and we let him in. I took a Polaroid picture of the office before we started looking for the Ellsberg papers so we could put everything back just as it was before. But there was nothing of Ellsberg's there. There was nothing about psychiatry, no one file of sick people, only bills. It looked like an import-export office more than a psychiatrist's. The only thing with the name of Ellsberg in it was the doctor's telephone book. I took a photo of this so that we could bring something back. Before leaving I took some pills from Dr. Fielding's briefcase—vitamin C, I think—and spread them all over the floor to make it look like we were looking for drugs.

Eduardo was waiting for us outside. He was supposed to be keeping watch on Dr. Fielding so he could let us know if the doctor was returning to his office, but Eduardo had lost Dr. Fielding and he was nervous. A police car appeared as we drove away and it trailed behind us for three or four blocks. I thought to myself that the police car was protecting us. That is the feeling you have when you are doing operations for the government. You think that every step has been taken to protect you.

Back at the hotel, Barker, Felipe, and I felt very bad. It was our first opportunity, and we had failed; we hadn't found anything.

"Yes, I know, but they don't know it," Eduardo said, and he congratulated us all. He said, "Well done," and then he opened a bottle of champagne. And he told us, "This is a celebration. You deserve it."

I told Diego and Barker that this had to have been a training mission for a very important mission to come or else it was a cover operation. I thought to myself that maybe these people already had the papers of Ellsberg. Maybe Dr. Fielding had given them out and for ethical reasons he needed to be cov-

ered. It seemed that these people already had what we were looking for because no one invites you to have champagne and is happy when you fail.

The whole thing was strange, but Eduardo was happy so we were happy.
He thanked us and we left for the airport. We took the plane back to Miami
and we never talked about this thing until we were all together in the District of Columbia jail.

In Miami I again told my CO about Eduardo. I was certain then that the
Company knew about his activities. But once again my CO did not pursue
the subject.

Meanwhile, Hunt started to do more and more things that convinced us of
his important position in the White House. Once he called Barker and told
him the President was about to mine Haiphong Harbor. He asked us to prepare letters and a rally of support in advance. It was very impressive to us
when the announcement of the mining was made several days later.

I made a point of telling my CO at our next meeting that Hunt was involved in some operations and that he was in the White House, even if they
said he wasn't. After that the CIA chief of the Western Hemisphere asked me
for breakfast at Howard Johnson's on Biscayne Boulevard, and he said he
was interested in finding out about Howard Hunt's activities. He wanted me
to write a report. He said I should write it in my own hand, in Spanish, and
give it to my CO in a sealed envelope. Right away I went to see my CO. We
are very close, my CO and I, and he told me that his father had once given
him the advice that he should never put anything in writing that might do
him any harm in the future. So I just wrote a cover story for the whole thing.
I said that Hunt was in the Mullen Company and the White House and things
like that that weren't important. What I really thought was that Hunt was
checking to see if I could be trusted.

Little by little I watched Eduardo's operation grow. First Barker was
given $89,000 in checks from Mexican banks to cash for operational money.
And then Eduardo told Barker to recruit three more men, including a key
man. He signed up Frank Sturgis and Reinaldo Pico, and then Eduardo flew
down to talk to our friend Virgilio Gonzales, who is a locksmith, before recruiting him. Finally orders come for us to report to Washington. The six of
us arrived in Washington on May 22 and checked into the Manger Hay-
Adams Hotel in time for Eduardo's first briefing.

By that time Liddy, whom we had known as George from the Fielding
break-in, was taking a visible role in the planning. Eduardo had started calling him "Daddy," and the two men seemed almost inseparable. We met Mc-
Cord there for the first time. Eduardo said he was an old man from the CIA
who used to do electronic jobs for the CIA and the FBI. We did not know

his whole name. Eduardo just introduced him as Jimmy. He said we would be using walkie-talkies, and Jimmy was to be our electronics expert. There was also a boy there who had infiltrated the McGovern headquarters.

There was no mention of Watergate at that meeting. Eduardo told us he had information that Castro and other foreign governments were giving money to McGovern, and we were going to find the evidence. The boy was going to help them break into the McGovern headquarters, but I did not pay much attention. They didn't need me for that operation so I had some free time.

During the day I went off to see the different sights around Washington. I like those things—particularly the John Paul Jones monument and the Naval Academy in Annapolis. Remember that, prior to this, all of my operations for the United States were maritime.

After three days Eduardo aborted the McGovern operation. I think it was because the boy got scared. Anyway, Eduardo told us all to move into the Watergate Hotel to prepare for another operation. We brought briefcases and things like that to look elegant. We registered as members of the Ameritus Corporation of Miami, and then we met in Eduardo's room.

Believe me, it was an improvised briefing. Eduardo told us he had information that Castro money was coming into the Democratic headquarters, not McGovern's, and that we were going to try to find the evidence there. Throughout the briefing, McCord, Liddy, and Eduardo would keep interrupting each other, saying, "Well, this way is better," or, "That should be the other way around."

It was not a very definite plan that was finally agreed upon, but you are not too critical of things when you think that people over you know what they are doing, when they are really professionals like Howard Hunt. The plan called for us to hold a banquet for the Ameritus Corporation in a private dining room of the Watergate. The room had access to the elevators that ran up to the sixth floor where the Democratic National Committee Headquarters are located. Once the meal was underway, Eduardo was to show films and we were to take the elevator to the sixth floor and complete the mission. Gonzales, our key man, was to open the door; Sturgis, Pico, and Felipe were to be lookouts; Barker was to get the documents; I was to take the photographs and Jimmy (McCord) was to do his job.

We were all ready to go, but the people in the DNC worked late. Eduardo was drinking lots of milk. He has ulcers, so he was mixing his whiskey with the milk. We waited and waited. Finally, at 2:00 A.M., the night guards said we had to leave the banquet hall. So then there was a discussion. Eduardo said he would hide in the closet of the banquet room with Gonzales, the key man, while the guard let the rest of us out. As soon as the coast was clear, they would let us back in. But then they couldn't open the door.

It is difficult for me to tell you this story. I do not want it to become a laughing matter. More than thirty people are in jail already, and a lot of people are suffering. I spent more than fifteen months in jail, and you must understand that this is a tragedy. It is not funny. But you can imagine Eduardo, the head of the mission, in the closet. He did not sleep the whole night. It was really a disaster.

So, more briefings, and we decided to go the next night. This time the plan was to wait until all the lights had gone out on the sixth floor of the Watergate and then go in through the front door.

They gave us briefcases, and I remember that there was a Customs tag hanging on Eduardo's case, so I pulled it off for him. He got real mad. He said that every time he did something he did it with a purpose. I could not see the purpose, but then I don't know. Maybe the tag had an open sesame command to let us in the doors.

Anyway, all seven of us in McCord's army walked up to the Watergate complex at midnight. McCord rang the bell, and a policeman came and let us in. We all signed the book, and McCord told the man we were going to the Federal Reserve office on the eighth floor. It all seemed funny to me. Eight men going to work at midnight. Imagine, we sat there talking to the police. Then we went up to the eighth floor, walked down to the sixth—and do you believe it, we couldn't open that door, and we had to cancel the operation.

I don't believe it has ever been told before, but all the time while we were working on the door, McCord would be going to the eighth floor. It is still a mystery to me what he was doing there. At 2:00 A.M. I went up to tell him about our problems, and there I saw him talking to two guards. What happened? I thought. Have we been caught? No, he knew the guards. So I did not ask questions, but I thought maybe McCord was working there. It was the only thing that made sense. He was the one who led us to the place and it would not have made sense for us to have rooms at the Watergate and go on this operation if there was not someone there on the inside. Anyway, I joined the group, and pretty soon we picked up our briefcases and walked out the front door.

Eduardo was furious that Gonzales hadn't been able to open the door. Gonzales explained he didn't have the proper equipment, so Eduardo told him to fly back to Miami to get his other tools. Before he left the next day, Barker told Gonzales that he might have to pay for his own flight back to Miami. I really got mad and told Barker I resented the way they were treating Gonzales. I was a little hard with Barker. I said there wasn't adequate operational preparation. There was no floor plan of the building; no one knew the disposition of the elevators, how many guards there were, or even what time the guards checked the building. Gonzales did not know what kind of door he was supposed to open. There weren't even any contingency plans.

Barker came back to me with a message from Eduardo: "You are an operative. Your mission is to do what you are told and not to ask questions."

Gonzales got back from Miami that night with his whole shop. I've never seen so many tools to open a door. No door could hold him. This time everything worked. Gonzales and Sturgis picked the lock in the garage exit door; once inside, they opened the other doors and called over the walkie-talkie: "The horse is in the house." Then they let us in. I took a lot of photographs—maybe thirty or forty—showing lists of contributors that Barker had handed me. McCord worked on the phones. He said his first two taps might be discovered, but not the third.

With our mission accomplished, we went back to the hotel. It was about 5:00 A.M. Eduardo said he was happy. But this time there was no champagne. He said we should leave for Miami right away. I gave him the film I had taken and we left for the airport.

There were things that bothered me about the operation, but I was satisfied. It is rare that you are able to check the effect of your work in the intelligence community. You know, they don't tell you if something you did is very significant. But we had taken a lot of pictures of contributions, and I had hopes that we might have done something valuable. We all had heard rumors in Miami that McGovern was receiving money from Castro. That was nothing new. We believe that today.

A couple of weeks later I was talking with Felipe de Diego and Frank Sturgis at our real-estate office when Barker burst in like a cyclone. Eduardo had been in town, and he had given Barker some film to have developed and enlarged. Barker did not know what the film was, and he had taken it to a regular camera shop. And then Eduardo had told him it was the film from the Watergate operation. Barker was really excited. He needed us to come with him to get it back. So we went to Rich's Camera Shop, and Barker told Frank and me to cover each door to the shop in case the police came while he was inside. I do not think he handled the situation very well. There were all these people and he was so excited. He ended up tipping the man at the store $20 or $30. The man had just enlarged the pictures showing the documents being held by a gloved hand and he said to Barker: "It's real cloak-and-dagger stuff, isn't it?" Later that man went to the FBI and told them about the film.

My reaction was that it was crazy to have those important pictures developed in a common place in Miami. But Barker was my close friend, and

I could not tell him how wrong the whole thing was. The thing about Barker was that he trusted Eduardo totally. He had been his principal assistant at the Bay of Pigs, Eduardo's liaison with the Cubans, and he still believed tremendously in the man. He was just blind about him.

It was too much for me. I talked it over with Felipe and Frank, and decided I could not continue. I was about to write a letter when Barker told me Eduardo wanted us to get ready for another operation in Washington.

When you are in this kind of business, and you are in the middle of something, it is not easy to stop. Everyone will feel that you might jeopardize the operation. "What to do with this guy now?" I knew it would create a big problem so I agreed to go on this last mission.

Eduardo told us to buy surgical gloves and forty rolls of film with thirty-six exposures on a roll. Imagine, that meant 1,440 photographs. I told Barker it would be impossible to take all those pictures. But it did seem to mean that what we got before encouraged Eduardo to go back for more.

We flew into National Airport about noon on June 16, and Barker and I went off to rent a car. In the airport lobby, Frank Sturgis ran into Jack Anderson, whom he had known since the Bay of Pigs, when Anderson wrote a column about him as a soldier-adventurer. Frank introduced Gonzales to Anderson, and he gave him some kind of excuse about why he was in town.

On our way to the Watergate, we made some jokes about the car Barker had rented. It gave me a premonition of a hearse. The mission was not one I was looking forward to.

Eduardo was waiting for us at the Watergate. This time he had two operations planned, and we were supposed to perform them both that night. There was no time for anything, it was all rush.

We went to eat at about five o'clock. Barker ate a lot and when he came back he felt really bad. I was not feeling too good myself. I had just gotten my divorce that day and had gone from the court to the airport and from the airport to the Watergate. The environment in each one of us was different, but the whole thing was bad; there was tension in those people.

Liddy was already in the room when Eduardo came in to give the briefing. Eduardo was wearing loafers and black pants with white stripes. They were very shiny. Liddy was not happy with those pants. He criticized them in front of us and he told Eduardo to go change them.

So Eduardo went and changed his pants. The briefing he gave when he came back was very simple. He said we were going to photograph more documents at the Democratic headquarters and then move on to another mission at the McGovern headquarters after that. McCord was critical of the second operation. He said he didn't like the plan. It was very rare to hear

McCord talking because usually he didn't say anything and when he did talk he only whispered.

Before we left, Eduardo took all of our identification. He put it in a brief-case and left it in our room. He gave Sturgis his Edward J. Hamilton identification that the CIA had provided to him before, and he gave us each $200 in cash. He said we should use it as a bribe to get away if we were caught. Finally, he told us to keep the keys to our room, where he had left the identification. I don't know why. Even today, I don't know. Remember, I was told in advance not to ask about those things.

McCord went into the Watergate very early in the evening. He walked right through the front door of the office complex, signed the book, and, I'm sure, went to the eighth floor as he had before. Then he taped the doors from the eighth floor to the bottom floor and walked out through the exit door in the garage. It was still very early, and we were not going to go in until after every-one left the offices. We waited so long that Eduardo went out to check if the tapes were still there. He said they were but when we finally got ready to go in, Virgilio and Sturgis noticed that the tape was gone, and a sack of mail was at the door.

So we said, well, the tape has been discovered. We'll have to abort the operation. But McCord thought we should go anyway. He went upstairs and tried to convince Liddy and Eduardo that we should go ahead. Before mak-ing a decision, they went to the other room; I believe they made a phone call, and Eduardo told us to go ahead.

McCord did not come in with us. He said he had to go someplace. We never knew where he was going. Anyway, he was not with us, so when Vir-gilio picked the locks to let us in, we put tape on the doors for him and went upstairs. Five minutes later McCord came in, and I asked him right away: "Did you remove the tapes?" He said, "Yes, I did."

But he did not, because the tape was later found by the police. Once in-side, McCord told Barker to turn off his walkie-talkie. He said there was too much static. So we were there without communications. Soon we started hearing noises. People going up and down. McCord said it was only the peo-ple checking, like before, but then there was running and men shouting, "Come out with your hands up or we will shoot!" and things like that.

There was no way out. We were caught. The police were very rough with us, pushing us around, tying our arms, but Barker was able to turn on his walkie-talkie, and he asked where the police were from. And then he said, "Oh, you are the metropolitan policemen who catch us." So Barker was cool. He did a good job in advising Eduardo we were caught.

I thought right away it was a set-up or something like that because it was so easy the first time. We all had that feeling. They took our keys and found the identification in the briefcase Eduardo had left in our room.

McCord was the senior officer, and he took charge. He was talking loudly now. He told us not to say a thing. "Don't give your names. Nothing. I know people. Don't worry, someone will come and everything will be all right. This thing will be solved."

Nixon and Arms Control

PAUL H. NITZE

I had a uniquely long and close association with Richard Nixon that began back in the late 1940s, when Nixon was a freshman Congressman from California and I was Director of Policy Planning for the State Department in the Truman Administration, and ended when he was President. Nixon was one of some 40 Congressmen who had accompanied Christian Herter on a fact-finding mission to Europe to assess at firsthand the need of the Western European countries for a helping hand from the United States in the wake of World War II. The need was indeed desperate, both economically and politically. A close friend of mine, Philip Watts, served as the Executive Secretary of the Herter Commission.

When the Commission returned to Washington, Watts told me that most of the Congressmen were wholly ignorant in the field of foreign affairs and only vaguely interested in learning anything about the subject. He told me there was one exception, a Congressman named Richard Nixon who struck him as being smart, energetic, and interested in learning about the world. That was the first I had heard of Richard Nixon.

A couple of years later, Nixon, at this time planning to run against Helen Gahagan Douglas to be U.S. Senator from California, asked Phil, who had attached himself to Nixon as a personal adviser, to recommend someone to brief him on foreign affairs. Nixon wanted a better grasp of foreign affairs than he then had. Phil suggested that Nixon talk to me, and so arrangements were made for the three of us to have a series of Thursday night dinners together at his house at which I should be given an opportunity to go over the ins and outs and pros and cons of the various foreign policy issues.

At the time Nixon was best known for his role in the Alger Hiss investigation, and that experience had left a deep mark on him thereafter. It was a topic he enjoyed talking about—as I soon discovered firsthand. At our first dinner session, Nixon demonstrated a somewhat limited attention span. I began by talking about NATO and was about 20 minutes into my exposition when he found it necessary to bring up some recollection from his own career to bring the focus back on himself. He interrupted me and said, "Now that reminds me of an incident during the Hiss investigation . . ." Away he vent for the rest of the evening with a monologue on the Hiss trial. The same thing happened at our next dinner. That time I was describing the situation in the Middle East and again he interrupted and went off on another monologue on Hiss. I don't remember if we ever made it to a third dinner or not. He could be self-absorbed, but while he listened, he seemed to learn fast.

As I later remarked in my own memoirs,[1] what fascinated me about Nixon were the several opposing facets of his personality. To understand him, one had to appreciate the role that Eisenhower played in his life. To advance his career, Nixon had passed himself off as Eisenhower's protégé, though I seriously doubt Ike ever really thought of Nixon in those terms. What endeared Eisenhower to the American people was his apparent sincerity, which derived from his uncanny ability to believe in two mutually contradictory and inconsistent propositions at the same time. While he would declare nuclear war "unthinkable," in the next breath he would give his JCS detailed instructions on how they should go about fighting one. It was this "sincere" inconsistency that impressed Nixon with its effectiveness and, considering himself to be generally more intelligent than Eisenhower, he reasoned that if Ike could reconcile two mutually inconsistent propositions, he could do so with three or four. As a result, Nixon wound up never really being sure of what he believed, though to many he came across as sincerely believing what he said.

My relationship with Nixon was never particularly close. By the time he and I came to know each other, we were in opposite political parties. When he came into office as Eisenhower's Vice President, I was still Director of Policy Planning at State, but soon moved over to the Department of Defense, at the suggestion of Secretary of State John Foster Dulles who wanted a Republican helping him with policy.

After he had won his election to the Presidency in 1968, Nixon invited me to come to his office one morning at 9:30. I was still Deputy Secretary of Defense (this was during the transition period between Administrations) and as I recall it I presumed he wished to discuss three yachts the Navy maintained for the President's exclusive use, the expenses for which had been noted in the press. Nixon was on the telephone when I was ushered in, and he continued to accept one call after another while keeping a beady eye on me. It became evident to me that he wished to determine whether he could psychologically dominate me to a point where he could count on my total loyalty to him as a person, not just to him as President. I was not about to give him such loyalty and became angry that he should presume I could be persuaded to agree. The meeting ended by me rising to my feet and saying I had

[1]*From Hiroshima to Glasnost* (New York: Grove Weidenfeld, 1989).

significant matters to attend to. Nixon never held that sternness against me; to the contrary, he seemed to respect me for it.

I saw no personal reason why he would be interested in including me in his Administration, and there were political reasons why he might not. I was a Democrat and had served in every Democratic Administration since Franklin Roosevelt. In fact, I had served under John Kennedy as Secretary of the Navy and under Lyndon Johnson as Undersecretary of Defense. I was surprised in the summer of 1969 when his then Secretary of State William Rogers asked me if I was interested in serving as Ambassador to West Germany. While I was very much interested in the post, both this nomination and a subsequent proposal that I serve as Ambassador to Japan fell through due to a previous falling out on my part with Senator Bill Fullbright, who was head of the Foreign Relations Committee that handled the matter. Once the nominations fell through, I went back to my private life, and the Nixon Administration went on with trying to run the country. Among the things absorbing me in those days was arms control.

At the outset of his Presidency, I doubted Nixon's interest in negotiating an arms deal with the Soviet Union. Too much else was crowding his agenda including Vietnam, a weakening of our strategic military defenses vis-à-vis the Soviet Union, and economic problems. Arms control seemed to take a back seat to these other pressing problems. However, within a few months of taking office, Nixon found himself face to face with the arms control problem. The issue was not arms control in particular, but the status of our antiballistic missile (ABM) program, which was coming up for a vote in Congress.

The ABM program was meant to help protect American cities from nuclear attack by shooting down nuclear missiles while they were still in the air. While it was a simple idea, it was very complicated in practice. It required a great deal of sophisticated technology; we had been working on such a program since the late 1950s. Opponents of the program, mainly in the Senate, wanted to kill it. Whereas a few years earlier Congress had been a big supporter of the program, even voting unsolicited money for it, there was now a movement afoot to get rid of it. Some believed that pursuing the ABM program would escalate the arms race, ignoring the fact that the Soviets had long had a vigorous ABM program underway; others insisted we were wasting our time on a program which, in their estimation, would never work.

Nixon made it clear that he needed the ABM authorization bill to pass because he wanted to enter into negotiations with the Soviets on jointly limiting ABM defenses in the interests of stabilizing the strategic nuclear balance between the United States and the Soviet Union. However, he did not see how he could negotiate with any hope that the Soviets would make reasonable concessions if the Senate had killed the program. Judging from my own experience with the Russians, I shared Nixon's concern, and agreed that the United States would be in an exceedingly difficult position in the negotiations if the authorization bill failed to clear the Senate.

I felt strongly about the need to keep the ABM program alive, so I joined with my close friend and former boss, former Secretary of State Dean Acheson, and with Albert Wohlstetter, a brilliant physics professor from the University of Chicago, to fight for it. We organized the Committee to Maintain a Prudent Defense Policy as a lobbying group. It was a shoestring effort that had no ties to either party and it did not accept money from anyone connected with the defense industry. Despite a minute budget (half of which I personally contributed), we were surprisingly effective in getting our message out and in running rings around the opposition in our testimony before Congress. Apparently, we also grabbed the attention of the Nixon Administration.

During the ABM debate, Secretary of State Rogers called me again, this time to ask if I was interested in serving as a member of the arms control negotiating delegation that would tackle working out an agreement with the Soviet Union—the SALT I process. The head of the delegation was to be Gerard Smith, whom Nixon had picked as his Director of the Arms Control and Disarmament Agency (ACDA), which at that time was part of the State Department. The job Rogers was proposing to me would be that of representing Secretary of Defense Melvin Laird on the team. Laird had already agreed to the nomination. I was interested in the job. I had worked on nuclear arms control since the 1950s, and most recently in the Johnson Administration when we had hammered out the original proposals for the SALT process. Unfortunately, the 1968 Soviet invasion of Czechoslovakia had prevented further progress.

Bill Rogers arranged for me to meet with Nixon and his then National Security Adviser, Henry Kissinger, in the President's Oval Office in the White House. Rogers was not to be with us. It had been some time since I had seen and talked to Nixon personally; I found him little changed. The meeting was a memorable one. Nixon began the conversation by expressing his reservations about both Bill Rogers and Gerard Smith.

"Paul," I recall him saying, "I very much want you to take this job. I have no confidence in Bill Rogers nor do I have complete confidence in Gerry Smith. I don't think they understand the arms control problem. So I want you to report anything you disapprove of directly to me." I was supposed to see to it that the delegation did not go beyond its instructions. President Nixon then went on to describe the back channel Joint Chiefs of Staff communications network I was to use.

I was angered by this attempt to compromise my loyalty before I had even joined the delegation. As I recall it, I told Nixon, "Smith is head of the delegation and the delegation can only function effectively if there is teamwork and trust within it. If I am to be a member of the delegation, it will be as a member of Gerry Smith's team and not as someone reporting to someone else. And in any case, Smith reports to the Secretary of State, who must have complete confidence in what Smith reports. That's the way it has to work!"

Nixon refused to see it my way. He repeated, in sharp terms, the same suggestion I had just refused. I refused to budge on the matter. Smith had to have complete control and the loyalty of his team if he was to be effective. Nixon finally abandoned the attempt to create a separate line to the delegation. He simply told me that I knew how to use the JCS channel of direct communication if I ever felt the need to use it. That ended the interview; however, it gave me a foretaste of the frustrating back-channel diplomacy Kissinger and Nixon were to conduct without informing us as we labored in Helsinki to try to hammer out the basics of the SALT I treaty.

Nixon created other problems for the team. Both the U.S. and Soviet delegations agreed there should be no "linkage" or trade-offs between the negotiations and outside issues such as Berlin, Vietnam, or the Middle East where U.S. and Soviet interests were in conflict. Nixon had other ideas. He intended to exploit direct linkage, although he did not say so at the time. I suspect this was behind many of the concessions he made in SALT I. He was desperate to do something about Vietnam, and he may have felt he had a better chance of getting Soviet cooperation on it by making concessions on strategic weapons.

There were also problems in the way Nixon tried to control the negotiations themselves. Nixon had such a passion for secrecy and such a lack of confidence in the reliability of what he considered the bureaucracy that not even Gerry Smith was kept precisely informed of what was happening at the Presidential level. This went to such lengths that at discussions at the highest levels (where unknown to us many of the key concessions were being made) Nixon would rely on the Soviet interpreters rather than on the more competent American ones, whose notes might be made available to others on the U.S. side. As a result, there were no precise U.S. records of what was being said in these critical discussions. Even the less precise memoranda of the discussions, subsequently dictated by a member of Kissinger's staff, were not made available outside the White House. It was not even the practice to give a full oral briefing to those who had a need to know. Not only did this leave members of the delegation in the dark much of the time, it also deprived the President and his immediate advisers of the available expertise to fine-comb the relevant detail. Such practices led to unnecessary difficulties, some very significant, in parrying Soviet strategy and negotiating tactics.

Eventually, Nixon's conduct caught up with the negotiations. A couple of years later, in 1973, I was still a surviving member of the U.S. arms delegation, this time working on the sequel treaty, SALT II. Late that year, I came to the conclusion that as long as the Watergate scandal dragged on, serious arms control negotiations were unlikely, if not impossible. Initially, the Soviets had found it hard to imagine that a President of Nixon's power and prestige could ever be in serious political trouble at home. But as time went on, they began to realize Nixon was in a weakened position. They were fully prepared to exploit that weakness in the expectation that eventually he would make concessions to improve his image at home and salvage his Presidency. I believed they were not too far off the mark. Nixon, as the Soviets seemed to observe, had given in on the SALT I Interim agreement at a time when his political position had been markedly stronger. Little wonder that they now expected him to do so again. As the Watergate scandal loomed ever larger, I concluded it was destroying the prospects for a sensible and sane SALT II accord.

By this time I was also beginning to wonder whether I was making an effective contribution by staying with the delegation. I had serious differences with some of our positions, as well as the overall direction of the Administration. As a government official, I could not speak out on the issues; as a private citizen, I would be under fewer constraints and could put my views before a wider audience in the hopes of influencing the ultimate course of national policy. I had not yet decided to resign, but I began to look on resignation as an option to be considered.

At the White House the deepening gloom of Watergate was taking a heavy toll on Nixon himself and on the credibility of his Administration. Many associated with it, including some who had nothing to do with Watergate, found their reputations tarnished. I had known Nixon a long time, so I was familiar with his behavior. I believed that in an effort to rescue his Administration and to rally public opinion behind him before impeachment proceedings began, he would make imprudent concessions to the Soviet Union in SALT II to strike a deal. He would then attempt to use this seeming success to back his claim that his leadership was essential to the long-range future of the United States and of the world as a whole.

I realized that if I resigned at this point, it would be seen merely as an act of protest. My resignation would have no immediate impact on the conduct of policy, nor would it prevent Nixon from taking some improvident step to save his Presidency. But I could function no longer under the steadily darkening cloud of Watergate. I had to do something to escape from the con-

tamination that was enveloping the Executive Branch. Resignation seemed
the only course to take.

On May 28, 1974, I wrote Secretary Schlesinger of my decision to resign. The same day I wrote President Nixon, proposing to him that my resignation take effect on May 31. A week passed and I heard nothing. Then
another. I ended up sending a second letter on June 14, this time saying simply that I unilaterally terminated my appointment, effective that day. So
there would be no misunderstanding of the motive behind my action, I also
issued a press release that voiced my deeply felt concern over the current situation and the debilitating effects it was producing.

Shortly thereafter, Kissinger and Nixon set off for their scheduled Summit meeting with Brezhnev in Moscow, where arms control topped the
agenda. Contrary to the impression left by Kissinger in his book *Years of Upheaval,* it was never my intent to time my resignation to coincide with the
Summit and undercut or embarrass him or his boss in those talks. I had tried
to resign weeks earlier and Nixon had paid me no heed. Moreover, what damage may have been done to the U.S. negotiating position was done by Nixon
himself, not by others. The erosion of Nixon's credibility and standing in the
eyes of the American people was an accomplished fact. Nixon's Presidency
was already morally bankrupt and mortally wounded.

In the end, Nixon's handling of arms control reflected his Presidency. He
had shown he was willing to use his office, in this case arms control and national security, for short-term domestic political gain. In doing so he put his
personal interest above that of the American people he had been elected to
serve. It was the same weakness that was to destroy his Presidency. Nixon
had a complex personality. He had great energy and disposition to act. Sometimes he displayed acute judgment and considerable courage. At other times
he let his ambitions and combativeness overcome the ethical standards that
his devout mother had attempted to inculcate into his character. He was a
complex and most interesting man.

PART 2

NIXON:
THE ORIGINAL
ANNOTATED
SCREENPLAY

Nixon

Editor's Note: *This is the shooting script used in filming* Nixon. *Inevitably, during the course of filming, changes were made when the director or actors found it necessary to modify lines. Also, scenes are sometimes shot out of chronological order, and only during the final editing process is the determination made as to how the footage plays best. Finally, the editing process itself results in changes, as the director seeks to arrange and present the material in a manner that meets his creative instincts and experience as a storyteller. Thus, this annotated script may vary in some instances from the film.*

PROLOGUE

A PROLOGUE APPEARS on black screen:

This film is an attempt to understand the truth of Richard Nixon, thirty-seventh President of the United States. It is based on numerous public sources and on an incomplete historical record.

In consideration of length, events and characters have been condensed, and some scenes among protagonists have been conjectured.[1]

---

[1] The portrait of Richard Nixon that emerges in this screenplay is based on extensive research by the writers, Stephen J. Rivele, Christopher Wilkinson, and Oliver Stone, who studied books, articles, and material about Nixon or written by the former President, by those who worked with and for him, and by others who interviewed or studied him. The writers have also drawn on tape-recorded conversations made by President Nixon during his presidency. These sources are listed in the bibliography that follows the script. In addition, throughout this project Oliver Stone talked at length with many people who knew Richard Nixon personally during his long political career and who were familiar with the events portrayed.

This film is not a documentary; rather, it is a dramatic interpretation of the life of a man who had a tremendous impact on American politics and history. In the interests of filmic form, it has been necessary to make both aesthetic and budgetary decisions in selecting material. There is no intention here to revise history; rather, events have been examined, condensed, and encapsulated based on existing research and dramatic demands. In a few instances where facts are in dispute, the writers have used reasonable speculation arising from the information available. This annotated script reflects a sampling of the historical material on which the writers drew in creating this story of Richard Nixon.

On a portable screen we read the famous words from Matthew: "What shall it profit a man if he shall gain the whole world and lose his own soul?" This FADES into:

A BLACK AND WHITE 16-mm sales training FILM.[2] At the moment, the sales manager, BOB, is chatting with EARL, a rookie salesman.

BOB

Sure you've got a great product, Earl. But you have to remember what you're really selling. (*then*) Yourself.

SCENE ONE[3]

INT. WATERGATE HOTEL–CONFERENCE ROOM–NIGHT

Seven men in shirts and ties are seated around a table in the darkened room. They are smoking Cuban cigars, idly watching the film.

TITLE: "JUNE 17, 1972." Then: "THE WATERGATE HOTEL"

A BUSBOY yawns as he clears away the remains of dinner. A WAITER starts pouring Margaritas from a pitcher.

A balding man in his early fifties tosses a five onto the table. He is HOWARD HUNT.

HUNT

Just leave it.

---

[2]On the film viewed by the burglars, see E. Howard Hunt, *Undercover: Memoirs of an American Secret Agent* (New York: Berkley, 1974), p. 223; G. Gordon Liddy, *Will: The Autobiography of Gordon Liddy* (New York: St. Martin's Press, 1980), p. 230; and Jim Hougan, *Secret Agenda: Watergate, Deep Throat, and the CIA* (New York: Random House, 1984), p. 141. The film was actually used in the May 26 break-in attempt. The burglars posed as executives of Ameritas, Inc. Hunt rented the film, which he called a "travelogue."

[3]The break-ins at the Democratic National Committee offices at the Watergate Office Building in Washington, D.C. on May 28, 1972 and June 17, 1972 have been compressed and dramatized in this scene. Full accounts of these events are given in Liddy, *Will*, pp. 223–246; Hunt, *Undercover*, pp. 219–243; and James W. McCord, Jr., *A Piece of Tape: The Watergate Story: Fact and Fiction* (Washington, DC: Media Services, 1974), pp. 24–36. See also United States Senate, *The Final Report of the Select Committee on Presidential Campaign Activities* [hereafter: Select Committee, *Final Report*], June 1974 (Washington, DC: Government Printing Office, 1974), pp. 27–31; and Hougan, *Secret Agenda*, pp. 139–260.

The waiter puts down the pitcher, picks up the five, and follows the busboy out of the room.

The moment the door closes behind them, GORDON LIDDY is on his feet, locking the door. OTHER MEN are visible, putting on jackets, securing technical equipment from briefcases and bags. They are: FRANK STURGIS, BERNARD BARKER, EUGENIO MARTINEZ, VIRGILIO GONZALES, and JAMES MCCORD.

LIDDY (CHECKS HIS WATCH)

Zero-one-twenty-one. Mark.

Sturgis rolls his eyes, drains his Margarita. Liddy pulls a wad of cash from his pocket, starts passing out hundred-dollar bills to his men.[4]

LIDDY

Just in case you need to buy a cop. But don't spend it all in one place. We're going to do McGovern's office later tonight.[5]

McCord shakes his head.

LIDDY

Orders from the White House, partner.[6]

Liddy bypasses Hunt, who is browsing a folded Spanish-language paper.

---

[4]For Liddy passing out money, see Liddy, *Will*, pp. 331–332; Hunt, *Undercover*, p. 240. The money was in sequentially numbered $100 bills. For this, see Hunt, *Undercover*, p. 240n; Hougan, *Secret Agenda*, p. 214; and Select Committee, *Final Report*, p. 31.

[5]Liddy had planned a break-in at George McGovern's headquarters for the same night as the Watergate break-in. See Liddy, *Will*, p. 324 passim; Hunt, *Undercover*, pp. 236–237; Stephen E. Ambrose, *Nixon: The Triumph of a Politician 1962–1972* (New York: Simon & Schuster, 1987), p. 558; and Select Committee, *Final Report*, p. 27.

[6]On Liddy being instructed by the White House to gather intelligence on Sen. George McGovern (when McGovern was considered either the likely Democratic Party nominee to run against Nixon or a stalking horse for Sen. Edward Kennedy), see the testimony of Gordon Strachan, an aide to White House Chief of Staff Bob Haldeman, *Hearings Before the Senate Select Committee on Presidential Campaign Activities* [hereafter: *Senate Watergate Committee Hearings*], Book 6, p. 2455. Strachan testified that he called Liddy to his White House office in April 1972 and gave him the message from Haldeman that he was "to transfer whatever capability he had from Muskie to McGovern, with particular interest in discovering what the connection between McGovern and Senator Kennedy was."

LIDDY

Howard . . . What the hell? What're you doing?

HUNT

Dogs . . . Season starts tomorrow. (*off Liddy's look*) It keeps me calm. I don't like going back into the same building four times.[7]

Liddy mutters something didactic in German.

HUNT

Mein Kampf?

LIDDY *(TRANSLATES TO ENGLISH)*

"A warrior with nerves of steel is yet broken by a thread of silk." Nietzsche.[8]

HUNT

Personally I'd prefer a greyhound with a shot of speed.

LIDDY *(TO ALL)*

Remember—listen up! Fire team discipline in there at all times. Keep your radios on *at all times* during the entire penetration.[9] Check yourselves. Phony

---

[7]The burglars had attempted to break into the DNC three times in May: the 26, 27, and 28. On the 28 they succeeded in entering the DNC where they planted bugs and photographed documents. For this, see Hougan, *Secret Agenda,* pp. 139–157; Hunt, *Undercover,* pp. 227–228; Liddy, *Will,* 320–321; and Select Committee, *Final Report,* pp. 28–31.

[8]Liddy's German obsession is well documented. He speaks some German, is an admirer of German culture, attended a high school taught by German Benedictine monks, some of whom spoke little English, and he says in *Will:* "When I organize, I am inclined to think in German terms" (p. 203). He also says that he was entranced as a child by Nazi martial music, sought out German playmates, and listened with them breathlessly to Hitler's speeches ("He [Hitler] sent an electric current through my body . . . I realized suddenly that I had stopped breathing" [pp. 22–23]). It is also noted that Liddy collected German weapons, and often sang German marching songs (including the Nazi anthem, "Die Fahne Hoch" [p. 400]). He named his surveillance plan ODESSA after the German World War II veterans' group. The plan called for an *"einsatzgruppe,"* or Nazi-style assassination squad. He referred to Attorney General John Mitchell as *"mein general"* (with a hard G), even to his face.

[9]In fact, James McCord, the wireman of the group, turned off his radio, making it impossible for Liddy to warn the burglars that the police had arrived. This and other actions and omissions on McCord's part have raised questions about the true nature of his role in the break-in. For a discussion of this see Carl Oglesby, *The Yankee and Cowboy War: Conspiracies from Dallas to Watergate* (Kansas City: Sheed Andrews and McFeel, 1976), pp. 265–302; Hougan, *Secret Agenda,* pp. 192–204. On the other hand, many who are knowledgeable about the Watergate break-in have concluded that the amateurism and incompetence of those involved should not be elevated into a conspiracy based on this all-too-apparent ineptitude. See Fred Emery, *Watergate: The Corruption of American Politics and the Fall of Richard Nixon* (New York: Times Books, 1994), one of the few books that includes material based on an interview with McCord.

ID's, no wallets, no keys. We rendezvous where? The Watergate, Room 214. When? At zero-three-hundred.

                              STURGIS
Yawohl, mein fartenfuhrer.

                    LIDDY *(NARROWING, WAVING HIS GUN)*
Don't start with me, Frank, I'll make you a new asshole.

                         HUNT *(RISING PAST THEM)*
Let's get the fuck out of here, shall we ladies?

                              LIDDY
Anything goes wrong, head for your homes, just sit tight—you'll hear from me or Howard.

                         HUNT *(ASIDE)*
Personally I'll be calling the President of the United States.

A nervous chuckle as Hunt follows Liddy out the main door. The rest exit through the door behind the screen.

The FILM is ending. Bob puts a hand on Earl's shoulder.

                               BOB
And remember, Earl: Always look 'em in the eye. (*to the camera*) Nothing sells like sincerity.

A BLACK SCREEN as the film rattles out, followed by a RADIO REPORT over the darkened room, the sounds of doors closing.

                         RADIO REPORT *(v.o.)*
Five men wearing surgical gloves and business suits, and carrying cameras and electronic surveillance equipment, were arrested early today in the headquarters of the Democratic National Committee in Washington. They were unarmed. Nobody knows yet why they were there or what they were looking for . . .[10]

---

[10]Liddy, *Will,* pp. 236–237, writes that the purpose of the break-in was to repair a faulty bug on Larry O'Brien's phone, and "to find out what O'Brien had of a derogatory nature" about Nixon or his people. McCord's testimony confirms this as the reason for the entry. *Senate Watergate Committee Hearings,* Book 1, pp. 107–108. More recently, however, Liddy has stated that he may have been misled as to the real purpose of the break-in, but students of the events find Liddy's revisionism dubious.

FADE IN TO:

SCENE TWO

EXT. THE WHITE HOUSE—NIGHT—1973

TITLES RUN—A raw November night. We are looking through the black iron bars of the fence towards the facade of the Executive Mansion. A LIGHT is on in a second floor room.

We move towards it through the bars, across the lawn. Dead leaves blow past. A SUBTITLE READS: "NOVEMBER 1973"

A black LIMOUSINE slides up to the White House West Wing. An armed GUARD with a black DOBERMAN approaches.

The window opens slightly. The Guard peers in. Then, he opens the door.

> GUARD
> Good evening, General Haig.

GENERAL ALEXANDER HAIG gets out, walks up the steps. He carries a manila envelope. As he enters the White House, we hear an AUDIO MONTAGE of NEWS REPORTERS from the previous year. The VOICES fade in and out, overlap:[11]

> REPORTERS *(v.o.)*
> Judge John Sirica today sentenced the Watergate burglars to terms ranging up to forty years . . . The White House continues to deny any involvement . . .

SCENE THREE

INT. THE WHITE HOUSE—VESTIBULE—NIGHT

HAIG enters, starts up the stairs. The mansion is dark, silent. Like a tomb.

---

[11]The series of "V.O." (voice-over) statements occurred on the following dates: Sirica sentenced the Watergate burglars—March 23, 1973; Haldeman and Ehrlichman resigned—April 30, 1973; Dean testified before Senate Watergate Committee—June 25–29, 1973; Butterfield revealed the White House taping system—July 16, 1973; Nixon fired Cox—October 20, 1973; Judge Sirica first ordered the President to turn over tapes—August 29, 1973; and Sirica was first informed about the tape gap by White House lawyers the day before Thanksgiving, 1973.

REPORTERS *(v.o.: CONTINUES)*

Presidential counsel John Dean testified before the Senate Watergate Committee that the scandal reaches to the highest levels . . .

MOVING: A low-angle shot of HAIG's spit-shined shoes moving down the long corridor of the second floor of the Residence.

REPORTERS *(v.o.: CONTINUES)*

Presidential aides Haldeman and Ehrlichman were ordered to resign today . . . In a stunning announcement, White House aide Alexander Butterfield revealed the existence of a secret taping system . . .

CLOSE: on the manila envelope in Haig's hand.[12]

REPORTERS *(v.o.: CONTINUES)*

The President has fired the Watergate Special Prosecutor, Archibald Cox, provoking the gravest constitutional crisis in American history . . .

Haig stops at a door, quietly knocks. No answer.

REPORTERS *(v.o.: CONTINUES)*

Judge Sirica has ordered the President to turn over his tapes . . .

Haig opens the door.

SCENE FOUR

INT. THE WHITE HOUSE—LINCOLN SITTING ROOM—NIGHT

The room is small, austere, dominated by a portrait of LINCOLN over the fireplace. HAIG stands in the doorway, holding the envelope.

HAIG

These are the tapes you requested, Mr. President.[13]

---

[12]For Haig having custody of the tapes in November 1973 see Haig's testimony before the Grand Jury, December 5, 1973, House Judiciary Committee ("HJC"), *Statement of Information,* Book IX (Part 1), pp. 385–387; see also Richard Nixon, *RN: The Memoirs of Richard Nixon* (New York: Touchstone, 1990), pp. 999–1000; and Emery, *Watergate,* p. 369.

[13]For Haig urging Nixon to listen to the tapes, see Stephen E. Ambrose, *Nixon: Ruin and Recovery 1973–1990* (New York: Simon & Schuster, 1991), pp. 157–158; Carl Bernstein and Bob

RICHARD NIXON is in shadow, silhouetted by the fire in the hearth. The air-conditioning is going full blast.

Haig crosses the room, opens the envelope, takes out a reel of tape.

Nixon sits in a small armchair in a corner. A Uher tape recorder and a head-set are on an end table at his elbow. Next to it is a large tumbler of Scotch.

Haig hands the envelope containing the tapes to Nixon.

NIXON

This is June twentieth?[14]

HAIG

It's marked. Also there's June twenty-third. And this year—March twenty-first. Those are the ones . . .

Nixon squints at the label in the firelight.

HAIG

. . . the lawyers feel . . . will be the basis of the . . . proceedings.[15]

Nixon tries to thread the tape.

NIXON

Nixon's never been good with these things.[16]

Woodward, *The Final Days* (New York: Touchstone, 1974), p. 44; and Nixon, *RN*, pp. 999–1000.

[14]On October 1, 1973, Nixon's secretary, Rose Mary Woods, told the President she might accidentally have caused a small gap in a tape while transcribing its contents. On November 21, 1973, the fact that there was an 18 1/2-minute gap on the tape of June 20, 1972, in the conversation between the president and Haldeman was disclosed to Judge Sirica, who appointed an advisory panel to examine the tapes. See Stanley I. Kutler, *The Wars of Watergate: The Last Crisis of Richard Nixon* (New York: Knopf, 1990), pp. 429–431.

[15]The President's lawyers, Fred Buzhardt and James St. Clair, discussed the June 23, 1972, tape of the conversations between the President and Haldeman with Haig at length. This June 23 tape would be considered the "smoking gun," i.e., the evidence needed to show that Nixon had been personally involved in a criminal obstruction of justice relating to the Watergate cover-up. See Alexander M. Haig, Jr., *Inner Circles, How America Changed the World, a Memoir* (New York: Warner, 1992), pp. 472–486.

[16]For Nixon's habit of talking about himself in the third person, see Michael Korda, "Nixon, Mein Host," *New Yorker*, May 2, 1994, pp. 20–30; Jeb Stuart Magruder, *An American Life:*

He drops the tape on the floor.

                            NIXON

Cocksucker!

Haig picks up the tape. Then he steps to the table, reaches for the lamp.

                            HAIG

Do you mind?

Nixon gestures awkwardly. Haig turns on the lamp. For the first time we can see Nixon's face: he hasn't slept in days, dark circles, sagging jowls, five-o'-clock shadow. He hates the light, slurs a strange growl—the effect of sleeping pills.

                            HAIG

Sorry . . .

                    NIXON *(GESTURES)*

. . . go on.

Haig threads the tape. Nixon, looking at it, remembers.

                            NIXON

. . . Y'know Al, if Hoover was alive none of this would've happened. He would've protected the President.

                            HAIG

Mr. Hoover was a realist.

                            NIXON

I trusted Mitchell. It was that damn big mouth wife of his.

                            HAIG

At least Mitchell stood up to it.

One Man's Road to Watergate (New York: Atheneum, 1974), p. 168; and Fawn Brodie, *Richard Nixon: The Shaping of His Character* (New York: W. W. Norton, 1981), pp. 22–23. Also, many members of Nixon's staff mentioned his awkwardness with mechanical things during conversations with Oliver Stone.

NIXON

Not like the others—Dean, McCord, the rest . . . We never got our side of the story out, Al. People've forgotten. I mean: "Fuck you, Mr. President, fuck you Tricia, fuck you Julie!" and all that shit, just words, but what violence! The tear gassing, the riots, burning the draft cards, Black Panthers—we fixed it, Al, and they hate me for it—the double-dealing bastards. They lionize that traitor, Ellsberg, for stealing secrets, but they jump all over me 'cause it's Nixon (*repeats*) . . . They've always hated Nixon.

Haig finishes threading.

HAIG

May I say something, Mr. President?

NIXON

There's no secrets here, Al.

HAIG

You've never been a greater example to the country than you are now, sir, but . . . but you need to get out more, sir, and talk to people. No one I know feels . . . close to you.

Nixon looks at him, moved by his concern.

Nixon (Anthony Hopkins) with Alexander Haig (Powers Booth), John Ehrlichman (J.T. Walsh), Chuck Colson (Kevin Dunn), and John Mitchell (E.G. Marshall)

NIXON

I was never the buddy-buddy type, Al. You know, "Oh I couldn't sleep last night, I was thinking of my mother who beat me"—all that kinda crap, you know the psychoanalysis bag . . . My mother . . . The more I'd spill my guts, the more they'd hate me. I'd be what . . .*pathetic!* If I'd bugged out of Vietnam when they wanted, do you think Watergate would've ever happened? You think the Establishment would've given a shit about a third-rate burglary? But did I? Quit? Did I pull out? (*he stares, waits*)

HAIG

No, sir, you did not.

NIXON

Damn right. And there's still a helluva lotta people out there who wanna believe . . . That's the point, isn't it? They wanna believe in the President.

He suddenly tires of talking, rubs his hands over his face.

HAIG

You're all set, sir. Just push this button. Good night, Mr. President.

NIXON

You know, Al, men in your profession . . . you give 'em a pistol and you leave the room. (*Haig: "I don't have a pistol."*) 'Night, Al . . .

Haig quietly closes the door. Nixon takes a generous slug of Scotch. Then he looks down at the tape recorder. He puts on the UHER headset, and hits the "fast forward" button: high-speed VOICES.

NIXON

Goddamn!

He hits "stop," puts on his eyeglasses, studies the recorder a moment. Pushes the "play" button. VOICES. Barely audible at first. Nixon leans closer, listening.

NIXON (*ON TAPE*)

They did what?! I don't understand. Why'd they go into O'Brien's office *in the first place?*

HALDEMAN (*ON TAPE*)

Evidently to install bugs and photograph documents.

FLASHBACK TO:

SCENE FIVE[17]

INT. EXECUTIVE OFFICE BLDG.–PRESIDENT'S OFFICE–DAY (1972)

SUBTITLE READS: "JUNE 1972."

NIXON's hideaway office.[18] BOB HALDEMAN, his crew-cut, hard-edged chief of staff, sits across the desk, a folder open on his lap. Nixon, at his desk, seems a healthier man than in the previous scene. Also there are JOHN EHRLICHMAN, portly domestic advisor, and JOHN DEAN, blond, gentrified legal counsel.

                    NIXON *(CONT'D)*
But O'Brien doesn't even use that office. The Democrats've moved to Miami. There's nothing there!

                    HALDEMAN
It was just a fishing expedition. Apparently it was their fourth attempt at the DNC. (*Nixon: "Their fourth!"*) It's possible they were looking for evidence of an illegal Howard Hughes donation to the Democrats, so the Democrats couldn't make an issue of your Hughes money.[19]

---

[17]This scene of the President meeting with his staff is a composite of many meetings, extending over several months. During the period immediately following the arrests of the burglars at the Democratic headquarters, it was principally Haldeman who discussed what had happened with the President. However, Haldeman was receiving information from Mitchell, Ehrlichman, Colson, and Dean, which he in turn imparted to the President. See Nixon, *RN*, pp. 625–646. In the Sources and Acknowledgments of his memoirs, *RN*, Nixon states that, in addition to the public transcripts of his recorded conversations, he asked Mrs. Marjorie Acker of his staff "to type transcripts as well of the tapes of every conversation (he) had with H. R. Haldeman, John Ehrlichman, and Charles Colson for the month after (his) return to Washington following the break-in, June 20–July 20, 1972." These transcripts of taped conversations on which Nixon relied for his book have never been made public.

[18]The building next to the White House, and within its grounds, is known as the Executive Office Building (often called the "EOB"). The President liked to get out of the White House and away from the Oval Office, and often worked in his smaller office on the first floor of the EOB. Most of the White House staff was located in the EOB.

[19]For an in-depth discussion of the Hughes donation to Nixon, see Oglesby, *The Yankee and Cowboy War*, pp. 171–224. Also see Ambrose, *Nixon: The Triumph of a Politician 1962–1972*, pp. 570–571; and Warren Hinckle and William Turner, *The Fish Is Red: The Story of the Secret War Against Castro* (New York: Harper & Row, 1981), p. 301.

Alexander Butterfield, Oliver Stone, and J.T. Walsh (as John Ehrlichman) on the set.

NIXON

Contribution! It was a legal contribution. Who the hell authorized this?[20] Colson?

EHRLICHMAN (SHAKES HIS HEAD)

Colson doesn't know a thing about it; he's pure as a virgin on this one. It's just not clear the burglars knew what they were looking for. They were heading to McGovern's office later that night.

---

[20]Only recently has it been documented that someone above Jeb Magruder, who was Deputy Director of the Committee to Re-Elect the President ("CREEP"), actually authorized the June 17 break-in at the Watergate. Magruder admitted his approval in 1973. In a 1987 press conference, Bob Haldeman said, "To this day, no one knows who ordered the break-in." See also Ambrose, *Nixon: The Triumph of a Politician 1962–1972,* p. 562; H. R. Haldeman, *The Ends of Power* (New York: Times Books, 1978), pp. 119–135. Haldeman appears to have forgotten that in fact he ratified and approved Liddy's general intelligence-gathering activities on April 4, 1972; a document showing his ratification was located in the National Archives in 1992. See Emery, *Watergate,* pp. 103–105, and *Watergate,* the six-hour television documentary broadcast by The Discovery Channel. In addition, Haldeman overlooked his own diary, which reports that John Mitchell admitted to both Haldeman and John Dean that he had approved Liddy's plans. See H. R. Haldeman, *The Haldeman Diaries: Inside the Nixon White House* (New York, Putnam's, 1994), p. 618; and John Dean, "Ghosts in the Machine," *Rolling Stone,* Sept. 8, 1994, pp. 47–49. None of this, however, constitutes direct evidence that either Haldeman or Mitchell personally approved the break-in itself, but this information, if known at the time, could have been the basis to indict and convict them for involvement in criminal conspiracy relating to the Watergate break-in.

NIXON

Jesus! Did Mitchell know?

EHRLICHMAN

Mitchell's out of his mind right now. Martha just put her head through a plate-glass window.

NIXON

Jesus! Through a window?

HALDEMAN

It was her wrist. And it was through a plate-glass door.

EHRLICHMAN

Anyway, they had to take her to Bellevue. Maybe she'll stay this time.[21]

A beat.

NIXON

Martha's an idiot, she'll do anything to get John's attention. If Mitchell'd been minding the store instead of that nut, Martha, we wouldn't have that kid Magruder runnin' some third-rate burglary![22] Was he smoking pot?

EHRLICHMAN

Mitchell?

NIXON

No! Magruder! That sonofabitch tests my Quaker patience to the breaking point.

---

[21]For Martha's injury, see Emery, *Watergate,* p. 203; Winzola McClendon, *Martha: The Life of Martha Mitchell* (New York: Random House, 1979), pp. 10–14; Haldeman, *The Haldeman Diaries,* p. 475. Martha was forcibly sedated and taken secretly to a hospital. Sources conflict on when and where she was hospitalized; however, the incident with the plate-glass door took place in California. The White House put out a story that she had been institutionalized. See Emery, *Watergate,* p. 203; and McClendon, *Martha,* pp. 13, 267–268. John Mitchell told *Newsweek* that he had attempted twice to have Martha institutionalized. See McClendon, *Martha,* pp. 267–268. Martha threatened on many occasions to commit suicide. See McClendon, *Martha,* pp. 233–244, 266, 296–298, 316, 323, 332, 347–348.

[22]For Nixon's views of Martha Mitchell, see Nixon, *RN,* p. 649; Ambrose, *Nixon: The Triumph of a Politician 1962–1972,* pp. 570–571; and McClendon, *Martha,* p. 386. In his diary, Nixon wrote, "Without Martha, I am sure that the Watergate thing would never have happened."

DEAN

The bigger problem I see is this guy who was arrested, McCord—James Mc-Cord—he headed up security for the Committee to Re-Elect.[23] He turns out to be ex-CIA.

NIXON

"Ex-CIA"? There's no such thing as "ex-CIA," John—they're all Ivy League Establishment. Is he one of these guys with a beef against us?

EHRLICHMAN

McCord? . . .

NIXON

Find out what the hell he was doing at "CREEP." This could be trouble. These CIA guys don't miss a trick. This could be a set-up.

INTERCUTS of all these people arise as the scene runs—McCord, Liddy, Magruder, Mitchell, Martha, Hunt, etc.

HALDEMAN (WITH A LOOK TO EHRLICHMAN)
We feel the bigger concern is Gordon Liddy . . .

NIXON

That fruitcake![24] What about him?

HALDEMAN

Well, you know, sir, he's a nut. He used to work here with the "Plumbers" and now he's running this Watergate caper. You remember his plan to firebomb the Brookings using Cubans as firemen? He wanted to buy a damned fire truck! Magruder thinks he's just nutty enough to go off the reservation.

NIXON

What's Liddy got?

---

[23]For a discussion of McCord's background, including his CIA career and his work as security chief for CREEP, see Oglesby, *The Yankee and Cowboy War*, pp. 265–302; for McCord as CREEP security chief, see also Nixon, *RN*, p. 628; Hougan, *Secret Agenda*, p. 57; and Emery, *Watergate*, p. 78.

[24]On the June 23, 1972, tape transcript, Nixon actually calls Liddy "nuts." See Watergate Special Prosecution Force transcript, June 23, 1972, National Archives; see also New York *Times, The End of a Presidency* (New York: Bantam, 1974), p. 330.

HALDEMAN

Apparently he was using some campaign cash that was laundered for us through Mexico.[25] The FBI's onto it. We could have a problem with that.

DEAN

. . . But it'll just be a campaign finance violation . . .

HALDEMAN

. . . And if Liddy takes the rap for Watergate, we can take care of him . . .[26]

NIXON *(LOOKING AT HIS WATCH)*

I don't have time for all this shit! *(to Haldeman)* Just handle it, Bob! Keep it out of the White House. What else? Kissinger's waiting—he's gonna throw a tantrum again if I don't see him, threatening to quit . . . again. *(sighs)*

EHRLICHMAN *(RELUCTANT)*

Well, sir . . . it turns out—one of the people implicated is still, you see, on our White House payroll.

NIXON

Who? Not another Goddamn Cuban?

HALDEMAN

No, sir. A guy named Hunt.[27]

Nixon stops, stunned.

NIXON

Hunt? Howard Hunt?

---

[25]On laundering the campaign cash through Mexico, see Emery, *Watergate*, pp. 111–112; Carl Bernstein and Bob Woodward, *All the President's Men* (New York: Touchstone, 1974), pp. 37–41, 53–55; Haldeman, *The Haldeman Diaries*, pp. 474–475; Hunt, *Undercover*, p. 240n; and Select Committee, *Final Report*, p. 37.

[26]According to Nixon, "Ehrlichman had come up with the idea of having Liddy confess; he would say he did it because he wanted to be a hero at the CRP. . . . Then, Haldeman said, our people would make an appeal for compassion on the basis that Liddy was a poor, misguided kid who read too many spy stories." See Nixon, *RN*, p. 635. A tape of this conversation between Haldeman and Nixon is available in the National Archives, but no transcript has ever been presented.

[27]For Hunt being on the White House payroll, see Nixon, *RN*, p. 514; Bernstein and Woodward, *All the President's Men*, p. 133; Emery, *Watergate*, pp. 33–34; and Ambrose, *Nixon: The Triumph of a Politician 1962–1972*, p. 566.

EHRLICHMAN

He left his White House phone number in his hotel room.[28]

HALDEMAN

He works for Colson.[29] He used him on the Pentagon Papers. We're trying to figure out when he officially stopped being a White House consultant. After the arrest he dumped his wiretapping stuff into his White House safe.

NIXON *(INCREDULOUS)*

Howard Hunt is working for the White House? No shit! This is Goddamn Disneyland! Since when?

EHRLICHMAN

Chappaquiddick. You wanted some dirt on Kennedy. Colson brought him in.[30]

DEAN

You know Hunt, sir?

NIXON *(PERTURBED)*

On the list of horribles, I know what he is. And I know what he tracks back to. (*then*) You say he was involved in the Plumbers?

---

[28]Howard Hunt's White House phone number was found in the address book of one of the Watergate burglars, along with a check to Hunt's country club that Hunt wanted mailed from out of state by one of the burglars. The police found this evidence in the Watergate Hotel room where the burglars were staying, and Ehrlichman was informed of this by the Secret Service. See Emery, *Watergate,* p. 150.

[29]On Hunt working for Colson, see Emery, *Watergate,* pp. 33–34, 49–50; Charles W. Colson, *Born Again* (Old Tappan, NJ: Chosen Books, 1976), pp. 60–61; Hougan, *Secret Agenda,* pp. 32–33; Hunt, *Undercover,* p. 146 passim.

[30]For Colson using Hunt to get dirt on Teddy Kennedy, see Hougan, *Secret Agenda,* pp. 34–35; Emery, *Watergate,* pp. 52–53; and Hunt, *Undercover,* pp. 159–161. Although Colson originally brought Hunt to the White House to work on the Pentagon Papers, he also used Hunt to work on the Chappaquiddick matter long after the incident itself, which had occurred on July 19, 1969. For the investigation of Chappaquiddick by Nixon, see Tony Ulasewicz with Stuart A. McKeever, *The President's Private Eye: The Journey of Detective Tony U. from N.Y.P.D. to the Nixon White House* (Westport, CT: MACSAM, 1990). Nixon employed Ulasewicz and paid him with campaign funds; Ulasewicz spent several years investigating Sen. Edward Kennedy as well as other matters for the Nixon White House.

> HALDEMAN

Definitely. Colson had him trying to break into Bremer's apartment after Bremer shot Wallace, to plant McGovern campaign literature.[31]

> NIXON *(LOFTY)*

I had nothing to do with that. Was he . . . in the Ellsberg thing?

> HALDEMAN

Yes, you approved it, sir.[32]

> NIXON

I did?

> HALDEMAN

It was right after the Pentagon Papers broke. They went in to get his psychiatric records.

> NIXON

Fucking hell.

> HALDEMAN

We were working on China . . .

Nixon has taken a seat, shaken. He stares right at us as we:

SHARP CUT BACK TO:

---

[31]On the plan to plant McGovern literature in Bremer's apartment, see Hunt, *Undercover,* pp. 216–218; Emery, *Watergate,* pp. 115–117; Liddy, *Will,* p. 309; Bernstein and Woodward, *All the President's Men,* pp. 326–330; and Stephen Lesher, *George Wallace, American Populist* (New York: Addison-Wesley, 1994); Lesher states at pp. 565–566, n. 148: ". . . a month before the Watergate break-in, the president ordered his subordinates to enter the apartment of the man who had just shot a presidential candidate, plant phony evidence, possibly affect the outcome of the nominating and electoral process, and perhaps skew the conclusions that investigators might reach concerning the safety of all future campaigners. The episode brands Nixon as a morally bankrupt felon who made it clear that any act, regardless of its illegality, would be condoned and protected if it served the president's ambitions."

[32]On Nixon approving the break-in at Dr. Fielding's office, see Emery, *Watergate,* pp. 61–62; Haldeman, *The Ends of Power,* p. 115; Nixon, *RN,* p. 514. In his memoirs, Nixon wrote that he could not recall whether or not he knew about the Fielding break-in in advance, but stated that had he known he would not necessarily have disapproved it.

SCENE SIX

INT. OVAL OFFICE–DAY–(1971)

The PRESIDENT'S MEN are gathered in somber silence, sharing front page copies of the New York Times. *SUBTITLE READS: "JUNE 1971–A YEAR EARLIER"*

INSERT HEADLINE: "Secret Pentagon Study Details Descent into Vietnam"; "Pentagon Papers Expose Government Lies."

The technique we've established of an AUDIO MONTAGE of REPORTERS' VOICES continues over the scene.

> REPORTERS *(v.o.)*
> The New York *Times* began publishing today the first in a series of *forty-seven volumes* of top secret Pentagon Papers relating to the war in Vietnam. The papers reveal a systematic pattern of government lies about American involvement in the war . . .

NIXON throws down the paper in disgust and attempts to feed his Irish setter, KING TIMAHOE, a biscuit, as HENRY KISSINGER paces the room, the most upset of all.

Filming an Oval Office meeting

KISSINGER

Mr. President, we are in a revolutionary situation. We are under siege—Black Panthers, Weathermen; the State Department under Rogers is leaking like a sieve. And now this insignificant little shit, Ellsberg, publishing all the diplomatic secrets of this country, will destroy our ability to conduct foreign policy![33]

NIXON (*FEEDING THE DOG*)

Here, Tim . . . Tim. I'm as frustrated as you, Henry, but don't you think this one's a Democrat problem. They started the war; it makes them look bad.

Kissinger lowers his voice for effect, pounds the desk.

KISSINGER

Mr. President, how can we look the Soviets or the Chinese in the eye now and have any credibility when any traitor can leak! Even the Vietnamese, tawdry little shits that they are, will never—*never*—agree to secret negotiations with us. This makes you look like a *weakling,* Mr. President.[34]

HALDEMAN

He's right about one thing, sir. I spoke with Lyndon. This Pentagon Papers business has knocked the shit out of him. Complete collapse, massive depression.[35] He feels the country is lost, that you as President can't govern anymore.

Nixon is bent from the waist, stiffly extending the biscuit, but the dog still won't come.

NIXON (*IRRITATED*)

Goddamn! How long have we had this fucking dog?! Two years, he still doesn't come! We need a dog that looks happy when the press is around.

EHRLICHMAN

Well, he's photogenic. Let's try dog bones?

---

[33]For Nixon's and Kissinger's reaction to the Pentagon Papers, see Tom Wicker, *One of Us: Richard Nixon and the American Dream* (New York: Random House, 1991), pp. 640–646; Ambrose, *Nixon: The Triumph of a Politician 1962–1972*, p. 447; Nixon, *RN,* pp. 508–515; and Haldeman, *The Haldeman Diaries,* p. 300. Haldeman characterized Kissinger's tirade as "beyond belief."

[34]On Kissinger calling Nixon a "weakling," see Ambrose, *Nixon: The Triumph of a Politician 1962–1972,* p. 447; and Emery, *Watergate,* pp. 43–44.

[35]On Johnson's collapse, see Haldeman, *The Haldeman Diaries,* p. 302.

KISSINGER *(END OF HIS PATIENCE)*

Mr. President, the Vietnamese, the Russians . . .

Nixon finally throws the biscuit at the dog, glares at Kissinger.

NIXON *(TO EHRLICHMAN)*

Fuck it! He doesn't like me, John! *(to Kissinger)* It's your fault, Henry.

KISSINGER

I beg your pardon—

NIXON

It's your people who are leaking to the *Times.* Wasn't this Ellsberg a student of yours at Harvard? He was your idea; why are you suddenly running for cover?

KISSINGER

He was, he was. We taught a class together at Harvard. But you know these back-stabbing Ivy League intellectuals, they can't . . .

NIXON *(COLD)*

No, Henry, I don't.

KISSINGER

He's turned into a drug fiend, he shot people from helicopters in Vietnam, he has sexual relations with his wife in front of their children.[36] He sees a shrink in L.A. He's all fucked up. Now he's trying to be a hero to the liberals . . . If he gets away with it, everybody will follow his lead. He must be stopped at all costs.

COLSON

Sir, if I might?

---

[36]For the language of Kissinger's tirade about Ellsberg, see Ambrose, *Nixon: The Triumph of a Politician 1962–1972,* p. 447; Aitken, *Nixon,* pp. 420–421; Wicker, *One of Us,* p. 643; Seymour M. Hersh, *The Price of Power: Kissinger in the Nixon White House* (New York: Summit, 1983), pp. 383–387. See also John Dean, "Ghosts in the Machine," *Rolling Stone,* Sept. 8, 1994, and the letters page, *Rolling Stone,* Oct. 4, 1994, where Dean wrote: "By chance I happened to run into Dan Ellsberg in Washington just after I wrote of this conversation, so I asked him about Kissinger's charges. 'Absolutely untrue—all of them,' Dan said. 'In fact, claiming that I shot peasants is a horrible thing to say, it is the antithesis of my life. The contention is absurd. I find it particularly offensive because it is so contrary to what I believe.' "

NIXON

Go, Chuck.

COLSON

For three years now I've watched people in this government promote themselves, ignoring your orders, embarrassing your administration. It makes me
sick! We've played by the rules and it doesn't work!

MITCHELL *(TO NIXON)*

We can prosecute the New York *Times,* go for an injunction . . .

NIXON

. . . but it's not, bottom-line, gonna change a Goddamn thing, John. The question is: How do we screw Ellsberg so bad it puts the fear of God into all leak-
ers?

COLSON

Can we link Ellsberg to the Russians?

NIXON

Good, I like that. The other issue is: How the hell do we plug these leaks once
and for all? Who the hell's talking to the press? *(he looks directly at Henry)*
Henry, for two Goddamn years you've put wiretaps on your own people.[37]

KISSINGER

To protect you, Mr. President.

COLSON *(INTERJECTS)*

To protect yourself is more like it. The pot calling the kettle . . .

Kissinger throws COLSON a vicious look, while Nixon ignores it.

KISSINGER *(ASIDE)*

Who are you talking to like this, you insignificant shit . . .

---

[37]On Kissinger wiretapping his staff, see Hersh, *The Price of Power,* pp. 86–97; Walter Isaacson, *Kissinger: A Biography* (New York: Simon & Schuster, 1992), pp. 212–231; Kutler, *The
Wars of Watergate,* pp. 119–120; United States Senate, *Chronology of Events Relative to the
Seventeen Wiretaps and Pertinent Documents, in Dr. Kissinger's Role in Wiretapping: Hearings Before the Senate Foreign Relations Committee,* 93rd Congress, 2nd Session (Washington,
DC: Government Printing Office, 1975); and *Halperin v. Kissinger,* 606 F2d 1192 (1979) at
1196.

NIXON

. . . and what do we get for it? Gobs and gobs of bullshit, gossip, *nothing!* Someone is leaking. We've got to stop the leaks, Henry, at any cost, do you hear me? Then we can go for the big play—China, Russia.

COLSON

Mr. President, we can do this ourselves. The CIA and the FBI aren't doing the job. But we can create our own intelligence unit—right here, inside the White House.

A slow move in on Nixon as he thinks about it.

NIXON

Well, why not?

HALDEMAN

Our own intelligence capability—to fix the leaks?

COLSON

Yeah, like plumbers.[38]

Nixon smiles.

NIXON

I like it. I like the idea.

EHRLICHMAN

Is it legal? (*a beat*) I mean has anyone ever done it before?

NIXON

Sure. Lyndon, JFK, FDR—I mean, Truman cut the shit out of my investigation of Hiss back in '48.[39]

---

[38]On the creation of the Plumbers, see Select Committee, *Final Report,* pp. 12–17; Ambrose, *Nixon: The Triumph of a Politician 1962–1972,* p. 465; Nixon, *RN,* p. 514; Emery, *Watergate,* pp. 53–54; and Hougan, *Secret Agenda,* pp. 35–37.

[39]See United States House of Representatives, *Committee on Un-American Activities, Hearings on Proposed Legislation to Curb or Control the Communist Party of the United States,* 80th Congress, 2nd Session (Washington, DC: Government Printing Office, 1948). Richard Nixon was a member of the House Un-American Activities Committee (HUAC), and he often referred to these hearings held February 5–20, 1948, during his Presidency.

MITCHELL

It was illegal, what he did.

NIXON

You know, this kinda thing, you gotta be brutal. A leak happens, the whole damn place should be fired. Really. You do it like the Germans in World War II. If they went through these towns and a sniper hit one of them, they'd line the whole Goddamned town up and say: "Until you talk you're all getting shot." I really think that's what has to be done. I don't think you can be Mr. Nice-guy anymore . . .

COLSON

Just whisper the word to me, sir, and I'll shoot Ellsberg myself.

EHRLICHMAN

We're not Germans, sir . . .

NIXON

Ellsberg's not the issue. The Pentagon Papers aren't the issue. (*almost to himself*) It's the lie.

A pause. Everyone in the room chews on this for a moment. MITCHELL, the oldest in the group, smokes on his pipe, stoned-faced.

John Mitchell with his pipe

MITCHELL

The lie?

NIXON

You remember, John, in '48—no one believed Alger Hiss was a Communist. Except me. They loved Hiss just like they love this Ellsberg character. East Coast, Ivy League. He was their kind.[40] I was dirt to them. Nothing.

As they talk, a MONTAGE arises of ALGER HISS and the days of old—the photographs of the notorious 1948 Hiss case: HISS, CHAMBERS, the YOUNGER NIXON with the microfilm; a headline reading "HISS FOUND GUILTY"; TRUMAN, ELEANOR ROOSEVELT, a beaming EISENHOWER shaking Nixon's hand.

MITCHELL *(TO THE ROOM)*

And Dick beat the shit out of them.

NIXON

But I wouldn't have if Hiss hadn't lied about knowing Chambers. The documents were old and out of date, like these Pentagon Papers. The key thing we proved was that Hiss was a liar. Then people bought that he was a spy. *(then)* It's the lie that gets you.

MITCHELL *(TO THE ROOM)*

Hiss was protecting his wife. I've always believed that.

NIXON *(CRYPTICALLY)*

When they know you've got something to protect, that's when they fuck you!

HALDEMAN

What's this faggot, Ellsberg, protecting?[41]

COLSON

His liberal elitist friends. His Harvard-Ph.D.-I-shit-holier-than-thou attitude.

Kissinger waits. Nixon acknowledges him. The camera is moving tighter and tighter on the President. His expression is furious, his words violent.

---

[40]For Nixon comparing Ellsberg to Hiss, see Haldeman, *The Haldeman Diaries,* pp. 302–303, 313.

[41]For Kissinger's characterization of Ellsberg as a "pervert" and a "sexual weirdo," see n. 3.

NIXON *(CONT'D)*

Alright, Henry—we're gonna go your way. Crush this Ellsberg character the same way we did Hiss!

KISSINGER *(INTERJECTS)*

There's no other choice.

NIXON

We're gonna hit him so hard he looks like everything that's sick and evil about the Eastern Establishment. *(To Colson)* You and your "plumbers" are gonna find the dirt on this guy—let's see him going to the bathroom in front of the American public! And when we finish with him, they'll crucify him!

FLASH CUT TO:

SCENE SEVEN

INT. FIELDING PSYCHIATRIST OFFICE—NIGHT (1971)

SUBTITLE READS: "ELLSBERG'S PSYCHIATRIST'S OFFICE—1971"

ANOTHER BREAK-IN is in effect. LIDDY in wig, thick glasses, false teeth, and THREE CUBANS (Barker, Martinez from Watergate, and de Diego, not at Watergate) are visible, moving through, smashing up the office. In CLOSE-UPS, we see hands jerking open filing cabinets, pulling the drawers out of desks.[42]

REPORTERS *(V.O. CONT'D)*

The Nixon Administration responded by filing an injunction against the New York *Times* to prevent further publication . . . President Nixon condemned the Pentagon Papers as the worst breach of national security in U.S. history . . . Daniel Ellsberg, who leaked the papers, was charged today in federal court . . .

---

[42]For a full discussion of the Fielding break-in, and Liddy's and Hunt's roles therein, see *United States v. Ehrlichman,* 546 F2d 910 (1976); Liddy, *Will,* pp. 222–235; Hunt, *Undercover,* pp. 162–174; and Hougan, *Secret Agenda,* pp. 42–49.

While this is going on, a powerful FLASHBULB keeps popping. The pho-
tographer, looking for evidence, suddenly catches his partner in the light, his
startled face buried beneath a 70's wig—HOWARD HUNT. Hunt is pissed:
"Fuck you—gimme that fucking film!"

BACK TO:

SCENE EIGHT

INT. EXECUTIVE OFFICE BLDG.—PRESIDENT'S OFFICE—DAY (1972)

RESUME—CLOSE on NIXON remembering Howard Hunt, as HALDEMAN
looks on.

                            NIXON
Howard Hunt? . . . Jesus Christ, you open up that scab . . . and you uncover
a lot of pus.[43]

                          HALDEMAN
What do you mean, sir?

Nixon chooses not to answer.

                            NIXON
Where's Hunt now?

                          EHRLICHMAN
In hiding. He sent Liddy to talk to me.

                            NIXON
And?

                          EHRLICHMAN
He wants money.[44]

---

[43]This reference is on the June 23, 1972, tape transcript. Also see Emery, *Watergate*, p. 190.

[44]This is a composite reference. Liddy first mentioned to John Dean his need to help his men on
June 19, 1972, two days after the arrest. Dean told Liddy there was nothing the White House
could do. Liddy then spelled out to campaign officials Robert Mardian and Fred La Rue the de-

NIXON

Pay him.

EHRLICHMAN

Pay him? I told him to get out of the country.[45] It's crazy to start . . .

NIXON

What the hell are you doing, Ehrlichman—screwing with the CIA? I don't care how much he wants—pay him.

HALDEMAN

But what are we paying him for?

NIXON

Silence!

HALDEMAN

But sir, you're covered—no one here gave orders to break into the damned Watergate. We're clean. It's only the Ellsberg thing, and if that comes out, it's "national security."

NIXON

"Security" is not strong enough.

---

tails of his need for bail, attorneys' fees, and support money for the men arrested at the Watergate Select Committee, *Final Report,* pp. 40–41. Dean conveyed this information to Ehrlichman. On Hunt's blackmail demands, see Aitken, *Nixon,* p. 478; Hunt, *Undercover,* pp. 275–277, 295; Liddy, *Will,* pp. 257, 265–266, 276; Oglesby, *The Yankee and Cowboy War,* pp. 48–62; Emery, *Watergate,* pp. 200–201, 226–228, 260; and Select Committee, *Final Report,* "Payoffs to Watergate Defendants," pp. 51–62. On the White House tape transcripts of March 21, 1973, Dean stated several times that the White House was being "blackmailed" by Hunt and the others. See White House Tape Transcript, March 21, 1973, National Archives or House of Representatives, *Transcripts of Eight Recorded Presidential Conversations, Hearings Before the Committee on the Judiciary,* 93rd Congress, Second Session, e.g., pp. 91, 92, 93.

[45]Dean testified that Ehrlichman told him to order Hunt to leave the country. See testimony of John Dean, June 25, 1973, *Senate Watergate Committee Hearings,* Book 3, p. 934; see also John W. Dean, III, *Blind Ambition* (New York: Simon & Schuster, 1976), pp. 102–103, 238–239. The Watergate Special Prosecutor's Office indicted and convicted John Ehrlichman for his role in the cover-up, specifically stating in the indictment that charged Ehrlichman with perjury and conspiracy to obstruct justice that "On or about June 19, 1972, JOHN D. EHRLICHMAN met with John W. Dean, III, at the White House in the District of Columbia, at which time EHRLICHMAN directed Dean to tell G. Gordon Liddy that E. Howard Hunt, Jr., should leave the United States." Dean's testimony was corroborated at the trial by Hunt and an FBI agent. Notwithstanding his conviction in 1975, Ehrlichman denies he ordered Hunt out of the country. See John Ehrlichman, *Witness to Power: The Nixon Years* (New York: Simon & Schuster, 1982), p. 348. Most commentators agree with Dean. See, for example, Emery, *Watergate,* p. 165; Bernstein and Woodward, *All the President's Men,* p. 132.

Director Oliver Stone talks with Anthony Hopkins (as Nixon) on the set

HALDEMAN

How 'bout a COMINT classification. We put it on the Huston plan. Even the designation is classified.

NIXON

"National priority."

EHRLICHMAN

"Priority?" How about "secret, top secret"?

DEAN

I was thinking "sensitive."

NIXON

"National security priority restricted and controlled secret."

HALDEMAN

We'll work on it. I say we cut ourselves loose from these clowns and that's all there is to it.

(A beat. Nixon looks out at the Rose Garden)

NIXON

It's more than that. It could be more than that. I want Hunt paid.

EHRLICHMAN

Uh, we've never done this before, sir . . . How do we pay? In . . . hundreds?
(*smirks*) Do you fill a black bag full of unmarked bills?

NIXON (*SNAPS*)

This is not a joke, John!

EHRLICHMAN

No, sir.

NIXON

We should set up a Cuban defense fund on this; take care of all of them.

HALDEMAN

Should we talk to Trini about paying these guys? Or maybe Chotiner?

NIXON

No, keep Trini out of this.[46] Chotiner's too old. And for God's sake, keep Colson out. (*including Dean*) It's time to baptize our young counsel. That means
Dean can never talk about it. Attorney-client privilege. Get to it. And Dean—
you stay close to this.

DEAN

Yes, sir, don't worry—

Prompted, Ehrlichman and Dean leave. When the door closes:

NIXON

Bob, did I approve the Ellsberg thing? You know, I'm glad we tape all these
conversations because . . . I never approved that break-in at Ellsberg's psychiatrist. Or maybe I approved it after the fact? Someday we've got to start
transcribing the tapes . . .[47]

---

[46]Trini is a composite character. Richard Nixon had a number of male friends who were successful businessmen and with whom he spent time.

[47]According to the National Archives, the repository of the Nixon tapes, the White House taping system consisted of a network of seven stations maintained and operated by agents of the
Technical Security Division of the Secret Service. The system was installed in several segments.
In February 1971, seven microphones were placed in the Oval Office, with five in the President's
desk and one on each side of the fireplace. Two other microphones were placed in the Cabinet
Room under the table near the President's chair. All nine devices were wired directly to a Sony
800B recorder in an old locker room in the basement of the White House. In April 1971, four

HALDEMAN

You approved that before the fact, because I went over it with you. But . . .

NIXON

Uh, no one, of course, is going to see these tapes, but . . .

HALDEMAN

That's right, and it's more a problem for Ehrlichman. He fixed Hunt up with the phony CIA ID's,[48] but . . . what else does Hunt have on us?

Again, Nixon chooses not to answer.

NIXON

We've got to turn off the FBI. You just go to the CIA, Bob, and tell Helms that Howard Hunt is blackmailing the President. Tell him that Hunt and his Cuban friends know too damn much, and if he goes public, it would be a fiasco for the CIA. He'll know what I'm talking about.[49]

HALDEMAN *(STILL CONFUSED)*

All right.

NIXON

Play it tough. That's the way they play it and that's the way we're going to play it. Don't lie to Helms and say there's no involvement, but just say this is sort of a comedy of errors, bizarre, without getting into it. Say the President be-

---

microphones were installed in the President's EOB office, with three concealed under the top of the President's desk and a fourth in the knee well of the desk. In addition to microphones monitoring these rooms, the President's telephones in the Oval Office, the EOB office, and the Lincoln Sitting Room of the White House were wired. In May 1972, the President had his study in Aspen Lodge at Camp David wired, as well as his telephones. The system in the Oval Office, the EOB, and the Camp David study were sound activated. The telephone taps engaged when a call was placed. The sound quality of most recordings is relatively poor, although the National Archives has made some efforts to improve it.

[48]For Ehrlichman's role in gaining CIA cooperation for Liddy and Hunt, see Liddy, *Will*, p. 222; and Hougan, *Secret Agenda*, p. 34. See, generally, United States House of Representatives, *Inquiry into the Alleged Involvement of the Central Intelligence Agency in the Watergate and Ellsberg Matters, Hearings Before the Special Subcommittee on Intelligence of the Committee on Armed Services*, 94th Congress, First Session (Washington, DC: Government Printing Office, 1975).

[49]Nixon's instruction to Haldeman to go to Helms is on the June 23, 1972, tape transcript. Also see Emery, *Watergate*, p. 190; Brodie, *Richard Nixon*, p. 495; and Ambrose, *Nixon: Ruin and Recovery 1973–1990*, pp. 27–28.

lieves it's going to open up the whole Bay of Pigs thing again.[50] Tell Helms he should call the FBI, call Pat Gray, and say that we wish for the sake of the country—don't go any further into this hanky-panky, period![51]

HALDEMAN

The Bay of Pigs? . . . That was Kennedy's screwup. How does that threaten us?

NIXON

Just do what I say, Bob.

HALDEMAN

Yes, sir, but . . . do you think Gray'll go for it?

NIXON

Pat Gray'll do anything we ask him. That's why I appointed him.

HALDEMAN

He'll need a pretext. He'll never figure one out for himself.

NIXON *(SIGHS)*

Christ, you're right—Gray makes Jerry Ford look like Mozart. (*then*) Just have Helms call him. Helms can scare anybody.

HALDEMAN

The only problem with that, sir—it gets us into obstruction of justice.

NIXON

It's got nothing to do with justice. It's national security.

HALDEMAN

How is this national security?

---

[50]On the June 23, 1972, tape Nixon refers to the Bay of Pigs and its connection to Watergate repeatedly. This subject will be covered in greater detail in subsequent notes. Haldeman says he eventually came to believe the reference was actually to the JFK assassination. See Haldeman, *The Ends of Power,* pp. 37–40: "It seems that in all those Nixon references to the Bay of Pigs, he was actually referring to the Kennedy assassination" (p. 39).

[51]This material is taken from the June 23, 1972, tape transcript.

NIXON

Because the President says it is. My job is to protect this country from its enemies, and its enemies are inside the walls.

Pause. Haldeman is perplexed.

NIXON

I suppose you thought the Presidency was above this sort of thing.

HALDEMAN

Sir?

NIXON

This isn't a "moral" issue, Bob. We have to keep our enemies at bay or our
whole program is gonna go down the tubes. The FBI is filled with people
who're pissed that I put Gray in and not one of their own. Vietnam, China, the
Soviet Union: when you look at the big picture, Bob, you'll see we're doing a
hell of a lotta good in this world. Let's not screw it up with some shit-ass, third-
rate burglary.

HALDEMAN

I'll talk to Helms. (*looks at his watch*) Oh, Pat asked if you're coming to the
Residence for dinner tonight.

NIXON

No, no, not tonight. Don't let her in here; I have too much to do.

HALDEMAN

Yes, sir. I'll talk to Helms, and, uh . . . what's our press position on this Watergate thing? What do I tell Ziegler to tell them?

SCENE NINE

INT. THE WHITE HOUSE—LINCOLN SITTING ROOM—NIGHT (1973)

RESUME SCENE—NIXON takes another drink, looks up at Lincoln's portrait.

NIXON (*ON THE TAPE, YELLING*)

Tell 'em what we've always told 'em! Tell 'em anything but the Goddamn truth!

As the tape grinds on with hard-to-hear DIALOGUE, Nixon searches through a drawer in the rolltop desk next to the fireplace. He finds a small vial of pills, fumbles with the cap. He rips the cap off, the pills scattering on the desk.

NIXON

Shit!

He begins scooping them back into the bottle, his hands trembling with the effort.

NIXON *(MUMBLES)*

Put me in this position . . . Expose me like this.

He downs a couple of pills with the Scotch.[52]

NIXON

Why don't they just fucking shoot me?

Nixon takes another drink, looks down.

SHARP CUT BACK TO:

SCENE TEN

INT. TV STUDIO—NIGHT—(1960)

DOCUMENTARY FOOTAGE—JOHN F. KENNEDY looking straight at the camera. Tanned, impeccable, confident.

KENNEDY

I do not think the world can exist in the long run half-slave and half-free. The real issue before us is how we can prevent the balance of power from turning against us . . . If we sleep too long in the sixties, Mr. Khrushchev will "bury" us yet . . . I think it's time America started moving again.

DISSOLVE TO:

----

[52]For Nixon's use of drugs and alcohol, see Brodie, *Richard Nixon,* pp. 21, 166–167, 337, 461, 474, 477; Aitken, *Nixon,* pp. 343–346; Ambrose, *Nixon: The Triumph of a Politician 1962–1972,* pp. 84–85; Wicker, *One of Us,* pp. 392–395; and Bernstein and Woodward, *All the President's Men,* pp. 104, 395, 424.

NIXON does not look well. His clothes are baggy, and he has a slight sheen of perspiration around his lower lip. He seems uncomfortable in his movements, robotic, falsely aggressive with his raised eyebrow and glaring demeanor. (The following essences are taken from four debates and various campaign material; in using a documentary "JFK," we will be cutting around him when off-debate material is used.)

NIXON

. . . When it comes to experience, I want you to remember I've had 173 meetings with President Eisenhower, and 217 times with the National Security Council. I've attended 163 Cabinet meetings. I've visited fifty-four countries and had discussions with thirty-five presidents, nine prime ministers, two emperors, and the Shah of Iran . . .

SCENE ELEVEN

INT. TV STUDIO–CONTROL ROOM–NIGHT

PAT NIXON, a year older than Dick, watches her champion through the glass booth. The "Mona Lisa" of American politics, she projects deep admiration for, and pride in, her husband. But now she appears perturbed by what she's seeing.

A younger HALDEMAN sits watching the debates on monitors with HERB KLEIN, press secretary, and OTHERS in the Nixon circle. Through the glass we see the CANDIDATES.

MURRAY CHOTINER, campaign manager, overweight and bow-tied, moves down the row of monitors holding a cigar. He manages to drop ashes on an attractive KENNEDY STAFFER.

CHOTINER

Excuse me, sweetheart.

As he sits next to Haldeman, Nixon drones on.

NIXON *(ON TV MONITOR)*

Let's take hydroelectric power. In our administration, we've built more . . .

CHOTINER *(PRIVATELY)*

Jesus Christ, has he told them how many pushups he can do yet? What the hell happened to him?

HALDEMAN

He just got out of the hospital, Murray, and he hasn't taken an hour off during the campaign, thanks to you.

CHOTINER

You could've at least gotten him a suit that fit, for Christ's sake, and slapped some makeup on him. He looks like a frigging corpse!

NIXON *(TV)*

. . . When we consider the lineup of the world, we find there are 590 million people on our side, 800 million people on the Communist side, and 600 million who are neutral. The odds are 5 to 3 against us . . .

HALDEMAN

He wouldn't do the makeup. Said it was for queers.

JFK's face is on the monitors now.

CHOTINER

Kennedy doesn't look like a queer, does he? *(then)* He looks like a God.

HALDEMAN

Murray, it's not a beauty contest.

CHOTINER

We better hope not.

PAT *(UPSET)*

What are you doing to him, Murray?! Look at him—he's not well. He doesn't have to debate John Kennedy.

HALDEMAN

Mrs. Nixon, we didn't . . .

CHOTINER

Pat, baby, listen, when it comes to . . .

PAT

He can win without doing this.

KENNEDY *(TV)*

. . . in attacking my resolve, Mr. Nixon has carefully avoided mentioning my position on Cuba . . .

HALDEMAN

Oh shoot! He's going to do it! Here it comes.

KENNEDY *(TV)*

. . . As a result of administration policies, we have seen Cuba go to the Communists . . . eight jet minutes from the coast of Florida! Castro's influence will spread through all of Latin America. We must attempt to strengthen the democratic anti-Castro forces in exile. These fighters have had virtually no support from our government!

HALDEMAN *(WHISPERS TO KLEIN, CHOTINER)*

Sonofabitch! He was briefed last week by the CIA. He's using it against us! He knows we can't respond.[53]

CHOTINER

It's a disgrace.

MODERATOR

Mr. Nixon?

NIXON looks, astounded, at JFK. He fumbles his response.

NIXON

I think . . . I think . . . that's the sort of very dangerous and irresponsible suggestion that . . . helping the Cuban exiles who oppose Castro would, uh . . . not only be a violation of international law, it would be . . .

---

[53]On Kennedy using the CIA briefing on Cuba in the debate, see Nixon, *RN*, pp. 220–221; Oglesby, *The Yankee and Cowboy War*, p. 57; Stephen E. Ambrose, *Nixon: The Education of a Politician 1913–1962* (New York: Simon & Schuster, 1987), pp. 592–593. Also see the debate transcripts: *The Joint Appearances of Senator John F. Kennedy and Vice President Richard M. Nixon: Presidential Campaign of 1960* (Washington, DC: Government Printing Office, 1961). Nixon wrote that this was the only time in the campaign he was personally angry with Kennedy.

HALDEMAN *(CLOSES HIS EYES)*

He's treading water. Don't mention Khrushchev.

NIXON

. . . an open invitation for Mr. Khrushchev to become involved in Latin America. We would lose all our friends in Latin America.

KLEIN

He just violated national security, Dick! Attack the bastard!

KENNEDY

I, for one, have never believed the foreign policy of the United States should be dictated by the Kremlin. As long as . . .

Klein hangs his head; Chotiner shares a look with Haldeman.

The young Kennedy staffers applaud gleefully.

NIXON *(v.o.)*

The sonofabitch stole it![54]

SCENE TWELVE

INT. AMBASSADOR HOTEL—SUITE—LOS ANGELES—DAWN (1960)

NIXON stands at the center of a room crowded with his MEN. He is despondent, astounded. PAT NIXON watches silently, bitter, nearly in tears.

CHOTINER

He carried every cemetery in Chicago! And Texas—they had the Goddamned cattle voting!

The final ELECTION FIGURES are coming in over the television. They show Kennedy with a 120,000-voter margin—34.2 to 34.1 million—and run down the electoral college votes.

---

[54]On the charge that Kennedy stole the 1960 election, see Wicker, *One of Us*, pp. 251–253; Brodie, *Richard Nixon*, p. 433; Ambrose, *Nixon: The Education of a Politician 1913–1962*, p. 606; Aitken, *Nixon*, pp. 289–290; and Nixon, *RN*, p. 224.

CHOTINER

Closest election in history, Dick, and they stole it. Sonofabitch!

NIXON

He outspent us and he still cheated. A guy who's got everything. I can't believe it. We came to Congress together. I went to his wedding. We were like brothers, for Christ's sake.

Pat leaves abruptly; she can't take it anymore. Chotiner looks at Dick as if he were incredibly naive. HALDEMAN and KLEIN are at a table, reams of returns before them.

KLEIN

We've got the figures, Dick! The fraud is obvious—we call for a recount.[55]

HALDEMAN

Nobody's ever contested a presidential election.

CHOTINER

Who's going to do the counting? The Democrats control Texas, they control Illinois.

KLEIN

We shift 25,000 votes in two states, and . . .

CHOTINER

How long would that take? Six months? A year?

HALDEMAN

Meanwhile, what happens to the country?

NIXON

That bastard! If I'd called his shot on Cuba I would've won. He made me look soft.

KLEIN *(READING TRANSCRIPT)*

"I feel sorry for Nixon because he does not know who he is, and at each stop he has to decide which Nixon he is at the moment, which must be very exhausting."—Jack Kennedy.

---

[55]On the question of Nixon demanding a recount, see Brodie, *Richard Nixon,* p. 433; Aitken, *Nixon,* pp. 290–291; Ambrose, *Nixon: The Education of a Politician 1913–1962,* p. 606; Nixon, *RN,* pp. 224–225; and Richard M. Nixon, *Six Crises* (New York: Touchstone, 1990), p. 395 passim.

CHOTINER

Bullshit!

The CAMERA is driving in on Nixon building to a rage. Klein knows how to get to him.

KLEIN *(READING)*

"Nixon's a shifty-eyed, Goddamn liar. If he had to stick to the truth he'd have very little to say. If you vote for him you ought to go to hell!"—Harry S. Truman . . . That's what killed us, Dick, not Cuba—the personality problem. Are we gonna let these sonofabitch Democrats get away with this?

HALDEMAN *(SOTTO VOCE)*

You know, Herb, it's not the time. . . .

Nixon in close-up, inner demons moving him. A brief IMAGE of something ugly . . . in Nixon. Himself, perhaps, drenched in blood, or death imagery.

NIXON

Goddamn Kennedy! Goes to Harvard. His father hands him everything on a silver platter! All my life they been sticking it to me. Not the right clothes, not the right schools, not the right family. And then he *steals* from me! I have *nothing* and *he steals.* (softly, lethal) . . . And he says I have "no class." And they love him for it. It's not fair, Murray, it's not fair.

CHOTINER

Dick, you're only forty-seven. You contest this election, you're finished. You gotta swallow this one. They stole it fair and square.

Nixon looks at him, broken-hearted. He controls his reaction, and exits the room.

CHOTINER

We'll get 'em next time, Dick.

KLEIN

What makes you think there's gonna be a next time, Murray?

Chotiner picks up the corner of a campaign poster with Nixon's face on it, the name in bold below.

CHOTINER

Because if he's not President Nixon, he's nobody.

SCENE THIRTEEN

INT. AMBASSADOR HOTEL–CORRIDOR & SUITE–DAWN

NIXON crosses the corridor which is subdued in the morning light. He hesitates at the door, knocks softly.

PAT NIXON stirs quietly as her husband walks to her bed. They occupy separate beds.

NIXON

We lost . . .

PAT *(BITTERLY)*

I know . . .

NIXON

It's hard to lose . . .

She reaches out to touch him. He allows himself to be touched. It seems that, between them, intimacy is difficult.

PAT

It makes us human . . .

NIXON

It's not fair, Buddy.[56] I can take the insults; I can take the name-calling. But I can't take the losing. I hate it.

PAT

We don't *have* to put ourselves through this again, Dick.[57]

---

[56] For Pat's nickname, Buddy, see Brodie, *Richard Nixon,* pp. 27, 149; and Roger Morris, *Richard Milhous Nixon: The Rise of an American Politician* (New York: Henry Holt, 1994), Pat's yearbook photograph following p. 496.

[57] For Pat's attitude toward Nixon running for office again after the 1960 defeat, see Brodie, *Richard Nixon,* pp. 454–455; Julie Nixon-Eisenhower, *Pat Nixon: The Untold Story* (New York: Simon & Schuster, 1986), p. 204; and Aitken, *Nixon,* p. 298.

NIXON

What do you mean? We worked for it. We earned it. It's ours.

PAT

It is. We know that. (*then*) And it's enough that we know. Just think of the girls. They're still young. We never see them. I lost my parents. I don't want them to lose theirs; I don't want them to grow up without a mother and father . . .

NIXON

Maybe I should get out of the game. What do you think, Buddy? Go back to being a lawyer and end up with something solid, some money at the end of the line . . . You know I keep thinking of my old man tonight. He was a failure too.

PAT

You're not a failure, Dick.

NIXON

You know how much money he had in the bank when he died? (*beat*) Nothing. He was so damned honest . . . (*then*) But I miss him. I miss him a hell of a lot.

He seems about to cry. Pat reaches out and cradles his head on her shoulder. On his eyes we:

CUT TO:

SCENE FOURTEEN

EXT. NIXON GROCERY STORE—DUSK (1925)

A few gas pumps in front, overlooking a dry western, Edward Hopper landscape. A run-down residence at the back. A large man in a bloody butcher's apron, FRANK NIXON (46), crosses.

SCENE FIFTEEN

INT. NIXON GROCERY STORE—DUSK

HAROLD (16), tall, handsome, walks in whistling. He winks at RICHARD (12), who is sorting fruit in the bins. HANNAH (39), a dour but gracious Quaker woman, is behind the counter with a CUSTOMER.[58]

RICHARD *(WHISPERS)*

What'd he say?

HAROLD

What do you think? He said in life there's no free ride.

RICHARD

What'd you say?

HAROLD

I said I didn't need a ride. *(flashes a smile)* I need a suit.

Richard buries his face in his hands.

RICHARD

Oh, no, Harold. He doesn't respond well to humor. *(looks at his Mother, worried)* . . . Maybe if you talk to Mother she can . . .

HAROLD

I'd rather get a whipping than have another talk with her. *Anything* but a talk with her.

Richard is terrified Mom might overhear:

RICHARD

Shhhh!

But it's too late. Hannah looks over, very sharp, as her customer departs:

---

[58]For the formative years of Richard Nixon, and the influence on him of his family, see generally Bela Kornitzer, *The Real Nixon: An Intimate Biography* (New York: Rand McNally, 1960).

HANNAH

Richard . . . come with me, would you . . .

RICHARD *(SURPRISED, ALOUD)*

Why me?

SCENE SIXTEEN

INT. NIXON HOUSE–KITCHEN–DUSK

RICHARD, obediently seated, pays his Mother heed. He seems a gloomy, unsmiling child in her presence. We sense that this is familiar territory for both. HANNAH, very quiet, penetrating with her gaze.[59]

HANNAH

Because Harold tests thy father's will is no reason to admire him. Let Harold's worldliness be a warning to thee, not an example.

---

[59]For an in-depth discussion of Nixon's relationship with his mother, see Brodie, *Richard Nixon,* especially pp. 53–63. Also see Morris, *Richard Milhous Nixon,* pp. 40–86; Wicker, *One of Us,* pp. 28–32; Aitken, *Nixon,* pp. 196–197, 223–224, 339–340; Bruce Mazlish, *The Leader, the Led, and the Psyche: Essays in Psychohistory* (Hanover, MA: Wesleyan University Press, 1990), pp. 207–210; and Ambrose, *Nixon: The Education of a Politician 1913–1962,* pp. 22–32.

Nixon meets with his Cabinet

RICHARD

Yes, Mother . . .

HANNAH

Harold may have lost touch with his Bible, but thou must never lapse.

Then, she extends her hand.

HANNAH

Now, give it to me . . .

Richard is about to plead ignorance.

HANNAH

Do not tell a lie, Richard . . . The cornsilk cigarette Harold gave thee behind the store this morning.

RICHARD *(LYING)*

I don't . . . have them. Mother . . . I swear, I . . . didn't smoke.

HANNAH *(WITHDRAWING)*

I see . . . Well then, Richard, we have nothing more to talk about, do we?

RICHARD *(FEARFUL, BLURTS OUT)*

Please, Mother, it . . . it was just one time, Mother, I'm . . . I'm sorry.

HANNAH

So am I. Thy father will have to know of thy lying.

RICHARD *(TERRIFIED)*

No, no! Please, don't. Don't tell him. I'll never do it again. I promise. I promise . . . *(on the edge of tears)* Please, Mama . . .

HANNAH *(PAUSE)*

I expect more from thee, Richard.

He buries his head in her skirt. The faintest smile on Hannah's face as she pockets the cigarette.

RICHARD

Please! I'll never let you down again, Mother. Never. I promise.

HANNAH

Then this shall be our little secret. (*She lifts his face to hers.*) Remember that I see into thy soul as God sees. Thou may fool the world. Even thy father. But not me, Richard. Never me.

RICHARD

Mother, think of me always as your faithful dog . . .[60]

SCENE SEVENTEEN

INT. NIXON HOUSE—KITCHEN—NIGHT

HANNAH puts the food on the table as FRANK NIXON, sleeves rolled up, waits at the head of the table, fuming. ARTHUR (6) and DONALD (9) join RICHARD and HAROLD. (The fifth brother, Edward, has not yet been born.)

Hannah takes the remaining food to TWO HOBOS who are standing outside the kitchen door. Harold reaches for his spoon impatiently.

FRANK

Don't you dare, Harold!

HAROLD *(A LITTLE LAUGH)*

I just thought, since the food was here . . .

HANNAH

We haven't said grace yet. Richard.

RICHARD *(NERVOUSLY)*

Is it my turn?

Hannah nods. Richard puts his hands together, trying to please.

RICHARD

Heavenly Father, we humbly thank—

FRANK *(INTERRUPTS)*

I'll do it. There's a coupla things I wanna say.

---

[60]For Nixon referring to himself as his mother's "dog," see Morris, *Richard Milhous Nixon*, p. 73. This actually appeared in a letter the ten-year-old Nixon wrote to his mother, which he closed, "Your good dog, Richard."

                          HANNAH
Could thou at least remove thy apron, Frank?

                          FRANK
This blood pays the bills, Hannah. I'm not ashamed of how I earn my money.
(*clears his throat*) Heavenly Father, you told Adam in the Garden, after that
business with the snake, that man would have to earn his way by the sweat of
his face. Well, as far as I can tell, Father, what was true in Eden is true in Whittier, California. So we ask you now to remind certain of our young people . . .
(*glares at Harold*) That the *only* way to get a new suit to go to the promenade
with Margaret O'Herlihy, who happens to be a Catholic by the way, is to *work
for it.* (*then*) Amen.

Little cute-faced Arthur looks up.

                          ARTHUR
I like Margaret O'Herlihy too. She's very pretty. Can we pray now?

The boys start giggling.

                          HANNAH
Arthur!

                          FRANK
You think this is funny? (*then*) Pretty soon you boys are gonna have to get out
there and scratch, 'cause you're not gonna get anywhere on your good looks.
Just ask those fellas . . .

*Frank waves to the Hobos, now squatting and wolfing down the food. They
look up, embarrassed.*

                          FRANK
Charity is only gonna get you so far—even with saints like your mother around.
Struggle's what gives life meaning, not victory—struggle. When you quit strug-
gling, they've beaten you, and then you end up in the street with your hand out.

Frank begins eating; the rest follow.

                          NIXON *(v.o.)*
My mother was a saint, but my old man struggled his whole life. You could call
him a little man, a poor man, but they never beat him. I always tried to remember
that when things didn't go my way . . .

SCENE EIGHTEEN

EXT. WHITTIER FOOTBALL FIELD—DAY (1932)

FOOTBALL MONTAGE: RICHARD (19), 150 pounds, is on the defensive line as the ball is hiked. ("Let's get fired up!") He gets creamed by a 200-pound offensive tackle. He jumps up, no face guard, hurting, and resets. AD LIB football chatter. We can tell from Richard's cheap uniform that he is a substitute. But:

We go again. And again. Building a special RHYTHM of JUMP CUTS show-ing Nixon getting mauled each time. He doesn't have a chance, this kid, but he has pluck. And he comes back for more. And more.[61]

This image of pain and humiliation should weave itself in and out of the film in repetitive currents. As we CUT TO:

SCENE NINETEEN

OMIT #19

SCENE TWENTY

INT. HILTON HOTEL—BALLROOM—NIGHT (1962)

We move down past a blizzard of balloons and confetti blown by a hotel air-conditioner to a huge "NIXON FOR GOVERNOR" banner.

NIXON thrusts his arms in the air—the twin-V salute. The CROWD cheers wildly. SUBTITLE READS: "CALIFORNIA GOVERNORSHIP, 1962."

---

[61]Nixon's Whittier football teammate, Richard Harris, reports that the coach, "Chief" New-man, a full-blooded Indian, needed a sturdy wall of resistance against which to try out his new plays. Dick Nixon volunteered for this unrewarding and painful assignment. Harris says he ad-mired Dick's courage as he was mauled, slammed back, and knocked down, all in the cause of building a better first string. See Kornitzer, *The Real Nixon,* p. 110.

SCENE TWENTY-ONE

INT. HILTON HOTEL—SUITE—NIGHT

NIXON is slumped in an armchair, feet on a coffee table, holding a drink, going through defeat once again.

HALDEMAN stares glumly at the TV. PAT sits across the room in grim silence.

ON TV—a NEWSCASTER stands in front of a tally board with the network logo: "Decision '62."

NEWSCASTER
President Kennedy has called Governor Pat Brown to congratulate him . . .

HALDEMAN
Are we making a statement?

NEWSCASTER
ABC is now projecting that Brown will defeat Richard Nixon by more than a quarter of a million votes.

NIXON holds up his drink to the screen. Moves to a piano.

NIXON
Thank you, Fidel Castro.

PAT
You're not going to blame this on Castro, are you?

NIXON
I sure am. The Goddamned missile crisis united the whole country behind Kennedy. And he was supporting Brown. People were scared, that's why.[62]

PAT
I suppose Castro staged the whole thing just to beat you.

---

[62]Nixon laid much of the blame for his defeat in 1962 on the missile crisis. See Ambrose, *Nixon: The Education of a Politician 1913–1962*, p. 668; Aitken, *Nixon*, p. 204; and Nixon, *RN*, p. 244.

NIXON

Buddy, before you join the jubilation at my being beaten again, you should remember: People vote not out of love, but *fear.* They don't teach that at Sunday School or at the Whittier Community Playhouse!

HALDEMAN *(INTERJECTS)*

I should go down and check in with our people.

Haldeman leaves quickly.

ON TV: GOVERNOR BROWN steps to the podium. A band plays "Happy Days Are Here Again."

PAT *(BACK AT DICK)*

I'm glad they don't. You forget I had a life before California, a rough, rough life. Life isn't always fair, Dick . . .

Nixon drowns her out, playing the piano (well) and singing along bitterly.

NIXON

"—the skies above are clear again. Let's sing a song of cheer again—" . . . Cocksucker!

Pat turns off the TV.

NIXON *(CONTINUES TO PLAY)*

Don't you want to listen to Brown's victory speech?

PAT

No. I'm not going to listen to any more speeches ever again.

NIXON

Amen to that.

PAT

It's over, Dick.

NIXON

I'll concede in the morning.

PAT

Not that. *(then)* Us.

Nixon stops playing, looks at her.

PAT (COLDLY)

I've always stood by you. I campaigned for you when I was pregnant. During Checkers, when Ike wanted you out, I told you to fight. This is different, Dick. You've changed. You've grown more . . . bitter, like you're at war with the world. You weren't that way before. You scare me sometimes . . . I'm fifty years old now, Dick. How many people's hands have I shaken—people I didn't like, people I didn't even know. It's as if, I don't know, I went to sleep a long time ago and missed the years between . . . I've had enough.

He moves towards her awkwardly. Pat struggles. She goes to a window, her back to him. She is not one to enjoy "scenes." She tends to accommodate to others to preserve an aura of happiness.

NIXON (CONFUSED)

What are you saying? What are you talking about?

PAT

I want a divorce.[63]

NIXON

My God—divorce?
(*beat*)
. . . What about the girls?

PAT

The girls will grow up. They only know you from television anyway.

NIXON

It would ruin us, Buddy, our family.

PAT

You're ruining us. If we stay with you, you'll take us down with you. (*beat*) This isn't political, Dick. This is our life.

NIXON

Everything's political, for Christ's sake! I'm political. And you're political too!

---

[63]On Pat threatening to divorce Nixon, see Brodie, *Richard Nixon*, p. 466; and Bernstein and Woodward, *The Final Days*, p. 165.

Dick and Pat (Joan Allen) at daughter Tricia's wedding

PAT

No, I'm not! I'm finished.

*She is very serious. He sees it. It terrifies him. The same withdrawal he ex-
perienced from his mother.*

NIXON

This is just what they want, Buddy. Don't you see? They want to drive us apart.
To beat us. We can't let them do it. We've been through too much together,
Buddy . . . We belong together.

PAT *(IRONIC)*

That's what you said the first time we met. You didn't even know me.

*MARRIAGE MONTAGE: During this scene we have a series of SHOTS of
their courtship—the Whittier College campus, 1930s Los Angeles; driving in
a car together; the wedding; the FIRST CHILD; the Pacific NAVAL CAPTAIN
underneath a palm tree; running as a first-time CONGRESSMAN with Pat;
the EISENHOWER years . . .*

NIXON *(VERY TENDER)*

Oh, yes I did. I told you I was gonna marry you, didn't I? On the first date . . .
I said it because I knew . . . I knew you were the one . . . so solid and so strong

. . . and so beautiful. You were the most beautiful thing I'd ever seen . . . I don't want to lose you, Buddy, ever . . .

INTERCUT WITH:

NIXON seeking tenderness. He puts a hand on her arm. He tries gently to pull her towards him, to kiss her.

PAT

Dick, don't . . .

NIXON

Buddy, look at me . . . just look at me. Do you really want me to quit?

She stares out the window. A long moment.

PAT

We can be happy. We really can. We love you, Dick. The girls and I . . .

NIXON

If I stop . . . there'll be no more talk of divorce?

A long moment. She finally turns her eyes to him, assenting.

NIXON

I'll do it. (*waves his hand*) No more.

PAT

Are you serious?

NIXON

Yeah . . . I'm out.

PAT

Is that the truth?

NIXON

I'll never run again. I promise.

SHARP CUT TO:

SCENE TWENTY-TWO

INT. HILTON HOTEL—HALLWAY—NIGHT

NIXON stalks down the hallway, fuming. HALDEMAN walks alongside.

NIXON

Where are they?

HALDEMAN *(WORRIED, POINTS TO A DOOR)*

Dick, you don't have to make a statement. Herb covered it for you.

NIXON

No![64]

He bursts through the door into:

SCENE TWENTY-THREE

INT. HILTON HOTEL—PRESS CONFERENCE—BALLROOM—NIGHT

A noisy CROWD of REPORTERS reacts, excitedly, to NIXON'S fast entry. The smell of blood in the air.

TIME CUT TO:

NIXON at the podium.

NIXON

. . . I believe Governor Brown has a heart, even though he believes I do not. I believe he is a good American, even though he feels I am not. I am proud of the fact that I defended my opponent's patriotism; you gentlemen didn't report it but I am proud I did that. And I would appreciate it, for once, gentlemen, if you would write what I say.

(time dissolve)

. . . For sixteen years, ever since the Hiss case, you've had a lot of fun—a lot

---

[64]On Nixon's decision to talk to the press after the 1962 defeat, see Ambrose, *Nixon: The Education of a Politician 1913–1962*, pp. 668–671; Nixon, *RN*, pp. 244–246; and Aitken, *Nixon*, p. 304.

of fun. But recognize you have a responsibility, if you're against a candidate, to give him the shaft, but if you do that, at least put one lonely reporter on the campaign who will report what the candidate says now and then . . .

HALDEMAN glances at KLEIN.

NIXON

. . . I think all-in-all I've given as good as I've taken. But as I leave you I want you to know—just think how much you're going to be missing: you won't have Nixon to kick around anymore. Because, gentlemen, this is my last press conference . . .

A FEW REPORTERS shout questions. There is a loud confusion, but Nixon has vanished.

KLEIN

What the hell was that?

HALDEMAN *(BEAT)*

Suicide.

CUT TO:

NIXON HISTORICAL MONTAGE:

A grainy "NEWSREEL" treats NIXON as political history, now over. The ANONYMOUS REPORTERS return—YOUNG NIXON, in his Navy uniform, is campaigning in California in the 1940s against Voorhis and Douglas.

REPORTER 1 *(v.o.)*

We can now officially write the political obituary of Richard Milhous Nixon . . .[65] He came into being as part of the big post-war 1946 Republican sweep of the elections. People were weary of the New Deal and FDR's big government . . .

Images of FDR, TRUMAN, and ACHESON, early Cold War imagery—the Soviets, Berlin.

---

[65]Five nights after Nixon's 1962 defeat, ABC Television broadcast a program entitled "The Political Obituary of Richard Nixon." See Nixon, *RN*, pp. 246–247; Ambrose, *Nixon: The Education of a Politician 1913–1962*, p. 673; and Aitken, *Nixon*, p. 306. The version contained in this script is not intended to reflect the actual contents of that program.

REPORTER 1 *(v.o.)*

. . . The United States had been a strong ally of the Soviet Union, which had lost more than twenty million people in its fight against Nazism. But Nixon, coming from the South Pacific war, won his first term in the House by freely associating his liberal opponent, Jerry Voorhis, with Communism.

Images of Voorhis, Hoover . . . NIXON working a CROWD, standing on the tailgate of a station-wagon, debating Voorhis.

REPORTER 2 *(v.o.)*

For Nixon, politics was war. He didn't have opponents, he had enemies. He didn't run against people, he ruined them . . . He won his California seat in the U.S. Senate in 1950 in a vicious campaign against liberal congresswoman and movie actress, Helen Gahagan Douglas . . .

NEWSFILM of NIXON and CHOTINER at a rally with PAT. Images of DOUGLAS follow. CAMPAIGN WORKERS handing out smear literature.

NIXON *("NEWSFILM LOOK")*

How can Helen Douglas, capable actress that she is, take up so strange a role as a foe of Communism? Why, she's pink right down to her underwear . . .

REPORTER 3 *(v.o.)*

. . . Nixon quickly became the Republicans' attack dog. He tore into Truman for losing Mainland China in 1949, and blamed the war in Korea on a weak foreign policy . . . His speeches, if more subtle than those of his Republican ally, Joe McCarthy, were just as aggressive . . .

Nixon at another rally with Pat.

NIXON *("NEWSFILM LOOK")*

. . . I promise to continue to expose the people that have sold this country down the river! Until we have driven all the crooks and Communists and those that have helped them out of office!!

Images of Truman, the hydrogen bomb, the Rosenbergs, Klaus Fuchs, Oppenheimer, the Chinese taking over in 1949 . . . Mao.

NIXON *("NEWSFILM LOOK")*

The direct result of Truman's decisions is that China has gone Communist. Mao is a monster. Why?! Why, Mr. Acheson?! Who in the State Department is watching over American interests?! Who has given the Russians the atomic bomb?! . . . Today the issue is slavery! The Soviet Union is an example of the slave state in its ultimate development. Great Britain is halfway down the same road; powerful interests are striving to impose the British socialist system upon the people of the United States!

REPORTER 2 *(v.o.)*
. . . Nixon became one of the leading lights on the notorious House Un-American Activities Committee, questioning labor leaders, Spanish Civil War veterans, Hollywood celebrities . . .

NIXON *(QUESTIONING WITNESS)*
Can you tell me today the names of any pictures which Hollywood has made in the last five years showing the evils of totalitarian Communism?

NIXON surrounded by REPORTERS outside the HUAC hearing room.

REPORTER 4 *(v.o.)*
. . . but it was the Alger Hiss case that made Nixon a household name . . .

IMAGES of Alger Hiss's career: clerking for Oliver Wendell Holmes; with FDR at Yalta, with Churchill, with Stalin.

REPORTER 4 *(v.o.)*
. . . One of the architects of the United Nations, intimate of FDR and Oliver Wendell Holmes, Alger Hiss was a darling of the liberals. *(then)* But Whittaker Chambers, a former freelance journalist, said he was a Communist.

WHITTAKER CHAMBERS testifying before HUAC.

CHAMBERS *(TV INTERVIEW)*
. . . if the American people understood the real character of Alger Hiss, they would boil him in oil . . .

REPORTER 4 *(v.o.)*
. . . Hiss claimed he was being set up by Nixon and J. Edgar Hoover to discredit the New Deal's policies. The case came down to an Underwood typewriter, and a roll of film hidden in a pumpkin patch.

DOCUMENTARY IMAGE—A DETECTIVE-TYPE reaches into a hollowed-out pumpkin and pulls out microfilm . . . In his congressional office, NIXON ex-

amines the film with a magnifying glass, playing to the cameras with a deadly serious mien . . . Shots of MRS. HISS, the Underwood typewriter.

REPORTER 4 (v.o.)

. . . Years later the Freedom of Information Act revealed that the film showed a report on business conditions in Manchuria, and fire extinguishers on a U.S. destroyer.[66] None of these documents was classified. Were they planted by Chambers, who seemed to have a strange, almost psychotic fixation with Alger Hiss?

NIXON ("NEWSFILM")

I asked Hiss if he'd ever known Chambers before. When he said 'no,' that's when I knew he was lying. That's when I knew I had him . . . He was twisting, turning, evading, changing his story to fit the evidence he knew we had . . . But I tell you this: I vow that we're going to go after everyone responsible for selling this country down the river . . .

NIXON points to a headline—"Hiss Convicted."

REPORTER 1 (v.o.)

After two confusing trials, Hiss went to jail for perjury. To the right wing, Nixon was a hero and a patriot. To the liberals, he was a shameless self-promoter who had vengefully destroyed a fine man. Eleanor Roosevelt angrily condemned him. It was to become a pattern: you either loved Richard Nixon or you hated him.

A brief IMAGE here that will recur throughout the film. An image of evil—call it "The Beast."

REPORTER 2 (v.o.)

Driven by demons that seemed more personal than political, his rise was meteoric. Congressman at 33, senator at 35, Eisenhower's vice-presidential candidate at 39. Then came the Checkers Crisis . . . Nixon was accused of hiding a secret slush fund. About to be kicked off the ticket by Ike, he went on national television in an unprecedented appearance . . .

INTERCUT Checkers speech—NIXON, looking and sounding like Uriah Heep, pleads with the American people on TV, as PAT sits uncomfortably in an armchair nearby.

---

[66]For an in-depth discussion of the contents of the Pumpkin Papers, see John Chabot Smith, *Alger Hiss: The True Story* (New York: Holt, Rinehart and Winston, 1976), pp. 331–354.

NIXON *(ON TV)*

. . . so now what I am going to do is to give this audience a complete financial history. Everything I've earned, everything I've spent, everything I owe . . .

Nixon forces a smile. Pat is clearly in pain, mortified.

REPORTER 2 *(v.o.)*

The list included their house, their Oldsmobile, Pat's Republican cloth coat, and lastly, in what was to become history—a sentimental gift from a Texas businessman . . .

NIXON *(ON TV)*

You know what it was? It was a little cocker spaniel dog. Black and white spotted. And . . . our little girl, Tricia, the six-year-old, named it "Checkers." And you know, the kids love that dog and we're going to keep it . . .

Pat Nixon listens to the "Checkers" speech

REPORTER 4 *(v.o.)*

Fifty-eight million people saw it. It was shameless. It was manipulative.
(then)
It was a huge success!

DOCUMENTARY REPLACEMENT–Nixon with Ike in triumph. A clip of Eisenhower praising Nixon. Nixon and Pat standing up to rock-throwing STU-DENTS in Venezuela. Pointing his finger at KHRUSHCHEV in the Kitchen Debate.

REPORTER 3 *(v.o.)*

Eisenhower put Nixon back on the ticket . . . Responding to attacks on Truman, Acheson, and the entire Democratic Party for betraying American principles in China, Korea, and elsewhere—it was two-time Democratic presidential candidate, Adlai Stevenson, who perhaps best summed up the national unease with Richard Nixon . . .

DOCUMENTARY–SHOTS of ADLAI STEVENSON campaigning in '52 and '56 against IKE. Images of JOE MCCARTHY precede. The HERBLOCK CARTOON of Nixon crawling out of the sewer system. Others of his cartoons follow.[67]

STEVENSON *(RADIO V.O.)*

. . . This is a man of many masks. Who can say they have seen his real face? He is on an ill-will tour, representing McCarthyism in a white collar. Nixonland has no standard of truth but convenience, and no standard of morality except the sly innuendo, the poison pen, the anonymous phone call; the land of smash and grab and anything to win . . . "What, ultimately, shall it profit a man if he shall gain the whole world and lose his own soul?"

Ending with more recent SHOTS of Nixon campaigning in '60 and '62. As the IMAGES spot out in newsreel style:

REPORTER 4 *(v.o.)*

It was a great story of its time and, in California where it started, it has come to a crashing end. It is too bad in a way, because the truth is, we never knew who Richard Nixon really was. And now that he is gone, we never will . . .

---

[67]For a selection of Herblock's Nixon cartoons, see Herbert Block, *Herblock's State of the Union* (New York: Simon & Schuster, 1972).

"March of Time"-type music as we SLOWLY FADE INTO:

> NIXON *(v.o.)*

"Your father stinks" . . . They actually said this to Tricia. Two girls wearing Kennedy pins. At Chapin!

SCENE TWENTY-FOUR

INT. FIFTH AVE APARTMENT—NEW YORK CITY—NIGHT (1963)

A New York cocktail party. Society DAMES. Rich, conservative BUSINESS-MEN, platters of martinis and hors d'oeuvres carried by white-gloved BLACK BUTLERS. The fashions are Balenciaga and Courreges, tipping to the shorter hemlines; the mood is smoky and upbeat, the folks pressed into airtight packs of loud conversation.

NIXON is talking to JOHN MITCHELL (54), his wife MARTHA (40's), and TWO OTHER ASSOCIATES of the law firm he has joined.

> NIXON *(ANGUISHED)*

She was crying when she came home *(shakes his head)*. She was devastated.

> MARTHA

Poor little Tricia! Well, that's New York—makes for a tougher animal later in life.

> NIXON *(TO THE OTHER LAWYERS)*

I told her, her daddy couldn't even get a Goddamned job in this city when I got out of Duke. Every white-shoe lawyer firm turned me down. Didn't have the right "look." Hell, I couldn't even get into the FBI.

> MITCHELL *(INDICATING)*

Dick, we should catch Rocky 'fore he leaves.

NELSON ROCKEFELLER, Governor of New York, dominates the room. Big smile, horn-rimmed glasses. Next to him is HAPPY, his new wife, much younger.

> NIXON *(GLANCING)*

Well, he can walk in this direction too.

MARTHA

Did you catch that picture of you in the *News* last week, Dick? You were stand-ing in a crowd on Fifth Avenue, and you were looking straight ahead, and every-one else was looking the other way like you'd just farted or something. (*laughs*) It said: "Who Remembers Dick Nixon?" I was screaming. It was so funny!

NIXON

Yeah, that was hilarious, Martha. (*for the others*) They were all looking the other way 'cause they were waiting for the light to change. I called AP on that—typ-ical of the press in this country, they wouldn't correct it. That or they print the retraction right next to the girdle ads.

LAWYER

Oh, I've read some very nice things about you.

MARTHA (*PUTS HER HAND ON NIXON'S ARM*)

Maybe where you come from. But where I come from, Dick Nixon is as misun-derstood as a fox in a henhouse. And you know why? (*they all wait*) Because, honey, they all think your smile and your face are never in the same place at the same time. (*nervous laughter*) You and me—we gotta work on that, sweetie . . .

MITCHELL (*GUIDING DICK AWAY*)

Someone freshen Martha's drink. I think she's down a quart.

MARTHA

Well, zippety-fucking-doo-dah!

Mitchell moves Nixon away towards the Rockefeller GROUP.

MITCHELL

Sorry, Dick. She's a little tipsy.

NIXON

You mean *smashed!* She called up at *midnight* last week. Talking a bunch of crap! Pat can't stand her.

MITCHELL

It's a thing she does. She talks at night.

NIXON

Talks all day too! How the hell can you put up with her, John?

MITCHELL *(SHEEPISHLY)*

What the hell—I love her. And she's great in bed.

Rockefeller holds court, not immediately noticing Nixon.

ROCKEFELLER

. . . There are no guarantees in politics. I'm going to roll the dice with everyone else.

HENRY KISSINGER (40's), intense, holds a martini.

KISSINGER

Well, if a Rockefeller can't become President of the United States, what's the
point of democracy? *(laughter)*

NIXON

The point of democracy is that even the son of a grocer can become president. *(laughs)*

ROCKEFELLER

And you came damn close, too, Dick.

As Rocky clutches Dick, who doesn't like to be touched:

ROCKEFELLER

Howya doin'! New York treating you okay? I'm sorry I haven't been able to
see you at all . . .

NIXON *(CUTTING OFF THE APOLOGY)*

Well enough. You're looking "happy," Nelson. *(with a look to Happy)*

ROCKEFELLER

Oh, Happy! *(introduces his new wife)* Dick Nixon . . . You remember him.

NIXON

Hi, Happy. Well, you're obviously making him happy.

ROCKEFELLER

Repartee, Dick—very good. Hey, I feel ten years younger! It makes a helluva
difference, let me tell ya! How's the lawyer life?

NIXON

Never made so much money in my life. But my upbringing doesn't allow me to enjoy it. I did get to argue a case before the Supreme Court.

ROCKEFELLER

Won or lost?

NIXON

Lost.

ROCKEFELLER

Someday, Dick.

OTHERS are pressing in on Rockefeller, who is obviously the "star" of the party, so there is pressure to talk fast.

NIXON

But being out of the game gives me time to write.

ROCKEFELLER

To what?

NIXON

Write. You know, a book. I'm calling it "Six Crises." It's a good thing, Rocky— take some time off to write.

ROCKEFELLER *(SHAKING ANOTHER HAND)*

Hiya, fellow . . . What were they?

NIXON

What?

ROCKEFELLER

The "crises"?

NIXON

"Checkers" of course, Hiss, Ike's heart attack, Venezuela, the Kitchen Debate, and Kennedy.

ROCKEFELLER

Sounds like you got a crisis syndrome. Aren't you exaggerating a bit, Dick?
Call it three-and-a-half, maybe four . . .

NIXON *(LAUGHS AWKWARDLY)*

Let's wait and see how you survive *your* first crisis, Rocky . . .

ROCKEFELLER

Whatcha mean by that?

NIXON

You know: how the voters are gonna play your divorce.

*Rockefeller, who still clutches the visibly uncomfortable Nixon, gives him a
squeeze before finally releasing him.*

ROCKEFELLER

Don't you worry about it, fellah, and I won't. *(about to rejoin his wife)*

NIXON *(SMILING)*

Well, in any case, Rocky, I'll send you my book. "Six Crises."

ROCKEFELLER *(PAUSES, ASIDE)*

Whatcha predicting—your boy Goldwater's going to split the party?

NIXON

Some say *you* are, Rocky.

ROCKEFELLER

The Republican Party was never a home to extremists. You should know better. This guy's as stupid as McCarthy, and McCarthy never did you any good
in the long run, now did he?

*A pause. It lands home on Dick. Rockefeller turns to Kissinger, who's been
listening.*

ROCKEFELLER

Hey, you know Henry Kissinger—he's down from Harvard. On my staff, foreign policy whiz . . .[68]

---

[68]For Kissinger as Rockefeller's adviser, see Nixon, *RN,* p. 340; Henry Kissinger, *White House
Years* (New York: Little, Brown, 1979), pp. 4–5; and Aitken, *Nixon,* p. 363. Also note: Mitchell
introduced Kissinger to Nixon on November 25, 1968.

NIXON *(SHAKES HANDS)*

No, but I liked your book on nuclear weapons. We have similar views on the balance of power . . .

ROCKEFELLER

Well, that's wonderful. So get me this "crisis" thing, Dick; I'll be glad to take a look at it.

He raps Nixon one more time on the shoulder and moves off into a waiting GROUP.

NIXON

. . . as the old alliances crumble.

KISSINGER

Finally someone who's noticed! I'm a great admirer of yours too, Mr. Nixon. You are an unusual politician. We share a mutual idol—"Six Crises" sounds like a page from Churchill.

NIXON

Churchill, DeGaulle, Disraeli. They all went through the pain of losing power.

KISSINGER *(SMILES)*

But they all got it back again, didn't they? *(proffering a card)* We should have lunch sometime.

TIME CUT:

NIXON and MITCHELL move to the edges of the PARTY, which is now diminishing. They bypass PAT, who is absently staring off in conversation with MARTHA and SEVERAL OTHER LADIES who lunch . . . Nixon looks back at ROCKEFELLER leaving—KISSINGER hovering near him.

NIXON *(SEETHING)*

Rocky's full of shit! No way he's going to get nominated west of the Hudson with a new wife. He's gonna be drinking Scotches in retirement at some God-damn country club with the rest of the Republicans.

> ### MITCHELL
> Goes to show you all the moolah in the world can't buy you a brain.

> ### NIXON *(SNAGS A DRINK FROM A PASSING TRAY)*
> Well, he seems to have bought Kissinger.

> ### MITCHELL
> The Jewboy's a Harvard whore with the morals of an eel—sells himself to the highest bidder.

> ### NIXON *(BRAYS LOUDLY)*
> You're the one who should be in politics, John. You're tougher than I am. You never crack.

> ### MITCHELL
> That'll be the day.

> ### NIXON
> Let's get out of here; it's too painful. I hate it. (*then*) We went bowling last weekend. Next weekend we're going to the zoo. Whoever said there was life after politics was full of shit.

> ### MITCHELL
> Make some money, Dick, prove yourself to the Wall Street crowd and let Goldwater and Rockefeller take the fall against Kennedy.

Nixon looks at him.

> ### NIXON
> Yeah. John, I'm in hell. (*then*) I'll be mentally dead in two years and physically dead in four.[69] I miss—I don't know—making love to the people. I miss—entering a room. I miss—the pure "acting" of it. John, I've got to get back in the arena.

On Pat glancing over:

CUT TO:

---

[69]Ambrose, *Nixon: The Triumph of a Politician 1962–1972,* p. 63; and Wicker, *One of Us,* p. 275; see also Nixon interview, New York *Times,* April 20, 1964.

SCENE TWENTY-FIVE

INT. DALLAS CONVENTION SITE—DAY (1963)

SPOTLIGHT on a sexy Studebaker car of the era. A DRUM ROLL, and suddenly out of the various apertures of the car pop six half-naked HOSTESSES doing the twist. Wild cheers.

The ANNOUNCER describes the new gimmicks on the car (AD LIB) as we swing to reveal NIXON, looking uncomfortable in a Stetson cowboy hat shaking hands with AUTOGRAPH SEEKERS and car buffs, posing for cheesecake photographs. A banner behind him reveals: "Dallas Welcomes Studebaker Dealers." [70]

The Studebaker GIRLS are fanning out through the sales booths, whistling, swinging whips, as a large man in a Stetson, JACK JONES,[71] *accompanied by a suave-looking Cuban-born businessman, TRINI CARDOZA, breaks through the autograph hounds to rescue Nixon.*

                         JONES
That's enough now, let him be. He's just like you and me, folks, just another lawyer . . . Let's go, let's go, break it up . . .

Moving Nixon out of there.

                         NIXON
Thanks, Jack. You sure throw a helluva party.

                         JONES
Party ain't started yet, Dick. Got these gals coming over to the ranch later for a little private "thing," y'know . . . There's some fellows I want you to meet.

                         NIXON
Well, uh, Trini and I have an early plane. We were hoping to get back to New York in time for . . .

---

[70]Nixon attended a convention in Dallas on November 21, 1963. For this, see Wicker, *One of Us,* p. 267; Ambrose, *Nixon: The Triumph of a Politician 1962–1972,* pp. 31–32; Nixon, *RN,* pp. 251–252.

[71]Jack Jones is a composite and fictional character. Richard Nixon knew, and befriended, a number of wealthy businessmen during his career.

TRINI

It'll be okay, Dick; these guys are interesting . . . real quiet. And the girls are too.

JONES

Y'know, it's not every day we Texans get to entertain the future President of the United States.

NIXON

Like you said Jack, I'm just a New York lawyer now.

JONES *(CHUCKLES, WITH A LOOK TO TRINI)*

We'll see about that.

New FANS circle up, their WIVES giggling.

FANS

Oh, Mr. Nixon, could you sign . . . ? My wife and I think you are just the greatest. Please run again . . .

More fans flood in, encircling him. On Trini and Jack watching this.

SCENE TWENTY-SIX

EXT. JONES RANCH—DAY

An entire LONGHORN STEER turns on a spit in a large barbecue pit, basted by black SERVANTS. We see a sprawling Spanish-style RANCH HOUSE in the countryside. The parking area looks like a Cadillac dealership. The CROWD is a mixture of CORPORATE EXECUTIVES, CUBANS, and COWBOY-TYPES, some WIVES.

TRINI is talking to TWO of the DANCERS, nodding his head in NIXON's direction. They look, and smile at him.

Across the lawn, Nixon smiles back awkwardly as JACK JONES nudges him. They both eat steaks and corncobs.

JONES

I know for a fact the one with the big tits is a Republican, and she'd do anything for the Party.

                              NIXON
She's quite pretty.

                              JONES
Her name's Sandy . . .

Trini joins them, bringing the girls.

                              NIXON
By the way, Jack, this looks like a pretty straightforward transaction to me,
but we should get into it soon—take just a few minutes, maybe up at the
house . . .

                    JONES (TO TRINI, COMING UP)
He's all business, ain't he, Trini? (*to Dick*) Dick, we could've had our own Goddamn lawyers handle this deal. We brought you down here 'cause we wanted
to talk to you . . .

                              TRINI
Dick, this is Teresa, and this is Sandy.

                              TERESA
Hi . . . Dick.

                              SANDY
Hi.

                              NIXON
Hello . . .

Pause.

                    SCENE TWENTY-SEVEN

                    INT. JONES RANCH–DAY

*A walk-in stone fireplace dominates the room; the heavy beams hung with
black wrought-iron candelabras. Thick cigar smoke impregnates the air; the
crowd has substantially thinned to the heaviest hitters. The MEN, now in shirt-
sleeves, drink from bottles of bourbon . . .*

A man—MITCH—emerges from one of the side rooms with a DANCER.

Off to the side in a semi-private alcove, SANDY, the dancer, tries to make conversation, but NIXON is showing her a picture of his kids.

NIXON

That's Julie . . . and that's Tricia. She, uh, reminds me a little bit of you . . .

SANDY *("INTERESTED")*

Oh yeah . . . she really is . . . wholesome.[72]

Trini interjects, trying to help out.

TRINI

So what's up? . . . Uh, I get the feeling Sandy really likes you, Dick.

SANDY

I like that name, *Dick.*

TRINI

Why don't you two disappear in the bedroom there. Come back in half an hour . . .

---

[72]ALTERNATE VERSION

SANDY

She really is . . . wholesome. So, what's it like to be so famous—a vice-president and all?

NIXON

Uh, it's not like that Sandy. You see, the reason I got into politics in the first place was . . . well, to do something for the people . . . to change things. And what's really amazing about my story . . . it's not so different from anyone else's . . . I came from the wrong side of the tracks, you know, I grew up a butcher's son . . . And I think that's the great thing about America—that you can turn your life around. You can't do that anywhere else in the world, Sandy, believe me, and I've traveled everywhere—(genuinely) but here you can change . . . You can make a difference.

Trini interjects. Sandy seems bored.

TRINI

So . . . what are you two talking about? (to Dick) You know there's more privacy back in the . . .

NIXON

No, Trini, we're fine right here . . .

NIXON

Uh . . . Trini.

Trini smiles and, leaving Dick the playing field, vanishes. Sandy, feeling the vacuum, holds Nixon's hand.

SANDY

What do you say? Do you like me, Mister *Vice* President?

Nixon swallows hard, blushing now. He sweats, very uncomfortable with this intimacy.

NIXON *(CROAKS)*

Yes, of course. But . . . uh . . .

A brief IMAGE flashes by—beastlike, offensive, unworthy.

NIXON

. . . I don't really know you yet, Sandy . . . What do you like? I mean, what kind of clothes do you like? Do you like blue . . . red?

SANDY

Oh, I like satin, I like pink . . .

NIXON

What kind of, uh . . . music do you like?

SANDY

I like jazz . . .

NIXON

Yeah . . . Guy Lombardo . . .

SANDY

Elvis I like too.

NIXON

Oh yeah, he's good.

Sandy puts her hand on his face and head.

SANDY

. . . but it depends what I'm doing to the music, *Dick* . . .

NIXON

Uh, is your mother . . . still alive?

SANDY

Yeah, she lives in Dallas . . .

NIXON

She must be very attractive. Would she like an autograph? She might remember me . . . Where's Trini? (*looking around desperately*)

TIME CUT TO:

SCENE TWENTY-EIGHT

Later. The crowd has thinned further to a hard-core dozen. The last man—
Mitch—comes from the inner bedrooms, zipping up; the Servants, chasing out
the straggling Girls. Another round of drinks is served. The cigars are out.

JONES

Hell, Kennedy's pissed Cuba away to the Russians. And he don't know what
the hell he's doing in Vietnam. These are dangerous times, Dick, especially
for business . . .[73]

NIXON

Agreed.

A CUBAN in an Italian suit, one part sleazy, another part dangerous, steps
from the shadows.[74]

---

[73]For the anti-Kennedy sentiment in Dallas at this time, see Ambrose, *Nixon: The Triumph of
a Politician,* pp. 31–32; Peter Dale Scott, *Deep Politics and the Death of JFK* (Berkeley: University of California Press, 1993), pp. 214, 292; and Nixon, *RN,* p. 252.

[74]A note on the possible relationship between Texas oil men, anti-Castro Cuban exiles, and the
JFK assassination: In 1962, Kennedy removed Texas oil's exemption from taxes on repatriated
and foreign-invested revenues, causing a drop in oil company profits from 30% to about 15%,
and infuriating the owners. Then in 1963 he introduced legislation that would have sharply reduced the 27.5% depletion allowance, an even bigger potential loss. See J. Gary Shaw, *Cover-
Up* (Cleburne, TX: J. Gary Shaw, 1976), p. 170.

On November 21, 1963, in Dallas, a leading Texas oil man gave a party that reportedly was
secretly attended by J. Edgar Hoover. Nixon also attended this gathering. See Shaw, *Cover-*

CUBAN

We know what you tried to do for Cuba, Mr. Nixon. If you'd been elected in '60, we know Castro'd be *dead* by now.[75]

NIXON shares a look with TRINI.

NIXON

Gentlemen, I tried. I told Kennedy to go into Cuba. He heard me and he made his decision. I appreciate your sentiments, I've heard them from many fine Cuban patriots, but it's nothing I can do anything about. Now, it's a long drive back to Dallas tonight, and Trini and I have got an early flight tomorrow to New York . . .

JONES *(INTERRUPTING)*

Dick, these boys want you to run. (*The "boys" mutter in unison.*) They're serious. They can deliver the South and they can put Texas in your column. That would've done it in '60.

Up, pp. 182–183. Hoover had several important and influential friends in the Texas oil community. See Anthony Summers, *Official and Confidential: The Secret Life of J. Edgar Hoover* (New York: Putnam's, 1993), pp. 180–190, 232–235, 263–264. According to Summers, ". . . the (Texas oil) milieu was infested with organized crime figures." The Senate reported that 20% of their leasing business was owned by the Genovese crime family (Ibid., p. 233). Texas oil men also owned the Del Charro Hotel and the Del Mar racetrack in California where Hoover stayed and gambled.

Some of these Texas oil men were extreme right-wingers, with ties to the John Birch Society, the American Nazi Party, and radical anti-Castro Cubans. The name of one of them was in the address book of Jack Ruby (the murderer of Lee Harvey Oswald), and Ruby had visited with this man the day before the assassination. See Bernard Fensterwald, *Coincidence or Conspiracy* (New York: Zebra, 1977), pp. 571–575. On November 8, 1963, Oswald wrote a cryptic letter that the FBI believed may have been addressed to one of these oil men. See Henry Hurt, *Reasonable Doubt: An Investigation into the Assassination of John F. Kennedy* (Holt, Rinehart and Winston, 1985), p. 236.

The oil men contributed heavily to Nixon's campaigns, and one financed the anti-Kennedy ad in the Dallas Morning *News* on November 22, 1963. On November 21, 1963, one of the oil men was visited by Eugene Hale Brading (a.k.a. Jim Braden), a Mafia bagman who was arrested the next day in Dealey Plaza. See Seth Kantor, *Who Was Jack Ruby?* (New York: Everest House, 1978), p. 35. Brading also met with Ruby before the assassination (Ibid., p. 37).

Texas oil money helped fund the most radical and violent anti-Castro Cuban groups in South Florida, Texas, and Louisiana. See Hinckle and Turner, *The Fish Is Red*, p. 202; Scott, *Deep Politics and the Death of JFK*, pp. 212–221. The oil companies allowed the exiles to use their offshore platforms as staging areas for raids into Cuba. This alignment of right-wing Texas oil men, radical anti-Castro Cubans, and organized crime figures represented what one scholar calls an anti-Kennedy coalition. See Scott, *Deep Politics and the Death of JFK*, pp. 211–225.

[75]Nixon wrote in 1964 that as Vice President he felt "we must do whatever was necessary to rid Cuba of Castro and Communism." See Richard Nixon, "Cuba, Castro and John F. Kennedy," *Reader's Digest*, November 1964, p. 291.

NIXON

Only if Kennedy dumps Johnson.

JONES

That sonofabitch Kennedy is coming back down here tomorrow. Dick, we're willing to put up a shitpot fulla money to get rid of him—more money'n you ever dreamed of.

NIXON

Nobody's gonna beat Kennedy in '64 with all the money in the world.

A beat.

CUBAN

Suppose Kennedy don't run in '64?

Nixon looks at him. A subconscious IMAGE again—something slimy, reptilian.

NIXON

Not a chance.

CUBAN

These are dangerous times, Mr. Nixon. Anything can happen.

Another pause. Nixon gathers together his papers and briefcase.

NIXON

Yes, well . . . Gentlemen, I promised my wife. I'm out of politics.

MITCH *(INSOLENT SMILE)*

You just came down here for the weather, right, Mr. Nixon?

NIXON

I came down here to close a deal for Studebaker.

TRINI

What about '68, Dick?

NIXON

Five years, Trini? In politics, that's an eternity.

JONES

Your country needs you, Dick.

Nixon shakes his hand, departs.

NIXON

Unfortunately, the country isn't available right now.

SCENE TWENTY-NINE

EXT. LOVE FIELD—DAY (1963)

A CROWD is waiting for Air Force One. People hold banners, signs: "Dallas Loves JFK," "We Love You Jackie."

A Cadillac pulls up at the far corner of the tarmac. NIXON gets out with CARDOZA. They walk toward a small executive PLANE.

Nixon pauses, looks up. He feels something ominous in the air.

NIXON

Trini, let's get out of here fast. Go check on the pilot, or they'll hold us up till he's out of the airport.

As Trini hurries off to the plane, Nixon takes one last look up at his fate written in the soft white clouds over Dallas. As we:

CUT TO:

SCENE THIRTY

DOCUMENTARY—JOHN KENNEDY coming off the plane at Love Field with JACKIE, waving to the crowd. The sound of a rushing, monstrous engine. Then wind.

CUT TO:

SCENE THIRTY-ONE

INT. NIXON'S FIFTH AVENUE APARTMENT—DAY (1963)

NIXON sits, subdued, in an armchair in a small study, caught between the fire in the grate, the TELEVISION images of the assassination, and the phone call he's on.

NIXON (LOW-KEY)
Look, Edgar, these guys were really strange, I mean, y'know . . . extremists, right-wing stuff, Birchers . . . Yeah? (*listens several beats*)[76]

PAT, smoking nervously, watches from another chair. Newspapers are strewn all around.

DOCUMENTARY IMAGES on the TV show a grieving JACKIE, BOBBY, TEDDY, and the TWO CHILDREN.

NIXON
I see . . . Oswald's got a Cuba connection . . . to Castro? I see. A real Communist. That makes sense. Thank you, Edgar.

He hangs up. It's evident he's still puzzled, but wants to believe.

NIXON
Hoover says this Oswald checks out as a beatnik-type, a real bum, pro-Castro . . .

TV images of BOBBY KENNEDY.

PAT
Dick, you should call Bobby.

NIXON
He doesn't want me at the funeral.[77]

---

[76]For Nixon's call to Hoover after the JFK assassination, see Wicker, *One of Us,* pp. 267–268; Nixon, *RN,* p. 252; Ambrose, *Nixon, The Triumph of a Politician 1962–1972,* p. 32.

[77]Nixon was not invited to JFK's funeral. He had to arrange to attend through Texas Congressman Pat Hillings. See Aitken, *Nixon,* p. 317.

                              PAT

You don't have to go.

                    NIXON *(GLANCES AT TV)*

De Gaulle's gonna be there. And Macmillan. And Adenauer. Nixon can't *not*
be there.

                              PAT

Then call him. I'm sure it was an oversight.

                             NIXON

No. It's his way. He hates me. Him and Teddy. They always hated me.

                              PAT

They've lost their brother. You know what that means, Dick.

Nixon sighs, watches the TV—images of a touch football game in Hyannis Port.

SHARP CUT BACK TO:

                  SCENE THIRTY-TWO

              INT. NIXON HOUSE—BEDROOM—DAY (1925)

*ARTHUR NIXON (7) cries in pain. RICHARD (12) helps FRANK, his father,
hold him on the bed as a DOCTOR twists a long needle into the base of
Arthur's spine.*[78]

                            ARTHUR

Daddy! Please! Make it STOP!!!

Arthur's eyes roll onto Richard for help, Richard can't bear it, pulls away.

---

[78]Sources disagree on the exact cause of Arthur's death; Nixon himself gave several different versions of it during his lifetime. For a discussion of it, see Brodie, *Richard Nixon*, pp. 506–507; Morris, *Richard Milhous Nixon*, pp. 83–84; Aitken, *Nixon*, pp. 25–26; Ambrose, *Nixon: The Education of a Politician 1913–1962*, pp. 41–43; and Mazlish, *The Leader, the Led, and the Psyche*, pp. 204–205.

SCENE THIRTY-THREE

INT. NIXON HOUSE—PARLOR—DAY (1925)

FRANK comes down the narrow stairs, shocked, fighting tears. HANNAH sits reading her Bible. The BOYS linger nervously around their made-up cots in the parlor.

FRANK *(SOBS)*
The doctors are afraid the little darling is going to die . . .

SCENE THIRTY-FOUR

INT. ARTHUR BEDROOM—DAY

ARTHUR laps at some tomato gravy on toast, which makes him happy. His face is angelic, as if he were getting better.

HANNAH feeds him, cleans his lips with a napkin, as RICHARD sits close by, squeezing Arthur's hand, puzzled by it all. FLASHES run through his head—Arthur sitting on his lap, learning to read; Dick swinging Arthur by his arms. DON and HAROLD are also there. The Doctor has gone.

ARTHUR *(LOW)*
Thank you, Mama, I feel better . . . I'm sleepy.

HANNAH *(REMOVING THE FOOD)*
We'll let thee rest now, my little angel.

She tucks him in. He yawns. The brothers are awkward, ready to leave. Arthur turns his loving eyes on Richard.

ARTHUR
Richard, don't you think . . . I should say a prayer before I sleep?

Richard is awkward, stutters.

HANNAH *(NEARLY CRACKING)*
Yes, Arthur, I do . . .

He smiles at her, then:

ARTHUR *(MURMURS)*

If I should die before I wake, I pray the Lord my soul to take . . .

He slips off, into a coma.

Richard watches, devastated.

SCENE THIRTY-FIVE

INT. NIXON HOUSE–PARLOR–ANOTHER DAY

RICHARD runs to his mother, HANNAH, who is coming down the stairs with FRANK. She seems very shaken, but quiet, off in another world. The moment Richard reaches her, throwing his arms around her skirt, she snaps him back. A harsh, angry voice.

HANNAH

No! . . . No. Don't . . .

Richard is shocked as his mother sweeps by in her private grief.

SCENE THIRTY-SIX

INT. NIXON STUDY–NEW YORK APARTMENT–DAY

RESUME NIXON–his face lost in the silence of the memory. The television SOUNDS fade back in alongside PAT's voice.

TV IMAGE–LYNDON JOHNSON being sworn in.

NIXON

. . . if I'd been president, they *never* would have killed me.

Pat is bewildered by the statement.

PAT *(o.s.)*

Dick? Are you going to call?

He looks at her, absent.

PAT

Bobby?

He looks back at the TV screen.

NIXON *(QUIETLY)*

No . . . I'll go through Lyndon. We'll be invited.

We flash suddenly to Kennedy's head being blown apart. Then back to JOHNSON as we:

CUT FORWARD TO:

SCENE THIRTY-SEVEN

SUBTITLE READS: "FIVE YEARS LATER—1968"

DOCUMENTARY IMAGE—CLOSE on LYNDON JOHNSON announcing:

JOHNSON

. . . accordingly, I shall not seek, and I will not accept, the nomination of my party for another term as your president . . .

CUT TO:

SCENE THIRTY-EIGHT

INT. NURSING HOME—DAY

HANNAH NIXON, in her seventies.

REPORTER 1 *(v.o.)*

. . . Johnson's withdrawal resurrects Richard Nixon as a strong Republican candidate against the war. His mother, Hannah Nixon, just before her death last year, commented on her son's chances . . .

REPORTER 2 *(OFF)*

Mrs. Nixon, do you think your son will ever return to politics?

HANNAH
I don't think he has a choice. He was always a leader.

REPORTER 2 (*OFF*)
Do you think he'd make a great president, Mrs. Nixon?

HANNAH (*UNSMILING*)
. . . if he's on God's side, yes . . .

SCENE THIRTY-NINE

EXT. NEW YORK APARTMENT BUILDING—DAY (1968)

REPORTERS flock outside the building as NIXON and his GROUP exit their car, trying to ignore the press.

SCENE FORTY

INT. NIXON APARTMENT—DAY (1968)

NIXON enters, ebullient, with MITCHELL, HALDEMAN, ZIEGLER, taking off their winter coats.

MITCHELL
Jesus, Dick, never seen anything like it! Even the Goddamn *Times* is saying you got it.

HALDEMAN
Vietnam's gonna put you in there this time, chief.

ZIEGLER
We got the press this time!

NIXON
And we got the "big mo"! We're back!

PAT (*o.s.*)
So? You've decided?

They turn. PAT is in the corridor.

PAT

Were you planning to tell me?

NIXON

We . . . haven't announced anything . . . uh . . .[79]

She's walking away, cold. Dick follows, with a look to his men.

NIXON

Uh, wait . . .

MITCHELL

You need her, Dick—in '60 she was worth five-, six million votes.

NIXON

Don't worry—I'll use the old Nixon charm on her.

As he goes:

HALDEMAN *(TO THE OTHERS)*

The old Nixon charm? Who could resist that.

SCENE FORTY-ONE

INT. NIXON BEDROOM—DAY

NIXON enters. PAT is mechanically taking his identical grey suits from the closet and laying them on the bed.

NIXON

Buddy? . . .

PAT

You should be going . . . the primaries are soon, aren't they? New Hampshire. . . .

NIXON

They love you, Buddy. They need you, too.

---

[79]Note: Nixon had already entered the presidential primaries before Johnson resigned. The chronology has been compressed for dramatic purposes.

PAT

I don't want *them* to love me.

NIXON

I need you out there. It won't be like the last time. The war's crippled the Democrats. I can win . . . We deserve it. Yeah, it's ours Buddy—*at last.* Nobody
knows that better than you. Frank Nixon's boy.

Pat slows her packing. Nixon takes her hand.

NIXON

Remember what Mom said? We're not like other people, we don't choose our
way. We can really *change things,* Buddy. We've got a chance to get it right.
We can change America!

She stops, looks at him, feels his surge of power.

NIXON

It was our dream too, Buddy, together . . . always.

PAT

Do you really want this, Dick?

NIXON

This. Above all.

PAT

And then you'll be happy?

The briefest smile opens her face. He takes the inch, presses in, hugs her.

NIXON

Yes . . . you know it! Yes . . . I will. Yeah!

PAT (*IN HIS EMBRACE*)

Then I'll be there for you.

NIXON (*EXULTANT*)

You're the strongest woman I ever met. I love you, Buddy.

PAT

Can I just ask for one thing?

NIXON

Anything.

PAT

Will you . . . would you kiss me?

He does so with all the earnestness he is capable of.

SCENE FORTY-TWO

INT. TELEVISION STUDIO—DAY (1968)

NIXON, fielding questions, is on a small stage, surrounded by a STUDIO AU-DIENCE in a semi-circle. A mike is around his neck, no separation from the people. PAT sits behind him, a campaign smile painted on. Nixon is visible to us on TV monitors inside an engineer's booth.[80]

NIXON *(ON TV)*

I would never question Senator Kennedy's patriotism. But going around the country promising *peace at any price* is *exactly* what the North Vietnamese want to hear!

Cheers, applause.

HALDEMAN *(TO THE TV DIRECTOR)*

Cue the crowd. Go to the women's group. Get the bald guy, he's great . . .

NIXON *(TV)*

I, unlike Senator Kennedy, have a *plan* to end the war. But not for peace at any price, but *peace with honor!*

INTERCUT:

---

[80]For a discussion of Nixon's television appearances, see Joe McGinniss, *The Selling of the President* (New York: Penguin, 1988), pp. 97–111. This scene is a composite of many of Nixon's appearances during the 1968 campaign as described by McGinniss.

SCENE FORTY-THREE

EXT. LA COSTA COUNTRY CLUB–ESTABLISHING–DAY

SCENE FORTY-FOUR

EXT. PRIVATE PATIO–LA COSTA COUNTRY CLUB–DAY

J. EDGAR HOOVER (60's), short and fat, covered with steam-room sweat, looks like a Roman emperor, as he watches the television intermittently, taking pictures of CLYDE TOLSON (50's), his long-time friend and associate. Tolson has a towel around his waist and one over his head.

> CLYDE *(SARCASTIC)*
> What do you think this plan is, Edgar? A nuclear attack?

> HOOVER
> He's lying, Clyde. Always has. That's why Nixon's always been useful. Hold still. And take your hand off your hip.

JOAQUIN, a very young, near-naked Hispanic boy, comes in with refreshments: orange slices, fruit, and pastel drinks with parasols.

INTERCUT TO:

SCENE FORTY-FIVE

INT. TV STUDIO–DAY

RON ZIEGLER checks his scripts as NIXON continues on the other side of the glass.

> DIRECTOR *(TURNS)*
> Who's next?

> ZIEGLER
> The Negro. We gotta have a Negro.

A BLACK MAN appears on the monitors.

Nixon answers questions (with Pat) before a TV studio audience during the 1968 campaign

BLACK MAN

Mr. Nixon . . . (Nixon: "Yes, sir!") You've made a career out of smearing people as Communists. And now you're building your campaign on the divisions in this country. Stirring up hatred, turning people against each other . . .

Ziegler and HALDEMAN are apoplectic.

HALDEMAN

What the *fuck's* he doing? He's making a speech.

ZIEGLER

Cut him off!

DIRECTOR

I can't cut him off! This isn't Russia!

The Black Man turns to the studio audience.

BLACK MAN

You don't want a real dialogue with the American people. This whole thing's been staged. These aren't real people. You're just a mouthpiece for an agenda that is hidden from us.

HALDEMAN *(SCREAMING)*

Go to commercial!

DIRECTOR

There are no commercials. You bought the whole half hour, baby . . .

The Black Man is walking down the aisle toward Nixon.

BLACK MAN *(IMPASSIONED)*

When are you going to tell us what you really stand for? When are you going to take the mask off and show us who you really are?

Close on Nixon's upper lip, sweating.

Haldeman watches intently.

HALDEMAN

It's a high, hard one, chief. Park it.

Nixon gathers himself, looks firmly at the Black Man.

NIXON

Yes, there are divisions in this country (Black Man: "Who made them—you made them!") . . . but I didn't create them. The *Democrats did!* If it's dialogue you want, you're more likely to get it from me than from the people who are burning down the cities! Just think about that . . . The great Doctor King said the same things. You know, young man, who a great hero is— Abraham Lincoln. Because he stood for common ground, he brought this country together . . .

The audience applauds. Haldeman punches Ziegler's arm.

HALDEMAN

I love that man! I love him. (*then*) Fire the sonofabitch who let that agitator in!

ZIEGLER *(RELIEVED)*

Okay, go to the little girl. Can he see the little girl?

DIRECTOR

She's right down front.

NIXON

I don't know if you can see her, but there's a little girl sitting down here with a sign. Could you hold that up, sweetheart?

ZIEGLER

Bag the guy. Take the sign!

The Camera cuts to a LITTLE GIRL holding a hand-lettered sign.

NIXON

The sign has on it three simple words. "Bring-us-together!" That is what I want, and that is what the great silent majority of Americans want!

The audience loves it. APPLAUSE signs light up.

NIXON (SHOUTS OVER)

And that's why I want to be president. I want to bring us together!

SCENE FORTY-SIX

EXT. PATIO–LA COSTA COUNTRY CLUB–DAY

Like a lizard, HOOVER eyes JOAQUIN, the Hispanic boy.[81]

TOLSON

. . . give me a break, Mary.

NIXON (V.O.: CONTINUES)

You all know me. I'm one of you. I grew up a stone's throw from here on a little lemon ranch in Yorba Linda . . .

HOOVER (MIMICS)

It was the poorest lemon ranch in California, I can tell you that. My father sold it before they found oil on it.

---

[81]On Hoover's alleged homosexuality, see Anthony Summers, *Official and Confidential*, pp. 80–88, 91–95, 240–248, 253–258, 377–378; Scott, *Deep Politics and the Death of JFK*, pp. 144–146; Curt Gentry, *J. Edgar Hoover: The Man and the Secrets* (New York: W. W. Norton, 1991), pp. 159, 179–180, 192, 240, 531; Ovid Demaris, *The Director: An Oral Biography of J. Edgar Hoover* (New York: Harper's, 1975), pp. 30, 93, 109–110; and Athan Theoharis, *J. Edgar Hoover, Sex, and Crime* (Chicago: Ivan R. Dee, 1995), pp. 11–17, 20–23, 33–52, 55, 167.

NIXON *(v.o.)*

It was the poorest lemon ranch in California, I can assure you. My father sold it before they found oil on it.

TOLSON *(MIMICS)*

But it was all we had.

NIXON *(v.o.)*

. . . but it was all we had.

HOOVER

You're new. What's your name?

JOAQUIN

Joaquin, Mr. Hoover.

Hoover selects an orange slice, puts one end between his teeth. Wiggles it. Joaquin bends over, bites off the other end. Tolson looks peeved.

NIXON *(v.o.)*

My father built the house where I was born with his own hands. Oh, it wasn't a big house . . .

HOOVER

Turn this crap off, Clyde. It's giving me a headache . . . You may go, Joaquin.

He takes a drink off Joaquin's tray as Clyde turns off the TV. Joaquin vanishes.

HOOVER

I want to see him tomorrow, Clyde.

CLYDE

Edgar, think twice. He works in the kitchen.

HOOVER

Not Joaquin, you idiot. Nixon. Did you hear what he said in Oregon? About me having too much power.

CLYDE

It's between Nixon and a Kennedy again, Edgar . . . Who do you want?

HOOVER

Kennedy—never. He'll fry in hell for what he did to me. But Nixon don't know that, which is why I'm gonna have to remind him he needs us a helluva lot more'n we need him.

SCENE FORTY-SEVEN

EXT. DEL MAR RACETRACK—STARTING GATE—DAY

THOROUGHBREDS explode out of the chutes.

SCENE FORTY-EIGHT

EXT. DEL MAR RACETRACK—CLUBHOUSE—DAY

A private box just above the finish line. HOOVER raises his binoculars, watching the race. He is wearing a white tropical suit, Panama hat, white shoes. CLYDE is dressed similarly.

JOHNNY ROSELLI, white hair, deep tan, sharp dresser, sits with him in the box, spots someone . . .[82]

ROSELLI

Your boy's on the way up . . . I met him years ago. In Havana.

ON THE TRACK: TWO HORSES are in a terrific stretch drive.

HOOVER watches impassively.

ANNOUNCER *(O.S.: FRANTIC)*

And down the stretch they come. It's Sunday's Chance Son and Olly's Boy dueling for the lead . . .

---

[82]On Hoover's relationship with Roselli, see Summers, *Official and Confidential,* pp. 233, 241–242.

CLOSE: OLLY'S BOY puts a nose in front of SUNDAY'S CHANCE.

HOOVER

He's folding, Johnny.

ON THE TRACK: Sunday's Chance is tiring, falling behind Olly's Boy.

ROSELLI

You just wait a second.

CLOSE: On Olly's Boy's bandaged front legs. Then, Olly's Boy's right fore-leg snaps. It sounds like a rifle shot.

Olly's Boy goes down over his shoulder. The JOCKEY is thrown across the track.

The CROWD is stunned. Sunday's Chance wins easily.

Hoover turns to Roselli.

TOLSON

A bit extreme, isn't it?

ROSELLI

It's the drama. (*gestures to the crowd*) The crowd loves that shit. Hey! There's Randolph Scott. You might like that guy, friend of mine. Wanna meet him, Edgar?

SHOUTING and CHEERS behind them. They turn. NIXON is making his way down the aisle, waving to the crowd. He is followed by HALDE-MAN.

Hoover passes Roselli a ticket.[83]

HOOVER

Not now, Johnny. Cash this for me, would you?

---

[83]On Hoover's gambling, see Summers, *Official and Confidential*, pp. 234–235, 239–241, 429–430; Scott, *Deep Politics and the Death of JFK*, p. 205; Demaris, *The Director*, pp. 17–18.

ROSELLI

It's a two-dollar bet, Edgar. You got thousands coming on this . . . what the fuck?

HOOVER

I told you, just cash it, Johnny. And don't swear around me . . .

A beat. Roselli crosses Nixon, who enters the box.[84]

NIXON

Edgar, wonderful to see you. Clyde . . . hi.

TOLSON

Mr. Nixon . . .

HOOVER

Thank you for coming, Dick.

NIXON

Winning?

HOOVER

Actually, I've just had a bit of luck.

ANNOUNCER *(o.s.)*

The management of Del Mar is saddened to announce that Olly's Boy will have to be destroyed . . .

Groans from the crowd.

NIXON

Oh, my goodness . . .

HOOVER

How about you? Are you going to win?

NIXON

You should ask Bobby.

---

[84]For Nixon's relationship with Hoover, see Wicker, *One of Us,* pp. 625–626; Summers, *Official and Confidential,* pp. 385–399; Scott, *Deep Politics and the Death of JFK,* pp. 112, 208, 218.

TOLSON (SARCASTIC)

. . . little Bobby.

HOOVER

Would you walk with me down to the paddock? I'd like to look at the horses for the eighth.

NIXON

Can't we just talk here? I've got the police chiefs in San Diego.

Hoover moves close.

HOOVER (WHISPERS)

I'm trying to spare you an embarrassment. Johnny Roselli is on his way back here.

Nixon looks sick.

NIXON

Roselli? Johnny Roselli?

HOOVER

Yes. Your old friend from Cuba.

NIXON

I never met the man.

HOOVER

I know you've been very careful not to. That's why I'm concerned.

Nixon glances at Hoover. Hoover smiles.

SCENE FORTY-NINE

EXT. DEL MAR RACETRACK—PADDOCK—DAY (1968)

Moving with NIXON, HOOVER and TOLSON along the rail outside the walking ring. FBI AGENTS have cleared a circle around them. The HORSES for the next race are being saddled. Nixon waves and smiles to PATRONS of the track.

HOOVER

You'll win the nomination.

NIXON

It could be '60 all over again, Edgar. Bobby's got the magic, like a Goddamn rock star. They climb all over each other just to touch his clothes! He'll ride his brother's corpse right into the White House.

TOLSON

Ummm . . .

HOOVER *(NODS)*

If things remain as they are . . . He's got the anti-war vote.

NIXON

Or he'll *steal* it like his brother. He's a mean little sonofabitch, Edgar . . . He had the IRS audit my *mother* when she was dying in the nursing home . . .

HOOVER

I know . . .

TOLSON *(CASUALLY)*

. . . Somebody should shoot the little bastard.

NIXON

I wanna fight just as dirty as he does.

TOLSON

. . . Use his women.

NIXON

. . . Any information you have, Edgar. The sonofabitch is *not* gonna steal from me again! Can you back me up on this? Can I count on your support?

HOOVER *(AMUSED)*

I look at it from the point of view that the system can only take so much abuse. It adjusts itself eventually, but at times there are . . . savage outbursts. The late "Doctor" King for example. A moral hypocrite screwing women like a degenerate tomcat, stirring up the blacks, preaching against our system . . . (shakes his head) Sometimes the system comes close to cracking.

Hoover stops in front of a huge GELDING, pats his muzzle.

HOOVER
We've already had one radical in the White House. I don't think we could survive another.

Nixon feels uncomfortable. Images, vague, disturbing. Even the nostrils on the horse seem to be emitting a devil's fire, and the noises of the snorting animal magnify . . .

NIXON (A BEAT)
Yeah, well, as I said, Edgar . . .

HOOVER (PRECISELY)
You *asked* if you could count on my support . . . As long as I can count on yours.

NIXON (V.O.: ON TAPE)
The old queen did it on purpose.

SCENE FIFTY

INT. THE WHITE HOUSE—LINCOLN SITTING ROOM—NIGHT (1973)

RESUME SCENE—NIXON listens as the tape rolls.

NIXON (ON TAPE)
He wasn't protecting me. He was putting me on notice.

HALDEMAN (ON TAPE)
What? That he knew Johnny Roselli? Hoover knew a lot of gangsters.

NIXON (ON TAPE)
Yeah, but Roselli wasn't just any gangster. He was the gangster who set up Track 2 in Cuba.[85]

---

[85]For a discussion of Track 2, its history and implications, see Brodie, *Richard Nixon,* pp. 392–413; Scott, *Deep Politics and the Death of JFK,* pp. 111–113, 305–306; Claudia Furiati, *ZR Rifle: The Plot to Kill Kennedy and Castro* (Melbourne, Australia: Ocean Press, 1994), pp. 127–131. For a U.S. Senate investigation of Track 2, see United States Senate, *Alleged Assassination Plots Involving Foreign Leaders* (Washington, DC: Government Printing Office, 1975), pp. 181–190. See also Michael R. Beschloss, *The Crisis Years* (New York: HarperCollins, 1991), pp. 134–137, 685–687.

The President at his desk

SCENE FIFTY-ONE

INT. EXEC OFFICE BLDG.–PRESIDENT'S OFFICE–NIGHT (1972)

NIXON and HALDEMAN are alone. The lights are on. Nixon's had a couple of drinks. The talk is a little looser.

> HALDEMAN *(CONFUSED)*
> I don't understand. Track 2's Chile?

> NIXON
> Chile, Congo, Guatemala, Cuba. Wherever there's a need for an Executive Action capability, there's a Track 2. In Cuba, Track 1 was the Bay of Pigs invasion. Track 2 . . . it was our idea.
> *(stands)*
> We felt the invasion wouldn't work unless we got rid of Castro. So we asked ourselves—who else wants Castro dead? The Mafia, the money people. So we put together Track 2 . . .[86]

---

[86]For a discussion of the CIA-Mafia plots to kill Fidel Castro, see United States Senate, *Alleged Assassination Plots Involving Foreign Leaders,* pp. 67–84; Oglesby, *The Yankee and Cowboy War,* pp. 47–80; Hinckle and Turner, *The Fish Is Red,* pp. 26–29, 34–36, 73–79, 271–279; Thomas Powers, *The Man Who Kept the Secrets: Richard Helms and the CIA* (New York: Knopf, 1979), pp. 126–131, 146–158, 287–294; David C. Martin, *Wilderness of Mirrors* (New

CUBA MONTAGE

Images begin to project from that long-ago time. A YOUNGER NIXON. Macho Cuban "FREEDOM FIGHTERS" in the Keys and Guatemala. The CIA, the MOB—including JOHNNY ROSELLI. FAT CATS and CASINO BOSSES shaking hands with young Nixon on his visit in the 40's.[87] A Rum and Coca-Cola SONG plays.

NIXON *(SOFTLY)*

The first assassination attempt was in '60, just before the election.

HALDEMAN *(STUNNED)*

Before?! Eisenhower approved that?

NIXON

He didn't veto it.[88] *(then)* I ran the White House side. The mob contact was Johnny Roselli. *(then)* One of the CIA guys was that jackass, Howard Hunt.

HALDEMAN

Jesus!

NIXON

And not just Hunt. Frank Sturgis, all those Cubans. All of them in the Watergate. They were involved in Track 2 in Cuba. *(then)* Hunt reported to my

---

York: Harper & Row, 1980), pp. 121–124, 138–141, 145, 146, 151–153, 219–221; Jim Hougan, *Spooks* (New York: Morrow, 1978), pp. 332–348. See also Claudia Furiati, *ZR Rifle:The Plot to Kill Kennedy and Castro* (Melbourne, Australia: Ocean Press, 1994). The Brazilian journalist has analyzed long secret files of the Cuban government and states:

> Let's get to the final conclusions. The Cuban State Security Department has concluded that those responsible for Kennedy's assassination are David Phillips, as the promoter of ZR Rifle; and Santos Trafficante, as the coordinator of the Mafia participation in the operation. And those who fired the shots were Cubans from the "elite troops" in exile. The day of the assassination they were deployed in groups, together or separate, forming a triangle of fire, and one of these groups was under the direct orders of Jack Ruby. And who was the ultimate author of this entire scheme? Richard Helms, the brain of the CIA.

Id. at 135.

[87]Nixon visited Havana in 1940 and considered setting up his law practice there. See Hinckle and Turner, *The Fish Is Red*, p. 290.

[88]For Eisenhower not vetoing Track 2, see United States Senate, *Alleged Assassination Plots Involving Foreign Leaders*, pp. 11–12, 64–66, 108–109; and Oglesby, *The Yankee and Cowboy War*, p. 58.

military aide. But I met with him several times as Vice President.[89] That's what worries the shit out of me. I don't know how much Hunt knows. Or the Cubans.

                              HALDEMAN

So? You wanted Castro dead. *Everybody* wanted Castro dead. If Hunt and the others are CIA, why don't we just throw this back in the CIA's lap? Let Richard Helms take the fall?

                         NIXON (*PAUSE*)

Because . . . because Dick Helms knows too much . . . If anyone in this country knows more than I do, it's Hoover and *Helms!* You don't *fuck* with Dick Helms! Period . . .

Pause.

                              HALDEMAN

Alright. But why, if Kennedy is so clean in all this, didn't *he* cancel Track 2?

                               NIXON

Because he didn't even know about it.[90] The CIA never told him, they just kept it going. It was like . . . it had a life of its own. Like . . . a kind of "beast" that doesn't even know it exists. It just eats people when it doesn't need 'em anymore. (*drops back in his chair*) Two days after the Bay of Pigs, Kennedy called me in. He reamed my ass . . .

DOCUMENTARY INTERCUT: Brief, moving, live-action image of JOHN KENNEDY.

---

[89]Nixon was the "action officer" for the Bay of Pigs operation. Howard Hunt was the chief political officer. See Hunt, *Undercover,* p. 131 ("Secretly . . . he [Nixon] was the White House action officer for our covert project . . . General Robert Cushman had urged me to inform him of any project difficulties the Vice President might be able to resolve.") Cushman was a long-time Nixon military adviser, whom Nixon would appoint as CIA deputy director. CIA agent David Phillips was the chief military officer for the operation. See David Phillips, *The Night Watch: 25 Years of Peculiar Service* (New York: Atheneum, 1977), p. 91n. Phillips writes it was Cushman who told him that Nixon was the action officer. For Nixon's role in the Bay of Pigs, also see Hinckle and Turner, *The Fish Is Red,* pp. 21–22; Peter Wyden, *Bay of Pigs: The Untold Story* (New York: Simon & Schuster, 1979), pp. 27–30; and Oglesby, *The Yankee and Cowboy War,* p. 58.

[90]Note: Recently Judith Exner, an intimate of President Kennedy, has indicated that Kennedy did know of the plan to use the Mafia to kill Castro as early as the fall of 1960. She also suggests that his brother, Robert, also knew of the CIA-Mafia plot. See Anthony Summers, *Conspiracy* (New York: Paragon House, 1989), pp. 527–528.

NIXON (*CONTINUED*)

. . . he'd just found out about Track 2.

HALDEMAN

You never told him?

NIXON (*SOFTLY*)

I didn't want him to get the credit. He said I'd stabbed him in the back. Called me a two-bit grocery clerk from Whittier.

Nixon's face expresses the deep hurt of that insult.

NIXON

That was the last time I ever saw him.

IMAGE—the "Beast"—an image of Kennedy perverted, his head blown off . . .

HALDEMAN

If they didn't tell Kennedy about Track 2, how did Hoover find out?

NIXON

He had us bugged. Christ, he had everybody bugged. Yeah, he was gonna support me in '68, but he was also threatening me. (*then*) That was Hoover: he'd give you the carrot, but he'd make damn sure the stick went right up your ass.

Chief of Staff Bob Haldeman (James Woods)

SCENE FIFTY-TWO

INT. AMBASSADOR HOTEL—PANTRY (1968)—DOCUMENTARY

DOCUMENTARY FOOTAGE of chaos in the pantry. The camera is jostled. Women screaming. A man is being wrestled to the floor.

ROBERT KENNEDY lies there, mortally wounded.[91]

NIXON (v.o.)

When I saw Bobby lying there on the floor, his arm stretched out like that . . .

SCENE FIFTY-THREE

INT. EXECUTIVE OFFICE BLDG.—PRESIDENT'S OFFICE—NIGHT (1973)

RESUME SCENE—NIXON and HALDEMAN

NIXON

. . . his eyes staring . . . (*then*) I knew I'd be president. (*beat*) Death paved the way, didn't it? Vietnam. The Kennedys. It cleared a path through the wilderness for me. Over the bodies . . . Four bodies.

Haldeman corrects him.

HALDEMAN

You mean two . . . two bodies?

SCENE FIFTY-FOUR

INT. THE WHITE HOUSE—LINCOLN SITTING ROOM—NIGHT (1973)

HALDEMAN (v.o. on tape)

You mean two . . . two bodies?

---

[91]For a dramatic account of this tragic event, see Bill Eppridge (photographs) and Hays Gorey (text), with foreword by President Bill Clinton, *Robert Kennedy The Last Campaign* (New York: Harcourt Brace, 1993).

RESUME SCENE—NIXON *takes a slug of Scotch, then he rubs the bridge of his nose, looks up at the portrait of Lincoln. A pause, softly to Mr. Lincoln.*

NIXON (SLURS)

How many did you have? Hundreds of thousands . . . Where would we be without death, hunh Abe?

Nixon stands, steadies himself.

NIXON (SOFTLY)

Who's helping us? Is it God? Or is it . . . Death?

CUT BACK TO:

SCENE FIFTY-FIVE

EXT. SANITARIUM CABIN—PORCH—ARIZONA—DAY (1933)

A lunar landscape—barren, scorched, silent. Suddenly, violent, desperate COUGHING.

HAROLD NIXON (23) *is doubled over the railing, a long string of bloody mucus hanging from his lips. He is shockingly emaciated—the last stages of tuberculosis. HANNAH NIXON, in background attending TWO OTHER PATIENTS, looks on at Harold.*

RICHARD (19) *hurries out of the cabin with a cotton cloth. He holds HAROLD until he stops heaving. Then, he wipes his mouth.*

HAROLD (GASPS)

. . . that was a whopper.

Richard carefully folds the cloth, drops it into a metal container that is already full of them. He stands there, helpless, a solemn boy.

HAROLD (PANTING)

Hey . . . you'll be able to do it now.

RICHARD

What . . . ?

HAROLD

Go to law school. Mom and Dad'll be able to afford it now . . .

Richard looks at him in horror.

HAROLD

Mom expects great things from you . . .

RICHARD

Harold . . . can I get you anything?

Harold throws a loving arm around Richard, who tenses. We sense that Harold in some way could have helped Richard, taught him to laugh a bit.

HAROLD *(A GENTLE SMILE)*

Relax, Dick, it's just me . . . The desert's so beautiful, isn't it? *(then)* I want to go home, Dick. Time to go home.

RICHARD *(STIFFLY)*

You're not gonna quit on me, are you, Harold?

Harold looks out over the landscape. Silence.

SCENE FIFTY-SIX

INT. NIXON HOUSE—PARLOR—NIGHT (1933)

RICHARD sits staring into the fire. He still wears his black suit from Harold's funeral.[92] HANNAH enters quietly.

HANNAH

Richard?

He looks up at her.

---

[92]For Harold's death, see Brodie, *Richard Nixon,* pp. 92–99; Morris, *Richard Milhous Nixon,* pp. 146–148; Ambrose, *Nixon: The Education of a Politician 1913–1962,* pp. 57–58; and Mazlish, *The Leader, the Led, and the Psyche,* p. 58.

                              RICHARD

I can't . . .

                              HANNAH

Thou must.

She moves closer. Casting a shadow over his face.

                              HANNAH

It's a gift, Richard. This law school is a gift from your brother.

                         RICHARD *(BITTER)*

Did he have to *die* for me to get it?!

                              HANNAH

It's meant to make us stronger. (*kneels*) Thou art stronger than Harold . . .
stronger than Arthur. God has chosen thee to survive . . .

                              RICHARD

What about happiness, Mother?

                              HANNAH

Thou must find thy peace at the center, Richard. Strength in this life. Happiness in the next.

DISSOLVE TO:

                    SCENE FIFTY-SEVEN

              INT. REPUBLICAN CONVENTION—NIGHT (1968)

*ON RICHARD NIXON (55)—in his prime. A profile of his face—as the vast
crowd goes berserk. Nixon absorbs the adoration: at last, he has arrived. He
looks down at someone in the audience. Points, smiles, waves.*

*Then he steps forward, thrusts his arms in the air—the twin-V salute. The
cheers rattle the hall as PAT and their DAUGHTERS join him, followed by
Vice President SPIRO AGNEW and his FAMILY. Nixon puts his arm around
Pat. She waves. The crowd is on its feet.*

NIXON *(PRIVATELY TO PAT)*

Now tell me you didn't want this, Buddy.

Pat smiles back at him, caught up in it. Then she kisses him on the cheek.

TIME CUT TO:

NIXON addresses the DELEGATES (A COMPOSITE OF NIXON SPEECHES).

NIXON

It's time for some honest talk about the problem of law and order in the United States. I pledge to you that the current wave of violence will not be the wave of the future! (*vast APPLAUSE.*)

INTERCUT WITH:

DOCUMENTARY FOOTAGE–1. Civil war. Tanks in the streets of DETROIT. 2. A BLACK PANTHER safe-house in flames surrounded by FBI AGENTS.

NIXON *(v.o.)*

. . . The long dark night for America is about to end . . . Let us begin by committing ourselves to the truth—to find the truth, to speak the truth. And to live the truth . . . A new voice is being heard across America today: it is not the voice of the protestors or the shouters, it is the voice of a majority of Americans who have been quiet Americans over the past few years . . . a silent majority.

DOCUMENTARY FOOTAGE–3. GEORGE WALLACE whips a DIXIE CROWD into a frenzy. 4. The WOUNDED KNEE SIEGE is under way–FBI AGENTS and LOCAL MILITANTS pour fire in on the INDIAN MILITANTS. 5. The YIPPIE DEMONSTRATORS outside the CHICAGO DEMOCRATIC CONVENTION. Chicago POLICE wade in with nightsticks, tear gas.

NIXON *(AT THE PODIUM)*

Who are they? Let me tell you who they are—they're in this audience by the thousands, they're the workers of America, they're white Americans and black Americans . . .

We cut among the DELEGATES, seeking to show the face of a populace that is torn by civil war.

NIXON (CONT'D)

. . . they are Mexican Americans and Italian Americans, they're the great silent majority, and they have become angry, finally; angry not with hate but angry, my friends, *because they love America and they don't like what's happened to America these last four years!* We will regain respect for America in the world. A burned American library, a desecrated flag . . . Let us understand: North Vietnam cannot defeat or humiliate the United States. Only Americans can do that!

This brings the house down! As we:

CROSSCUT TO:

DOCUMENTARY FOOTAGE–6. CHICAGO is now a full-scale POLICE RIOT. The COPS have lost all control, swinging nightsticks wildly, breaking heads, dozens of arrests.

Closing on NIXON at the podium.

NIXON

Let's face it. Most Americans today, in a crisis of spirit, are simply fed up with government at all levels. All the Great Society activists are lying out there in wait, poised to get you if you try to come after them: the professional welfareists, the urban planners, the day-carers, the public housers. The costly current welfare system is a mess, and we are on the brink of a revolt of the lower middle class. The bottom line is—no work, no welfare. Our opponents have exaggerated and over-emphasized society as the cause of crimes. The war on poverty is not a war on crime, and it is no substitute for a war on crime. (*pause*) I say to you, tonight we must have a new feeling of responsibility, of self-discipline. We must look to renew state and local government! We must have a complete reform of a big, bloated federal government. The average American is just like the child in the family. You give him some responsibility and he is going to amount to something. If you make him completely dependent and pamper him, you are going to make him soft, and a very weak individual.

NIXON (CONT'D)

I begin with the proposition that freedom of choice in housing, education, and jobs is the right of every American. A good job is as basic a civil right as a good education. On the other hand, I am convinced that while legal segregation is totally wrong, forced integration of housing or education is just as wrong! We simply have to face the hard fact that the law cannot go beyond what the people are willing to support. This was true as far as Prohibition was concerned. It is far more true with regard to education and housing . . . Yet those of us in public service know—we can have full prosperity in peacetime . . . Yes, we can cut the defense budget. We can reduce conventional forces in Europe. We can restore the national environment. We can improve health care and make it available more fairly to all people. And yes, we can have a complete reform of this government. We can have a new American Revolution.

CROSSCUT TO:

DOCUMENTARY FOOTAGE—7. The young CHICAGO DEMONSTRA-TORS are chanting rebelliously at POLICE.

> DEMONSTRATORS
> The whole world is watching! The whole world is watching!

DOCUMENTARY FOOTAGE—8. A B-52 unloads BOMBS and NAPALM over jungle.

SUBTITLE READS: "LAOS—SECRET BOMBING CAMPAIGN, 1969–70; 242,000 MISSIONS."

CUT TO:

SCENE FIFTY-EIGHT

OMIT #58

SCENE FIFTY-NINE

EXT. THE WHITE HOUSE—NIGHT

The lights are blazing late with war talk.

Nixon lectures his Cabinet about leaks

SCENE SIXTY

INT. SIDE OFFICE—THE WHITE HOUSE—NIGHT

In a small paneled room, the talk is angry: BILL ROGERS, Secretary of State, MEL LAIRD, Defense Secretary, to one side; KISSINGER with HAIG, seen earlier, but now Kissinger's assistant, to the other side of the desk, as NIXON listens; HALDEMAN takes notes. ZIEGLER looks on. Though a stand-up chart displays a large map of Cambodia's border with South Vietnam, we may note there are no military personnel in the room.

> ROGERS

. . . It'd be a disaster for us, Mr. President. There's a lot of sympathy out there for Cambodia, a tiny, neutral Buddhist nation. There'd be protests in the streets, right out on your front lawn . . .

> LAIRD

. . . Building this Cambodian army up will be harder even than the Vietnamese army. They have no tradition of . . . The government there would collapse if we . . .

Nixon's eyes narrow, furious.

NIXON

So you're saying, "Do nothing"—that's what you're saying. The same old shit. Well, that's not good enough. I'm sick of being pushed around by the Vietnamese like some pitiful giant. They're using our POWS to humiliate us. What we need now is a bold move into Cambodia; go right after the VC base camps, make 'em scream. That's what I think. You, Henry?

A pivotal moment for Henry. Nixon is clearly scrutinizing Kissinger, who glances at his rivals.

KISSINGER

Well, as you know, most of my staff have weighed in against this "incursion." They believe it will fail to achieve anything fundamental militarily, and will result in crushing criticism domestically . . .

NIXON *(INTERRUPTS)*

I didn't ask what your staff thinks, Henry. What do you think?

KISSINGER *(PAUSE)*

What I think is . . . they're *cowards.* Their opposition represents the cowardice of the Eastern Establishment. They don't realize as you do, Mr. President, that the Communists only respect strength, and they will only negotiate in good faith if they fear the "madman," Richard Nixon.[93]

Nixon lets a dark smile curl one side of his mouth.

NIXON

Exactly! We've got to take the war to them. Hit 'em where it hurts—right in the *nuts.* More assassinations, more killings. Right, Al?

HAIG

That's what they're doing.

NIXON

These State Department jerks, Bill, don't understand; you got to electrify people with bold moves. Bold moves make history, like Teddy Roosevelt—"T.R."—rushing up San Juan Hill. Small event but dramatic. People took notice.

---

[93]For the so-called madman theory, see Wicker, *One of Us*, pp. 134, 424, 581; Ambrose, *Nixon: The Triumph of a Politician 1962–1972*, p. 224; and Hersh, *The Price of Power*, pp. 607–608, 614–615, 619–620.

ROGERS

They'll take notice all right.

NIXON

The fact is if we sneak out of this war, there'll be another one a mile down the road. (*pause*) We bite the bullet here. In Cambodia. We blow the *hell* out of these people!

ZIEGLER

So what should we tell the press?

SCENE SIXTY-ONE

DOCUMENTARY FOOTAGE–9. Bombs dropping over Cambodia.

DOCUMENTARY FOOTAGE–10. Combined U.S. and SOUTH VIET-NAMESE TROOPS invade CAMBODIA.

SUBTITLE reads: "APRIL 1970"

NIXON *(v.o.)*

Tonight, American and South Vietnamese units will attack the headquarters for the entire Communist military operation in South Vietnam. *This is not an invasion of Cambodia.* We take this action not for the purpose of expanding the war into Cambodia, but for the purpose of ending the war in Vietnam . . .

CROSSCUT TO:

DOCUMENTARY FOOTAGE–11. The Administration Building at BERKELEY is burning. POLICE in riot gear move in. A BATTLE between STUDENTS and POLICE is taking place.

REPORTER *(v.o.)*

Across the country, several hundred universities are in turmoil as students battle police in protest against the invasion of Cambodia . . .

CUT TO:

DOCUMENTARY FOOTAGE–11. KENT STATE UNIVERSITY–(1970) A phalanx of NATIONAL GUARDSMEN advances. They look very young and scared. A CROWD of STUDENTS taunts them.

NIXON (*V.O.: A SPEECH*)

When I think of those kids out there. Kids who are just doing their duty . . .

CROSSCUT TO:

SCENE SIXTY-TWO

INT. THE WHITE HOUSE—EAST ROOM—DAY

The end of a ceremony for a released VIETNAM POW. NIXON, with JULIE, stands before emotional WIVES, DEFENSE DEPARTMENT EMPLOYEES, and UNIFORMED OFFICERS. The POW sits in a wheelchair at NIXON's elbow, emaciated, the blue ribbon of the CMH around his neck. PAT is also there.

NIXON (*CONTINUES*)

I'm sure they're scared. I was when I was there. But when it really comes down to it . . .(*turns to the POW*). . . you have to look up to these men. They're the greatest!

Applause. The POW manages a smile.

DOCUMENTARY FOOTAGE—An ugly stand-off. The STUDENTS confront the GUARDSMEN, jeering. The GUARDSMEN lower their bayonets.

STUDENTS (*CHANTING*)

One-two-three-four. We don't want your fucking war.

Someone throws a rock.

BACK TO SCENE:

NIXON (*CONTINUES*)

You see these bums,[94] you know, blowing up the campuses, burning books and so forth. They call themselves "flower children." Well, I call them spoiled rotten. And I tell you what would cure them—a good old-fashioned trip to my Ohio father's woodshed. That's what these bums need!

---

[94]Nixon referred to the students as "bums" during an off-the-cuff talk with Pentagon employees. See Wicker, *One of Us,* p. 585; Ambrose, *Nixon: The Triumph of a Politician 1962–1972,* p. 348; and Aitken, *Nixon,* p. 403.

DOCUMENTARY FOOTAGE—More STUDENTS are throwing rocks. The GUARDSMEN are momentarily panicked, confused.

Then, suddenly: they open fire. A melee. Screaming. STUDENTS running.

Then: half a dozen BODIES lie on the ground. A young WOMAN crouches over a BODY, crying.

REPORTER 1 (v.o.)

Today, less than twenty-four hours after President Nixon called them "bums," four students were shot dead at Kent State University in Ohio.

SCENE SIXTY-THREE

EXT. POTOMAC RIVER—YACHT SEQUOIA—NIGHT

NIXON sits at the head of an outdoor dinner table with HALDEMAN, EHRLICHMAN, ZIEGLER, KISSINGER. They are being served steaks by MANOLO, Nixon's Cuban valet.

REPORTER 1 (v.o.)

Enraged student groups across the country are calling for a general strike tomorrow to shut down the *entire* university system until the Vietnam War is ended.

MITCHELL joins them.

NIXON (GRIM)

How many?

MITCHELL

Four. Two boys. Two girls. And eight wounded.

NIXON

Jesus Christ!

MITCHELL

One of the fathers was on TV saying, "My child was not a bum." And it's playing like gangbusters. Hell, Hoover told me one of the girls was a nymph.

NIXON

Shit, the press doesn't care about the facts. Cronkite's sticking it to me. It's their first big hit on Richard Nixon.

ZIEGLER

The governor says they were rioting.

EHRLICHMAN

The governor's full of shit. Most of them were changing classes.

NIXON

Oh, I suppose you would've just let them take over. These aren't fraternity pranks, John. It's anarchy. A revolution!

EHRLICHMAN

I don't know if I'd go that far, sir.

NIXON

Why not?

EHRLICHMAN

Is the war worth it? Is it worth a one-term presidency? Because I think right now that's what we're looking at.

NIXON

I will not go down as the first American president to lose a war! Going into Cambodia, bombing Hanoi, bombing Laos—it buys us time so we can get out and give the South Vietnamese a fighting chance.

KISSINGER

Exactly, sir. That is your historical contribution: to lead boldly in an era of limits.

NIXON (DRINKS)

No one understands!—even my own men. What do you think the Communists respond to? Honesty, liberal guilt, soul-wringing crap, fathers on TV crying? Hell no! I understand the Communist mind, I've studied it for thirty years. They grasp "realpolitik" better than any of us, right, Henry? (Henry nods). We gotta make 'em think we're just as tough as they are—that Nixon's a mad bomber, he might do *anything!* I played a lot of poker in World War II (Haldeman and Ehrlichman know the story), and I won big, and let me tell you this—unpredictability is our best asset. That redneck, Johnson, left me a shitty hand and I'm bluffing. I've got to play the hawk in Vietnam and the dove in China. And if we keep our heads, we can win this thing.

ZIEGLER

What? Win Vietnam, sir?

ALL

No . . .

NIXON

No! But what we can do with Vietnam, Ron, is drive a *stake* through the heart of the Communist alliance! Henry's already getting strong signals from the Chinese. They hate the Viets more than the Russians, and they're worried about a unified Vietnam. The Russians hate the Chinese and are supporting the Viets, you understand? If we stick it out in Vietnam . . . we'll end up negotiating separately with both the Chinese *and* the Soviets. And we'll get better deals than we ever dreamed of from *both* . . . (*Kissinger nods*) *That's* triangular diplomacy, gentlemen.

KISSINGER

Exactly, yes, Mr. President. That is my contention.

NIXON

That's what geopolitics is *about*—the *whole world linked* by self-interest . . . You tell me, Ron, how the hell I can explain *that* on television to a bunch of simple-minded reporters and weeping fucking mothers!

ZIEGLER

But what am I telling the press about Kent State?

NIXON

Tell 'em what you like; they'll never understand anyway.

EHRLICHMAN

Excuse me . . . Are you talking about recognizing China, Mr. President? That would cost us our strongest support.

NIXON

No . . . I can do this because I've spent my whole career building anti-Communist credentials.

HALDEMAN
If Johnson or Kennedy'd tried it, they'd have crucified them, and rightfully so!

MITCHELL
It's damned risky, Mr. President. Why don't we wait till the second term?

HALDEMAN
This will get him a second term.

NIXON *(REPEATS)*
This will get me a second term. Damn it, without risk, there's no heroism. There's no history. I, Nixon, was born to do this.

KISSINGER
Mr. President, this cannot be breathed! *Especially* to our secretary of state— that cretin Rogers . . .[95] The Chinese would never trust us again. The *only* way, I *emphasize only way,* to pull this off is in secret.

NIXON *(CACKLES)*
This is a major coup, gentlemen—our own State Department doesn't even know. And if it leaks out of here tonight *(pause, he eyes them)* . . .

Pause. Discomfort.

HALDEMAN
Well, one way or the other, Kent State is *not good.* We have to get out in front of this thing. The PR is going to murder us.

NIXON
Money. Follow the money. *(Haldeman: "Sir?")* These kids are being manipulated by the Communists. Like Chambers and Hiss.

MITCHELL *(SMOKING HIS PIPE)*
This isn't '48, Dick. They'll never buy it.

NIXON *(ANGRY)*
How do you know that, John? Did we *try*? Are we just giving up like the rest of 'em. What's Hoover found, for God's sake?

---

[95]Kissinger's feud with Rogers is well documented. See, for example, Hersh, *The Price of Power,* pp. 111–114; Ehrlichman, *Witness to Power,* pp. 296–300; and Isaacson, *Kissinger,* pp. 195–198, 209–211, 420–421, 474–475.

HALDEMAN

Well, he called the other day, sir. He asked for President Harding.

Laughter around the table.

KISSINGER

He's an idiot . . .

HALDEMAN

Seriously, sir, he's gotta go . . .

NIXON

We can't touch Hoover—

EHRLICHMAN

I thought the gloves were off.

NIXON

—as long as he's got secret files on everybody. I don't want 'em used against us.[96] (*frustrated*) What about the CIA?! Helms's done nothing for us. I want to see him.

HALDEMAN

Done.

MITCHELL

With Hiss, Mr. President, you had the microfilm, you had the lie. With the students, we got no proof.

NIXON

The soldiers were provoked. The students started it, for Christ's sake!

EHRLICHMAN

Sir, there's dead American kids here. Let's say we don't apologize for Kent State, but maybe we could have a national prayer day . . .

---

[96]For Nixon's fear of Hoover's secret files, see Wicker, *One of Us,* pp. 647–648; Summers, *Official and Confidential,* pp. 371–372, 398; and Emery, *Watergate,* p. 114.

> HALDEMAN

. . . never complain, never explain, John . . .

> NIXON (*YELLS*)

I tell you, the soldiers were *provoked*. Now stop this pussyfooting around. (*irritated*) Dead kids! How the hell did we ever give the Democrats a weapon like this? (*then*) I mean, if Cambodia doesn't work, we'll bomb Hanoi if we have to.

They all look at him. He is resolute.

> NIXON

That's right! And if necessary, I'll drop the big one.

> KISSINGER

We have to entertain the possibility . . .

Nixon looks down at his steak. It is oozing blood. Too much blood—something is very wrong. He shoots back, momentarily terrified.

> NIXON

Goddamn it! Who the hell cooked this steak? (*yells*) Manolo, there's blood all over my plate!

NIXON throws down his knife and fork and walks off.

SCENE SIXTY-FOUR

EXT. YACHT SEQUOIA—NIGHT (LATER)

NIXON is on the bow, alone, watching the city slip by. MITCHELL slides up beside him, offering him a freshened drink.

> MITCHELL

You all right?

> NIXON

My brother Harold was about the same age as those kids, John. Tuberculosis got him.

MITCHELL

It wasn't your fault. The soldiers were just kids, too. They panicked.

NIXON

They were throwing *rocks,* John, just rocks. They don't think I feel . . . but I feel too much sometimes. I just can't let a whole policy get dominated by our sentimentality.

MITCHELL

You're doing the right thing, Dick . . . don't let 'em shake you.

NIXON

It broke my heart when Harold died.

MITCHELL

That was a long time ago.

Nixon looks out at the water.

NIXON

I think that's when it starts. When you're a kid. The laughs and snubs and slights you get because you're poor or Irish or Jewish or just ugly. But if you're intelligent, and your anger is deep enough and strong enough, you learn you can change these attitudes by excellence, gut performance, while those who have everything are sitting on their fat butts . . . (*then*) But then when you get to the top, you find you can't stop playing the game the way you've always played it because it's a part of you like an arm or a leg. So you're lean and mean and you continue to walk the edge of the precipice, because over the years you've become fascinated by how close you can get without falling . . . I wonder, John, I wonder . . .[97]

Mitchell puts his hand on Dick's shoulder.

MITCHELL

Get off that. That leads nowhere. You should offer condolences to the families of those kids.

---

[97]For the origin of this speech, see Brodie, *Richard Nixon,* pp. 25–26; and Wicker, *One of Us,* p. 9.

NIXON

Sure, I'd like to offer condolences.

He shrugs off Mitchell's hand and walks down the deck into the shadows.

NIXON

But Nixon can't.

SCENE SIXTY-FIVE

INT. LIMOUSINE—THE WHITE HOUSE—DAY

*Leaving the WHITE HOUSE, NIXON looks out at ANGRY DEMONSTRA-
TORS giving him the finger, shaking placards—"IMPEACH NIXON" (spelled
with a swastika), "PEACE NOW." With him are HALDEMAN and EHRLICH-
MAN.*

HALDEMAN (WITH CLIPBOARD)

. . . and we've got the economic guys at five. The Dow lost another 16 points.
They're going to want a decision on the budget. Sir? . . . Are we holding the
line on a balanced budget?

Eric Hamburg with co-author Christopher Wilkinson in the "Oval Office"

NIXON *(PREOCCUPIED)*

No . . . a little deficit won't hurt. Jesus, they're serious. Why're we stopping?

HALDEMAN *(TO THE DRIVER)*

Run 'em over.

The presidential limousine has a difficult time negotiating its way through the BLOCKADING BUSES. A MAN with a NIXON mask runs up to the window and peers in, before being peeled off by SECRET SERVICE. It is an ugly, violent scene, but Nixon seems to delight in the threat of action. He's in an upbeat mood.

NIXON

Get that little fucker! Great tackle! Reminds me of my days at Whittier. Most of these kids are useless.

HALDEMAN

Probably flunking, nothing to do except come down here and meet girls. Henry's out there with them.

NIXON

There's a poison in the upper classes, Bob. They've had it too soft. Too many cars, too many color TVs . . .

HALDEMAN

Don't forget the South, sir, the West. Filled with good football colleges, straight kids. There's more of 'em with you than against you. Not like these mudmutts.

NIXON

It's the parents' fault really.

EHRLICHMAN

Let's not forget they're just kids, they don't vote.

HALDEMAN

It's the fall of the Roman Empire, are you blind? And we're putting fig leaves on the statues . . .

PROTESTOR

Ho, Ho, Ho Chi Minh is going to win!

HALDEMAN

Get that fucker!

A glum moment. Haldeman stares at him. A PROTESTOR waves a Vietcong flag in Nixon's face. He gets pulled off the limo.

NIXON *(EXHILARATED)*

But, hell, this is *nothing* compared to Venezuela. When I was Vice President, Ike sent me down there like a blocking back. They threw rocks, broke out our windows, almost overturned the car. Read *Six Crises,* Bob. Boy, Pat was brave!

HALDEMAN

Yeah, we've got to get our vice president off the golf course and back out there on the college circuit. That's top priority.

EHRLICHMAN

He's in the dumps, sir. Agnew. Every time you have him attack the press, they give it back to him in spades. He's become the most hated man in America.

NIXON *(CHUCKLES)*

Yeah, good old Spiro. Well, better him than me. What the hell is he but an insurance policy?[98]

HALDEMAN

We gotta keep reminding those media pricks, if Nixon goes they end up with Agnew. (*They all laugh.*)

EHRLICHMAN

He's begging for a meeting, chief. He wants to go overseas for a while.

NIXON

Well, no place where they speak English. That way we can always say he was misquoted. (*emits a high, manic laugh*)

The PROTESTORS are frustrated as the limousine breaks through.

---

[98]For Nixon's view of Agnew as his insurance against impeachment, see Ehrlichman, *Witness to Power,* p. 143; and Emery, *Watergate,* pp. 301, 381.

SCENE SIXTY-SIX

INT. CIA HEADQUARTERS—LOBBY—DAY (1970)

The SEAL of the CIA: "You shall know the truth and the truth shall make you free." We CRANE BACK, revealing that the seal is on the floor of the LOBBY as NIXON strides in with his ENTOURAGE.[99]

LT. GENERAL ROBERT CUSHMAN hurries out, ruffled, to meet NIXON.

CUSHMAN

Mr. President, I don't know what to say. As soon as we learned from the Secret Service you were en route, the Director was notified. He should be here any minute.

NIXON

Where the hell is he?

CUSHMAN

Uh, he's rushing back from his tennis game, sir . . .

NIXON (IMPATIENT)

So . . . Let's go . . .

CUSHMAN *(WALKING WITH NIXON)*

He told me to take you to his conference room.

NIXON

No. His office. (*aside*) I want a very private conversation. I don't want to be bugged.

CUSHMAN

Then his office will be fine.

———————

[99]Note: Nixon's visit to CIA headquarters actually took place on March 7, 1969, and was not a surprise. See *Public Papers of the Presidents, Richard Nixon 1969* (Washington, DC: Government Printing Office, 1971), pp. 202–204. This and the following scenes dramatize and interpret a number of events that took place in the White House and in telephone conversations among the President, members of the White House staff, and the CIA.

SCENE SIXTY-SEVEN

INT. OPERATIONS CENTER & HELMS'S OFFICE—DAY

They walk past ANALYSTS laboring in isolation behind Plexiglass walls; the hum of computers, a dark austerity to the place. They all glance up as NIXON strides past.

                           NIXON
How's the job coming, Bob?

                         CUSHMAN
Frankly sir, it stinks. I have no access. I'm lucky Helms lets me have a staff.

                    NIXON *(OMINOUS)*
We'll see about that . . .

               CUSHMAN *(SENSING CHANGE)*
He's nervous, sir. He's heard you're looking for a new director.

                           NIXON
Well, he certainly isn't acting like it.

                         CUSHMAN
That's Helms. He's "sang froid," a world-class poker player.

                NIXON *(UNDER HIS BREATH)*
Yeah? Well, I own the fucking casino.

SCENE SIXTY-EIGHT

INT. HELMS'S OFFICE—DAY

A DUTY OFFICER opens the door of the director's office with a flourish. Nixon catches RICHARD HELMS throwing his trench coat and tennis racket on a chair, obviously hurrying in from a secret door. Helms spots Nixon, extends his hand with a reptilian smile.[100]

---

[100]For a discussion of Nixon's relationship with Helms, see Powers, *The Man Who Kept Secrets,* pp. 200–203; and Emery, *Watergate,* p. 22. Haldeman notes the "unspoken feud between CIA Director Richard Helms and Nixon." Haldeman corroborates his firsthand knowledge by citing Watergate Committee Co-Chairman Howard Baker, who looked into the relationship and found "Nixon and Helms have so much on each other, neither of them can breathe." Haldeman, *The Ends of Power,* pp. 25–27.

HELMS

I'm honored, Dick, that you've come all this way out here to Virginia to visit us at last.

NIXON

My friends call me "Mister President."

HELMS

And so shall I. (*to Cushman*) Arrange for some coffee, would you General Cushman?

Cushman stares back a beat, bitterly. Nixon signals to Haldeman and Ehrlichman that he, too, wants to be alone. The door closes.

NIXON

Robert Cushman is a lieutenant general in the Marine Corps, the Deputy Director of the CIA . . . and this is what you use him for?

HELMS

I didn't choose him as my deputy, Mr. President. You did.

Nixon paces the office, which is festooned with photos, awards, and an abundance of flowers, particularly orchids. A collector.

NIXON

You live pretty well out here. Now I understand why you want to keep your budgets classified.

Helms sits on a settee, a hard-to-read man.

HELMS

I suppose, "Mister President," you're unhappy that we have not implemented your Domestic Intelligence plan, but . . .[101]

NIXON

You're correct. I'm concerned these students are being funded by foreign interests, whether they know it or not. The FBI is worthless in this area. I want your full concentration on this matter . . .

---

[101]For a discussion of Nixon's proposals to deal with domestic intelligence, see Select Committee, "The Huston Plan," *The Final Report*, pp. 3–7.

HELMS

Of course we've tried, but so far we've come up with nothing that . . .

NIXON *(STERN)*

Then find something. And I want these leaks stopped. Jack fucking Anderson, the New York *Times,* the State Department—I want to know who's talking to them.

HELMS

I'm sure you realize this is a very tricky area, Mr. President, given our charter and the congressional oversight committees . . .

NIXON

Screw congressional oversight. I know damn well, going back to the 50's, this agency reports what it wants, and buries what it doesn't want Congress to know. Pay close attention to this.

Nixon fixes him with his stare. Helms clears his throat.

HELMS

Is there something else that's bothering you, Mr. President?

NIXON

Yes . . . It involves some old and forgotten papers. Things I signed as Vice President. I want the originals in my office and I don't want copies anywhere else.[102]

Now knowing Nixon's cards, Helms relaxes—about an inch.

HELMS

You're referring, of course, to chairing the Special Operations Group as Vice President.

NIXON

Yes . . .

---

[102]On Nixon's efforts to secure documents concerning CIA plots to assassinate foreign leaders, see Nixon, *RN,* p. 515; Brodie, *Richard Nixon,* pp. 494–496; and Powers, *The Man Who Kept Secrets,* pp. 254–255, 368. Nixon states in his memoirs that, despite all of his efforts, he was never satisfied Helms had turned over all the documents he sought. An example of the efforts to obtain documents is set forth in Part III of this book: a tape-recorded conversation made by Ehrlichman of a conversation with Helms.

Helms wanders over to his prize orchids, fingers them.

HELMS

As you know . . . that was unique. Not an operation as much as . . . an organic phenomenon. It grew, it changed shape, it developed . . . insatiable, devouring appetites. (*then*) It's not uncommon in such cases that things are not committed to paper. That could be very . . . embarrassing.

Nixon is embarrassed, and does not like it. Suddenly, the Beast is in the room.

HELMS (*REMINDING HIM*)

I, for one, saw to it that my name was never connected to any of those operations.

On Nixon, waiting.

HELMS (*FISHING*)

Diem? Trujillo? Lumumba? Guatemala? Cuba? . . .[103] It's a shame you didn't take similar precautions, Dick.

NIXON (*VERY UNCOMFORTABLE*)

I'm interested in the documents that put your people together with . . . the others. All of them . . .

A beat. This is the fastball. Helms pours himself a coffee.

HELMS

President Kennedy threatened to smash the CIA into a thousand pieces. You could do the same . . .

NIXON

I'm not Jack Kennedy. Your agency is secure.

---

[103]On the Castro assassination plots, see Brodie, *Richard Nixon,* pp. 392–413, 492–496 (see also Brodie's sources, pp. 543–546 and 551–554); Scott, *Crime and Cover-up: The Dallas-Watergate Connection,* pp. 47–49 passim, p. 112; Hinckle and Turner, *The Fish Is Red,* pp. 21–60, 106–109, 173–184; Powers, *The Man Who Kept Secrets,* p. 234 passim; Oglesby, *The Yankee and Cowboy War,* pp. 52–53; United States Senate, *Alleged Assassination Plots Involving Foreign Leaders,* pp. 229–234 passim; Hougan, *Spooks,* pp. 332–348. For an overview of the CIA's war against Castro, see Hinckle and Turner, *The Fish Is Red,* and United States Senate, *Alleged Assassination Plots Involving Foreign Leaders,* pp. 71–179, which also discusses Track 2 within the context of CIA activities.

HELMS *(STIRS THE COFFEE)*

Not if I give you all the cards . . .

NIXON

I promised the American people peace with honor in Southeast Asia. That could take time—two, maybe three years . . . In the meantime, your agency will continue at current levels of funding.

HELMS *(SIPS HIS COFFEE)*

Current levels may not be sufficient.

NIXON

The President would support a reasonable request for an increase.

Helms smiles.

HELMS

And me? . . .

NIXON

Firing you, Mr. Helms, wouldn't do any good. Of course you'll continue as DCI. You're doing a magnificent job.

HELMS

And of course I accept. I'm flattered. And I want you to know, I work for only one president at a time.

NIXON

Yes. And you will give General Cushman full access.

HELMS *(GRUDGINGLY ACCEPTS THAT)*

It will take a little time, but I'll order a search for your papers. Though it does raise a disturbing issue.

NIXON

What?

HELMS

Mr. Castro.

NIXON *(TENSE)*

Yes.

HELMS

We have recent intelligence that a Soviet nuclear submarine has docked at Cienfuegos.[104]

NIXON

Well, we'll lodge a formal protest.

HELMS

I don't think we can treat this as a formality. Mr. Kennedy made a verbal promise to the Russians not to invade Cuba. But you authorized Dr. Kissinger to put this *in writing.*[105]

Nixon is taken aback by Helms's inside knowledge.

NIXON

Are you tapping Kissinger?

HELMS

My job, unpleasant sometimes, is to know what others don't want me to know.

NIXON *(COLD)*

Not if you have spies in the White House, it isn't your job.

HELMS

It is not my practice to spy on the president. Doctor Kissinger manages to convey his innermost secrets to the world at large on his own.

NIXON *(ABSORBS THIS)*

Mr. Helms, we've lived with Communism in Cuba for ten years . . .

HELMS

. . . But it has never been the policy of this government to accept that. And it is certainly not CIA policy.

---

[104]For a discussion of the Cienfuegos incident, see Nixon, *RN,* pp. 486–489; Ambrose, *Nixon: The Triumph of a Politician 1962–1972,* pp. 381–383; Kissinger, *The White House Years,* pp. 635–652; Hersh, *The Price of Power,* pp. 250–257.

[105]On Kissinger putting the pledge not to invade Cuba in writing, see Ambrose, *Nixon: The Triumph of a Politician 1962–1972,* pp. 380–381; Kissinger, *The White House Years,* pp. 632–635.

                                   NIXON

CIA policy? The CIA has no policy, Mr. Helms. Except what I dictate to you
. . . (*beat, they stare at each other*) I try to adjust to the world as it is today,
not as you or I wanted it to be ten years ago.

                                   HELMS

Is that why you and Kissinger are negotiating with the Chinese?

A beat. Nixon stares.

                                   HELMS

This is an extremely dangerous direction, Mr. President. Terrible consequences
can result from such enormous errors of judgment.

                                   NIXON

But . . . if we were able to separate China from Russia once and for all, we
can—we could create a balance of power that would secure the peace into
the next century.

                                   HELMS

By offering Cuba to the Russians as a consolation prize?

                                   NIXON

Cuba would be a small price to pay.

                                   HELMS

So President Kennedy thought.

*A disturbing image suddenly appears in Nixon's mind—KENNEDY with his
head blown off in Dallas. Followed by an IMAGE of his own death. In a cof-
fin.*

*The smell of the orchids in the room is overwhelming. Nixon feels himself
dizzy.*

                                   NIXON

I never thought Jack was ready for the presidency. But I would never, never
consider . . . (*then*) His death was awful, an awful thing for this country. (*then*)
Do you ever think of death, Mr. Helms?

HELMS

Flowers are continual reminders of our mortality. Do you appreciate flowers?

NIXON

No. They make me sick. They smell like death . . . I had two brothers die young. But let me tell you, there are worse things than death. There is such a thing as evil.

HELMS

You must be familiar with my favorite poem by Yeats? "The Second Coming"?

NIXON

No.

HELMS

Black Irishman. Very moving. "Turning and turning in the widening gyre / The falcon cannot hear the falconer / Things fall apart, the center cannot hold / Mere anarchy is loosed upon the world / And everywhere the ceremony of innocence is drowned / The best lack all conviction, while the worst are full of passionate "intensity" . . . But it ends so beautifully ominous—"What rough beast, its hour come round at last / Slouches toward Bethlehem to be born?" . . . Yes, this country stands at such a juncture.

On Nixon, as we CUT TO:

SCENE SIXTY-NINE

INT. THE WHITE HOUSE–NIXON BEDROOM–NIGHT

NIXON has just returned from a dinner party, his tuxedo coming off, on the phone, a Scotch in hand, in high spirits. A series of JUMP CUTS of his phone self follows:

NIXON

It was sudden death, Trini, but I think I kicked Helms's ass. (*laughs*) Yeah, and Kissinger's running around like a scared chicken right now; he doesn't know who's gonna grab his power. Yeah . . . you should see him. I call Haig, Kissinger shits! (*laughs*)

JUMP CUT TO:

NIXON *(ON PHONE)*

Did you see the look on Hoover's face? He was redder than a beet. That little closet fairy's got no choice. He hates McGovern and Kennedy so much, he's got to love me. And Lyndon?

PAT enters, in a nightdress, smoking.

PAT

He looked old, didn't he?

NIXON *(HARDLY NOTICING)*

I asked him, "Lyndon, what would you do, on a scale of one to ten?" And he said, "Bomb the shit out of Hanoi, boy! Bomb them where they live." . . . John, do you think I was too soft on TV?

JUMP CUT TO:

NIXON

Bob, I want to get on this energy thing tomorrow—we really have to rethink our needs to the end of the century. Let's do it at 1:00. And don't forget the budget boys. I'm gonna carve the shit out of 'em. *(beat)* Well, no, clear the afternoon and tell Trini I'll be in Key Biscayne by 4:00 . . . No, alone . . . Pat's staying here with the girls.

Pat approaches, nuzzles him. She seems a little strange, tipsy . . . but sexy in her nightdress.[106]

PAT

I'd like to go with you.

HALDEMAN *(O.S.)*

Hello?

NIXON *(TO PAT)*

Uh, you should check with Bob . . . *(to Bob)* Listen, Bob, I'll call you in the morning.

---

[106]On Nixon's marital problems, see Bernstein and Woodward, *The Final Days,* pp. 165–166; and Brodie, *Richard Nixon,* pp. 331–332, 466–470. On Nixon not sleeping in the same bed with his wife, at least after he left the White House, see Ambrose, *Nixon: Ruin and Recovery 1973–1990,* p. 476. For a general discussion of this relationship, see Lester David, *The Lonely Lady of San Clemente: The Story of Pat Nixon* (New York: Thomas Y. Crowell, 1978).

He hangs up, awkward.

> NIXON

Hi, Buddy. What are you doing in here?

> PAT

I've missed you.

> NIXON *(SUSPECTING DRINK ON HER BREATH)*

Are you okay?

> PAT

Why don't we go down to Key Biscayne together? Just the two of us.

> NIXON

Because . . . I have to relax.

> PAT

I was thinking tonight—do you remember, Dick . . . ? Do you remember when you used to drive me on dates with the other boys? You didn't want to let me out of your sight.

> NIXON

Yeah, sure, a long time ago.

> PAT

Yes, it's been a long time . . . (*a signal given*)

He recoils, embarrassed. A slight sweat.

> NIXON

I don't need that, Buddy. I'm not Jack Kennedy.

> PAT *(REBUFFED, DISTANT)*

No, you're not. So stop comparing yourself to him. You have no reason to . . . You have everything you ever wanted. You've earned it. Why can't you just enjoy it?

> NIXON

I do. I do. In my own way.

PAT

Then what are you scared of, honey?

NIXON

I'm not scared, Buddy. (*a pause*) You don't understand. They're playing for keeps, Buddy. The press, the kids, the liberals—they're out there, trying to figure out how to tear me down.

PAT

They're all your enemies?

NIXON

Yes!

PAT

You personally?

NIXON

Yes! This is about me. Why can't you understand that, you of all people? It's not the war—it's Nixon! They want to destroy Nixon! And if I expose myself even the slightest bit they'll tear my insides out. Do you want that? Do you want to see that, Buddy? It's not pretty.

PAT

Sometimes I think that's what you want.

NIXON

You've been drinking. What the hell are you saying? Jesus, you sound like them now! . . .(*a beat, quietly*) I've gotta keep fighting Buddy, for the *country*. These people running things, the elite . . . they're soft, chickenshit faggots! They don't have the long-term vision anymore. They just want to cover their asses or meet girls or tear each other down. Oh, God, this country's in deep trouble, Buddy . . . and I have to see this through. Mother would've wanted no less of me . . . I'm sorry, Buddy.

Pat stands, about to leave.

PAT

I just wish . . . you knew how much I love you, that's all. It took me a long time to fall in love with you, Dick. But I did. And it doesn't make you happy. You want *them* to love you . . .

Pat waves outward, indicating the world, the public.

NIXON *(INTERJECTS)*

No, I don't. I'm not Jack . . .

PAT

But they never will, Dick. No matter how many elections you win, they never will.

She leaves. He is left in the middle of the room. He shuffles to the phone, picks it up.

SCENE SEVENTY

INT. THE WHITE HOUSE—KITCHEN—NIGHT

NIXON *(v.o.)*

Manolo! Where the hell are you?

The lights come on, revealing MANOLO SANCHEZ, the valet, in the doorway, wearing bathrobe and slippers.

MANOLO

I was asleep, Mr. President. What can I get you?

NIXON

Just . . . uh . . . you know.

MANOLO

Of course.

Manolo moves to a cabinet on the far side of the pantry. Takes out a bottle of Chivas, puts ice into a tumbler.

NIXON

Do you miss Cuba, Manolo?

MANOLO

Yes, Mr. President.

NIXON
We let you down, didn't we. Your people.

MANOLO
That was Mr. Kennedy.

NIXON
You don't think he was a hero?

Manolo pours Nixon a drink.

MANOLO *(SHRUGS)*
He was a politician.

NIXON *(SWALLOWS THE DRINK)*
Did you cry when he died?

MANOLO
Yes.

NIXON
Why?

MANOLO
I don't know. *(then)* He made me see the stars . . .

NIXON *(LOOKS OUTSIDE, TO HIMSELF)*
How did he do that? *(then)* All those kids . . . Why do they hate me so much?

SCENE SEVENTY-ONE

EXT. LINCOLN MEMORIAL—PRE-DAWN

*NIXON gets out of the front of the presidential LIMOUSINE. MANOLO fol-
lows.[107]*

---

[107]For a discussion of Nixon's visit to the Lincoln Memorial, see Aitken, *Nixon,* pp. 406–408; Ambrose, *Nixon: The Triumph of a Politician 1962–1972,* pp. 355–356; Nixon, *RN,* pp. 461–466; and Wicker, *One of Us,* pp. 634–635. The aide who would discover the President was roaming the city was Egil "Bud" Krogh, who told the story on camera in the television documentary *Watergate* on The Discovery Channel. The documentary also contains footage of Nixon's visit and Haldeman's efforts to get the President back to the White House.

Nixon looks up: a surreal scene. The Lincoln Memorial has been turned into a pagan temple. FIRES burn on the broad marble steps, half-naked KIDS sleep on filthy blankets below the immense columns. Hendrix plays faintly on a portable radio. Nixon starts up the steps, picking his way among the sleeping forms.

He passes a GIRL, tripping, eyes closed, twirling a long scarf over her head. He stares at her, steps on a sleeping bag.

STUDENT 1

Fuck, man. That's my fuckin' leg—

The BOY's jaw drops. Nixon towers over him. An apparition.

NIXON

You just go back to sleep now, young fella.

STUDENT 1 (RUBS HIS EYES)

Whoa, this is some nasty shit . . .

Nixon reaches the top of the monument. Taped to one of the pillars is a poster: Nixon scowling, and the motto "Would You Buy A Used Car From This Man?"

Nixon peers at it, moves inside. He looks up at LINCOLN in the eerie firelight. Banners with peace signs have been draped over his shoulders, bunches of flowers between his fingers.

HALF A DOZEN STUDENTS are talking among themselves. They see Nixon, stop. Stunned. Nixon strides toward them.

NIXON

Hi, I'm Dick Nixon.

STUDENT 2

You're shittin' me.

NIXON

Where you from?

STUDENT 2

Syracuse.

NIXON

The Orangemen! Now there's a football program. Jim Brown. And that other tailback . . . The one with the blood disease . . .

STUDENT 2

Ernie Davis.

NIXON

Right, right. I used to play a little ball myself at Whittier. (*laughs nervously*) Of course, they used me as a tackling dummy . . .

A self-possessed YOUNG WOMAN abruptly interrupts.

YOUNG WOMAN

We didn't come here to talk about football. We came here to end the war.

NIXON (CHASTENED)

Yes, I understand that.

Pause. Nobody responds.

NIXON

Probably most of you think I'm a real SOB. I know that. But I understand how you feel, I really do. I want peace too, but peace with honor.

STUDENT 3

What does that mean?

NIXON

You can't have peace without a price. Sometimes you have to be willing to fight for peace. And sometimes to die.

STUDENT 3

Tell that to the GIs who are going to die tomorrow in Vietnam.

STUDENT 2

What you have to understand, Mr. Nixon, is that we are willing to die for what we believe in.

NIXON (LOOKS UP AT LINCOLN)

That man up there lived in similar times. He had chaos and civil war and hatred between the races . . . Sometimes I go to the Lincoln Room at the White
House and just pray. You know, the liberals act like idealism belongs to them,
but it's not true. My family went Republican because Lincoln freed the slaves.
My grandmother was an abolitionist. It was Quakers who founded Whittier,
my hometown, to abolish slavery. They were conservative Bible folk, but they
had a powerful sense of right and wrong . . . Forty years ago I was looking,
as you are now, for answers. (then) But you know, ending the war and cleaning up the air and the cities, feeding the poor—my mother used to feed hobos
stopping over at our house—none of it is going to satisfy the spiritual hunger
we all have, finding a meaning to this life . . .

HALDEMAN arrives with SEVERAL SECRET SERVICE AGENTS, looking
very worried. The crowd around Nixon has grown much larger.

HALDEMAN

Mr. President!

NIXON

It's okay, Bob, we're just rapping, my friends and I. We actually agree on a lot
of things . . .

YOUNG WOMAN

No, we don't! You're full of shit! You say you want to end the war, so why don't
you? My brother died over there last November. Why? What good was his
death?

NIXON

I know. I know. I've seen a lot of kids die too, in World War II.

STUDENT 2

Come on, man—Vietnam ain't Germany. It doesn't threaten us. It's a civil war
between Vietnamese.

NIXON

But change always comes slowly. I've withdrawn more than half the troops.
I'm trying to cut the military budget for the first time in thirty years. I want an
all-volunteer army. But it's also a question of America's credibility, our position in the world . . .

> YOUNG WOMAN

You don't want the war. We don't want the war. The Vietnamese don't want the war. So why does it go on?

Nixon hesitates, out of answers.

> YOUNG WOMAN

Someone wants it . . . (*a realization*) You can't stop it, can you. Even if you wanted to. Because it's not *you.* It's the system. And the system won't let you stop it . . .

> NIXON

There's a lot more at stake here than what you want. Or even what I want . . .

> YOUNG WOMAN

Then what's the point? What's the point of being president? You're power-less.

The girl transfixes him with her eyes. Nixon feels it. The nausea of the Beast makes him reel. The students press on him from all sides.

> NIXON (*STUMBLING*)

No, no. I'm not powerless. Because . . . because I understand the system. I believe I can control it. Maybe not control it totally. But . . . tame it enough to make it do some good.

> YOUNG WOMAN

It sounds like you're talking about a wild animal.

> NIXON

Maybe I am..

A silence. Nixon looks at her.

Haldeman and the SECRET SERVICE MEN fill the succeeding beat of si-lence by moving Nixon off. He allows himself to be herded, waving absently to the protestors.

> HALDEMAN

We really must go, Mr. President.

NIXON *(TO ALL)*

Don't forget, the most important thing in life is your relationship with your Maker . . . *(over his shoulder to all)* Don't forget to be on God's side.

This doesn't go down well with the protestors. ("Bullshit!")

As Nixon is led down the steps to the limousine:

NIXON

She got it, Bob. A nineteen-year-old college kid . . .

HALDEMAN

What?

NIXON

She understood something it's taken me twenty-five fucking years in politics to understand. The CIA, the Mafia, the Wall Street bastards . . .

HALDEMAN

Sir?

NIXON *(CLIMBING INTO THE LIMO, MUTTERS)*

. . . "The Beast." A nineteen-year-old kid. She understands the nature of "the Beast." She called it a wild animal.

The door closes. The LIMOUSINE is whisked away under searchlights and heavy security.

SUBTITLE READS: "JUNE 1971-A YEAR LATER"

DOCUMENTARY FOOTAGE—The White House is still ·ringed. ARMED TROOPS patrol Pennsylvania Avenue. The BUSES are drawn up. SMOKE is in the air. The SOUNDS of cherry bombs going off. Signs that read: "End the war! Throw the fascists out! Dick Nixon before he dicks you."

SCENE SEVENTY-TWO

EXT. THE WHITE HOUSE—ROSE GARDEN—DAY

Inside the barricades, a fairyland. A white lattice gazebo draped with flowers. TRICIA's wedding is in preparation. GROUNDSKEEPERS and various PERSONNEL lay out the carpet to the altar.

Nixon and H.R. Haldeman at Tricia's wedding

SCENE SEVENTY-THREE

INT. EXECUTIVE OFFICE BUILDING–PRESIDENT'S OFFICE–DAY

J. EDGAR HOOVER joins NIXON, pulling on his wedding tuxedo, at a window, looking out at the PROTESTORS. Intermittently, Hoover helps him with his clothes.

NIXON *(MUSING)*

There must be a quarter-million out there, Edgar. They've been at it now for a year. Young kids just like Tricia. I don't know. Do you think they have a point, Edgar? Maybe this whole damned system of government is . . .

HOOVER *(SUSPECTING 'SOFTNESS')*

Remember what Lenin said in 1917, Mr. President: "The power was lying in the streets just waiting for someone to pick it up." The Communists have never been closer. Now is the time to go back to the old themes. The ones that made you president. Let the Communists know you're onto them.

NIXON *(LAUGHS)*

The little bastards think they can ruin Tricia's wedding by dancing naked in the Reflecting Pond.

HOOVER

Don't listen to 'em, don't quit. Remember—Kennedy, Bobby, and King were against the war. Where are they now? Don't give 'em a Goddamn inch on the war. President Johnson bombed Laos for years and nobody knew or said a thing. How the hell the *Times* ever got ahold of this Ellsberg stuff is a disgrace!

NIXON

We can't keep a Goddamn secret in this government, Edgar. They're stealing papers right out of this office.

HOOVER

Johnson had the same damned problem till he bugged his own office.

NIXON *(NODS)*

We took his system out.

HOOVER

That was a mistake. The White House was full of Kennedy people then. It still is.

NIXON

Who do you think is behind it?

HOOVER

Well, you have CIA people all over this place. Helms has seen to that.[108] (*beat, Nixon remains poker-faced*) Then there's Kissinger's staff. Kissinger himself, I believe, may be the leaker.

NIXON *(STUNNED)*

Kissinger?

HOOVER

He's obsessed with his own image. He wants his Nobel Peace Prize a little too much. As the late "Doctor" King proved—even an ape can win a prize with good press.

---

[108]On the question of CIA infiltration of the White House, see Summers, *Official and Confidential*, p. 409; Scott, *Deep Politics and the Death of JFK*, pp. 305–306; Oglesby, *The Yankee and Cowboy War*, p. 273 passim; Haldeman, *The Ends of Power*, p. 109 passim, 204, 138–147; and Hougan, *Secret Agenda*, pp. 58–59.

NIXON

Jesus, I'd like to book him into a psychiatrist's office. He comes in here rant-
ing and raving, dumping his crap all over the place . . .[109] Could you prove it,
Edgar?

HOOVER

I always get my man.

NIXON

Yeah, you do. (then) I'd be bugging myself, Edgar . . . Who'd get the tapes?

HOOVER

No one. Your property. It would prove your case. Why do you think Kissinger's
taping your calls?[110] For history. His word against yours—and right now he's
got the records.

Nixon is stung by the comparison, fussing with his bow tie. Hoover helps him.

NIXON

This damned tie . . . Will you help me, Edgar? (then) Churchill used to say to
me, "If you want your own history written properly, you must write it yourself"
. . . (starts out) All right, Edgar, but just don't let it come back and haunt me.[111]

HOOVER (A REMINDER)

It won't. As long as I'm here.

---

[109]For Kissinger's mood swings, his threats to resign, and Nixon's concern that he needed psychiatric care, see Ehrlichman, *Witness to Power*, p. 307 ("Nixon wondered aloud if Henry
needed psychiatric care."); Ambrose, *Nixon: The Triumph of a Politician 1962–1972*, pp.
489–490; Haldeman, *The Haldeman Diaries*, pp. 234–256 (for example); Hersh, *The Price of
Power*, pp. 227, 232, 383–384, 475, 618, 638; Isaacson, *Kissinger*, pp. 585–586, 589–590,
671–672.

[110]Kissinger routinely recorded his calls and had members of his staff listen on "dead key" ex-
tensions. See Hersh, *The Price of Power*, pp. 318–319, 398–399; Isaacson, *Kissinger*, p. 600;
and Bernstein and Woodward, *The Final Days*, pp. 190–191. Dead keys and recording of telephone calls were common in the Nixon White House; for example, Haldeman, Ehrlichman, and
Colson all had recording equipment connected to their telephones and selected (often self-serving) tapes of recorded conversations surfaced during the Watergate investigations relating to
themselves. Like Kissinger, Haldeman had a dead key on his telephone so aides could listen. See
testimony of Gordon Strachan, *Senate Watergate Committee Hearings*, Book 6, p. 2506.

[111]On Hoover wiretapping for Nixon, see Summers, *Official and Confidential*, pp. 395–399; Gentry, *J. Edgar Hoover*, pp. 632–640, 672–674, 690.

Nixon absentmindedly shows Hoover through a small door into his BATH-ROOM ... There is an awkward pause, as both men are too proud to pretend they are cramped in this place together. Hoover clears his throat and exits the regular door. As we hear the Love Theme from "Doctor Zhivago":

CUT TO:

SCENE SEVENTY-FOUR

INT. EAST ROOM—DAY

The White House GUARDS wear German comic opera uniforms including tall cylindrical hats with beaks. We see champagne, white lace, the MUSI-CIANS wearing morning coats. HOOVER and TOLSON are together, very happy. To the sound of wedding MUSIC, NIXON takes a turn with his daughter, TRICIA, in gown. He has never seemed happier.

NIXON
I am very proud of you today, princess. Very.

The President dances with the bride (Marley Shelton)

When one of the GROOMSMEN cuts in, Nixon asks several OTHERS to dance. He retreats to JULIE's side. Julie says something sweet but unheard to him.

PAT is at a window, upset, looking out at the PROTESTORS as Julie comes over to get her.

JULIE

Come on, Mother, join the . . . *(sees her look)* What's the matter?

PAT

We're just not going to buckle to these people.

Pat puts on her party face and rejoins the crowd.

SCENE SEVENTY-FIVE

INT. THE WHITE HOUSE—CABINET ROOM—DAY (1971)—RAIN

CABINET MEMBERS chat, lean back in their chairs, smoking, as NIXON suddenly erupts into the room, a focused fury on his face. He sits, slams the New York Times down. CLOSE—we can make out the words "Pentagon Papers."[112]

NIXON

Gentlemen, we've had our last damned leak! This is no way to run a Goddamn government. We're going to prosecute the hell out of Ellsberg and anyone else who wants to leak. And that means any one of you who crosses the line, I'm personally going after . . .

INTERCUTTING among the faces—KISSINGER predominant. Nixon glances in his direction, pauses on him.

NIXON

The permissiveness of this era is over. The belts are coming off and people are gonna be taken to the woodshed. This government cannot survive with a counter-government inside it. I know how traitors operate—I've dealt with them all my life. This bullshit to the effect—some stenographer did it, some

---

[112] For a record of Nixon's speech to the Cabinet, see Haldeman, *The Haldeman Diaries*, pp. 309–311; see also Emery, *Watergate*, p. 48.

President Nixon and his Cabinet

stenographer—that's never the case. It's never the little people—little people do not leak. It's always a sonofabitch like Ellsberg who leaks! The Harvard He-brew boys with the private agendas who wanna be heroes.

Nixon grabs the paper, shakes it.

NIXON

Ellsberg did this "for the good of the country." I suppose you've never heard that one before. Alger Hiss and the Rosenbergs said the same damn crap, and you know what happened to them—ol' Sparky got 'em. They've always underestimated Nixon, the intellectuals. Well, we're gonna let them know we can fight just as dirty. This is sudden death, gentlemen. We're gonna get 'em on the ground, stick in our spikes and twist, show 'em no mercy!

Nixon looks around the room. The Cabinet members are stunned.

NIXON

This administration is a Goddamn disaster. We got bums out there at the gates. We've got thirty-eight of forty pieces of our domestic legislation defeated in Congress. Unless we turn things around, we'll all be looking for jobs next year. (*then*) Starting today, nobody in this room talks to the press without clearing it first with Haldeman. That means a complete freeze on the New York *Times,*

CBS, Jack fucking Anderson, and the *Washington Post!* From now on, Haldeman is the Lord High Executioner. So don't you come whining to me when he tells you to do something, 'cause that's me talking. And if you come to me, I'll be tougher than he is. Anybody tries to screw us, his head comes off. Do you understand? Good day, gentlemen . . .

He walks out, leaving them stunned and silent.

                                   HALDEMAN
Well, I guess that's it for today's meeting . . .

SCENE SEVENTY-SIX

INT. POULTRY PROCESSING PLANT—MIAMI—NIGHT

A chicken's head flies off. The CUBAN CROWD is going crazy as a FIGHTING COCK is moving in for the kill. The ring is surrounded by impromptu bleachers, the walls lined with metal cages filled with chickens. The slaughterhouse is adjacent.

HOWARD HUNT stands at the edge of the crowd, holding a greasy wrapper of churos, as the fight ends.

Cheers and groans. Fistfuls of money are exchanged.

FRANK STURGIS turns from the ring, makes his way to Hunt, hands him a twenty.[113]

---

[113]This scene is a dramatized conceptualization of the events. Hunt met with the Cubans in April 1971. Initially he spoke with Barker and Martinez at the Bay of Pigs memorial in Miami. This meeting took place two months before the release of the Pentagon Papers and the formation of the Plumbers. See Hougan, *Secret Agenda,* p. 29. While conspiracy students find this interesting, Hunt writes he was simply in Florida "in connection with my work on the HEW account" for Mullen & Company and at "Dorothy's [his wife's] suggestion" he got in touch with Barker to renew old friendships. See Hunt, *Undercover,* pp. 143–144. Barker testified before the Senate Watergate Committee that this first meeting with Hunt on April 17, 1971, was "nothing" and merely a reunion. See testimony of Bernard Barker, *Senate Watergate Committee Hearings,* Book 1, pp. 374–375. Martinez, on the other hand, insists the purpose of Hunt's visit was recruitment: "He said he wanted to meet with the old people. It was a good sign. We did not think he had come to Miami for nothing." See Eugenio Martinez, "Mission Impossible," *Harper's,* October 1974, p. 51; and Hougan, *Secret Agenda,* p. 29.

For the hiring of Sturgis and the Cubans, see Hougan, *Secret Agenda,* pp. 27–30; Aitken, *Nixon,* pp. 62–64; Emery, *Watergate,* p. 63; and Eugenio Martinez, "Mission Impossible" *Harper's,* October 1974. Note: Liddy was not at the recruitment meeting.

STURGIS

How the fuck did you know?

HUNT

Injections. Even this noble sport's been fixed. (*pockets the twenty*) Seen the guys?

STURGIS

They're around.

Sturgis snags a piece of churo, swallows it.

STURGIS

Why, you got a customer?

HUNT

The White House.

STURGIS (*STOPS*)

You're fucking me.

Oliver Stone, E. Howard Hunt, and co-producer Eric Hamburg on the set

HUNT

We're gonna be plumbers, Frank. We're gonna plug leaks.

STURGIS

Who we working for?

HUNT

A guy named Gordon Liddy. Thinks he's Martin Borman. You wanna meet him? (*He motions.*)

GORDON LIDDY comes out of the edges of the crowd, shakes hands with Sturgis.

HUNT

Gordon Liddy . . . Frank Sturgis.

They turn the handshake into a parallel of the cock fight, iron grips subtly crushing the other's hand.

LIDDY (*AFTER THEY BREAK*)

Y'ever hold your hand over a fire? (*pulls out a Zippo lighter*)

HUNT

That's okay, Gordon. (*motions him off*)

As Liddy drifts off:

STURGIS

Where'd you find him?

HUNT

Just don't tell him to do anything you don't really want him to do.

STURGIS

So, does Tricky Dick know about this?

HUNT

I won't tell him if you won't.

The HANDLERS throw TWO NEW FIGHTING COCKS into the ring. They start to rip at each other.

HUNT (*CHEWING ON HIS CHURO*)

The claws are out, Frank.

SCENE SEVENTY-SEVEN

INT. FIELDING PSYCHIATRIST OFFICE—NIGHT (1971)

As seen before: a GLASS shatters, a CROWBAR jacks open the door marked: "Dr. Lewis J. Fielding, Psychiatrist."

NIXON *(v.o.)*

History will never be the same.

Cabinets full of pills are overturned. The disguised HUNT and LIDDY, with the three CUBANS, go to work. A FILE FOLDER is ripped from a cabinet. In the flashlight beam the file reads "Daniel Ellsberg." A VOICE calls out: "Howard, I got it!"

NIXON *(v.o.)*

We've taken a step into the future. We have changed the world.

"America the Beautiful" MUSIC takes us into:

SCENE SEVENTY-EIGHT

INT. MAO TSE-TUNG'S OFFICE—BEIJING—DAY (1972)

SUBTITLE READS—"FEBRUARY 1972"

NIXON beams, standing under a huge red flag bearing the hammer and sickle. The "America" theme is being played on traditional Chinese instruments as CHINESE PHOTOGRAPHERS are allowed to take stiff portraits. The MEN chit-chat.[114]

NIXON

I must say you look very good, Mr. Chairman.

---

[114]For Nixon's meeting with Mao, see Kissinger, *The White House Years,* pp. 1060–1062; Nixon, *RN,* pp. 561–563.

Nixon, Henry Kissinger (Paul Sorvino), Mao Tse-tung (Ric Young), Chou En-lai (Li-Ren Yin) at the summit with translator (Bai Ling)

MAO

Looks can be deceiving . . .

NIXON

We know you've taken a great risk in inviting us here.

MAO stares at Nixon and replies in Chinese, which the INTERPRETER repeats:

MAO *(HALF SMILES)*

I took no risk. I'm too old to be afraid of what anyone thinks.

Nixon forces a rigid smile as they move to chairs.

TIME CUT TO:

MAO and NIXON are seated in armchairs opposite each other, KISSINGER and CHOU EN-LAI to either side of Mao. An INTERPRETER between. In media res:

MAO

Don't ever trust them. They never tell the truth or honor their commitments. Vietnamese are like Russians. Both are dogs.

NIXON *(CLEARS HIS THROAT)*

Mr. Chairman, there is an old saying: The enemy of my enemy is my friend.

MAO *(SMILES)*

That has the added virtue of being true.

Mao doesn't seem to be taking any of this too seriously: in fact, he seems a little medicated.

KISSINGER

You know, Mr. Chairman, at Harvard I used your writings in my class.

MAO

What a waste of time. My writings mean absolutely nothing.

KISSINGER

But your writings have changed the world, Mr. Chairman.

MAO

Fung pi! (*Bullshit!*) I've only managed to change a few things around the city of Beijing. (*then: to Kissinger*) I want to know your secret.

KISSINGER

Secret, Mr. Chairman?

MAO

How a fat man gets so many girls.

Mao howls at his own joke.

KISSINGER

Power, Mr. Chairman, is the ultimate aphrodisiac. (*laughter*)

MAO *(TURNS TO NIXON)*

You know, I voted for you in your last election.

NIXON *(SELF-EFFACING)*

I was the lesser of two evils.

A moment. Mao levels a gaze at him, deadly serious.

MAO

You're too modest, Nixon. You're as evil as I am. We're both from poor families. But others pay to feed the hunger in us. In my case, millions of reactionaries. In your case, millions of Vietnamese.

NIXON *(TAKEN ABACK)*

Civil war is always the cruelest kind of war.

MAO

The real war is in us. *(then)* History is a symptom of our disease.

CUT FORWARD TO:

SCENE SEVENTY-NINE

DOCUMENTARY FOOTAGE–THE BOMBING OF HANOI ... SUBTITLE READS: "CHRISTMAS 1972." HUNDREDS OF B-52 STRIKES, BOMBS POURING OVER THE CITY.

Kissinger, Mao, Nixon, Chou En-lai, in Beijing

REPORTER *(V.O. BBC ACCENT)*

In a surprise Christmas bombing of Hanoi, President Nixon today delivered more tonnage than was used at Dresden in World War II . . . It is, without doubt, the most brutal bombing in American history.

CROSSCUT:

DOCUMENTARY FOOTAGE—1. HANOI—the devastation of the city. It's on fire. Bodies are being carried from a collapsed HOSPITAL. 2. The USA—in contrast, shots in the media of Christmas trees (Rockefeller Center, etc.); families shopping; a children's choir singing "Gloria in Excelsis Deo."

REPORTERS *(v.o.)*

. . . This Christmas bombing has shaken up the Paris peace talks and created a huge amount of criticism across the globe. Newspapers are calling it a "Stone Age tactic," and Nixon, a "maddened tyrant" . . . Nixon's only response: "When the Vietnamese take the peace talks seriously, I'll stop."

STOCK FOOTAGE—moving through a bank of clouds towards the sun.

SCENE EIGHTY

INT. AIR FORCE ONE—MAIN CABIN—SUNSET (1972)

NIXON is looking out the window, PAT next to him. HALDEMAN and EHRLICHMAN are out of earshot.

PAT

Penny for your thoughts.

NIXON

Is that adjusted for inflation? (*She laughs.*) Think of the life Mao's led. In '52 I called him a monster. Now he could be our most important ally. (*then*) Only Nixon could've done that.

PAT

You're a long way from Whittier.

A beat. He shares her look.

NIXON

Yes . . . yes, I am.

Pat puts her hand on his hand.

PAT

Congratulations, Dick.

NIXON *(SMILES)*

How am I going to break this to Bob Hope?

KISSINGER walks into the cabin.

KISSINGER

We've got the Russians where we want them! They're calling us. We will have a SALT treaty with them this year.

HALDEMAN

In time for the election? Brezhnev's tough. He knows McGovern's right on our ass . . .

KISSINGER

He doesn't have a choice! He has to shift missiles from Europe to the Chinese border. With one stroke, the balance of power moves completely in our favor. This is a coup, Mr. President!

EHRLICHMAN

For you, Henry? Nobel Peace Prize, maybe . . . *(sees the look on Nixon's face)*

NIXON

Not for the Pentagon it isn't. I'm kissing Mao's ass. And the press is gonna find some way to shaft Nixon on this one.

PAT

It's not the press that matters. Nixon's wife is proud of him.

He squeezes her hand.

HALDEMAN

And his staff. Come on, the copy they were filing from China was great.

NIXON

Wait till the Mai-tais wear off.

EHRLICHMAN

The country's loving it.

NIXON

The hard-core four million "Nixon nuts" aren't gonna go for it . . . They'll say I sold out to the Communists.

KISSINGER

You'll pick up the middle on this one—the Jews and Negroes.

NIXON

Jews and Negroes don't win elections, Henry. Better to hang them around the Democrats' necks.

HALDEMAN

The Jews aren't the middle, Henry. They're the far left.

NIXON

You're talking too much about black Africa, Henry. It's killing us with the rednecks.

HALDEMAN

The blacks are lost, the "schwartzes" are gone . . .

NIXON

Don't let it lose us the right-wing vote . . .

A silence as the sour notes depress everyone.

NIXON *(FEELING THE DEFLATION)*

Hey, I sound like my father now. Let's have a drink!

Pat smiles. ZIEGLER pokes his head in.

ZIEGLER

Mr. President, the press guys asked if you could come back for a minute.

NIXON

The hell with 'em.

KISSINGER

I'll go back, Mr. President.

Everyone glares at Henry.

ZIEGLER

No, they want you, Mr. President. I really think it would be a good move.

Nixon puts aside his drink, gets up.

NIXON

Gentlemen, I go now to discover the exact length, width, and depth of the shaft.

SCENE EIGHTY-ONE

INT. AIR FORCE ONE—PRESS CABIN—SUNSET

NIXON closes the door behind him, turns.

DOZENS of REPORTERS stand, burst into applause.

He is momentarily stunned, then he moves down the aisle. Shaking hands. The reporters continue applauding. Nixon, for once, is deeply moved. On the sound of applause, we:

CUT TO:

SCENE EIGHTY-TWO

EXT. JONES RANCH—TEXAS—DAY (1972)

REPORTER'S VOICE

J. Edgar Hover is dead at the age of seventy-seven. The legendary crime buster served his country as Director of the FBI for almost half a century, from 1924 to 1972.

An enormous BRAHMA BULL, red-eyed, snorting, thrashes viciously against the reinforced walls of its pen. NIXON and JACK JONES watch as SECRET SERVICE hover nearby.[115]

JONES *(v.o.)*

There's two kinds of bulls, Dick. Your good bull and your bad bull. This here's a bad bull. You piss him off, he'll kill everything in his path. Only way to stop him is to shoot him.

A WRANGLER climbs carefully into the chute. The Brahma lunges for him.

JONES

Eddie, you be damned careful with that beast. His nuts are worth a helluva lot more'n yours.

He leads Nixon down the steps.

JONES *(CAGEY)*

So, what's this about, Dick?

NIXON

It's me or Wallace, Jack. Wallace's third party is only going to help McGovern. I need your support.

JONES

Well, you sure been chock full of surprises so far, "Mister President."

SCENE EIGHTY-THREE

INT. JONES RANCH—LIVING ROOM—DAY (1972)

NIXON and HALDEMAN are standing by the hearth. The years have gone by but, in different clothing and hairstyles, it is much the same group of a

---

[115]Shortly after his return from China, Nixon flew to Floresville, Texas, where he met at a ranch with some two hundred Gulf Coast money men, including leading Texas oil executives, with some of whom he had met in Dallas in November 1963. See Ambrose, *Nixon: The Triumph of a Politician 1962–1972,* p. 534. See also H. R. Haldeman, *The Haldeman Diaries: Inside the Nixon White House–The Complete Multimedia Edition* [on CD-ROM] (Santa Monica, CA: Sony Electronic Publishing, 1994), where Haldeman reports that Nixon traveled to the Floresville ranch of Secretary of the Treasury, John Connally, the former Governor of Texas.

DOZEN BUSINESSMEN gathered around, drinking Jack Daniels and smoking cigars. Among them we recognize the CUBAN and MITCH. It's heated.

JONES

It looks like to me we're gonna lose a war for the first Goddamn time and, Dick, Goddamnit, you're going along with it, buying into this Kissinger bullshit— "détente" with the Communists. "Détente"—it sounds like two fags dancing.

NIXON

Jack, we're not living in the same country you and I knew in '46. Our people are just not gonna sacrifice in major numbers for war. We can't even get 'em to accept cuts in their gas tanks. Hell, the Arabs and the Japanese are bleeding the shit out of our gold . . .

JONES

And whose fault is that? If we'd won in Vietnam . . .

NIXON

It's nobody's fault, Jack. It's change—which is a fact of history. Even that old cocksucker Hoover's dead. Things change.

An uncomfortable silence. A servant brings coffee to Nixon, but Haldeman cuts him off. No one gets close to his guy.

MITCH

So . . . how's the food over there in China, Mr. Nixon?

NIXON

Free, if you're the president. (*nervous laughter*)

MITCH

What are you going to do about this Allende fellow nationalizing our businesses in Chile? You gonna send Kissinger down there?

NIXON

We're gonna get rid of him—Allende, I mean—just as fast as we can. He's on top of the list.

MITCH

How about Kissinger along with him?

NIXON

Kissinger's misunderstood. He pretends to be a liberal for his Establishment friends, but he's even tougher than I . . .

CUBAN

So Kissinger stays. Just like Castro, Mr. Nixon?

NIXON

Yeah, he stays . . .

An uncomfortable silence. Jones walks closer to Nixon.

JONES

Desi's got a point. What the hell we gonna do about the Communists right here in our backyard?!

NIXON

What do you mean, Jack?

JONES

I mean I got federal price controls on my oil. The ragheads are beating the shit out of me. And I got your EPA environment agency with its thumb so far up my ass it's scratching my ear.

HALDEMAN

Gentlemen, I think it's about time for us to be getting to the airport.

NIXON

Let him finish, Bob.

JONES

. . . And now I have a federal judge ordering me to bus my kids halfway 'cross town to go to school with some nigger kids. I think, Mr. President, you're forgetting who put you where you are.

NIXON

The American people put me where I am.

Jones smirks. They all smirk. A dreadful moment.

JONES

Really? Well, that can be changed.

Dead silence. Nixon moves closer to Jones.

NIXON

Jack, I've learned that politics is the art of compromise. I learned it the hard way. I don't know if you have. But I tell you what, Jack . . . If you don't like it, there's an election in November. You can take your money out into the open, give it to Wallace . . . How 'bout it Jack? Are you willing to do that? Give this country over to some poet-pansy socialist like George McGovern?

Nixon is right in Jones's face now.

NIXON

Because if you're uncomfortable with the EPA up your ass, try the IRS . . .

JONES

Well, Goddamn. Are you threatening me, Dick?

NIXON *(SOFTLY)*

Presidents don't threaten. They don't have to. *(then)* Good day, gentlemen.

As he walks out with Haldeman, there is a stone silence.

SCENE EIGHTY-FOUR

EXT. TEXAS LANDSCAPE–DAY

As the PRESIDENTIAL CAR pulls away in a three-car entourage, we hear:

REPORTERS *(v.o.)*

. . . With George Wallace out of the race, paralyzed by an assassin's bullet, Richard Nixon has crushed George McGovern in the 1972 presidential election. It is the second biggest landslide in American history, but . . .

SCENE EIGHTY-FIVE

EXT. AIR FORCE ONE–DAY (STOCK FOOTAGE)

The plane flying through clouds. A royal feeling.

REPORTERS *(v.o.)*

. . . the Democrats have increased their majority in the House and the Senate. As the new term begins, there is mounting evidence of strong hostility to President Nixon's mandate for a "New American Revolution." However, it does not seem that the Watergate investigations have, up to now, damaged Nixon politically in any significant way . . .

SCENE EIGHTY-SIX

INT. AIR FORCE ONE–PRESIDENT'S CABIN–NIGHT

NIXON looks out the window, turns to HALDEMAN next to him, making notes on his ubiquitous clipboard. ZIEGLER is nearby.

NIXON

You know, they all miss the point. Probably our biggest achievement as an administration, when it's all said and done, isn't China or Russia. It's pulling out of Vietnam without a right-wing revolt.

HALDEMAN

I believe you're right, boss.

NIXON

. . . but even the presidency isn't enough anymore . . .

HALDEMAN

Sir?

NIXON

The presidency by itself won't protect us, Bob. We're beyond politics now . . .

Haldeman is puzzled. EHRLICHMAN enters the cabin, excited, extending a cable. He is followed by long-haired JOHN DEAN.

EHRLICHMAN

Sir, just in from Paris—the Vietnamese have accepted Henry's peace proposal. The bombing worked! They're caving.

Nixon reads Kissinger's cable, but he doesn't express any happiness.

HALDEMAN *(EXCITED)*

Congratulations, boss (*handshake offered*)—a great victory! The madman theory wasn't so crazy after all.

NIXON *(TO HIMSELF)*

This could be it . . . this could be it. Four long years . . .

EHRLICHMAN

Henry's on his way back to meet us. He wants to make sure he gets in all the photographs. Incidentally . . . maybe this isn't the right time but . . . uh, you should know . . . Bill Sullivan over at the FBI got back to us with his report on Kissinger.

Nixon looks up, interested.

EHRLICHMAN *(NODS)*

Yeah . . . Sullivan thinks Henry's leaking. He's the one . . .[116]

HALDEMAN

Yeah, I knew it. I knew it from '69 on, and I said it all along, didn't I . . .

Nixon's expression changes totally, narrowing, cold.

NIXON

No, you didn't, Bob . . .

EHRLICHMAN

Looks like he talked to Joe Kraft . . . and to the *Times.* Told them he was dead set against the bombing and that you were . . . "unstable." Claims he has to handle you "with kid gloves" . . .

Waiting on Nixon, who goes into some inner state alone, dark brows furrowing with built-up rage.

HALDEMAN *(HIS DARKER SIDE EMERGING)*

So that explains his press notices. Working both sides of the fence: Jewboy Henry, always trying to get his Nobel Prize, get laid . . .

---

[116]On Kissinger as a leaker, see Ambrose, *Nixon: Ruin and Recovery 1973–1990,* pp. 41, 43; Ehrlichman, *Witness to Power,* pp. 302–303, 310; Hersh, *The Price of Power,* pp. 160, 205n, 254, 379–380, 397, 597, 603–604; and Isaacson, *Kissinger,* pp. 189, 200, 228–229, 232–233, 292, 306–307.

NIXON *(IN HIS OWN WORLD)*

My God, my God! He talked to the New York *Times?*

HALDEMAN

We ought to fire his whining ass. Right now when he's on top. You know what—it'll set the right example for the rest of this administration.

EHRLICHMAN

I would personally enjoy doing that, sir.

NIXON (CONFLICTED)

No, no. He's our only "star" right now. He'd go crying straight to the press. He'd crucify us—the sonofabitch! . . . (*lethal*) Get someone from on our staff on his ass. Tap his phones. I want to know everyone he talks to.[117]

HALDEMAN

Then we'll see how long the Kissinger mystique lasts.

In a foul mood now, paranoia setting in like a storm cloud on his face, Nixon shifts back to Dean, who is scared of this Nixon and tries to pacify him.

NIXON

So, what about those Watergate clowns, John? This fucking Sirica's crazy. Thirty-five-year sentences! There were no weapons. Right? No injuries. There was no success! It's just ridiculous.

DEAN

Sirica's just trying to force one of them to testify. But they're solid.

NIXON

Then what about this *Washington Post* crap? Woodwind and Fernstein? (*Ziegler corrects him, "Bernstein"*) Who the fuck are they? (*to Haldeman*) Bob, are you working on revoking the *Post*'s television license?[118] (*Haldeman nods, "Yes sir, I am."*) Good.

---

[117]For Kissinger as a target of White House wiretaps, see Hersh, *The Price of Power,* p. 391.

[118]See Bernstein and Woodward, *All the President's Men,* pp. 220–221; see also the transcript of the September 15, 1972, conversation among the President, Haldeman, and Dean, National Archives.

> ### DEAN
>
> Well, they're trying to connect Bob and John to a secret fund, but they don't have much.[119]

> ### HALDEMAN *(WITH A LOOK TO EHRLICHMAN)*
>
> They don't have anything on us.

> ### DEAN
>
> The FBI's feeding me all their reports. I didn't think you should lose any more sleep on it, sir.

> ### NIXON *(MUTTERS, RELIEVED)*
>
> Good man, John, good man.

They all fall silent, feeling that false sense of security as the sound of the jet engines takes over. Suddenly, there is an air pocket and they rock back and forth.

SCENE EIGHTY-SEVEN

INT. THE WHITE HOUSE—PRESS CONFERENCE—EAST ROOM—DAY

SUBTITLE READS: "JANUARY 1973."

NIXON is concluding his statement to the PRESS, HALDEMAN in the background with ZIEGLER.

> ### NIXON
>
> . . . I can therefore announce that our long and tragic involvement in Vietnam is at an end. Our mission is accomplished, we have a cease-fire, our prisoners of war are coming back, and South Vietnam has the right to determine its own future. We have peace with honor.

The REPORTERS are immediately on their feet. A MONTAGE of QUICK CUTS follows to give the impression of a hostile and never-ending barrage of questions without satisfactory answers.

---

[119]For a discussion of the secret fund, see Bernstein and Woodward, *All the President's Men*, pp. 101–101, 170–193, 195–198.

Oliver Stone with Anthony Hopkins (as Nixon) preparing for a press conference scene

REPORTER 1 *("DAN RATHER"-TYPE)*

Sir, isn't it true little has been achieved in this peace agreement that the Communists have not been offering since 1969? That in fact your administration has needlessly prolonged the war and, at certain stages, has escalated it to new levels of violence?

JUMP TO:

REPORTER 2 *("LESLIE STAHL"-TYPE)*

Mr. President, what is your reaction to James McCord's statement that high White House officials were involved in the Watergate break-in?

JUMP TO:

REPORTER 3 *("SAM DONALDSON"-TYPE)*

Sir, the *Washington Post* is reporting that Mr. Haldeman and Mr. Ehrlichman have secretly disbursed up to $900,000 in campaign funds. Is there any truth to that?[120]

---

[120]For the $900,000 disbursement, see Bernstein and Woodward, *All the President's Men,* p. 195. This story was originally reported by the New York *Times.* Woodward and Bernstein had established that the fund contained at least $350,000, and perhaps as much as $700,000. Senator George McGovern stated on *Meet the Press* that the fund was controlled first by Mitchell and later by Ehrlichman-Haldeman.

NIXON (*SNAPS*)

I've said before and I'll say again: I will not respond to the charges of the *Washington Post.* Nor will I comment on a matter that's currently before the courts.

REPORTER 4

Do you intend to cooperate with Senator Ervin's committee?

REPORTER 5

Will you agree to the appointment of a special prosecutor?

The questions flood in. Nixon is overwhelmed. He gathers his papers and starts to move off. A darkly funny thing happens: ZIEGLER wanders into his path, almost colliding. Nixon, pissed, grabs Ziegler by the shoulders, spins him back towards the REPORTERS, and pushes him at them. Ziegler stumbles, looks confused.[121]

SCENE EIGHTY-EIGHT

INT. OVAL OFFICE—THE WHITE HOUSE—DAY (1973)

NIXON storms into his office, picking up an ashtray and hurling it across the room—it shatters against a wall. Everyone in the room with him—KISSINGER, HALDEMAN, EHRLICHMAN—is stunned.

NIXON

I end the longest war in American history and they keep harping on this chickenshit! You know who's behind this, don't you—it's Teddy Kennedy! He drowns a broad in his car and he can't run for president.

EHRLICHMAN

He got pretty burned at Chappaquiddick.

NIXON

My point exactly! Somebody had to *die* before his shit got in the papers! Fucking Kennedys get away with everything. Do you see me screwing everything that moves? (*then*) For Christ's sake! I *did* what the New York *Times* editorial page said we should do! I ended the war, I got SALT I with the Russians,

---

[121]This incident actually occurred in New Orleans in August 1973. See Ambrose, *Nixon: Ruin and Recovery 1973–1990,* p. 210.

I opened China! So why are these cocksuckers turning on me? Because they don't like the way I look. Where I went to school.

HALDEMAN

Because they're not Americans.

NIXON

Right. They don't trust! They don't trust America!

HALDEMAN (VENTING WITH HIM)

Why would they?! Who the hell's Sulzberger anyway? Their parents are gold traders from Eastern Europe. They buy things. They come to Jew York City[122] and they buy up things. One of the things they buy is the New York *Times.* (*glares at Kissinger*) And you know what? Be proud because they'll never trust you, sir, because we speak for the average American.

Ehrlichman shares a look with Kissinger as Nixon and Haldeman feed into each other.

NIXON

You know why they're turning on me? They're not *serious* about power, that's why. They're playing with power. They're forgetting the national interest. In the old days, people knew how to hold power, how to set limits. They wouldn't have torn this country apart over a third-rate burglary. All they care about now are their egos, looking good at cocktail parties . . .

HALDEMAN

. . . beating out the other papers, chasing girls . . .

NIXON

. . . worrying whether someone said something "nice" about them. All short-term, frivolous bullshit; Ben Bradlee worrying about Teddy Kennedy liking him . . .

Kissinger tries to get the focus back.

KISSINGER

Mr. President, I feel we're drifting toward oblivion here. We're playing a to-tally reactive game; we've got to get ahead of the ball. (*pause, in an embar-*

---

[122]For anti-Semitism within the Nixon inner circle, see Hersh, *The Price of Power,* pp. 84–86, 135, 213–214, 603; Isaacson, *Kissinger,* pp. 148, 494, 560–562, 635.

rassed voice) We all know you're clean . . . Right? So let's do a housecleaning. Take the gloves off.

Haldeman shares a look with Ehrlichman. Is he referring to them? Nixon turns slowly on Kissinger, cryptic.

NIXON

Housecleaning? It would be ugly, Henry, really ugly . . .

KISSINGER

But it must be done; your government is paralyzed.

NIXON

All kinds of shit would come out. Like the Ellsberg thing. You knew about that Henry, didn't you?

KISSINGER *(VAGUE)*

I . . . I heard something . . . It sounded idiotic.[123]

NIXON

Idiotic? Yes, I suppose it was.

EHRLICHMAN

But you're the one who said we should expose him as some kind of sex fiend. Someone took you literally.

KISSINGER *(STUNG, AND SUDDENLY KNOWLEDGEABLE)*

I never suggested for some *imbeciles* to go break into a psychiatrist's office. How stupid of . . .

NIXON

That doesn't matter now, Henry. The point is, you might lose some of your media-darling halo if the press starts sniffing around our dirty laundry.

---

[123]For the possibility of Kissinger's advance knowledge of the Fielding break-in, see Hersh, *The Price of Power*, p. 391n. (Hersh cites the private notes of a Kissinger aide who reports that Kissinger was being kept informed of the Plumbers' activities.)

KISSINGER (*INDIGNANT*)

I had nothing to do with that, sir, and I resent any implication . . .

NIXON

Resent it all you want, Henry, but you're in it with the rest of us. Cambodia, Ellsberg, the wiretaps you put in.[124] The President wants you to know you can't just click your heels and head back to Harvard Yard. It's your *ass* too, Henry, and it's in the wind twisting with everyone else's.

A stony silence. The men, all clenched jaws, wait. Kissinger, icily, clicks his heels and withdraws.

KISSINGER (*AT THE DOOR*)

Mr. Nixon, it is possible for even a president to go too far.

NIXON

Yeah . . .

Nixon laughs maniacally. JOHN DEAN crosses in as Kissinger exits. Dean closes the door behind him.

HALDEMAN

You played it perfectly, sir—cocksucker! He's going to think twice before he leaks again.

NIXON (*EXULTANT*)

He'll be looking in his toilet bowl every time he pulls the chain.

They laugh madly, like hatters at a tea party.

DEAN (*WORRIED*)

Mr. President, Hunt wants more money. Another hundred-and-thirty thousand.

NIXON

Son of a bitch.

---

[124]For Kissinger's wiretaps, see Hersh, *The Price of Power*, pp. 82–87, 89–97, 193–197, 318–326, 398–401; Isaacson, *Kissinger*, pp. 145, 230–232, 388, 493; and Ambrose, *Nixon: Ruin and Recovery 1973–1990*, pp. 134, 156, 214, 352–353, 370, 419.

DEAN

He says if he doesn't get it right away, he's going to blow us out of the water.[125] And he means it. Ever since his wife died in the plane crash, he's been over the edge.[126]

NIXON

Pay him. Pay him what he wants.

HALDEMAN

We've got to turn the faucet off on this thing. It's out of control . . . (*as he crosses Dean, sotto voce*) You might burden just me with this in the future.

NIXON

It's Helms—it's got to be.

---

[125]A conversation of this nature actually took place on March 21, 1973, between Dean and the President. See Watergate Special Prosecutor's Office Transcripts, National Archives; and Dean, *Blind Ambition*, pp. 192, 196.

[126]The most in-depth discussion of the plane crash in which Dorothy Hunt died is contained in Oglesby, *The Yankee and Cowboy War,* pp. 225–264. Also see Colson's views on the crash in *Time,* July 8, 1974: "I don't say this to my people. They'd think I'm nuts. I think the CIA killed Dorothy Hunt." For Hunt's explanation of why his wife was carrying $10,000 in $100 bills at the time of her death, see Hunt, *Undercover,* pp. 282–283. The Watergate Special Prosecutor's Office reviewed the FBI's and other investigations of this crash and found nothing sinister relating to the crash per se. See Watergate Special Prosecutor's Office files, National Archives.

Nixon confronts Kissinger with staff

HALDEMAN

We could leverage Helms.

NIXON

How?

HALDEMAN

When I met with him, he said . . .

SCENE EIGHTY-NINE

INT. CIA–HELMS'S OFFICE–DAY (FLASHBACK)

HELMS, sitting across from HALDEMAN.

HALDEMAN

. . . this entire affair, the President wants you to know, is related to the Bay of Pigs, and if it opens up . . .

Helms grips the arms of his chair, leans forward excitedly, and yells at Haldeman.

HELMS

The Bay of Pigs had nothing to do with this! I have no concern about the Bay of Pigs!![127]

Haldeman is shocked by Helms's violent reaction, but remains very cool.

HALDEMAN

This is what the President told me to relay to you, Mr. Helms.

HELMS *(SETTLING BACK)*

All right . . .

---

[127]For Helms's reaction, see Brodie, *Richard Nixon,* p. 496; Haldeman, *The Ends of Power,* pp. 37–38; Ehrlichman, *Witness to Power,* p. 350; Aitken, *Nixon,* p. 478; Emery, *Watergate,* pp. 192–193: "Turmoil in the room, Helms gripping the arms of the chair leaning forward and shouting . . ." (Ibid., p. 192).

SCENE NINETY

INT. OVAL OFFICE–DAY (1973)

RESUME SCENE–HALDEMAN, EHRLICHMAN, DEAN, and NIXON.

HALDEMAN *(FISHING)*

. . . I was wondering what's such dynamite in this Bay of Pigs story?[128] (*Nixon stares, nothing*) . . . although it was clearly effective, because all of a sudden it was no problem for Helms to go to the FBI and try to put a lid on Watergate.[129]

NIXON

What about the documents he promised?

HALDEMAN

He'll give us the documents. (*then*) But I think he should be offered the ambassadorship to Iran. Then he'll go without a whimper.[130]

Nixon stares at him, distracted.

---

[128]Haldeman, *The Ends of Power,* p. 38. "Before the meeting . . . Haldeman had gone into Ehrlichman's office and said, 'Guess what? It's Bay of Pigs time again.' Ehrlichman replied, 'This time you're going to push the red button, not me' " (Emery, *Watergate,* p. 192). For a discussion of "what's such dynamite in this Bay of Pigs story," see Peter Dale Scott, *Crime and Coverup: The Dallas-Watergate Connection* (Berkeley: Westworks, 1977). Also see Oglesby, *The Yankee and Cowboy War,* pp. 48–64.

[129]For Helms going to the FBI, see Emery, *Watergate,* p. 193; and Nixon, *RN,* p. 642. Helms prepared a memorandum of his activities that was provided to Congress. See House Judiciary Committee, "Events Following the Watergate Break-in, June 17, 1972–February 9, 1973," *Statement of Information,* Book II, Hearings Before the Committee on the Judiciary, 93rd Congress, Second Session (Washington, DC: Government Printing Office, 1974), pp. 458–459. Helms would later testify that Haldeman's reference to the Bay of Pigs ". . . was incoherent, I simply mean that, because I really didn't understand what he was talking about as far as the Bay of Pigs was concerned. I don't know whether he really understood himself. He was making an aversion *(sic)* to it, and I don't know why he was doing it, and I don't know to this day why." See Helms's testimony, Special Subcommittee on Intelligence, *Inquiry into the Alleged Involvement of the Central Intelligence Agency in the Watergate and Ellsberg Matters,* Hearings Before the Special Subcommittee on Intelligence of the Committee on Armed Services, House of Representatives, 94th Congress, First Session (Washington DC: Government Printing Office, 1975), p. 93.

[130]On Helms becoming ambassador to Iran, see Haldeman, *The Haldeman Diaries,* p. 540; Hougan, *Secret Agenda,* pp. 231–232; and Powers, *The Man Who Kept Secrets,* pp. 242–243, 363. On the references to ambassadorships and campaign contributions, see Select Committee, *Final Report,* pp. 492–505 and Maurice H. Stans, *The Terrors of Justice: The Untold Side of Watergate* (New York: Everest House, 1978), p. 405.

NIXON

I promised Iran to Townsend.

HALDEMAN

Put Townsend in Belgium; it's available.

NIXON

Townsend gave us 300 grand. Belgium's not worth more than 100, 150 . . .

EHRLICHMAN

What about England?

NIXON

Forget it. Ehrenberg's paid three times that much . . .

HALDEMAN

Helms wants Iran or there might be problems. All his old CIA buddies are over there making a fortune off the Shah.

NIXON

For God's sake, when does this end?!

DEAN *(SUDDENLY)*

Executive clemency . . .

NIXON

What?

DEAN

Hunt has nothing to lose now. Pardon all of them. Nobody's going to investigate a crime for which the criminals have already been pardoned.[131]

NIXON

I like that. That's a solution.

EHRLICHMAN

It'll never wash. Pardoning them means we're all guilty. The people, the press will go nuts.

---

[131]Note: Dean never actually made this suggestion. On executive clemency for Hunt and the other burglars, see Emery, *Watergate,* pp. 209, 233–234, 305, 329; Ehrlichman, *Witness to Power,* p. 355; Bernstein and Woodward, *The Final Days,* pp. 91–93; and Bernstein and Woodward, *All the President's Men,* pp. 312, 331.

NIXON

And what am I supposed to do? Just sit here and watch them coming closer? Eating their way to the center. (*paces*) Lyndon bugged! So did Kennedy! FDR cut a deal with Lucky Luciano. Christ, even Ike had a mistress! What's so special about me? (*then*) What about Lyndon? He could make a couple of calls to the Hill and shut this whole thing down. Did anyone talk to him?

HALDEMAN (*HESITANT*)

I did. He hit the roof. No dice. He says if you come out with the story about how he bugged your plane, he's going to reveal . . . (*he looks at Ehrlichman and Dean, pauses*)[132]

We CUT ACROSS the room from Ehrlichman's point of view as Haldeman whispers the rest of the message in Nixon's ear.

Nixon's face goes ashen.

NIXON (*LOW KEY*)

All right . . . all right.

He walks to the window.

NIXON (*TO HIMSELF*)

I don't know, I don't know . . . I just know we've made too many enemies.

EHRLICHMAN

Sir, Bob and I are gonna have to testify before Ervin's Committee.

NIXON

No, you're not! You're going to claim executive privilege and you're going to stonewall it all the way—plead the Fifth Amendment.[133] I don't give a shit. They can't force the President's people to testify.

EHRLICHMAN

Executive privilege will make it look like we're covering up.

---

[132]On the Nixon/LBJ threats, see Ambrose, *Nixon: Ruin and Recovery 1973–1990,* pp. 50–51.

[133]This is found on the March 21, 1973, tape transcript. See Watergate Special Prosecutor's Office Transcripts, National Archives. Also see Bernstein and Woodward, *The Final Days,* p. 127.

NIXON

We are covering up! For some petty, stupid shit. (*then*) There are things I can say—when other people say them, they'd be lies. But when I say them nobody believes me anyway . . .

Pause. A look between Haldeman and Ehrlichman, puzzled.

DEAN

Then we're going to have to give them Mitchell.

Nixon turns, stunned.

NIXON

Mitchell? Mitchell's . . . family.

DEAN

Either it goes to Mitchell or it comes here.

Nixon looks like he's been punched in the stomach.

HALDEMAN (*SOFTLY*)

John's right. It's not personal, boss. It's just the way the game is played. Sometimes you have to punt.

Nixon looks out the window. Suddenly, he looks very old and very tired in the gray Washington light.

NIXON

Jesus, I'm so Goddamn worn out with this . . .

SCENE NINETY-ONE

INT. THE WHITE HOUSE–CORRIDOR–DAY

HALDEMAN and EHRLICHMAN leave the President's office. They're pensive, on the move. They come to a huddle next to a window in an isolated alcove.

EHRLICHMAN

Who's gonna tell Mitchell?

HALDEMAN

You do it.

EHRLICHMAN

Why me?

HALDEMAN

'Cause he hates you. It's worse when you get it from someone you trust.

EHRLICHMAN

He's wrong, you know—about Kennedy, LBJ, Truman.

HALDEMAN

How so?

EHRLICHMAN

Sure, they did stuff, but nothing like this, Bob. Forget Watergate, the break-ins, the Enemies List. You got an attempted firebombing at the Brookings Institution,[134] planting McGovern stuff on the guy that shot Wallace,[135] trying to slip LSD to Jack Anderson.[136]

HALDEMAN

The "Old Man" plays politics harder than anybody else.

EHRLICHMAN

You think this is just about politics?

They go inanimate as a White House STAFFER passes.

---

[134]On the plan to firebomb the Brookings Institution, see Dean, *Blind Ambition*, pp. 45–48; Ehrlichman, *Witness to Power*, p. 403; Liddy, *Will*, p. 237; Bernstein and Woodward, *All the President's Men*, pp. 324–325; and Emery, *Watergate*, p. 48. See also Nixon, *RN*, p. 512, where Nixon admits he wanted a document taken from the Brookings Institution ". . . even if it meant having to get it surreptitiously."

[135]For the plan to break into Bremer's apartment and plant left-wing literature, see Bernstein and Woodward, *All the President's Men*, pp. 326–330; Emery, *Watergate*, pp. 115–117; and Hunt, *Undercover*, pp. 216–218. See also n. 30.

[136]For Hunt's and Liddy's discussion of plans to drug or murder Jack Anderson, see Liddy, *Will*, pp. 286–291; and Hougan, *Secret Agenda*, pp. 207–208.

EHRLICHMAN (*PRIVATELY*)
You think LBJ would ever have asked Hunt to forge a cable implicating John Kennedy in the assassination of the President of Vietnam?[137](*whispering fiercely*) How long have you know him, Bob? Twenty years? (*then*)
You ever shake hands with him? You ever have a real conversation with him? We don't have a clue what's going on inside that man.[138] And look what we're doing for him . . .

Ehrlichman glances around to make sure no one is listening. He leans close.

EHRLICHMAN
This is about Richard Nixon. You got people dying because he didn't make the varsity football team. You got the Constitution hanging by a thread because the "Old Man" went to Whittier and not to Yale. (*then*) And what the hell is this "Bay of Pigs" thing—he goes white every time it gets mentioned?

Haldeman, more bothered than he pretends, looks around.

HALDEMAN
It's a code or something.

EHRLICHMAN
I figured that out.

HALDEMAN (*LOW WHISPER*)
I think he means the Kennedy assassination.[139]

EHRLICHMAN
Yeah?

HALDEMAN
They went after Castro. In some crazy way it got turned on Kennedy. I don't think the "P" knows what happened, but he's afraid to find out. It's got him shitting peach pits.

---

[137]For Hunt's forging of the Diem cables, see Emery, *Watergate,* pp. 71–73; Ambrose, *Nixon: Ruin and Recovery 1973–1990,* pp. 26, 113, 133, 140; Bernstein and Woodward, *All the President's Men,* p. 306; and Oglesby, *The Yankee and Cowboy War,* pp. 59–60.

[138]For Nixon's personal relationships with Haldeman and others, see Ambrose, *Nixon: The Triumph of a Politician 1962–1972,* pp. 410–411; Ehrlichman, *Witness to Power,* p. 77; and Haldeman, *The Ends of Power,* pp. 65, 74, where he writes, "He didn't see me as a person or even, I believe, as a human being."

[139]For Haldeman's view of the "Bay of Pigs" as a code for the JFK assassination, see Haldeman, *The Ends of Power,* pp. 38–40.

EHRLICHMAN

Christ, we created Frankenstein with those fucking Cubans.

Haldeman sighs, lets his guard down.

HALDEMAN

Eight words back in '72—"I covered up. I was wrong. I'm sorry"—and the American public would've forgiven him. But we never opened our mouths, John. We failed him.

EHRLICHMAN

Dick Nixon saying "I'm sorry"? That'll be the day. The whole suit of armor'd fall off.

HALDEMAN

So you tell Mitchell . . .

SCENE NINETY-TWO

EXT. WASHINGTON D.C. BRIDGE—NIGHT

JOHN DEAN stands at the center of the bridge, looks down at the Potomac.

REPORTER *(v.o.)*

Lyndon Johnson passed away today at 74—one of the most tragic of American presidents . . .

HUNT *(o.s.)*

You're early, John.

Dean jumps. Turns. HOWARD HUNT is standing behind him.[140]

---

[140]Note: This scene is a dramatized composite of events. In fact, Dean spoke directly with Hunt on only a few occasions to say hello to him at the White House. Hunt's demands for money were directed at Colson, and then through intermediaries to Ehrlichman. Responses were communicated through intermediaries, namely Hunt's attorney, and attorneys for the Nixon Re-election Committee. The basis for this encapsulated scene is the series of threats and demands that Hunt made, and Dean's response to them. Although at one point, according to Colson, Hunt asked to see Dean, Dean declined to go, and asked Colson to go instead. Colson was advised not to go by his former law partner, Dave Shapiro. Shapiro went in his place. Colson, however, had several telephone conversations with Hunt (which Colson recorded), and Colson did meet with Hunt's lawyer, William Bittman, to discuss clemency for Hunt. See Dean, *Blind Ambition*, pp. 192–200; Emery, *Watergate*, pp. 226–228 passim, 260; Colson, *Born Again*, p. 93; Hunt, *Undercover*, pp. 276, 295. See also Select Committee, *Final Report*, pp. 55–70.

                              DEAN
I was sorry to hear about your wife.

                         HUNT *(A LOOK)*
Yes . . . I got the money.

                              DEAN
The President would like to know if that was the last payment.

                              HUNT
I'll bet he would.

                              DEAN
Is it?

                         HUNT *(A BEAT)*
In Richard Nixon's long history of underhanded dealings, he has never gotten
better value for his money. If I were to open my mouth, all the dominoes would
fall.

Hunt starts to walk away.

                              DEAN
Can I ask you a question?

Hunt turns.

                              DEAN
How the hell do you have the temerity to blackmail the President of the United
States?

                              HUNT
That's not the question, John. The question is: Why is he paying?

                              DEAN
To protect his people.

                              HUNT
I'm one of his people. The Cubans are his people. And we're going to jail for
him.

DEAN

Howard, you'll serve no more than two years, then he'll pardon you.

HUNT (*LIGHTS HIS PIPE*)

John, sooner or later—sooner I think—you are going to learn the lesson that has been learned by everyone who has ever gotten close to Richard Nixon. That he's the darkness reaching out for the darkness. And eventually, it's either you or him. Look at the landscape of his life and you'll see a boneyard.

Hunt throws the match into the river.

HUNT

. . . And he's already digging your grave, John.

SCENE NINETY-THREE

INT. THE WHITE HOUSE—CORRIDOR—DAY

JOHN DEAN, looking glum, walks down the corridors for his meeting with the President. Passing the SECRETARIES who look at him—that furtive look of people who sense crisis.

REPORTERS *(v.o.)*

FBI Director-designate, L. Patrick Gray, shocked the Senate by revealing that John Dean has been secretly receiving FBI reports on Watergate . . . Gray also said that Dean lied when he claimed Howard Hunt did not have an office in the White House . . .

SCENE NINETY-FOUR

INT. THE WHITE HOUSE—OVAL OFFICE—DAY

SUBTITLE READS: "MARCH 1973"

DEAN is explaining his new outlook to a quiet NIXON.[141]

---

[141]Note: Much of this conversation is adapted from the March 21, 1973, tape transcripts of meetings among Nixon, Dean, and, later, Haldeman. See *Transcripts of Eight Recorded Presidential Conversations, Hearings Before the Committee on the Judiciary,* House of Representatives, 93rd Congress, Second Session, pp. 79–145.

Nixon and John Dean (David Hyde Pierce) in the Oval Office

DEAN

. . . this is the sort of thing Mafia people can do—washing money, and things like that. We just don't know about these things because we're not criminals.

On Nixon listening behind his desk, hands cupped over his mouth, frown across his face–the classic Nixon image of a deep thinker. The CAMERA drops to his desk. And moves towards a MIKE drilled in the edge of the desk.

INTERCUT TO:

SCENE NINETY-FIVE

INT. FILE ROOM–BASEMENT–DAY

A bank of TAPE RECORDERS labelled "Oval Office," "Lincoln Room," "Phones 1–6," "EOB," is rolling. BACK TO SCENE AT OPTION:

NIXON

How much do you need?

DEAN

Uh, I would say these people are going to cost a million dollars over the next two years . . .

NIXON

We could get that.

DEAN

Uh huh . . .

NIXON

We could get a million dollars. We could get it in cash. I know where it could be gotten.

INTERCUT: the TAPE rolling.

DEAN (PAUSE)

I'm still not confident we can ride through this. Some people are going to have to go to jail. Hunt's not the only problem. Haldeman let me use the $350,000 cash fund in his safe to make the payments. Ehrlichman had a role, a big role, in the Ellsberg break-in.[142] And I'm . . . uh, I think it's time we begin to think in terms of cutting our losses.

NIXON (WORRIED ABOUT DEAN)

You say, John, cut our losses and all the rest. But suppose the thing blows and they indict Bob and the others. Jesus, you'd never recover from that, John. It's better to fight it out instead, and not let people testify . . .

DEAN

Sir, I still don't think, uh, we can contain it anymore. There's a cancer on the presidency. And it's growing. With every day that . . .

NIXON

Jesus, everything is a crisis among the upper intellectual types, the softheads. The average people don't think it's much of a crisis. For Christ's sake it's not Vietnam . . . no one's dying here. Isn't it ridiculous?

DEAN

I agree it's ridiculous but—

---

[142]Liddy states it was Ehrlichman who applied to the CIA for technical assistance for the burglars (see Liddy, *Will*, p. 222: "In fact . . . it was John Ehrlichman who secured this cooperation from the CIA.") and who approved the original plan to break into the Fielding office. Ehrlichman also received copies of photographs taken inside the office. See Hougan, *Secret Agenda*, pp. 47–48. Also, the Plumbers' activities were regularly reported to him. See Bernstein and Woodward, *All the President's Men*, p. 215.

                              NIXON

I mean, who the hell cares about this penny-ante shit. Goldwater put it right.
He said: "Well for Christ's sakes, everybody bugs everybody else; we know
that." . . . It's the cover-up, not the deed that's really bad here. (*then*) If only
Mitchell could step up and take the brunt of it; give them the hors d'oeuvre
and maybe they won't come back for the main course. That's the tragedy in
all this. Mitchell's going to get it in the neck anyway. It's time he assumed responsibility.

Dean has a nervous look in his eye.

                              DEAN

He won't. He told Ehrlichman he won't.

*A lightning-like IMAGE reveals MITCHELL, responding to EHRLICHMAN.
This is Nixon's mind at work.*

                            .MITCHELL

You tell Brother Dick I got suckered into this thing by not paying attention to
what these bastards were doing. I don't have a guilty conscience . . . And he
shouldn't either.

*Nixon glances towards the microphone as he moves around the desk to get
closer to Dean.*

                      NIXON (LOUD AND CLEAR)

He's right. Maybe it's time to go the hang-out route, John. A full and thorough
investigation . . . We've cooperated with the FBI, we'll cooperate with the Senate. What do we have to hide?

                       DEAN (PROMPTED)

No, we have nothing to hide.

                      NIXON (REPEATING)

We have nothing to hide. (*then*) But the only flaw in the plan is that they're not
going to believe the truth. That is the incredible thing!

*Dean, who is worried about his own hide if the truth comes out, sees the point
of this.*

DEAN

I agree. It's tricky. Everything seems to lead back here, and, uh . . . people would never understand.

Nixon awkwardly puts his arm around Dean's shoulder. Dean begins to sense a betrayal in the offing.[143]

NIXON

John, I want you to get away from this madhouse, these reporters, and go up to Camp David for the weekend. And I want you to write up a report. I want you to put everything you know about Watergate in there. Say: Mr. President, here it all is.

Another lightning-like IMAGE is Nixon's worst fear—JOHN DEAN is at a table, plea-bargaining with TWO PROSECUTORS, their backs to us.

DEAN *(v.o.)*

You want me to put it all in writing? Over my signature?

NIXON *(v.o.)*

Nobody knows more about this thing than you do, John.

A pause.

DEAN

I'm not going to be the scapegoat for this.[144] Haldeman and Ehrlichman are in it just as deep as me.

NIXON

John, you don't want to start down that road. I remember what Whittaker Chambers told me back in '48—and he was a man who suffered greatly—he said, "On the road of the informer, it's always night." (*then*) This is beyond you or even me. It's the country, John. It's the presidency.

DEAN

I understand that, sir.

---

[143]For Dean's sense that he was being set up, see Dean, *Blind Ambition*, p. 214; Emery, *Watergate*, p. 276; and Ambrose, *Nixon: Ruin and Recovery 1973–1990*, p. 92.

[144]For Dean refusing to be the scapegoat for Watergate, see Dean, *Blind Ambition*, pp. 269–270, 277; Emery, *Watergate*, p. 336; and Haldeman, *The Haldeman Diaries*, pp. 650–651.

NIXON

Good. You know how I feel about loyalty. I'm not going to let any of my people go to jail. That I promise you. (*moves closer*) The important thing is to keep this away from Haldeman and Ehrlichman. I'm trusting you to do that, John. I have complete confidence in you.

Off Dean's face we:

CUT TO:

SCENE NINETY-SIX

TELEVISION SCREEN–NIXON–NIGHT (1973)

NIXON on the TV screen, shaken, ashen-faced.

NIXON

I was determined that we should get to the bottom of Watergate, and the truth should be fully brought out no matter who was involved . . .

SCENE NINETY-SEVEN

INT. CIA–HELMS'S OFFICE–NIGHT (1973)

RICHARD HELMS, absently watching NIXON on TV, carries a handful of documents to a CIA incinerator. He drops them in the fire, watches them burn.[145]

NIXON (*ON TV, STRUGGLES*)

Today, in one of the most difficult decisions of my presidency, I accepted the resignations of two of my closest associates—Bob Haldeman and John Ehrlich-

---

[145]Richard Helms left the CIA in early 1973. Most likely, Helms's successor, James Schlesinger, was installed in the Director's office by the time Haldeman, Ehrlichman, and Dean were fired by the President on April 30, 1973. This scene dramatizes the order by Helms, shortly before leaving office, to destroy a large number of important files. For this see Powers, *The Man Who Kept Secrets,* p. 272; and Hougan, *Secret Agenda,* pp. 231–233, 303. See also Select Committee, *Final Report,* where committee member Sen. Howard Baker states his individual views and reports: "Shortly before Director Helms left office, and approximately one week after Senator Mansfield's letter requesting that evidentiary material be retained, Helms ordered that the tapes (from the CIA's central taping system) be destroyed." Select Committee, *Final Report,* p. 1131.

man—two of the finest public servants it has been my privilege to know . . .
The counsel to the President, John Dean, has also resigned.

CLOSE on Helms burning documents.

SCENE NINETY-EIGHT

LIMBO—HALDEMAN watches TV, his WIFE and CHILDREN next to him. He thinks back to:

INT. EXEC. OFFICE BLDG.—NIXON OFFICE—NIGHT (FLASHBACK)

Haldeman's mind—the last one-on-one session. HALDEMAN leaves the office, looking back over his shoulder at NIXON alone in the gathering shadows.

HALDEMAN

More light, chief?

NIXON (DISTRACTED, WAVES)

No . . .

Haldeman exits.

BACK TO SCENE:

NIXON (v.o.)

. . . There can be no whitewash at the White House . . . two wrongs do not make a right. I love America. God bless America and God bless each and every one of you.

HALDEMAN (TO HIMSELF)

Six . . . six bodies.

His wife puts her hand on his knee in support. He squeezes her hand.

SCENE NINETY-NINE

LIMBO—EHRLICHMAN also watches, with FAMILY.

SCENE ONE HUNDRED

INT. THE WHITE HOUSE—OVAL OFFICE—NIGHT

NIXON sits at his desk, holding a rigid expression.

FLOOR MANAGER *(o.s.)*

And . . . we're clear.

We stay on Nixon as the film lights go off, leaving him in shadow. He is devastated.

ALEXANDER HAIG, Nixon's new chief-of-staff, seen earlier, watches Nixon for a moment, turns to the VIDEO CREW.

Nixon deep in thought

HAIG (SOFTLY)

Out.

SCENE ONE HUNDRED ONE

INT. THE WHITE HOUSE—DINING-ROOM—NIGHT (1973)

NIXON at one end of the lengthy table, PAT at the other eat, in a dreadful silence, attended by MANOLO and SERVANTS who move nervously, anxious to have the dinner over with.

PAT (AT LAST)

I'm giving a tea for the wives of the POWs.

Nixon doesn't respond.

PAT

Are you going to Key Biscayne?

Nixon doesn't look up.

NIXON

Yes.

PAT

When?

NIXON

Tomorrow.

PAT

Ron told me that Bob Haldeman's been calling. But you won't talk to him . . . If he's convicted, will you pardon him?

NIXON

No.[146]

---

[146]For Nixon refusing to pardon Haldeman, see Nixon, *RN*, p. 1079; Emery, *Watergate*, p. 498; and Haldeman, *The Ends of Power*, p. 313. Ehrlichman claims that although he was trying to assist Haldeman in reaching the President about pardons for everyone involved by calling Julie, he did not ask for a pardon himself, since that would have been an admission of guilt. See Ehrlichman, *Witness to Power*, p. 410.

She looks at him.

> PAT
>
> . . . Why are you cutting yourself off from the rest of us? (*then*) Can't we dis-
> cuss this?

Nixon slowly sets his spoon down. An icy stare.

> NIXON
>
> What exactly did you want to discuss, Pat?

> PAT
>
> You. What you're doing—

> NIXON (*INTERRUPTS*)
>
> And what *am* I doing?

> PAT
>
> I wish I knew. You're hiding.

> NIXON
>
> Hiding what?

> PAT
>
> Whatever it is you've always been hiding. You're letting it destroy you, Dick.
> You won't even ask for help. You're destroying *yourself*, Dick.

Nixon pauses, rings the dinner bell. MANOLO reappears at the door.

> NIXON
>
> Mrs. Nixon is finished.

Pat looks as if she's been slapped; slowly puts down her silverware.
MANOLO clears away her plate.

> PAT
>
> I'm the only one left, Dick. If you don't talk to me, you . . .

> NIXON
>
> Brezhnev's coming in three days. I don't want to deal with *them*. And *him*. And
> *you.*

Pat sits rigid for a moment.

                              PAT

How much more? How much more is it going to cost? When do the rest of
us stop paying off your debts?

Nixon puts down his fork, embarrassed. Manolo has beaten a hasty retreat.

                            NIXON

I'd like to finish my dinner in peace. It's not too much to ask.

Pat stands slowly.

                              PAT

No, it isn't. I won't interfere with you anymore. I'm finished trying.

                            NIXON

Thank you.

                      PAT *(INCREDULOUS)*

Thank you? *(then)* Dick, sometimes I understand why they hate you.

*Nixon watches her walk out the door. Then, he picks up his fork and contin-
ues eating.*

              SENATOR SAM ERVIN *(V.O.: DRAWLS)*

The Senate Select Committee on Watergate will come to order . . .

A gavel POUNDS O.S.

              SCENE ONE HUNDRED TWO

          INT. THE WHITE HOUSE–HAIG'S OFFICE–DAY

NIXON STAFFERS are gathered around Haig's TV set as we:

CROSSCUT TO:

The President's Counsel John Dean

SCENE ONE HUNDRED THREE

INT. COMMITTEE CHAMBER–(SEEN ONLY ON TV)–DAY (1973)

JOHN DEAN reads his statement to the COMMITTEE. Conservatively groomed, horn-rimmed glasses, shorter hair, Dean speaks in a monotone. A pretty blond woman, his WIFE, sits noticeably behind him.

> DEAN *(ON TV)*
> . . . it was a tremendous disappointment to me because it was quite clear that the cover-up, as far as the White House was concerned, was going to continue . . .

> STAFFERS
> Lying sack of shit! Little mommy's boy—go tell the teacher, will ya . . .

HAIG looks at Dean on TV, shakes his head, disgusted, and goes out.

HAIG

The weasel's got no proof. Just remember that it's still an informer's word against the President's.

SCENE ONE HUNDRED FOUR

INT. THE WHITE HOUSE—CORRIDOR—DAY

HAIG walking past STAFF into the Oval Office:

DEAN *(DRONING ON, V.O./TV)*

. . . it was apparent to me I had failed in turning the President around . . . I reached the conclusion that Ehrlichman would never admit to his involvement in the cover-up . . . I assumed that Haldeman would not, because he would believe it a higher duty to protect the President . . .

SCENE ONE HUNDRED FIVE

INT. THE WHITE HOUSE—OVAL OFFICE—DAY (1973)

HAIG slides into the room where NIXON and LEONID BREZHNEV, Premier of the USSR, are engaged in a friendly meeting through an INTERPRETER. ANDREI GROMYKO completes the glum Soviet threesome.

BREZHNEV *(IN RUSSIAN)*

. . . Mao told me in 1963: "If I have nuclear weapons, let 400 million Chinese die, 300 million will be left." *(leans closer)* Mao suffers from a mental disorder; we know this a long time in my country. *(then)* This is the man you want to be your ally?

NIXON

He was *your* ally for twenty years, Leonid.

BREZHNEV *(MAKES A FUNNY GESTURE)*

Yes, yes, Dick. Life is always the best teacher, you know this—and you too will discover how treacherous he can be. But it must not interfere with the building of a SALT II treaty between our great countries. Peace in our era is possible . . .

Nixon looks to Haig, who whispers something in his ear.

NIXON

Excuse me, Mr. Chairman.

Nixon and Haig move to a corner of the room, whisper.

BREZHNEV *(TO GROMYKO)*

If Haldeman and Ehrlichman are indicted, it will wound him, perhaps fatally.

GROMYKO

That depends on who they believe—Nixon or Dean.

Brezhnev looks at Nixon, who is visibly shaken.

BREZHNEV *(SHAKES HIS HEAD)*

Incredible. He looks like a man with little time left.

*Nixon meets with Soviet leader Leonid Brezhnev
(Boris Sichkin)*

SCENE ONE HUNDRED SIX

INT. THE WHITE HOUSE—NIXON BEDROOM—NIGHT (1973)

Nixon's daughter, JULIE, earnest, bright-eyed, looks at her Father.

> JULIE *(HESITANTLY)*
Did you . . . Daddy? Did you cover it up?

NIXON looks at her steadily.

> NIXON
Do you think I would do something like that, honey?

Julie shakes her head vigorously, then puts her hands to her eyes.

> JULIE
Then you can't resign! You just can't. You're one of the best presidents this country's ever had! You've done what Lincoln did. You've brought this country back from civil war! You can't let your enemies tear you down! *(calmer)* You've got to stay and fight. I'll go out there and make speeches, Dad. No one knows the real you. How sweet you are, how nice you are to people. I'll tell them.

She embraces him almost desperately, kissing him on the forehead, crying.

> JULIE
Daddy, you are the most decent person I know.

> NIXON *(OVER HER SHOULDER)*
I hope I haven't let you down.

> JULIE *(HUGGING HIM THROUGH HER TEARS)*
They just don't know; they don't know the real you.

On Nixon—CLOSE.

SCENE ONE HUNDRED SEVEN

INT. THE WHITE HOUSE—PAT'S BEDROOM—DAY (1973)

PAT is still wearing her nightdress, coffee and cigarette in hand, as her press secretary, HELEN SMITH, runs through a sheaf of papers. A TELEVISION drones in the background.

Nixon and Brezhnev with translator (Raissa Danilova)

SMITH *(CHEERY)*
. . . and on Friday we have the high-school students from Ohio, Saturday is
the Women's National Republican Club . . .

NEWSCASTER 1 *(V.O.)*
In a development that could break Watergate wide open, former White House
aide, Alexander Butterfield, testifying today before the Senate Select Committee, revealed the existence of a taping system that may have recorded conversations in the White House, the EOB, and the Camp David retreat . . .[147]

Pat glances up over the top of her glasses.

SMITH *(CONTINUES)*
And on Sunday you're saying hello to the VFW Poppy Girl . . .

She realizes Pat is not listening.

SMITH
Mrs. Nixon. . . . ?

---

[147]For Butterfield revealing the existence of the taping system, see Sam Dash, *Chief Counsel: Inside the Ervin Committee—The Untold Story of Watergate* (New York: Random House, 1976),
pp. 176–188. See also Emery, *Watergate*, p. 367; Ambrose, *Nixon: Ruin and Recovery
1973–1990*, pp. 193–194; and Kutler, *The Wars of Watergate*, pp. 368–369.

Close: on Pat as she slowly raises a hand to her lips.

NEWSCASTER 1 *(v.o.)*

White House sources say that for the past three years, President Nixon has recorded virtually every conversation he has had, including those with his staff, and even members of his own family . . .

Pat is horrified.

SCENE ONE HUNDRED EIGHT

INT. THE WHITE HOUSE–PRESIDENT'S BEDROOM–DAY

NIXON sits in his bed, alone, still in his pajamas. It's clear he hasn't slept. He looks shell-shocked.

NEWSCASTER 1 *(v.o.)*

This is a stunning revelation. If such tapes exist, they could tell us once and for all: What did the President know and when did he know it . . .

The CAMERA closing on NIXON. His deepest secrets are now being revealed. He begins coughing violently. He tries to cover his mouth, but notices now that his hand and the sheets around him are covered with blood.[148] He screams, terrified.

NIXON

Oh God—Pat!

HARD CUT TO:

SCENE ONE HUNDRED NINE

INT. BETHESDA NAVAL HOSPITAL CORRIDOR–DAY (1973)

NIXON on a gurney, being wheeled down a hospital corridor. PAT, wearing dark sunglasses, is with him, very concerned. A plastic mask is over his face.

---

[148]For Nixon's pneumonia attack, see Ambrose, *Nixon: Ruin and Recovery 1973–1990*, pp. 191–192; Aitken, *Nixon*, p. 498; and Nixon, *RN*, pp. 898–899.

He struggles to get up, but a NURSE gently presses him back down. SECRET SERVICE AGENTS surround the gurney. HAIG clears the corridors nervously.

HAIG

Clear the path! The President is coming through. Clear a path. I'm in charge here.

PAT gets the DOCTOR's attention on the move.

PAT *(PRIVATELY)*

Is it TB?

DOCTOR

No.

PAT

He's sure he has tuberculosis.

DOCTOR

No, it's an acute viral pneumonia *(lowers his voice)*. But that's not what we're worried about. We found an inflammation in his left leg. It's phlebitis . . .

CLOSE on Nixon, eyes closed; the overhead lights reflect in the mask.

REPORTERS *(v.o.)*

Watergate Special Prosecutor Archibald Cox has broadened his investigation to include President Nixon's business dealings and house payments. Nixon apparently paid no income tax in the years 1970, '71, and '72 . . .[149] and may have illegally used government funds to improve his San Clemente Western White House.

HAIG holds open the doors as the ORDERLIES push Nixon into the respiratory unit.

---

[149]For a discussion of the revelation that Nixon failed to pay taxes, see Lowell P. Weicker, Jr. with Barry Sussman, *Maverick: A Life in Politics* (New York: Little, Brown, 1995), pp. 89–97.

SCENE ONE HUNDRED TEN

INT. BETHSEDA NAVAL HOSPITAL—RESPIRATORY UNIT—DAY

A DOCTOR and NURSE remove the mask from NIXON'S face.

REPORTERS *(v.o.)*
Attorney General Elliot Richardson will present evidence to a grand jury that
Vice President Agnew is guilty of bribery, extortion and tax evasion . . .

*Nixon immediately starts gasping. He again tries to rise, but hands push him
back. The doctor fits the mouthpiece of a respirator into Nixon's mouth. Images of the Beast pervade the room.*

Nixon begins breathing . . . His eyes going past PAT to . . .

*IMAGES OF THE PAST—OF HIS PARENTS, FRANK, HANNAH, LITTLE
ARTHUR, HAROLD . . . THE GROCERY STORE.*

INTERCUT WITH:

SCENE ONE HUNDRED ELEVEN

EXT. STREET—DAY

*MARTHA MITCHELL is acting strangely behind enormous sunglasses—at an
impromptu interview on the STREET.*

MARTHA
. . . Can you keep a secret, honey? 'Tween you, me, and the gatepost, Tricky
Dick *always* knew what was going on . . . every last Goddamn detail. And my
husband's not taking the rap this time . . . They know they can't shut me up,
so they'll probably end up killing me, but I depend on you, the press, to protect me . . . and my husband, because that's what it's going to come to . . .[150]

INTERCUT WITH:

---

[150]For Martha's attitude toward Nixon, see Bernstein and Woodward, *All the President's Men*,
p. 300; and McClendon, *Martha*, pp. 221–226.

SCENE ONE HUNDRED TWELVE

EXT. STREET–DAY

JOHN MITCHELL, angry, beleaguered, bypasses cameras outside a COURT-HOUSE.

> MITCHELL
> She doesn't know what she's talking about. Stop bothering her. She's not well. Hell, she's nuts—you bastards've seen to that. (*brushing past another question*) You can stick it right back up your keester fella. Our marriage is finished, thank you very much . . . (*pushes on*)

BACK TO:

SCENE ONE HUNDRED THIRTEEN

NIXON IN THE HOSPITAL, BREATHING.

> REPORTER *(v.o.)*
> Archibald Cox declared war on President Nixon today by issuing a subpoena for nine of the President's tapes . . .

> NIXON *(v.o., YELLS)*
> Never! Over my dead body!

SCENE ONE HUNDRED FOURTEEN

INT. THE WHITE HOUSE–WEST WING CORRIDOR–DAY (1973)

NIXON, his leg swollen, limps down the corridor, furious. HAIG walks with him, ZIEGLER and the lawyer, BUZHARDT, bringing up the rear. HAIG clears the corridor of potential eavesdroppers.

> NIXON
> It's the President's personal property! I will never give up my tapes to a bunch of Kennedy-loving Harvard Democrat cocksuckers!

HAIG

This could trigger the impeachment. They'll go to the Supreme Court next.

NIXON

Let 'em try! I appointed three of those bastards! I'm not giving 'em my tapes!

HAIG

Can the president afford to ignore a subpoena?

NIXON

Who the fuck does Cox think he is? (*fumes*) I never made a dime from public office! I'm honest. My dad died broke. You know the sonofabitch went to law school with Jack Kennedy? . . . The last gasp of the Establishment! They got the hell kicked out of 'em in the election, so now they gotta squeal about Watergate cause we were the first real threat to them in years. And by God, Al, we would have changed it, changed it so they couldn't have changed it back in a hundred years, if only . . .

HAIG

Congress is considering four articles of impeachment, sir.

NIXON

For what?!

BUZHARDT

Sir, the charges are serious—first, abuse of power; second, obstruction of justice; third, failure to cooperate with Congress; and last, bombing Cambodia . . .

NIXON

They can't impeach me for bombing Cambodia. The President can bomb anybody he wants.

ZIEGLER

That's true . . .

BUZHARDT

Sir, we'll win that one, but the other three . . .

NIXON

You know, Fred, they sell tickets.

ZIEGLER

Sir?

NIXON

They sell tickets to an impeachment. Like a fucking circus . . . Okay, so they impeach me. Then it's a question of mathematics. How many votes do we have in the Senate?

A beat. Then:

HAIG

About a dozen.

NIXON *(WOUNDED)*

A dozen? I got half of 'em elected. I still got the South and Goldwater and his boys. I'll take my chances in the Senate.

ZIEGLER

We should . . .

HAIG

Then we'll have to deal with the possibility of removal from office, loss of pension, possibly . . . prison.

NIXON

Shit, plenty of people did their best writing in prison. Gandhi, Lenin . . .

ZIEGLER

That's right.

NIXON *(BEAT, GLOWERS DARKLY)*

What I know about this country, I . . . I could rip it apart. If they want a public humiliation, that's what they'll get. But I will *never* resign this office. Where the fuck am I?

They look at him strangely. They've stopped at the doors of the East Room. The SOUND of VOICES and a VIOLIN playing inside.

NIXON *(TO ZIEGLER)*

What's in there?

ZIEGLER

POWs. And their families.

NIXON

So I'm supposed to be . . .

ZIEGLER

Compassionate. Grateful.

NIXON

Proud?

ZIEGLER *(CONFUSED)*

Sir?

NIXON

Of them.

ZIEGLER

Yes, yes.

NIXON *(BACK TO HAIG, BITTERLY)*

Fire him.

HAIG

Who?

NIXON

Cox! Fire him.[151]

HAIG

But he works for the Attorney General. Only Richardson can fire him.

BUZHARDT *(CONCERNED)*

Sir, if I may . . . echo my concern . . .

NIXON *(IGNORING BUZHARDT, TO HAIG)*

Then tell Richardson to fire him.

---

[151]On Nixon's decision to fire Cox, see Ambrose, *Nixon: Ruin and Recovery 1973–1990*, pp. 224, 225, 232–233, 241–242, 247–250; Kutler, *The Wars of Watergate*, pp. 405–410, 426, 442; Bernstein and Woodward, *The Final Days*, pp. 69–76; and Emery, *Watergate*, pp. 378, 385, 390.

> HAIG

Richardson won't do that. He'll resign.

> NIXON

The hell he will! Fire him too. If you have to go all the way down to the janitor at the Justice Department, fire the sonofabitch! And . . .

> ZIEGLER

He's asked for it.

> HAIG

May I just say something, sir? I think you should welcome the subpoena. The tapes can only prove that Dean is a liar.

> ZIEGLER

That's right, sir.

A moment.

> NIXON

There's more . . . there's more than just me. You can't break, my boy, even when there's nothing left. You can't admit, even to yourself, that it's gone, Al. (*pointing to the East Room*) Do you think those POWs in there did?

> ZIEGLER

No, sir . . .

> NIXON

Now some people, we both know them, Al, think you can go stand in the middle of the bullring and cry, "Mea culpa, mea culpa," while the crowd is hissing and booing and spitting on you. But a man doesn't cry. (*then*) I don't cry. You don't cry . . . You fight!

INTERCUT soft IMAGES over NIXON being pounded at FOOTBALL . . .

Nixon straightens himself, puts on a smile, nods to Ziegler. Ziegler opens the door. A ROAR of CHEERS and MARTIAL MUSIC greets the President, as he disappears inside.

SCENE ONE HUNDRED FIFTEEN

TV SCREEN—NBC LOGO—LIMBO

ANNOUNCER *(v.o.)*
We interrupt this program for a special report from NBC News.

A REPORTER appears, stunned.

REPORTER *(v.o.)*
The country tonight is in the midst of what may be the most serious constitutional crisis in history. In the wake of Vice President Spiro Agnew's forced resignation on charges of corruption, President Nixon has fired Special Prosecutor Archibald Cox.[152]

DOCUMENTARY IMAGES—ARCHIBALD COX walking in the street, having heard the news, smiling.

REPORTER *(v.o., CONT'D)*
Attorney General Elliot Richardson has resigned rather than comply with the President's order, and Deputy Attorney General William Ruckelshaus was fired when he refused to carry out the order . . .

DOCUMENTARY IMAGES—FBI AGENTS carrying boxes of files out of the Special Prosecutor's office. RUCKELSHAUS getting into a car, refusing to comment. ELLIOT RICHARDSON moving down a gauntlet of REPORTERS. We CUT BACK to the REPORTER on camera, grim.

REPORTER *(ON TV, CONT'D)*
Tonight, the country, without a Vice President, stands poised at a crossroads—has a government of laws become a government of one man?

SCENE ONE HUNDRED SIXTEEN

EXT. THE WHITE HOUSE—NIGHT—1973

As before, the black iron bars. The facade of the mansion. The light in the second floor. We move in slowly.

---

[152]For a discussion of the "Saturday Night Massacre," see Emery, *Watergate,* pp. 397–401; Ambrose, *Nixon: Ruin and Recovery 1973–1990,* pp. 247–253; and Kutler, *The Wars of Watergate,* pp. 406–414.

SCENE ONE HUNDRED SEVENTEEN

INT. THE WHITE HOUSE—LINCOLN SITTING ROOM—NIGHT (1973)

NIXON is really drunk now, listening to some GIBBERISH on the tape. We move in on his profile, framed by Lincoln in the background. We should not be able to make out the voices—occasional words like "Castro," "Kennedy." But that's about it . . . nothing more. And as we move closer on Nixon, bleary-eyed, we should feel he has no idea, either, of what he's listening to. It's just . . . noise. PAT's voice cuts in. She's standing at the doorway. She's been drinking too, but is sharp.

PAT

They're like love letters. You should burn them.[153]

Nixon, startled, tries to shut off the tape, but he hits the wrong button and we hear high-speed VOICES in reverse.

PAT

Why didn't you?

NIXON *(SLURS)*

You can't expect me to explain that to you.

PAT

What matters to me is whether you understand it.

A beat. He finally gets the tape stopped.

NIXON

They're evidence. You can't legally destroy evidence.

Pat stares at him.

PAT

You don't expect me to believe that for one minute, do you? *(then)* Does it matter what's on them? Really? . . . Murder, Dick? Sex? Your secrets, your fantasies? Or just me and you and . . .

---

[153]For Mrs. Nixon's view of the tapes as love letters, and her belief they should have been destroyed, see Bernstein and Woodward, *The Final Days*, p. 166; and Nixon-Eisenhower, *Pat Nixon*, pp. 380, 409–410.

                              NIXON

Don't be ridiculous!

                               PAT

I remember Alger Hiss. I know how ugly you can be—you're capable of
anything. But you see, it doesn't really matter, at the end of the day, what's
on them. Because you have absolutely no remorse. No concept of remorse. You want the tapes to get out, you want them to see you at your
worst . . .

                              NIXON

You're drunk! (*Pat laughs, "Yeah, I am."*) No one will ever see those tapes. Including you!

A beat.

                               PAT

And what would I find out that I haven't known for years. (*then*) What makes
it so damn sad is that you couldn't confide in any of us. You had to make a
record . . . for the whole world.

                              NIXON

They were for me. They're mine.

                               PAT

No. They're not *yours*. They *are* you. You should burn them.

*She turns and walks out. Nixon is turbulent, upset. He turns and suddenly
sees the ghost of his young mother, HANNAH, sitting there in the shadows,
staring at him.*[154]

He jumps. Those eyes of hers. Penetrating, gazing right through him.

                             HANNAH

What has changed in thee, Richard . . . When thou were a boy . . .

                       NIXON (*BLURTS OUT*)

No! Please! Don't talk to me! Anything . . . but *don't talk to me.*

---

[154]For Nixon's emotional state at this period, see Bernstein and Woodward, *The Final Days*,
pp. 32, 395, 403–404; Emery, *Watergate*, p. 408; and Aitken, *Nixon*, pp. 531–534.

A SHARP CUT snaps us from this reverie, and Nixon is alone in his sitting room, the door closed, the VOICE on the tape droning. He downs pills with the Scotch.

NIXON *(V.O. ON TAPE)*

. . . these guys went after Castro. Seven times, ten times . . . What do you think—people like that, they just give up? They just walk away? *(then)* Whoever killed Kennedy came from this . . . this *thing* we created.[155] This Beast . . . That's why we can't let this thing go any farther . . .

He looks over at the recorder, slowly turning. He pushes "Stop" and then runs it back on "Rewind." High-speed voices. He pushes "Stop" again. A series of TIME CUTS shows Nixon getting drunker. Playing sections of the tape. The camera closes on the tape machine. It's all a blur as we hear a HUM growing louder and louder, as we inch in on an abstract CLOSE-UP of the TAPE moving across the capstan.[156]

REPORTER *(v.o.)*

In the latest bombshell, the President's lawyers revealed that there is an eighteen-and-a-half-minute gap in a critical Watergate tape . . .

---

[155]For the possibility of a connection between Track 2 and the JFK assassination, see Haldeman, *The Ends of Power*, pp. 38–40. "It is possible that . . . when Nixon said, 'It's likely to blow the whole Bay of Pigs' he might have been reminding Helms, not so gently, of the cover-up of the CIA assassination attempts on . . . Fidel Castro—a CIA operation that may have triggered the Kennedy tragedy . . ." (Ibid., p. 40). See also United States Senate, *Alleged Assassination Plots Involving Foreign Leaders,* pp. 67–84, 181–190; Brodie, *Richard Nixon,* pp. 392–413; Scott, *Deep Politics,* pp. 111–113, 305–306; Oglesby, *The Yankee and Cowboy War,* pp. 47–80; Hinckle and Turner, *The Fish Is Red,* pp. 26–29, 34–36, 73–79, 271–279; Powers, *The Man Who Kept Secrets,* pp. 126–131, 146–158, 287–294; Hougan, *Spooks,* pp. 332–348; and Martin, *Wilderness of Mirrors,* pp. 121–124, 138–141, 145, 146, 151–153, 219–221.

[156]On Nixon's responsibility for erasing the tape, see Bernstein and Woodward, *The Final Days,* p. 352n; Emery, *Watergate,* pp. 414–418; Haldeman, *The Ends of Power,* pp. 16–17. A panel of experts appointed by the court determined that the 18 1/2-minute gap was created by hand operation of the tape player controls and was the result of multiple, deliberate erasures. For this, see Emery, *Watergate,* p. 418; Bernstein and Woodward, *All the President's Men,* p. 333; and Ambrose, *Nixon: The Triumph of a Politician 1962–1972,* pp. 277–278. Earlier, Nixon had suggested fabricating evidence, in the form of a dictabelt. For this, and his attitude toward the tapes as evidence, see Bernstein and Woodward, *The Final Days,* p. 27; Emery, *Watergate,* p. 412; and Haig, *Inner Circles,* pp. 426–427.

SCENE ONE HUNDRED EIGHTEEN

INT. THE WHITE HOUSE–WEST WING–DAY (1974)

A frenzy of paperwork as the PRESIDENT'S LAWYERS–BUZHARDT and ST. CLAIR–sit hunched around a table piled with transcripts, helped by TWO YOUNG ASSISTANTS.

NIXON is aghast as he reads some of the highlighted sections. HAIG and ZIEGLER attend.[157]

REPORTER 1 *(v.o.)*
. . . In an attempt to head off impeachment proceedings, the President has agreed to release transcripts of forty-six taped conversations . . .

REPORTER 2 *(v.o.)*
. . . In a simple ceremony, Gerald Ford was sworn in as Vice President. A long-time, popular member of Congress, Ford reinforces a sense of . . .

REPORTER 3 *(v.o.)*
. . . citing White House wrong-doing, the judge has dismissed all charges against Daniel Ellsberg.

REPORTER 4 *(v.o.)*
. . . the grand jury has indicted former Nixon aides Bob Haldeman, John Ehrlichman, and former Attorney General John Mitchell . . .

Nixon shakes the paper in the faces of Buzhardt and St. Clair.

NIXON
You're lawyers. How can you let this shit go by! *(points)* Look! This? Nixon can't say this.

---

[157]For the tape transcripts as edited and released by the White House, see New York *Times, The End of a Presidency.* For a discussion of these transcripts, see Ambrose, *Nixon: Ruin and Recovery 1973–1990,* pp. 335–336, 414; and Bernstein and Woodward, *The Final Days,* p. 125 passim. When the House Judiciary Committee later compared the transcripts with the original tape recordings, they found the White House–prepared transcripts were unreliable, if not fraudulent. Indeed, the production of these untrustworthy transcripts would be included in the Articles of Impeachment against Nixon by the House of Representatives. See House Judiciary Committee, *Impeachment of Richard M. Nixon, President of the United States, Report of the Committee on the Judiciary,* House of Representatives, August 20, 1972 (Washington, DC: Government Printing Office, 1974), pp. 203–205.

                    BUZHARDT
You did say it, sir.

                      NIXON
Never. I never said that about Jews!

Buzhardt glances at St. Clair.

                    BUZHARDT
We could check the tape again, sir.

                      NIXON
You don't need to check the tape. I know what I said.

He grabs the Magic Marker out of the lawyer's hand and furiously blacks out an entire section.

                      NIXON
And this?! Good Lord, have you lost your mind? Nixon can't say this. "Niggers"!

                     ZIEGLER
Well, we could delete it.

                    ST. CLAIR
We're doing the best we can, sir.

                      NIXON
Well it's not good enough . . .

                    ST. CLAIR
We can black it out.

                     ZIEGLER
Or we could write "expletive deleted."

                      NIXON
. . . and get rid of all these "Goddamns" and "Jesus Christs"!

                    ST. CLAIR
Sir, all these deletion marks in the transcripts will make it look like you swear all the time.

Nixon grows cold, stares steadily at St. Clair.

NIXON

For Christ's sake, it soils my mother's memory. Do you think I want the whole Goddamn world to see my mother like this? Raising a dirty mouth!

BUZHARDT

But sir, we'll have to start over from the beginning. We don't have the staff to . . .

Nixon loses it, sweeps the piles of transcripts off the table. They fly around the office.

NIXON *(SCREAMS)*

Then start over! The world will see only what I show them. From page one!

SCENE ONE HUNDRED NINETEEN

INT. THE WHITE HOUSE—OVAL OFFICE—NIGHT (1974)

NIXON sits at his desk, grimacing tightly into the TV CAMERA. Next to him is a stack of blue binders emblazoned with the presidential seal.

NIXON

Good evening, my fellow Americans. Tonight I'm taking an action unprecedented in the history of this office . . .

SCENE ONE HUNDRED TWENTY

INT. THE WHITE HOUSE—HAIG'S OFFICE—NIGHT (1974)

KISSINGER and HAIG watch NIXON on television. They share a drink.

NIXON *(ON TV, CONTINUES)*

. . . an action that will at last, once and for all, show that what I knew and what I did with regard to the Watergate break-in and cover-up were just as I have described them to you from the very beginning . . .

> HAIG

He's completely lost touch with reality.

> NIXON (ON TV, CONT'D) . . .

I had no knowledge of the cover-up until John Dean told me about it on March twenty-first. And I did not intend that payment to Hunt or anyone else be made . . .

> KISSINGER

Can you imagine what this man would have been had he ever been loved?

> NIXON (ON TV, CONT'D)

. . . because people have got to know whether or not their President is a c rook. Well, I am not a crook. I have never made a dime from public service . . .

> KISSINGER

Oh God, I'm going to throw up.

> HAIG

They'll crucify him . . .

Kissinger turns to Haig.

> KISSINGER

Does anybody care anymore? (*then*) What happens after . . . ?

They share a look.

INTERCUT TO:

SCENE ONE HUNDRED TWENTY-ONE

INT. THE WHITE HOUSE—PAT'S BEDROOM—NIGHT

PAT sits alone, drinking, as the television drones on with the latest invasion of her privacy. As we move in, we see the spirit drawn out of her. She seems numb.

SCENE ONE HUNDRED TWENTY-TWO

DOCUMENTARY IMAGE—EXT. THE WHITE HOUSE—NIGHT (1974)

REPORTERS *(v.o.)*

The Supreme Court ruled today eight-to-zero that President Nixon's claims of "executive privilege" cannot be used in criminal cases, and that he must turn over all subpoenaed tapes . . . a firestorm on Capitol Hill as . . .[158]

SCENE ONE HUNDRED TWENTY-THREE

INT. THE WHITE HOUSE—CORRIDORS & STAIRS—NIGHT (1974)

SUBTITLE READS: "JULY 1974," over EMPTY SHOTS of an EMPTY HOUSE, filled with gloom and dread. The FOOTSTEPS of two silhouettes crack the silence as they make their way towards the Lincoln Sitting Room. It is an eerie echo of the film's opening shots of the White House. The silhouettes now become apparent as GENERAL HAIG and HENRY KISSINGER.

REPORTERS *(v.o.)*

. . . The House Judiciary Committee has voted twenty-seven-to-eleven to recommend impeachment to the full House. The deliberations now go to the House floor . . . In its report, the Committee offers evidence that Nixon obstructed justice on at least thirty-six occasions, that he encouraged his aides to commit perjury, and that he abused the powers of his office . . . In a separate report, the Senate Select Committee details the misuse of the IRS, the FBI, the CIA and the Justice Department. It denounces the Plumbers, and it raises the question of whether the United States had a valid election in 1972.[159]

HIGH ANGLE—Haig knocks and enters the Lincoln Sitting Room. A shaft of LIGHT from inside zigzags the darkness. And we hear a snatch of LOUD MUSIC before the door is closed.

---

[158]See *United States v. Nixon,* 418 U.S. 683 (1974).

[159]See House Judiciary Committee, *Impeachment of Richard M. Nixon, President of the United States, Report of the Committee on the Judiciary,* House of Representatives, August 20, 1972.

SCENE ONE HUNDRED TWENTY-FOUR

INT. THE WHITE HOUSE—LINCOLN SITTING ROOM—NIGHT (1974)

NIXON sits in his chair in a suit and tie, listening to "Victory at Sea" at top volume. In front of him is a picture album—1922 portraits of the NIXON FAM-ILY—HAROLD holding ARTHUR. RICHARD stares glumly at the camera between HANNAH and FRANK.

GENERAL HAIG, with KISSINGER behind, approaches with some papers held out in his hand. Nixon sees them, turns down the hi-fi.

NIXON

"Victory At Sea," Al . . . Henry. The Pacific Theater. Christ, you can almost feel the waves breaking over the decks.

HAIG

I'm afraid we have another problem, Mr. President.

He hands him a paper. Nixon glances at it.

HAIG

June twenty-third, '72, sir. The part that's underlined. Your instructions to Haldeman regarding the CIA and the FBI.[160]

---

[160]Haig writes that it was the following "devastating exchange" between Haldeman and the President that troubled the lawyers:

> PRESIDENT: When you get in—when you get in . . . say: Look, the problem is that this will open the whole Bay of Pigs thing, and the President just feels that, uh, without going into the details—don't, don't lie to them to the extent to say there's no involvement, but just say this is a comedy of errors, without getting into it, the President believes that this is going to open the whole Bay of Pigs thing up again. And, uh, because these people are plugging for [unintelligible] and that they should call the FBI in and [unintelligible] don't go any further into this case period! . . . Well, can you get it done?
> HALDEMAN: I think so. (Haig, *Inner Circles,* p. 475)

Nixon would write in his memoirs that, when ordering Haldeman to use the CIA to block the FBI, he recalled the difficulty that Ehrlichman had encountered in getting the Bay of Pigs material from the CIA (see Part III of this book) even with a Presidential request. Thus, Nixon says,

> I saw that Howard Hunt would give us a chance to turn Helms' extreme sensitivity about the Bay of Pigs to good advantage. I was not sure whether the CIA actually had any bona fide reason to intervene with the FBI. There was enough circumstantial evidence to suggest they might. But, in any case, Howard Hunt would provide a good way of suggesting that they do. If the CIA would deflect the FBI from Hunt, they would thereby protect us from the only White House vulnerability involving Watergate that I was worried about exposing—not the break-in, but the political activities Hunt had undertaken for Colson. (Nixon, *RN,* p. 641)

                              NIXON

So?

                              HAIG

Your lawyers feel it's the . . . "smoking gun."

                              NIXON

It's totally out of context. I was protecting the national security, I never intended—

                              HAIG

Sir, the deadline is today.

                              NIXON

Can we get around this, Al?

                              HAIG

It's the Supreme Court, sir; you don't get around it.

Nixon, silenced, looks down at the paper in his hands and sighs.

                              HAIG

If you resign, you can keep your tapes as a private citizen . . . You can fight
them for years.

                              NIXON

And if I stay?

A long moment.

                              HAIG

You have the army.

Nixon looks up at him, then over at Henry.

                              NIXON

The army?

                              HAIG

Lincoln used it.

NIXON

That was civil war.

HAIG

How do you see this?

Nixon closes his eyes. Haig takes the transcript back.

HAIG

We can't survive this, sir. They also have you instructing Dean to make the payoff to Hunt.[161]

NIXON

There is nothing in that statement the President can't explain.

HAIG

Sir, you talked about opening up the whole "Bay of Pigs" thing again.[162]

NIXON

That's right . . .

HAIG

Three days before, on the June twentieth tape—the one with the eighteen-minute gap—

NIXON *(INTERRUPTS)*

I don't know anything about that.

HAIG *(CONTINUES)*

. . . You mentioned the "Bay of Pigs" several times. Sooner or later they're going to want to know what that means. They're going to want to know what was on that gap . . .

---

[161]This is a reference to the March 21, 1973, conversation between the President and Dean.

[162]Nixon writes in his memoirs that he started thinking about the Bay of Pigs on June 20, 1972, and he says he had a "new idea for handling the public relations aspect of the Watergate incident." He would call his friend Bebe "Rebozo and have him get the anti-McGovern Cubans in Miami to start a public bail fund for their arrested countrymen and make a big media issue out of it." Nixon says he wanted "to revive the Democrats' inept handling of the Bay of Pigs." See Nixon, *RN*, p. 635.

NIXON

It's gone. No one will ever find out what's on it.

Haig moves closer and leans down, very low, whispers.

HAIG

They might . . . if there were another . . . recording.

Nixon glances up at him.

HAIG

We both know it's possible. (*then*) I know for a fact it's possible.[163]

Nixon stares up at him.

HAIG

I've spoken to Ford . . . And there's a very strong chance he'll pardon you . . .[164]

Haig hands him a letter of resignation.

INSERT: "I hereby resign the office of President of the United States."

---

[163]Haig does not claim knowledge that such a tape exists. The possibility of another copy of the tape existing is educated speculation. See Hougan, *Secret Agenda,* pp. 50–55; Summers, *Official and Confidential,* pp. 407–408; Haldeman, *The Ends of Power,* pp. 138–147. For infiltration of the White House by other government agencies, see Hougan, *Secret Agenda,* pp. 41–56, 66–76; Emery, *Watergate,* pp. 33–34; and Powers, *The Man Who Kept Secrets,* pp. 258–264.

A senior military intelligence officer has said that normal practice in the case of such taping systems was to strike one copy from the master tape and then to seal the master away in a federal storage facility for safekeeping. He insists it is highly unlikely that the tapes to which Nixon listened were the master copies and that no other copies were made. Summers and Hougan contend that the FBI and the CIA had access to the tapes in the White House storage room.

However, for there to be such a duplicate copy of the June 20 tape (and this fact was not revealed when the gap was discovered) would have required many persons with no apparent motive to lie to commit perjury during weeks in open court and private sessions, proceedings, and investigations conducted by the Watergate Special Prosecutor's Office, as well as by Judge Sirica, regarding missing and erased tapes. This subject was probed in great depth in an attempt to account for all known and possible copies of the tapes. See files of the Watergate Special Prosecution Force, National Archives; John J. Sirica, *To Set the Record Straight: The Break-in, the Tapes, the Conspirators, the Pardon* (New York: W. W. Norton, 1979), pp. 189–199; and Richard Ben-Veniste and George Frampton, Jr., *Stonewall: The Real Story of the Watergate Prosecution* (New York: Simon & Schuster, 1977), pp. 158–186.

[164]For Haig and the Nixon pardon by Ford, see Emery, *Watergate,* pp. 460–462; Ambrose, *Nixon: Ruin and Recovery 1973–1990,* pp. 406–409; Bernstein and Woodward, *The Final Days,* pp. 324–326; Ehrlichman, *Witness to Power,* pp. 410–411; Haig, *Inner Circles,* pp. 513–515, 518–519.

HAIG

This is something you will have to do, Mr. President. I thought you would rather do it now . . . I'll wait outside.

Haig drifts out as Kissinger comes out of the shadows. Nixon looks down blankly at the sheet of paper in front of him.

KISSINGER

May I say, sir, if you stay now it will paralyze the nation and its foreign policy . . .

Nixon looks up at Kissinger. The Judas himself—at least one of them. There is irony here that is apparent to Nixon but not Kissinger.

NIXON

Yes, you always had a good sense of timing, Henry. When to give and when to take. How do you think Mao, Brezhnev will react? (*sitting up, suddenly intense*) Do you think this is how they'll remember me, Henry, after all the great things you and I did together? As some kind of . . . of . . . crooks?

KISSINGER (*PREPARED RESPONSE*)

They will understand, sir. To be undone by a third-rate burglary is a fate of biblical proportions. History will treat you far more kindly than your contemporaries.

NIXON

That depends who writes the history books. I'm not a quitter . . . but I'm not stupid either . . . A trial would kill me—that's what they want. (*with some satisfaction*) But they won't get it.

He signs the resignation paper. A pause. It lies there.

KISSINGER (*GRANDIOSELY*)

If they harass you, I, too, will resign. And I will tell the world why.

NIXON

Don't be stupid. The world needs you, Henry; you always saw the big picture. You were my equal in many ways. (*then*) You're the only friend I've got, Henry . . .

KISSINGER

You have many friends . . . and admirers . . .

NIXON

Do you ever pray? You know . . . believe in a Supreme Being?

KISSINGER

Uh . . . not really. You mean on my knees?

NIXON

Yes. My mother used to pray . . . a lot. It's been a long time since I really prayed. (*a little lost*) Let's pray, Henry; let's pray a little.

As Nixon gets down on his knees, Kissinger perspires freely. He clumsily follows the President down to the floor.[165]

NIXON

. . . Uh, I hope this doesn't embarrass you.

KISSINGER

Not at all. This is not going to leak, is it?

NIXON (LOOKS AT HENRY)

Don't be too proud; never be too proud to go on your knees before God.

He prays silently, then suddenly, he sobs.

NIXON

Dear God! Dear God, how can a country come apart like this! What have I done wrong . . . ?

Kissinger is experiencing pure dread, his shirt soaked with sweat. He opens his eyes and peeks at Nixon.

NIXON

. . . I opened China. I made peace with Russia. I ended the war. I tried to do what's right! Why . . . why do they hate me so!

---

[165]For Kissinger and Nixon praying together, see Ambrose, *Nixon: Ruin and Recovery 1973–1990*; Richard M. Nixon, *In the Arena: A Memoir of Victory, Defeat, and Renewal* (New York: Pocket Books, 1990), p. 97; Nixon, *RN,* 1076–1077; Bernstein and Woodward, *The Final Days,* pp. 422–424; Emery, *Watergate,* pp. 474–475; Henry Kissinger, *Years of Upheaval* (Boston: Little, Brown, 1982), pp. 1207–1210.

A silence. Nixon wraps his arms across his chest and rocks back and forth in an upright fetal position. Kissinger, looking very distressed, reaches over and touches the President, trying awkwardly to console him.

NIXON *(WOOZILY AT HIS HANDS)*

It's unbelievable, it's insane . . .

On that note, we:

CUT TO:

SCENE ONE HUNDRED TWENTY-FIVE

EXT. THE WHITE HOUSE—CORRIDORS AND ENTRY—NIGHT (1974)

A solitary SENTINEL—a Marine Guard—stands at strict attention, eyes forward, as we hear the VOICES of:

The THREE SILHOUETTES of NIXON, KISSINGER, and HAIG walking out. HIGH ANGLES allow us to hear their VOICES echoing off the empty rooms, and sometimes catch a glimpse of a passing face. From the voice we can tell that Nixon has resumed his customary bluffness, a sense of bravado in the face of defeat.

NIXON *(OFF)*

. . . they smelled the blood on me this time, Al. I got soft. You know . . . that rusty, metallic smell . . .

HAIG *(OFF)*

I know it well, sir.

NIXON *(OFF)*

It came over from Vietnam, you know.

HAIG *(OFF)*

Sir?

NIXON *(OFF)*

That smell. I mean, everybody suffered so much, their sons killed. They need to sacrifice something, y'know, appease the gods of war—Mars, Jupiter. I am that blood, General. I am that sacrifice, in the highest place of all . . . All leaders must finally be sacrificed.

They turn a corner, come into more light.

NIXON
Things won't be the same after this. I played by the rules, but the rules changed right in the middle of the game . . . There's no respect for American institutions anymore. People are cynical, the press—God, the press—is out of control, people spit on soldiers, government secrets mean nothing . . .

Nixon separates from Haig and Kissinger who bid him a last "Mr. President."

NIXON (REMOTE)
I pity the next guy who sits here . . . Goodnight, gentlemen . . .

Haig and Kissinger depart.

Nixon shuffles back, alone, coming to a stop in front of a larger-than-life, full-length oil portrait of JOHN F. KENNEDY. Nixon studies the portrait, pads closer. Looks up.

NIXON
When they look at you, they see what they want to be.(*then*) When they look at me, they see what they are . . .[166]

PAT, overhearing, comes from the shadows in a nightgown. She looks weary, crazed.

PAT
Dick, please don't . . .

He half turns to her. He is unshaven, eyes red-rimmed, a wounded animal who can no longer defend himself.

NIXON
I can't . . . I just don't have the strength anymore . . .

---

[166]For Nixon talking to the portraits in the White House, see Bernstein and Woodward, *The Final Days*, p. 395; Emery, *Watergate*, p. 408; and Aitken, *Nixon*, pp. 531–534. (Note: The writers are indebted to Tom Wicker for this phrasing of Nixon's comparing himself to JFK.)

His voice trails off. For a moment, it looks like he's going to collapse. Pat moves towards him to support him.

PAT

It'll be over soon.

NIXON

No . . . it's going to start now . . . (*looks into her eyes*) If I could just . . . If I could just . . . sleep.

PAT

There'll be time for that . . .

He's barely aware of her.

NIXON

Once . . . when I was sick, as a boy . . . my mother gave me this stuff . . . made me swallow it . . . it made me throw up. All over her . . . I wish I could do that now . . .

Pat puts her arm around him.

NIXON

I'm afraid, Buddy . . . There's darkness out there.

Pat is crying now. She tries to soothe him, strokes his brow like a sick child.

NIXON

I could always see where I was going. But it's dark out there. God, I've always been afraid of the dark . . . Buddy . . .

Nixon breaks down. She slowly leads him up the grand staircase—into the shadows of history.

SCENE ONE HUNDRED TWENTY-SIX

INT. THE WHITE HOUSE—EAST ROOM—DAY

The EPILOGUE and END CREDITS run over NIXON as he addresses the assembled WHITE HOUSE STAFF. PAT and the FAMILY flank him.

Nixon's farewell speech to his staff

NIXON

. . . I remember my old man. I think they would've called him a little man, common man. He didn't consider himself that way. He was a streetcar motorman
first, and then he was a farmer, and then he had a lemon ranch. It was the poorest lemon ranch in California, I assure you. He sold it before they found oil on it.

*IMAGES of FRANK and HANNAH NIXON now arise in Nixon's conscious-
ness—a past he could never really connect his own life to. As if it were a story-
book, a fabled America that never was. The MUSIC should, in a sense, ac-
centuate this divorce of sentiment from reality.*

NIXON (CONT'D)

. . . and then he was a grocer. But he was a great man because he did his job,
and every job counts up to the hilt, regardless of what happens . . . Nobody
will ever write a book, probably, about my mother. Well, I guess all of you would
say this about your mother: my mother was a saint. And I think of her, two boys
dying of tuberculosis and seeing each of them die, and when they died . . .
Yes, she will have no books written about her. But she was a saint . . . But
now, however, we look to the future.

*Nixon is holding himself together by sheer force of will. Many members of his
STAFF are weeping. He pulls an old well-leafed book open, puts a set of eyeglasses on to read from it, the first time he's ever worn them in public.*

NIXON (CONT'D)

. . . I remember something Theodore Roosevelt wrote when his first wife died. He was still a young man, in his twenties, and this was in his diary—"T.R."— . . . "She was beautiful in face and form and lovelier still in spirit . . . When she had just become a mother, when her life seemed to be just begun, and when the years seemed so bright before her, then by a strange and terrible fate death came to her. And when my heart's dearest died, the light went from my life forever . . ." That was "T.R." in his twenties. He thought the light had gone from his life forever.

He puts down the book, nearly cracking.

NIXON

. . . But of course he went on, to become president, sometimes right, sometimes wrong, always in the arena, always vital . . . We sometimes think, when things happen that don't go the right way, we think that when someone dear to us dies, when we lose an election, when we suffer a defeat, that all is ended . . . but that's not true. It is only a beginning, always; because the greatness comes not when things always go good for you, but the greatness comes, and you're really tested, when you take some knocks, some disappointments, when sadness comes . . . Because only if you have been in the deepest valley can you ever know how magnificent it is to be on the highest mountain . . . To have served in this office is to have felt a very personal sense of kinship with each and every American. In leaving it, I do so with this prayer: May God's grace be with you in all the days ahead.

SCENE ONE HUNDRED TWENTY-SEVEN

EXT. THE WHITE HOUSE—DAY

A MARINE CORPS HELICOPTER waits at the end of a red carpet. NIXON and PAT make their way towards it, followed by the FAMILY.

NIXON (V.O. CONT'D)

. . . Remember: always give your best, never get discouraged, never be petty. Always remember: Others may hate you, but those who hate you don't win unless you hate them . . . and then you destroy yourself.

They climb the steps and Nixon turns on the top step and smiles bravely. Then he waves good-bye.

NIXON *(v.o. cont'd)*

... Only then will you find what we Quakers call "peace at the center." *Au revoir*—we'll see you again!

He raises his arms in his characteristic twin-V salute. And we FADE OUT.

EPILOGUE runs over a DARK SCREEN.

EPILOGUE

Nixon always maintained that if he had not been driven from office, the North Vietnamese would not have overwhelmed the South in 1975.[167] In a sideshow, Cambodian society was destroyed and mass genocide resulted. In his absence, Russia and the United States returned to a decade of high-budget military expansion and near-war. Nixon, who was pardoned by President Ford, lived to write six books and travel the world as an elder statesmen. He was buried and honored by five Presidents on April 26, 1994, less than a year after Pat Nixon died.

We include a DOCUMENTARY CLIP of his FUNERAL, eulogized by President CLINTON, the four other PRESIDENTS alongside him. ROBERT DOLE eulogizes him as a "great American."

EPILOGUE *(cont'd)*

For the remainder of his life, Nixon fought successfully to protect his tapes. The National Archives spent fourteen years indexing and cataloguing them.[168] Out of four thousand hours, only sixty hours have been made public.

We end on an IMAGE OF YORBA LINDA, CALIFORNIA ... turn of the twentieth century where it began. We focus on the faces of the early pioneers who settled the land—we drift over the faces of HANNAH and FRANK, in their stern postures—past the BROTHERS, including the two deceased ones ... to little RICHARD, eyes all aglow with the hopes of the new century.

THE END

---

[167]For Nixon's view of the fall of Saigon, see Nixon, *In the Arena*, p. 27; and Nixon, *RN*, p. 889.

[168]For a discussion of the history of the Nixon tapes, which the Congress directed the National Archives to release over 20 years ago, see Seymour Hersh, "Nixon's Last Cover-up: The Tapes He Wants the Archives to Suppress," *New Yorker,* May 1994; and "Nixon's Last Trump," *Harper's,* August 1994, pp. 33–44. Litigation is pending in Washington, D.C., to force the public release of the Nixon tapes relating to "abuse of office."

Cast and Character List

RICHARD NIXON	*Anthony Hopkins*
PAT NIXON	*Joan Allen*
H.R. HALDEMAN	*James Woods*
JOHN EHRLICHMAN	*J.T. Walsh*
HENRY KISSINGER	*Paul Sorvino*
ALEXANDER HAIG	*Powers Boothe*
JOHN DEAN	*David Hyde Pierce*
JOHN MITCHELL	*E.G. Marshall*
MARTHA MITCHELL	*Madeline Kahn*
RON ZIEGLER	*David Paymer*
HERB KLEIN	*Saul Rubineck*
CHUCK COLSON	*Kevin Dunn*
MANOLO SANCHEZ	*Tony Plana*
J. EDGAR HOOVER	*Bob Hoskins*
MURRAY CHOTINER	*Fyvush Finkel*
JOHNNY ROSELLI	*Tony Lo Bianco*
GORDON LIDDY	*John Diehl*
HOWARD HUNT	*Ed Harris*
FRANK STURGIS	*Robert Beltran*
BILL ROGERS	*James Karen*
MEL LAIRD	*Richard Fancy*
JULIE NIXON	*Annabeth Gish*
TRICIA NIXON	*Marley Shelton*
FRANK NIXON	*Tom Bower*
HANNAH NIXON	*Mary Steenburgen*
RICHARD NIXON @12	*Corey Carrier*
RICHARD NIXON @19	*David Barry Gray*
DONALD NIXON	*Sean Stone*
ARTHUR NIXON	*Joshua Preston*
HAROLD NIXON @16	*Tony Goldwyn*
HAROLD NIXON @23	*Tony Goldwyn*
JACK JONES	*Larry Hagman*
TRINI CARDOZA	*Dan Hedaya*
CUBAN MAN	*John Bedford Lloyd*
MITCH	*O'Neal Compton*
FAN #1	*Harry Murphy*
FAN #2	*Suzanne Schnulle Murphy*
SANDY	*Bridgitte Wilson*
CONVENTION ANNOUNCER	*Mike Kennedy*
TERESA	*Pamela Dickerson*

CLYDE TOLSON	*Brian Bedford*
JOAQUIN	*Wilson Cruz*
VERNON WALTERS	*Roy Barnitt*
RICHARD HELMS	*Sam Waterston*
LEONID BREZHNEV	*Boris Sichkin*
ANDREI GROMYKO	*Fima Noveck*
RUSSIAN INTERPRETER	*Raissa Danilova*
JAMES MCCORD	*Ron Von Klaussen*
FRED BUZHARDT	*George Plimpton*
NELSON ROCKEFELLER	*Ed Herrmann*
MAO TSE-TUNG	*Ric Young*
CHINESE INTERPRETER	*Bai Ling*
BETHESDA DOCTOR	*Bill Bolender*
FLOOR MANAGER	*Michael Kaufman*
JFK DOUBLE	*James Kelly*
PROTESTER #1	*Wass Stevens*
REPORTER #1	*John Tenney*
REPORTER #2	*Julie Araskog*
REPORTER #3	*Ray Wills*
REPORTER #4	*John Bellucci*
REPORTER #5	*Zoey Zimmerman*
STAFFER #1	*John Stockwell*
STAFFER #2	*Charlie Haugk*
STUDENT #1	*Breck Wilson*
STUDENT #2	*Peter Carlin*
YOUNG WOMAN	*Joanna Going*
BLACK ORATOR	*James Pickens*
WHITE HOUSE SECURITY	*Mark Steines*
COCK HANDLER #1	*Humberto Martinez*
SECRET SERVICE AGENT	*Tom Nicoletti*
SECRET SERVICE AGENT	*Chuck Pfeiffer*
WEDDING GUEST	*Phyllis Samhaber*
KISSINGER DATE	*Nicole Nagle*
STUDIO AUDIENCE #1	*Diane Armbuster*
GREETER	*Jesus Cabildo*
BULL RIDER	*Scott Giliis*
HAPPY ROCKEFELLER	*Annette Helde*
PARTY GUEST #1	*Paul Boyle*
PARTY GUEST #2	*Jaxon Redding*
RINGMASTER	*Albert Leon*
CUBAN PLUMBER	*Lenny Vullo*
FOOTBALL COACH	*Jack Wallace*
ASST. COACH	*James Raskin*
FOOTBALL PLAYER	*Ian Calip*

BOB	*John Cunningham*
MAUREEN DEAN	*Donna Dixon*
WOMAN STAFFER #1	*Jenne Lee*
STUDENT #4	*Michelle Matheson*
ROSEMARY WOODS	*Mary Rudolph*
SPIRO AGNEW	*Bob Marshall*
YOUNG PAT NIXON	*Julie Condra Douglas*
EARL	*John C. McGinley*
VIRGILIO GONZALES	*Enrique Castillo*
CUBAN PLUMBER	*Victor Revees*
EUGENIO MARTINEZ	*Kamar de los Reyes*
HELEN SMITH	*Marilyn Rockafellow*
LAWYER AT PARTY	*Howard Platt*

Bibliography

BOOKS

Aitken, Jonathan. *Nixon: A Life*. Washington, DC: Regnery, 1993.

Ambrose, Stephen E. *Nixon: The Education of a Politician 1913–1962*. New York: Simon & Schuster, 1987.

Ambrose, Stephen E. *Nixon: The Triumph of a Politician 1962–1972*. New York: Simon & Schuster, 1989.

Ambrose, Stephen E. *Nixon: Ruin and Recovery 1973–1990*. New York: Simon & Schuster, 1991.

Ben-Veniste, Richard, and George Frampton, Jr. *Stonewall: The Real Story of the Watergate Prosecution*. New York: Simon & Schuster, 1977.

Bernstein, Carl, and Woodward, Bob. *All the President's Men*. New York: Touchstone, 1974.

Bernstein, Carl, and Woodward, Bob. *The Final Days*. New York: Touchstone, 1974.

Beschloss, Michael R. *The Crisis Years*. New York: HarperCollins, 1991.

Block, Herbert. *Herblock's State of the Union*. New York: Simon & Schuster, 1972.

Brodie, Fawn. *Richard Nixon: The Shaping of His Character*. New York: W. W. Norton, 1981.

Colodny, Len, and Gettlin, Robert. *Silent Coup: The Removal of a President*. New York: St. Martin's Press, 1991.

Colson, Charles W. *Born Again*. Old Tappan, NJ: Chosen Books, 1976.

Dash, Samuel. *Chief Counsel: Inside the Ervin Committee—The Untold Story of Watergate*. New York: Random House, 1976.

Dean, John W., III. *Blind Ambition*. New York: Simon & Schuster, 1976.

Dean, John W., III. *Lost Honor*. Los Angeles: Stratford Press, 1982.

de Toledano, Ralph. *Nixon*. New York: Duell, Sloan and Pierce, 1960.

Demaris, Ovid. *The Director: An Oral Biography of J. Edgar Hoover*. New York: Harper's, 1975.

Ehrlichman, John. *Witness to Power: The Nixon Years*. New York: Simon & Schuster, 1982.

Emery, Fred. *Watergate: The Corruption of American Politics and the Fall of Richard Nixon*. New York: Times Books, 1994.

Eppridge, Bill, and Hays, Gorey, with President Bill Clinton. *Robert Kennedy The Last Campaign*. New York: Harcourt, Brace, 1993.

Fensterwald, Bernard. *Coincidence or Conspiracy?* New York: Zebra, 1977.

Frost, David. *I Gave Them a Sword: Behind the Scenes of the Nixon Interviews*. New York: Morrow, 1978.

Furiati, Claudia. *ZR Rifle: The Plot to Kill Kennedy and Castro*. Melbourne, Australia: Ocean Press, 1994.

Garza, Hedda (compiler). *The Watergate Investigation Index: Senate Select Committee Hearings and Reports on Presidential Campaign Activities*. Wilmington, DE: Scholarly Resources, 1982.

Garza, Hedda (compiler). *The Watergate Investigation Index: House Judiciary Com-

mittee Hearings and Report on Impeachment. Wilmington, DE: Scholarly Resources, 1985.

Gentry, Curt. *J. Edgar Hoover: The Man and the Secrets.* New York: W. W. Norton, 1991.

Haig, Alexander M., Jr. *Caveat.* New York: Macmillan, 1984.

Haig, Alexander M., Jr. (with Charles McCarry). *Inner Circles: How America Changed the World.* New York: Warner, 1992.

Haldeman, H. R. *The Ends of Power.* New York: Times Books, 1978.

Haldeman, H. R. *The Haldeman Diaries: Inside the Nixon White House.* New York: Putnam's, 1994.

Hersh, Seymour M. *The Price of Power: Kissinger in the Nixon White House.* New York: Summit, 1983.

Hinckle, Warren, and Turner, William. *The Fish Is Red: The Story of the Secret War Against Castro.* New York: Harper & Row, 1981.

Hougan, Jim. *Secret Agenda: Watergate, Deep Throat, and the CIA.* New York: Random House, 1984.

Hougan, Jim. *Spooks.* New York: Morrow, 1978.

Hunt, E. Howard. *Undercover: Memoirs of an American Secret Agent.* New York: Berkley, 1974.

Hurt, Henry. *Reasonable Doubt: An Investigation into the Assassination of John F. Kennedy.* New York: Holt, Rinehart and Winston, 1985.

Isaacson, Walter. *Kissinger: A Biography.* New York: Simon & Schuster, 1992.

Johnson, Haynes. *The Bay of Pigs: The Leaders' Story of Brigade 2506.* New York: W. W. Norton, 1964.

Kantor, Seth. *Who Was Jack Ruby?* New York: Everest House, 1978.

Kissinger, Henry. *White House Years.* Boston: Little, Brown, 1979.

Kissinger, Henry. *Years of Upheaval.* Boston: Little, Brown, 1982.

Kornitzer, Bela. *The Real Nixon: An Intimate Biography.* New York: Rand McNally, 1960.

Kutler, Stanley I. *The Wars of Watergate: The Last Crisis of Richard Nixon.* New York: Knopf, 1990.

Liddy, G. Gordon. *Will: The Autobiography of G. Gordon Liddy.* New York: St. Martin's Press, 1980.

Lukas, Anthony. *Nightmare: The Underside of the Nixon Years.* New York: Viking Press, 1976.

Magruder, Jeb Stuart. *An American Life: One Man's Road to Watergate.* New York: Atheneum, 1974.

Mankiewicz, Frank. *Perfectly Clear: Nixon from Whittier to Watergate.* New York: Popular Library, 1974.

Martin, David C. *Wilderness of Mirrors.* New York: Harper & Row, 1980.

Mazlish, Bruce. *The Leader, the Led, and the Psyche: Essays in Psychohistory.* Hanover, MA: Wesleyan University Press, 1990.

McClendon, Winzola. *Martha: The Life of Martha Mitchell.* New York: Random House, 1979.

McCord, James W., Jr. *A Piece of Tape: The Watergate Story: Fact and Fiction.* Rockville, MD: Washington Media Services, 1974.

McGinniss, Joe. *The Selling of the President*. New York: Penguin, 1988.

Morris, Roger. *Haig: The General's Progress*. New York: Playboy, 1982.

Morris, Roger. *Richard Milhous Nixon: The Rise of an American Politician*. New York: Henry Holt, 1994.

New York Times. *The End of a Presidency*. New York: Bantam, 1974.

Nixon, Richard M. *1999: Victory Without War*. New York: Touchstone, 1989.

Nixon, Richard M. *In the Arena: A Memoir of Victory, Defeat, and Renewal*. New York: Pocket Books, 1990.

Nixon, Richard M. *Six Crises*. New York: Touchstone, 1990.

Nixon, Richard M. *The Real War*. New York: Touchstone, 1990.

Nixon, Richard M. *RN: The Memoirs of Richard Nixon*. New York: Touchstone, 1990.

Nixon, Richard M. *Seize the Moment: America's Challenge in a One-Superpower World*. New York: Simon & Schuster, 1992.

Nixon-Eisenhower, Julie. *Pat Nixon: The Untold Story*. New York: Simon & Schuster, 1986.

Oglesby, Carl. *The Yankee and Cowboy War: Conspiracies from Dallas to Watergate*. Kansas City: Sheed Andrews and McFeel, 1976.

Oudes, Bruce (ed.). *From: The President: Richard Nixon's Secret Files*. New York: Harper & Row, 1989.

Phillips, David Altee. *The Night Watch: 25 Years of Peculiar Service*. New York: Atheneum, 1977.

Powers, Thomas. *The Man Who Kept the Secrets: Richard Helms and the CIA*. New York: Knopf, 1979.

Price, Ray. *With Nixon*. New York: Viking Press, 1977.

Schudson, Michael. *Watergate in American History*. New York: Basic Books, 1992.

Scott, Peter Dale. *Crime and Cover-up: The Dallas-Watergate Connection*. Berkeley: Westworks, 1977.

Scott, Peter Dale. *Deep Politics and the Death of JFK*. Berkeley: University of California Press, 1993.

Shaw, J. Gary. *Cover-Up*. Cleburne, TX: J. Gary Shaw, 1976.

Shawcross, William. *Sideshow: Kissinger, Nixon and the Destruction of Cambodia*. New York: Touchstone, 1987.

Sirica, John J. *To Set the Record Straight: The Break-in, the Tapes, the Conspirators, the Pardon*. New York: W. W. Norton, 1979.

Smith, John Chabot. *Alger Hiss: The True Story*. New York: Holt, Rinehart and Winston, 1976.

Strober, Gerald S., and Strober, Deborah Hart. *Nixon: An Oral History of His Presidency*. New York: HarperCollins, 1994.

Summers, Anthony. *Conspiracy*. New York: Paragon House, 1989.

Summers, Anthony. *Official and Confidential: The Secret Life of J. Edgar Hoover*. New York: Putnam's, 1993.

Sussman, Barry. *The Great Cover-Up: Nixon and the Scandal of Watergate*. Arlington, VA: Seven Locks Press, 1992.

Theoharis, Athan (ed.). *From the Secret Files of J. Edgar Hoover.* Chicago: Ivan R. Dee, 1991.

Theoharis, Athan. *J. Edgar Hoover, Sex, and Crime.* Chicago: Ivan Dee, 1995.

Thompson, Hunter S. *Fear and Loathing on the Campaign Trail.* San Francisco: Straight Arrow, 1973.

Vidal, Gore. *An Evening with Richard Nixon.* New York: Random House, 1972.

Ulasewicz, Tony (with Stuart A. McKeever). *The President's Private Eye: The Journey of Detective Tony U. from N.Y.P.D. to the Nixon White House.* Westport, CT: MACSAM, 1990.

White House Historical Association. *The Living White House.* Washington, DC: National Geographic Society, 1991.

White House Historical Association. *The White House, an Historic Guide.* Washington, DC: National Geographic Society, 1991.

Weicker, Lowell P., Jr. *Maverick: A Life in Politics.* Boston: Little, Brown, 1995.

Wicker, Tom. *One of Us: Richard Nixon and the American Dream.* New York: Random House, 1991.

Wills, Gary. *Nixon Agonistes: The Crisis of the Self-Made Man.* New York: New American Library, 1971.

Wyden, Peter. *Bay of Pigs: The Untold Story.* New York: Simon & Schuster, 1979.

ARTICLES

Dean, John. "Ghosts in the Machine." *Rolling Stone,* Sept. 8, 1994, pp. 47–49.

Hersh, Seymour M. "Nixon's Last Cover-up: The Tapes He Wants the Archives to Suppress." *New Yorker,* May 1994.

Korda, Michael. "Nixon, Mein Host." *New Yorker,* May 2, 1994.

Martinez, Eugenio. "Mission Impossible." *Harper's,* Oct. 1974.

Nixon, Richard. "Cuba, Castro and John F. Kennedy." *Reader's Digest,* Nov. 1964.

"Nixon's Last Trump." *Harper's,* Aug. 1994.

"Richard M. Nixon: His Place in History." *U.S. News and World Report,* May 2, 1994, pp. 25–27.

Stacks, John F. "Victory in Defeat." *Time,* May 2, 1994, pp. 26–29.

"The Legacy of Richard Nixon." *Newsweek,* May 2, 1994, pp. 20–30.

Time, July 8, 1974. (Colson interview)

CD-ROM

Haldeman, H. R. *The Haldeman Diaries: Inside the Nixon White House—The Complete Multimedia Edition.* Santa Monica, CA: Sony Electronic Publishing, 1994.

TV/VIDEOS

Nixon, PBS documentary.

Nixon-Frost Interviews (originally broadcast May 1977).

"Richard M. Nixon: His Life and Times," ABC News.

The Final Days (based on the Woodward/Bernstein book), teleplay by Hugh White-more, directed by Richard Pearce.

"The Haldeman Diaries," Nightline, ABC News.

Watergate, The Discovery Channel.

Watergate (two-part symposium), The Discovery Channel.

"Watergate: The Secret Story," Mike Wallace, CBS News.

GOVERNMENT DOCUMENTS

The Joint Appearances of Senator John F. Kennedy and Vice President Richard M. Nixon: Presidential Campaign of 1960. Washington, DC: Government Printing House, 1961.

United States House of Representatives, *Transcripts of Eight Recorded Presidential Conversations, Hearings Before the Committee on the Judiciary,* House of Representatives, 93rd Congress, 2nd Session. May–June 1974. Washington, DC: Government Printing Office, 1975.

United States House of Representatives, *Statements of Information, Books I through XII, and Appendix, Hearings Before the Committee on the Judiciary,* House of Representatives, 93rd Congress, Second Session. May–June 1974. Washington, DC: Government Printing Office, 1974.

United States House of Representatives, *Impeachment of Richard M. Nixon, President of the United States, Report of the Committee on the Judiciary,* House of Representatives, 93rd Congress, Second Session. August 20, 1974. Washington, DC: Government Printing Office, 1974.

United States House of Representatives, *Inquiry into the Alleged Involvement of the Central Intelligence Agency in the Watergate and Ellsberg Matters, Hearings Before the Special Subcommittee on Intelligence of the Committee on Armed Services,* House of Representatives, 94th Congress, First Session. Washington, DC: Government Printing Office, 1975.

United States House of Representatives, *Committee on Un-American Activities, Hearings on Proposed Legislation to Curb or Control the Communist Party of the United States,* House of Representatives, 80th Congress, Second Session. Washington, DC: Government Printing Office, 1948.

United States Senate, *Select Committee on Presidential Campaign Activities, Hearings, Books 1 through 23,* 93rd Congress, First and Second Sessions, 1973, 1974. Washington, DC: Government Printing Office, 1974.

United States Senate, *The Final Report of the Select Committee on Presidential Campaign Activities, June 1974.* Washington, DC: Government Printing Office, 1974.

United States Senate, *Alleged Assassination Plots Involving Foreign Leaders: An Interim Report of the Select Committee to Study Government Operations with Respect to Intelligence Activities.* Washington, DC: Government Printing Office, 1975.

United States Senate, *Chronology of Events Relative to the Seventeen Wiretaps and Pertinent Documents, in Dr. Kissinger's Role in Wiretapping: Hearings Before the Senate Foreign Relations Committee,* 93rd Congress, Second Session. Washington, DC: Government Printing Office, 1975.

COURT CASES

Halperin v. Kissinger, 606 F2d 1192 (1979).
United States v. Mitchell, et al., 559 F2d 31 (1976).
United States v. Ehrlichman, et al., 546 F2d 910 (1976).
United States v. Richard Nixon, 418 U.S. 683 (1974).

PART 3

WATERGATE DOCUMENTS AND TAPES

Editor's Note on Watergate Documents and Tapes: *It has always been a mystery why President Nixon chose to tape his conversations. Perhaps for history, perhaps to help him write his memoirs, perhaps to protect himself. We may never know all of his reasons. But we can be fairly certain that he never expected his tapes to be made public or to be published in newspapers and books.*

Actually, it is a misconception to think the Nixon tapes are in fact public. Out of some 4,000 hours of tapes at the National Archives, only about 60 hours of conversations have been made public. To the end of his life, Richard Nixon fought in court to keep the tapes secret, a battle that still goes on. Even those that have been "released" to the public can only be heard in one place, on headsets at the National Archives facility in College Park, Maryland. They have never been heard by the vast majority of the American public. And many of them have never even been published.

We are including here a sampling of documents and tapes from the Nixon White House. They provide glimpses and insights into the inner workings of Nixon and his staff, and the mentality that prevailed in his inner circle. We have included documents ranging from personal handwritten notes to internal memos, from humorous to deadly serious.

We have also included transcripts of a small sampling of the Nixon tapes. Some of these have rarely been seen before. We have included pre-Watergate conversations from 1971, including a discussion of how to use "thugs" and "murderers" to break up protest demonstrations, and an example of Nixon's obsession with Daniel Ellsberg and the leaked "Pentagon Papers." We also include the famous "smoking gun" tape of June 23, 1972, which led to Nixon's resignation from office. And we include John Dean's famous "cancer on the Presidency" meeting of March 21, 1973, where he urged Nixon to end the cover-up. Also included is a Nixon strategy session with Haldeman and Ehrlichman on April 14, 1973, trying desperately to figure out a way to create scapegoats and save themselves. As the President put it, "Give 'em an hors d'oeuvre and maybe they won't come back for the main course." Sixteen days later, Nixon announced their resignations. Sixteen months later, Nixon himself was gone.

Contents:
Watergate Documents and Tapes

DOCUMENTS

"H" [BOB HALDEMAN] to "C" [Dwight Chapin] with "Words to remember."

TAPE OF TELEPHONE CONVERSATION (April 24, 1971) between John Ehrlichman and Richard Helms relating to Bay of Pigs documents.

PAT BUCHANAN MEMO of June 9, 1971, to the president regarding Teddy Kennedy.

MEMORANDUM from Donald Santerelli of June 15, 1971, to Egil Krogh showing how Gordon Liddy got a job at the White House.

LETTER OF RECOMMENDATION for Gordon Liddy to be admitted to the D.C. Bar from John Ehrlichman (although Ehrlichman knows Liddy has broken into Dr. Fielding's office).

CHUCK COLSON MEMO of August 11, 1971, regarding Ellsberg attack.

EHRLICHMAN MEMO to the president of October 27, 1971, regarding the removal of J. Edgar Hoover from the FBI.

JOHN MITCHELL'S February 1972 handwritten **letter** of resignation as attorney general and Richard Nixon's handwritten response. Also a post-1972 election letter from Mitchell to Nixon, with Nixon's notes on the letter to Haldeman.

MEMO of March 17, 1972, from Haldeman to Ehrlichman that shows Ehrlichman's open moves to get rid of Mitchell.

MEMO from the president to Ehrlichman re "Kennedy's Thirteen Greatest Mistakes" and Dean being the only one who understands the Hiss Case.

SELECTED MEMOS from the Watergate Special Prosecutor's files regarding Higby interview (October 18, 1973), Hunt interviews on July 3 and 19, 1973, and sampling of computer-generated "WSPF Chronological Report—Hunt on Ehrlichman."

TAPES

NIXON, Haldeman meeting, May 5, 1971.

NIXON, Mitchell, Haldeman, and Ehrlichman, July 6, 1971.

EXCERPTS of conversations of Nixon and Haldeman, June 23, 1972.

NIXON, Dean, and Haldeman, March 21, 1973.

NIXON, Haldeman, and Ehrlichman, April 14, 1973.

THE WHITE HOUSE
WASHINGTON
DATE:_____

TO: C

FROM: BOB HALDEMAN

FYI_____   PLEASE HANDLE_____

OTHER:

Words to remember.

H

THE WHITE HOUSE
WASHINGTON

A large part of political life consists not so much in doing things yourself as in imparting the right tone to things that are going to happen anyway.

EYES ONLY - ~~SECRET~~   4/24/71 (?)
                                          12³⁰ pm

Conversation with Richard Helms

E   Ehrlichman
H   Helms

E   Dick, John Ehrlichman.

H   Good morning to you.

E   How are you, sir.

H   I'm alright. On these matters we discussed the other
             day -- have you got a pencil?
             Let's start with the Bay of Pigs because that's the thing
             in which we have a larger interest than any of these other
             items. First off we do not in the agency anywhere either
             in John McCon'e's files or Allen Dulles' files or any place
             else a copy of that Green Committee report chaired by
             General Taylor.

E   OK.

H   The only... when I consulted with all my ~~xxxxixix~~ associates
             the only thing they could come up with was that either
             General Taylor himself might have a copy or that the only
             copy in existence was given to McGeorge Bundy whom
             you know was in Henry Kissinger's spot at that time.

E   OK

H   In that sense trying to be helpful as to where we might
             look. But I don't think there were very many copies
             of it if I understand this correctly.

E   OK

H   Secondly, we do have a copy of the Kirkpatrick report that
             you asked about. And that is something that in connection
             with which I'm going to take you up on a suggestion you made
             to me that when we get a little further down the line you drop
             by here some ~~xxxx~~ morning and have a look at what some
             of these things are and you can make your own judgment
             about what whether you want them or don't want them.

SANITIZED COPY   DECLASSIFIED
                              E.O. 12356, Sect. 3.4
                              NSC ltr. 1/22/90 F88-1627
                              By NdH   NARA Date 5-30-90
                              (MR NLN 89-4)

-2-

E   Fair enough

H   And how much of them you want because you know
         the gentleman's style and ~~thxxcapacxty~~ capacities a
         lot~~s~~ better than I do and I think there's going to have
         to be some subjective judgments made here as
         to whether some of this is worth doing or not.

E   I'll do that.

H   Then I also located another ~~oxx~~ report on the Bay of Pigs

                              which might give a sort of
         a round picture of what this operation was all about and
         may in many ways be an easier thing for you and the President
         to handle than some of these other things.

E   Good

H   OK, so much for that. Now on the Cuban missile crisis.
         We have an excellent report that was put together by the
         community working together on the intelligence
         community's activities in connection with the Cuban
         missile crisis. It's a summary plus three volumes.
         But that's all that we have. The policy matter -- the
         messages between Kennedy and Khrushchev and all the
         Scali(?) business and all that stuff I'm sure you have to get
         through the State Department. We certainly don't have it
         here.

E   OK

H   That will save you some time if you head yourself in that
         direction. As far as the Lebanon landing is concerned,
         we have a couple of estimates that we made around about
         that period, you know, sort of giving an indication of
         what was going on in that part of the world but we don't
         have any policy documents of any kind that anybody can
         find so I guess that's a State plus JCS problem.

E   OK

H   Then the last item is what we choose to call the Diem
         episode. And on that we have indeed here a chronological
         report of you know the events of the time and how one thing
         relates to another.

EDITOR'S NOTE: The text missing from line 9 was deleted by the CIA.

- 3 -

H It's the kind of thing, however, which comes along with that other report of things that you'd probably want to look at it to see if it was satisfactory -- at least it is available. And I suggest that we do this when --- as soon as you return from the West Coast. If you'll give me a call we can arrange a time for you to come by and I'll have the stuff spread out and so forth and explain to you what it is.

E I'll do that

H John, I have one thing I'd like to take up with you and if you're going to speak with the President on the plane and so forth I'd like you to have this in the forefront of your mind. Obviously, I'm going to hand this stuff over for the President, but I'd be terribly glad if you would get his backing not to share it with a lot of the staff over there. For example, I know Howard Hunt has been doing some work. There's nothing he'd like better than, as an old agency hand to run around in some of the soiled linen there is around here, in the garbage cans and so forth. That you could well understand.

E Well, I tried to reassure you on that and I was very sincere about it and I've talked with Henry since about this whole thing and he and I are going to visit on the plane on this trip about the way that we can safeguard this.

H Because it really is basically an agency document. To be returned to us after the President has had his will with it. I think we'd have to be the ultimate custodian... There are so many names of people and events and so forth it's just the dirty linen being washed in its ultimate, particularly on the Bay of Pigs.

E Well I understand that and I will certainly talk with the President in those terms.

H Thank you very much. You did give me that assurance but I simply wanted to come back to it because now that I've had a chance to look at it I'm much more up-tight about it than I was before.

E I understand perfectly and I will talk to both Henry and the President in those terms and that I'll be in touch with you when I get back. And thanks for your timely response.

-4-

H   Not at all. We're right behind you.

* * *

THE WHITE HOUSE
WASHINGTON
DATE _____

TO: *Attorney General*
FROM: BOB HALDEMAN

| FYI_____ | PLEASE HANDLE_____ |

OTHER:

Personal

Eyes Only

CONFIDENTIAL

CONFIDENTIAL

THE WHITE HOUSE

WASHINGTON

DETERMINED TO BE AN
ADMINISTRATIVE MARKING
E.O. 12065, Section 6-102
By ~~PP~~_____NARS, Date _1- 15-82_

~~CONFIDENTIAL~~   June 9, 1971

MEMORANDUM FOR: THE PRESIDENT

FROM: PATRICK J. BUCHANAN

SUBJECT: EMK - POLITICAL MEMORANDUM

A careful analysis of news clippings of recent weeks, coupled
with reports of recent days, removes, I think, vestigal doubts
that <u>EMK is running actively for the Presidency.</u>

<u>Items:</u>

        Last night on the Elizabeth Drew show, Kennedy pointedly
refused to issue any Sherman statements. In April, for the first
time, he stated "I am keeping my mind open" about the nomination.
ABC finds that he has written to former top aides indicating he is
assessing the situation. Humphrey thinks he is a potential active
candidate, as does Muskie. Daley, according to HHH, is "strong
for Teddy." Riesel claims nearly all the top AFL-CIO types,
excepting Meany, are holding back, waiting for Teddy; the same
is true of many political pros around the country, according to
Jerry Greene. Andrew Tully said a month or more ago that
anyone who doesn't think Teddy is running "suffers from rocks
in the head," and Andy Biemiller of AFL-CIO indicates that if a
fellow does not think Kennedy is running, he is "nuts".

        Buchanan's View: Kennedy is keeping his options open --
against the possibility that RN may be so strong by summer '72
that the nomination will not be worth anything. In which event,
he can stay out. However, <u>at this point, he and his people have
obviously concluded RN can be beaten -- and they are not about
to sit this one out -- risking spending eight years outside the
inner circle</u> of power of a President Humphrey or a President Muskie.
If Kennedy believes the Democrats can win -- as he quite apparently
does now -- he will go after the nomination. If he thinks the Democrats
by spring of 1972 are sure losers, he can yet stand off.

~~CONFIDENTIAL~~

2

Hard Evidence:

Mankiewicz, Salinger, Goodwin and Walinsky have all
hooked up (CSM) with sure-loser George McGovern. These are
not idealistic school boys willing to spend a year of their lives
on an ideological lark. They are interested in power -- there
is no power to be had by going the route with George McGovern.

It appears they have been given the go-sign by Kennedy
to join McGovern, that the purpose is to serve (a) as a "holding
operation" for the Kennedy staff, (b) to make top Kennedy
personnel familiar with all the levers of state Democratic power
when Kennedy makes his move and (c) to elevate McGovern in the
polls and start cutting Humphrey and Muskie down to size where
they can't be nominated.

McGovern is now moving in line with this strategy, with
his overt violation of O'Brien's 11th Commandment and attack
on HHH and Muskie for opposition to the Mansfield Amendment.
Last night, Kennedy himself had the needle out for some of the
"older" voices locked in the thinking of the past -- and he
mentioned, specifically, the opposition to Mansfield Amendment
as his basis -- refusing, however, to name names.

Also, in line with the strengthening of the weak sister,
McGovern, is the emergence of candidates Jackson and Mills --
both of whom will corral conservative Democrat delegates who
might otherwise be in the Muskie or Humphrey Camp.

Kennedy Strategy:

Avoid the early primaries in which the left-handers
McGovern, Bayh, Hughes, etc. will all be knocked out of the
box in the early innings -- freeing up their "Kennedyites" for the
switch to Teddy. Maneuver to guarantee that neither Muskie nor
Humphrey moves into the convention with the nomination locked
up. Hold open the option of going into the California Primary
itself -- if that is necessary to halt the momentum of a Muskie
or Humphrey. Nearing convention time -- have the left candidates,
one-by-one, throw their support to Teddy and Teddy emerge as

3

the single champion of that wing of the party -- with good labor
backing, with good machine backing, and with young, poor,
black unanimous behind his candidacy.

Muskie versus Kennedy:

        Since November Muskie has lost almost 40 percent of
his first-choice support among Democrats, dropping from 33-21.

        Between March and May, Muskie's 1 point lead among
Democrats over Kennedy (26-25) disappeared into an eight point
deficit (29-21).

        Among Independents -- Muskie's long suit -- his March
lead over Kennedy of 18 points (31-13) was sliced all the way to
four points (19-15).

        Muskie still has tremendous support among Democratic
Party leaders -- Kennedy, from the polls, next to nothing -- but
Kennedy support among the rank-and-file Democrats, his ability
to attract publicity and generate excitement and the support of the
ideologically committed give him more than enough to balance off
his weakness with the pros.

        Impossible for me to believe the Kennedyites, who believe
RN is vulnerable, are going to sit by and watch a Muskie or Humphrey
take the prize in August -- and perhaps the Presidency, thus putting
off the "Restoration" for four years, possibly eight, possibly forever.

The Kennedy Assets:

        These are well known. Charm, "commitment", affinity
with the young, polish, Kennedy looks, mystique, the Myth, charisma
along the campaign trail; he generates enormous excitement -- as is
attested by GOPers traveling with him.

Deficiencies:

        1. Even his best friends never accused Kennedy of being
an intellectual. On the Drew show, he tended to retreat into the New
Left cliches, "we can build a better America," material, which

4

reflects a lack of depth. Further, he tends to react somewhat
hotly to attack. (PJB suggestion is that it might be well to have
hang one or two on him -- from the Vice President or Dole --
taking some particular excessive statement, and really putting
it to him, to ascertain how he handles himself. This would
perhaps best be done by a moderate-liberal Senator who would
unleash a stinging attack on him -- away from the Senate floor --
before television, about two-minutes of good work -- then we could
see how he reacts.)

    2. His far-left foreign policy positions, which win him
the plaudits of the New Left journalists and fellow travelers in the
media -- should be portrayed as shocking, alarming, frightening,
dangerous to the peace, inviting war in Europe, "immature" and
irresponsible. Not, of course, from here -- but in backgrounders
with press, he should be portrayed as too reckless, too immature,
too irresponsible, at his age, to be President of the United States.
This fits hand in globe with the impression he has left upon much
of the country and the center of the Democratic Party in the wake
of Chappaquiddick.

    It is the quiet constant repetition of private and public
comments like, "Sure, Muskie is strong but this 'indecisive' thing
is killing him" that is itself injuring Muskie's chances. He has
been unable to shake the "indecisive" charge with which we have --
with his help -- tagged him.

    3. His far left social policy positions should be broadcast
and re-broadcast. He has the Left and the Radical Kids. We don't
and won't get a one. The effort should be to identify him with them,
to associate him with them, to tie him to them.

    No matter that EMK is adored by the Party's Left, we have
a serious problem only if he gets well with the Party's Center. The
more he acts like Brother Bobby the better off we are; the less he
acts like brother John, the better off we are.

    4. Socially, Kennedy is out of touch with the political mood.
The Jet Set, Swinger, See-Through Blouse cum Hot Pants crowd,
the Chappaquiddick Hoe-down and Paris highjinks -- the more
publicity they all get, the better. (The pictures of the Kennedy
sisters, in mod attire, at the Kennedy Center, did them no good.)

5

Chappaquiddick:

This, of course, will be kept in the public mind by the press -- speculating on whether it is helping or hurting EMK. We ought to stay miles away from it -- indicating even in private, "it's hard to say the effect; we don't know."

Racial Issue:

Kennedy's support of the social-engineering Ribicoff Plan should be emphasized -- and a check made to determine how many of his own children go to integrated schools -- and then this fact, if relevant, placed in Monday, or some publication to get attention. Monday could investigate this -- if Kennedy is guilty of hypocrisy on the question -- this made known.

The Democratic Right:

EMK openly endorsed the left-wing Mayoral candidate who lost to Rizzo in the primary by a whopping margin. The President might well congratulate Rizzo -- if and when he wins the Mayorality -- and try to wean some of these tough-line conservative Mayor types to a position of neutrality in a Kennedy-RN contest.

They have no reason to love EMK -- and it would appear to me that this effort would be at least as worthwhile as the effort to woo labor chieftains equally locked into the Democratic Party.

JFK:

Since EMK will be trafficking on the JFK myth, it would be well to document JFK's tough line on Defense, foreign policy, Vietnam, Europe, etc. over against EMK's positions -- to provide conservative Democrats with some rationale for abandoning the little brother of their hero.

Some of the above are tactical gestures, rather than strategic planning. But the main objective, again, is to keep Kennedy out on the Far Left of his Party -- to prevent his major inroads into the center -- so that if he is the nominee against the President -- we have a clear shot at all those conservative Democrats, who make

up an integral part of the Nixon Majority. If he is nominated, it
should be by the Left Wing of his Party so that LBJ, the South,
and the Conservative Democrats will feel they have been run
over top of by the unrepresentative radicals and the elite.

Form DJ-150
(Ed. 4-26-65)

UNITED STATES GOVERNMENT   DEPARTMENT OF JUSTICE

Memorandum

TO   : Egil Krogh   DATE: June 15, 1971
         Deputy Assistant to the President

FROM : Donald E. Santarelli
         Associate Deputy Attorney General

SUBJECT: Gordon Liddy

Wally Johnson and I rode home with the Attorney General
after the testimonial dinner. The Attorney General was most
explicit in his response to our inquiry about the Liddy status
to the affect that the decision had been made to take Liddy
aboard at the White House on the issues of narcotics, bombing
and guns, and the Treasury Department performance on those
subjects and that the decision to do so should be implemented
immediately. When we indicated that it seemed to be languishing,
he was very strong in instructing us to follow through with
you to see that it occurred. When I told him I thought you
needed more muscle to accomplish it, he said why did you not
come to me with that information sooner. He then added that
you should go to whomever it is you need to to accomplish that
end and that you had his support in doing so. He concluded
the discussion with the admonition to "get it done".

Liddy file.

THE WHITE HOUSE

WASHINGTON

June 6, 1972

Dear Mr. Morris:

Mr. Gordon Liddy served as a member of the Domestic Council's staff from July 1971 to December 1971.

He was a very effective member of the staff and undertook numerous difficult assignments with great skill. He possesses a keen legal mind and is certainly highly qualified for the practice of law. He has approached all problems, even the most sensitive, with the highest sense of integrity.

He would be a very able member of the Bar here in the District of Columbia.

Sincerely,

John D. Ehrlichman
Assistant to the President
for Domestic Affairs

Mr. William H. Morris,
Director
National Conference of Bar Examiners
333 N. Michigan Avenue
Chicago, Illinois 60601

THE WHITE HOUSE
WASHINGTON

DETERMINED TO BE AN
ADMINIS.RATIVE MARKING
E.O. 120:5, Section 6-102
By_____MAR, Date_1-22-82

CONFIDENTIAL

CONFIDENTIAL
EYES ONLY

August 11, 1971

MEMORANDUM FOR: H. R. HALDEMAN

FROM: CHARLES COLSON

SUBJECT: Attached Memo

I have prepared the attached memo in very guarded terms. I
think it is important to everyone that I not appear to be going
around anyone's end and I therefore have written this with a
view to other people reading it.

My own feeling, as I told you, is that Bud was straining to
come up with every possible reason why nothing was going
to happen including how the FBI isn't functioning the way it
should, that the CIA and the FBI do not work together and on
and on and on. I just have intuitive feelings that this is all
going to peter out; nothing is going to happen. If there has
been a conscious decision that this is what we want, fine.
If not, I would hate to see a political opportunity missed by
default.

The P raised this with me today.
His feelings are very clear. I did
NOT indicate that I thought there
was any foot dragging or any
real problem because I don't
want to end-run and my
concerns may be unfounded. I
did say we were holding back until
after the VN elections.

THE WHITE HOUSE

WASHINGTON

~~CONFIDENTIAL~~

EYES ONLY

August 11, 1971

MEMORANDUM FOR: H. R. HALDEMAN

FROM: CHARLES COLSON

SUBJECT: Pentagon Papers

Bud Krogh gave me a full briefing this week on where things
stand on the Ellsberg matter and the Pentagon Papers issue.

As you know, we have had two objectives: the first to discredit
publicly the Ellsberg conspiracy; the second to encourage the
disclosure of information which discredits the Kennedy/Johnson
Administration and its appointees. Bud said that he will have
a complete report in the next few days for Ehrlichman, which
I will review. He indicated, however, that the conclusion will
be that at the moment there is not a basis for establishing
"an Alger Hiss type" case against Ellsberg, that the evidence
is scanty and unreliable. As to the locksmith story which I
was asked to get out, Bud indicates that there simply is not
enough there to work with. Moreover, he understands that the
Ellsberg case is not to be pushed either publicly or legally until
after the Vietnamese elections. I read from Bud's oral report
that it looks highly unlikely that at this point we will be able to
make much of a case -- certainly not for the next two months.

As you know, I think the real political payoff from this whole
controversy will be realized from the planned House and Senate
investigations into the origins of the Vietnam War. We can feed
"our" people with information which will devastate the Democrats.
As to this, Bud indicates that the same ground rules apply, that is
we should not encourage Congressional hearings and we should not
start feeding out information about the Diem coup or other similar
events until after the Vietnamese elections.

2.

The obvious bind that we are in is that the Democrats are now
trying to low key what had been heralded as a major investigation
into the origins of the war. I am convinced that they have sensed
that there is nothing but political trouble for them in such hearings.
We, on the other hand, because of the election apparently cannot
do much ourselves. Bud's feeling was that this would rule out
any activities this fall inasmuch as the election comes in October
and at that point the Congress will be pressing to adjourn.

As far as Congressional activities are concerned, therefore, we
presumably will have to wait for next year; the Pentagon Papers
will then be old news and it will be very difficult in my opinion
to crank up much in the way of hearings. The Democrats will
fight it hard in an election year.

I have suggested to Bud that Howard Hunt go through the material
that Bud has been assembling. Howard has the instincts for the
juggler and if any case can be made by fact or by innuendo, I
think Howard will pick it up.

My own reading from this is that we are not going to be able to
exploit either the substance of the Pentagon Papers or the Ellsberg
case in the way we had hoped. Bud's analysis of the facts so far and
the timing of the Vietnamese elections clearly work against us.

After the elections, we can do some good by selectively leaking
out some material such as the Diem coup information, but unless
we have Congressional hearings which we will have to encourage,
we cannot make a major national impact.

*Co~ ~~~~ π file
E safe*

October 27, 1971

MEMORANDUM FOR   THE PRESIDENT

FROM   JOHN EHRLICHMAN

SUBJECT   Director of the FBI

Last week you requested the Attorney General to provide
you with a proposed scenario with regard to the Director.

Attached are his suggestions, none of which are
particularly novel.

Also attached is a letter from Director Hoover and an article
by William Buckley which you may find of interest.

Edgar, as you can imagine I've been giving your situation a great
deal of thought. I am absolutely delighted that you have weathered
the attacks upon you and the Bureau so well. The Princeton
symposium, the various articles and stories that have run have only
scratched you in minor ways.

In thinking through your future I have concluded that you must stay
as Director of the Bureau through November of 1972. I hope you will
agree to do so because I think it's very unrealistic to even contemplate
your replacement in the meantime. Anyone who is selected as your
replacement would immediately become a political issue, would undergo
a bruising confirmation process and both he and the Bureau would be
hurt in the process.

This next year is going to be a highly political year. We must figure out
some way to keep the FBI out of the political crossfire. I have
concluded that the best way to do this is for you to say right now,
publicly, that you have decided to serve one more year, until just after
the Inauguration in January of 1973, and that then you will retire on
"senior status". You would obviously be available to the Bureau and
the government as a special consultant, and could provide for an orderly
transition for the new Director.

This timing would permit whoever is elected President in November to
announce your replacement, thereby taking your replacement's identity
out of the political campaign.

Between now and November you can be thinking about who a replacement
might be. If we can agree on a replacement we can keep it secret, and
begin to prepare the way for the new man. Obviously, if I am reelected,
your replacement would be someone who would carry on your tradition.
On the other hand, if the Democrats were to prevail in November of
1972, the Bureau would be subject to some Director that neither of us
would like.

I sincerely think that this is in our mutual best interests and in the best
interest of the Bureau. I've sifted through every conceivable alternative
and option and I know that you should and must do it this way.

JOHN EDGAR HOOVER
DIRECTOR

Federal Bureau of Investigation
United States Department of Justice
Washington, D. C.

October 26, 1971

PERSONAL ATTENTION
BY LIAISON

Honorable John D. Ehrlichman
Assistant to the President
The White House
Washington, D. C.

Dear Mr. Ehrlichman:

Since you were interested in the letter
which I wrote to Duane Lockard, Department of
Politics, Princeton University, I am enclosing
herewith a column which appeared yesterday in
The Evening Star by William F. Buckley, Jr.,
which, I think, pretty well exposes the type of
"kangaroo court" which this Princeton group is
holding at the end of this week.

Sincerely,

J. Edgar Hoover

Enclosure

SCENARIO FOR CONVERSATION WITH THE DIRECTOR

Unfortunately the attacks upon the Director have resumed and can be expected to increase. (John Ehrlichman is collecting the applicable material)

While in the past attacks came from the left, since the Sullivan affair, some are now coming from people on the right who worked with Sullivan in the anti-communism field. These same people and others are questioning the nature of the liaison between the Bureau and the CIA as it affects our national security capacity.

For the two reasons set forth below it is vital that a date be set for the retirement of the Director.

> 1. The retirement should take place when the Director is at the top of his career and not after he becomes the center of controversy.

> 2. With the political campaign coming on shortly, the opposition will use its attacks against the Director to get at the President as a candidate.

The staging of the retirement should provide the Director with full honors (medal, dinner, etc.)

The Director should be asked to accept a position as Consultant to the President and the Bureau with compensation to be worked out at the highest available level.

The Director would maintain an office within the Bureau space at the Justice Department and retain his secretary and be provided with a car and driver and whatever backup help he might need for his consultant work.

If all goes well to this point, it may be advisable to discuss Pat Gray as a successor and the concept of getting him aboard at the Bureau in the near future so that the transition would be as smooth as possible.

THE ATTORNEY GENERAL
WASHINGTON

February 15, 1972

Dear Mr. President

For the reasons we have discussed, I hereby submit my resignation from the office of Attorney General, effective March 1, 1972.

It has been a great privilege to serve in your Cabinet and Administration, and for this opportunity and experience I am most appreciative.

Respectfully submitted

John Mitchell

THE WHITE HOUSE
WASHINGTON
February 5, 1972

Dear John -

In my 25 years in public life I have found there are very few indispensable men.

In the campaign of 1968 and in our first three years you have been one of those rare men.

My only regret is that you are also the indispensable man to run the campaign of 1972.

But fortunately we will still be working together in the same cause

I can't pay you what
you are worth. But if just plain
"thank you" will do — you have
that a Thousand fold —
(and Martha too!)

Dick

H
12/6/72

Twenty Broad Street

November 27, 1972

Dear Mr. President,

      Thank you for taking time to write your
kind note of November 16th. Needless to say, I
have taken great personal satisfaction in the
magnitude of your landslide, but cannot attribute
your accomplishments, even in part, to the factor
you describe.

      My purpose in burdening you with this
response is to set the record straight from my
vantage point.

      No political campaign, and certainly not
our campaign in 1972, could possibly result in the
extraordinarily broad-based support that you received
from the American people. Simply put, your landslide
resulted from the voters' acceptance of Richard Nixon
as the personification of one they want to hold the
office of the Presidency.

      The voters' perception of a President is
analogous to our American jury system. Jurors do not
always understand all of the ramifications of a case
but they do come up with the proper verdict.
Similarly, the voters cannot understand all of the
brilliance of your foreign policy or many of the nuances
of your economic policy, but they can perceive the
total accomplishment and accept it as in their interest
and in the interest of the USA.

H — a brilliant perception. P

- 2 -

Another ingredient that must be considered as contributing substantially to your victory was your political astuteness. I am sure you will agree that one cannot succeed as a President during a single term, and certainly not in this day and age be re-elected, without a full understanding of the surrounding political forces. You have had a full and complete understanding of such forces during your entire term, perhaps more comprehensive than anyone else in the country.

I cannot sign off without relating this last point to our friends in the media. During most of your tenure they have written and spoke of your seclusion in the White House -- out of touch with the American people. It must now come as a great shock to these pundits to realize, if not admit, that Richard Nixon was the one that really had hold of the pulse of the people and that they were the ones who saw the American public from behind blinders.

As to your next four years, Mr. President, I have no concern, and every expectation, the foundations put in place during the first four provide a great base upon which to build and I am sure that you will so do.

Respectfully,

John N. Mitchell

The President
The White House
Washington, D. C. 20500

THE WHITE HOUSE

WASHINGTON

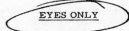

March 17, 1972

MEMORANDUM FOR :   JOHN EHRLICHMAN

FROM :   H. R. HALDEMAN

You once wrote me a memo which you said was difficult to write,
but which contained some things you felt needed to be said regarding
my operation and the general situation with regard to the planning
for the President.

I feel now that I should do likewise for you, regarding your relationship with the Committee for the Re-Election of the President, and
the President's Campaign Manager. I realize I may be treading on
dangerous ground and that this may be a futile exercise, or even
counterproductive, but I have some concerns which I think should
be expressed.

In recent weeks, I've seen several examples of indications of a
problem, and have learned of several others. Perhaps they are
isolated and insignificant, but on the other hand, if they are in-
dicative of the present situation in a growing trend, I think we need
to take some action to correct the problem.

I was quite disturbed with the results of the meeting we had in my
office awhile back with John Mitchell, Fred Malek, and Ken Cole.
You will recall that at that meeting, you took a totally negative
position and quite severely criticized Mitchell directly, as well as
laying some strenuous objections and obstructions in the way of the
development of Malek's campaign role.

The role John is trying to develop for Malek may well not be the best
way to handle things, but it is the result of an honest and sincere
effort to try to make the operation as fully as effective as possible,
and it seems to me that all of us should approach it in that constructive
sense, and do everything we can to make it succeed, rather than simply
to criticize it.

what is it ?

2

?

Somewhat more disturbing, is the tone and possibly also the content, of your February 23rd memorandum to John Mitchell regarding the Committee. A memorandum, which I understand, was ultimately not sent to John, but rather to Jeb Magruder, and was subsequently answered by Jeb Magruder - only partially satisfactorily - I would guess.

*not at all
satisfactory,
unwilling
to admit
there's a
problem
at 1701*

As to the substance of that letter, the challenge you make to Magruder's involvement in the development of substantive policy, would be entirely appropriate if, in fact, Jeb were involved. However, it's my understanding that Ken Cole has been working with Jeb for a long time and has presumably kept you advised of his discussions and actions.

No

The Committee's material on issues may, indeed, be terrible. But, we ought to at least consider the possibility that that's a reflection of the input they've been given from those better able to outline the issues and our positions on them.

*Detail our
inputs
&
The
product*

This seems to fall dangerously close to the old "we - they" situation that has arisen in the past. I think it's imperative that we all consider ourselves part of the Committee for the Re-Election of the President and not consider it as a separate entity which is in some way, an enemy of the White House.

I understand there was some problem on the briefing sessions set up in early March for members of the Committee in the Roosevelt Room. I'm told that the meeting was set up by Ed Harper, at your request, that Stein and Krogh both briefed the group, that you arrived at the meeting, declined Harper's offer to brief, left a half hour later, and then told John Mitchell that "Magruder's meeting was poorly arranged and hadn't permitted you an opportunity to speak". It's quite possible that my information is faulty, but whether it is or not, the fact that there's a flap here at all, indicates some lack of positive coordination and cooperation.

yes

Never

I also understand there's a problem regarding campaign advertising. Jeb says that you've told him that the advertising stinks, and that you've quoted me as agreeing that it stinks. I'm not sure I went quite that strong. I have had some disagreements with some of the advertising, although some of it, I think, is very good. In every case where I have disagreed, I have told the people at the Committee, what my disagreement was, why I felt that way, and what I thought should be

3

done to correct it. I feel that all of us should be free to criticize, but should do it in a way that leads to a better result.

I understand that Ed Harper has told Jeb that you are setting up a review committee to analyze campaign advertising and that this committee consists of you, Ray Price and Bill Safire. I think this is a good idea, if you are analyzing the advertising on the basis of content. I think we're going to get into a problem if you decide to analyze it on the basis of appeal, and if that is your intention, you should meet jointly with the campaign advertising review group, rather than separately. I'm sure that if this is approached right, Pete Dailey and the advertising people will welcome constructive criticism and review. On the other hand, if they are simply required to submit their product to a senior review committee, and then told ~~ that it's no good, we aren't going to help them much.

Each of the above problems is probably petty and minor in itself, but taken together, they may indicate a general problem of the relationship between you and the Domestic Council vs. Mitchell and the Re-Election Committee. If there is such a problem, I would deeply hope that it can be ironed out quickly because cooperation both ways is extremely important. If there is anything I can do to help in the process, I would, of course, be most happy to do so. If you would prefer that I keep my nose out of the problem, I would be happy to do that, and once again, I apologize for writing this at all, but hope you will give it some serious consideration. The principle thing that concerns me is tone and attitude. The specifics can all be worked out if the basic approach is on the right grounds.

THE WHITE HOUSE

WASHINGTON

Camp David
March 4, 1973

MEMORANDUM FOR JOHN EHRLICHMAN

FROM THE PRESIDENT

I note that the TIMES is starting a series of articles by John
Hebers in which he is interviewing the most liberal political
science professors around the country on the point as to whether
or not the President is usurping power -- Henry Steele Commager,
of course, and people like that are his main sources. Obviously
they are going to come down hard on the fact that we are going far
beyond what any previous Administration has done in extending the
Presidential power.

As you are, of course, aware - this is really nonsense. For
example, in terms of withholding, the fact that we are withhholding
approximately half what our predecessors did in the sixties is one
which should be gotten across in any discussion of this matter.
With regard to the use of the FBI, etc., it can be pointed out that
we have not only gotten rid of the survelliance conducted by the
Department of Defense but that we have had less taps for national
security purposes authorized by the FBI than any previous Administration. And then, of course, make the subtle point that the highest
number of taps was when Bobby Kennedy was Attorney General and,
incidentally, that was before the war in Vietnam had headed up. Also
point out the fact that the war period was one where such taps were
particularly necessary and now they will recede even more. The
main point of this discussion, however, is to get across the fact that
it was during the Kennedy Administration and the Johnson Administration
that the FBI was used for survelliance on newsmen and everybody else.

In this respect, if you will look at the chapter in Smith's book on
"Kennedy's Thirteen Greatest Mistakes," dealing with the steel strike
there is a fascinating page in which he tells about how Bobby Kennedy
had FBI agents rout newspapermen out of bed in the middle of the night
and put them under grilling as to what they knew about a possible price
rise by steel companies. This kind of thing, of course, goes far beyond
anything we have attempted in the national security area.

- 2 -

On the matter of Executive Privilege, it should be pointed out
that far from being more restricted we are being more communica-
tive. We never withhold information - all we do is to question under
proper circumstances how the information is to be given and still
maintain the position of separation of power. Here, I would go back
very candidly to the Hiss Case example that I have often used which
nobody but Dean seems to have taken the trouble to read and understand. Basically, what happened in the Case is that Truman, the
day the hearings began, issued an Executive Order prohibiting all
 cooperation by the FBI, the Justice Department and other government
agencies with the investigation. We ran into a total stone wall in a
case in which what was involved was not espionage by one political
party against another but espionage against the nation itself. We
nevertheless were able to conduct the investigation with our own
small staff and break the case open even after the Justice Department
tried to drop it.

Now at this time we have not only cooperated with the Justice Department
in an investigation; we have made our own investigation; and in addition
we have offered to cooperate with the Congress in furnishing information
under proper circumstances. For example, we tried desperately to
get this kind of cooperation during the Hiss Case and got nothing but a
stone wall. The FBI totally refused to talk to us. I think this should
be prepared in a very good op-ed piece and smack it into the Times at
an appropriate time to keep the record straight. Give me a report as
to who this assignment is being given to and what you think of the idea.

WATERGATE SPECIAL PROSECUTION FORCE   DEPARTMENT OF JUSTICE

Memorandum

TO   : Files   DATE: October 18, 1973

FROM : Henry L. Hecht *HLH*   *Fk: Higb, WF*

SUBJECT: Interview of Larry Higby, former Assistant to H. R. Haldeman

On October 5, 1973, Hecht and Horowitz interviewed
Larry Higby who was accompanied by his attorney, Al. Philip Kane.
Horowitz advised Higby of his constitutional rights which Higby
said he understood fully. Higby was advised that we were not
taping the interview but Hecht was taking notes.

Kane reviewed part of the statement of his client from
Higby's interview of July 30, 1973, at this Office. Kane
asserted that Strachan worked for Haldeman in the political
field and that Higby worked on internal matters of administration. Higby met daily with Strachan at 8:15 a.m. to pass on
orders from Haldeman. Higby substantially conceded that he
was a superior to Strachan but he also explained the fact of
his giving out orders from Haldeman as occasioned by the
physical proximity of his office to Haldeman's office. Higby
said that Strachan and he were able to tell when the other
person was on the phone. One example of his hierarchial
relationship with Strachan was that the latter had complained
to Higby that he was often unavailable when Strachan wanted to
send messages to Haldeman.

The Opponent's List

When shown Dean Exhibit 60, Higby said that he recognized
it as the large list of opponents maintained in Joanne Gordon's
office. Gordon occasionally sent around additions to the list
which were retained by Strachan. Higby said that he had no
occasion to refer to this large list and was not certain if
Haldeman referred to it.

2

On one occasion Colson sent a memorandum to Haldeman complaining that friends of the White House were not being invited to White House dinners. Higby thereafter attempted to implement a procedure to assure that the opponent's list and the contact books were regularly checked. When the staff sent memoranda, Higby checked to see if Colson's list had been consulted. Before social invitations were taken into the President, Higby determined whether Butterfield had checked the list with Colson. Higby stated that Haldeman may have known of Colson's complaints because Rosemary Woods did not always cooperate on checking with Colson's list. Haldeman may have spoken to Rosemary Woods on this subject.

After being shown Dean's memorandum of August 16, 1971, headed "Dealing with our political enemies," Higby said he was familiar with the memorandum. At the request of Haldeman in about June 1971, Dean, as well as other staff members under line authority of Haldeman, had sent to Haldeman memoranda concerning what their respective staffs could do to "maximize the President's incumbency." Higby said that Dean's reply was six or seven pages long and listed hundreds of little details. In response to Kane's question as to whether we had this memorandum, Horowitz replied that neither Horowitz nor Hecht had been shown that document or reviewed it. Higby said that one portion of Dean's memorandum mentioned special projects and that another portion might have concerned actions against major Democratic contributors. Higby said that Haldeman contemplated meeting with every line officer such as Colson, Malek, Dean, Chapin, and Butterfield to discuss their respective suggestions. Accordingly, Higby said that he believed that following receipt of the June 1971, memorandum Haldeman and Dean met alone to discuss how the White House could be sure not to favor Democrats and could be sure to pursue Democrats fully if they were already in trouble.

With respect to the August 16, 1971 memorandum itself, Higby said that he "must have seen it". The original probably was returned to Dean by writing Dean's name in the corner. Higby said that he was aware that Dean was responsible for the area of the political enemies project and that he recalled the language of "using the available Federal machinery." Higby attributed the phrase "screwing our enemies" to Strachan. Higby said that he was not certain whether Dean had reviewed the question with "a number of persons possessed with expertise in the field." On the question of "project coordinators" for Dean's project Higby said that he would have suggested Nofziger who, he knew, had been concerned with Huntley's "Big Sky" project in the Summer of 1971.

3

Higby said that one follow-up on this question of maximizing the incumbency came from Malek. Malek proposed a program of "Grantsmanship" in which a congressman who was running for election would announce grants for his district. Malek also had an operation called "government responsiveness effort" in which Federal agencies were instructed particularly to be responsive to inquiries by congressmen who were running for office.

Higby said that Strachan asked Dean to get a small list of names to Haldeman for the project. When Strachan was unsuccessful in getting Dean to act, he asked Higby to do so; and Higby did call Dean. Higby said that his call to Dean on this matter referred back to the August 16, 1971 memo. Dean was responsible for the project in part, because Dean occupied the position of counsel and thus could give more color of independence of the White House. Higby said that his office used a 7-day suspense file and that Dean's memo would have been placed in this file. Higby recalled that Haldeman asked him for the list from Dean.

After being shown the memorandum of September 14, 1971, from Dean to Higby, Higby said that he saw this memo. He was not sure whether Haldeman had stressed that the memo was an "eyes only" matter but Higby recalled it was sensitive. Higby was not sure what the additional materials referred to in the memorandum were.

Higby said that he had reviewed his files which are maintained in Room 522 in the White House and then saw the original of the September 14 memo and a xeroxed copy in Buzhardt's office. On the original copy in the files, Haldeman had written "Go." Higby presumes that this was sent back to Dean.

Higby suggested that the list of 20 names attached to the memorandum of September 9, 1971 could have been the other attachment on the September 14 memorandum. Following the return of Dean's memorandum of September 14, 1971, with the indication of "Go," Higby did ask Strachan about Dean's progress on the harrassment project. Strachan reported that Dean was not doing anything.

4

After being shown Dean Exhibit 52, Higby said that he recalled discussing with Strachan the need to get a list of those who went to the Muskie weekend in Kennebunkport, Maine and it was in reference to this that Strachan produced the "fat cats" memorandum.

Higby said that he recalled that names were continually added to the opponent's list and that he sent the memo labeled Dean Exhibit 51.

Higby said that he discussed with Haldeman Dean's failure to get anything done on the political enemies project, a phrase he used with Strachan, and that Haldeman showed interest in this problem. When Dean did not produce, Higby sent action items to Dean's deputy Fielding.

Chet Huntley

After being shown Dean Exhibit No. 53, Higby said that
he did not recall discussing this memorandum with Strachan.
Higby did discuss with Strachan Nofziger's desire to see that
the Government dragged its feet on a project that Huntley
sponsored. Higby said that the copy of this memorandum at the
White House indicates that it is Dean's handwriting on the top
of the October 26 memorandum stating, "start confidential file."
The notation on the October 19, 1971, memorandum says "agree."

The IRS

Higby said that he discussed the IRS with Haldeman and
understood that Dean would be the liaison. There was concern
that the IRS was not politically responsive, e.g. Democratic
contributors were never being audited. Upon occasion names
were referred to Dean to see if there was a possibility to
initiate audits. Higby said also that if a prominent figure
was having difficulty with the IRS the White House was informed.
As examples Higby cited John Wayne, Billy Graham, and Dr. Riland
(see below)

Higby said that he personally had contacted persons with
the IRS on three occasions. Higby called Roger Barth(whom
Higby knew to have contact with White House)on behalf of
Haldeman to get certain special forms for Haldeman to use to
report his income tax. Second, Higby called Barth to set up
an appointment for Barth to meet with Haldeman. Barth thereafter came to the White House and advised Haldeman on his tax

5

return. (Higby stated that IRS sent over people to help
White House staff with tax returns.) Third, Higby asked
Barth for copies of Higby's own tax returns for the last
5 years in order to compute income averaging.

Higby said that Dean and Haldeman met to discuss
a talking paper that Dean had prepared on the IRS. Haldeman
returned the talking paper to Dean with a notation to the
effect that Dean should follow up on the matter and "see
how things go." Higby said that Haldeman was to meet with
the secretary of the Treasury or the then Commissioner of
IRS, Johnnie Walters, but he was not sure if those meetings
took place.

Higby did discuss with Haldeman Dean's inactivity in
general, and his inactivity in getting the IRS to be responsiv·
to White 'ouse demands. Higby says that such discussion was in
the context of why someone whose name had been passed on to
Dean was not being audited. Dean's typical response was that
the fault lay with the personnel at IRS.

Higby recalled that during the year 1971, he received
three or four requests from Haldeman to "see if Dean can get
an audit on so and so." Higby then called Dean to get the
audit started by passing on Haldeman's order to "see what
could be done." Higby doubted that he placed these items in
the suspense file as they were usually oral requests from
Haldeman.

Higby did recall that Larry O'Brien's name came up with
respect to the fact that he was being paid by a firm of the
Ford Foundation, while serving as DNC Chairman. Higby said
that the information probably came from Colson and there was
the suggestion that the information might be leaked.

     Higby was requested to review his notes of meetings with
Haldeman from 1971 and 1972 for any discussions of tax activity.

     With respect to Billy Graham, Higby said that Dean sent
a memorandum to Higby on which Higby placed a comment, sent
the memorandum to Haldeman; and Haldeman said the matter was
"covered." With respect to John Wayne, Higby said the matter
of the Wayne investigation came to Haldeman's attention and
that Dean may have reported to Higby that it was only a routine

6

matter. With respect to Riland, Higby said that it was
probably Rosemary Woods who brought the matter to Haldeman's
attention. Higby had no knowledge of C. Arnhol Smith.
With respect to Greene of Newsday, Higby said that Haldeman
and Ziegler were disgusted by Greene's hatchet job on Rebozo.

cc:
   Chron
   File - the original
   Frampton
   Hecht
   Horowitz

MEMORANDUM

TO: The Files   DATE: July 3, 1973

FROM: Phil Heymann

SUBJECT: Interview With Howard Hunt

On Friday, June 29, 1973, Neal, Heymann, Vorenberg, Silbert, Glanzer, and Campbell met with Howard Hunt and his attorney, Bill Bittman. In a later session of about twenty minutes to a half-hour, Heymann met alone with Hunt and Bittman.

Jim Vorenberg first asked if Hunt knew anything about the letter from a prisoner at Danbury called Normal Carl McKenzie who claimed to have an important document from Hunt. Hunt explained that McKenzie had seen him reading the ACLU report and had fabricated from there with the ACLU report as his "important document."

Heymann asked to go through the details of the Fielding break-in with Hunt. Asked about the report that four wiretaps (Ellsberg, Sheahan, Tad Szulk, and Beecher) had been involved in the Plumbers operation, Hunt responded that they had ordered none but that he recalled FBI reports which at least indicated a tap on Ellsberg's phone. In particular, there was a call to his psychiatrist saying how relieved he was to have done what he planned to do with the Pentagon Papers. Hunt knew nothing of an alleged picture of Ellsberg's house in Cambridge or a Plumbers document called "Locksmith" -- he said. He denied any memory of discussing the Fielding break-in with Colson on any occasion. Heymann referred to a document sent to Colson by Hunt mentioning this possibility (a break-in) but Hunt did not admit any recollection of it. Pressed on where the money came from for the trip to California, Hunt responded that as far as he knew it came from Krogh to Liddy and that was it. His only recollection of Colson's involvement was a statement, "I don't want to know anything about that" by Colson when Hunt tried to show him the pictures after the trip out to California. Hunt said after one such trip

Chenow had typed a full report prepared by him and Liddy. The
purpose of the Ellsberg operation was described as learning
more about Ellsberg's motivation, particularly in light of
suspicion that he might have an insanity defense available
because of drug use or otherwise.

Neal asked about Hunt's statement that he had spent
several weeks going over available documents after coming on
the job July 6th. In particular, Neal asked for an explanation of the July 7th contact with the CIA to obtain equipment
and disguises. Hunt explained that shortly after going to
work for Mr. Colson, Hunt had learned that a man named De Mott
had called Hunt's employer at Mullin and Co. (Bennett) and
said that he had lots of information bearing on Ted Kennedy
and Chappaquiddick. De Mott was a former employee of Bennett
at the Department of Transportation. When Hunt told Colson
of Bennett's call, Colson asked him to check it out but with
no possible identification of the check with the White House.
Colson suggested trying the CIA. Hunt said that could not be
done on a person-to-person basis; it would require a call from
the White House. Later, about July 20th, either Carl Wagner
or General Cushman's secretary from the CIA called Hunt and
told him to come over where everything would be arranged. On
July 22nd, Hunt saw Cushman, explained his need of a disguise
and "pocket litter" and was told to just tell Wagner what he
needed. A man named "Steve" handled the false documentation.

The disguises obtained on that occasion were used when
Hunt went to see Dita Beard, when he first checked out the
layout of Fielding's office, and in the Fielding break-in and
the Watergate break-ins (where they were used by others).
There is no explanation of why De Mott was reinterviewed after
his Ulasewicz visit.

Neal asked Hunt about a meeting in January or February,
1972, where he introduced Liddy to Colson. Liddy's plans were
stalled to Hunt's knowledge, and Liddy thought he might get
them off the ground by meeting Colson. Hunt arranged the
interview but says that he sat at the rear of a very large
room and did not overhear what was said. On the way out,
according to Hunt, Liddy said that he thought things might
now be under way. It is presumably after this meeting that
Colson called Magruder urging him to speed up his consideration
of Liddy's plans.

- 2 -

Neal pressed very hard on Hunt's claim that he did not
hear what was said at the meeting asking whether this was
possible in light of his interest in the subject, the fact
that Liddy and Colson had never met, and the size of the room.
Hunt insisted it was,

7c

After the prosecution team had met briefly with the Grand
Jury, Heymann met again with Hunt and Bittman to review a
number of other questions. Hunt listed the activities he had
engaged in for the White House: De Mott, Fielding, Dita
Beard, the forged Vietnam cables (for Colson), and Watergate.
He also listed the abortive assignments he had received or
which had fallen through on their own: a planned entry into
McGovern headquarters which fell through when Thomas Gregory
(a spy in, first, Muskie and then McGovern headquarters)
backed out; an assignment from Colson to go into Bremmer's
apartment and find out whether there was any connection between
Bremmer and liberal causes (called off hours later by Colson
after Hunt had urged the difficulty of the task); the Greenspun
affair.

Hunt explained the last as follows. Robert Bennett called
Hunt in and said that he had heard that Greenspun had enough
information on Muskie to sink him. Bennett represented Howard
Hughes' interests in Las Vegas and was calling this to Hunt's
attention because he associated Hunt with Colson. Although
Hunt knew that Colson was in this line of work and that Bennett
expected him to take it to Colson, Hunt claims that he never
told Colson but instead went to Liddy. Later, Hunt was introduced by Bennett to a Ralph Wintee, an ex-FBI man who was
Chief of Security for the Hughes interests. Hunt said more
information was necessary and Wintee said he would check this
out further through Intertel (the private security agency
used by Hughes). Later, Hunt and Liddy arranged a meeting
with Wintee in Los Angeles where Wintee produced a floor plan
of Greenspun's newspaper plant but no further indication as to
what was in Greenspun's safe. The plan was never used and
nothing further was done according to Hunt.

- 3 -

      Hunt was also the courier for information received in
early 1972 from an individual known as "Fat Jack" who was
placed in Muskie headquarters. Hunt passed the information
to Liddy. Heymann inquired about the following list of events,
all of which Hunt said he had nothing to do with: a wiretap
on Ellsberg, Szulk, and Sheahan; the wiretap on Joseph Kraft;
break-ins in the Chilean Embassy; the Daniel Rather burglary;
and the burglary at the NAACP Legal Defense Fund (which
Vorenberg pursued in some detail with Hunt).

cc: Messrs. Cox, Ruth, Neal,
     Merrill, and Bakes

                          - 4 -

Hunt witness file

Files   July 19, 1973

Phil Bakes

E. Howard Hunt

On Monday, July 16, 1973, Heymann, Merrill and Bakes interviewed Hunt.

Hunt does not specifically remember the July 28 memorandum to Colson but has no doubt that he wrote it. There was, he says, a very intense interest in Ellsberg; and he clearly remembers that Ellsberg was indicted about one month before July 28 memorandum. He can't remember whether the "impetus" for Ellsberg "operation" came from Colson, the "covert press man," or Room 16, the Plumbers office of David Young headed by Egil Krogh. He remembers being hired by Colson because of work he could do in (1) general problem of leaks, (2) the Pentagon Papers and Ellsberg and (3) work on matters of national security and origins of Vietnam War. Around the same day he was hired, July 6 or 7, he met Ehrlichman very briefly with Colson and Ehrlichman indicated that he knew about Hunt and his background. Hunt says Ehrlichman and he did not discuss CIA assistance at this time. Hunt says that his CIA background was the decisive factor in his being hired, but did not know that he would be used as a covert operator. Instead, he claims that the impetus for his involvement in covert operations came from his superiors, i.e., Colson. He thought most of his work would be on Vietnam but first realized he would be asked to do covert work when Colson asked him to interview Clifton De Motte about Kennedy.

About 2 or 3 days after being hired, Colson requested him to interview De Motte. Hunt said he'd need a disguise and Colson said he'd take care of it through CIA. Hunt says there was no discussion of CIA assistance for Hunt in his presence before this time. Shortly thereafter, Hunt got a call from Karl Wagner of CIA, General Cushman's assistant, and an appointment was arranged for Hunt to see Cushman.

Hunt was detailed to the Plumbers group and he may have
had Colson informed of his work on the Plumbers. He remembers
a very intense concern and dislike or resentment of Ellsberg
on the part of Colson, Krogh, Young, and he and Liddy shared
this feeling. He remembers that Young, Krogh and Liddy used
to have very technical legal discussions concerning the indictment itself and he recalls Mardian's name arising in these
discussions. He can't accurately and precisely recall the
substance of those conversations because he is not a lawyer
and did not fully understand the details. But he clearly
remembers that Liddy was very displeased with the indictment
itself on legal grounds, and there was concern among all of
them that the trial itself might be very damaging to the
Nixon administration because Ellsberg would make a martyr of
himself. There was also concern that, since the FBI investigation had learned Ellsberg had experimented once with LSD,
he might be dabbling in other "mind-expanding drugs," and
might go berserk at the trial and embarrass the government.
It was this fear which prompted Hunt to recommend that Ellsberg
not be tried, but Liddy told him that the case had gone too
far to stop it now. In this connection, there was a belief
that a public relations attack should be mounted against
Ellsberg in order to destroy his public image, especially
with the election year coming up.

Hunt was reading daily FBI reports concerning the Ellsberg
investigation and the concern was that Ellsberg would embarrass
the President at the trial. Hunt believes these reports were
being transmitted from Mardian to Krogh and perhaps Young.
He specifically and clearly remembers what he firmly believes
was a wiretap report, in which Ellsberg was talking to Dr. Fielding
and told Fielding that he felt better now that he had released
Pentagon Papers. He knows the name was Fielding. He also
remembers that there was an FBI attempt to interview Dr. Fielding.
In reading these FBI files, Hunt was trying to determine whether
Ellsberg was prosecutable, i.e., whether Ellsberg would embarrass
the President or the government at trial.

He vaguely recollects some rumor he heard at that time
that the Soviet Embassy received a set of the Pentagon Papers
and also that Ellsberg had kept company with a Swedish girl
and a West Indian girl. Hunt said he speculated then that
perhaps Ellsberg was involved with others who were foreigners
and who might be using Ellsberg to their own advantage. He
also speculated that perhaps Ellsberg was working with others
from U.S.A. like Halperin and Gelb.

2

His first introduction to Plumbers was when Joan Hall, Colson's secretary, called him and told him to go see Krogh and Krogh and he attended a meeting with representatives of DOD, DOS, CIA, FBI on the subject of government leaks. A day or two later he saw Colson and Colson told him that a new fellow named Liddy had started at EOB 16. He went down there and said it looked like a war room and had charts on wall with names of investigations or current matters and one of these was on Daniel Ellsberg. David Young maintained these charts.

Hunt presumes that if the material in 7-28-71 Colson memo was secured, it would be used for "covert press" operations, i.e., leaks or planted stories and also that it might be used at Ellsberg's trial, at least for cross-examination purposes. He says Colson was the "covert pressman" at White House and generally remembers that Colson "hated" Ellsberg and wanted to "get the son of a bitch." They never thought Ellsberg was working as a foreign agent, but at the early stages he himself might have felt that perhaps Ellsberg was involved with others.

He remembers meeting with Doctor Malloy prior to the August 23 reconnaisance trip to California, and there was no mention of Ellsberg being involved with any foreign governments. He does remember asking Malloy what a psychiatrist does with an inactive file. He asked Malloy this in order to determine if Fielding still had file on Ellsberg. Malloy said it depended on the doctor. Hunt says that the original idea for a CIA profile was his and Young fouled through on it as a good idea. Hunt believed that a psychological assessment would help him (Hunt) figure out how to "get" Ellsberg. Everyone in EOB was talking about Ellsberg in enemy terms and a psychological assessment would help him "work against Ellsberg." For example, he wanted to see if Ellsberg was psychologically vulnerable, and a sexually disturbed, an exhibitionist, a drug user, etc. He thought that if damaging stuff could be found it could be given out to press and therefore undercut any possibility that Ellsberg would be admired by the American people. Hunt said he, of course, wouldn't give the material out himself, but that it would go through Colson and Ehrlichman.

The first trip to L.A. for reconnaisance was done under their true names and registered in hotel under true names. On this trip they took pictures outside the building and also inside the office itself after Hunt introduced himself as a doctor to a cleaning lady in Spanish. He used the tobacco pouch camera for this.

3

On their return, Liddy and he wrote a detailed report
or memorandum describing precisely how the job would be done,
that it would be a break-in, and the plan described a contingency means of escape if in fact they were discovered while
inside of Fielding's office. They recommended Labor Day
weekend as the best time to do it because everyone would be
gone at that time and the memo included a budget of around
two to three thousand dollars. The memo was directed to
Krogh and Young, typed by Kathleen Chenow, and later they
had a meeting in EOB 16 conference room where he and Liddy
talked to Krogh and Young about the memo and the planned
break-in. They discussed it precisely and specifically in
terms of a break-in, and mentioned the Cubans.

After the meeting, Liddy said they had the go-ahead and
Liddy said to have Barker advance the money to fly Barker,
Diego and Martinez to L.A. and he'd be reimbursed in cash in
L.A. Hunt remembers waiting in EOB 16 with Liddy. Their
bags were packed and a short time before their plane was to
take off, Krogh hurried in, said "here's the money, get going"
and handed Liddy an envelope. Hunt and Liddy immediately
left for Dulles Airport.

After job was finished, Liddy called Krogh from hotel,
and they caught the first plane East to get out of L.A. and
landed in New York Saturday night, stayed at the Pierre Hotel
and then flew to D.C. on a shuttle the next day, which was
Sunday. Monday morning, Hunt went to the White House and
early in morning brought the pictures of the file drawers
to Colson to show them to him and tell him what he was doing
over the weekend. When Colson came in Hunt said: "I have
photos about our activities this weekend." Colson said: "I
don't want to see them and Colson went into his office.

Hunt would stop in Colson's office most everyday to drop
off memos to Colson and to pick up memos from Colson. He
remembers sending a memo to Colson regarding the "California
job" which was probably mentioned in the context of his complaint that David Young was not a "doer" and EOB 16 operation
did not move fast enough on things. He believes he sent this
memo after Fielding break-in. He assumes Colson knew about
the Fielding break-in before it occurred because of Colson's
conversations with Krogh.

Hunt's files with all his carbons of memos he wrote to
Colson was in his third floor EOB office safe but are not part
of material recovered from the safe and now in hands of prosecutors. He believes someone destroyed that file.

cc: Files   P. Bakes
     Chron   G. Frampton
     P. Heymann   P. Rient
     B. Merrill

-WSPF CHRONOLOGICAL REPORT-

COMPLETE   COLLECTION ------------ TO 05/07/74

HUNT **ON EHRLICHMAN**

CHRONOLOGICAL REPORT   PAGE   1

DATE OF EVENT: NA 000000

    HUNT HAD NO CONTACT WITH STRACHAN. HE KNOWS THE NAME BECAUSE
STRACHAN WAS EMPLOYED AT THE WHITE HOUSE WHILE HUNT WAS A PART-TIME
WHITE HOUSE EMPLOYEE. LIDDY MENTIONED STRACHAN AS A MAN WHO WORKED
EITHER FOR EHRLICHMAN OR HALDEMAN BUT NOT IN CONNECTION WITH THE
ACTIVITIES HUNT WAS UNDERTAKING WITH LIDDY. HUNT GUESSES THAT
STRACHAN SCREENED CORRESPONDENCE, POLICY PAPERS AND THINGS LIKE THAT
FOR HALDEMAN.
    SOURCE: HUNT, HOWARD MARCH 29, 1973
    SOURCE-REF: DCGJ ███████
    RECORD CONTROL NO: 76-2945

DATE OF EVENT: MAY 1, 1970-JULY 6, 1971 700501

    AFTER RETIREMENT FROM CIA, HUNT TOOK POSITION FOR FIRM
MAINTAINING CLOSE RELATIONSHIP WITH CIA. SOME MONTHS AFTER JOINING
THAT FIRM, HUNT APPROACHED BY COLSON TO BECOME CONSULTANT TO
EXECUTIVE OFFICE OF THE PRESIDENT. HUNT CHOSEN BECAUSE OF HIS
INTELLIGENCE BACKGROUND. HIS EMPLOY- MENT APPROVED BY EHRLICHMAN AND
HALDEMAN.
    SOURCE: HUNT, HOWARD SEPTEMBER 24, 1973 WASHINGTON, DC
    SOURCE-REF: SELECT COMMITTEE TRANSCRIPT P. 7577-7578
    RECORD CONTROL NO: 73-11803

DATE OF EVENT: JUNE-JULY 1971 710600

    COLSON OFFERED HUNT WHITE HOUSE POSITION, INDICATING SPECIAL
INTEREST IN HUNT'S INVESTIGATIVE BACKGROUND AND HUNT'S INVOLVEMENT IN
POLITICAL ACTION OPERATION. HUNT ALSO INTERVIEWED BY EHRLICHMAN.
    SOURCE: HUNT, HOWARD SEPTEMBER 24, 1973 WASHINGTON,DC
    SOURCE-REF: SELECT COMMITTEE TRANSCRIPT P. 7586-7587
    RECORD CONTROL NO: 73-11822

DATE OF EVENT: JUNE 13-20, 1971-UNKNOWN 710613

    HUNT RECEIVED NO INFORMATION FROM MARDIAN AT TIME MARDIAN WAS
HEAD OF   INTERN████AL SECURITY DIVISION. HUNT SAW INFORMATION CROSS
HUNT'S DESK THAT HAD BEEN SENT BY MARDIAN TO OTHERS WITHIN THE
PLUMBERS UNIT AND OUTSIDE. INFORMATION WAS ADDRESSED PRINCIPALLY TO
KROGH AND EHRLICHMAN, INFORMATION RELATED MAINLY TO ELLSBERG AFFAIR,
AND PROBLEMS OF LEAKS.
    SOURCE: HUNT, HOWARD SEPTEMBER 25, 1973 WASHINGTON, DC
    SOURCE-REF: SELECT COMMITTEE TRANSCRIPT P. 7868
    RECORD CONTROL NO: 73-12292

CHRONOLOGICAL REPORT   PAGE   2

DATE OF EVENT: JULY 6, 1971—MARCH 29, 1972 710706

   HUNT PUT IN CONTACT WITH CUSHMAN RATHER THAN HELMS. HUNT/COLSON
CONVERSATION REGARDING ACQUISITION OF TECHNICAL MATERIAL. CUSHMAN'S
ASSISTANT, WAGNER, CALLED HUNT SHORTLY THEREAFTER TO SCHEDULE MEETING
WITH CUSHMAN. THIS WAS IN RESPONSE TO PHONE CALL CUSHMAN HAD RECEIVED
FROM EHRLICHMAN. HUNT CANNOT REMEMBER SUBSTANCE OF HUNT/CUSHMAN
CONVERSATION.
   SOURCE: HUNT, HOWARD SEPTEMBER 24, 1973 WASHINGTON, DC
   SOURCE—REF: SELECT COMMITTEE TRANSCRIPT P. 7751-53
   RECORD CONTROL NO: 73-11961

DATE OF EVENT: JULY 6, 1971 710706

   ON JULY 6, 1971, COLSON HIRED HUNT. HUNT HAD MET COLSON AND
EXPRESSED HIS DISSATISFACTION WITH WORKING FOR MULLEN COMPANY, AND
COLSON INDICATED THERE MIGHT BE AN OPENING AT THE WHITE HOUSE. THEY
HAD A NUMBER OF DISCUSSIONS OVER HIS EMPLOYMENT, CULMINATING IN THE
HIRING OF HUNT AS A CONSULTANT FOR THE WHITE HOUSE. COLSON TOOK HUNT
TO MEET EHRLICHMAN (ON JULY 5 OR 6, 1971) WHO READ HIS RESUME. HUNT
THINKS THAT COLSON SAID, "JOHN, THIS IS HOWARD HUNT OF WHOM WE HAVE
BEEN TALKING, AND I BROUGHT HIM OVER TO MEET YOU." EHRLICHMAN WAS
AWARE OF HIS CIA BACKGROUND. COLSON INDICATED THAT EHRLICHMAN WAS
THE ONE WHO WOULD MAKE THE FINAL DECISION.
   SOURCE: HUNT, HOWARD ████████████████
   SOURCE—REF: ████████████████████████████
   RECORD CONTROL NO: 76-297

   HUNT MET EHRLICHMAN ONLY ONCE IN HIS LIFE, IN JUNE ON THE DAY
WHEN HUNT'S (EMPLOYMENT) BEGAN AT THE WHITE HOUSE. HUNT NEVER HAD ANY
OTHER CONVERSATION WITH EHRLICHMAN.
      COMMENTS: HUNT WAS TAKEN ON AS A CONSULTANT AT THE WHITE
      HOUSE ON JULY 6, 1971, ████ORDEMANN DECEMBER 8, 1973
   SOURCE: HUNT, HOWARD MAY 2, 1973
   SOURCE—REF: DCGJ ████
   RECORD CONTROL NO: 76-2548

DATE OF EVENT: AFTER JULY 6, 1971 710707

   THE OPERATIONAL DIRECTION OF THE (ROOM 16) GROUP (HUNT, YOUNG,
LIDDY) WAS PROVIDED BY KROGH WHO WAS EHRLICHMAN'S PRINCIPAL DEPUTY.
KROGH TOLD LIDDY AND HUNT THAT THERE WAS AN INTENSE AMOUNT OF
INTEREST IN ELLSBERG (AT THE WHITE HOUSE). HUNT'S INITIAL WORK ON
THE PENTAGON PAPERS INVOLVED THOROUGHLY FAMILIARIZING HIMSELF WITH
THOSE PORTIONS WHICH HAD APPEARED IN THE PRESS.
   SOURCE: HUNT, HOWARD MAY 2, 1973
   SOURCE—REF: DCGJ ██████
   RECORD CONTROL NO: 76-2550

CHRONOLOGICAL REPORT   PAGE   3

AFTER ELLSBERG WAS INDICTED THE WHITE HOUSE RECEIVED ON A DAILY
BASIS REPORTS FROM THE FBI AND OTHER LAW ENFORCEMENT AGENCIES.   THERE
WERE WEEKLY SUMMARIES AND COMPILATIONS, SOME ELABORATELY INDEXED.
HUNT HAD ACCESS TO THIS MATERIAL ON A ROUTINE BASIS AND BECAME
FAMILIAR WITH THE CASE ITSELF.   SOME OF THE FBI REPORTS DEALT AT
GREAT LENGTH WITH (ELLSBERG'S) BACKGROUND, ALLEGATIONS CONCERNING HIS

MORAL CHARACTER, SOME RATHER BIZARR SEXUAL PRACTICES, A VERY UNUSUAL
LIFE STYLE.   A PICTURE OF A MAN BEGAN TO EMERGE THAT EVOKED INTEREST
ON THE PART OF CERTAIN WHITE HOUSE OFFICIALS, INCLUDING KROGH, YOUNG,
LIDDY, AND TO THE EXTENT THAT HE WAS A WHITE HOUSE OFFICIAL, HUNT.
AT THAT TIME THERE WAS SOME CONCERN ABOUT THE APPROPIRATENESS OF
PROSECUTING ELLSBERG AND HIS ASSOCIATES AND HUNT SHARED THAT CONCERN.
HE FELT THAT (ELLSBERG) WOULD PROBABLY BECOME A MARTYR.   THE
GOVERNMENT WAS CONTEMPLATING A MAJOR PROSECUTION, WHICH IN FACT HAS
EVOLVED, AND KROGH, WHO WAS A LAWYER, SUGGESTED IT WOULD BE WELL IF A
JUDGEMENT COULD BE MADE ON ELLSBERG'S SANITY AND PROSECUTABILITY. TO
THAT END EXTRACTS WERE MADE OF MATERIAL DEALING WITH ELLSBERG'S
PECULIAR BACKGROUND.   THEY READ THESE EXCERPTS AND CONCLUDED THAT THE
BEST SOURCE ON ELLSBERG WOULD BE WHATEVER FILES (FIELDING) HAD
MAINTAINED WHILE ELLSBERG WAS UNDER ANALYSIS.   HUNT DOESN'T KNOW WHO
MENTIONED THE POSSIBILITY OF A BAG JOB ON (FIELDING'S) OFFICE FIRST,
BUT IT BECAME A TOPIC OF LOW-KEY CONVERSATION AROUND THE OFFICE.   A
BAG JOB IS A TERM USED BY THE FBI AND CIA MEANING AN ENTRY OPERATION.
HUNT WAS FAIRLY NEW TO THE WHITE HOUSE AND SAID IF THEY WANTED THE
MATERIALS WHY COULDN'T THEY SIMPLY GET THE FBI TO PROCURE IT.   LIDDY
(SAID) THAT IN THE LAST FIVE OR SIX YEARS, UNDER HOOVER'S AEGIS, THE
FBI HAD CEASED TRAINING AGENTS IN ENTRY OPERATIONS AND THE CADRE
MAINTAINED FOR THIS TYPE OF OPERATION WAS NO LONGER IN EXISTENCE.
HUNT SUGGESTED THE SECRET SERVICE AND LIDDY REPLIED THAT THE WHITE
HOUSE DID NOT HAVE SUFFICIENT CONFIDENCE IN THE SECRET SERVICE TO
ENTRUST THEM WITH THIS SORT OF TASK.
          COMMENTS: ELLSBERG WAS INDICTED ON JUNE 28, 1971, BUT HUNT
          DID NOT GO TO THE WHITE HOUSE UNTIL JULY 6, 1971. ORDEMANN
          DECEMBER 10, 1973
     SOURCE: HUNT, HOWARD MAY 2, 1973
     SOURCE-REF: DCGJ ████████
     RECORD CONTROL NO: 76-2551

DATE OF EVENT: PRIOR TO JULY 22, 1971 710721

     ON JULY 22, 1971 HUNT MET WITH GENERAL CUSHMAN. PRIOR TO THIS
MEETING, HUNT WAS EITHER TOLD BY COLSON'S SECRETARY THAT HE WOULD BE
HEARING FROM CUSHMAN, OR HUNT RECEIVED A CALL FROM CUSHMAN'S
EXECUTIVE ASSISTANT, CARL WAGNER.   DURING THE COURSE OF HIS MEETING,
IT WAS APPARENT THAT CUSHMAN HAD CONVERSED WITH EHRLICHMAN PRIOR TO
THE MEETING. CUSHMAN MENTIONED THAT EHRLICHMAN HAD CALLED.   HUNT TOLD
CUSHMAN OF HIS NEED FOR CERTAIN ITEMS OF PHYSICAL DISGUISE.   HUNT
EXPLAINED THAT IT WAS A ONE-TIME INTERVIEW OF PERSON WHOSE IDEOLOGY
WAS QUESTIONABLE AND IT WAS A HIGHLY SENSITIVE AND CONFIDENTIAL
MISSION.
     SOURCE: HUNT, HOWARD ████████
     SOURCE-REF: ██████████████████
     RECORD CONTROL NO: 76-306

CHRONOLOGICAL REPORT   PAGE   4

DATE OF EVENT: JULY 28, 1971 710728

AFTER THE JULY 28, 1971 MEMO, LIDDY AND HUNT MADE A PROPOSAL TO
KROGH AND YOUNG THAT FIELDING'S OFFICE BE ENTERED ILLEGALLY TO FIND
ELLSBERG'S FILE. KROGH AND YOUNG RESPONDED THAT A FEASIBILITY-
VULNERABILITY STUDY SHOULD BE MADE FIRST. HUNT DOES NOT KNOW IF THIS
WAS DISCUSSED WITH EHRLICHMAN. KROGH DID NOT IMMEDIATELY APPROVE THE
PLAN, BUT SOME TIME LATER CAME BACK AND SAID IT WAS ALL RIGHT TO GO
AHEAD.
   SOURCE: HUNT, HOWARD ███████████
   SOURCE-REF: ████████████████
   RECORD CONTROL NO: 76-313

DATE OF EVENT: AUGUST 24, 1971 710824

MEMO DATED AUGUST 24, 1971 FROM EHRLICHMAN TO COLSON (EXHIBIT 2)
REFERS TO AN "ATTACHED MEMORANDUM BY HUNT THAT SHOULD BE USEFUL IN
CONNECTION WITH THE RECENT REQUEST THAT WE GET SOMETHING OUT ON
ELLSBERG." HANDWRITTEN ON THE MEMO IS "DELIVER TO TERHORST 8/26."
HUNT STATES THAT THE HANDWRITING IS NOT COLSON'S. HUNT HAD A
CONVERSATION WITH COLSON ABOUT GETTING TOGETHER WITH JERRY TERHORST
IN CONNECTION WITH THE BOUDIN ARTICLE THAT HUNT WAS WRITING.
TERHORST IS A NEWSPAPER REPORTER.
   SOURCE: HUNT, HOWARD ███████████
   SOURCE-REF: ████████████████
   RECORD CONTROL NO: 76-312

DATE OF EVENT: AUGUST 26, 1971 710826

IN AUGUST 26, 1971 MEMO FROM YOUNG TO EHRLICHMAN, SUBJECT:
"STATUS OF INFORMATION WHICH CAN BE FED INTO CONGRESSIONAL
INVESTIGATION ON PENTAGON PAPERS AFFAIR." EHRLICHMAN REFERS TO THE
SPEED WITH WHICH ELLSBERG'S IMAGE SHOULD BE ALTERED. ALSO REFERENCE
TO HUNT/LIDDY PROJECT NUMBER ONE AND HOW ITS PRODUCTS COULD BE USED
IN CONJUNCTION WITH CONGRESSIONAL INVESTIGATION. A BUCHANAN MEMO
CAUTIONING ATTACKING ELLS- BERG THROUGH THE PRESS IS REFERRED TO.
HUNT DOES NOT KNOW OF THE BUCHANAN MEMO NOR WAS HE EVER AWARE THAT
BUCHANAN HAD BEEN SOLICITED TO TAKE ON ELLSBERG INVESTIGATION BUT HAD
DECLINED.
   SOURCE: HUNT, HOWARD SEPTEMBER 25, 1973 WASHINGTON, DC
   SOURCE-REF: SELECT COMMITTEE TRANSCRIPT P. 7947-48
   RECORD CONTROL NO: 73-12105

DATE OF EVENT: AUGUST 27, 1971 710827

AUGUST 27, 1971, MEMO FROM EHRLICHMAN TO COLSON ENTITLED "HUNT-
LIDDY SPECIAL PROJECT NO. 1" (EXHIBIT NO. 81) CONCERNING HOW
MATERIALS FROM SPECIAL PROJECT NO. 1 SHOULD BE USED. HUNT ASSUMES
SPECIAL PROJECT NO. 1 TO BE FIELDING ENTRY, SINCE HUNT AND LIDDY HAD
JUST RETURNED FROM RECONNAISSANCE OF FIELDING'S OFFICE.
   SOURCE: HUNT, HOWARD SEPTEMBER 24, 1973 WASHINGTON, DC
   SOURCE-REF: SELECT COMMITTEE TRANSCRIPT P. 7609-7610
   RECORD CONTROL NO: 73-11907

CHRONOLOGICAL REPORT   PAGE   5

DATE OF EVENT: AUGUST 27—SEPTEMBER 3, 1971 710827

    HUNT ASSUMES THAT EHRLICHMAN ALSO CONSIDERED REPORT SINCE
FINDINGS WERE THAT SECURE ENTRY COULD BE MADE.
  SOURCE: HUNT, HOWARD SEPTEMBER 25, 1973 WASHINGTON, DC
  SOURCE—REF: SELECT COMMITTEE TRANSCRIPT P. 7871—72
  RECORD CONTROL NO: 73—12217

DATE OF EVENT: SEPTEMBER 3, 1971—UNKNOWN 710903

    AFTER ELLSBERG BREAKIN, LIDDY AND HUNT SUBMITTED REPORT TO
KROGH. HUNT DOES NOT KNOW IF REPORT WENT TO EHRLICHMAN.
  SOURCE: HUNT, HOWARD SEPTEMBER 24, 1973 WASHINGTON, DC
  SOURCE—REF: SELECT COMMITTEE TRANSCRIPT P. 7739
  RECORD CONTROL NO: 73—11922

DATE OF EVENT: ON OR AFTER SEPTEMBER 5, 1971 710905

    HUNT HAS NO KNOWLEDGE THAT ANYONE ELSE (OTHER THAN KROGH AND
YOUNG) WAS ADVISED OF THE (FIELDING) OPERATION AFTER IT WAS
COMPLETED. ON ONE OCCASION HE ATTEMPTED TO DISCUSS IT WITH COLSON,
BUT WAS UNSUCCESSFUL. HE ENTERED COLSON'S OFFICE ON MONDAY OR
TUESDAY, THE DAY FOLLOWING THEIR (HUNT AND LIDDY'S) RETURN TO
WASHINGTON (THE DAY FOLLOWING SEPTEMBER 4 OR 5) AND WAITED UNTIL
COLSON CAME IN. HUNT HAD A PHOTOGRAPH OF THE RIFLED SAFE IN HIS
HAND. WHEN COLSON CAME IN HUNT SAID HE HAD SOMETHING THAT MIGHT BE
OF INTEREST TO COLSON HAVING TO DO WITH HUNT'S ACTIVITIES THIS PAST
WEEKEND. COLSON SAID HE DIDN'T WANT TO HEAR ANYTHING ABOUT THEM AND
WENT ON INTO HIS OFFICE. HUNT DID NOT HAVE A CONVERSATION WITH
EHRLICHMAN CONCERNING THIS BREAK—IN AND NEVER HEARD OF LIDDY HAVING
ONE. EHRLICHMAN NEVER DIRECTED HUNT PERSONALLY NOT TO COMMIT SUCH AN
ACT AGAIN. HUNT IS NOT INNOCENT OF WHAT EHRLICHMAN HAS SAID IN THE
NEWSPAPER. HE HAS BEEN STUDYING IT ALL MORNING. HE CONSTRUES WHAT
HE HAS READ ABOUT EHRLICHMAN'S REFUSAL TO PARTICIPATE IN ANOTHER
OPERATION IN THE TERMS THAT HE PROBABLY SIMPLY TOLD KROGH TO FORGET
ABOUT IT, DON'T DO SOMETHING LIKE THE FIELDING ENTRY AGAIN. HUNT
DIDN'T SPEAK TO EHRLICHMAN ABOUT THIS. JACKSON HAD NO KNOWLEDGE OF
THIS OPERATION.
  SOURCE: HUNT, HOWARD MAY 2, 1973
  SOURCE—REF: DCGJ ███████████
  RECORD CONTROL NO: 76—2581

DATE OF EVENT: APRIL 1972 720400

    LIDDY TOLD HUNT THAT FOREIGN MONEY COMING INTO DNC. LIDDY
RECEIVED INFORMATION FROM GOVERNMENT AGENCY, BUT DID NOT SPECIFY
WHICH AGENCY. HUNT BELIEVED THAT INFORMATION CAME FROM FBI, BUT HAD
NO INDEPENDENT COROBORATION, DID NOT MAKE INQUIRY. THERE WERE TWO
CHANNELS OF REPORTING FROM FBI TO WHITE HOUSE. ONE WAS HOOVER
CHANNEL TO EHRLICHMAN AND KROGH; SECOND WAS CHANNEL TO LIDDY FROM
MARDIAN AND FROM FORMER ASSOCIATES OF LIDDY AT FBI. HUNT TOLD LIDDY
FOREIGN MONIES FROM CUBA.
  SOURCE: HUNT, HOWARD SEPTEMBER 24, 1973 WASHINGTON, DC
  SOURCE—REF: SELECT COMMITTEE TRANSCRIPT P. 7698—7700
  RECORD CONTROL NO: 73—12075

CHRONOLOGICAL REPORT   PAGE   6

DATE OF EVENT: JUNE 17, 1972-UNKNOWN 720617

DURING WATERGATE INVESTIGATION HUNT ADVISED GOVERNMENT OF TWO
NOTEBOOKS MISSING FROM HUNT'S WHITE HOUSE SAFE. OTHER ITEMS MISSING
FROM SAFE THAT HUNT DID NOT INFORM GOVERNMENT OF WERE: ITEMS THAT
DEAN AND EHRLICHMAN GAVE GRAY; FOLDER CONTAINING CHRONOLOGICAL NOTES
HUNT MADE FROM CONVERSATIONS WITH LIDDY ABOUT GEMSTONE PLAN; SURGICAL
GLOVES.
   SOURCE: HUNT, HOWARD SEPTEMBER 25, 1973 WASHINGTON, DC
   SOURCE-REF: SELECT COMMITTEE TRANSCRIPT P. 7912-7914
   RECORD CONTROL NO: 73-12057

DATE OF EVENT: NOVEMBER, 1972 721100

IN NOVEMBER, 1972 TELEPHONE CONVERSATION WITH HUNT, COLSON TRIED
TO CLOSE HUNT OFF AS HUNT BEGAN TO OPEN WATERGATE DOOR IN
CONVERSATION. HUNT CONSIDERS COLSON'S REPEATED CLOSING OF DOOR SELF-
SERVING, CONSIDERED IT SELF-SERVING DURING COURSE OF CONVERSATION.
HUNT HAD NO IDEA HE WAS BEING SET UP. BEFORE TODAY, HUNT TOLD
MEMBERS OF COMMIT- TEE'S STAFF THAT HE BELIEVED HE WAS BEING SET UP
BY COLSON. IN CONVERSATION WITH COLSON, HUNT REFERRED TO "THE GUYS
WHO ARE REALLY RESPONSIBLE". HUNT MEANT MITCHELL, MAGRUDER, DEAN;
NOT EHRLICHMAN, WHO APPROVED HUNT'S EMPLOYMENT INITIALLY; NOT COLSON
BECAUSE HUNT WAS ADDRESSING COLSON. HUNT WANTED MONEY FOR LEGAL FEES
FOR DEFENSE.
   SOURCE: HUNT, HOWARD SEPTEMBER 25, 1973 WASHINGTON, DC
   SOURCE-REF: SELECT COMMITTEE TRANSCRIPT P. 7880-83
   RECORD CONTROL NO: 73-12231

WHITE HOUSE TAPES
(WATERGATE SPECIAL PROSECUTION FORCE FILE SEGMENT)

TRANSCRIPT OF CONVERSATION*
May 5, 1971
9:35–10:15 AM
Participants: President Nixon, H.R. Haldeman

Conversation No.: 491-014

SANITIZED COPY
Transcript of a recording of a meeting between the president and H. R. Haldeman on May 5, 1971, in the Oval office from 9:55 a.m. to ?
SANITIZED COPY

Nixon, Haldeman Meeting, May 5, 1971, 9:55 a.m. to ?

Music

HALDEMAN: . . . Mitchell in today?

PRESIDENT: Picked up them all right.

HALDEMAN: Yesterday.

PRESIDENT: How's he's do—great? What was the situation today? Did they have any more actions?

HALDEMAN: Uh, there's gonna be a, they're going to . . .

PRESIDENT: March on the Capitol?

HALDEMAN: Uh, . . . be at the Congress at noon when the thing . . .

PRESIDENT: (*Unintelligible*)

HALDEMAN: Well, that's the plan, uh, whether they do it never can quite sure. But they, they've followed the plan pretty much up to now. It's (*Tape Noise*) the theory is they're gonna . . .

---

*This transcript was prepared during the Watergate investigations by officials involved in those inquiries and was located among the Records of the Watergate Special Prosecution Force (Record Group 460) in the custody of the National Archives. The National Archives has not attempted to correct or improve the transcript.

PRESIDENT: Demonstrate up there, at the Capitol?

HALDEMAN: From twelve noon until the People's Peace Treaty is signed, you see, they're demanding that the Congress sign this. This is this peace treaty that they've signed with North Vietnam. (*Laughs*)

PRESIDENT: Hmm. (*Tape Noise*)

HALDEMAN: They've got no (*Tape Noise*) special permit. Best estimate is 2,000 demonstrators. Trouble very likely.

PRESIDENT: Good.

HALDEMAN: They've planned two meetings tonight to plan demon . . .

PRESIDENT: That was last night.

HALDEMAN: . . . to plan demonstration activities. We don't, I haven't had a late reading on, on that. (*Tape Noise*) They just granted the federal employees' permit, after all. They're, before they'd left the stand they couldn't get a base for an injunction apparently, so they didn't get . . .

PRESIDENT: All right.

HALDEMAN: . . . one. So . . .

PRESIDENT: (*Unintelligible*) out here today?

HALDEMAN: . . . that's—in and out here today. There'll also be the students of Shelton College . . .

PRESIDENT: Where the hell is that?

HALDEMAN: . . . on the, on the sidewalk in front of the White House. It's in New Jersey. They're then demonstrating in favor of the war. Heh. They're gonna, heh, they're gonna be on our side of the street and the other people are gonna be in the park.

PRESIDENT: That's fine. Probably a new college of some sort.

HALDEMAN: It's—I'm afraid it has somethin' to do with Carl McIntyre.

PRESIDENT: Oh, be suspicious, yeah.

HALDEMAN: Yeah, McIntyre's having a victory thing next Saturday. Sunday. This coming Sunday. Victory by the Fourth of July. It's, it's a . . .

PRESIDENT: Can we get in there with those Government employees. Is there any way to?

HALDEMAN: I guess you can't.

PRESIDENT: I'd sure get a lot of pictures and everything.

HALDEMAN: Sure, are.

PRESIDENT: You know, just get guys with, with news cam—, news things, so that they don't . . .

HALDEMAN: No, they have a plan to do anything (*Tape Noise*).

PRESIDENT: We sure have good intelligence, don't we?

HALDEMAN: Heh, heh.

PRESIDENT: (*Tape Noise*) Don't know, don't know what's been happenin'.

HALDEMAN: They, can, uh, picked up . . .

PRESIDENT: (*Unintelligible*)

HALDEMAN: . . . in a sweep yesterday, they arrested Abbie Hoffman. They got Dr. Spock, as you know, the day before. They got Al Hubbard, the, uh, veterans' guy that, that had . . . pos—the black who had posed as a . . .

PRESIDENT: Yeah.

HALDEMAN: . . . Army, as an Air Force captain and then turns out not to have been a captain.

PRESIDENT: Sargeant is he a, is he one of 'em?

HALDEMAN: He—they arrested him.

PRESIDENT: I'll be damned.

HALDEMAN: So they scooped up, they, they got all these people in these nets, you know. Th-th-they'd taken one in a fish net. They also discovered, much to their horror, they got two or three *Washington Star* reporters and a couple of *Life* reporters.

PRESIDENT: And the *Washington Post* reporter I noticed has wrote an article this morning.

HALDEMAN: Well . . .

PRESIDENT: They let 'em out. In case . . .

HALDEMAN: Oh yeah.

PRESIDENT: Let out. Check that.

HALDEMAN: Well, the *Life* reporter, *Life* reporters didn't go out. They were delighted to be in. I think there's a *Life* photographer in there, too. So they're getting a lot of pictures (*Tape Noise*) instance, well, we had a big—did you read about the nude dance. That was one the big things in the stockade is that a lot, men and women took off all their clothes and did a, did a, uh, some sortta (*Tape Noise*) operation.

PRESIDENT: Well, the reporters certainly—they've got to damned well understand that if they're in there and they're told to move and don't, they're gonna get picked up too.

HALDEMAN: That's the sce- . . .

PRESIDENT: I noticed the *Post* is, is screamin' about it. Nicolas Von Hoffman, the nut.

HALDEMAN: Oh, I know.

PRESIDENT: Jesus Christ. Why do they carry that son-of-a-bitch?

HALDEMAN: Well now, because he says the kind of things they like to say. He says it with total irresponsibility.

PRESIDENT: That's right. They had a reporter in here said he was a Vietnam Marine veteran, an associate editor of the society page of the damned thing.

HALDEMAN: Is that right.

PRESIDENT: (*Tape Noise*) They had him all over the place.

HALDEMAN: But . . .

PRESIDENT: They let him out just as soon as they found out who they were, right?

HALDEMAN: Should have missed (*Tape Noise*).

PRESIDENT: (*Tape Noise*) The whole business about repression and so forth, don't you think it's, on that side—inci-incidentally, has anybody thought, you know, I, I, I mean it may be that you guys went ahead (*Unintelligible*), maybe it occurred to you that, to, to put some of these guys in sp—why doesn't somebody introduce a resolution. If you can't get a resolution, perhaps circularize a letter supporting the President on the handling of the demonstrations. You know we—or something like that. Or if you want to, praising the chief of police, or praising the Attorney General. See what I mean? Couldn't you (*Unintelligible*)—have any speeches been made yet supporting us or on this, uh? . . .

HALDEMAN: Yeah. (*Tape Noise*) The speeches don't do any damn . . .

PRESIDENT: (*Unintelligible*) do

HALDEMAN: No.

PRESIDENT: Maybe a resolution.

HALDEMAN: A resolution or a letter might.

PRESIDENT: Maybe, maybe it isn't worth the bother. I just thought that it might, . . .

HALDEMAN: . . . It might get them thinking about it.

PRESIDENT: That's my point.

HALDEMAN: Right.

PRESIDENT: I think really that— . . .

HALDEMAN: Even Sam Ervin got up and went, went through a big pretension of praising the, the, the whole operation, Justice, the Administration, the police. Everybody heard.

PRESIDENT: That right?

HALDEMAN: Yeah, he's the great defender of constitutional liberties and all . . .

PRESIDENT: Yeah.

HALDEMAN: . . . that stuff.

PRESIDENT: Wh—what'd he praise?

HALDEMAN: The handling of the demonstration overall, the whole, you, you know, there was a very— (*Tape Noise*) it was a sweeping praise type.

PRESIDENT: Yeah. Well, . . .

HALDEMAN: It all went . . .

PRESIDENT: One thing we, uh, one thing I was gonna say, th-th-th-th, Pat went down to the Senate wives and (*Tape Noise*) ate at a luncheon and she said they were all (*Tape Noise*) on our side, left and right. She said Mrs. Ervin, Mrs. Stennis came through the line and she said, "You know, the President has saved our country."

HALDEMAN: (*Unintelligible*)

PRESIDENT: They really think this is good. I mean, we may have more goin' for us than we think here, Bob. Yah. We shouldn't be frightened about it. That's my point. Let me put it this way, let me put it this way: I know, I know what it is that you're gonna run into on this. You're gonna run into people that—the overreaction thing and all that sort of thing. My point, you're gonna get accustomed to that. No way that you're gonna avoid it.

HALDEMAN: That's right.

PRESIDENT: So therefore, play it hard. Play it responsibly, but play it hard and don't back off from it. Now, they can—you see, they're all, they'll all think back to the San Jose thing, you know, and forgetting that San Jose was fine except for the God damned silly speech, you know. Covering that getaway from it, we got out (*Unintelligible*) home free. We had it all on our side.

HALDEMAN: Nobody's raised that analogy and I think—there's been no . . .

PRESIDENT: Well.

HALDEMAN: . . . thought of backing off.

PRESIDENT: Don't back.

HALDEMAN: It's been all, the whole line has been . . .

PRESIDENT: . . . firm.

HALDEMAN: Stay firm.

PRESIDENT: Stay firm and get credit for it. That's my point. See, I don't want to make an accident out of it. I don't want to be doing on the basis, well, we're sorta sitting here embattled and doing the best we can. I think the idea here is to lead a noble—you see maybe, you, it may be that we're setting an example, Bob, for, uh, for universities, for other cities, and so forth and so on. Right? (*Tape Noise*) Let 'em look here. These people try somethin', bust 'em. (*Unintelligible Noise*) general attitude of your people.

HALDEMAN: Yeah.

PRESIDENT: Convinced?

HALDEMAN: I think . . .

PRESIDENT: . . . we ought to go forward.

HALDEMAN: Yeah. We, we stay with that all the way. There's no—

PRESIDENT: In other words, let's be proud of what we're doing, not that we're—I think Ziegler is 'cause I . . .

HALDEMAN: I think there're some folks out there to tear down the Vietcong flags today.

PRESIDENT: Good.

HALDEMAN: There'll be some confrontation on that in the, in the Hill thing. That's, we're, we're trying for that. Would be good. And, uh, (*Tape Noise*) of the Vietcong flags. There's been some play. *Newsweek* ran some big color stuff. I think they, I don't think realized that they were . . .

PRESIDENT: Yeah.

HALDEMAN: . . . doing them a disservice because I think the *Newsweek* coverage hurt the demonstra—we have them—, cause they showed this guerilla theatre stuff with their faces all painted up and, and Vietcong flags and this kinda thing in color. Uh, very vivid color pictures.

PRESIDENT: Um-hmm.

HALDEMAN: So . . .

PRESIDENT: Hmm. You have 'em on that (*Unintelligible*)?

HALDEMAN: Yeah, (*Unintelligible*) Uh, . . .

PRESIDENT: (*Tape Noise*) take a look. (*Unintelligible; Tape Noise*)

HALDEMAN: That was the first of last week's stuff. We don't have any this week, uh.

PRESIDENT: Don't you think they'll have quite a bit this week too?

HALDEMAN: Oh sure. They'll have to.

PRESIDENT: Even though it came out . . .

HALDEMAN: I would guess th-th-th, what *Time, Newsweek* covers this week would probably be Chief Wilson. (*Tape Noise*) Unless somethin' happens the latter part the week, some new story, but, uh, they have to go pretty much with what's in by Wednesday. (*Unintelligible; Tape Noise*) decision and I would think that might be the, might be the story. Maybe not.

PRESIDENT: (*Tape Noise; Unintelligible*) an awfully good job.

[*Pause. Tape Noise*]

HALDEMAN: Heh-heh. Damn Colson thing.

PRESIDENT: He do something else?

HALDEMAN: Yeah. Uh, Muskie sent those oranges down to the veterans in the, the group on Saturday I mean.

PRESIDENT: Yeah.

HALDEMAN: He didn't, he didn't go down himself, but he's sent oranges.

PRESIDENT: Colson ordered some oranges for him?

HALDEMAN: Colson sent oranges down yesterday.

(*Laughter*)

HALDEMAN: (*Laughing*) From Muskie.

PRESIDENT: Is it out?

HALDEMAN: I don't know whether it's out yet or not. They'll get it out.

(*Laughter*)

PRESIDENT: (*Laughing*) He just ordered 'em.

HALDEMAN: (*Laughing*) Yeah. He's got an awful lot of cases of oranges at the— I don't know how the hell he does that stuff, but he—it's good, you know, he's been around the District here so long, he has a lot of contacts and, he, he, as a local guy he can get stuff done here, but—and he's got no—and he's—gonna get caught at some of these things.

PRESIDENT: (*Unintelligible*) admit it.

HALDEMAN: Well he has, he has been caught.

PRESIDENT: It's all right?

HALDEMAN: But, he's, he's got a lot done that he hasn't been caught at and, uh, he, he gets those guys, you know, something like that going. (*Tape Noise*) of course this is uh—we got some stuff that he doesn't know anything about too through, uh, . . .

PRESIDENT: Huston?

HALDEMAN: No, through Chapin's crew and, and Ron Walker and the advance men we got, we got, uh,—see our plant's in the, . . .

PRESIDENT: What do you do?

HALDEMAN: . . . in the (*Unintelligible*), . . .

PRESIDENT: (*Unintelligible*)?

HALDEMAN: . . . and some of our—guess you've gotta—what we've got is a, is a guy that nobody, none of us knows except Dwight—

PRESIDENT: Um-hum.

HALDEMAN: Who is a, uh, and, and, who is just completely removed. There's no contact at all. Who has a mobilized a crew of about—I don't what it is. He's, he's starting to build it now. We're gonna use it for the campaign next year.

PRESIDENT: (*Unintelligible*)

HALDEMAN: Yeah.

PRESIDENT: Are they really any good?

HALDEMAN: In fact this guy's a real conspirator-type who, who can sorta . . .

PRESIDENT: Like Huston then?

HALDEMAN: Thug type guy, no, his, he's a stronger guy than Huston. Huston is a, is a—stay in back room.

PRESIDENT: Yeah.

HALDEMAN: This is the kinda guy can get out and tear things up.

PRESIDENT: What do they what do they do with, uh, do they just, uh, . . .

HALDEMAN: They get in and—they were the ones that did the, the Nixon signs, for instance, when Muskie was in New Hampshire.

PRESIDENT: Oh did they?

HALDEMAN: And, uh . . .

PRESIDENT: Everybody thought that was great.

HALDEMAN: They, you know—things of that sort. They, there some of that, and then they're, they're the, they're gonna stir up some of this Vietcong flag business as Colson's gonna do it through hardhats and legionnaires. What Colson's gonna do on it, and what I suggested he do, and I think that they can get a, away with this, do it with the Teamsters. Just ask them to dig up those, their eight thugs.

PRESIDENT: Yeah.

HALDEMAN: Just call, call, uh, what's his name.

PRESIDENT: Fitzsimmons.

HALDEMAN: Is trying to get—play our game anyway. Is just, just tell Fitzsimmons . . .

PRESIDENT: They, they've got guys who'll go in and knock their heads off.

HALDEMAN: Sure. Murderers. Guys that really, you know, that's what they really do. Like the Steelworkers have and—except we can't deal with the Steelworkers at the moment.

PRESIDENT: No.

HALDEMAN: We can deal with the Teamsters. And they, you know, . . .

PRESIDENT: Yeah.

HALDEMAN: . . . it's the regular strikebusters-types and all that and they (*Tape Noise*) types and this and then they're gonna beat the shit out of some of these people. And, uh, and hope they really hurt 'em. You know, I mean go in with some real—and smash some noses. (*Tape Noise*) some pretty good fights.

PRESIDENT: I take it you can (*Unintelligible*) picture of the guy in the *Post* that the reporter (*Tape Noise; Unintelligible*) back injured and all.

HALDEMAN: I didn't see that. I must admit Buchanan said in his summary—it's obvious the *Post* is going for a Pulitzer prize on their coverage of the thing or something because they're just spilling it . . .

PRESIDENT: Yeah.

HALDEMAN: . . . by the ton with all these (*Tape Noise*) picture stories and everything else.

PRESIDENT: (*Tape Noise*) just don't want to overplay it. They'll just get, the country'll just get a belly full of these people.

HALDEMAN: (*Tape Noise*) yeah.

PRESIDENT: (*Tape Noise*) How did it handle it last night?

HALDEMAN: (*Tape Noise*) had, had some good footage of the big mob out on the Justice Department thing and, and . . .

PRESIDENT: Some close-up?

HALDEMAN: . . . (*Tape Noise; Unintelligible*) Fortunately, they're all just really bad lookin' people. There's no, there's no, uh, semblance of respectability.

PRESIDENT: (*Unintelligible*) on this. There was some veterans either.

HALDEMAN: No. I didn't. There's not. Rennie Davis has, has been spokesman and, and he's as good for us and he's a convicted conspirator and, uh, (*Tape Noise*) discredited.

PRESIDENT: Hmm.

HALDEMAN: I think getting Abbie Hoffman and, and this John—the other—they got . . .

PRESIDENT: (*Unintelligible*)

HALDEMAN: . . . another of the Chicago Seven guys. Uh, (*Tape Noise*) amounts to anybody, but they got him. But that sorta takes . . .

PRESIDENT: Aren't the Chicago Seven all Jews? Davis' a Jew, you know.

HALDEMAN: I don't think Davis is.

PRESIDENT: Hoffman, Hoffman's a Jew.

HALDEMAN: Abbie Hoffman is and that's so

PRESIDENT: (*Tape Noise*) John Luzens or Leubens or . . .

HALDEMAN: (*Unintelligible*)

PRESIDENT: . . . the other one they got.

HALDEMAN: (*Tape Noise*) is.

PRESIDENT: About half of these are Jews.

HALDEMAN: (*Tape Noise*) they got one shot of a policeman clubbing a guy. (*Tape Noise*) it doesn't do us any good; but they're, you know, you can't avoid that. They're bound to get one somewhere along the line. Most of it was very much the other way.

PRESIDENT: (*Tape Noise*) inevitable, Bob. How the hell do you expect the poor God damned policemen—

HALDEMAN: They've got to do it and I think people probably recognize that and there wasn't, th—we don't have the thing like in Chicago, if you remember . . .

PRESIDENT: Hmm.

HALDEMAN: . . . that it w-; it was a totally different kind of thing. There the policemen were just, they were really ruthless. They had good reason to be.

PRESIDENT: Sure.

HALDEMAN: But these cops don't come . . .

PRESIDENT: And even then, and you'd better remember, (*Unintelligible*) the public supported.

HALDEMAN: Then . . .

PRESIDENT: The public supported. We were, we thought the public was not on their side, the public was on their side.

HALDEMAN: With the cops all the way.

PRESIDENT: You bet your life. And at this time, the public's gonna be on the side of—I think the speeches Congressmen and Senators give—well for me, they won't come but for me, but they could come out for Wilson, couldn't they?

HALDEMAN: Yeah.

PRESIDENT: And, uh . . .

HALDEMAN: I (*Unintelligible*) get 'em, you know, somehow. (*Unintelligible*)

PRESIDENT: Yeah. Okay.

HALDEMAN: This is the thing on the, uh (*Tape Noise*) employees for peace thing. They, uh, (*Tape Noise*) over five hundred people on, and, uh, five hundred permits so they've got to do it under law.

PRESIDENT: For five hundred?

HALDEMAN: Yeah. Court (*Tape Noise*) can't get an injunction because we have to show that it represents a clear threat to security of the White House.

PRESIDENT: Forget it. Forget it.

HALDEMAN: And this doesn't, so—

PRESIDENT: Just don't pay any attention to that. We can't (*Unintelligible; Tape Noise*) I'll be over there. That's no problem. There's one place Chapin screwed (*Unintelligible*) is getting (*Unintelligible*) God damn it if there are any State Department people there. And I bet I—I'd just like to know. (*Unintelligible*) if they're HEW, to hell with it, that's all.

HALDEMAN: What it's generally gonna be is all the activities at HEW (*Unintelligible*) College people are gonna start this Thursday and go through Saturday. So they aren't gonna be out there today.

PRESIDENT: Oh boy. (*Unintelligible*) All those preacher types without their (*Unintelligible*).

HALDEMAN: (*Tape Noise*) Immediate victory in Vietnam, (*Tape Noise*) a military victory in Vietnam.

(*Pause; Background Noise*)

PRESIDENT: (*Unintelligible*) on Saturdays.

HALDEMAN: Not really.

PRESIDENT: No, I mean it changed. I mean the attitudes change. Two weeks ago everybody was worried about the   **RESTRICTED-"D"**   and so forth and this week they're on the side of the cops. See what I mean? People, people there.

HALDEMAN: Why . . .

PRESIDENT: (*Tape Noise*) They weren't too much on the side of the veterans either.

HALDEMAN: That same thing as that poll of ours which shows the shift back to 48–40 approval of Vietnam, the President's handling of Vietnam.

PRESIDENT: Yeah, uh-huh. (*Tape Noise*)

HALDEMAN: You know, it shifted just the other way, just that week of the veterans' . . .

PRESIDENT: That the vets . . .

HALDEMAN: . . . demonstration.

PRESIDENT: That's, that's awful.

HALDEMAN: (*Tape Noise*) That's really what happened. It sure shows that, the effect of, uh, of the television barrage and was just all it can be. That's the only way they knew anything . . .

PRESIDENT: (*Unintelligible*)

HALDEMAN: . . . about the vets 'cause the papers didn't give 'em that much, that much of a play outside of, out . . .

PRESIDENT: Outside of Washington. That's right. That was a hell of a television show.

HALDEMAN: Yeah. (*Tape Noise*) and that was before, that article was taken before they threw the medals over the fence which was the most effective appearing (*Tape Noise*) on T.V.

PRESIDENT: (*Tape Noise*) Oh, yeah. The lunge around the—the drop. That's right. (*Tape Noise; Unintelligible*) to show it the day before the medal (*Unintelligible; Tape Noise*) The poll indicates that was . . .

HALDEMAN: Well, our poll indicated they were two-to-one against the, the demonstrations before this happens, before any s-s-, of this stuff. (*Tape Noise*) I think you're gonna have to, have to—it's more than two. It's almost three.

PRESIDENT: Um-hum.

HALDEMAN: (*Tape Noise*) I think more now. (*Tape Noise; Unintelligible*) . . .

PRESIDENT: Does know anybody gonna be around today. Did you look—I hope they're keepin' the flags up. (*Tape Noise*) That ought to be a national—cause I suggested to the Legion and VFW should have that was a national project. Defend the flags. Anybody that would tear it down—you know, that's, that's part of their drill anyway. Wouldn't that be a good idea? (*Tape Noise; Unintelligible*) Just gonna be the end. These people got a flag upside down, you know, burning it and so forth. The hell with it. You let 'em start on that—

HALDEMAN: Um-hum.

PRESIDENT: . . . (*Tape Noise; Unintelligible*)

HALDEMAN: Yeah.

PRESIDENT: (*Tape Noise*) cool Spring. It's, it's never . . .

HALDEMAN: It's supposed to warm up now today.

PRESIDENT: Is it?

HALDEMAN: And, uh— (*Tape Noise*) it's up to seventy.

PRESIDENT: I wonder if the Congress, uh, today will really get a belly full of these people.

HALDEMAN: Well, I hope so.

PRESIDENT: If they could just move in into the halls of Congress somewhere, have they thought of that.

HALDEMAN: (*Tape Noise*) Congressional Police are probably gonna try and—the Capitol Police will turn 'em over to us (*Tape Noise*) know what their plan is, least did as of, first thing this morning.

PRESIDENT: (*Tape Noise*) Did that thing about that, that story about the bomb under the bridge ever get out?

HALDEMAN: It turned out that it wasn't a live bomb, just a fake, (*Tape Noise*) went down and tested it and it was no (*Unintelligible*).

PRESIDENT: Just a fake. (*Unintelligible; Tape Noise*)

HALDEMAN: (*Unintelligible; Tape Noise*) see these people run. And they (*Tape Noise*) don't even know what they . . . Really impatient.

HALDEMAN: On that— (*Tape Noise*) Yeah. Their technique was theoretically non-violent, but transient stuff they don't regard as violent. (*Tape Noise*) God Almighty.

PRESIDENT: That's the worst thing I ever heard of. (*Tape Noises*) It's—he said the Congress is mad again. (*Unintelligible*)—well, they're not—this is really their first run at the Congress en masse. They didn't have a their, th-, last week, they just went—a few of 'em.

HALDEMAN: That's right. They didn't have any demonstration—well, the veterans' thing, uh . . .

PRESIDENT: No, the majority of the pain though was at, was after the veterans' thing.

HALDEMAN: Yeah and that was small groups.

PRESIDENT: That was small groups.

HALDEMAN: Sort of marauding bands. I don't know, (*Tape Noise*) they may decided to crank it up.

PRESIDENT: (*Tape Noise*) supposed to be the big day. Anyway, that's what I have on the calendar. May 5th.

HALDEMAN: Oh yeah. This was gonna be the big day.

PRESIDENT: (*Tape Noise*) situation reporters have been scooped up alright. (*Unintelligible*)

HALDEMAN: (*Tape Noise*) say that again.

PRESIDENT: Reporters would be in—it's the logical thing. They're there to cover—

HALDEMAN: They just circle them, you know, which has been the tactic they've used. They get a group, order them to disperse. If they don't then they circle 'em and arrest everybody inside the circle. And they, the thing is they'd move 'em fast onto the vans, and uh, (*Tape Noise*)—they, now they've changed that tactic now. They won't any more press because the press has got all these lit—they'll show the badge of course. Unless he wants to be arrested and some of them probably wanted to be. Some of them probably purposely didn't show . . .

PRESIDENT: Sure.

HALDEMAN: . . . their badge.

PRESIDENT: They wanted to be—so they can get all the (*Unintelligible*) for the Pulitzer Prize.

HALDEMAN:

PRESIDENT:

HALDEMAN: **RESTRICTED-"D"**

PRESIDENT:

HALDEMAN:

PRESIDENT:

HALDEMAN:

PRESIDENT:

HALDEMAN:

PRESIDENT: **RESTRICTED-"D"**

HALDEMAN:

PRESIDENT:

HALDEMAN:

PRESIDENT: on these meetings today (*Unintelligible; now Background Noises*).

HALDEMAN: Yeah, uh,—

PRESIDENT: Incidentally—

HALDEMAN:

PRESIDENT: **RESTRICTED-"D"**

HALDEMAN:

PRESIDENT: **RESTRICTED-"D"**   what else is, uh,—with regard to the (*Unintelligible*).

HALDEMAN: Saw him for a few minutes.

PRESIDENT: (*Unintelligible*) Left for New York. (*Unintelligible*)

HALDEMAN: Mitchell. He wanted to catch up. That, that was just your weekly get-together that we had scheduled for yesterday.

PRESIDENT: Well let's leave it up to him. He might have some (*Unintelligible*)

HALDEMAN: Okay.

PRESIDENT: I know, uh,—

(*Pause; Writing Sounds*)

HALDEMAN: Uh (*Tape Noise*) Pete Peterson. And then this group that's goin' into this Business Council thing.

PRESIDENT: (*Tape Noise; Unintelligible*) head of the Business Council, Bob? Connally? Who else?

HALDEMAN: Connally, Shultz, Stans, the Vice President and Pete Peterson.

PRESIDENT: (*Tape Noise*) what—I can't see that there's much I can say to them. They all have their own speeches to make. (*Tape Noise*) I think it gives them—the Business Council's importance too much . . .

HALDEMAN: Yeah.

PRESIDENT: . . . for me to spend that much time to talk to (*Unintelligible*)

HALDEMAN: It was just a, you know . . .

PRESIDENT: Well, wh-what's the line, er, has been what the line is? Connally's?

HALDEMAN: (*Tape Noise*) to get Connally in and, and still not necessar—we don't have to do the Lockheed thing.

PRESIDENT: (*Tape Noise*) I figure the Lockheed thing doesn't have to be done us. I don't have to anyway, (*Unintelligible*)

HALDEMAN: No, I know.

PRESIDENT: I want Connally to do it in Treasury.

HALDEMAN: Well, I could get Connally in to get it done.

(*Pause*)

HALDEMAN: (*Tape Noise; Unintelligible*) That oughta do it, anyway, stay out of it, that's one more day's st . . .

PRESIDENT: I . . .

HALDEMAN: . . . I don't think a leak gonna do that much good. He said he'd announce Tuesday or Wednesday.

PRESIDENT: Yeah. I think you could have done the thing—I, I think you're right. I think the leaks thing is worth—they have most anything (*Unintelligible*) the papers have had it anyway. It's a bunch a—

HALDEMAN: It's . . .

PRESIDENT and HALDEMAN talk at once.

HALDEMAN: . . . day after day. One more day isn't gonna make that much difference probably.

PRESIDENT: (*Tape Noise*) Peterson want to talk about to talk about the Japan trade thing? Does this—does he say he doesn't know about the day that, uh . . .

HALDEMAN: (*Tape Noise*) He's at a critical stage. Needs to consult prior to taking any further action.

PRESIDENT: Yeah. (*Tape Noise*) because we don't have anybody in the cabinet that's sorta guiding him. So he gets down to me all the time. See it's (*Tape Noise*) he's like Kissinger who sets his own (*Tape Noise*) understanding of the whole thing. So, so (*Tape Noise*) kinda the area he's in. Well, we used to have Flanigan—Flanigan's the one to stick with.

HALDEMAN: Okay.

PRESIDENT: Flanigan's better.

HALDEMAN: We'll try and do these this morning and keep the afternoon clear then.

PRESIDENT: (*Tape Noise; Unintelligible*) Peterson on two important things—I, I don't think he's a hell of a lot of value, so, uh,—if Connally wants to come over, any time. (*Tape Noise*) I think would probably just as soon not come today. He's busy with his (*Tape Noise*).

HALDEMAN: Yeah. There's, there's no pressure on . . .

PRESIDENT: I'll meet with Mitchell. I think if possible I'd let him, I'd let him ride today. You could do it tomorrow. Why don't you have him come—could have one at 10:30 and one at 11.

(*Background Noise During Next Segment*)

PRESIDENT: Okay. Huh?

PRESIDENT
or
HALDEMAN: (*Unintelligible*) Connally. Connally if he wants to come see me.

HALDEMAN: Can you get him in.

PRESIDENT: Yeah.

HALDEMAN: . . . (*Unintelligible*)

(End of Background Noise)

PRESIDENT: Boy it's really a clear day.

HALDEMAN: Yeah.

PRESIDENT: On the agriculture thing—do I speak outside?

HALDEMAN: No.

PRESIDENT: To the dinner or . . .

HALDEMAN: No, you, you . . .

PRESIDENT: What do I do then?

HALDEMAN: You—you go over to the Agriculture Department on a Friday morning.

PRESIDENT: Oh *(Unintelligible)*

HALDEMAN: Seminar that you just open. And then they have greetings from Henry Kissinger or somebody, you know, and that. Uh, . . .

PRESIDENT: But what do I have to—

PRESIDENT
and
HALDEMAN: Both talk at once

PRESIDENT: . . . Expect a speech then? Do I have to give something?

HALDEMAN: Remarks. Just, just . . .

PRESIDENT: What in the hell is out there? I don't have to go out there today, do I?

HALDEMAN: That's something—I don't know what that is, no *(Unintelligible)*.

(Background Noise During Next Segment)

PRESIDENT: Hold the door. Now if God damn it, I can, I don't want to *(Unintelligible, Background Noise)*, Bob. We went through this before.

HALDEMAN: No, this is, this *(Unintelligible)*. This is the, the, uh,—

(End of Background Noise)

PRESIDENT: What is it, just a "during each Administration, men are chosen top civil servants (*Unintelligible*)" (*Tape Noise*) not going to comment upon it.

HALDEMAN: This is the one where you don't . . .

PRESIDENT: I don't want to say a word. Now . . .

HALDEMAN: You've never done the ceremonies.

PRESIDENT: I'll do the ceremony. Just leave . . .

HALDEMAN: We're only doing just (*Unintelligible*) . . .

PRESIDENT: (*Unintelligible*) introduce you to the Chairman and (*Unintelligible*). Then the boys will want, "You might wish to comment." "No, no, no, no, no, no, no, I'm not gonna c-,"—see I don't want to a speech about these men. I don't want to do it. They can send it over for your signature to the heads of (*Tape Noise; Unintelligible*) by the appropriate Department heads. That's—

HALDEMAN: Well, nothing good.

PRESIDENT: Sure. Now, then. Oh, with regard to this thing here in August, uh,

HALDEMAN: (*Unintelligible*) presentation

PRESIDENT: Of the, of the just presenting the awards. And get the God damned people out, you know. I mean, I don't want the, you know, the reporters chewin' their gum and waiting for me to say something profound.

HALDEMAN: Well there's nothing to say that's . . .

PRESIDENT: You know really it isn't going to me lose anyway, Bob. Just present the awards. Very nice picture story. That's all. And then, and tell 'em there's not going to be any comments. If, if the reporters—let's let Ollie take a picture. Can we do that this time? I mean, you have so many coming in of, of the press pool.

HALDEMAN: You don't have to say anything. There's no, you know, uh—

PRESIDENT: Okay. We'll go over it tomorrow. Good, this is (*Unintelligible*). Maybe (*Unintelligible*).

(*Door closes. End of conversation. Eight counter units of background noise until end of tape.*)

WHITE HOUSE TAPES
(WATERGATE SPECIAL PROSECUTION FORCE FILE SEGMENT)

TRANSCRIPT OF CONVERSATION*
JULY 6, 1971
11:47 AM–12:45 PM
PARTICIPANTS: PRESIDENT NIXON, JOHN N. MITCHELL,
JOHN D. EHRLICHMAN, H.R. HALDEMAN

Conversation No.: 538-015
Nixon, Mitchell, Haldeman and Ehrlichman—July 6, 1971

NIXON: Uh, I wanted to, uh, check with you before you had left. Because you won't be back for a week. And—

MITCHELL: It'll, it'll be, be, well, it's not quite two weeks. But it's close to it. The 24th, I'll be back.

NIXON: But with regard to, uh, where we stand. I'll be in California through the 19th, or the 20th, I guess is that it?—Are we still doing that thing

HALDEMAN: It says here . . .

NIXON: . . . Senator?

HALDEMAN: The 20th.

NIXON: Well, we'll come right back from there, I guess, right, then we'd come back and uh, uh, the uh, uh, have you talked to John about this Ells—this, uh—not Ellsberg thing.

MITCHELL: Cook.

NIXON: The, the Mathias thing. The rest of the papers.

SEVERAL UNIDENTIFIED SPEAKERS: No, I have not, I don't know I haven't. I know—uh, Mardian—Mardian (*Unintelligible*)

---

*This transcript was prepared during the Watergate investigations by officials involved in those inquiries and was located among the Records of the Watergate Special Prosecution Force (Record Group 460) in the custody of the National Archives. The National Archives has not attempted to correct or improve the transcript.

MITCHELL: And there's to be a meeting with Mathias the 8th—I don't know why he postponed it so long—with Mardian and people from DOD, I guess that's it. State's not involved—to get into this. Mathias is playing a little cat and mouse game—wouldn't see them before the 8th to get into the background of how they got them from Ellsberg, what they are and get them returned.

NIXON: Well, the problem that we have on those is not that, these, these are papers from the NSC, is that correct? Y'see—that's what I'm concerned about. These are papers—that's why State should be in on it. These are papers that involves memorandas apparently that Rogers is supposed to have written to the NSC, or to me or to somebody.

MITCHELL: They are they are the Nixon papers. As far as I know he has not described them.

HALDEMAN: How did they get—

NIXON: How did they get out of the NSC file, that's my point. And, and, and then, are we—that's the, that's the investigation that's got to be given the highest priority immediately now.

HALDEMAN: . . . they don't necessarily.

NIXON: Now here's—

HALDEMAN: . . . could have come out of an NSC file, the NSC could have got you've gotta, got a Defense file, out of a State file—or out of an NSC file—

MITCHELL: Aw come on, bullshit.

NIXON: Sure. Rogers sent papers to me. I'm not sure that Defense would have them.

HALDEMAN: No, but then State would.

NIXON: Fine, fine, all right. States, that's my point. State's got to get in on it. Henry's—you gotta check Lynn and, uh, this fellow Cwok—what's his name? Is that his name?

MITCHELL: Cook.

NIXON: Cook. He was there right? Is he one that had access to this stuff?

HALDEMAN: He had access to the Vietnam studies in the—uh,

NIXON: Yeah.

MITCHELL: (*Unintelligible*)

HALDEMAN: . . . since '69 when at State. Yeah.

EHRLICHMAN: I don't think we really know what—we don't know what they are.

(*Unintelligible*)

MITCHELL: No. The only information I have and it's what, apparently, he told Mel Laird and it was the fact that they were Nixon papers.

EHRLICHMAN: And that they came from Ellsberg?

MITCHELL: Yes. Ells—Ellsberg.

NIXON: Ellsberg.

MITCHELL: Ellsberg. That's correct.

EHRLICHMAN: But that's all you can tell me.

MITCHELL: Well, as I say, he—

NIXON: Well, in any event, when you say Nixon papers—Are these papers—not apparently from me, if, uh, or, or are they?

MITCHELL: No. I understood—

NIXON: I don't see how they could be—

MITCHELL: —that they were—

NIXON: . . . because I, I've scared Henry within an inch of his life from the time he's been here. He's never going to get anything from me out on anything.

EHRLICHMAN: Well, I gather these are to or from you—one or the other. And—

NIXON: It wouldn't be from me. They're not from me, John, because they're written from Henry. You know what I mean. The NSC—that's the way it's done.

MITCHELL: I, I understood it as being during the Nixon Administration.

NIXON: Correct.

MITCHELL: That's as much information as I have on it.

NIXON: We'll know in a couple of days.

MITCHELL: The 8th's—

NIXON: If he makes good on it. But in any case, if Ellsberg's sources are contemporary.

MITCHELL: I, I believe that.

NIXON: And if they're—and the main point I would to get at when I've got—I think we've got to get at the conspiracy angle here. Uh, Ellsberg is not a lone operator. Ellsberg is a, he's a,—I don't know who's in it. Maybe Lynn is in it. Maybe Cook is in it. Uh. I'm not speaking just to the New York Times—I understand they're going to do something about Sheehan—whatever his name is. That's uh, but, but he's uh, he's a party once removed. But we have got to get at the people . . .

MITCHELL: (*Unintelligible*)

NIXON: . . . who are conspirators in it—because that's one thing we find the public supports—the public want, the people they want Ells, Ellsberg prosecuted probably because of his, because they, they understand, that threat. They may not want a newspaper—they maybe want a newspaper to publish it, but they don't want, they don't want a guy to steal it. That's the, that's the general thing that I see from everything that I've been able to pick up here—

MITCHELL: We've had a crew—

NIXON: I think if we could get a, the conspiracy thing—Now, the other thing, John. I think it's, I think we need cooperation from Hoover, uh, in terms of, uh— This has to be tried in the, in the papers, in the newspapers, you understand what I mean? Let me say that there is, uh, the, uh, maybe, I don't mean Ellsberg, Ellsberg now has already been indicted, or has he?—No.

MITCHELL: Yes. He's under indictment.

NIXON: —been charged—

MITCHELL: No, he's indicted. He's—been indicted by a grand jury.

NIXON: Yeah, yeah. I see. Indicted. Well, the point is that, that, uh, as far as the others are concerned, the way really, to get the conspiracy out is to get it out through papers, through Congressional sources, through, uh, newspapers and so forth and so on, and smoke them out that way. Uh, it's the only we were, we were able to crack the Hiss case and the Bentley case. In other words, we could, and then, we didn't have the cooperation of the government. They were fighting us, but we God damn well (*Unintelligible*) got it out. And in this instance, these fellows have all put themselves above the law and, uh, including apparently, including two or three of Henry's staff and by God we're going to go after 'em because there's just too much stuff in there now that I don't want another one of his boys to leak it out. That's why,—I, John, you cannot assume that Henry's staff didn't do this. Now, I've had Haig in here right now and Haig says he couldn't believe Lynn did anything. Lynn has left. Now he's over working for Richardson. I'd get him in and I'd question him. Did you do this? And I'd polygraph him. I think we've got to do that for Lynn. I think you've got to do it to—for Cook. Because we've got to find out whether people currently in, who, who, Jesus he's still in the government. Now, Richardson isn't going to like it, but I, I don't know how, what else we can, we can do to, to get at this thing. Uh, the uh, think, the Ellsberg prosecution—it's a—you've got a pretty good man on it, have you? Who's that?

MITCHELL: Well, it's under Mardian's department and—we've got . . .

NIXON: Is that Mardian?

MITCHELL: . . . and we've got some of the better people . . .

NIXON: Good, well

MITCHELL: . . . working on it. A fell by the name of Vincent. They've, we've been—we've had a crew working over the weekend with DOD on this conspiracy concept . . .

NIXON: Have you?

MITCHELL: . . . that we put together.

NIXON: How, what kind of cooperation are you getting from them, John? Is it—

MITCHELL: DOD?

NIXON: Yeah.

MITCHELL: Good . . .

NIXON: Now, Laird . . .

MITCHELL: . . . as, as, far as, as far as we can tell.

NIXON: is Laird?

HALDEMAN: It's Buzhardt

NIXON: y'see, ya see, ya see, Laird's gone, but Laird sat in here as you recall and said he had all this thing—that he thought it was a conspiracy and so forth but they've got a much bigger outfit working on this than Edgar Hoover has.

MITCHELL: I know they have. But I want to tell you, Mr. President—after Mel Laird said that that day, I asked Buzhardt over the next day and they weren't even close to it. They had Cook and Ellsberg—those are the only two . . .

NIXON: Is that right?

MITCHELL: . . . two they had.

NIXON: they are? Just bulling?

MITCHELL: But, uh, they are, of course, these obvious leaks that go back into the Halperins, or the or Larry Lynn or the rest of them and that's what they've been working on over the weekend and I'll have a briefing on that today.

NIXON: John, would you like—do you think it would be well to put, uh, to put uh, for you to put some—oh, maybe that isn't the place for it. Maybe the place for it's up in a committee of Congress. Let Ichord and his bear cats go after it. Uh, what I'm getting at is, that, uh, you've got the Ellsberg case. I, I'm not so interested in getting out and indicting people and then having our mouths shut. I'm more interested in frankly, getting the story out, see the point? That's even on the Ellsberg thing. I'm not so sure that I'd would. That I'd want him tried, convicted—we had to do that because he's admitted—but as long as we can, uh—

MITCHELL: Well, uh, we have Ellsberg back into some of our domestic Communists.

NIXON: Have you?

MITCHELL: Yes.

NIXON: You really have?

MITCHELL: Yup.

NIXON: Domestic Communists—now, that's that's great. That's the kind of thing we need.

MITCHELL: That's right. And we're putting the story together. He's been, attended meetings out in Minnesota and, uh, for this Communist lawyer in a trial out there and we're putting all that together. We're gettin'—

NIXON: Is that, is that the result of Hoover or the Defense Department, do you think?

MITCHELL: You mean the information?

NIXON: Yeah.

MITCHELL: It, it came out of a U.S. Marshal out in Minnesota who, uh . . .

NIXON: Oh?

MITCHELL: . . . recognized the guy and recognized his background . . .

NIXON: Great

MITCHELL: . . . and had, had him under surveillance at one of those meetings.

NIXON: Mm Hmm.

HALDEMAN: Shouldn't somebody get at—I assume they keep the files on all those taps when we were running all those people through.

NIXON: You know that's—

MITCHELL: Halperin—

HALDEMAN: This—In light of this, some of that stuff may be a hell of a lot more meaningful now . . .

MITCHELL: I

HALDEMAN: . . . than it was then.

MITCHELL: I, I, I've had them reviewed in the Bureau.

HALDEMAN: There were a lot of conversations with Sheehan in them, to my recollection.

NIXON: Were there?

HALDEMAN: I think there were. I may be wrong but I sure think there was. And nobody would agree—

(*Several Talking At Once*)

NIXON: In light of current history who's got the time to read it. I haven't, I naturally never saw any of that stuff.

HALDEMAN: Well some of it may have been gobbledy gook at the time but it may—

MITCHELL: Well, a, Bob is right. You never know what those taps mean . . .

NIXON: No.

MITCHELL: . . . until it relates to . . .

NIXON: No.

MITCHELL: . . . something. And they're being reviewed.

EHRLICHMAN: John, don't you think that, uh, we could get ourselves into a, into a dilemma if Mardian begins to develop evidence on this conspiracy and we want to go on a non-legal approach—either leaks or through the Ichord committee. If it, if it gets too—if, if, if the Justice . . .

NIXON: too far down the track

EHRLICHMAN: . . . (*Unintelligible*) . . . too much in the predominance so to speak in the development of this—

MITCHELL: Well, it's my idea that we should only pick out the hard cases to try where we know we can get convictions.

NIXON: John what is your feeling on—speaking of hard cases, now—uh. Or, are you, do you say that you're gonna, they're having a grand jury—do you, did somebody told me that Cheean or Sheehan—

EHRLICHMAN: Yeah, Mardian told me that.

MITCHELL: Well, we're running a grand jury in, in Boston which doesn't necessarily relate to anybody.

NIXON: I see.

MITCHELL: It relates to the overall case.

NIXON: Now, on Sheehan. Let's talk about that. Is that smart? Just, just being quite candid. Is it smart to go after Sheehan? My feeling, off the top of my head, is to convict that son of a bitch before a committee.

MITCHELL: Shehan?

NIXON: Make him the (*Unintelligible*) Here's the point. Uh. Let me say that, uh let me, let me recap in my own mind the whole attitude on the whole thing on this. First, and despite all the beating and so forth you've taken, you did the right, we've done exactly the right thing up to this point. You had to get that case to court. It had to go to the Supreme Court and when you read those, when you read the, the the opinions—as even Scotty Reston agreed—it, it gave them goddam little comfort.

MITCHELL: This is the general census in the newspapers now which I think is right . . .

NIXON: Right, that's right.

MITCHELL: . . . which I think is right and great.

NIXON: But my point is that it had to be done. On the, on the other, on the next point, however, I think that having done that and now, now, we've got to continue to protect the security of these, these things—having in mind our own security—but, not recognizing that there is, in my view, I think there is—I, I won't say there, but there's very, it seems to me, pretty good evidence of a conspiracy. Do you feel there's a conspiracy?

MITCHELL: Well, yes.

NIXON: I don't just don't know.

MITCHELL: Well, I know there's a conspiracy, uh, because of the fact that, uh, our East Coast conspiracy people in Massachusetts are the ones that are, have been distributing the documents . . .

NIXON: Uh, huh.

MITCHELL: . . . which we will be able to develop. Uh. With respect to, uh Ellsberg and the papers that Mathias has, obviously, there's somebody else other than Ellsberg is taking them out of the government and uh, we may have some problems finding that guy, but hopefully we will be able to. That guy or guys. Let me put out one other factor in here. I don't know whether you noticed it, but uh, this statement that I put out with respect to the court decision, that the court decision spoke for itself . . .

NIXON: Yes, yes (*Noise*) but you were going to—

MITCHELL: . . . but that it reserved all of our criminal approaches and . . .

NIXON: That's exact, that's exactly right.

MITCHELL: No, what we have got going there is the *Post* has fallen over and laying dead. They, y' know, they're talking to McComber. They want to give him back those sensitive documents and everything else.

NIXON: You've gotta watch (*Unintelligible*)

MITCHELL: And they want to give McComber back all the sensitive documents.

NIXON: (*Unintelligible*)

MITCHELL: Now, the reason for this is, and I've just let it sit there, is that if we ever convicted the, the *Post* or Katie Graham she'd lose all of her television and radio licenses.

NIXON: (*Unintelligible*)

MITCHELL: . . . and radio licenses so I've just let this thing sit there and let 'em sweat . . .

NIXON: Great.

MITCHELL: . . . and, let 'em sweat. But uh, I think personally feel at this time that it would be a mistake if we start indicting newspapers Now, what, what I have

NIXON: . . . You're right about that.

MITCHELL: . . . what I have structured . . .

NIXON: Try em in the papers

MITCHELL: . . . oh yes (*Unintelligible*) now what I have done is, is get these grand juries going so we can get all of this information and hold it. Keep the investigation going and then make our determinations as to who we want to indict and who we don't want to indict. We don't have to bring down an indictment out of the grand jury if we, if we don't want to. Uh, so that we can put the mosaic together and then have another look at it and see where we're gonna go. And I have of course a hold on everything—not to put out anything which won't— out of the grand jury. There'll be no indictments, no bringing Sheehan before the grand jury or anything like that until we put the pieces together and see what we've got.

NIXON: What we would like, what I would like, John, is this I would like to have a, see, I'm keeping up, get a, and I've gotta see somebody in Rose on something, just a little peek, and I want to see Flanigan very briefly before I leave, we can walk out to the airfield, well, it's not important, and I'll let you know when it's ready.

UNIDENTIFIED: Right, right

NIXON: And the other thing is, I think right now I have a feeling you're in an excellent position to go forward letting the leaks and everything else out which would indicate that these bastards are guilty as hell and uh, I, uh, can, cannot wait for, uh, the conviction of Ellsberg and so forth (*Unintelligible*)

MITCHELL: No, I, I quite agree.

NIXON: I think, we've got, I think the conspiracy side of that's why I hope, I think, I think we've got to go out. If you would tell Hoover to work people (*Unintelligible*) Defense outfit and push Laird, is it, or or whoever it is—Buzhardt.

MITCHELL: I believe Buzhardt (*Unintelligible*)

NIXON: Make that son of a bitch get it done. Tell him we want it done. I'm cutting off. I've—I find shocked amazement to find that this stupid Administration sold this classified (*Unintelligible*) and everything else. Now, we're gonna start getting tough. Where are those names? Now I asked for those names this morning.

UNIDENTIFIED: (*Unintelligible*)

NIXON: None of you asked what I want. I want them on my desk. Every former ten Johnson Administrator who's not in the government I want his God damned name (*Unintelligible*) so we can removed. I was out for eight years. I've never, they refused me CIA briefings. What the hell, it would have beautiful opportunity to have offered—

MITCHELL: (*Unintelligible*)

NIXON: That's right. But does this sound like a good game plan? We're going to keep this one step away from me. (*Unintelligible*) relation. I'll, I'll know what's going on and (*Unintelligible*) Buchanan knows how to tell

MITCHELL: I hope they won't be using Victor Lasky.

NIXON: Lasky? You mean as a leaker?

MITCHELL: Yes.

HALDEMAN: He's a leaker of last resort. If nobody else'll print it, Lasky will. (*Laughs*)

EHRLICHMAN: Who will uh, who will manage this grand jury while you're gone?

NIXON: Mardian.

EHRLICHMAN: Mardian?

MITCHELL: Mardian and Kleindienst. But, thank God, as, as I say, this is a fact finding expedition to put together the mosaic and not to take any action at all without my approval.

EHRLICHMAN: Good.

NIXON: Y'know—

(*30 second deletion*)

[*This is a WSPF 30-second deletion from the transcript. However, the tape recording contains this segment with 9 seconds of unintelligible conversation withdrawn by the National Archives.*]

NIXON: It shows you the pay-off, though, uh the *Washington Post* and the *Times* both have swamped slop over, uh, beautiful stories on Gurfein and that, I mean son of a bitch of a Republican. There were others. There'll be no more.

HALDEMAN: Of course, I realize that undoing there'll be no (*Unintelligible*)

MITCHELL: Probably would have, Gurfein probably would have consulted you.

NIXON: That's right. Well, enjoy your trip.

You'll follow up then with Laird, and you, and you press hard Buzhardt. In other words, play the game in a public vein. Take off Sheehan, you figure that if we knock too hard it's gonna—What do you think? What's it (*Unintelligible*)

MITCHELL: I think we ought to see what the whole picture is. We know what Sheehan has done, but we don't know how deeply he was involved with Ellsberg. Uh. He is—

EHRLICHMAN: Will he—do you have any reason to think he'd testify?

MITCHELL: Sheehan?

EHRLICHMAN: Yeah.

MITCHELL: No. I wouldn't want him to testify because if he did, he'd ask for immunity and that would be the end of it.

EHRLICHMAN: That's right.

MITCHELL: And we can get the testimony out, we know

EHRLICHMAN: You can never, you can never get Sheehan except on the testimony of uh witnesses on the, uh well, uh, on the committee or on testimony of others, others, limited, and so forth and so on.

MITCHELL: Well—

HALDEMAN: All we'd have to do get maybe somebody who received the stuff.

EHRLICHMAN: Plenty of people, people have been convicted without (*Unintelligible*) it's a terrible lesson.

MITCHELL: **RESTRICTED-"D"**

UNIDENTIFIED: Well, I suppose, (*Unintelligible*)

HALDEMAN: She has no expectation.

MITCHELL: No, none of them have any immunity explicit or (*Unintelligible*)

NIXON: We're we're . . .

EHRLICHMAN: We're going to have to gather this information in that's available to the President.

MITCHELL: All right. Dick Moore has been working on some of this. He's got a lot of the background memoranda.

EHRLICHMAN: He'll be (*Unintelligible*)

MITCHELL: (*Unintelligible*)

EHRLICHMAN: He can't (*Unintelligible*)

MITCHELL: Yeah.

Editor's Note: *The following are excerpts of taped conversations made on June 23, 1972. These excerpts are taken from transcripts prepared by the Watergate Special Prosecutor's office and the White House. The revelation of these conversations would result in the resignation of Richard Nixon as President. Most commentators at the time concluded that these conversations were the "smoking gun," meaning the evidence needed to convict Mr. Nixon of obstruction of justice.*

THE OVAL OFFICE—JUNE 23, 1972

[Mid-Morning]

HALDEMAN: Now, on the investigation, you know, the Democratic break-in thing, we're back in the problem area because the FBI is not under control, because Gray doesn't exactly know how to control it, and they have, their investigation is now leading into some productive areas, because they've been able to trace the money, not through the money itself, but through the bank, you know, sources—the banker himself. And, and it goes in some directions we don't want it to go. Ah, also there have been some things like an informant came in off the street to the FBI in Miami who was a photographer or has a friend who is a photographer who developed some films through this guy Barker and the films had pictures of Democratic National Committee letterhead documents and things. So it's things like that that are filtering in. Mitchell came up with yesterday, and John Dean analyzed very carefully last night and concludes, concurs now with Mitchell's recommendation that only way to solve this, and we're set up beautifully to do it, ah, in that and that the only network that paid any attention to it last night was NBC—they did a massive story on the Cuban thing.

PRESIDENT: That's right.

HALDEMAN: That the way to handle this now is for us to have Walters call Pat Gray and just say, "Stay to hell out of this—this is business here we don't want you to go any further on it."

PRESIDENT: What about Pat Gray—you mean Pat Gray doesn't want to?

HALDEMAN: Pat does want to. He doesn't know how to, and he doesn't have, he doesn't have any basis for doing it. Given this, he will then have a basis. He'll call Mark Felt in, and the two of them—and Mark Felt wants to cooperate because he's ambitious—

PRESIDENT: Yeah.

HALDEMAN: He'll call him in and say, "We've got the signal from across the river to put the hold on this." And that will fit rather well because the FBI agents who are working this case, at this point, feel that's what it is. This is CIA.

PRESIDENT: But they've traced the money to 'em?

HALDEMAN: Well they have, they've traced it to a name, but they haven't gotten to the guy yet.

PRESIDENT: Would it be somebody here?

HALDEMAN: Ken Dahlberg.

PRESIDENT: Who the hell is Ken Dahlberg?

HALDEMAN: He gave $25,000 in Minnesota and the check went direct to this, to this guy Barker.

PRESIDENT: Maybe he's a . . . bum. He didn't get this from the Committee though, from Stans?

HALDEMAN: Yeah. It is. It's directly traceable and there's some more through some Texas people in—that went to the Mexican bank which can also be traced to the Mexican bank. They get their names today. And . . .

PRESIDENT: Well, I mean, there's no way . . . I'm just thinking if they don't cooperate, what do they say? They, they, they were approached by the Cubans. That's what Dahlberg has to say, the Texans too. Is that the idea?

HALDEMAN: Well, if they will. But then we're relying on more and more people all the time. That's the problem. And, they'll stop if we could, take this other step.

PRESIDENT: All right, fine.

HALDEMAN: And, and they seem to feel the thing to do is get them to stop?

PRESIDENT: Right, fine.

HALDEMAN: They say the only way to do that is from White House instructions. And it's got to be to Helms and to, ah, what's his name . . . ? Walters.

PRESIDENT: Walters.

HALDEMAN: And the proposal would be that Ehrlichman and I call them in, and say, ah . . .

PRESIDENT: All right, fine.

HALDEMAN: . . . and say, ah . . .

PRESIDENT: How do you call him in, I mean you just, well, we protected Helms from one hell of a lot of things.

HALDEMAN: That's what Ehrlichman says.

PRESIDENT: Of course, this is a, this is a Hunt, you will—that will uncover a lot of things. You open that scab there's a hell of a lot of things and we just feel that it would be very detrimental to have this thing go any further. This involves these Cubans, Hunt, and a lot of hanky-panky that we have nothing to do with ourselves. Well, what the hell, did Mitchell know about this thing to any much of a degree?

HALDEMAN: I think so. I don't think he knew the details, but I think he knew.

PRESIDENT: He didn't know it was going to be handled though, with Dahlberg and the Texans and so forth? Well who was the asshole that did. (*Unintelligible*) Is it Liddy? Is that the fellow? He must be a little nuts.

HALDEMAN: He is.

PRESIDENT: I mean he just isn't well screwed on is he? Isn't that the problem?

HALDEMAN: No, but he was under pressure, apparently, to get more information, and as he got more pressure, he pushed the people harder to move harder on . . .

PRESIDENT: Pressure from Mitchell?

HALDEMAN: Apparently.

PRESIDENT: Oh, Mitchell, Mitchell was at the point, that you made on this, that's exactly what I need from you is on the—

HALDEMAN: Gemstone, yeah.

PRESIDENT: All right, fine. I understand it all. We won't second-guess Mitchell and the rest. Thank God it wasn't Colson.

HALDEMAN: The FBI interviewed Colson yesterday. They determined that would be a good thing to do. To have him take an interrogation, which he did, and that, the FBI guys working on the case had concluded that there were one or two possibilities, one, that this was a White House, they don't think that there is anything at the Election Committee, they think it was either a White House operation and they had some obscure reason for it, non political, or it was a . . .

PRESIDENT: Cuban thing—

HALDEMAN: Cubans and the CIA. And after their interrogation of Colson, yesterday, they concluded it was not the White House, but are now convinced it is a CIA thing, so the CIA turnoff would . . .

PRESIDENT: Well, not sure of their analysis, I'm not going to get that involved. I'm [*Unintelligible*].

HALDEMAN: No, sir. We don't want you to.

PRESIDENT: You call them in. Good. Good deal. Play it tough. That's the way they play it and that's the way we are going to play it.

HALDEMAN: Okay. We'll do it.

[*Later in conversation President raises following:*]

PRESIDENT: When you get in these CIA people, say Look, the problem is that this will open the whole, the whole Bay of Pigs thing, and the President just feels that, without going into the details—don't, don't lie to them to the extent to say no involvement, but just say this is a comedy of errors, without getting into it, the President believes that this is going to open the whole Bay of Pigs things up again. And because these people are plugging for [*Unintelligible*] and that they should call in the FBI and say "Don't go any further into this case period!"

[*IMMEDIATELY PRIOR TO HELMS/WALTERS–HALDEMAN/EHRLICH-MAN MEETING AT WHITE HOUSE*]

PRESIDENT: . . . very bad to have this fellow Hunt, you know, it's, he, he knows too damn much and he was involved, who happen to know that. And that it gets out that the whole, this is all involved in the Cuban thing, that it's a fiasco, and that it's going to make the FB, ah CIA look bad, it's going to make Hunt look bad, and it's likely to blow the whole Bay of Pigs thing which we think would be very unfortunate for the CIA and for the country at this time, and for American foreign policy, and he just better tough it and lay it on them. Isn't that what you . . .

HALDEMAN: Yeah, that's, that's the basis we'll do it on and just leave it at that.

PRESIDENT: I don't want them to get any ideas we're doing it because our concern is political.

HALDEMAN: Right.

PRESIDENT: And at the same time, I wouldn't tell them it is not political . . .

HALDEMAN: Right.

PRESIDENT: I would just say, Look, it's because of the Hunt involvement . . .

[CONVERSATION IN EOB OFFICE IMMEDIATELY FOLLOWING HELMS/WALTERS–HALDEMAN/EHRLICHMAN MEETING AT WHITE HOUSE]

HALDEMAN: Well, it was kind of interesting. Walters made the point, and I didn't mention Hunt, I just said that the thing was leading into directions that were going to create potential problems because they were exploring leads that led back into areas that would be harmful to the CIA and harmful to the government. I didn't have to do any explaining.

[Telephone call interruption]

HALDEMAN: Walter's got it. I think Helms did too. But he said, I've had no—

PRESIDENT: God damn, he'd better.

HALDEMAN: Gray called Helms and said I think we've run right into the middle of a CIA operation.

PRESIDENT: Gray said that?

HALDEMAN: Yeah. And he said we're on hold, nothing we've done at this point, and Helms told him don't worry, but Gray says it sure looks to me like it is a CIA job, and that was the end of that conversation. I told Helms that the problem is it tracks back to the Bay of Pigs, and it tracks back to some others, the leads run out to people who had not involvement in this, except by contacts and connections, but it gets to the areas that are liable to be raised. The whole problem [*Unintelligible*] Hunt. So at that point he kind of got the picture. He said, he said we'll be very happy to be helpful [*Unintelligible*] handle anything you want. I would like to know the reason for being helpful, and I made it clear to him he wasn't going to get explicit [*Unintelligible*] generality, and he said fine. And Waters agreed. Walters is going to make a call to Gray. That's the way we put it and that's the way it was left.

PRESIDENT: How does that work though, how, they've got to [*Unintelligible*] somebody from the Miami bank.

HALDEMAN: Right. The point John makes, the Bureau is going on, on this, because they don't know what they are uncovering, so they continue to pursue it. They don't need to because they already have their case as far as the charges against these men are concerned, and as they pursue it. They don't need to because they already have their case as far as the charges against these men [*Unintelligible*] and ah, as they pursue it [*Unintelligible*] exactly, but we didn't in any way say we [*Unintelligible*]. One thing Helms did raise. He said, Gray—he asked Gray why they thought they had run into a CIA thing and Gray said because of the characters involved and the amount of money involved, a lot of dough. [*Unintelligible*] and ah, [*Unintelligible*].

PRESIDENT: [*Unintelligible*].

HALDEMAN: Well, I think they will.

PRESIDENT: If it runs [*Unintelligible*] what the hell who knows [*Unintelligible*] contributed CIA.

HALDEMAN: Ya, it's money, CIA gets money [*Unintelligible*] I mean their money moves in a lot of different ways, too.

Transcript of a recording of a meeting among the President, John Dean, and H. R. Haldeman, in the Oval Office, on March 21, 1973, from 10:12 to 11:55 A. M.

PRESIDENT: John, sit down, sit down.

DEAN: Good morning.

PRESIDENT: Well, what is the Dean summary of the day about?

DEAN: John caught me on the way out and asked me about why Gray was holding back on information, if that was under instructions from us. And it, uh, it was and it wasn't. Uh, it was instructions proposed by the Attorney General, consistent with your press conference statement that no further raw data was to be turned over to the . . .

PRESIDENT: Full committee.

DEAN: . . . full committee.

PRESIDENT: Right.

DEAN: And that was the extent of it. And Gray, himself, is the one who reached the conclusion that no more information be turned over; he'd turned over enough. Uh, so this is again Pat Gray making decisions on his own as to how to handle his hearings. He has been totally unwilling all along to take any guidance, any instruction. We don't know what he is going to do. He is not going to talk about it. He won't review it, uh, and I don't think . . .

PRESIDENT: Right.

DEAN: . . . he does it to harm you in any way, sir.

PRESIDENT: He's just quite stubborn and—he's quite stubborn; also he isn't very smart. You know he and I—

DEAN: He's bullheaded.

PRESIDENT: He's smart in his own way, but . . .

DEAN: Yeah.

PRESIDENT: . . . but he's got that typical, "Well, by God, this is right and they're not going to do it."

DEAN: That's why he thinks he'll be confirmed, because he thinks he's being, he's being his own man. He's being forthright, honest. He's feels he has turned over too much and so it's a conscious decision that he is harming the Bureau by doing this and so he's not going to—

PRESIDENT: (*Sighs*) I hope to God that we can get off (*Unintelligible*) though today, this is because the White House told him to do this and that other thing. And also, I told Ehrlichman, I don't see why our little boys can't make something out of the fact that, God darn it, this is the, this is the, the only responsible decision you could possibly make. The FBI cannot turn over raw files. Has anybody made that point? I've tried . . .

DEAN: Sam Ervin has made that point himself.

PRESIDENT: Did he?

DEAN: Uh, in fact, in reading the transcript of Gray's hearings, Ervin tried to hold Gray back from doing what he was doing at the time he did it. Uh, I thought it was very unwise. I don't think that anyone is criticizing . . .

PRESIDENT: Well, let's say—

DEAN: . . . your position on it.

PRESIDENT: Let's make the point, let's make the point that the raw files cannot be turned over. Well, I think that point should be made.

DEAN: That, that—

PRESIDENT: (*Background Noises*) We are standing for the rights of innocent individuals. The American Civil Liberty Union is against it. We're against it. (*Unintelligible*) tradition, and it will continue to be the tradition that all files are—I'd like to turn them (*Unintelligible*) let them see what is in one.

DEAN: How damaging—

PRESIDENT: Any further word on, on Sullivan? Is he still—

DEAN: Yeah, he's, he's going to be over to see me today, this morning, hopefully, sometime. Uh—

PRESIDENT: As soon as you get that, I'll be available to talk to you this afternoon.

DEAN: All right, sir.

PRESIDENT: I'll be busy until about one o'clock; after that we can contact. Anytime you're through I would like to see whatever thing he has. Well, he's got something, but I'd like to just see what it is.

DEAN: Uh, the reason I thought we ought to talk this morning is because in, in our conversations, uh, uh, I have, I have the impression that you don't know everything I know . . .

PRESIDENT: That's right.

DEAN: . . . and it makes it very difficult for you to make judgments that, uh, that only you can make . . .

PRESIDENT: That's right.

DEAN: . . . on some of these things and I thought that—

PRESIDENT: You've got, in other words, I've got to know why you feel that, uh, that something . . .

DEAN: Well, let me . . .

PRESIDENT: . . . that, that we shouldn't unravel something.

DEAN: . . . let me give you my overall first.

PRESIDENT: In other words, you, your judgment as to where it stands, and where we go now—

DEAN: I think, I think that, uh, there's no doubt about the seriousness of the problem we're, we've got. We have a cancer—within, close to the Presidency, that's growing. It's growing daily. It's compounding, it grows geometrically now because it compounds itself. Uh, that'll be clear as I explain you know, some of the details, uh, of why it is, and it basically is because (1) we're being blackmailed; (2) uh, people are going to start perjuring themself very quickly that have not had to perjure themselves to protect other people and the like. And that is just—and there is no assurance—

PRESIDENT: That it won't bust.

DEAN: That, that won't bust.

PRESIDENT: True.

DEAN: So, let me give you the sort of basic facts, talking first about the Watergate; and then about Segretti; and then about some of the peripheral items that, uh, have come up. First of all, on, on the Watergate: How did it all start, where did it start? It started with an instruction to me from Bob Haldeman to see if we couldn't set up a perfectly legitimate campaign intelligence operation over at the Re-election Committee.

PRESIDENT: Hmm.

DEAN: Not being in this business, I turned to somebody who had been in this business, Jack Caulfield, who is, I don't know if you remember Jack or not. He was your original bodyguard before . . .

PRESIDENT: Yeah.

DEAN: . . . they had . . .

PRESIDENT: Yeah.

DEAN: . . . candidate, candidate . . .

PRESIDENT: Yeah.

DEAN: . . . protection, an old New York City policeman.

PRESIDENT: Right, I know, I know him.

DEAN: Uh, Jack had worked for John and then was transferred to my office. I said, "Jack, come up with a plan that, you know, is a normal infiltration, I mean, you know, buying information from secretaries and all that sort of thing." He did, he put together a plan. It was kicked around, and, uh, I went to Ehrlichman with it. I went to Mitchell with it, and the consensus was that Caulfield wasn't the man to do this. Uh, in retrospect, that might have been a bad call, 'cause he is an incredibly cautious person and, and wouldn't have put the situation to where it is today.

PRESIDENT: Yeah.

DEAN: All right, after rejecting that, they said, "We still need something," so I was told to look around for somebody that could go over to 1701 and do this. And that's when I came up with Gordon Liddy, who—they needed a lawyer. Gordon had an intelligence background from his FBI service. I was aware of the fact that he had done some extremely sensitive things for the White House while he'd been at the White House, and he had apparently done them well. Uh, going out into Ellsberg's doctor's office . . .

PRESIDENT: Oh, yeah.

DEAN: . . . and things like this. He'd worked with leaks. He'd, you know, tracked these things down. Uh, and (*Coughs*) so the report that I got from Krogh was that he was a hell of a good man and, not only that, a good lawyer, uh, and could set up a proper operation. So we talked to Liddy. Liddy was interested in doing it. Took, uh, Liddy over to meet Mitchell. Mitchell thought highly of him because, apparently, Mitchell was partially involved in his ev—coming to the White House to work for, for Krogh. Uh, Liddy had been at Treasury before that. Then Liddy was told to put together his plan, you know, how he would run an intelligence operation. And this was after he was hired over there at the, uh, the Committee. Magruder called me in January and said, "I'd like to have you come over and see Liddy's plan."

PRESIDENT: January of '72?

DEAN: January of '72. (*Background Noises*) Like, "You come over to Mitchell's office and sit in on a meeting where Liddy is going to lay his plan out." I said, "Well, I don't really know as I'm the man, but if you want me there I'll be happy to." (*Clears Throat*) So, I came over and Liddy laid out a million dollar plan that was the most incredible thing I have ever laid my eyes on. All in codes, and involved black bag operations, kidnapping, providing prostitutes, uh, to weaken the opposition, bugging, uh, mugging teams. It was just an incredible thing. (*Clears Throat*)

PRESIDENT: But, uh . . .

DEAN: And—

PRESIDENT: . . . that was, that was not, uh . . .

DEAN: No.

PRESIDENT: . . . discussed with . . .

DEAN: No.

PRESIDENT: . . . other persons.

DEAN: No, not at all. And—

PRESIDENT: (*Unintelligible*)

DEAN: Uh, Mitchell, Mitchell just virtually sat there puffing and laughing. I could tell 'cause after he—after Liddy left the office I said, "That's the most incredible thing I've ever seen." He said, "I agree." And so then he was told to go back to the drawing boards and come up with something realistic. So there was a second meeting. Uh, they asked me to come over to that. I came into the tail end of the meeting. I wasn't there for the first part. I don't know how long the meeting lasted. Uh, at this point, they were discussing again bugging, kidnapping and the like. And at this point I said, right in front of everybody, very clearly, I said, "These are not the sort of things (1) that are ever to be discussed in the office of the Attorney General of the United States"—where he still was—"and I am personally incensed." I was trying to get Mitchell off the hook, uh, 'cause—

PRESIDENT: I know.

DEAN: He's a, he's a nice person, doesn't like to say no under—when people he's going to have to work with.

PRESIDENT: That's right.

DEAN: So, I let, I let it be known. I said, "You all pack that stuff up and get it the hell out of here 'cause we just, you just can't talk this way in this office and you shouldn't, you shouldn't, you should re-examine your whole thinking." Came back—

PRESIDENT: Who else was present? Be-, besides you—

DEAN: It was Magruder, Magruder—

PRESIDENT: Magruder.

DEAN: Uh, Mitchell, Liddy and myself. I came back right after the meeting and told Bob, I said, "Bob, we've got a growing disaster on our hands if they're thinking this way," and I said, "The White House has got to stay out of this and I, frankly, am not going to be involved in it." He said, "I agree John." And, I thought, at that point the thing was turned off. That's the last I heard of it, when I thought it was turned off, because it was an absurd proposal.

PRESIDENT: Yeah.

DEAN: Liddy—I did have dealings with him afterwards. We never talked about it. Now that would be hard to believe for some people, but, uh, we never did. Just the fact of the matter.

PRESIDENT: Well, you were talking about other things.

DEAN: Other things. We had so many other things.

PRESIDENT: He had some legal problems at one time.

DEAN: Now (*Coughs*)—

PRESIDENT: But you were his advisor, and I, I understand how you could have some, uh, what cam—what are they campaign laws—I knew that was you, you have—Haldeman told me you, that you were heading all of that up for us. Go ahead.

DEAN: Now. (*Clears Throat*). So, Liddy went back after that and it was over, over at, uh, 1701, the Committee, and I, this is where I come into having put the pieces together after the fact as to what I can put together what happened. Liddy sat over there and tried to come up with another plan that he could sell. (1) They were talk-ing, saying to him he was asking for too much money, and I don't think they were discounting the, the illegal points at this, after—you know. Jeb is not a lawyer and he didn't know whether this was the way the game was played or not, and what it was all about. They came up with, apparently, another plan, uh, but they couldn't get it approved by anybody over there. So, Liddy and Hunt apparently came to see Chuck Colson, and Chuck Colson picked up the telephone and called Magruder and said, "You all either fish or cut bait. Uh, this is absurd to have these guys over there and not using them, and if you're not going to use them, I may use them." Things of this nature.

PRESIDENT: When was this?

DEAN: This was apparently in February of '72.

PRESIDENT: That could be. Colson know what they were talking about?

DEAN: I can only assume, because of his close relationship with . . .

PRESIDENT: Hunt.

DEAN: . . . Hunt, he had a damn good idea of what they were talking about, a damn good idea. He would probably deny it, deny it today and probably get away with denying it. But I, uh, I still—

PRESIDENT: Unless Hunt—

DEAN: Unless Hunt, uh, blows on him—

PRESIDENT: But then Hunt isn't enough. I takes two doesn't it?

DEAN: Probably. Probably. But Liddy was there also and if, if Liddy were to blow—

PRESIDENT: Then you've got a problem—I was thinking (*Unintelligible*) the criminal liability goes.

DEAN: Yeah.

PRESIDENT: Okay.

DEAN: I'll go back over that, and tell (*Noise*) you where I think the, the soft spots are.

PRESIDENT: Colson then, then Colson then, do you think was the, uh, was the person who . . .

DEAN: I think he . . .

PRESIDENT: . . . pushed?

DEAN: I think he helped to get the push, get the thing off the dime. Now something else occurred, though—

PRESIDENT: Did Colson—did he talk to anybody here?

DEAN: No. I think this was an independent . . .

PRESIDENT: Did he talk to Haldeman?

DEAN: No. I don't think so. Now, but here's the other thing, where the next thing comes in the chain: I think that Bob was assuming that they had something that was proper over there, some intelligence gathering operation that Liddy was operating. And through Strachan, uh, who was his tickler, uh, he started pushing them . . .

PRESIDENT: (*Sighs*) yeah.

DEAN: . . . to get something, to get some information and they took that as a signal—Magruder took that as a signal to probably go to Mitchell and say, "They're pushing us like crazy for this from the White House." And so Mitchell probably puffed on his pipe and said, "Go ahead." And never really reflected on what it was all about. So, they had some plan that obviously had, I gather, different targets they were going to go after. They were going to infiltrate, and bug, and do all this sort of thing to a lot of these targets. This is knowledge I have after the fact. (*Coughs*) And, apparently, they, uh, they, they had, they had after they had initially broken in and bugged the Democratic National Committee they were getting information. The information was coming over here to Strachan. Some of it was given to Haldeman. Uh, there is no doubt about it. Uh—

PRESIDENT: Did he know what it was coming from?

DEAN: I don't really know if he was, sir.

PRESIDENT: Not necessarily.

DEAN: Not necessarily. That—not necessarily. Uh—

PRESIDENT: Strachan knew what it was from.

DEAN: Strachan knew what it was from. No doubt about it, and whether Strachan— I've never wanted to press these people on these points because it . . .

PRESIDENT: Yeah.

DEAN: . . . it hurts them to, to give up that next inch. So I had to piece things together. All right, so, Strachan was aware of receiving information, reporting to Bob. At one point Bob even gave instructions to change their capabilities from Muskie to McGovern, and had passed this back through Strachan to Magruder and, and apparently to Liddy, and Liddy was starting to make arrangements to go in and bug the uh, uh, McGovern operation. They had done prelim- . . .

PRESIDENT: They had never bugged Muskie, though, did they?

DEAN: No, they hadn't but they had a, they had, uh, they'd . . .

PRESIDENT: (*Unintelligible*).

DEAN: . . . infiltrated it by a, a, they had . . .

PRESIDENT: A secretary.

DEAN: . . . a secretary and a chauffeur. Nothing illegal about that.

PRESIDENT: I suppose you're—

DEAN: Now, so the information was coming over here and then, uh, I finally, after— the next point in time where I became aware of anything was on June 17th, when I got word that there had been this break-in at the Democratic National Committee and somebody from the Committee had been caught, uh, from our Committee had been caught in the DNC. And I said, "Oh, my God, that, I can only," you know, if, instantly putting the pieces together—(*Coughs*)

PRESIDENT: You knew what it was.

DEAN: I knew what it was. So I called Liddy, uh, on that Monday morning, and I said, "Gordon" I said, "first, I want to know if anybody in the White House was involved in this." And he said, "No." And they weren't. I said, "Well, I want to know how in God's name this happened." And he said, "Well, I was pushed without mercy by Magruder to get in there, get more information—that the information, it was not satisfactory. Magruder said, 'The White House is not happy with what we're getting.' "

PRESIDENT: The White House?

DEAN: The White House. Yeah, Uh—

PRESIDENT: Who do you think was pushing him?

DEAN: Well, I think it was probably Strachan thinking that Bob wanted things, (*Cough*) and, because because I have seen that happen on other occasions where things have been said to be of very prime importance when they really weren't.

PRESIDENT: Why (*Unintelligible*) I wonder? I'm just trying to think as to why then. We'd just finished the Moscow trip. I mean, we were—

DEAN: That's right.

PRESIDENT: The Democrats had just nominated Mc G-, McGovern. I mean, for Christ's sakes, I mean, what the hell were we—I mean, I can see doing it earlier but I mean, now let me say, I can see the pressure, but I don't see why all the pressure would have been on then.

DEAN: I don't know, other than the fact that, uh, they might have been looking for information about . . .

PRESIDENT: The convention.

DEAN: . . . the conventions.

PRESIDENT: Well, that's right.

DEAN: Because, I understand, also after the fact, that there was a plan to bug Larry O'Brien's suite down in Florida.

PRESIDENT: Yeah.

DEAN: Uh, so, uh, Liddy told me, that uh, you know, this is what had happened and, and this is why it had happened.

PRESIDENT: Liddy told you he was planning—where'd you learn there was such a plan—from whom?

DEAN: Beg your pardon.

PRESIDENT: Where did you learn of the plans to bug Larry O'Brien's suite?

DEAN: From Magruder, after the, long after the fact.

PRESIDENT: Oh, Magruder, he knows.

DEAN: Yeah. Magruder is totally knowledgeable on the whole thing.

PRESIDENT: Yeah.

DEAN: All right, now, we've gone through the trial. We've—I don't know if Mitchell has perjured himself in the Grand Jury or not. I've never—

PRESIDENT: Who?

DEAN: Mitchell. I don't know how much knowledge he actually had. I know that Magruder has perjured himself in the Grand Jury. I know that Porter has perjured himself, uh, in the Grand Jury.

PRESIDENT: Porter (*Unintelligible*).

DEAN: He's one of Magruder's deputies.

PRESIDENT: Yeah.

DEAN: Uh, that they set up this scenario which they ran by me. They said, "How about this?" I said, "Well, I don't know. I, you know, if, if this is what you're going to hang on, fine." Uh, that they—

PRESIDENT: What did they say before the Grand Jury?

DEAN: They said, they said, as they said before the trial and the Grand Jury, that, that, uh, Liddy had come over as, as a counsel and we knew he had these capacities to, you know, to do legitimate intelligence. We had no idea what he was doing. He was given an authorization of 250,000 dollars . . .

PRESIDENT: Right.

DEAN: . . . to collect information, because our surrogates were out on the road. They had no protection. We had information that there were going to be demonstrations against them, that, uh, uh, we had to have a plan to get information as to what liabilities they were going to be confronted with . . .

PRESIDENT: Right.

DEAN: . . . and Liddy was charged with doing this. We had no knowledge that he was going to bug the DNC. Uh—

PRESIDENT: Well, the point is, that's untrue.

DEAN: That's right.

PRESIDENT: Magruder did know that—

DEAN: Magruder was specifically instructed him to go back in the DNC.

PRESIDENT: He did?

DEAN: Yes.

PRESIDENT: You know that? Yeah, I see. Okay.

DEAN: Uh, (*Pause*) I honestly believe that no one over here knew that. I know, uh, as God is my maker, I had no knowledge that they were going to do this.

PRESIDENT: Bob didn't either (*Unintelligible*).

DEAN: Uh, but, you know, (*Unintelligible*)

PRESIDENT: (*Unintelligible*) Bob, Bob—he wouldn't—

DEAN: Bob I don't believe specifically knew they were going in there.

PRESIDENT: I don't think so.

DEAN: I don't think he did. I think he knew there was a capacity to do this, but he wouldn't, wasn't giving it specific direction.

PRESIDENT: Strachan, did he know?

DEAN: I think Strachan did know.

PRESIDENT: They were going back into the DNC? Hunt never entered DNC.

DEAN: All right, so—uh, those people are in trouble as a result of the Grand Jury and the trial. Mitchell, of course, was never called during the trial. Now—

PRESIDENT: Mitchell has given a sworn statement?

DEAN: Yes, sir.

PRESIDENT: To the Bureau?

DEAN: To the Grand Jury—

PRESIDENT: Did he go before the Grand Jury?

DEAN: He had, we had a, an arrangement whereby he went down to, with several of the—because it was, you know, the heat of this thing and the implications on the election, we made an arrangement where they could quietly go into the Department of Justice and have one of the Assistant U.S. Attorneys come over and take their testimony and then read it before the Grand Jury. Uh—

PRESIDENT: That was (*Unintelligible*).

DEAN: Although I—that's right. Mitchell was actually called before the Grand Jury. The Grand Jury would not settle for less. The jurors wanted him.

PRESIDENT: And he went.

DEAN: And he went.

PRESIDENT: Good.

DEAN: Uh, I don't know what he said. Uh, so I've never seen a transcript of the Grand Jury. Now (*Sighs*) what, what has happened post—June 17? Well, it was, I was under pretty clear instructions (*Laughs*) not to really investigate this, that this was something that just could have been disastrous on the election if it had—all hell had broken loose, and I worked on a theory of containment . . .

PRESIDENT: Sure.

DEAN: . . . to try to hold it right where it was.

PRESIDENT: Right.

DEAN: There's no doubt, I, I, uh, that, uh, I was totally aware what the Bureau was doing at all times. I was totally aware of what the Grand Jury was doing.

PRESIDENT: You mean—

DEAN: I knew what witnesses were going to be called. I knew what they were going to be asked, and I had to. There just—

PRESIDENT: Why did Petersen play the, play the game so straight with us?

DEAN: Because Petersen is a soldier. He played—he kept me informed. He told me when we had problems, where we had problems, and the like. Uh, he believes in, in, in you. He believes in this Administration. This Administration has made him. Uh, I don't think he's done anything improper, but he did make sure the investigation was narrowed down to the very, very . . .

PRESIDENT: Right.

DEAN: . . . fine . . .

PRESIDENT: Right.

DEAN: . . . criminal things, which was a break for us. There's no doubt about it.

PRESIDENT: He honestly feels that he did an adequate job?

DEAN: He, uh, they ran that investigation out to the fullest extent they could follow a lead (*Coughs*) and that was it.

PRESIDENT: But the point is, where I suppose he could be criticized for not doing an adequate job is why didn't he call Haldeman? Why didn't he get a statement from Colson? Or they did get Colson?

DEAN: That's right. But see, the thing is, is based on their FBI interviews, there was no reason to follow up. There were no leads there. Colson said, "I have no knowledge of this" to the FBI. Uh, Strachan said, "I have no knowledge of—" you know. They didn't ask Strachan any Watergate questions. They asked him about Segretti. Uh, they said, "What's your connection with Liddy?" and he just said, "Well, I, you know. I just, met him over there," and they never really pressed him. They didn't, you know, they—look, Strachan appeared, uh, as a result of some coaching, he could be the dumbest paper pusher in the bowels of the, the White House. All right, now, post-June 17th, these guys immediately—it is very, very (*Laughs*) interesting—Liddy, for example, the Friday before—uh, on I guess it was the, uh, on the 15th, uh, 16th, uh, of, uh, June—had been in Henry Petersen's office with another member of my staff on campaign compliance (*Laughs*) problems, uh, joking. After the incident, he went, he ran, uh, Kleindienst down at Burning Tree Country Club and told (*Laughs*) him that "You've got to get my men out of jail," which was kind of a—Kleindienst said, "Now, you get the hell out of here, kid, uh, uh, whatever you've got to say, just say to somebody else. Don't bother me," and—but this has never come up.

PRESIDENT: Yeah.

DEAN: Uh, Liddy said, said that, you know—they all got counsel instantly and said that, you know, "We'll, we'll ride this thing out." All right, then they started making demands; "We've got to have attorneys' fees. Uh, we don't have any money ourselves, and if—you are asking us to take this through the election." All right, so arrangements were made through Mitchell, uh, initiating it, in discussions that—I was present—that these guys had to be taken care of. Their attorneys' fees had to be done. Kalmbach was brought in. Uh, Kalmbach raised some cash. Uh, they were, uh, you know—

PRESIDENT: They put that under the cover of a Cuban Committee or (*Unintelligible*).

DEAN: Yeah, they, they had a Cuban Committee and they had—some of it was given to Hunt's lawyer, who in turn passed it out. This, you know, when Hunt's wife was flying to Chicago with ten thousand, she was actually, I understand after the fact now, was going to pass that money to, uh, one of the Cubans, to meet him in Chicago and pass it to somebody there.

PRESIDENT: Why didn't she (*Unintelligible*) maybe—well, whether it's maybe too late to do anything about it, but I would certainly keep that, (*Laughs*) that cover for whatever it's worth.

DEAN: I'll . . .

PRESIDENT: Keep the Committee.

DEAN: Af-, after, well, that, that, that's the most troublesome post-thing, uh, because (1) Bob is involved in that; John is involved in that; I'm involved in that; Mitchell is involved in that. And that's an obstruction of justice.

PRESIDENT: In other words the fact that, uh, that you're you're, you're taking care of the witnesses.

DEAN: That's right, uh—

PRESIDENT: How was Bob involved?

DEAN: Well, th-, they ran out of money over there. Bob had three hundred and fifty thousand dollars in a safe over here that was really set aside for polling purposes. Uh, and there was no other source of money, so they came over here and said, "You all've got to give us some money."

PRESIDENT: Right.

DEAN: I had to go to Bob and say, "Bob, you know, you've got to have some—they need some money over there." He said "What for?" And so I had to tell him what it was for 'cause he wasn't about to just send money over there willy-nilly. And, uh, John was involved in those discussions, and we decided, you know, that, you know, that there was no price too high to pay to let this thing blow up in front of the election.

PRESIDENT: I think you should handle that one pretty fast.

DEAN: Oh, I think—

PRESIDENT: That issue, I mean.

DEAN: I think we can.

PRESIDENT: So that the three-fifty went back ov-, over here.

DEAN: That's alright. I think we can too.

PRESIDENT: Who else is?

DEAN: But, now, here, here's what's happening right now.

PRESIDENT: Yeah.

DEAN: What sort of brings matters to the—this is (1) this is going to be continual black-mail operation by Hunt and Liddy and the Cubans. No doubt about it. And McCord . . .

PRESIDENT: Yeah.

DEAN: . . . who is, who is another one involved. McCord has asked for nothing. Uh, McCord did ask to meet with somebody, and it was Jack Caulfield, who is his old friend, who'd gotten him hired over there. And, when, when, when Caulfield had him hired, he was a perfectly legitimate security man. And he wanted to know, well, you know, (*Coughs*) he wanted to talk about commutation, and things like that. And as you know Colson has talked to, indirectly to Hunt about commutation. (*Clears Throat*). All these things are bad, in, in, in that they are problems, they are promises, they are commitments. They are the very sort of thing that the Senate is going to be looking most for. I don't think they can find them, frankly.

PRESIDENT: Pretty hard.

DEAN: Pretty hard. Damn hard. It's all cash. Uh—

PRESIDENT: Well, I mean, pretty hard as far as the witnesses are concerned.

DEAN: That's right. Now, the blackmail is continuing. Hunt called one of the lawyers from the Re-election Committee on last Friday to meet with him on—over the weekend. The guy came in to me, to see me to get a message directly from Hunt to me, for the first time.

PRESIDENT: Is Hunt out on bail?

DEAN: Pardon?

PRESIDENT: Is Hunt on bail?

DEAN: Hunt is on bail. Correct. Uh, Hunt now is demanding another seventy-two thousand dollars for his own personal expenses; another fifty thousand dollars to pay his attorneys' fees; a hundred and twenty some thousand dollars. Wants it, wanted it by the close of business yesterday. 'Cause he says, "I'm going to be sentenced on Friday, and I've got to be able to get my financial affairs in order." I told this fellow O'Brien, "You came—all right, you came to the wrong man, fellow. I'm not involved in the money. Uh, I don't know a thing about it, can't help you." Said, "You better scramble around elsewhere." Now, O'Brien is, O'Brien is, is a ball player. He's been, he carried tremendous water for us. Uh—

PRESIDENT: He isn't Hunt's lawyer, is he?

DEAN: No, he is, he is our lawyer at the Re-election Committee.

PRESIDENT: I see, good.

DEAN: So he's safe. There's no problem there. But it raises the whole question of Hunt now has made a direct threat against Ehrlichman, as a result of this. This is his blackmail. He says, "I will bring John Ehrlichman down to his knees and put him in jail. Uh, I have done enough seamy things for he and Krogh, uh, that they'll never survive it."

PRESIDENT: What's that, on Ellsberg?

DEAN: Ellsberg, and apparently some other things. I don't know the full extent of it. Uh—

PRESIDENT: I don't know about anything else.

DEAN: I don't know either, and I (*Laughs*) hate to learn some of these things. So that's, that's that situation. Now, we're at the soft points. How many people know about this? Well, uh, well, let me go one step further in this, this whole thing. The Cubans that were used in the Watergate were also the same Cubans that Hunt and Liddy used for this California Ellsberg thing, for the break-in out there.

PRESIDENT: Yeah.

DEAN: So they're, they're aware of that. How high their knowledge is, is something else. Hunt and Liddy, of course, are totally aware of, of, of it, and the fact that, uh, it was right out of the White House.

PRESIDENT: I don't know what the hell we did that for.

DEAN: I don't either.

PRESIDENT: What in the name of God did that—

DEAN: Mr. President, there have been a couple of things around here that I have gotten wind of. Uh, there was at one time a desire to do a second-story job on the Brookings Institute where they had the Pentagon Papers. Now I flew to California because I was told that John had instructed it and he said, "I really hadn't. It's a mis-impression, that for Christ's sake, turn it off." And I did. I came back and turned it off. Because, you know the, when you, you know, if the risk is minimal and the, and the gain is fantastic, it's something else. But with a low risk and uh, no gain, uh, hey, it's just, uh, it's not worth it. Well—who knows about this all now? All right, you've got (*Clears Throat*) the Cubans' lawyer's a man by the name of Rothblatt, who is a no-good, publicity-seeking, son-of-a-bitch, to be very frank about it. He has had to be turned down and tuned off. He was canned by his own people 'cause they didn't trust him. They were trying to run a different route than he wanted to run. He didn't want them to plead guilty. He wants to represent them before the Senate. So, F. Lee Bailey, who was the partner of one of the, one of the men representing McCord, uh, got in and, and cooled Rothblatt down. So, F. Lee B-, Bailey's got knowledge. Uh, Hunt's lawyer, a man by the name of Bittman, who's an excellent criminal lawyer from the Democratic era of Bobby Kennedy, he's got knowledge. Uh—

PRESIDENT: Do you think, do you think, that he's got some? How much?

DEAN: Well, everybody—not only, all the, all the direct knowledge that Hunt and Liddy have, as well as all the hearsay they have.

PRESIDENT: I (*Unintelligible*).

DEAN: Uh, you've got the two lawyers over at the Re-election Committee who did an investigation to find out the facts. Slowly, they got the whole picture. They're, uh, they're solid, but they're—

PRESIDENT: But they know.

DEAN: But they know. Uh, you've got, then, an awful lot of—all the principals involved know. Uh, Hunt—some people's wives know.

PRESIDENT: Sure.

DEAN: Uh, there's no doubt about that. Mrs. Hunt was the savviest woman in the world. She had the whole picture together.

PRESIDENT: Did she?

DEAN: Yeah, it, uh—apparently, she was the pillar of strength in that family before the death, and, uh—

PRESIDENT: Great sadness. The basis, as a matter of fact (*Clears Throat*) there was some discussion (*Unintelligible*) uh, Hunt's problems after his wife died and I said, of course, commutation could be considered on the basis of his wife, and that is the only discussion I ever had in that light.

DEAN: Right. Uh, so that's, that's it. That's the, the extent of the knowledge. Now, where, where are the soft spots on this? Well, first of all, there's the, there's the problem of the continued blackmail . . .

PRESIDENT: Right.

DEAN: . . . which will not only go on now, it'll go on when these people are in prison, and it will compound the obstruction of justice situation. It'll cost money. It's dangerous. Nobody, nothing—people around here are not pros at this sort of thing. This is the sort of thing Mafia people can do: washing money, getting clean money, and things like that, uh—we're—we just don't know about those (*Noise*) things, because we're not used to, you know—we are not criminals and not used to dealing in that business. It's, uh, it's, uh—

PRESIDENT: That's right.

DEAN: It's tough thing to know how to do.

PRESIDENT: Maybe we can't even do that.

DEAN: That's right. It's a real problem as to whether we could even do it. Plus there's a real problem in raising money. Uh, Mitchell has been working on raising some money. Uh, feeling he's got, you know, he's got one, he's one of the ones with the most to lose. Uh, but there's no denying the fact that the White House, and uh, Ehrlichman, Haldeman, Dean are involved in some of the early money decisions.

PRESIDENT: How much money do you need?

DEAN: I would say these people are going to cost, uh, a million dollars over the next, uh, two years.

(*Pause*)

PRESIDENT: We could get that.

DEAN: Uh, huh.

PRESIDENT: You, on the money, if you need the money, I mean, uh, you could get the money. Let's say—

DEAN: Well, I think that we're going—

PRESIDENT: What I mean is, you could, you could get a million dollars. And you could get it in cash. I, I know where it could be gotten.

DEAN: Uh, huh.

PRESIDENT: I mean it's not easy, but it could be done. But, uh, the question is who the hell would handle it?

DEAN: That's right, uh—

PRESIDENT: Any ideas on that?

DEAN: Well, I would think that would be something that Mitchell ought to be charged with.

PRESIDENT: I would think so, too.

DEAN: And get some, get some pros to help him.

PRESIDENT: Let me say, there shouldn't be a lot of people running around getting money. We should set up a little—

DEAN: Well, he's got one person doing it who I'm not sure is—

PRESIDENT: Who is that?

DEAN: He's got Fred LaRue, uh, doing it. Now Fred started out going out trying to . . .

PRESIDENT: No.

DEAN: . . . solicit money from all kinds of people. Now, I learned about that, and I said, "My God" . . .

PRESIDENT: No.

DEAN: . . . "It's just awful. Don't do it."

PRESIDENT: Yeah.

DEAN: Uh, people are going to ask what the money is for. He's working—apparently he talked to Tom Pappas.

PRESIDENT: I know.

(*Noise*)

DEAN: And Pappas has, uh, agreed to come up with a sizeable amount, I gather, from, from . . .

(*Noise*)

PRESIDENT: Yeah.

DEAN: . . . Mitchell.

PRESIDENT: Yeah, well, what do you need, then? You need, uh, you don't need a million right away, but you need a million. Is that right?

DEAN: That's right.

PRESIDENT: You need a million in cash, don't you? If you want to put that through, would you put that through, uh—this is thinking out loud here for a moment—would you put that through the Cuban Committee?

DEAN: Umm, no.

PRESIDENT: Or would you just do this through a (*Unintelligible*) that it's going to be, uh, well, it's cash money, and so forth. How, if that ever comes out, are you going to handle it? Is the Cuban Committee an obstruction of justice, if they want to help?

DEAN: Well, they've got a pr-, they've got priests, and they—

PRESIDENT: Would you like to put, I mean, would that, would that give a little bit of a cover, for example?

DEAN: That would give some for the Cubans and possibly Hunt.

PRESIDENT: Yeah.

DEAN: Uh, then you've got Liddy and—McCord is not, not accepting any money. So he's, he is not a bought man right now.

(*Pause*)

PRESIDENT: Okay.

DEAN: All right. Let, let me, uh

PRESIDENT: Go ahead.

DEAN: . . . continue a little bit here now. The, uh, I, when I say this is a growing cancer, uh, I say it for reasons like this. Bud Krogh, in his testimony before the Grand Jury, was forced to perjure himself. Uh, he is haunted by it. Uh, Bud said, "I haven't had a pleasant day on the job."

PRESIDENT: Huh, said what?

DEAN: He said, "I have not had a pleasant day on my job." Uh, he's talked, apparently, he said to me, "I told my wife all about this," he said. "The, uh, the curtain may ring down one of these days, and, uh, I may have to face the music, which I'm perfectly willing to do." Uh—

PRESIDENT: What did he perjure himself on, John?

DEAN: His, did, uh, did he know the Cubans? He did. Uh—

PRESIDENT: He said he didn't?

DEAN: That's right. They didn't press him hard, or that he—

PRESIDENT: He might be able to—I'm just trying to think. Perjury is an awful hard rap to prove. He could say that I (*Pause*) hmm, well, go ahead.

DEAN: (*Coughs*) Well, so that's, that's the first, that's one perjury. Now, Mitchell and, and, uh, Magruder are potential perjuries. There is always the possibility of any one of these individuals blowing. Hunt, Liddy. Liddy's in jail right now; he's serving his—trying to get good time right now. I think Liddy is probably, in his, in his own bizarre way, the strongest of all of them. Uh, so there's, there is that possibility.

PRESIDENT: Well, your, your major, your major guy to keep under control is Hunt.

DEAN: That's right.

PRESIDENT: I think. Because he knows . . .

DEAN: He knows so much.

PRESIDENT: . . . about a lot of other things.

DEAN: He knows so much. Right. Uh, he could sink Chuck Colson. Apparently, apparently, he is quite distressed with Colson. He thinks Colson has abandoned him. Uh, Colson was to meet with him when he was out there, after, now he had left the White House. He met with him through his lawyer. Hunt raised the question he wanted money. Colson's lawyer told him that Colson wasn't doing anything with money, and Hunt took offense with that immediately, that, uh, uh, that Colson had abandoned him. Uh—

PRESIDENT: Don't you, just looking at the immediate problem, don't you have to have—handle Hunt's financial situation . . .

DEAN: I, I think that's—

PRESIDENT: . . . damn soon?

DEAN: That is, uh, I talked to Mitchell about that last night—

PRESIDENT: (*Unintelligible*)

DEAN: And, and, uh, I told—

PRESIDENT: (*Unintelligible*) may—after all, you've got to keep the cap on the bottle that much . . .

DEAN: That's right; that's right.

PRESIDENT: . . . in order to have any options.

DEAN: That's right.

PRESIDENT: Either that or let it all blow right now.

DEAN: Well, that, you know, that's the, that's the question. Uh—

PRESIDENT: Now, go ahead. The others. You've got Hunt . . .

DEAN: All right, now we've got—

PRESIDENT: . . . you've got Krogh, and you've got—

DEAN: Now we've got Kalmbach (*Coughs*).

PRESIDENT: Yeah, that's a tough one.

DEAN: Kalmbach received . . .

PRESIDENT: (*Unintelligible*)

DEAN: . . . at the close of the, of the, uh, '68 campaign, in January of '69, he got a million seven dollars, uh, a million seven hundred thousand dollars to be custodian for. That came down from New York. It was placed in safe deposit boxes here. Uh, some other people were on the boxes, and ultimately, the money was taken out to California. All right, there is knowledge of the fact that he did start with a million seven. Several people know this. Now, since '69, he's spent a good deal of this money and, and, uh, accounting for it is going to be very difficult for Herb. For example, he's spent—oh—close to five hundred thousand dollars on private polling. Now that just opens up a whole new thing. It's not illegal, but, uh, it's more of the same sort of thing.

PRESIDENT: I don't think that poses a hell of a problem, does it?

DEAN: No, I don't think so. Uh—

PRESIDENT: Practically everybody does polling.

DEAN: That's right, uh, it's not, there's nothing criminal about it. It was private polls. It was . . .

PRESIDENT: Nothing—

DEAN: . . . uh, proper money.

PRESIDENT: The law didn't, the law didn't (*Unintelligible*) . . .

DEAN: (*Coughs*)

PRESIDENT: . . . polled all through the years.

DEAN: That's right. Uh, he sent four hundred thousand dollars, as he's described to me, somewhere in the South for another candidate. I assume this was four hundred, uh, that went . . .

PRESIDENT: Wallace.

DEAN: . . . to Wallace. Right. Uh, he has maintained, uh, a, a man, who I only know by the name of "Tony," who is the fellow who did the, the Chappaquidick study and . . .

PRESIDENT: I heard about that.

DEAN: . . . other, other odd jobs like that. Nothing illegal . . .

PRESIDENT: Yeah.

DEAN: . . . uh, but closer. Uh, I don't know of anything that Herb has done that is illegal, other than the fact that he doesn't want to blow the whistle on a lot of people, and may find himself in a perjury situation.

PRESIDENT: Well, if he, uh, he could—because he will be asked about that money.

DEAN: He will. What'll happen is, when they call him up there—and he of course has no immunity, uh, they'll say, "How did you happen—how did you pay Mr. Segretti?" "Well, I had cash on hand." "Well, how much cash did you have on hand?"

PRESIDENT: Right.

DEAN: Uh, where does he go from there? "Where did you get the cash?"

PRESIDENT: Uh, huh.

DEAN: A full series of questions. His bank records indicate he had cash on hand, because some of these were set up in trustee accounts.

PRESIDENT: How would you handle him, then, John? For example, would you just have him put the whole thing out?

DEAN: (*Draws Breath*)

PRESIDENT: I don't think so. I mean I don't mind the five hundred thousand dollars and I don't mind the four hundred thousand dollars . . .

DEAN: No, that—

PRESIDENT: . . . for activities (*Unintelligible*).

DEAN: That, that, uh, that doesn't bother me either. There's—as I say, Herb's problems are . . .

PRESIDENT: There's a surplus—

DEAN: . . . politically embarrassing, but not as, not criminal.

PRESIDENT: Well, they're embarrassing, sure—he, he just handled matters that were between the campaigns, before anything was done. There were surveys, et cetera, et cetera, et cetera, et cetera. There is no need to account for that. No law requires him to account for that.

DEAN: Right. Uh, now—

PRESIDENT: The source of the money, there's no illegality in having a surplus, is there, in cash afterwards?

DEAN: No, the money—it has always been argued by Stans—came from pre-convention.

PRESIDENT: Pre-convention.

DEAN: For the—and pre-primary for the, for the, uh . . .

PRESIDENT: That's right.

DEAN: . . . '68 race.

PRESIDENT: That's right.

DEAN: It was just set aside.

PRESIDENT: That's right.

DEAN: Uh, that, that all can be explained. I think that the—

PRESIDENT: All right. How do your other vulnerabilities go together?

DEAN: The other vulnerabilities: We've got a, uh, runaway Grand Jury up in the Southern District.

PRESIDENT: Yeah, I heard.

DEAN: They're after Mitchell and Stans on some sort of bribe or influence peddling . . .

PRESIDENT: On Vesco.

DEAN: . . . with Vesco.

PRESIDENT: Yeah.

DEAN: Uh, they're also going to try to drag Ehrlichman into that. Apparently, Ehrlichman had some meetings with Vesco, also. Uh, Don Nixon, Jr., came in to see John a couple of times, uh, about the problem.

PRESIDENT: Not about the Complaint.

DEAN: That, there's uh—the fact of the matter is—

PRESIDENT: He came about a job.

DEAN: That's right. And, and, and, uh, I—

PRESIDENT: We're, it's—Ehrlichman's totally to blame on that.

DEAN: Yeah. Well, I think . . .

PRESIDENT: No White House (*Unintelligible*).

DEAN: No one has done anything for . . .

PRESIDENT: . . . Vesco.

DEAN: . . . Vesco.

PRESIDENT: . . . matter of—not for the prosecutor.

DEAN: No. (*Coughs*) The, uh—

PRESIDENT: Would Ehrlichman, incidentally, have to appear there?

DEAN: Before that Grand Jury? Yes. He could very well.

PRESIDENT: Uh, we couldn't presume immunity there?

DEAN: Not really. Uh, criminal charge—

PRESIDENT: Criminal charge—yeah. (*Unintelligible*) the charge is, mind you. Go ahead.

DEAN: Right. That's a little different. (*Clears Throat*) I think that would be dyna-mite to defend, uh . . .

PRESIDENT: Yeah.

DEAN: . . . against that.

PRESIDENT: Also, he, he distinguishes it. He says, "It's criminal charge; I'll be glad to go up." Use the Flanigan . . .

DEAN: Right.

PRESIDENT: . . . analogy.

DEAN: Right, uh, (*Clears Throat*) well, that's, that's pretty much the overall picture and probably the most troublesome thing—well, the Segretti thing. Let's get down to that. I think Bob has indicated to me he told you a lot of, of it, that he, indeed, did authorize it. He didn't authorize anything like ultimately evolved.

PRESIDENT: Yeah.

DEAN: He was aware of it. He was aware that Chapin and Strachan were looking for somebody.

PRESIDENT: Yeah.

DEAN: Again, this is one that, uh, it is potential that Dwight Cha-, Chapin could have a felony charge against him in this, because he's—

PRESIDENT: Felony?

DEAN: Felony. Because he has to, he has to disprove a negative. The negative is that he didn't control and direct Segretti.

PRESIDENT: Would the felony be in perjury again? Or—

DEAN: Uh, no. The felony this, in this instance being a potential use of the, one of the civil rights statutes, for anybody who interferes with a candidate for, uh, national office—not in, interferes with their campaign in any way.

PRESIDENT: Why isn't (*Unintelligible*) civil rights statute be used to pick up any of these clowns that were demonstrating against us, then?

DEAN: Well, I have, I've, I've argued that they use that for that very purpose. Uh—

PRESIDENT: Really?

DEAN: Yes, I have. And, uh—

PRESIDENT: We were, those were, uh, that was interfering with the campaign.

DEAN: That's exactly right. That's exactly right. But they—

PRESIDENT: The Segretti one, I think, uh, I'm not as concerned about that because it's so bad the way it's been put out on the PR side, then I think it will eventually end up on the PR side very confused. And it'll look bad when that's attributed, but I don't, I can't see the criminal thing, (*Clears Throat*) but I just may be wrong.

DEAN: Well, here, what really, what really bothers me is that this, this growing situation—as I say it is growing because of the, the continued need to provide support for the . . .

PRESIDENT: Right.

DEAN: . . . Watergate people who are going to . . .

PRESIDENT: Yeah.

DEAN: . . . hold us up for everything they've got . . .

PRESIDENT: That's right.

DEAN: . . . and the need for some people to perjure themselves as they go down the road here. Uh, if this thing ever blows, and we're in a cover-up situation, I think it'd be extremely damaging to you, uh, and uh, the, uh—

PRESIDENT: Sure.

DEAN: Uh—

PRESIDENT: The whole concept of Administration justice.

DEAN: That's right, uh—

PRESIDENT: We cannot have—

DEAN: That's what really troubles me. For example, what happens if it starts breaking, and they do find a criminal case against a Haldeman, a Dean, a Mitchell, an Ehrlichman? Uh, that is—

PRESIDENT: Well, if it really comes down to that, we cannot, maybe—we'd have to shed it in order to contain it again.

DEAN: (*Clears Throat*) That's right. I'm coming down to the—what I really think is that, that, Bob and John and John Mitchell and I should sit down and spend a day, or however long, to figure out (1) how this can be carved away from you, so it does not damage you or the Presidency. 'Cause it just can't. And it's not something, it, you're not involved in it and it's something you shouldn't—

PRESIDENT: That is true.

DEAN: I know, sir, it is. Well, I can just tell from our conversations that, you know, these are things that you have no knowledge of.

PRESIDENT: The absurdity of the whole damned thing . . .

DEAN: But it—

PRESIDENT: bugging and so on. Well, let me say I am keenly aware of the fact that, uh, Colson, et al, and so forth were doing their best to get information and so forth and so on. But they all knew very well they were supposed to comply with the law.

DEAN: That's right.

PRESIDENT: No question.

DEAN: Uh—

PRESIDENT: (*Unintelligible*) you think—you feel that really the man, the trigger-man was Colson on this end?

DEAN: Well, no. He was one of se-, he was just in the chain. He was, he helped push the thing.

PRESIDENT: Called him up and said, "We've got a, we've got (*Unintelligible*)" I don't know what the Christ he would be doing. Oh, I'll bet you, I know why. That was at the time of ITT. He was trying to get something going there because ITT—they were bugging us, I mean they were . . .

DEAN: Right.

PRESIDENT: . . . giving us hell.

DEAN: Well, I know, I know he used, uh—

PRESIDENT: Hunt to go out there?

DEAN: Hunt.

PRESIDENT: I knew about that.

DEAN: Yeah.

PRESIDENT: I did know about it at the time. I knew that there was, there was something going on there . . .

DEAN: Right.

PRESIDENT: . . . but I didn't know it was Hunt.

DEAN: Right. Uh, that's what re-, what really troubles me is, you know, (1) will this thing not break some day and . . .

PRESIDENT: Yeah.

DEAN: . . . the whole thing—domino situation.

PRESIDENT: Yeah.

DEAN: You know, they just, I think if it starts crumbling, fingers will be pointing, and—

PRESIDENT: That's right.

DEAN: Uh—

PRESIDENT: That's right.

DEAN: Bob will be accused of things he has never heard of . . .

PRESIDENT: Yeah.

DEAN: . . . and then he'll have to disprove it, and it'll just get nasty and it'll be a real, uh, real bad situation. And the person who will be hurt by it most will be you and . . .

PRESIDENT: Of course.

DEAN: . . . the Presidency, and I just don't think—

PRESIDENT: First, because I'm expected to know this, and I'm supposed to, supposed to check these things. And so forth . . .

DEAN: That's right.

PRESIDENT: and so on. But let's, let's, let's come back and go further. Sure. Yes, indeed. But what are your feelings, yourself, John? You know pretty well what they'll all say. What are your feelings toward the options?

DEAN: I am not confident that, uh, we can ride through this. I think there are, I think there are soft spots.

PRESIDENT: You used to feel comfortable.

DEAN: Well, I feel, I felt, I felt comfortable for this reason. I've noticed of recent since the publicity has increased on, on this thing again, with the Gray hearings, that everybody is now starting to watch out for their own behind. Uh—

PRESIDENT: That's right.

DEAN: Everyone's pulling in. They're getting their own counsel. More counsel are getting . . .

PRESIDENT: Right.

DEAN: . . . involved.

PRESIDENT: Right.

DEAN: Uh, you know, "How do I protect my ass?"

PRESIDENT: Well, they're scared.

DEAN: They're scared and that's just, you know, that's bad. We were able to hold it for a long time.

PRESIDENT: Yeah, I know.

DEAN: Uh, another thing is, you know, my facility now to deal with the multitude of people I have been dealing with has been hampered because of Gray blowing me up into the front page.

PRESIDENT: Your cover's broken.

DEAN: That's right and it's with, it was—

PRESIDENT: (*Unintelligible*) cover. All right. Now. So on. So, so, what you really come down to is, what in the hell, in the hell will you do? Let's, let us suppose that you and Haldeman and Ehrlichman and Mitchell say, uh, "We can't hold this." What, what then are you going to say? Are you going to put out a complete disclosure? Isn't that the best plan?

DEAN: Well, one way to do it is to—

PRESIDENT: That's by my view on it.

DEAN: One way to do it is for you to in-, tell the Attorney General that you can finally, you know, really, this is the first time you're getting all the pieces together.

Reel 2 Begins

DEAN: Uh—

PRESIDENT: Ask for another grand jury?

DEAN: Ask for another grand jury. The way it should be done though, is a way that—for example: I think that we could avoid, uh, criminal liability for countless people and the ones that did get it, it could be minimal.

Reel 1 Ends

(*Noise*)

PRESIDENT: How?

DEAN: Well, I think by just thinking it all through first, as to how some people could be granted immunity, uh . . .

PRESIDENT: Like Magruder?

DEAN: Yeah—to come forward. Uh, but some people are going to have to go to jail. That's the long and short of it, also.

PRESIDENT: Who? Let's talk about that.

DEAN: All right. Uh, I think I could, for one.

PRESIDENT: You go to jail?

DEAN: That's right.

PRESIDENT: Oh, hell no. I can't see how you can. But, I—no . . .

DEAN: Well, because . . .

PRESIDENT: I can't see how, that—let me say I can't see how a legal case could be made against you, J-, uh, John.

DEAN: It'd be, it'd be tough, but you know, uh . . .

PRESIDENT: Well.

DEAN: I can see people pointing fingers, you know, to get it out of their own—put me in the impossible position, disproving too many negatives.

PRESIDENT: Oh, no. Uh, let me say I—not because you're here—but just looking at it from a cold legal standpoint: You are a lawyer, you were a counsel—you were doing what you were doing as a counsel, and you were not, uh, . . .

DEAN: (*Clears Throat*)

PRESIDENT: doing anything like that. You mean—what would you go to jail on (*Unintelligible*)?

DEAN: The obstruc-, the obstruction of justice.

PRESIDENT: The obstruction of justice?

DEAN: That's the only one that bothers me.

PRESIDENT: Well, I don't know. I think that one, I think that, I feel could be cut off at the pass. Maybe the obstruction of justice . . .

DEAN: It could be a—you know how—one of the—that's, that's why—(*Sighs*)

PRESIDENT: Sometimes it's well to give them . . .

DEAN: (*Sighs*)

PRESIDENT: something, and then they don't want the bigger fish then.

DEAN: That's right. I think that, uh, I think that with proper coordination with the Department of Justice, Henry Petersen is the only man I know bright enough and knowledgeable enough in the criminal laws and the process that could really tell us how this could be put together so it did the maximum to carve it away with a minimum damage to individuals involved.

(*Noise*)

PRESIDENT: Petersen doesn't know the whole story?

DEAN: No, I know he doesn't now. I know he doesn't now. I am talking about somebody who I have over the years grown to have faith in. (*Banging Noises in Background*) (*Clears Throat*) It is possible that he'd have to, he'd have to, uh—put him in a very difficult situation as the Head of the Criminal Division of the United States Department of Justice, and the oath of office . . .

PRESIDENT: Tell me—talking about your obstruction of justice role, I don't see it. I can't see it. You're . . .

DEAN: Well, I've been a con-, I have been a conduit for information on, on taking care of people out there who are guilty of crimes.

PRESIDENT: Oh, you mean like the, uh, oh—the blackmail.

DEAN: The blackmail, right.

PRESIDENT: Well, I wonder if that part of it can't be, (*Pause*) I wonder if that doesn't—let me put it frankly: I wonder if that doesn't have to be continued?

DEAN: (*Clears Throat*)

PRESIDENT: Let me put it this way, let us suppose that you get, you, you get the million bucks and you get the proper way to handle it, and you could hold that side.

DEAN: Um huh.

PRESIDENT: It would seem to me that would be worthwhile.

DEAN: (*Clears Throat*)

PRESIDENT: Now we have . . .

DEAN: Well, that's, yeah that's . . .

PRESIDENT: One problem; you've got a problem here. You have the problem of Hunt and uh, his, uh, his clemency.

DEAN: That's right. And you're going to have the clemency problem for the others. They all would expect to be out and that may put you in a position that's just . . .

PRESIDENT: Right.

DEAN: untenable at some point. You know, the Watergate Hearings just over, Hunt now demanding clemency or he is going to blow. And politically it'd be impossible for, you know, you to do it. You know, after everybody . . .

PRESIDENT: That's right.

DEAN: I am not sure that you will ever be able to deliver on the clemency. It may be just too hot.

PRESIDENT: You can't do it till after the '74 elections, that's for sure. But even then . . .

DEAN: (*Clears Throat*)

PRESIDENT: your point is that even then you couldn't do it.

DEAN: That's right. It may further involve you in a way you shouldn't be involved in this.

PRESIDENT: No it's wrong, that's for sure.

DEAN: Well, whatever, you know, I, there've been some bad judgments made. There've been some necessary judgments made. Uh . . .

PRESIDENT: Before the election.

DEAN: Before the election and, in a way, the necessary ones, you know, before the election. There, you know, we've, this was to me there was no way

PRESIDENT: Yeah.

DEAN: that uh . . .

PRESIDENT: Yeah.

DEAN: But to burden this second Administration

PRESIDENT: We're all in on it.

DEAN: was something that, it's something that is not going to go away.

PRESIDENT: No it isn't.

DEAN: It is not going to go away, sir.

PRESIDENT: Not going to go away, it is, the idea that, uh, that, uh, well, that uh, that people are going to get tired of it and all that sort of thing . . .

DEAN: Anything will spark it back into life. It's got to be, uh, it's got to be . . .

PRESIDENT: Well, it's too much to the partisan interest of others to spark it back into life.

DEAN: And it seems to me the only way that . . .

PRESIDENT: Who else, though? Let's, let's leave you and I don't, I don't think on the, on, uh, on the obstruction of justice thing, I think that one we can handle. I, I don't know why I feel that way, but I . . .

DEAN: Well, it is possible that I . . .

PRESIDENT: I, I think you may be overplaying, but who else, uh, who else, who else do you think, has, uh

DEAN: Potential criminal liability?

PRESIDENT: Yeah.

DEAN: I think Ehrlichman does. I think that, uh, I think . . .

PRESIDENT: Why Ehrlichman? What'd he do?

DEAN: Because this conspiracy to burglarize the, uh, uh, Ellsberg office.

PRESIDENT: You mean, that, that is provided Hunt breaks

DEAN: Well, uh, the, the funny, let me say something interesting about that. Within the files . . .

PRESIDENT: Oh, I saw that. The picture.

DEAN: Yeah, the picture. That, see, that's not all that buried. And, while we can, we've got, I think we've got it buried, there is no telling when it's going to pop up. Uh, the Cubans, uh, could start this whole thing. Uh, when the Ervin Committee starts running down why this mysterious telephone was here at the White House, uh, listed in the name of a secretary, one of these, some of these secretaries have a little idea about this, and they can be broken down just . . .

PRESIDENT: Sure

DEAN: so fast. That's another thing I missed, missed in the cycle, in the circle. Uh, Liddy's secretary for example, is knowledgeable. Magruder's secretary is knowledgeable.

PRESIDENT: Sure.

DEAN: Uh . . .

PRESIDENT: So Ehrlichman on the, uh . . .

DEAN: But what I am coming to you today with is I don't have a plan of how to solve it right now, but I think it's at the juncture that we should begin to think in terms of, of how to cut the losses; how to minimize the further growth of this thing; rather than further compound it by, you know, ultimately paying these guys forever.

PRESIDENT: Yeah.

DEAN: I think we've got to look . . .

PRESIDENT: But at the moment, don't you agree that you'd better get the Hunt thing? I mean, that's worth it, at the moment.

DEAN: That, that's worth buying time on, right.

PRESIDENT: And that's buying time on, I agree.

DEAN: Uh, the, the Grand Jury is going to reconvene next week after Sirica sentences. Uh, but that's why I think that, you know, that John and Bob have met with me. They've never met with Mitchell on this. We've never had a real down and out with everybody, that, uh, has the most to lose. And the most, and it is the most danger for you to have them have criminal liability. I think Bob has a potential criminal liability, frankly, I think, in other words, a lot of these people could be indicted. They might never . . .

PRESIDENT: Yeah.

DEAN: might never, uh, be convicted; but just the thought of

PRESIDENT: Suppose . . .

DEAN: indictments . . .

PRESIDENT: Suppose that they are indicted in this. Suppose . . .

DEAN: I think that would be devastating.

PRESIDENT: Suppose the worst, that Bob is indicted and Ehrlichman is indicted. And I must say, maybe we just better then try to tough it through. You get my point.

DEAN: That's right. That . . .

PRESIDENT: If, if, if, for example, our, uh, our—say well, let's cut our losses and you say we're going to go down the road, see if we can cut our losses, and no more blackmail and all the rest, and the thing blows and they indict Bob and the rest. Jesus, you'd never recover from that, John.

DEAN: That's right.

PRESIDENT: It's better to fight it out instead. You see, that's the other thing, the other thing. It's better just to fight it out, and not let people testify, so forth and so on. Now, on the other hand, we realize that we have these weaknesses—that, uh, (Pause) we've got this weakness in terms of (Pause) blackmail.

DEAN: It's what, if we, you know, there, there are two routes, you know: One is to figure out how to cut the losses and, and, and minimize the, the human impact and get you up and out and away from it, in any way, uh, in, in a way that would never come back to haunt. Uh, that is one, one general alternative. The other is to go (Cough) down the road, just hunker down, fight it at every corner, every turn, uh, don't let people testify, cover it up is what we're really talking about. Just keep it buried, and just hope that we can do it, hope that we make good decisions at the right time, and keep our heads cool, uh, we make the right moves, uh . . .

PRESIDENT: And just take the heat.

DEAN: And just take the heat.

PRESIDENT: Now, with the second line of attack. You discussed this though I do want you to still consider my scheme of having y—, you brief the Cabinet, just in very general terms (*Unintelligible*) in very general terms, and maybe some, some very general statement with regard to my investigation. Answer questions, and to, and to basically on the question of what they told you, not what you know

DEAN: Right.

PRESIDENT: Haldeman is not involved. Ehrlichman . . .

DEAN: Oh, I can, you know, if, if we go that route, sir, I can, I can give a show that, you know, there's uh, we can sell, you know, just about like we were selling Wheaties on our position. There's no . . .

PRESIDENT: The problem that you have are these, uh, mine fields down the road. I think the most difficult problem is the, are the, are the, are the guys that are going to jail. I think you're right about that. I agree. Now. And also the fact that we're not going to be able to give them clemency.

DEAN: That's right. How long will they take? How long will they sit there? I don't know. We don't know, what they'll be sentenced to. There's always a chance . . .

PRESIDENT: Thirty years, isn't it? Maximum?

DEAN: It could be. You know, they haven't announced yet, but it, uh . . .

PRESIDENT: Isn't that what the potential is?

DEAN: Uh, it's even higher than that. It's about fifty years, with all the . . .

PRESIDENT: So ridiculous.

DEAN: Oh well, you know, what's so incredible is, the, these fellows who, who, sh . . .

PRESIDENT: People break and enter, and so forth, and get two years.

DEAN: Well, the other thing . . .

PRESIDENT: No, no weapons. No results. What the hell are they talking about?

DEAN: The, the individuals who are charged with shooting John Stennis are on the street. They were given, you know, uh, one was put on his personal recognizance rather than bond. They've got these fellows all stuck with hundred thousand dollar bonds. The same Judge—Sirica—let one guy, who, who's (*Laughs*) charged with shooting a United States Senator, out on the street.

PRESIDENT: Sirica did?

DEAN: Yeah. It's just, it's phenomenal.

PRESIDENT: I thought he was a hardliner judge.

DEAN: He's a, he's is just a, a peculiar animal, and uh, he set, set the bond for one of the others—I don't have all the facts, but he set the bond for one of the others—somewhere around fifty or sixty thousand dollars. But still, that guy is in, but didn't make bond, but you know, sixty thousand dollars as opposed to a hundred thousand dollars for these guys is phenomenal.

PRESIDENT: When could you have this meeting with these fellows, as I think that time is of the essence, in my opinion.

DEAN: (*Clears Throat*)

PRESIDENT: Could you do it this afternoon?

DEAN: Well, Mitchell isn't here, and . . .

PRESIDENT: Tomorrow?

DEAN: It might be, might be worth it to have him come down. And, now, I think that Bob and John did not want to talk to, to John about this, John Mitchell. And I don't believe they've had any conversations with him about it.

(*Loud Noises on Desk*)

DEAN: Bob and I have talked about just what we're talking about this morning. I told him I thought that you should have the facts, and he agrees. Cause we've got some tough calls down the road if we . . .

PRESIDENT: Let me say, though that Hunt (*Unintelligible*) (*Dragging Noise on Desk*) hard line, and that a convicted felon is going to go out and squeal (*Unintelligible*) (*Dragging Noise on Desk*) as we about this (*Unintelligible*) decision (*Unintelligible*) turns on that.

DEAN: Well, we can always, you know, on the other side, we can always charge them with blackmailing us, and it's, you know, this is absurd stuff they're saying and . . .

(*Pause*)

PRESIDENT: That's right. You see, even the way you put it out here, of course if it all came out, it may never, it may not never, never get there.

(*Haldeman Enters the Room*)

(*Loud Noises on Desk*)

PRESIDENT: I was talking to John about this, uh, this whole situation, and I think we, uh, so that we can get away from the bits and pieces that have broken out. He is right in having in, in, uh, recommending that, that, uh, that there be a meeting at the very first possible time. Ehrlichman, and now Ehrlichman's gone on to California but, uh, is today, uh, is tomorrow Thursday?

HALDEMAN: Uh, he John doesn't go until Friday.

DEAN: Friday ...

PRESIDENT: Well, in any event, could we do it. Thursday? This meeting: This meeting you can't do it today, can you?

DEAN: I don't think so. I was suggesting a meeting with Mitchell ...

PRESIDENT: Mitchell, Ehrlichman, yourself and Bob, that's all. Now, Mitchell has to be there because, uh, uh, he is seriously involved and, uh, we're trying to keep, uh, we've got to see how we, uh, how we handle it from here on. We are in the process of having to determine which way to go and, uh, John has thought it through, as well as he can. I do, I don't want Moore there on this occasion.

DEAN: No.

PRESIDENT: You haven't told Moore all of this, have you?

DEAN: Moore's got, uh, by being with me, has more bits and pieces. I've had to give him

PRESIDENT: Right.

DEAN: because he is making

PRESIDENT: Right.

DEAN: judgments that, uh ....

PRESIDENT: Well, the point is, once you get down to the PR, once you decide what you're going to do, then we can let him know, and so forth and so on. But it is the kind of thing, I think what really has to happen is for you to sit down with those three and for you to tell them exactly what you told me.

DEAN: Um huh.

PRESIDENT: It may take him about thirty-five or forty-five minutes. In other words he knows, John, uh, uh, knows about everything and also what all the, uh, what all the potential criminal liabilities are, you know, whether it's, uh, what's it like that thing, what about, uh obstruction . . .

DEAN: Obstruction of justice. Right.

PRESIDENT: So forth and so on. And, uh, the uh, I think, I think that's . . . Then we've got to, uh, see what the line is. Whether the line is one of continuing to, uh, run a, try to run a total stonewall, and take the heat from that, uh, having in mind the fact that, uh, there are vulnerable points there; the vulnerable points being that, well, the first vulnerable points would be obvious. In other words, it would be, if, uh, uh, one of the, uh, defendants, particularly Hunt, of course, who is the most vulnerable in my opinion, might, uh, blow the whistle, and he, he and his price is pretty high, but at least, uh, we should, we should buy the time on that, uh, as I as I pointed out to John. Apparently . . . Who, who is dealing with Hunt at the moment now that Colson's (*Unintelligible*)

DEAN: Well, uh, Mitchell's lawyer and, uh . . .

PRESIDENT: Colson's lawyer (*Unintelligible*)

DEAN: Colson's lawyer, both.

PRESIDENT: familiar with him. Hunt has at least got to know before he is sentenced that he's . . .

HALDEMAN: Who's Colson's lawyer? (*Characterization Deleted*) in his firm?

DEAN: Shapiro. Right. Who lied to the, you know, who just . . . The other day, he came up and . . .

HALDEMAN: Colson's told him everything, hasn't he?

DEAN: Yup, I gather he has. Uh, the other thing that bothered me about that is that he's, uh, a chatter. He came up to Fred Fielding, of my office, at Colson's going away party. I didn't go over there. It was over at the Blair House the other night. And he said to, uh, Fred, he said, "Well, Chuck has had some mighty serious words, with, uh, his, his friend Howard and had some mighty serious messages back." Now, you know, what's a lawyer how does he know what Fielding knows? Cause Fielding knows virtually nothing. (*Laughs*)

PRESIDENT: Well, anyway.

HALDEMAN: That's, that's where your dangers lie, is in all these stupid human errors developing.

PRESIDENT: That's very . . .

DEAN: That's . . . that's . . .

PRESIDENT: Well, the point is, Bob, let's face it, the secretaries know, the assistants know. There's a lot of the, many of the damn principals may be hard as a rock, but you never know when they're going to crack. But, so, we'll see, we'll see. First you've got the Hunt problem. That ought to be handled.

DEAN: Yeah.

PRESIDENT: Uh, incidentally, I do not think Colson should sit in this meeting. Do you agree?

DEAN: No. I would agree.

PRESIDENT: Okay. Uh, how then . . . who does sit and talk to Colson? Because somebody has to, shouldn't we talk to . . .

DEAN: Chuck, uh . . .

PRESIDENT: talks too much.

DEAN: (Sighs) I, I, you know, I like Chuck (Laughs) but, uh, I don't want Chuck, to know anything that I'm doing frankly. (Laughs)

PRESIDENT: All right.

HALDEMAN: I think that's right. I, I think you want to be careful not to give Chuck any more knowledge than he's already got.

DEAN: That's right.

PRESIDENT: Sure. Well . . .

DEAN: I wouldn't want Chuck to even know of the meeting, frankly.

PRESIDENT: Fortunately, fortunately, with Chuck, it is very, I, I talk to him about many, many political things, but I never talk about this sort of thing 'cause he's, uh, he's very harmful, I mean I don't think . . . he must be damn sure I don't know anything. And I don't. In fact, I'm rather surprised at what you told me today. From what you said, I gathered the impression, and of course, your, your, your analysis does not for sure, uh, indicate that Chuck knew that it was a bugging operation for certain.

DEAN: That's correct. I don't have . . .

PRESIDENT: On the other hand, on the other hand that,

DEAN: Chuck, Chuck denies that . . .

PRESIDENT: on the other hand, the other side of that is that Hunt had conversations with Chuck, and it may be that Hunt told Chuck that it was bugging, and so forth and so on.

DEAN: Um huh.

PRESIDENT: Is that correct?

DEAN: Um hum. They were very close. They, they talked too much, uh, about too many things.

PRESIDENT: Yeah.

DEAN: They were intimate on this sort of (*Coughs*)

HALDEMAN: Well then Chuck . . .

PRESIDENT: There's another thing you can't . . .

HALDEMAN: Chuck has a problem. Chuck loves,

PRESIDENT: Yeah.

HALDEMAN: he loves what he does.

PRESIDENT: Yeah.

HALDEMAN: He likes to talk about it.

PRESIDENT: He also is a name dropper. Chuck might have gone around and talked to Hunt and said "Well, I was talking to the President, and the President feels we ought to get information about this, or that or the other thing," and so forth and so on.

DEAN: Well, Liddy is the same way, and . . .

PRESIDENT: I have talked to, I have talked to . . . this and that and the other thing. I, I have never talked to anybody, but I have talked to Chuck and John and the rest and I am sure that Chuck may have, Chuck might have even talked to Hunt along those lines.

HALDEMAN: I would . . . well, anything could happen. I would doubt that.

DEAN: I would doubt that too.

HALDEMAN: I don't think he would. Uh, Chuck is a name dropper in one sense, but not in that sense.

PRESIDENT: Well, then do you think . . .

HALDEMAN: I think he very carefully keeps the President out of things.

(*Noise*)

PRESIDENT: Right.

HALDEMAN: Except when he's doing it, when he's very intentionally bringing the President in for, for the President's purposes.

PRESIDENT: He had the impression though, apparently, that he, he was the, as it turns out, really is, the trigger man. Uh, may of damn well have been the trigger man where he just called up and said, "Now look here Jeb, go ahead and get that information." And (*Unintelligible*) got to be a decision on it at that time. This is February.

DEAN: Yes sir, I figure it was some other . . .

PRESIDENT: It must be the . . . I . . . it must have been after . . .

DEAN: This was the call to Magruder from Colson saying "Fish or cut bait." Hunt and Liddy were in his office.

HALDEMAN: In Colson's office?

DEAN: In Colson's office. And he called Magruder and said, "Let's fish or cut bait on this operation. Let's get it going."

HALDEMAN: Oh, really?

DEAN: Yeah. This is . . . Magruder tells me this.

HALDEMAN: Of course. That . . .

PRESIDENT: Well, on the other hand . . .

HALDEMAN: Now wait, Magruder testified (*Unintelligible*).

(*Several Voices Unintelligible*)

DEAN: Chuck, Chuck, also told me that, uh, Hunt and Liddy were in his office and he made a call.

HALDEMAN: Oh, okay.

DEAN: So it did, it was corroborated by the, the principal.

HALDEMAN: Hunt and Liddy haven't told you that, though?

DEAN: No.

HALDEMAN: You haven't talked to Hunt and Liddy?

DEAN: I talked to Liddy once, right after the incident.

PRESIDENT: I'm sorry about that. All right, the point is, the point is this, that uh, it's now time, though, to, uh, that Mitchell has got to sit down, and know where the hell all this thing stands too. You see, John is concerned, as you know, Bob, about, uh, Ehrlichman, which, uh, worries me a great deal because it's a, uh, uh, a-, and this is why the Hunt problem is so serious, uh, because, uh, it had nothing to do with the campaign.

DEAN: Right, it, uh . . .

PRESIDENT: Properly, it has to do with the Ellsberg thing. I don't know what the hell, uh . . .

HALDEMAN: But why . . .

PRESIDENT: Yeah. Why . . . I don't know.

HALDEMAN: What I was going to say is . . .

PRESIDENT: What is the answer on that? How do you keep that out? I don't know. Well, we can't keep it out if Hunt . . . if . . . you see the point is, it is irrelevant. Once it has gotten to this point . . .

DEAN: You might, you might put it on a national security ground basis, which it really, it was.

HALDEMAN: It absolutely was.

DEAN: And just say that, uh . . .

PRESIDENT: Yeah.

DEAN: that this is not, you know, this was . . .

PRESIDENT: Not paid with CIA funds.

DEAN: Uh . . .

PRESIDENT: No, seriously, national security. We had to get information for national security grounds.

DEAN: Well, then the question is, why didn't the CIA do it or why didn't the FBI do it?

PRESIDENT: Because they were . . . we had to do it, we had to do it, on a confidential basis.

HALDEMAN: Because we were checking them?

PRESIDENT: Neither could be trusted.

HALDEMAN: Well, I think . . .

PRESIDENT: That's the way I view it.

HALDEMAN: That has never been proven. There was reason to question their

PRESIDENT: Yeah.

HALDEMAN: Position.

PRESIDENT: You see really, with the bombing thing and everything coming out, the whole thing was national security.

DEAN: I think we can probably get, get by on that.

PRESIDENT: I think on that one, I think you'd simply say this was a national security investigation that was conducted. And the same with the drug field with Krogh. Krogh could say I . . . if Krogh were to . . . if (*Unintelligible*) he feels that he perjured (*Unintelligible*) it was a national security matter. That's why . . .

DEAN: That's the way Bud rests easy, because he's, he's, he's convinced that he was doing it . . . he said there was treason about the country, and it could have threatened the way the war was handled. Uh, and by God . . .

PRESIDENT: Bud, Bud said this?

DEAN: Yes.

PRESIDENT: Well, Bud could say that and say this, it does involve . . . it was a national security and I was not in a position to divulge it. Well anyway, let's don't go beyond that. We're . . . forget . . . but I do think now we, uh, I mean, there is, there is a time, now when you don't want to talk to Mitchell. He doesn't want to talk, and the rest. But John is right. There must be a, must be a four way talk here of the particular ones that we can trust here. Uh, we've got to get a decision on it. It's not something that . . . you see you got two ways, basically. There are really only two ways you could go. You either decide the whole God damned thing is so full of problems with potential criminal liability which is what concerns me. I don't give a damn about the publicity. We could, we could rock that through, if we had to let the whole thing hang out. It would be a lousy story for a month. But I can take it. But the point is, I don't want any criminal liability. That's the thing that I am concerned about for members of the White House staff and I would trust for members of the Committee. And that means Magruder.

DEAN: Um.

PRESIDENT: Let's face it. He's the one that's, uh . . . I think Magruder is the major guy over there.

DEAN: I think he's got the most serious problem.

PRESIDENT: Yeah.

HALDEMAN: Well, then we talked about yesterday, you've got a, you got a question where your cut off point is. There is a possibility of cutting it at Liddy, where you are now.

PRESIDENT: Yeah.

HALDEMAN: But to accomplish that requires:

PRESIDENT: Requires what?

HALDEMAN: Requires continued perjury by Magruder.

PRESIDENT: Yeah. And it requires total . . .

DEAN: commitment . . .

PRESIDENT: Control, got total, got total control over all of the defendants, which . . . in other words (*Unintelligible*)

DEAN: The basic position . . .

HALDEMAN: They don't know anything beyond Liddy.

DEAN: Uh, no. Other than the fact, other than the fact that Liddy, they have hearsay, uh . . .

HALDEMAN: But we don't know about Hunt. Maybe Hunt has it tied in to Colson. We don't know that, though really.

DEAN: No.

PRESIDENT: I think Hunt knows a hell of a lot more.

DEAN: Yeah, I do too. And now what McCord . . .

HALDEMAN: You think he does? I am afraid you're right, but, uh, we don't know that.

PRESIDENT: I think we better assume it. I think Colson

DEAN: And he's playing hard ball, and he wouldn't play hard . . .

HALDEMAN: Is he?

DEAN: Yeah. He wouldn't play hard ball unless he were pretty confident that he could cause an awful lot of grief.

HALDEMAN: Really?

DEAN: Yeah.

PRESIDENT: He is playing hard boiled ball with regard to Ehrlichman, for example, and that sort of thing. He knows what he's got.

HALDEMAN: What's he planning on, money?

DEAN: Yeah, money and . . .

HALDEMAN: Really?

DEAN: Oh, yeah. He's uh . . .

PRESIDENT: It's a hundred and twenty thousand dollars. It's about what, about how much, which is easy. I mean, it's not easy to deliver, but it is easy to get. Uh, now, uh (*Nine Seconds of Silence*) If that, if what, if that, if that is the case, if it's just that way, then the thing to do is, if, if, the thing all, uh, cracks out . . . if, if for, if, for example, you say look we're not, we're not going to continue to try to, let's state it frankly . . . cut our losses . . . that's just one way you could go . . . on the assumption that we're, we, by continuing to cut our losses, we're not going to win. That in the end, we are going to be bled to death, and it's all going to come out anyway, and then you get the worst of both worlds. We are going to lose and people are going to . . .

HALDEMAN: And look (*Unintelligible*)

PRESIDENT: And we're going to look like we covered up. So that we can't do. Now. The other, the other, uh, the other line, however, uh, if you, if you take that line, that we're not going to continue to cut our losses, that means then we have to look square in the eye as to what the hell those losses are, and see which people can . . . so we can avoid criminal liability. Right?

DEAN: That's right.

PRESIDENT: And that means, we got to, we've got to keep it off of you, uh, which I, which I (*Unintelligible*) obstruction of justice thing. We've got to keep it off Ehrlichman. We've got to keep it, naturally, off of Bob, off Chapin, if possible, and Strachan. Right?

DEAN: Um hum.

PRESIDENT: And Mitchell. Right?

DEAN: Um hum.

PRESIDENT: Now.

HALDEMAN: And Magruder, if you can. But that's the one you pretty much have to give up.

PRESIDENT: But, but Magruder, Magruder, uh, uh, John's, Dean's point is that if Magruder goes down, he'll pull everybody with him.

HALDEMAN: That's my view.

PRESIDENT: Is it?

HALDEMAN: Yup. I think Jeb, I don't think he wants to. And I think he even would try not to, but I don't think he is able not to.

DEAN: I don't think he is strong enough, when it really . . .

HALDEMAN: Well, not that, not that . . .

PRESIDENT: Well, another way, another way to do it then Bob is to . . . and John realizes this . . . is to, (*Pause*) uh, continue to try to cut our losses. Now we have to look at that course of action. First, it is going to require approximately a million dollars to take care of the jackasses that are in jail. That could be, that could be arranged.

HALDEMAN or DEAN: Yeah.

PRESIDENT: That could be arranged. But you realize that after we're gone. I mean, assuming these (*Unintelligible*) are, they're going to crack, you know what I mean? And that'll be an unseemly story. Eventually, all the people aren't going to care that much.

DEAN: That's right. It's . . .

PRESIDENT: People aren't going to care.

DEAN: So much history will pass between then and now.

PRESIDENT: In other words, what we're talking about it no question. But the second thing is we're not going to be able to deliver on, on any kind of a, of a clemency thing. You know Colson has gone around on this clemency thing with Hunt and the rest.

DEAN: Hunt, Hunt is now talking in terms of being out by Christmas.

HALDEMAN: This year?

DEAN: This year. Uh, he was told by O'Brien, who is my conveyor of doom back and forth . . .

HALDEMAN: Yeah.

DEAN: uh, that, uh, hell, he'd be lucky if he were out a year from now, after the Ervin hearings were, uh, you know, over. He said, "How in the Lord's name could you be commuted that quickly?" He said, "Well, that's my commitment from Colson."

HALDEMAN: By Christmas of this year?

DEAN: Yeah.

HALDEMAN: See, that, that really, that's very believeable cause Colson

PRESIDENT: Do you think Colson could have told him . . .

HALDEMAN: Colson is an, is an . . . that's, that's your fatal flaw, really, in Chuck, is he is an operator in expediency, and he will pay at the time and where he is whatever he has to, to accomplish what he's there to do. And that's . . . I, I would believe that he has made that commitment if Hunt says he has. I would believe he is capable of saying that.

PRESIDENT: The only thing you could do with him would be to parole him for a period of time because of his family situation. But you couldn't provide clemency.

DEAN: No, I . . . uh, Kleindienst has now got control of the parole board, and he said that now we can, we can pull paroles off now where we couldn't before. So . . .

PRESIDENT: Well, parole . . .

HALDEMAN: Yeah, but Kleindienst always tells you that, and then never delivers.

PRESIDENT: Parole, parole. Let's talk candidly about that. Parole (*Unintelligible*) in human terms, and so forth, is something that I think in Hunt's case you could do Hunt, but you couldn't do the others. You understand?

DEAN: Well, so much depends upon how Sirica sentences. He can sentence, sentence in a way that, uh, makes parole even impossible.

PRESIDENT: Oh, he can?

DEAN: Sure. He can do all kinds of permanent sentences. Yeah. He can be a, just a son-of-a-bitch, uh, as far, as the whole thing.

(*Pause*)

HALDEMAN: Of course, can't you appeal on a, on an unjust sentence, as well as on an unjust conviction?

DEAN: You've got sixty days to ask the judge to review it. There is no appellate review of sentences.

HALDEMAN: There isn't?

DEAN: Not that I . . .

PRESIDENT: The judge can review it, yeah.

HALDEMAN: Only the sentencing judge can review his own sentence?

PRESIDENT: Coming back, though, to this. So you got that . . . the, uh, hanging over. Now. If, uh, you see if you let it hang there, the point is you could let all or only part . . . The point is, your feeling is that we just can't continue to, to pay the blackmail of these guys?

DEAN: I think that's our greatest jeopardy.

HALDEMAN: Yeah.

PRESIDENT: Now, let me tell you, it's

DEAN: 'Cause that is . . .

PRESIDENT: no problem, we could, we could get the money. There is no problem in that. We can't provide the clemency. The money can be provided. Mitchell could provide the way to deliver it. That could be done. See what I mean?

HALDEMAN: But, Mitchell says he can't, doesn't he?

DEAN: Mitchell says that, uh . . . well, Mitch . . . , that's, it's, you know, there has been an interesting thing, uh, phenomena all the way along on this, is that there have been a lot of people having to pull oars and not everybody pulls them all the same time, the same way, because their developed self-interests.

HALDEMAN: What John is saying is that everybody smiles at Dean and says, "Well, you better get something done about it."

DEAN: That's right.

PRESIDENT: (*Unintelligible*)

HALDEMAN: And Mitch . . . , Mitchell is leaving Dean hanging out on a . . . None of us, well maybe we're doing the same thing to you.

DEAN: That's right.

HALDEMAN: But I . . . let me say that, that I don't see how there's any way that you can have the White House, or anybody presently in the White House, involved in trying to gin out of this money.

DEAN: We are already deeply enough in that. That's the problem, Bob.

PRESIDENT: I thought you said you could handle the money?

DEAN: Well, in fact, that, uh, when . . .

PRESIDENT: Kalmbach?

DEAN: Well, Kalmbach, uh, was a . . .

HALDEMAN: He's not the one.

DEAN: No, but when they ran out of that money, as you know, they came after the three-fifty that was over here.

PRESIDENT: And they used that, right?

DEAN: And I had to explain what it was (*Laughs*) for, uh, before I could get the money.

PRESIDENT: Well, you said . . .

DEAN: Now, they . . . now, that . . . they . . .

HALDEMAN: That was put, that was, that was . . . in the first place, that was put back to LaRue.

DEAN: That's right.

HALDEMAN: where it belonged. It wasn't all returned in a lump sum. It was put back in pieces.

DEAN: That's right.

PRESIDENT: And then LaRue used it for this other purpose?

DEAN: That's right.

PRESIDENT: Well, I think they can get that.

HALDEMAN: And the balance was all returned to LaRue.

DEAN: That's right.

HALDEMAN: The problem is we don't have any receipt for that, do we. We have no way of proving that.

(*Pause*)

PRESIDENT: I (*Unintelligible*)

DEAN: And I think, I think that was because, you know, of self-interest over there. Mitchell would . . .

HALDEMAN: Mitchell told LaRue not to take it at all.

DEAN: That's right.

HALDEMAN: This is what you told me.

DEAN: That's right. And then you don't give them a receipt.

PRESIDENT: Well, then, but what happened? LaRue took it, and then what?

DEAN: Well, it was sent back to him because we just couldn't continue piecemeal giving, you know, I ask it . . . Every time I asked for it, I had to tell Bob I needed some, or something like that . . .

PRESIDENT: Yeah.

DEAN: and he had to get Gordon Strachan to go up to his safe and take it out and take it over to LaRue.

PRESIDENT: Yeah.

DEAN: This was just a forever operation.

PRESIDENT: Then what? Why didn't they take it all to him?

DEAN: I think it's sent over with him.

HALDEMAN: Well, we had been trying to get a way to get that money back out of here anyway.

PRESIDENT: Sure.

HALDEMAN: And what this was supposed to be was loans. This was . . .

PRESIDENT: Yeah.

HALDEMAN: immediate cash needs that was going to be re . . . , replenished. And Mitchell was arguing "You can't take the three-fifty back till it's all replenished." Isn't that right?

DEAN: That's right. Well—in the, uh . . .

HALDEMAN: And then they never replenished it, so we just gave it all back anyway.

PRESIDENT: I have a feeling we could handle this one. Well . . .

DEAN: Well, first of all, they'd have a hell of a time proving it. Uh, that's one thing. Uh . . .

PRESIDENT: Yeah, yeah . . . I just have a feeling on it. But let's now come back to the money, a million dollars, and so forth and so on. Let me say that I think you could get that in cash, and I know money is hard, but there are ways. That could be (*Unintelligible*). But the point is, uh, what would you do on that . . . Let's, let's look at the hard facts.

DEAN: I mean, that's been very interesting. That has been, thus far, the most difficult problem.

PRESIDENT: Why?

DEAN: They have been . . . that's why these fellows have been on or off the reservation all the way along.

PRESIDENT: So the hard place is this. Your, your feeling at the present time is the hell with the million dollars. In other words, you say to these fellows, "I am sorry, it is all off," and let them talk. Right?

DEAN: Well . . .

PRESIDENT: That, that's the way to do it, isn't it?

DEAN: That . . .

PRESIDENT: If you want to do it clean (*Unintelligible*)

HALDEMAN: See, then when you do it, it's a way you can live with. Because the problem with the blackmail, and that's the thing we kept raising with you when you said there's a money problem, when we need twenty thousand or a hundred thousand or something, was yeah, that's what you need today. But what do you need tomorrow and next year and five years from now?

PRESIDENT: How long?

DEAN: Well, that was just to get us through November seventh, though.

HALDEMAN: I recognize that's what we had to give

DEAN: Right.

HALDEMAN: to November seventh. There's no question.

DEAN: Except they could have sold . . . these fellows could have sold out to the Democrats for a fantastic amount.

PRESIDENT: Yeah, these fellows . . . but of course, you know, these fellows, though, as far as that plan was concerned.

HALDEMAN: But what is there?

PRESIDENT: As far as what happened up to this time, our cover there is just going to be the Cuban Committee did this for them up through the election.

DEAN: Well, yeah. We can put that together. That isn't, of course, quite the way it happened, but, uh . . .

PRESIDENT: I know, but it's the way it's going to have to happen.

DEAN: It's going to have to happen.

PRESIDENT: That's right. Finally, though, so you let it go. So what happens is then they go out and, uh, and they'll start blowing the whistle on everybody else. Isn't that what it really gets down to?

DEAN: Um hum.

PRESIDENT: So that, that would be the, the clean way, Right?

DEAN: Uh, . . .

PRESIDENT: Is that really you're . . . you, you really go so far as to recommend that?

DEAN: That . . . no, I wouldn't. I don't think, I don't think necessarily that's the cleanest way. One of the . . . I think that's what we all need to discuss; is there some way that we can get our story before a grand jury, and so, that they can have, have really investigated the White House on this . . . I mean, and I must, I must be perfectly honest, I haven't really thought through that alternative. We've been, you know, been so busy. (*Background Noise*)

PRESIDENT: John

DEAN: on the other containment situation

PRESIDENT: John Ehrlichman, of course, has raised the point of another grand jury. I just don't know how you're going to do it. On what basis. I, I could call for it, but I . . .

DEAN: That would be, I would think, uh . . .

PRESIDENT: The President takes the leadership and says, "Now, in view of all this, uh, stripped land and so forth, I understand this, but I, I think I want another grand jury proceeding and, and we'll have the White House appear before them." Is that right John?

DEAN: Uh huh.

PRESIDENT: That's the point you see. That would make the difference. (*Noise Banging on Desk*) I want everybody in the White House called. And that, that gives you the, a reason not to have to go up before the (*Unintelligible*) Committee. It puts it in a, in an executive session in a sense.

HALDEMAN: Right.

PRESIDENT: Right.

DEAN: Uh, well . . .

HALDEMAN: And there'd be some rules of evidence. aren't there?

DEAN: There are rules of evidence.

PRESIDENT: Both evidence and you have lawyers.

HALDEMAN: So you are in a hell of a lot better position than you are up there.

DEAN: No, you can't have a lawyer before a grand jury.

PRESIDENT: Oh, no. That's right.

DEAN: You can't have a lawyer before a grand jury.

HALDEMAN: Okay, but you, but you, you do have rules of evidence. You can refuse to talk.

DEAN: You can take the Fifth Amendment.

PRESIDENT: That's right. That's right.

HALDEMAN: You can say you forgot, too, can't you?

DEAN: Sure.

PRESIDENT: That's right.

DEAN: But you can't . . . you're . . . very high risk in perjury situation.

PRESIDENT: That's right. Just be damned sure you say I don't . . .

HALDEMAN: Yeah . . .

PRESIDENT: remember; I can't recall, I can't give any honest, an answer to that that I can recall. But that's it.

HALDEMAN: You have the same perjury thing on the Hill, don't you?

DEAN: That's right.

PRESIDENT: Oh hell, yes.

HALDEMAN: And, and they'll be doing things on (*Unintelligible*)

PRESIDENT: My point is, though . . .

HALDEMAN: which is a hell of a lot worse to deal with.

DEAN: That's right.

PRESIDENT: The grand jury thing has its, uh, uh, uh . . . view of this they might, uh. Suppose we have a grand jury proceeding. Would that, would that, what would that do to the Ervin thing? Would it go right ahead any way?

DEAN: Probably.

HALDEMAN: If you do it in executive . . .

PRESIDENT: But then on that score, though, we have . . . let me just, uh, run by that, that . . . you do that on a grand jury, we could then have a much better cause in terms of saying "Look this is a grand jury, in which, uh, the prosecutor . . ." How about a special prosecutor? We could use Petersen, or use another one. You see he is probably suspect. Would you call . . .

DEAN: No.

PRESIDENT: in another prosecutor?

DEAN: I'd like to have Petersen on our side, advising us (*Laughs*) frankly.

PRESIDENT: Frankly, well, Petersen is honest. Is anybody about to be, question him, are they?

DEAN: No, no, but he'll get a barrage when, uh, these Watergate hearings start.

PRESIDENT: Yes, but he can go up and say that he's he's been told to go further in the Grand Jury and go into this and that, and the other thing. Call everybody in the White House. I want them to come. I want the, uh, uh, to go to the Grand Jury.

DEAN: This may result . . . this may happen even without our calling for it, when, uh, when these, uh . . .

PRESIDENT: Vesco?

DEAN: No. Well, that's one possibility. But also, when these people go back before the Grand Jury, here, they are going to pull all these criminal defendants back in before the Grand Jury and immunize them.

PRESIDENT: And immunize them: Why? Who? Are you going to . . . on what?

DEAN: Uh, the U.S. Attorney's Office will.

PRESIDENT: To do what?

DEAN: To talk about anything further they want to talk about.

PRESIDENT: Yeah. What do they gain out of it?

DEAN: Nothing.

PRESIDENT: To hell with them.

DEAN: They, they're going to stonewall it, uh, as it now stands. Except for Hunt. That's why, that's the leverage in his threat.

HALDEMAN: This is Hunt's opportunity.

DEAN: This is Hunt's opportunity.

PRESIDENT: That's why, that's why . . .

HALDEMAN: God, if he can lay this . . .

PRESIDENT: that's why your, for your immediate thing you've got no choice with Hunt but the hundred and twenty or whatever it is. Right?

DEAN: That's right.

PRESIDENT: Would you agree that that's a buy time thing, you better damn well get that done, but fast?

DEAN: I think he ought to be given some signal, anyway, to, to . . .

PRESIDENT: Yes.

DEAN: Yeah . . . you know.

PRESIDENT: Well, for Christ's sakes, get it in a, in a way that, uh (*Pause*) who's, who's going to talk to him? Colson? He's the one who's supposed to know him.

DEAN: Well, Colson doesn't have any money though. That's the thing. That's been our, one of the real problems. They have, uh, been unable to raise any money. A million dollars in cash, or, or the like, has been just a very difficult problem as we've discussed before. Apparently, Mitchell has talked to Pappas, and I called him last . . . John asked me to call him last night after our discussion and after you'd met with John to see where that was. And I, I said, "Have you talked to, to Pappas?" He was at home, and Martha picked up the phone so it was all in, in code. "Did you talk to the Greek?" And he said, uh, "Yes, I have." And I said, "Is the Greek bearing gifts?" He said, "Well, I want to call you tomorrow on that."

PRESIDENT: Well, look, uh, what is it that you need on that, uh, when, uh, uh? Now look (*Unintelligible*) I am, uh unfamiliar with the money situation.

DEAN: Well that, you know, it, it sounds easy to do, apparently, until, uh, everyone is out there doing it and that's where our breakdown has, has come every time.

PRESIDENT: Well, if you had it, where would you, how would you get it to somebody?

DEAN: Well, I, uh, I gather LaRue just leaves it in mail boxes and things like that, and tells Hunt to go pick it up. Someone phones Hunt and tells him to pick it up. As I say, we're a bunch of amateurs in that business.

HALDEMAN: That was the thing that we thought Mitchell ought to be able to know how to find somebody who could do all that sort of thing, because none of us know how to.

DEAN: That's right. You got to wash money and all that sort, you know, if you get a hundred thousand out of a bank, and it all comes in serialized bills, and . . .

PRESIDENT: Oh, I understand.

DEAN: And that means you have to go to Vegas with it or a bookmaker in New York City, and I've learned all these things after the fact, it's (*Laughs*) great shape for the next time around

(*Laughter*)

HALDEMAN: Jesus.

PRESIDENT: Well, the main point now is, the people who will need the money (*Unintelligible*) well of course, you've got the surplus from the campaign. That we have to account for. But if there's any other money hanging around . . .

HALDEMAN: Well, but what about all the, what about the money we moved back out of the . . . here?

DEAN: Apparently, there's some there. That might be what they can use. Uh, I don't know how much is left.

PRESIDENT: Kalmbach must have some, doesn't he?

DEAN: Kalmbach doesn't have a cent.

PRESIDENT: He doesn't?

DEAN: See the new law . . .

HALDEMAN: No, see that three-fifty that we moved out was all we saved. Because they were afraid to because of this . . . that's what I mean; that's the trouble. We are so God damned square that (*Laughs*) we'd get caught on everything.

PRESIDENT: Well, could I suggest that this though, uh, now, let me, let, let me go back around . . . (*Unintelligible*) They will then, uh . . . (*Unintelligible*)

HALDEMAN: Be careful . . .

PRESIDENT: The, uh (*Pause*) the grand jury thing has appeal. Question is, uh . . . it, it at least says that we are cooperating

DEAN: Well . . .

PRESIDENT: with the Grand Jury.

DEAN: Once we, once we start down any route that involves the criminal justice system . . .

PRESIDENT: Yeah.

DEAN: you, you've got to have full appreciation of there is really no control over that.

PRESIDENT: No sir.

DEAN: Uh, while we did, uh, we had a, an amazing job of . . .

PRESIDENT: Yeah, I know.

DEAN: keeping the thing on the track before . . .

PRESIDENT: Straight.

DEAN: while the FBI was out there, all that . . . and that was, uh, only because . . .

PRESIDENT: Right.

DEAN: I had a (*Unintelligible*) of where they were going.

PRESIDENT: (*Unintelligible*) Right. Right. But you haven't got that now because everybody else is going to have a lawyer. Let's take the new Grand Jury. Uh, the new Grand Jury would call Magruder again, wouldn't it?

DEAN: But, based on what information it would? For example, what happens if Dean goes in and gives a story, you know, that here is the way it all came about. It was supposed to be a legitimate operation and it obviously got off the track. I heard of these horribles, told Haldeman that we shouldn't be involved in it. Then Magruder's going to have to be called in and questioned about all those meetings again and the like. And it begins to . . . again he'll begin to change his story as to what he told the Grand Jury the last time.

PRESIDENT: Well . . .

DEAN: That way, he's in a perjury situation.

HALDEMAN: Except, that's the best leverage you've got on Jeb . . . is that he's got to keep his story straight or he's in real trouble.

DEAN: That's right.

HALDEMAN: Unless they get smart and give him immunity. If they, immunize Jeb, then you have an interesting problem (*Pause*)

(*Tapping on Desk*)

PRESIDENT: He wouldn't

DEAN: Well, I think we have . . .

HALDEMAN: (*Unintelligible*) immunity

DEAN: we have control, we have control over who gets immunized.

HALDEMAN: Do we?

DEAN: Yeah, I think they wouldn't do that without our . . .

PRESIDENT: But you see, the Grand Jury proceeding (*Unintelligible*) sort of thing, you can go down that road and then . . . if . . . if they had . . . I'm just thinking of now how the President looks. We would be cooperating. We would be cooperating through the Grand Jury. Everybody would be behind us. That's the proper way to do this. It should be done through a grand jury, not up there in the kleig lights of the Committee, or . . .

DEAN: That's right.

PRESIDENT: Nobody's questioning if it's a grand jury, and so forth. So, and then we would insist on executive privilege before the Committee, flat out say, "No we won't do that. We're not going to do it. Matter before a grand jury," and that's that. You see . . .

HALDEMAN: All right, then you go to the next step. Would we then . . . the Grand Ju . . . , the Grand Jury meet in executive session?

DEAN: Yes sir, they're . . .

PRESIDENT: Always . . .

DEAN: secret sessions, they're secret.

HALDEMAN: Secret session . . .

PRESIDENT: Secret . . .

HALDEMAN: All right, then would we agree to release our statement, our Grand Jury transcripts?

DEAN: That's not, that's not for our . . . we don't have the authority to do that. That's up to the Court and the Court, thus far, has not released the ones from the last Grand Jury.

PRESIDENT: They usually are not.

DEAN: It would be highly unusual for a grand jury to come out. What would happen is . . .

HALDEMAN: But a lot of the stuff from the Grand Jury came out.

PRESIDENT: Leaks. Well . . .

DEAN: It came out of the U.S. Attorney's Office . . .

PRESIDENT: Yeah.

DEAN: more than the, the Grand Jury. We don't know. Some of the Grand Jurors may have leaked . . .

PRESIDENT: Right, right.

DEAN: it, but they were . . .

PRESIDENT: Bob, it's not so bad. It's just not the bad . . . or the worst place. But . . .

HALDEMAN: Well, what I was. I was going the other way there. I was going to . . . it might be to our interest to get it out.

PRESIDENT: Well, we, we could easily do that. Leak out certain stuff. We could pretty much control that. We've got much more control there. Now the other possibility is not to go to the Grand Jury. Then you've got three things. (1) You just say, "The hell with it, we can't raise the money, sorry Hunt, you can say what you want." And so Hunt blows the whistle. Right?

DEAN: Right.

PRESIDENT: All right, if that happens, then that raises some possibilities of other criminal . . . because he is likely to say a hell of a lot of things and he's certain to get Magruder on it.

DEAN: It'll get Magruder. It'll start the whole FBI investigation going again.

PRESIDENT: Yeah. So, uh, what else . . . it'll get Magruder; it could possibly get Colson. He's in that danger.

DEAN: That's right. Could get, uh . . .

PRESIDENT: Could get Mitchell. Maybe. No.

HALDEMAN: Hunt can't get Mitchell.

DEAN: I don't think Hunt can get Mitchell. Hunt's got a lot of hearsay.

PRESIDENT: Ehrlichman? He could on the other thing . . . except Ehrlichman (*Unintelligible*)

DEAN: Krogh, Krogh could go down in smoke. Uh . . .

PRESIDENT: Because Krogh, uh . . . where could anybody . . . but on the other hand, Krogh, just says he, uh, uh, Krogh says this is a national security matter. Is that what he says? Yeah, he said that.

DEAN: Yeah, but that won't sell, ultimately, in a criminal situation. It may be mitigating on sentences but it won't, uh, in the main matter . . .

HALDEMAN: Well, then that . . .

PRESIDENT: That's right. Try to look around the track. We have no choice on Hunt but to try to keep him . . .

DEAN: Right now, we have no choice.

PRESIDENT: But, but my point is, do you ever have any choice on Hunt? That's the point.

DEAN: (*Sighs*)

PRESIDENT: No matter what we do here now, John . . .

DEAN: Well, if we . . .

PRESIDENT: Hunt eventually, if he isn't going to get commuted and so forth, he's going to blow the whistle.

DEAN: What I have been trying to conceive of is how we could lay out everything we know (*Sighs*) in a way that, you know, we've told the Grand Jury or somebody else, so that if a Hunt blows . . .

PRESIDENT: Yeah.

DEAN: so what's new? You know, it's already been told to a grand jury, and they found no criminal liability, and they investigated it in full. We're sorry fellow . . .

PRESIDENT: That's right.

DEAN: Uh, we don't, it doesn't . . .

PRESIDENT: Including Ehrlichman's use of Hunt on the other deal?

DEAN: That's right.

PRESIDENT: You'd throw that out?

DEAN: Uh, well, Hunt will go to jail for that too . . . he's got to understand that.

PRESIDENT: That's the point too. I don't think that . . . I wouldn't throw that out. I think I would limit it to . . . I don't think you need to go into every God damned thing Hunt has done.

DEAN: No.

PRESIDENT: He's done some things in the national security area. Yes, true.

HALDEMAN: We've already said that. Anyway, I mean, we've laid the ground work for that.

DEAN: Uh huh.

PRESIDENT: But here is the point, John: So you go that . . . let's go to the other extreme, the other, the other angle is to decide on, well, if you open up the Grand Jury, first, it won't do any good; it won't be believed. And then you'll have two things going: The Grand Jury and you have the other thing. At least the Grand Jury appeals to me from the standpoint, it's the President makes the move. "Since all these charges have been bandied about, and so forth, the best thing to do is to . . . I have ordered, or I have asked the Grand Jury to look into any further charges. All charges have been raised." That's the place to do it and not before a committee of the Congress. Right?

DEAN: Um hum.

PRESIDENT: Then, however, we may say, Mitchell, et al., God we can't risk that, I mean, uh, all sorts of shit'll break loose there. Then that leaves you to your third thing. The third thing is just to continue to . . .

DEAN: Hunker down and fight it.

PRESIDENT: All right. If you hunker down and fight it, fight it and what happens?

DEAN: Your . . .

PRESIDENT: Your view is that, that is, is not really a viable option.

DEAN: It's a very . . . it's a high risk. A very high risk.

PRESIDENT: A high risk, because your view is that what will happen out of that is that it's going to come out. Somebody's . . . Hunt . . . something's going to break loose . . .

DEAN: Something is going to break and . . .

PRESIDENT: When it breaks it'll look like the President

DEAN: . . . is covering up . . .

Reel 2 Ends.

DEAN: Your . . .

PRESIDENT: Your view is that that is, is not really a viable option.

DEAN: In fact, it's a high risk. A very high risk.

PRESIDENT: A high risk, because your view is that what will happen out of that is that it's going to come out. Somebody's—Hunt—something's going to break loose . . .

DEAN: Something is going to break and . . .

PRESIDENT: When it breaks it'll look like the President . . .

DEAN: —is covering up—

PRESIDENT: is, has covered up a huge, uh, uh, this—Right?

DEAN: That's correct.

HALDEMAN: But you can't contain the charge.

PRESIDENT: That's not . . .

(*Noise*)

DEAN: I just don't . . .

PRESIDENT: You're, you're

DEAN: I don't think it's . . .

PRESIDENT: You now have, uh, moved away from the hunker down.

(*Noise*)

DEAN: Well, I've moved to the point that we've certainly got to take a, a harder look at the other alternative, which we haven't before.

PRESIDENT: The other alternatives.

DEAN: The other alternatives. Right

PRESIDENT: Three other choices, wouldn't you say? As a matter of fact, your m-, middle ground of Grand Jury. And then there's finally the other ground of—No, I suppose there's a middle ground.

DEAN: And I would—

PRESIDENT: or the middle grounds of a public statement, without a Grand Jury.

DEAN: What we need also, sir—

PRESIDENT: And also—

HALDEMAN: But John's view is if we make the public statement

PRESIDENT: Yeah.

HALDEMAN: that we talked—I raised that this morning, the, the thing we talked about last night.

PRESIDENT: Yeah.

HALDEMAN: If each of us

PRESIDENT: Yeah

HALDEMAN: make moves,

PRESIDENT: Yeah

HALDEMAN: He says that will immediately lead to a Grand Jury.

PRESIDENT: Fine—all right, fine.

HALDEMAN: As soon as we make that statement, they'll have to call a Grand Jury.

PRESIDENT: Then maybe we make the public statement before the Grand Jury, in order to—

HALDEMAN: So it looks like we are trying to do it over.

DEAN: All right, say all right, say here are public statements, and we want, we want, uh,

PRESIDENT: Yeah.

DEAN: full Grand Jury investigation

PRESIDENT: Yeah

DEAN: by the U.S. Attorney's Office

PRESIDENT: Curious to see whether this statement's, then, that's right. That I, but—And that we've said that the reason that we had delayed this is until after the sentencing. You see, the point is, the reason that time is of the essence, we can't play around with this, is that they're going to sentence on Friday. We're going to move the God damned thing pretty fast. See what I mean?

DEAN: That's right.

(*Pause*)

PRESIDENT: So we've got to act, we really haven't time to (*Unintelligible*)

DEAN: The other, the other thing is that the Attorney General could call Sirica, and say that. "The Government has some major developments that it's considering. Would you hold sentencing for two weeks?" If we set ourself on a course of action.

PRESIDENT: Yep, yep.

DEAN: Say, that "The sentencing may be in the wrong perspective right now. I don't know for certain, but I just think there are some things that, uh, I am not at liberty to discuss with you, that I want to ask that the, the court withhold two weeks sentencing."

HALDEMAN: So then the story is out: "Sirica Delays Sentencing Watergate For—"

DEAN: I think, I think that could be handled in a way between Sirica and Kleindienst that it would not get out.

PRESIDENT: No.

DEAN: Sirica tells me, I mean Kleindienst apparently does have good rapport with Sirica. He's never talked to him since this case has developed,

HALDEMAN
or
PRESIDENT: Why not?

DEAN: but, uh—

PRESIDENT: That's helpful. Kleindienst could say that he's, uh, he's working on something and would like, like, like to have a week. I wouldn't take two weeks. I would take a week.

DEAN: I'll tell you the person that I would, you know, I feel that, uh, we, we could use his counsel on this, because he understands the criminal process better than anybody over here does,

PRESIDENT: Petersen?

DEAN: is Petersen. It, it's awkward for Petersen. He's the head of the Criminal Division. But to discuss some of these things with him, we may well want to remove him from the head of the Criminal Division and say, (*Cough*) that, uh, "Rela-, related to this case, you will have no relation." Uh, and give him on some special assignment over here where he can sit down and say, "Yes, this is an, this is an obstruction, but it couldn't be proved," or so on and so forth. We almost need him out of there to take his counsel. That would, uh, I, I don't think he'd want that, but, uh, he is the most knowledgeable—

PRESIDENT: How could you get him out?

DEAN: I think an appeal directly to Henry, uh, that, uh

PRESIDENT: Why doesn't the President—could, could the President call him in as Special Counsel to the White—to the, to the White House for the purpose of conducting an investigation, represent—uh, you see, in other words—recommend that Dean,

DEAN: I have thought of that. I have thought of that.

PRESIDENT: have him as Special Counsel to represent to the Grand Jury and the rest.

DEAN: That is one possibility.

PRESIDENT: Yeah.

HALDEMAN: On the basis that Dean has now become a principal rather than a Special Counsel.

DEAN: Uh huh.

PRESIDENT: That's right.

DEAN: Uh huh.

PRESIDENT: And that he's a—

DEAN: And I, and I could recommend that to you.

PRESIDENT: He could recommend it, you could recommend it, and Petersen would come over and be the, uh—and I'd say, "Now—"

HALDEMAN: Petersen's planning to leave, anyway.

PRESIDENT: And I'd say, "Now,"

DEAN: Is he?

HALDEMAN: Yep—

PRESIDENT: "I want you to get—we want you to (1)—" We'd say to Petersen, "We want you to get to the bottom of the God damned thing, Call another Grand Jury or anything else." Correct? Well, now you've got to follow up to see whether Kleindienst can get Sirica to put off—Right? If that is, if we—Second, you've got to get Mitchell down here. You and Ehrlichman and Mitchell and let's—an—by tomorrow.

HALDEMAN: Why don't we do that tonight?

PRESIDENT: I don't think you can get him that soon, can you?

HALDEMAN: John?

PRESIDENT: It would be helpful if you could.

DEAN: I think it would be.

PRESIDENT: You need—

DEAN: Get him to come down this afternoon.

PRESIDENT: It would be very helpful to, to get it going. And, uh, uh, you know, and, uh, and then, uh—Actually, uh, I'm perfectly willing to meet with the group, or I don't know whether—

HALDEMAN: Do you think you want to?

PRESIDENT: Maybe have Dean report to me at the end, as to what are, as to what conclusions, et cetera, what you want to do. I think I should stay away from the Mitchell side of it at this point.

DEAN: Uh huh.

PRESIDENT: Do you agree?

DEAN: Uh huh.

PRESIDENT: and, uh—

DEAN: And I think, unless we see, you know, some sort of a reluctant dragon there—

HALDEMAN: You might try to meet with the rest of us, I, I'm, I'm not sure you'd want to meet with John in a group of us. (*Noise*) (*Pause*) Okay, let me see if I can get it done.

PRESIDENT: All right. Fine. That's it, my point is that, uh, we can, uh, you may well come—I think it is good, (*Noise*) frankly, to consider these various options. And then, once you, once you decide on the plan—John—and you had the right plan, let me say, I have no doubts about the right plan before the election. And you handled it just right. You contained it. Now after the election we've got to have another plan, because we can't have, for four years, we can't have this thing—you're going to be eaten away. We can't do it.

DEAN: —Well, there's been a change in the mood—

HALDEMAN: John's point is exactly right, that the erosion here now is going to you, and that is the thing that we've got to turn off, at whatever the cost and we've got to figure out where to turn it off at the lowest cost we can, but at whatever cost it takes.

DEAN: That's what, that's what we have to do.

PRESIDENT: Well, the erosion is inevitably going to come here, apart from anything, you know, people saying that, uh, well, the Watergate isn't a major concern. It isn't. But it would, but it will be. It's bound to be.

DEAN: We cannot let you be tarnished by that situation.

PRESIDENT: Well, I (*Unintelligible*) also because I—Although Ron Ziegler has to go out—They blame the (*Unintelligible*) on the White House (*Unintelligible*)

DEAN: That's right.

PRESIDENT: We don't, uh, uh, I say that the White House can't do it. Right?

HALDEMAN: Yeah.

DEAN: Yes, sir.

TRANSCRIPT OF A RECORDING OF A MEETING AMONG THE PRESIDENT, H.R.
HALDEMAN, AND JOHN EHRLICHMAN IN THE EXECUTIVE OFFICE BUILDING, APRIL 14,
1973, FROM 8:55 TO 11:31 A.M.

PRESIDENT: Jack, uh, do, uh, did you reach any conclusions as to, uh, where we are, recommendations?

EHRLICHMAN: No, no conclusions.

PRESIDENT: Uh—problems?

EHRLICHMAN: Dick Wilson, I think, is—has an interesting column this morning.

PRESIDENT: (*Unintelligible*).

EHRLICHMAN: Ah, yeah, it's, uh, uh, (*Noise*) money problem. He's been analyzing this money problem (*Unintelligible*).

HALDEMAN: (*Unintelligible*).

EHRLICHMAN: Oh, yeah, last night.

PRESIDENT: Wilson is in the Star.

EHRLICHMAN: Well then it is twice he made this point.

PRESIDENT: So what?

EHRLICHMAN: (*Unintelligible*). Argues that really the, the essence of this whole thing is too much money, too easily spent, and so on. And then he, uh . . .

(*Unintelligible*)

HALDEMAN: That's his great underlying, uh—

PRESIDENT: Yeah. That's what everybody—that's what—

HALDEMAN: No, not everybody. That's a, uh, one par—. . .

PRESIDENT: Well, Reston lies.

HALDEMAN: . . . one group thesis . . .

PRESIDENT: Yeah.

HALDEMAN: . . . that, uh, Reston . . .

PRESIDENT: That's right.

HALDEMAN: . . . Reston has on that side and point out (*Tape Noise*). And, the, the you know, his he, he, he carries it beyond—he says solving Watergate doesn't take care of it, but, uh, then there's, uh, all the money in—

PRESIDENT: Dick wants the President to speak out on the whole general issue of money and campaign and that sort of—

EHRLICHMAN: Basically that's—generally, but he, he gets specific on this. He says also (*Unintelligible*).

PRESIDENT: Is that what you think, go out and make a speech?

EHRLICHMAN: No, I'll tell you what I think. I think that the President's personal involvement in this is important. And I don't . . .

PRESIDENT: Yeah.

EHRLICHMAN: . . . I don't think it's a speech.

PRESIDENT: Well, that's the point. I think it's—there're other ways you can get at it. Now, I was thinking of the, uh—before we get into that though, let's get back—that's something we can get into later—I'd like to get—I'd like to go in, if I could, to what your conversation with Colson was and, uh, in essence. What, what was yours, what did he and the lawyer come to tell you about?

HALDEMAN: Hunt's visit.

EHRLICHMAN: That visit was to tell me that Hunt was going to testify on Monday afternoon.

PRESIDENT: How does he know that?

HALDEMAN: Um hmm.

PRESIDENT: How does, how does he get such information?

HALDEMAN: Why can't you use the tape?

PRESIDENT: Well—

EHRLICHMAN: It's an illegal tape.

HALDEMAN: No, it's not.

EHRLICHMAN: Yeah.

HALDEMAN: It is not.

PRESIDENT: That you tell somebody—

HALDEMAN: No, sir.

EHRLICHMAN: No beeper on it.

HALDEMAN: There is no beeper required. You check the Washington law.

PRESIDENT: Yeah.

HALDEMAN: District of Columbia is under federal law and the federal law does not require disclosure to the other party of the recording of phone conversations. The phone call was made to Magruder's lawyer's office which is also in the District of Columbia so both ends of the conversation were in the District of Columbia and there is no law requiring disclosure.

EHRLICHMAN: Well, that's interesting.

HALDEMAN: It's perfectly legal.

PRESIDENT: Well, anyway, anyway—

HALDEMAN: It can (or may) not be admissible, but it's legal.

PRESIDENT: That's interesting. That's a new one. (*Unintelligible*) beep every, every while then, now and then. I thought it was. However, I never heard anybody beepin', and hell—didn't you?

HALDEMAN: No. It all depends on where you are. Some—the basic law in most States is that you must disclose to the other party that you're recording the conversation.

PRESIDENT: Yeah. What is the situation—I might—I'll get past this in a hurry— what is the situation, John, in your opinion on what was Colson's and/or Shapiro's motive in building up the Magruder story? Maybe they believe it.

EHRLICHMAN: Their, their innuendo is that, that Mitchell has put Magruder up to this.

PRESIDENT: I guess not. Okay. There's the motive. Now, let me come to something else.

HALDEMAN: I don't believe that Magruder's—

PRESIDENT: I don't either. Not at all.

HALDEMAN: I don't believe Mitchell has tried to—

PRESIDENT: Huh?

HALDEMAN: I don't believe Mitchell tried to Magruder's faith 'cause he refers to Mitchell and now that I have decided to talk I am going to tell Mr. Mitchell and he's gonna be very unhappy with me 'cause he's told me not to.

PRESIDENT: (*Unintelligible*) tape, uh—

HALDEMAN: I did

PRESIDENT: And he's an emotional fellow who's ready to crack.

EHRLICHMAN: I, I really, I have no doubt that he's ready to talk.

PRESIDENT: What is he—he hasn't been subpoenaed yet, has he?

EHRLICHMAN: Well, he won't be. But he's already been there.

SEVERAL VOICES: (*Unintelligible*).

EHRLICHMAN: Dean doesn't think they'll give him a, a chance back unless he comes running at them and just and, uh, spills it.

HALDEMAN: 'Cause (A) they don't call the suspects and (B) they don't recall perjury witnesses.

PRESIDENT: Right. What would you do if you were his lawyer? Wouldn't you advise him to go in and try and purge himself, at least—get rid of one charge, doesn't he?

EHRLICHMAN: I'm not sure he's rid of it, but it certainly reduces it when he comes in voluntarily.

PRESIDENT: The way I understand it under the law, John, if he were to come to the . . .

EHRLICHMAN: But he's hooked.

PRESIDENT: . . . Grand Jury.

EHRLICHMAN: Yeah, but he's hooked, see. There's contrary evidence already . . .

PRESIDENT: Oh, I see.

EHRLICHMAN: . . . before the Grand Jury.

PRESIDENT: In other words—

EHRLICHMAN: If he did that—

PRESIDENT: Strachan—Strachan got in before there was (*Unintelligible*) evidence.

EHRLICHMAN: Exactly.

HALDEMAN: (*Unintelligible*)

PRESIDENT: Strachan?

HALDEMAN: No, (*Unintelligible*) . . .

PRESIDENT: (*Unintelligible*)

HALDEMAN: . . . Magruder.

EHRLICHMAN: And, and you take the circumstances, now . . .

PRESIDENT: They better have . . .

EHRLICHMAN: Yeah. If it's known, if it's known, for instance, that Hunt is going to come in and testify, then Magruder comes rushing in and says I want to tell all, it's, uh, you know—

PRESIDENT: Magruder's stuck on both counts.

EHRLICHMAN: Yeah, but I think he could improve it. I think he, he really could help to purge himself.

PRESIDENT: (*Unintelligible*). I've come to the—may I come to the other things that, uh, that you, uh, you talked to Colson about, uh? Hunt going to talk—what is Hunt going to say? Do we have any idea?

EHRLICHMAN: Yes.

PRESIDENT: He says, for example, will he say that Colson promised him clemency?

EHRLICHMAN: No. Apparently not.

PRESIDENT: And, uh, you see the, the only, the only possible involvement of the President in this is that. Now apparently, John, either you or Bob or Dean, somebody told me they said Cols-, told Colson not to discuss it with me.

EHRLICHMAN: I did.

PRESIDENT: You did. How did, bar-, how did it get to you then, John? How did you know that the, the matter had to be discussed with Bittman or something like that?

EHRLICHMAN: Well, I . . .

PRESIDENT: When did this happen?

EHRLICHMAN: I had . . .

PRESIDENT: I remember a conversation this day, it was about five thirty or six o'-clock, that Colson only dropped it in sort of parenthetically. He said, "I had a little problem today,"—and we were talking about the defendants—and I said, I sought to reassure him, you know, and so forth. And I said, "Well, that's"—told me about Hunt's wife—he said, "It's a terrible thing," and I said, "Obviously we'll do just, we will take that into consideration." And that was the total of the conversation.

EHRLICHMAN: Well, I had, uh, we had had a couple of conversations in my office—

PRESIDENT: With Colson?

EHRLICHMAN: With, or, I had with Colson. Yeah.

PRESIDENT: Well, how was . . .

EHRLICHMAN: And I, uh—

PRESIDENT: . . . who was getting, who was, was Bittman getting to Colson? Was that the point? Who, who—

EHRLICHMAN: Now Hunt, Hunt had written to Colson.

PRESIDENT: Oh?

EHRLICHMAN: Hunt wrote Colson a very I've-been-abandoned kind of letter.

PRESIDENT: Yeah. When was this, John?

EHRLICHMAN: I am sorry, I—

PRESIDENT: After the election?

EHRLICHMAN: Oh, yes. Yeah.

PRESIDENT: Oh, and Chuck Colson—you knew about this letter?

EHRLICHMAN: Colson come in to tell me about it. And he said, "What shall I do?" And I said, "Well, uh, better talk to him, I think somebody'd better talk to him—the guy is obviously very distraught . . ."

PRESIDENT: Right.

EHRLICHMAN: ". . . and, uh, feeling abandoned."

PRESIDENT: Right. Good advice.

EHRLICHMAN: And, uh, he said, "Well, what can, what can I tell him about, uh, clemency or pardon?" And I said, "You can't tell him anything about clemency or a pardon." And I said, "Under no circumstances should this ever be raised with the President."

PRESIDENT: Yeah. Told him not to raise it with me. Well, he raised it, I must say, in a tangential way. Now he denies that, as I understand it, that he said that he'd be out by Christmas. He says—

EHRLICHMAN: I never, I've never talked to Chuck about that, have you.

HALDEMAN(?): Yes and no.

PRESIDENT: What did he say he said?

Well, I'll tell you what I, what Dean, or somebody tells me he said he said. He said that he didn't—he just talked to, saw, saw Bittman casually, or on the phone or something of that sort.

EHRLICHMAN: Bittman?

PRESIDENT: That was it.

EHRLICHMAN: Oh.

PRESIDENT: And he said to Bittman . . .

EHRLICHMAN: Oh.

PRESIDENT: . . . he said, "I," he said, "I . . .

EHRLICHMAN: Well, now that . . .

PRESIDENT: . . . he said, "I . . .

EHRLICHMAN: . . . a difference.

PRESIDENT: Listen, I have written it. He said, "I, uh, I, uh, I, I know that, uh, I know about Hunt's concern about clemency. I, Chuck Colson, feel terrible about it, 'cause I knew his wife." And, uh, he said, "I will, will go to bat for him and I have reason to believe that my views would be, ah, listened to." Well it's the last part, part that, uh, might in any way remain, although . . .

EHRLICHMAN: He says he talked to Bittman and that he was very skillful . . .

PRESIDENT: That's right.

EHRLICHMAN: . . . in avoiding any commitment. He says Bittman . . .

PRESIDENT: (*Unintelligible*).

EHRLICHMAN: . . . Bittman was pitching 'em, but that he wasn't catching 'em. And . . .

PRESIDENT: (*Unintelligible*).

EHRLICHMAN: . . . he either has a tape of that meeting or a tape of the conversation or some such thing.

HALDEMAN: That's where he lost his thread, then. Yes, said you and Dean told him you, two promised clemency, and that he was smarter than you and, and didn't.

PRESIDENT: You haven't said you and Dean promised?

HALDEMAN: That Ehrlichman and Dean told him to promise . . .

PRESIDENT: Shit.

HALDEMAN: . . . (*Unintelligible*).

PRESIDENT: Well, anyway, whatever the case might be, uh, let me ask a question . . .

HALDEMAN: (*Unintelligible*) a little strange.

PRESIDENT: . . . does, does Hunt—well, just so that he, uh—does he, does, does, does he indicate that they, that Hu-, Hunt's going to talk to that subject for example—the promise of clemency?

EHRLICHMAN: Uh, he didn't say that. He didn't say that. I didn't ask him.

HALDEMAN: Well, going back to the basis, John—as I recall, they don't have anything to indi-—we don't know how they know Hunt's going to testify. We assume that Bittman told them . . .

EHRLICHMAN: Right.

HALDEMAN: . . . (A). (B) we don't, they don't have any indication, based on their knowledge that Hunt's going to testify, of what Hunt is going to testify to, except on the basis of Shapiro's meeting with Hunt . . .

EHRLICHMAN: The other day.

HALDEMAN: . . . the other day. And they're assuming that what Hunt told Shapiro is what he will tell the Grand Jury, but I don't know why they'd have any reason to assume that.

EHRLICHMAN: I don't, uh, uh,—Shapiro's general comment was that Hunt would corroborate a lot of McCord's hearsay . . .

PRESIDENT: Yeah.

EHRLICHMAN: . . . but that it also would be hearsay.

PRESIDENT: Alright. Hunt, however, and this is where Colson comes in, right? Hard. Hunt could testify on Colson's pressure.

HALDEMAN: Yeah. But what they, what they've said he's gonna test- . . .

PRESIDENT: Right.

HALDEMAN: . . . on the coverup, what he is gonna testify . . .

PRESIDENT: Now wait a minute . . .

HALDEMAN: (*Unintelligible*)

PRESIDENT: . . . I'm talking about something entirely different . . .

HALDEMAN: (*Unintelligible*)

PRESIDENT: . . . you're talking about when Colson . . .

HALDEMAN: (*Unintelligible*).

PRESIDENT: . . . Colson and Liddy were in the office and Colson, Colson picked up the phone and called Magruder.

HALDEMAN: That's right. Sure.

PRESIDENT: Now, there, uh, now Colson says that, uh, that they didn't discuss bugging at that point. Hunt could say, "I went in and I showed this whole plan to Colson and Colson phoned—picked up the phone . . .

EHRLICHMAN(?): That's right.

PRESIDENT: . . . and talked to Magruder."

EHRLICHMAN(?): True.

PRESIDENT: . . . does, does, does, does Colson realize his vulnerability there?

EHRLICHMAN: Well, course Colson claims he has no vulnerability, because when Hunt and Liddy come in to talk to him they talked in very general terms.

PRESIDENT: I understand that.

EHRLICHMAN: So, he . . .

PRESIDENT: I—

EHRLICHMAN: . . . doesn't acknowledge . . .

PRESIDENT: I—

EHRLICHMAN: . . . he doesn't acknowledge that there's any possibility—

PRESIDENT: I, I understand that, but I'm just simply saying, it's . . .

EHRLICHMAN: I think he's right.

PRESIDENT: . . . that Hunt and Liddy could . . .

EHRLICHMAN: That's true.

PRESIDENT: . . . could, could, could charge that—that's the point. They, they, they—if they talk, I would assume they would get into that point with them, any, any cross-examiner.

EHRLICHMAN: I, I've asked Colson specifically about that conversation and he maintains that they were talking, uh, in general terms about intelligence and when they said intelligence he meant one thing and apparently they meant another.

PRESIDENT: Question, uh, for example, uh, is, is Hunt preparing to talk on other activities that he engaged in?

EHRLICHMAN: Well, I couldn't, I couldn't derive that . . .

PRESIDENT: Umhmm.

EHRLICHMAN: (*Unintelligible*) at all.

PRESIDENT: For the White House and for the—you know?

EHRLICHMAN: I, I couldn't, I couldn't get that at all.

PRESIDENT: The U.S. Attorney, I would assume, would not be pressing (*Unintelligible*).

EHRLICHMAN: Ordinarily not.

PRESIDENT: (*Unintelligible*).

EHRLICHMAN: Now, McCord, McCord volunteered this Hank Greenspun thing, gratuitously apparently, not, not—

PRESIDENT: Could, can you tell me, is that a serious thing? Did, did they really try to get into Hank Greenspun?

EHRLICHMAN: I guess they actually got in.

PRESIDENT: What in the name of Christ, though, does Hank Greenspun got with— anything to do with Mitchell or anybody else?

EHRLICHMAN: Nothing. Well, now, Mitchell—

PRESIDENT: Hughes?

EHRLICHMAN: Here's—yeah, Hughes. And these two fellows, Colson and Shapiro, uh, uh—Colson threw that out.

PRESIDENT: Hughes on whom?

EHRLICHMAN: Well, you know the Hughes thing is cut into two factions . . .

PRESIDENT: I don't—

EHRLICHMAN: (A) and then the . . .

PRESIDENT: Uh, fighting—

EHRLICHMAN: . . . and then the other, and they're fighting.

PRESIDENT: Right.

EHRLICHMAN: Bennett, Senator Bennett's son, for whom Hunt worked . . .

PRESIDENT: Oh?

EHRLICHMAN: . . . represents one of those factions.

PRESIDENT: Yeah. So he ordered the bugging?

EHRLICHMAN: I don't know.

HALDEMAN: (*Unintelligible*).

EHRLICHMAN: . . . I know the . . .

SEVERAL VOICES: (*Unintelligible*).

EHRLICHMAN: . . . it's a bag job.

HALDEMAN: They busted his safe to get something out of it.

EHRLICHMAN: Now—

HALDEMAN: Wasn't that it? They flew out, broke his safe, got something out . . .

EHRLICHMAN: (*Unintelligible*).

HALDEMAN: . . . got on the airplane and flew away.

EHRLICHMAN: Now, as they sat there in my office . . .

PRESIDENT: There're others . . .

EHRLICHMAN: What?

PRESIDENT: . . . other delicate things, too. You've got, apart from my poor damn dumb brother, which unfortunately or fortunately was a long time ago, but, uh, more recently, you've got Herbert Humphrey's son works for him, and, of course, they're, they're tied in with O'Brien, I suppose. But maybe they were trying to get it for that reason.

EHRLICHMAN: I don't know why. The, the two of them put on a little charade for me in the office . . .

PRESIDENT: Shapiro and Colson?

EHRLICHMAN: . . . as we—yeah—as we talked about this, and it may have been genuine and it may not. But . . .

PRESIDENT: But they didn't know anything about it?

EHRLICHMAN: . . . but they—no—they said, one said to the other, "Say, that may have something to do with the New York Grand Jury," meaning the Vesco Grand Jury which is a runaway and which is into—

PRESIDENT: You think Colson knew about that?

EHRLICHMAN: I don't know. I don't say he knew about it. I said, he says he doesn't know even who Hank Greenspun is.

PRESIDENT: He should. Everybody knows he's the editor. His son, for Christ's sakes—

EHRLICHMAN: I, I'll take him at face value on that one, uh, uh, it isn't any other evidence.

PRESIDENT: You didn't know that either?

EHRLICHMAN: I, I know very well who he is.

PRESIDENT: Alright. Uh, let me just take a minute further and run out the Hunt thing, and then the Grand Jury. I just want to get all the pieces in my mind . . .

EHRLICHMAN: Sure.

PRESIDENT: . . . if I can.

EHRLICHMAN: Sure.

EHRLICHMAN: Uh, undoubtedly through Bittman.

PRESIDENT: Right.

EHRLICHMAN: Or Bittman through Shapiro.

PRESIDENT: Now why, why is Hunt testifying? Did he say? Or, uh, what . . .

EHRLICHMAN: He didn't say.

PRESIDENT: . . . (*Unintelligible*) about the—

EHRLICHMAN: He said—I'll tell you what he said and then I'll tell you what I think the fact is—he said Hunt was testifying because there was no longer any point in being silent. That, uh, uh, so many other people were testifying that there was no—he wasn't really keeping any secrets.

PRESIDENT: Yeah. Yeah.

EHRLICHMAN: Couldn't add much. Uh, my, my feeling is that Bittman got very antsy when this grand jury started focusing on the aftermath . . .

PRESIDENT: (*Unintelligible*) know what was involved

HALDEMAN: That's it exactly.

EHRLICHMAN: . . . and that he went to the U.S. Attorney and he said, "Maybe I can persuade my client to talk."

PRESIDENT: What does, uh, what do Colson, et al., Colson and Shapiro think we ought to do under these circumstances? Get busy and nail Wilson and, uh, nail Mitchell in a hurry? Is that what he means?

EHRLICHMAN: Yes.

PRESIDENT: How is that going to help?

EHRLICHMAN: Well, they feel that . . .

PRESIDENT: (*Unintelligible*) I just want to get the best effort.

EHRLICHMAN: . . . they feel that after Hunt testifies that the whole thing's going to fall in, in short order

PRESIDENT: Right.

EHRLICHMAN: That Mitchell and, uh, Magruder will involuntarily be, uh, uh, indicted.

PRESIDENT: Right.

EHRLICHMAN: (*Unintelligible*) say . . .

PRESIDENT: Right.

EHRLICHMAN: . . . that you have lost any possibly of initiative, so—for participation . . .

PRESIDENT: So, what does Colson . . .

EHRLICHMAN: (*Unintelligible*).

PRESIDENT: . . . want us to do?

EHRLICHMAN: He wants you to do several things. He wants you to persuade Liddy to talk.

PRESIDENT: Me?

EHRLICHMAN: Yes, sir. That's his—I didn't bring my notes, but basically—

PRESIDENT: Oh. Last night you didn't mention this, but that's alright.

EHRLICHMAN: Oh, I thought I had.

PRESIDENT: Maybe you did, maybe you did.

EHRLICHMAN: I didn't, I didn't . . .

PRESIDENT: (*Unintelligible*).

EHRLICHMAN: . . . in any event, he didn't—

PRESIDENT: I would bring, he-, le-, let Liddy in and tell him to talk?

EHRLICHMAN: You can't bring him in. He's in jail. But, uh—

PRESIDENT: Oh.

EHRLICHMAN: You would send, you'd send word to him, and of course wanting him to make full disclosure or in some way you would be activist on this score.

PRESIDENT: Yeah.

HALDEMAN: There's no, there's—that isn't—doesn't involve any real problem. As Dean points out, uh, Liddy is not talking 'cause he thinks he's supposed not to talk. If he is supposed to talk, he will. All he needs is a signal, if you want to turn Liddy up.

PRESIDENT: Yeah, oh—yeah. But the point that . . .

HALDEMAN: Face it, he believes—

PRESIDENT: . . . Colson wants is a public signal. Is that right?

HALDEMAN: No, he (*Unintelligible*).

PRESIDENT: A public signal (*Unintelligible*) what the hell do you do?

EHRLICHMAN: (*Unintelligible*) he wants to be able to—he wants you to be able to, to say afterward that you cracked the case.

PRESIDENT: Go ahead. What else?

EHRLICHMAN: Well, I forget what else. Do you remember, Bob? Uh, uh—

HALDEMAN: Well, that was basically (*Unintelligible*)

EHRLICHMAN: Basically, basically, uh, he, he feels that the next forty-eight hours are the, are the last chance . . .

PRESIDENT: Mmm-huh.

EHRLICHMAN: . . . for the White House to get out in front of this and that once Hunt goes on, then that's the ball game.

PRESIDENT: But you've got to be out in front earlier.

EHRLICHMAN: Well—

PRESIDENT: But, I mean, sorry, not earlier, but publicly.

EHRLICHMAN: Uh, either . . .

PRESIDENT: (*Unintelligible*)

EHRLICHMAN: . . . either publicly or with provable, identifiable steps which can be referred to later as having been the proximate cause.

PRESIDENT: He's just not talking because he thinks the President doesn't want him to talk? Is that the point?

EHRLICHMAN: He's—according to them . . .

PRESIDENT: (*Noise*) . . . Mitchell . . . (*Noise*) Mitchell's given him a promise of a pardon (*Tape Noise*) Bittman

EHRLICHMAN: Yeah, uh, no, according to, uh, uh, Colson and Shapiro. And I don't know where they get that.

PRESIDENT: Mitchell has promised Liddy a pardon?

EHRLICHMAN: Yes, sir. Other points that Colson may not have mentioned, uh, uh,—(*Tape Noise*)

PRESIDENT: I have an uneasy feeling that, that Magruder story may have been planted.

HALDEMAN: No.

PRESIDENT: Or is it true?

HALDEMAN: There, there's a third Magruder phone call which I haven't heard that, uh, uh, says . . .

PRESIDENT: Says he did talk to the press?

HALDEMAN: . . . says he did talk to a reporter on Monday—did not say any of the things he's, he's reported to have said, that what he, that—he said it wasn't an important conversation. He said the same—he gave the reporter the same line.

PRESIDENT: Yeah.

HALDEMAN: That, you know—but in listening to Magruder's thing . . .

PRESIDENT: Alright.

HALDEMAN: . . . I was convinced he wasn't completely telling the truth that he— in what he was saying. As you get into it, I'm convinced that his (*Unintelligible*) that part was pretty much . . .

PRESIDENT: Yeah.

HALDEMAN: . . . (*Unintelligible*).

PRESIDENT: Uh, but you come to this—all these pieces must be put together now. But you come to Magruder, uh, where the hell does Colson get such a thing? Uh, or is Colson a liar or—

EHRLICHMAN: Shapiro, Shapiro says he has a very good press contact who has proved very reliable to him and he says his, his practice in this town depends on his knowing what's going on. And he's (*Unintelligible*) press contact. This is one of the—and he's always found it to be—

PRESIDENT: He says that he's talked to Magruder and Magruder said that, that—?

HALDEMAN: Yeah. What they've now told us is we'll never get the transcript. That he—

PRESIDENT: Magruder, think Magruder may have done this?

EHRLICHMAN: I think Magruder may have talked, talked to somebody in the press and that, that was . . .

SEVERAL VOICES: (*Unintelligible*).

PRESIDENT: But, but in the great detail that Colson went into, that he nailed Bob Haldeman, I mean the way Colson did, he says he, he had Colson in the tube . . .

EHRLICHMAN: Yeah.

PRESIDENT: . . . but, but not in any way that was particularly, ah, bad. Right?

EHRLICHMAN: Well, I think, I think like so many things this got, this got planted as a little seed by Shapiro with Colson and that it grew and, uh, uh, uh—

PRESIDENT: Oh yeah?

EHRLICHMAN: Uh-huh. I'd, I'd just—

HALDEMAN: I would guess what's happened is he's got this report from—Colson does—from Danny Hofgren that at the bar in the Bahamas with (*Unintelligible*) or something (*Tape Noise*) one night said to Hofgren, "Jesus, everybody was involved in this." He didn't use the—

PRESIDENT: Uh hmm.

EHRLICHMAN: Everybody knew about it.

HALDEMAN: Mitchell, Haldeman, Colson, Dean, the President—

PRESIDENT: Magruder . . .

HALDEMAN: He, he specifically said the President.

PRESIDENT: . . . Magruder doesn't believe that, though, does he?

HALDEMAN: No. Ya know, I've got it, I've got . . .

SEVERAL VOICES: (*Unintelligible*).

PRESIDENT: I just wonder if he believes it. I'm curious because—do you think he believes it, John?

EHRLICHMAN: No. This tape's very convincing and Higby handled it so well that Magruder has closed all those doors now, with this tape.

PRESIDENT: What good will that do, John?

(Tape Noise)

EHRLICHMAN: Uh, sir, it beats the socks off him if he ever gets off the reservation.

PRESIDENT: Can you use the tape?

EHRLICHMAN: Well, no. You can use Higby.

PRESIDENT: Uh, Hunt's testimony on pay-off, of course, would be very important.

EHRLICHMAN: Right.

PRESIDENT: Is he prepared to testify on that?

EHRLICHMAN: I think so, that's what they say, that he will, and that he will implicate O'Brien and Parkinson. And, uh, then, of course, ah—

PRESIDENT: O'Brien and Parkinson?

EHRLICHMAN: The lawyers.

PRESIDENT: Were they the ones that talked to Hunt?

EHRLICHMAN: Well, he says they were and that they handed him the money. He in turn handed it to his wife and she was the, uh, go-between for the . . .

PRESIDENT: Yeah.

EHRLICHMAN: . . . Cubans.

PRESIDENT: For what purpose? That's the key to it all.

EHRLICHMAN: Well, I think, uh, he'll, he'll hook, hang 'em up on obstruction of justice.

PRESIDENT: Can Hunt do that?

HALDEMAN: How can he do that? Why would he simply—why doesn't he accomplish his purpose simply by saying they gave the money to handle their legal fees?

EHRLICHMAN: They're—all hang out there apparently.

PRESIDENT: Now this is . . .

HALDEMAN: I don't think—

PRESIDENT: . . . this, this is what Colson tells you guys?

HALDEMAN: That's right. I don't . . .

PRESIDENT: (*Unintelligible*).

HALDEMAN: . . . have any other information on this.

PRESIDENT: That, Hunt, that Hunt then is going to go. Well, now that, that, that raises the, the problem on,—with regard to Kalmbach. He has possible vulnerability as to whether he was aware, in other words, the motive, the motive—

EHRLICHMAN: This doesn't add anything to the Kalmbach problem at all.

PRESIDENT: What happened . . .

EHRLICHMAN: (*Unintelligible*).

PRESIDENT: . . . what happened on that?

EHRLICHMAN: Dean called Kalmbach.

PRESIDENT: And what did Dean call Kalmbach about?

EHRLICHMAN: And he said we have to raise some money in connection with the, the, uh, uh, aftermath, and I don't know how he described it to Herb. Uh, Herb said how much do you need, and, uh . . .

PRESIDENT: It was never discussed then?

EHRLICHMAN: . . . presumably Dean told him and Herb went to a couple of donors and got some money and sent it back.

HALDEMAN: Dean says very flatly that Kalmbach did not know the purpose, uh, for the money and has no problem.

PRESIDENT: Dean does know the purpose . . .

UNIDENTIFIED: Right.

PRESIDENT: . . . however. Hunt testifies—so, so basically then Hunt will testify that it was so-called hush money. Right?

EHRLICHMAN: I think so. Now that again, my water can't rise any higher than source.

PRESIDENT: I understand.

EHRLICHMAN: But that's that . . .

PRESIDENT: What is your, what is your . . .

EHRLICHMAN: . . . that's, that—

PRESIDENT: What does that serve him, let me ask, just to try to, uh . . .

EHRLICHMAN: Gen- . . .

PRESIDENT: . . . I mean, would it serve him?

EHRLICHMAN: The only thing it serves him is to, uh, uh . . .

PRESIDENT: Would it reduce his sentence?

EHRLICHMAN: . . . have his sentence remitted, that's all.

HALDEMAN: He'd be serving the same purpose by not saying it was hush money—by, by saying he gave it to "these guys that I had recruited for this job and I . . ."

PRESIDENT: I know.

HALDEMAN: ". . . felt badly about their family and," you know, "a great deal about it."

PRESIDENT: That's right, that's what it ought to be and that's got to be the story that, uh, and that . . .

HALDEMAN: (*Unintelligible*).

PRESIDENT: . . . that will be the defense of, uh, the people, right?

EHRLICHMAN: (*Unintelligible*) the only defense they have and so forth.

HALDEMAN: But that . . .

PRESIDENT: (*Unintelligible*).

HALDEMAN: . . . that was the line that he had used around here.

PRESIDENT: What?

HALDEMAN: That was the line that they used around here. That we've got to have money for their legal fees and family sup- . . .

PRESIDENT: Support them. Well, I heard something about that at a much later time.

HALDEMAN: Yeah.

PRESIDENT: And, frankly, not knowing much about obstruction of justice, I thought it was perfectly proper.

EHRLICHMAN: Well, it's like the . . .

PRESIDENT: Would it be perfectly proper?

EHRLICHMAN: . . . the defense of the . . .

PRESIDENT: Berrigans?

EHRLICHMAN: . . . the, uh, Chicago Seven.

PRESIDENT: The Chicago Seven?

HALDEMAN: They had a defense fund for everybody.

PRESIDENT: Not only a defense fund, Christ, they, they take care of the living expenses, too . . .

UNIDENTIFIED: Was there any—

PRESIDENT: . . . despite what all this crap about just legal fees, they take care of themselves. They raise—you remember the Scottsboro case? Christ. The, uh, uh, the Communist front raised a million dollars for the Scottsboro people. Nine hundred thousand went into the pockets of the Scotts-, er, uh, Communists.

HALDEMAN: (Laughs).

PRESIDENT: . . . so it's common practice.

EHRLICHMAN: Yeah.

PRESIDENT: Nevertheless, that's Hunt then saying about the payoff. Alright—Hunt, on other activities: uh, Hunt then according to Colson was not, uh—(Tape Noise) get into. What Colson meant about the door of the Oval Office.

EHRLICHMAN: Uh, I'll have to get back to you on that, 'cause Shapiro was there and I didn't want to get into it.

PRESIDENT: Right.

HALDEMAN: (Unintelligible).

PRESIDENT: He—

HALDEMAN: No, but it wasn't, it was in connection—

PRESIDENT: No, not—it was in an earlier conversation . . .

HALDEMAN: Your instructions said—

PRESIDENT: . . . about the Magruder conversation . . .

HALDEMAN: Yeah.

PRESIDENT: . . . when Colson was, uh—I think on the Magruder conversation, from what I have seen . . .

EHRLICHMAN: (*Unintelligible*).

PRESIDENT: . . . it seems to me that—

EHRLICHMAN: . . . 'cause Magruder doesn't got to the door of the Oval Office. He doesn't even come to visit me . . .

PRESIDENT: I know that.

EHRLICHMAN: . . . in the White House.

PRESIDENT: But he, he—it is Colson's, it is Colson's view that Magruder's talking would have the effect of bringing it there because of the—I think what he's really referring to, John, is that by reason of Colson, uh, by reason of Magruder nailing Haldeman and, er, and Colson, that that's the door to the Oval Office. I don't know what else because . . .

HALDEMAN: (*Unintelligible*).

PRESIDENT: . . . there's nobody else around, nobody physically around.

HALDEMAN: Magruder isn't going to nail Haldeman.

PRESIDENT: Well, let's see. I don't think so either, but—

HALDEMAN: (*Unintelligible*)

PRESIDENT: Well that is, that tape is, is invaluable, is it not?

EHRLICHMAN: Yeah, I suggest to Bob that he keep it.

HALDEMAN: And I disregard that as (*Unintelligible*).

EHRLICHMAN: (*Laughs*)

PRESIDENT: Let me just say a couple of things that we have to get there. We, we, uh . . .

HALDEMAN: Well, when we come to that, we'd take (*Unintelligible*).

PRESIDENT: . . . in regard to your, regard to your, uh, uh, your, your views and so forth and so on, now, uh I was told the other day, uh, last night, John, you and Bob or somebody—I guess you and I were talking about, uh, somebody going to see Mitchell. And you suggested Rogers. Got any other better names? Why did you . . .

EHRLICHMAN: Well, I've been up and down the list, and uh—

PRESIDENT: . . . why did you suggest Rogers?

EHRLICHMAN: Well, I suggested Rogers because—

PRESIDENT: First let me tell you—purpose of mission—tell me what it is, now.

EHRLICHMAN: The purpose of the mission is to go and bring him to a focus on this and I'd say, "The jig is up. And the President strongly feels that the only way that this thing can end up being even a little net plus for the Administration and for the Presidency and preserve some thread is for you to go in and, and, uh, voluntarily, uh, make a statement."

PRESIDENT: A statement that Haldeman, uh, has prepared.

EHRLICHMAN: Uh, uh, a, a sta-, statement that basically says . . .

HALDEMAN: No. He's got to go beyond that.

EHRLICHMAN: "I am, I am both morally and legally responsible."

PRESIDENT: Yeah.

EHRLICHMAN: Now, the reason for Rogers is that he's clean, number one . . .

PRESIDENT: Yeah.

EHRLICHMAN: . . . uh, he has been both, uh, Attorney General and has this other investigatory . . .

PRESIDENT: Right.

EHRLICHMAN: . . . and Senatorial background and so forth. And there isn't anybody that Mitchell trusts, except Haldeman.

PRESIDENT: He hates Rogers.

EHRLICHMAN: I understand.

HALDEMAN: Doesn't, doesn't trust Rogers but he would know if Rogers came . . .

EHRLICHMAN: That it was . . .

HALDEMAN: that it was you.

EHRLICHMAN: Now, the other, the only other alternative, going up and down the list—

HALDEMAN: Also, it from a public viewpoint Rogers is the dean of the Cabinet . . .

PRESIDENT: Yeah.

HALDEMAN: . . . and is the logical man as, as an attorney, and former Attorney General.

PRESIDENT: From a public viewpoint, that may be but, also . . .

EHRLICHMAN: Fifty reasons not to do this.

HALDEMAN: You've thought of those?

PRESIDENT: Oh, yeah. Yeah.

EHRLICHMAN: There, there, and there, there have consistently been—you go back through the history of this—

PRESIDENT: I know, but now is the time to do something. I agree with you.

EHRLICHMAN: Now is the only time, probably, and I'm, I'm persuaded by that argument.

PRESIDENT: Oh, I am too. I'm, I'm not,—I'm not arguing about not doing it . . .

EHRLICHMAN: I understand.

PRESIDENT: . . . I'm just trying to talk about the names

EHRLICHMAN: Okay. Uh, in, in going down the list, John Alexander is the only other one that I have come to that, that in any way could, could bridge it. Garment can't do it.

PRESIDENT: Now, let me give you another name . . .

EHRLICHMAN: Alright.

HALDEMAN: (*Unintelligible*) President.

PRESIDENT: . . . let me give you another name. Ken Rush. (*Unintelligible*). He's a fine lawyer, utterly clean. Uh, a long-time friend of Mitchell's—not a close friend, but he's known him, you know, in New York, uh, and that grew up there, they are, they, you know, they sort of—Rush would understand it all. Uh, Mitchell does not hate him—does trust him.

EHRLICHMAN: I don't know how able Rush is. I'd, uh—he's got—uh, I just don't know. Uh, another name—uh, two other names that have occurred to me that I'll throw out, uh, one is Elliot Richardson and the other is, uh, uh, Kleindienst. There is another possibility and that's Henry Petersen. Well, that of course . . .

PRESIDENT: Well—

EHRLICHMAN: . . . but he's in the prosecutorial end.

PRESIDENT: That's right.

EHRLICHMAN: And so is Kleindienst.

PRESIDENT: Yeah.

EHRLICHMAN: Well, that's the trouble.

PRESIDENT: Kleindienst, Kleindienst revealing to Mitchell the contents of the Grand Jury and all the rest . . .

EHRLICHMAN: Yeah.

PRESIDENT: . . . is wrong.

EHRLICHMAN: I, I must say I am impressed with the argument that the President should be personally involved in it at this stage.

PRESIDENT: Right. I agree.

EHRLICHMAN: Uh, old John, uh, Dean had a, had an interesting—got a phone call from him about 12:30.

PRESIDENT: (*Unintelligible*).

EHRLICHMAN: Oh, no. I was working on something I'll tell you about here.

PRESIDENT: What did you do?

EHRLICHMAN: Uh, well, not much last night.

PRESIDENT: You mean another subject?

EHRLICHMAN: Oh, no. No, this—

HALDEMAN: There is no other subject. (*Laughs*)

EHRLICHMAN: This week there's no other subject.

PRESIDENT: Yeah.

EHRLICHMAN: That, uh, no, I'll tell you. Last night when I got home I decided that, that, uh, I would sit down and try to put down on paper a report to you about what I have been doing since you asked me to get into this.

PRESIDENT: Right, right.

EHRLICHMAN: Uh, I am concerned about the overall aspect of this and then—I want to talk about that before we—

PRESIDENT: Yeah.

EHRLICHMAN: I don't know what your timing is like.

PRESIDENT: No problem.

EHRLICHMAN: We'll probably get back to it.

PRESIDENT: Uh, got plenty of time.

EHRLICHMAN: But, Dean called and he said, "Alright, here's a scenario." He said, "We've all been trying to figure out . . ."

PRESIDENT: Yeah.

EHRLICHMAN: ". . . how to make this go." He says, "The President calls Mitchell into his office on Saturday. He says, 'John, you've got to do this and here are the facts: bing, bing, bing, bing.' And then that's—you pull this paper out here. And you'd better go do this. And Mitchell stonewalls you. So then, John says, 'I don't know why you're asking me down here. You can't ask a man to do a thing like that. I need my lawyer. Uh, uh, I don't know what I'm facing? He says, 'You just really can't expect me to do this?' Uh, so the President says, 'Well, John, I have no alternative.' And with that, uh, uh, the President calls the U.S. Attorney and says, 'I, the President of the United States of America and leader of the free world want to go before the Grand Jury on Monday.' "

PRESIDENT: I won't even comment on that.

HALDEMAN: That's a silly (*Unintelligible*).

EHRLICHMAN: What I mean is, we're—typical of the thinking of—we're running out every, every line. So that was 12:30 this morning. I, uh, uh, but, but I . . .

PRESIDENT: I go before the Grand Jury—that's . . .

EHRLICHMAN: . . . I—

PRESIDENT: That's like putting Bob on national television uh . . .

HALDEMAN: With Dan Rather.

PRESIDENT: What?

HALDEMAN: With Dan Rather.

PRESIDENT: . . . well, well by putting it on national television period. When, uh, your, uh, when your, when your audience basically is not that big.

EHRLICHMAN: Well, let's, let's take it just as far as you calling Mitchell into the Oval Office, as a, as a . . .

(*Tape Noise*)

EHRLICHMAN: . . . essentially convinced that Mitchell was linchpin in this thing . . .

PRESIDENT: Right.

EHRLICHMAN: . . . and that if he goes down, it can rebound to the administration's advantage. If he doesn't then we're—

PRESIDENT: How can it rebound to our advantage?

EHRLICHMAN: That . . .

PRESIDENT: There's others . . .

EHRLICHMAN: . . . That. You have a report from me based on three weeks' work, that when you got it, you immediately acted to call Mitchell in as the, as the provable . . .

PRESIDENT: I see.

EHRLICHMAN: . . . wrong-doer . . .

PRESIDENT: I see.

EHRLICHMAN: . . . and you say, "My God, I've got a report here. And it's clear from this report that you are guilty as hell. Now, John, for Christ's sake go on in there and do what you should. And let's get this thing cleared up and get it off the country's back and move on." And, uh, uh—

HALDEMAN: Well, plus the given side of it is that that's the only . . .

PRESIDENT: Even way to—

HALDEMAN: . . . way to beat 'er down.

PRESIDENT: Well—

HALDEMAN: Now, from John Mitchell's own personal viewpoint that's the only salvation for John Mitchell. Can you see another way? And, obviously, once you have it, you've—he's got to admit it.

PRESIDENT: He's, he's not gonna make it, anyway.

HALDEMAN: Another factor in that to consider for what it's worth, is the point Connally made to me in that conversation we had on this.

PRESIDENT: I ought to talk to Mitchell?

HALDEMAN: I don't know whether he said this to you or not. He made the point that you had to get this laid out and that the only way it could hurt you is if it ultimately went to Mitchell. And that, that would be the one man you couldn't afford to let get hung on this.

PRESIDENT: Even worse than Hughes talk.

HALDEMAN: He thought so. Seemed to be . . .

PRESIDENT: (*Unintelligible*) That's true. Yeah.

HALDEMAN: . . . seemed to be, because he's the epitome of your . . .

PRESIDENT: Yeah.

HALDEMAN: . . . your hard line.

PRESIDENT: I think he's wrong about that. I think this is the the worst one, well, due, due to the closeness to the President at the time of the crime.

HALDEMAN: But—

PRESIDENT: Would you agree, John?

HALDEMAN: Well, what's bad—

EHRLICHMAN: That's the way I see it.

HALDEMAN: But, what Connally also said was unless it's the President himself who nails Mitchell, then the President is (*Unintelligible*).

EHRLICHMAN: Can I pull up this into the larger, in a larger picture? We've gotta live day to day through these things . . .

UNIDENTIFIED: Yeah.

EHRLICHMAN: . . . and forget, uh, the, uh, perspective that will be put on this period . . .

UNIDENTIFIED: Yeah.

EHRLICHMAN: . . . three months later.

PRESIDENT: The point is whether or not—I think I've got the larger picture—I think, I mean I, and I, in this regard, the point is this that the—we need some action before, uh—in other words, if, if it's like my, my feeling about having the Grand Jury do it and the court system do it rather than Ervin Committee—now we want the President to do it rather than the Grand Jury.

EHRLICHMAN: No.

PRESIDENT: And I agree with that.

EHRLICHMAN: Well, you're doing it in aid of the Grand Jury.

PRESIDENT: No. No. I didn't mean it. I didn't mean rather than the Grand Jury, but I mean to, to, to, to worm the truth—now look, I, I—the Grand Jury doesn't drag him in, he goes in as a result of the President's asking him to go in.

HALDEMAN: Okay. But while you're at that point could I argue a contrary view for a minute? 'Cause I don't agree with that.

PRESIDENT: Yeah.

HALDEMAN: I strongly feel, thinking it through, with all the stuff we talked about last night, that you don't want to rush in and that the solution here, if we can find it—maybe it's impossible, is . . .

PRESIDENT: Is for Mitchell to come voluntarily?

HALDEMAN: Well, or for Magruder to come voluntarily and nail Mitchell. But if the solution is—I agree that some sort of—

PRESIDENT: Where does Magruder come to? Me?

HALDEMAN: No. The, the U.S. Attorney. That—

PRESIDENT: Well, why does—why don't I urge Magruder to—I mean let me, let me look at this. The urging of Liddy to testify, the urging of Magruder to testify and Mitchell. John run those by, by—I didn't mean to stop your . . .

EHRLICHMAN: No, that's alright.

PRESIDENT: . . . your whole analysis but I think, I think I know what you're, what, what, what—isn't that really the essence of it?

EHRLICHMAN: I'm trying to write the news magazine story for next Monday . . .

PRESIDENT: Right.

EHRLICHMAN: . . . a week, Monday a week. And, if it is that "Grand Jury Indicts Mitchell" . . .

PRESIDENT: Right.

EHRLICHMAN: . . . "The White House main effort to cover up, uh, finally collapsed last week when the Grand Jury indicted John Mitchell and Jeb Magruder," . . .

PRESIDENT: Right.

EHRLICHMAN: . . . and uh, "Cracking the case was the testimony of a, a number of, uh, peripheral witnesses who—each of whom contributed to developing a, a uh, cross-triangulation and permitted the Grand Jury to analyze it," and so on and so forth. And then "the final, the final straw that broke the camel's back was, uh, an investigator's discovery of this and that and the other thing." That's one set of facts. Uh, uh, and then the tag on that is "The White House Press Secretary Ron Ziegler said that the White House would have no comment."

PRESIDENT: I know, I know. It can't be done.

EHRLICHMAN: The other one, the other one goes: "Events moved swiftly last week, after the President was presented with a report indicating that, uh, uh—for the first time—that, uh, uh suspicion of John Mitchell and, uh, Jeb Magruder as ringleaders in the uh, Watergate break-in were in fact substantiated by, uh, considerable evidence. Uh, the President then, uh, uh, dispatched so and so to do this and that and it"—maybe to see Mitchell or, or something of that kind and, uh, uh—" these efforts, uh, resulted in Mitchell going to the U.S. Attorney's office on Monday morning at nine o'clock, uh, asking to, uh, testify before the Grand Jury. Uh, uh, charges of cover-up, uh, by the White House were, uh, uh, materially dispelled by the diligent efforts of the President and his aides in, uh, moving on evidence which came to their hands in the, in the closing days of the previous week." Ah—

PRESIDENT: I, I'd buy that.

EHRLICHMAN: Okay.

PRESIDENT: You want to—so, we get down to the tactics.

EHRLICHMAN: Now, I've been concerned because since the end of March, I have turned up a fair amount of hearsay evidence that, that points at this guy. Now, just take—

PRESIDENT: And so did Dean . . .

EHRLICHMAN: And, and so did John.

PRESIDENT: . . . so did Dean.

EHRLICHMAN: Now, taking this—

PRESIDENT: Yet we've tried, very honestly, we've tried to, tried to look at it the best way we could. Maybe he couldn't, maybe he really didn't know.

EHRLICHMAN: Well, it's hearsay. And so, he . . .

PRESIDENT: That point.

EHRLICHMAN: . . . you don't hang a guy, you don't hang a guy necessarily—

PRESIDENT: And also, we are going to remember, Mitchell has denied it.

EHRLICHMAN: But I was, I st-, stood over there in Bob's office and listened to that tape of one of the co-actors saying, flat out on the tape, that he was guilty and that Mitchell was gonna, was going to fall and all that and I said to . . .

PRESIDENT: Did he say that? Did he say that?

HALDEMAN: Yeah.

PRESIDENT: Well, we can't—

EHRLICHMAN: . . . and, and I said to myself, "My God! I'm a, you know, I mean, I'm a United States citizen. I'm standing here listening to this, what is my duty?"

PRESIDENT: Well the point is you've now told me. That's the problem.

EHRLICHMAN: That's correct, that's correct.

PRESIDENT: You see, the diffe-, uh, uh, the uh, the problem of my position up to this time has been, quite frankly, nobody ever told me a God-damn thing . . .

EHRLICHMAN: That's right.

PRESIDENT: . . . that Mitchell was guilty.

EHRLICHMAN: That's right.

PRESIDENT: I mean, uh—

HALDEMAN: Well, we still don't know.

PRESIDENT: I, I . . .

HALDEMAN: I don't . . .

PRESIDENT: must say—

HALDEMAN: I, I will still argue that I think the scenario that was spilled, uh, spin, spun out, that Dean spun out to Mitchell is basically the right one . . .

PRESIDENT: Yeah.

HALDEMAN: . . . I don't think Mitchell did order the Watergate bugging and I don't think he was specifically aware of the Watergate bugging at the time it was instituted.

PRESIDENT: Well, let me—

HALDEMAN: I honestly don't.

PRESIDENT: That may be. Now . . .

HALDEMAN: I think that Mitchell . . .

PRESIDENT: . . . here's what he told . . .

HALDEMAN: . . . he had okayed that, but, uh, (*Unintelligible*).

PRESIDENT: . . . for your, for your information here's what he told Rebozo. He knows very well.

HALDEMAN: Mitchell?

PRESIDENT: That's why I asked, does it have to be a lawyer . . .

HALDEMAN: Mmm.

PRESIDENT: . . . to tell Mitchell.

HALDEMAN: Jeez, I wouldn't get Bebe into this.

PRESIDENT: I know.

HALDEMAN: Boy!

PRESIDENT: Well, anyway, let me tell you what he told Rebozo, uh, right afterwards—no, no, er a month ago—he said, he said—you know (*Unintelligible*) you know how he puffs on his pipe—"In the ITT thing, I may have perjured myself but I sure didn't on this God-damn thing."

HALDEMAN: Yeah.

PRESIDENT: There you are.

HALDEMAN: Okay. I still think that technically that may be correct.

EHRLICHMAN: I think so—'cause that's what he told Moore. And he believes that.

PRESIDENT: What did he say? Could he tell Moore?

EHRLICHMAN: Well, remember, I, he, I asked Moore to find out what Mitchell had testified to.

PRESIDENT: Yeah. Oh, yeah. That's right. And Moore heard the testimony and said well you're not—

EHRLICHMAN: He, he was never asked the right questions. Now, uh, uh, as far as he's concerned . . .

HALDEMAN: He probably didn't in the Grand Jury either.

EHRLICHMAN: That's right. As far as the quality of the evidence is concerned—

PRESIDENT: May I just, uh, digress for one point, that has nothing to do with this except that you've got to fight what's going on damn soon. It is essential that, uh, Roger's departure be delayed until this is over. Now, the hell with Henry on this. The point is, any member of the cabinet, except Kleindienst, leaving during this—there's no way that Dick is gonna leave anyway—and, uh, now you gotta talk to Hen-, you gotta just "And Henry it's not appealable." You just gotta say that, "Henry, there are bigger things here." With Rogers—

EHRLICHMAN: (*Unintelligible*).

PRESIDENT: Huh?

EHRLICHMAN: There's just gonna leave—

PRESIDENT: You're just gonna say—alright fine, then drop that and just say Rogers is gonna stay 'til this thing's over. Right John, you agree?

EHRLICHMAN: Absolutely.

PRESIDENT: Ya see, Rogers is gonna leave on the first of June, and, uh, but, uh, uh, he must—

EHRLICHMAN: We may be, we may be out of the woods by . . .

PRESIDENT: May be . . .

EHRLICHMAN: . . . it might be over by then.

PRESIDENT: . . . out of the woods? No.

HALDEMAN: I don't know.

EHRLICHMAN: Well, uh, to go back to . . .

PRESIDENT: Alright. We won't—

EHRLICHMAN: . . . the quality of the evidence—

PRESIDENT: . . . I only mentioned Bebe because (*Unintelligible*) let me—let's get— go ahead with your—

EHRLICHMAN: Well, all I was going to say is that—

PRESIDENT: Alright. I now have evidence, I am convinced . . .

EHRLICHMAN: But you, you don't have evidence if, uh, uh, if I—

PRESIDENT: I'm not convinced he's guilty . . .

EHRLICHMAN: That's it.

PRESIDENT: . . . but I am convinced that he ought to go before a Grand Jury.

EHRLICHMAN: Exactly. Uh, and, and, and it—what I did last night, or this morning, was to write out what would, uh, would in effect be a report to you . . .

PRESIDENT: Right.

EHRLICHMAN: . . . of, of this, of this . . .

PRESIDENT: Let me ask you whether—

EHRLICHMAN: . . . (*Unintelligible*) deliver it to you.

PRESIDENT: John—(*Pause*) Go see Mitchell.

HALDEMAN: (*Laughs*).

EHRLICHMAN: Uh, all I know about my relationship with Mitchell from his side is what others tell me. He has never, he's never, uh, never (*Unintelligible*).

PRESIDENT: The Mitchell problem, the Mitchell problem with Rogers has been totally created.

EHRLICHMAN: I see.

(*Privileged Material Deleted*)

PRESIDENT: . . . Let's come around, let's come around again though. You know the case. You've conducted the investigation for me. You have reported to me and I have asked you to go up and lay it on the ground to Mitchell and to tell Mitchell, look, there is only one thing that could save him. I think John's got to hear that kind of talk and I think he's got to hear it from somebody that doesn't have—I was thinking of bringing Rogers in and telling him all this stuff, but God-damn it, Mitchell will wind him around his finger.

EHRLICHMAN: Yeah, yeah.

PRESIDENT: . . . well, there's our problem.

EHRLICHMAN: If you want me to go, I'll go.

PRESIDENT: I think the message . . .

EHRLICHMAN: I don't know what he thinks—

PRESIDENT: . . . but the message to Garcia has got to be carried—

EHRLICHMAN: Bob, Bob has a pretty good feel of Mitchell's attitude toward me that I don't have.

PRESIDENT: Well, Mitchell's attitude toward you is not going to be personal—it isn't going to be any better for Rogers. It would be toward Rush . . .

EHRLICHMAN: Yeah, but how in the name of God can—

PRESIDENT: . . . Rush is smart and he is tough. He's a good man. And, uh, he's a man, incidentally that we can consider—

EHRLICHMAN: He can't argue the facts of this case, that's the point.

PRESIDENT: The point is, Rush is a man that I would cons-—if you need a special man in the White House—I was thinking last night that he is the best man I can think of . . .

EHRLICHMAN: (*Unintelligible*).

PRESIDENT: . . . to bring over to advise the President on this God-damn thing and—no, and examine all the White House things, to look at all the FBI files, to look at your report, Dean report, the FBI files and give me a report. He's articulate, he's, he's, uh, before television he's, uh, respected among, uh—he's one of the towering figures in the Ambassadorial world and in the bar. He is, he's no slouch.

EHRLICHMAN: Bobby?

PRESIDENT: And an outsider's—good God, it's going to take so long to—Rush, I trust. Rush is a friend. He's a total White House man and yet he is not, not tied into this.

EHRLICHMAN: He's exactly the kind of guy we need. Now, I don't know how he, he is in person—he hasn't practiced law for a long time. That's not, that's not an immediate drawback but, but, uh . . .

PRESIDENT: He has the lawyer's mind.

EHRLICHMAN: . . . you got to get him somebody to help him, like, uh, uh—

HALDEMAN: Haven't, though, haven't events overtaken that project?

PRESIDENT: Oh, no. No. No. No. No. Bob, for Christ's sake, will you—look, the point that I make is let's suppose they get Mitchell. Then they're going to say now what about Haldeman and what about Chapin, and what about Colson and the rest? I've got to have a report indicating—in other words, you've got all that whole Segretti crap in there. I want somebody to say, now look, here are the facts. None of the White House people were involved. There are no other higher-ups. The White House was not involved. Put a cap around it. And, and second . . .

EHRLICHMAN: More than that—

PRESIDENT: . . . and then face the Segretti crap.

EHRLICHMAN: I, I, in, in forcing this out, Dean remains a problem and, and, uh, here's—uh, let me just read you what I've come to on that . . .

PRESIDENT: Alright.

EHRLICHMAN: . . . "John Dean has not involved himself in this matter as your counsel for several months and properly so. I should not continue to fill in for him," meaning me, "for several reasons, including the impermissable demands on my time that are involved.

Reel 2 Begins

You need a full-time special counsel to follow these related problems who can advise you of the legal niceties from his experience in constitutional, criminal and governmental practice. I'll be happy to continue to consult with him, and so on. I do not recommend that Dean take a leave. That is neither in nor out. He has involved himself to the extent described above. Either that

Reel 1 Ends

requires dismissal or it does not. And that choice should be made at once. If he is discharged, the U.S. Attorney and the Grand Jury should treat him differently. But I think he's, he—you've got to bite the bullet on Dean, one way or the other, pretty quick.

PRESIDENT: Alright. But . . .

EHRLICHMAN: But recognize, uh, . . .

HALDEMAN: What did Dean say to . . .

EHRLICHMAN: . . . but recognize . . .

HALDEMAN: . . . what did Dean say to . . .

EHRLICHMAN: that kills him.

HALDEMAN: Dean's.

EHRLICHMAN: Yeah basically he says that kills him.

PRESIDENT: (*Unintelligible*).

HALDEMAN: Yeah.

PRESIDENT: (*Unintelligible*) and he got off with plea bargaining for a misdemeanor.

HALDEMAN: Sure.

PRESIDENT: A misdemeanor.

HALDEMAN: Yeah.

PRESIDENT: That's all the God-damn thing ever was.

HALDEMAN: Yeah. And he got an undetermined sentence that was suspended Friday.

PRESIDENT: That's right.

HALDEMAN: He never served an hour in jail.

PRESIDENT: Didn't serve in jail and then, but, but, not only—you see, Bob—

HALDEMAN: He was indicted on a felony . . .

PRESIDENT: He did not—indicted on a felony . . .

HALDEMAN: Pled to a—

PRESIDENT: Plea, plea-bargained to a misdemeanor, gets off with, uh, no sentence and so forth and, and Dash defends him and says that—and Lipschitz goes out and the Post prints reams of stuff that he . . .

HALDEMAN: (*Unintelligible*).

PRESIDENT: . . . is an honorable man and so forth. Now what really—

HALDEMAN: He had already been indicted on two other—

PRESIDENT: How in the hell, who got the, got that story out (*Unintelligible*).

HALDEMAN: Well, they, apparently, the two or three papers got wind of it, but the interesting thing is that Dash had made the moral judgment . . .

PRESIDENT: Earlier.

HALDEMAN: . . . that, that didn't disqualify him, he knew about it.

PRESIDENT: Right.

HALDEMAN: And Dash has a beautiful statement on the front page of the paper which is a man wouldn't be as good an investigator if he hadn't been in . . .

PRESIDENT: Unless he knew how to bug.

HALDEMAN: . . . (*Unintelligible*). No, unless he had—been in trouble a couple of, one or two times.

EHRLICHMAN: Ervin must have looked at that and . . .

SEVERAL VOICES: (*Unintelligible*).

HALDEMAN: . . . and he talked about . . .

EHRLICHMAN: (*Unintelligible*).

HALDEMAN: . . . man wouldn't have been a true campaigner if he hadn't had a prank or two once in a while.

PRESIDENT: Well, what I'm getting at is this, that uh, we're just talking here, not with Dean—we're talking about Dean naturally—you call my attention to Lipschitz' thing only I don't give a damn about the part of this with Hunt, Liddy, and the Cuban . . .

UNIDENTIFIED: True.

PRESIDENT: . . . (*Unintelligible*) are in this thing. It would be my (*Tape Noise*) a reasonable time had expired after the thing (*Unintelligible, With Tape Noise*) and before I leave office and they'll get off. You get them full pardons. That's what they have to have, John.

EHRLICHMAN: Right.

PRESIDENT: Do you agree?

EHRLICHMAN: Yep, I sure do. Well, you haven't asked me how I'd come out on this. I just, I just brought it to a focus. I think if you have to decide up or down on Dean now . . .

PRESIDENT: What do you think about that? Oh, let's see. What, what does Dean say when you tell him that?

EHRLICHMAN: He doesn't agree with that.

PRESIDENT: I know he doesn't agree, but what does he do?

EHRLICHMAN: He wants to stay and just disconnect himself from this case. And he says, "Yes, that's right, make your decision now, but make your decision that I should stay." He needn't decide that right this minute and I would encourage him not to . . .

PRESIDENT: I mean.

EHRLICHMAN: . . . but in talking about Rush, what relates to this general subject. I think I would pass it for the moment.

PRESIDENT: But the only thing that I was—yeah, I agree you should—

EHRLICHMAN: And, and, uh, get back to, get back to the Mitchell thing which really is, uh . . .

PRESIDENT: Like today. I know.

EHRLICHMAN: . . . uh, like this morning.

PRESIDENT: I don't think there's anybody that can talk to Mitchell except somebody that knows this case. Now, there's one or two people, I mean I—versed myself in it enough to know the God-damn thing, but I'm not sure that I want to know. I want to say Mitchell, "Now, look, I, I think that, I think that you're—the attorneys for the Committee, O'Brien—and I found out this, and I found out that, and I found out that, and the Grand Jury has told me this th-th-th-th-th-dee." I just don't know. I just don't—you know what I mean. They talk about my going out is, uh— but really, I am not trying to duck it. I, I don't mind, I've done unpleasant things and I'll take this in one minute. Uh, the thing, John, is that there's nobody really that can do it except you. And I know how Mitchell feels. But you conducted this investigation. I would—the way I would do it, Bob, you, you critique this, is I'd go up, and I'd say, . . .

HALDEMAN: Alright.

PRESIDENT: . . . "The President's asked me to see you." That you have come in today with this report; these are the cold facts indicating; of course, that this does not indicate that, but the Grand Jury is moving swiftly, Magruder will be indicted, you think. Under the circumstances, time is of the essence. You can't be in a position of having you (*Tape Noise*) the Grand Jury and (*Tape Noise*) (*Unintelligible*) "I am responsible, I did not know it. But I assume the responsibility. Nobody in the White House is involved," and so forth, and so on. "We did try to help these defendants afterwards, yes." He probably would not deny that anyway. He probably was not asked that at an earlier time. But the, just as the def-, just as any, the defendants are entitled to that sort of—

EHRLICHMAN: Well now you're, you're glossing it. Uh, I don't think he could do that.

PRESIDENT: All right.

EHRLICHMAN: I wouldn't want to, I wouldn't want to . . .

PRESIDENT: All right.

EHRLICHMAN: . . . have you . . .

PRESIDENT: Oh all right.

EHRLICHMAN: . . . (*Unintelligible*).

PRESIDENT: Fine, fine. What would you say to him?

EHRLICHMAN: I'd say (*Unintelligible*) . . .

PRESIDENT: Let me, let me hear your speech (*Unintelligible*).

EHRLICHMAN: I'd say, "The jig, you know, basically, the jig is up, John, and uh, I've listened to, uh, Magruder and, and, uh, uh, uh, he's gonna, he's in my opinion he's about to blow, uh, uh, and that's, that's the last straw." Uh—

PRESIDENT: And, also, Hunt is going to testify, Tuesday, Monday, we understand.

EHRLICHMAN: "We've got to, we've got to think of this thing from the standpoint of the President and I know you have been right along and that's the reason you've been conducting yourself as you have."

PRESIDENT: Right.

EHRLICHMAN: "It, it's now time, I think, to rethink what best serves the President and also what best serves you . . ."

PRESIDENT: Right.

EHRLICHMAN: ". . . in the ultimate outcome of this thing."

PRESIDENT: Right.

EHRLICHMAN: "And we have to, have to, recognize that you are not going to escape indictment. There's no way and . . ."

PRESIDENT: Because—yeah. Yeah.

EHRLICHMAN: ". . . the far better, far better that you should be prosecuted on an information from the U.S. Attorney based on your conversation with the U.S. Attorney, than on an indictment by a Grand Jury of, of 15 blacks and 3 whites, uh, after, uh, uh, this kind of uh, this kind of an . . .

PRESIDENT: Right.

EHRLICHMAN: ". . . investigation."

PRESIDENT: We're right on the door of the White House and we're trying to protect you.

EHRLICHMAN: "If, if the Grand Jury goes this way, you've been dragged in by the heels. Uh, if you go down first thing Monday morning, or yet this afternoon . . ."

PRESIDENT: This afternoon.

EHRLICHMAN: ". . . and talk to the U.S. Attorney, and say, 'Okay I want to make a statement,' then two things happen: one, you get credit for coming forward; two, you serve the President's interest. And, uh, I'm here in behalf of the President—"

HALDEMAN: Well, and three, you have the dignified opportunity to discuss this in, in the, office of . . .

EHRLICHMAN: Yeah.

HALDEMAN: . . . of Earl Silbert instead of in the third Washington jail.

EHRLICHMAN: "And, and I'm here at the President's request to ask you to do that . . ."

PRESIDENT: Yeah.

EHRLICHMAN: "He has reviewed the facts now . . ."

PRESIDENT: Right.

EHRLICHMAN: "He has no alternative, John . . .

PRESIDENT: Right.

EHRLICHMAN: ". . . but . . ."

PRESIDENT: Right.

EHRLICHMAN: ". . . to send me here and . . ."

PRESIDENT: Right.

EHRLICHMAN: ". . . ask you to do this."

PRESIDENT: Right, well, then, if you want to hear it personally, he, he, he, uh . . .

EHRLICHMAN: Pick up the phone.

PRESIDENT: No. Come down and see him.

HALDEMAN: I have a couple of modifications to that. One, a minor ques—not to what you say, but in setting it up. It would be helpful, in doing that, if I called Mitchell and said that the President wants you to talk with him. Then there's no question . . .

PRESIDENT: Right.

HALDEMAN: . . . in his mind . . .

PRESIDENT: That's right.

HALDEMAN: . . . that you're, you're operating . . .

PRESIDENT: Right.

HALDEMAN: . . . unilaterally.

EHRLICHMAN: Absolutely.

PRESIDENT: Right, right.

HALDEMAN: And, secondly, that if at all possible, he should come down here.

EHRLICHMAN: Why is that?

HALDEMAN: Well, my reason for it is, A, you get him here under your circum-stances. B, if you make your case, which you may (*Unintelligible*) at this point—

PRESIDENT: That's right.

HALDEMAN: . . . 'cause he may be on the same track.

PRESIDENT: Yeah.

HALDEMAN: . . . maybe at the same point.

PRESIDENT: Yeah.

HALDEMAN: If he is, you might be able then to swing a "let's get Silbert right now and go on over." Ah, he may say, I've got to talk to the President before I do this.

PRESIDENT: That's right.

HALDEMAN: And then run him in to do it.

PRESIDENT: Um, well, let me say, let me say this, uh, I've, I've run, run through my mind, uh, the, the thoughts. And believe me the idea of Rogers, as you, John, as Bob will tell you, is not, is not one that, uh, that I don't think is, is potentially good. I was hoping to get him in, in a bigger—but I, I know Rogers like the back of my hand and Rogers does not fight real, mean tough problems and he will not go.

HALDEMAN: The trouble with Rogers is that Mitchell will overrun him. Mitchell will say, "Bill, you're out of your fucking mind. If you knew what I knew—I mean those kids over at the White House are, are looking at me and, uh, and, uh—

PRESIDENT: What if you knew what I knew, what about them?

HALDEMAN: Well, he'd roll his eyes and, and Rogers wouldn't know one way or the other.

PRESIDENT: You see, John, somebody has to talk to him who knows the facts. That's the point.

HALDEMAN: And as I mentioned (*Unintelligible, With Tape Noise*) thing in your scenario that really worries me when you say I've listened to Magruder—

EHRLICHMAN: Well, all, all right, I can't say it quite that way

SEVERAL VOICES: (*Unintelligible*)

HALDEMAN: . . . what Magruder's gonna do.

EHRLICHMAN: I can say . . .

PRESIDENT: We have learned from . . .

EHRLICHMAN: I can, I—

PRESIDENT: . . . we have learned that Magruder is going to testify.

EHRLICHMAN: I can say, well, I can start out by saying, look, I can't vouch for any of this first-hand. A tremendous amount of what I know is second-hand, like my conversation with Paul O'Brien, but I have every reason to think that Magruder is in a frame of mind right now to go down there and tell everything he knows.

PRESIDENT: That Hunt's going to go Monday (*Unintelligible*) . . .

EHRLICHMAN: Hunt's going to go Monday.

PRESIDENT: . . . and Liddy, well, you can't say Liddy . . .

EHRLICHMAN: Well—

PRESIDENT: . . . maybe Mitchell has a feel—

EHRLICHMAN: I have, I have reason to think Liddy has already talked.

HALDEMAN: You know Rothblatt knows who (*Unintelligible*) Rothblatt. So they're obviously moving on the cover-up.

PRESIDENT: Yeah.

HALDEMAN: See, if Mitchell went in, that might knock that whole week into a cocked hat.

PRESIDENT: Why?

HALDEMAN: Well, what do they care about the cover-up any more? They—

PRESIDENT: Humph.

EHRLICHMAN: Well, they might, but they, but, you see, Mitchell—if Mitchell gave them a complete statement . . .

PRESIDENT: I wish they wouldn't, but (*Unintelligible*) they would, Bob.

EHRLICHMAN: . . . if Mitchell gave them a complete statement—

PRESIDENT: They shouldn't, I mean, you're right. I mean, the, the, the cover-up, he said that, uh—said well that basically it's a separate crime. Isn't that right, John?

EHRLICHMAN: Yes.

PRESIDENT: Do you think they would keep going on the cover-up even if Mitchell went in?

EHRLICHMAN: Well, I would assume so. I would certainly assume so. You see, they're got to explain to the Ervin Committee some day why they do things and they've got a hell of a lead. They're really not in shape to stop at this point. They would certainly be diverted.

HALDEMAN: (*Unintelligible With Tape Noise*) is this, that everything relating to this and all the fringes of it and all the, well, any other—

EHRLICHMAN: I think they're in a position to uh—I, I just don't know (*Unintelligible*)

HALDEMAN: Yeah, that's right.

EHRLICHMAN: (*Unintelligible*)

PRESIDENT: But the point is what, what they have that—they, their relations have been primarily with Dean.

HALDEMAN: I don't know about Colson.

EHRLICHMAN: I don't either.

HALDEMAN: Well, Dean is—

PRESIDENT: I have to bite the Dean bullet today.

EHRLICHMAN: I didn't say that. I didn't say that, but I think it, it is, it is a dependent question. And, uh, if you are in a situation where Mitchell stonewalls you . . .

PRESIDENT: Yeah.

EHRLICHMAN: . . . and walks out and says you know, to hell with you guys, I've got to, I've got to live my own life.

PRESIDENT: Well, let's say, uh, we could uh, uh, what, uh, I want to look at my watch, not because of an appointment.

EHRLICHMAN: You've got a dentist appointment.

PRESIDENT: (*Unintelligible*) I've been here since eight o'clock this morning.

EHRLICHMAN: That's why?

SEVERAL VOICES: (*Unintelligible*)

PRESIDENT: Don't worry about that. No, that's no problem. I could have got Haig to—but, I, uh, John Dean out of the Grand Jury.

EHRLICHMAN: Let me get around that by sug-, suggesting what I think his response would be.

PRESIDENT: Yeah.

EHRLICHMAN: His response will be, "Look, Ehrlichman, you're supposed to be a lawyer. You know better. To go to somebody who is a target in an inquiry of this kind and try to pressure into giving up his rights is very antithesis of what rights I would have if I were a defendant . . .

PRESIDENT: That's right.

EHRLICHMAN: "Uh, you're supposed to, you're in the executive branch, and a government official, you're supposed to tell me what, what all the chips are.

PRESIDENT: Uh, that, that chair's gone.

HALDEMAN: Oh.

SEVERAL VOICES: (*Unintelligible*)

HALDEMAN: . . . a couple and fall on the floor which would not be—

PRESIDENT: Go ahead Steve.

EHRLICHMAN: Uh, "you're supposed to tell me, uh, that I have a right to counsel and, uh, you know, read me the, the uh, Supreme Court thing (*Unintelligible*) and so forth. Instead of that, you just suggested that I, uh, I divest myself of all my rights, and, uh, and uh, you, uh, asked me down here for a highly improper conversation. You haven't even suggested that I bring my attorney. And I take it what you are doing, is, uh, you're acting as the, uh, prosecutor in this case." How do you come off doing that?

PRESIDENT: He won't do that, in my opinion. Uh I think he's more likely to say, "well God-damn it, look, John, we—don't you know that there are people in the White House that are deeply involved in this. Don't you know that Colson and Haldeman . . .

HALDEMAN: He may say this, yeah.

PRESIDENT: ". . . pressured this poor boy over here." I think Mitchell will take the offensive. Don't you agree? Bob?

HALDEMAN: You see, I'm not at all sure but what Mitchell may think I am involved. I'm sure he probably thinks Colson's involved, because Magruder has used that. I would guess that the line Magruder has used with Mitchell—and you might have to play Magruder's tape recording for him (*Unintelligible*)

EHRLICHMAN: Well I don't think, I don't think that'll happen. I just don't.

HALDEMAN: Well, I just—

PRESIDENT: Is Magruder planning to go see Mitchell?

HALDEMAN: Yes, sir, and it's—if he decides to go, if he decides to talk.

PRESIDENT: If he decides to talk, he's convinced . . .

HALDEMAN: And he's about on the verge, his—I, I assume from that conversation that what he has decided, he is either going to talk or he's going to take the Fifth. He's not going to lie, over and over.

PRESIDENT: But, they're not calling him—they may not call him back, that's always—

EHRLICHMAN: That's correct. (*Unintelligible*) Liddy will never try it.

PRESIDENT: Well the Fifth (*Unintelligible*).

HALDEMAN: Yeah.

EHRLICHMAN: He says, I know I'm going to be arrested. I know I'm on my way to jail. All right, if, if Mitchell comes back with a line like that, you're not serving the President, well, if you have made any kind of investigation surely you know people in the White House are involved.

PRESIDENT: What do you say?

EHRLICHMAN: I say, "look, John, we're past the point where we can be concerned about whether people in the White House are involved. We're not protecting the President by hoping this thing is going go go away."

PRESIDENT: The people in the White House are going to testify.

EHRLICHMAN: The thing is not going to go away, John, and by your sitting up there in New York and pretending that it is, it's just making it worse. And it's been getting steadily worse on account of your sitting up there for the last couple of months. We're at the point now where we have no choice but to ask you to do this.

HALDEMAN: We have a whole, and you could say, we have a whole series of people who have remained mum in order not to create problems for you, who, it's now clear, can no longer remain mum. They don't intend to create problems for you, but, I mean . . .

PRESIDENT: Like Hunt, Liddy?

HALDEMAN: No. I mean like Haldeman, Dean—

EHRLICHMAN: I could say that when I got into this I discovered that there were all kinds of people sitting around here who had bits of information. They were hanging on to them, because they didn't know where they led . . .

PRESIDENT: Well—

EHRLICHMAN: . . . and because they were afraid they would hurt John Mitchell. And I've had to put this whole thing together. And now, having put it together . . .

PRESIDENT: Yeah.

HALDEMAN: (*Unintelligible*) you guys received word he comes down—

EHRLICHMAN: . . . it, there's just no escape from it, just no escape.

HALDEMAN: And it's got to be proved whether, uh, any . . .

PRESIDENT: The adversary type. There's nobody that can do it—

HALDEMAN: He will be able to persuade anyone else there is a way.

PRESIDENT: But, there is nobody else that can do it. Also (*Pause*) let me digress a moment before we get to the (*Unintelligible*) of Mitchell. Another indication of the, the problem we've got here, uh, is—which is related to what we talked about last night—is to just to keep a, a posture vis-a-vis the Committee on this. Uh, I just think we are in an impossible position frankly, with regard to White House people not appearing before the Committee. Now you've gone over that with Ziegler and he still thinks we should stonewall it on those grounds.

HALDEMAN: That's right.

EHRLICHMAN: And I've, I have not talked with him at length for days.

PRESIDENT: Well, I hear you've got the—I, was just looking in the paper this morning—uh, Saxbe, Mathias, Johnny Rhodes, John Anderson, Aiken. Well, of course, two or three of those names are not new, but they're all there . . .

EHRLICHMAN: Yeah.

PRESIDENT: . . . they are trying to build that up as a chorus of Republicans and more will come.

EHRLICHMAN: They'll get five a day for the next month.

HALDEMAN: Bet they don't. Bet—what's interesting is on a universal chorus he must appear before the Committee.

PRESIDENT: Well—

HALDEMAN: Thus, if you've got some saying they've got to set up a way to take secret testimony . . .

HALDEMAN: Yeah, and it's a little difficult here because our people are trained to cooperate . . .

PRESIDENT: That's right.

HALDEMAN: . . . when Weicker's office calls.

PRESIDENT: You can say that, you can say Senator, now, uh, uh, we, we, we're not gonna turn this down unless you tell us to. And uh, and we just, just want you to know that uh, that uh, if you want us to go ahead, why we'll arrange for them to do it. But we want you to, for you to be told, uh, you know what I mean.

HALDEMAN: Use the specific call (*Unintelligible*)

PRESIDENT: Good reason to call him.

HALDEMAN: (*Tape Noise*) North Carolina this week.

PRESIDENT: (*Tape Noise*) we came full circle on the Mit-, on the Mitchell thing.

UNIDENTIFIED: Who?

PRESIDENT: On the Mitchell thing (*Unintelligible*) must come first . . .

HALDEMAN: Yeah.

PRESIDENT: . . . (*Tape Noise*) something today. We've got to make this move today. If it fails, uh, just to get back on position, I think you ought to talk to Magruder.

HALDEMAN: I agree.

PRESIDENT: And you tell Magruder, "Now Jeb, this evidence is coming in, you ought to go into the Grand Jury. Purge yourself if you're perjured, and tell this whole story."

EHRLICHMAN: I agree.

HALDEMAN: (*Unintelligible, With Tape Noise*)

PRESIDENT: The, we'll go—Bob, you don't agree with that?

HALDEMAN: Oh, I do.

PRESIDENT: Because I think we do have to. Third, we've got the problem—

HALDEMAN: Maybe you should talk to Jeb first, though.

PRESIDENT: (*Unintelligible*)

HALDEMAN: (*Unintelligible*) John?

EHRLICHMAN: Doesn't really matter, Bob, eh, either way . . .

PRESIDENT: Yeah.

EHRLICHMAN: . . . who is ever coming first.

PRESIDENT: But then, you see, you see the point is—

HALDEMAN: For God's sake, then don't use Jeb as a basis for the conversation.

PRESIDENT: Yeah. Say that the evidence is not Jeb. I'd just simply say that just a lot of other people with (*Unintelligible*) Jeb . . .

HALDEMAN: . . . although (*Unintelligible*).

PRESIDENT: . . . although he may blow (*Unintelligible*)

EHRLICHMAN: I can say, I can say that the the uh, uh, that I have, I have come to the conclusion that it is both John and Jeb who are liable—

PRESIDENT: Yeah.

EHRLICHMAN: . . . and, uh—

PRESIDENT: But no, I meant . . .

EHRLICHMAN: Yeah, go ahead.

PRESIDENT: I was going to say that we are not talking to you, John, just because Jeb is going to crack . . .

UNIDENTIFIED: Or that—

PRESIDENT: . . . or that Dean is going to the Grand Jury. It's past that point. They've got the case made.

HALDEMAN: That's right.

PRESIDENT: He'll say, "well I think they're bluffing here." What'll you say?

EHRLICHMAN: Uh, it isn't a question of bluffing. Uh, nobody's made any representations to us at all. Nobody's tried to bluff us . . .

PRESIDENT: Right.

EHRLICHMAN: Uh, it, it's just a question of putting together all the facts and that any time someone—if the U.S. Attorney's office goes through the process that I've gone through, he'll have all the facts. And there it'll be. And ya, you don't get it all from any one person. It's it's some from this one, some from that one. It's a typical, it's a typical case, Bob.

HALDEMAN: (*Unintelligible*)

PRESIDENT: How does Dean's, incidentally what is the, what is the, what is the liability or, uh, Hunt, or, uh—I'm thinking of the payoff thing . . .

EHRLICHMAN: Yeah.

PRESIDENT: . . . in this business,—somebody in, uh, Dean, Dean, uh, Dean asked, told me about the problem of Hunt's lawyer, uh, wanted—had gotten—this was a few weeks ago—needed, uh, needed sixty thousand or forty thousand dollars or something like that. You remember? He asked me about it and I said I, I don't know where you can get it. I said I would, uh, I mean, I frankly felt he might try to get it but I didn't know where. And then he left it up with Mitchell and Mitchell then said it was taken care of—am I correct? Is my recollection . . .

EHRLICHMAN: Yes, sir. (*Unintelligible*)

PRESIDENT: Is that approximately correct?

EHRLICHMAN: Yes, you could (*Unintelligible*).

PRESIDENT: Did he talk to you about that?

EHRLICHMAN: He talked to me about it. I said, John, I wouldn't have the vaguest notion where to get it.

PRESIDENT: Yeah—

EHRLICHMAN: I saw him later in the day. I saw Mitchell later in the day . . .

PRESIDENT: Yeah.

EHRLICHMAN: . . . Wednesday (*Unintelligible*)

PRESIDENT: What happened?

EHRLICHMAN: And he just said it's taken care of.

HALDEMAN: Mitchell raised the topic. He turned to Dean and said, "what have you done about, uh, that other problem?" And Dean said—he kind of looked at us—and then said, "well, uh, you know, I, I don't know." And Mitchell said, "Oh, I guess that's been taken care of. (*Tape Noise*) said apparently through LaRue.

PRESIDENT: (*Unintelligible*)

HALDEMAN: (*Tape Noise*) LaRue. Were you the one who told me?

EHRLICHMAN: Who told you?

HALDEMAN: . . . Oh, Dean told us. LaRue. He had, Dean had a long talk with LaRue and LaRue said, "this whole thing is ridiculous now" and said (*Unintelligible, With Tape Noise*) said, "yeah," he said, "If I were in charge of this now what I would do is I'd get a large bus and I'd put the President at the wheel and I'd throw everybody we've got around here in it and I'd drive up to the Senate and I'd have the President open the door and I'd say, you all get out and tell everything you know and I'll be back to pick you up when you're through." He said, "It's all out now and there's nothing we can do about it." And he, he said, "I can," he said, LaRue also said, "you know, I can't figure out how I got into this, uh, to begin with, but I, I, it seems to me all of us have been drawn in here in trying to cover up for John."

PRESIDENT: For Mitchell?

HALDEMAN: Yeah, which is exactly what's happened.

PRESIDENT: LaRue said that?

HALDEMAN: Yes.

PRESIDENT: He's right. (*Unintelligible*)

HALDEMAN: And if LaRue is called, LaRue is, is—intends to tell the truth about it.

PRESIDENT: Is he?

HALDEMAN: Yeah. Now, I—

PRESIDENT: Well, what will be his defense . . .

HALDEMAN: I don't know.

PRESIDENT: . . . about obstruction?

HALDEMAN: I don't know.

EHRLICHMAN: I don't think he has one.

HALDEMAN: If he doesn't intend—

PRESIDENT: No, well, no. His obstruction will be—LaRue'll, uh, that I was helping to get—

EHRLICHMAN: Ah, the way Dean talks LaRue wasn't even thinking about the message.

HALDEMAN: I don't think LaRue cares. I think LaRue's figured that the jig is up.

EHRLICHMAN: (*Tape Noise*) I—a bit of incidental intelligence that (*Unintelligible*) dropped yesterday with regard to Mardian. Just a small matter—went out to Phoenix (*Tape Noise*).—elaborate cover story, which he fed to the New York Times, which would lay it all back in the White House. (*Unintelligible With Tape Noise*) Just gonna know that if they do (*Unintelligible*) get screwed.

UNIDENTIFIED: —Yeah, they've gotten to—

EHRLICHMAN: It will only stand so long as Mitchell stands.

PRESIDENT: Why lay it at the White House?

EHRLICHMAN: That's all that—but I just don't know any other fact and, uh—

PRESIDENT: Well, he could lay it to the White House?

EHRLICHMAN: But bear in, bear in mind Shapiro was giving me this in a whole litany of things that were, that were persuasive and which . . .

PRESIDENT: Yep, yep.

HALDEMAN: I'm still afraid of Shapiro.

EHRLICHMAN: . . . what he said to me (*Unintelligible*) he's a scary guy.

HALDEMAN: (*Unintelligible*) I don't believe we can—

Reel 3 Begins

PRESIDENT: Uh, but what I meant on the Mardian, the point that, uh,—let me say, I don't think that Mardian or LaRue or Mitchell, uh, or Magruder or anybody want to hurt the President in this thing.

Reel 2 Ends

EHRLICHMAN: (*Unintelligible*)

HALDEMAN: I'm sure that's right.

PRESIDENT: Do you feel that way?

HALDEMAN: Yes sir.

PRESIDENT: Colson? How, how about Colson?

HALDEMAN: He, he—I (*Unintelligible*) said he'll do everything he can not to hurt the President.

PRESIDENT: Yeah. That has got to be the attitude of everybody because it isn't the man, it's the Goddamn office.

HALDEMAN: Sure. Sure.

PRESIDENT: But also it happens to be tr-, true. I mean I (*Unintelligible*) I knew about the son-of-a-bitch.

HALDEMAN: You don't have a, that doesn't apply and they didn't—I think rationalize to themselves that hurting or getting anybody else could be . . .

PRESIDENT: That's right.

HALDEMAN: . . . good for the President rather than bad. And that . . .

PRESIDENT: In other words—

HALDEMAN: . . . includes Ehrlichman, Haldeman . . .

PRESIDENT: Yeah.

HALDEMAN: . . . Dean . . .

PRESIDENT: Yeah.

HALDEMAN: . . . certainly Colson. Colson'd be at the top of that list. Colson first, then Haldeman, then Dean, then Ehrlichman.

PRESIDENT: You see I think a Mardian story to the Times will be, frankly, that Colson put the heat on.

HALDEMAN: Well, maybe, but he's gonna last. That could be where you—

PRESIDENT: Maybe Haldeman?

HALDEMAN: Mardian. No, Mardian, I don't think has any personal desire to get me. I think he would—I know he hates Colson.

PRESIDENT: Does he?

HALDEMAN: They all do. And any Mitchell person does, 'cause Mitchell did.

PRESIDENT: You can make, you see, you can make a hell of a circumstantial case on Colson. He's the guy that, you know, he's Dean's buddy, and uh, Liddy, he knew well, apparently knew well—

HALDEMAN: Wasn't Dean's buddy.

PRESIDENT: I'm sorry—I meant Hunt's buddy.

HALDEMAN: Yeah, right.

PRESIDENT: Of course, right. But you know, but, I mean, Colson is closer to this group of robbers than anybody else. That's the problem with Colson. Colson's got a very—

HALDEMAN: He has no tie to Liddy.

PRESIDENT: Oh, no, no. Okay.

HALDEMAN: You know, that is the (*Unintelligible*) he has no, no string to it. His string is to Hunt.

PRESIDENT: Well, then Hunt—

HALDEMAN: Hunt is the, Hunt is the central, uh, background figure that—

PRESIDENT: Is, uh, Hunt, uh, Hunt takes this money? (*Unintelligible*) he took it for what? To cover up?

HALDEMAN: Immunity. Bet Bittman's given immunity.

PRESIDENT: They're going to give Hunt immunity?

HALDEMAN: I don't know, maybe, I suppose.

EHRLICHMAN: I think that would be their deal.

PRESIDENT: Well, that's the standard— (*Unintelligible*) give him immunity for additional crimes?

EHRLICHMAN: He's convicted now, you see, so it would be for additional—

HALDEMAN: They haven't sentenced him.

EHRLICHMAN: That's right.

PRESIDENT: So they could give him immunity—

(*Unintelligible*)

PRESIDENT: . . . they could, they could, cut his sentence and give him immunity for the cover-up; the hush money; clemency. How do you handle the problem of clemency, John?

EHRLICHMAN: You'd have to stonewall that—it's, it's, it's—a cold fact, cold denial (*Unintelligible*)

HALDEMAN: Well, you don't handle it at all. That's Colson's main point because that's where it comes from.

EHRLICHMAN: That was the line of communication—

PRESIDENT: Colson to Bittman? Well, that's the only thing that we have on that, except Mitchell, apparently, had said something about clemency to people.

HALDEMAN: To Liddy.

PRESIDENT: And Mitchell has never, never disc—has he ever discussed clemency with you, Bob?

HALDEMAN: No.

PRESIDENT: Has he ever discussed it with you?

EHRLICHMAN: No.

PRESIDENT: Needless to say, not with me. The only terms (*Unintelligible*) we were all here in the room.

HALDEMAN: I think—

EHRLICHMAN: The only time—

HALDEMAN: . . . he may have said, well, you know, we've got to take care of these people, and, uh—

PRESIDENT: Yeah. Well, I understand that. But he's never said, "Look you're gonna get a pardon for these people when this is over." Never used any such language around here, has he, John?

EHRLICHMAN: Not to me.

HALDEMAN: I don't think so.

PRESIDENT: With Dean has he?

EHRLICHMAN: Well, I don't know.

HALDEMAN: That's a question (*Unintelligible*)

PRESIDENT: 'Cause Dean's never raised it. In fact, Dean told me an interesting thing I said, "Dean," I said, "John," I said, uh, "where's it all lead?" He said, "uh." I said "what's it going to cost? Now you could continue this of course." He said about a million dollars. I said facetiously, "Have you thought of this at all?" (*Unintelligible*) That's the point. That's the foul-up in the whole Mitchell arg-, Mitchell argument. Unless I could just up and say, "Look fellows, it, it's too bad and, and, and I, I, I could, I could give you executive clemency, like tomorrow. What the hell do you think, do you think, Dean, I mean do you think that, that—the point is, Hunt and the Cubans are going to sit on their ass in jail for four years and their families not taken care of? That's the point. Now where the hell do you get the money for that?" That's the reason this whole thing falls. I mean, uh, uh, it's, it's that, that, I mean, uh, that astonishes me about Mitchell and the rest.

EHRLICHMAN: Improbable.

PRESIDENT: Not only improbable, there's no way to get the money is there? Who was it, Tom Pappas they had to see me?

HALDEMAN: (*Unintelligible*) about the money.

PRESIDENT: Huh?

HALDEMAN: You didn't talk to him about the money?

PRESIDENT: I don't remember. You told me to see him. In fact, you said that he was helping on the—

HALDEMAN: But, yeah, but you were seeing him and you were seeing a number of contributors.

PRESIDENT: I know, I know and I said hell, I appreciate the work you're doing for us and I didn't mention what it was.

HALDEMAN: (*Unintelligible*)

PRESIDENT: Good old . . .

HALDEMAN: He was Mitchell's contact.

PRESIDENT: Good old Tom is raising money apparently, he's doing this, this thing—

HALDEMAN: That's right. I doubt that he is—

PRESIDENT: (*Unintelligible*) the word, the word never came up, but, uh, I said I appreciate what you're doing. I do, I do for the purpose of helping the poor bastards through the trial, but you can't after that, John. You can't or could you? I guess you could. Attorneys' fees? Could you, could you get a support program for these people for, for four years?

EHRLICHMAN: I haven't any idea. I have no idea.

PRESIDENT: Well, they've supported other people in jail . . .

EHRLICHMAN: (*Unintelligible*)

PRESIDENT: . . . for years.

EHRLICHMAN: The Berrigans or somebody.

PRESIDENT: Huh?

EHRLICHMAN: I say, I don't know how the Berrigan brothers and some of those . . .

PRESIDENT: They all have funds.

EHRLICHMAN: . . . operate. I think those they use—

PRESIDENT: Yes, there are funds, (*Unintelligible*) are developed. I guess that's true.

EHRLICHMAN: So that they—

PRESIDENT: But not to hush up.

EHRLICHMAN: That's right.

PRESIDENT: That's the point. All right. One final thing: Dean. You, you don't think we have to bite it today?

EHRLICHMAN: Well, I'm not so sure. Uh, I'd, I'd be inclined—say you are (*Unintelligible*). When you say bite it it's simply a matter of making a decision, in, in my opinion, uh—

PRESIDENT: Well, I've made a decision. I think he has to go.

EHRLICHMAN: Well, I'm not sure that's the right decision. It's uh, uh, uh, by, by framing the issue, I don't mean to imply that . . .

PRESIDENT: Oh, I see.

EHRLICHMAN: . . . that's the (*Unintelligible*).

PRESIDENT: I thought, no, no, I thought . . .

EHRLICHMAN: Uh, (*Unintelligible*)

PRESIDENT: When, when you said you didn't address it, I, I'm sorry, I thought that was one of the recommendations you had made.

EHRLICHMAN: No, no, my recommendation is that you recognize that, there's a go-no go decision that has to be . . .

PRESIDENT: Oh, I see.

EHRLICHMAN: . . . made right away.

PRESIDENT: Oh, alright, yeah.

EHRLICHMAN: You see, here's your situation as I—Look again—the big picture—You now are possessed of a body of fact.

PRESIDENT: That's right.

EHRLICHMAN: And you've got to, you can't just sit here.

PRESIDENT: That's right.

EHRLICHMAN: You've got to act on it.

PRESIDENT: Right.

EHRLICHMAN: . . . You've got to make some, you got to make some decisions and the Dean thing is one of the decisions that you have to make. Now you may decide—

PRESIDENT: [*On Telephone*] Bull, please. Steve Bull. [*To Ehrlichman*] (*Unintelligible*) Alright, fine, John.

EHRLICHMAN: Eh, eh—

PRESIDENT: . . . Then you're not . . .

EHRLICHMAN: Then you've got to dispose of it one way or the other. Uh, uh, there may be and, and, I'm, I'm—

(*Phone Rings*)

[*On Telephone*]

PRESIDENT: Yeah, put the, uh, that, uh, thing with, uh, uh, Haig, uh, back. What time you got now? Quarter after. I'll be there a few minutes late at the EOB.

[*Hangs Up Telephone*]

EHRLICHMAN: I'll tell you, I am still heavily persuaded that we affect the Grand Jury and U.S. Attorney treatment of Dean favorably by keeping him on.

PRESIDENT: Okay.

EHRLICHMAN: Uh, and that that's important. Now—

PRESIDENT: Why, why, do you say that? Because they like him?

EHRLICHMAN: No, no, not at all.

HALDEMAN: Because they can treat him differently as the President's counsel than—

EHRLICHMAN: As the dismissed President's counsel—

HALDEMAN: Exactly.

PRESIDENT: Yeah.

EHRLICHMAN: It's just that it's a very heavy psychological factor.

PRESIDENT: Well, this will be done, because there is another reason, too. It isn't like, it—Dean is not like Mitchell, now let's face it.

HALDEMAN: That's right.

PRESIDENT: Dean is not like Mitchell in the sense that Dean only tried to do what he could to pick up the Goddamn pieces and . . .

HALDEMAN: Certainly.

PRESIDENT: . . . everybody else around here knew it had to be done.

EHRLICHMAN: Certainly.

PRESIDENT: Uh, let's face it. I'm not blaming anybody else now.

HALDEMAN: I understand.

PRESIDENT: That was his job.

HALDEMAN: I understand.

EHRLICHMAN: I have, I have great trouble in (*Unintelligible*) that you could be involved in the light of the known involvement that he had . . .

PRESIDENT: After the?

EHRLICHMAN: . . . in the aftermath.

PRESIDENT: Right, but—

EHRLICHMAN: But—

HALDEMAN: The known involvement in the aftermath was for, uh, what was understood here to be the proper (*Unintelligible*)

EHRLICHMAN: That's half—

PRESIDENT: The question is motive.

HALDEMAN: That's right.

EHRLICHMAN: That's number one. Number two, there is nothing new about that.

PRESIDENT: That's right.

EHRLICHMAN: As I have developed in this thing—I'd like you to read this.

PRESIDENT: Yeah.

EHRLICHMAN: There were eight or ten people around here who knew about this, knew it was going on.

PRESIDENT: Yeah.

EHRLICHMAN: Bob knew, I knew, all kinds of people knew.

PRESIDENT: Well, I knew it. I knew it.

EHRLICHMAN: And it was not a question of whether—

PRESIDENT: (*Unintelligible*) I knew I must say though, I didn't know it, but I must have assumed it though, but you know, fortunately—and I thank you both for arranging it that way and it does show why the isolation of the President, isn't a bad position to be in.

EHRLICHMAN: (*Laughs*)

PRESIDENT: But the first time that I knew that they had to have the money was the time when, uh, Dean told me that they needed forty thousand dollars. I hadn't been rege-, I didn't, I just didn't, I closed my eyes, I couldn't read the Goddamn papers on those little envelopes. I didn't know about the envelopes and the (*Unintelligible*) and all that stuff.

EHRLICHMAN: Well, the, the . . .

PRESIDENT: But others did know.

EHRLICHMAN: . . . the point is that, that if Dean's, if the wrongdoing which justifies Dean's dismissal is his knowledge that that operation was going on . . .

PRESIDENT: Yeah.

EHRLICHMAN: . . . then you can't stop with him. You've got to go through the whole place wholesale.

PRESIDENT: Fire the whole staff.

EHRLICHMAN: That's right. It's, it's a question of motive. It's a question of role, and I don't think Dean's role in the aftermath, at least from the facts that I know now, achieves a level of wrongdoing that requires that you terminate him.

PRESIDENT: Nah.

EHRLICHMAN: . . . And, and, that, and this other thing—

PRESIDENT: I think you've made a very powerful point to me that, that—of course, you can be pragmatic and say, "Well, Christ, in fact Dean" and so forth—in other words cut your losses and get rid of 'em. I mean, give 'em an hors d'oeuvre and maybe they won't come back for the main course. Go out, John Dean. On the other hand, uh, it is true others did know, they did know.

EHRLICHMAN: But more than that—we've made Dean a focal point in the Gray process . . .

PRESIDENT: Right.

EHRLICHMAN: . . . And he will become a focal point in the Ervin process.

PRESIDENT: Well, we'll have—yes, except if—

HALDEMAN: Yeah, if, if goes on.

PRESIDENT: Yeah.

HALDEMAN: And if you dismiss him he'll still be a focal point.

EHRLICHMAN: He'll be a focal point. (*Unintelligible*)

HALDEMAN: He'll be a defrocked—with a less, with less protection, that's right.

EHRLICHMAN: And with less incentive.

PRESIDENT: Well, the point that I think, I think Dean—

HALDEMAN: That's also one of Dean's problem.

PRESIDENT: Dean's—

HALDEMAN: What Dean did was all proper . . .

PRESIDENT: Yeah.

HALDEMAN: . . . in terms of the higher good.

PRESIDENT: Dean—you've gotta have a talk with Dean. I feel that I should not talk to him.

EHRLICHMAN: I have talked to him.

PRESIDENT: But—I mean about motives.

EHRLICHMAN: I have talked to him.

PRESIDENT: What's he say about motives? He says it was hush up?

EHRLICHMAN: No. He says he knew, he, he had to know that people were, uh, trying to bring that result about . . .

PRESIDENT: Right.

EHRLICHMAN: . . . and he says, you know, the way I got into this was I would go to meetings in, in . . .

PRESIDENT: Right.

EHRLICHMAN: . . . campaign headquarters, uh, and, uh, uh, we'd get through the meeting and uh, Mitchell and LaRue would say to, to, uh, uh, I mean Mardian and LaRue would say to Mitchell, "Mitch, you've got to do something about this." And Mitchell's stock answer was to turn to John Dean.

HALDEMAN: Say what are you gonna do?

EHRLICHMAN: "What are you going to do?"

PRESIDENT: Jesus Christ.

EHRLICHMAN: And, uh, so John said, I got to be a kind of, kind of a water carrier. I'd come back from those meetings and I'd come in to see Bob, or me or somebody else . . .

PRESIDENT: Right.

EHRLICHMAN: . . . and say well, Mitchell's got this big problem. And then he'd say they'd say to me, well I don't know what I'll do about it.

PRESIDENT: When he came in to see Bob and you what would he say was the problem?

EHRLICHMAN: Uh, he'd say, these, these guys, uh, uh, Hunt's getting, uh, jittery and, uh, and says that he's got to have umpty-ump thousand dollars, and uh, Mitchell's terribly worried about it, and uh, uh—it, it was never expressed, but it was certainly understood . . .

PRESIDENT: Okay, on the question of motive then, though, (*Unintelligible*) those conversations to keep up (*Unintelligible*) that motive was never discussed.

EHRLICHMAN: Never discussed with me in those terms.

PRESIDENT: Right?

UNIDENTIFIED: Uh, right.

PRESIDENT: The motive was to help defendants who were, by golly, who had worked for the . . .

EHRLICHMAN: Well . . .

PRESIDENT: . . . campaign committee—

EHRLICHMAN: . . . it never really got that far because, uh, we uh, at least my, my conversation with John always was, "well, you know that's, that's interesting—I just don't know what to do for you."

PRESIDENT: Yeah. And, he may have gone further with you, Bob Did he?

HALDEMAN: No.

EHRLICHMAN: He, we referred him to Kalmbach.

HALDEMAN: You aimed him at Kalmbach.

EHRLICHMAN: Yeah.

HALDEMAN: I aimed him at Mitchell. I said, "John you can't come here and ask for help, we don't have any."

PRESIDENT: Yeah.

HALDEMAN: The one thing where it did go further, if you want to argue about it, it was in the sense that th-, the 350 . . .

PRESIDENT: At the end—

HALDEMAN: . . . which was not our money, we did move back over there.

PRESIDENT: For this purpose?

EHRLICHMAN: (*Unintelligible*) what it was.

HALDEMAN: Yeah, yeah.

PRESIDENT: Who asked for it?

HALDEMAN: Nobody.

PRESIDENT: I mean, eh, how did, who . . .

HALDEMAN: (*Unintelligible*) asked for that.

PRESIDENT: . . . who took the move on the 350?

HALDEMAN: I did.

PRESIDENT: How did you know that (*Unintelligible*)

HALDEMAN: Gordon Strachan . . .

PRESIDENT: . . . came to you?

HALDEMAN: . . . Gordon Strachan came to me after the election and said you have three hundred and fifty thousand . . .

PRESIDENT: Yeah.

HALDEMAN: . . . dollars in cash . . .

PRESIDENT: Oh . . .

HALDEMAN: . . . What do you want to do with it . . .

PRESIDENT: . . . this was not requested by LaRue?

HALDEMAN: No.

PRESIDENT: or Gordon?

HALDEMAN: No, the problem was getting them to take it back. They wouldn't take it.

EHRLICHMAN: 'Cause they didn't know how to (*Unintelligible*)

PRESIDENT: That money . . .

HALDEMAN: 'Cause LaRue didn't know what to do (*Unintelligible*)

PRESIDENT: . . . that, that money—

HALDEMAN: (*Unintelligible*) let him take it. LaRue wanted it . . .

PRESIDENT: Yeah.

HALDEMAN: . . . but Mitchell wouldn't let him take it.

PRESIDENT: Oh.

EHRLICHMAN: They just didn't know how to account for it.

PRESIDENT: Well, just frankly, he wouldn't have to account for it, in my opinion.

HALDEMAN: Well, but he didn't, he, he was—

PRESIDENT: 1970 money, for Christ's sakes.

HALDEMAN: (*Clears throat*) He said I have to account for it now because he's—Fred LaRue is in personal receipt after Grand Jury knowledge of three hundred and twenty-eight thousand dollars in cash delivered to him at night at his apartment by Gordon Strachan. Key witnesses to that transaction are Strachan and LaRue.

PRESIDENT: LaRue tells you, huh?

HALDEMAN: And Strachan just testified that that's what happened. Well, LaRue's got a problem. What did he do with it? At that point, it's income to him. He's got an IRS problem if he can't get it, get it—it's unaccounted.

PRESIDENT: He'll use it, what, what does he say? He says I used it for hush money?

HALDEMAN: I don't know what he'll say. He'll probably (*Tape Noise*) packaged it up—

PRESIDENT: Does that help any? That certainly doesn't help us.

HALDEMAN: Doesn't help anybody, but, uh, but, uh, you know—

PRESIDENT: The other thing he says, "Well I just, I, I've retained it in a fund for future campaigns."

HALDEMAN: No, can't show it, doesn't have it. I'm sure he doesn't have it.

EHRLICHMAN: I don't, I'm not sure either, but I assume that it went right out to, to pay these people, I, uh, that's, that's my assumption.

(*Unintelligible*)

EHRLICHMAN: Now Dean says this. He says we have only two problems with the aftermath in the White House. One is the fact that we made a referral to Kalmbach, but he said that can be explained. And, that's, that's no major problem. The other is the $350,000 and that can be explained and need not be a major problem if it's clearly explained. And we have no, no problem with the aftermath.

HALDEMAN: I'm running the three-fifty into my statement, but the question of whether we want it in.

PRESIDENT: Oh, yes. Put it in there.

HALDEMAN: Nobody knows about it—that's another bombshell.

PRESIDENT: (*Unintelligible*) I think it's been, there's been something written about it.

HALDEMAN: Well but, yeah, but not that I had it.

EHRLICHMAN: It is eleven o'clock.

PRESIDENT: All right. Eleven o'clock, that's when the armistice was signed, so off we go.

EHRLICHMAN: Uh, Mitchell is roughly two hours away at, at best. I could—

PRESIDENT: I think he's going to come down and do it today. I think—what—Bob, I think you have to go out and call him, now. And, uh, ask him if he can come down.

EHRLICHMAN: We'll send an airplane for him.

HALDEMAN: That'll take longer than his coming (*Unintelligible*)

PRESIDENT: Yeah.

HALDEMAN: And by the time we get a plane mobilized and up there it takes longer. We'll send it (*Tape Noise*) play golf or something.

PRESIDENT: I know, I know. He may be gone. But the point that I make is this, if, if he's out to play golf, we say we have, uh, we, we, have an urgent message for him and we say there've been some (*Tape Noise*) There have been some (*Unintelligible With Tape Noise*) on the Watergate thing.

HALDEMAN: And that hurry and come immediately.

PRESIDENT: (*Tape Noise*) should come down.

EHRLICHMAN: I think Bob's right.

PRESIDENT: Okay. Can you come down? If he says I can't come, then Ehrlichman should go up—

HALDEMAN: Then say to him well, John will come up. Where can you be re—

PRESIDENT: Yes. If he says well I've got a dinner tonight and I've got that, uh, say John—I mean this is the thing—John, this is very important. The President considers this of the highest urgency that you be aware of these developments. How's that sound to you?

UNIDENTIFIED: (*Unintelligible*)

EHRLICHMAN: Something that just can't be postponed any longer.

PRESIDENT: Can't be postponed and, uh, we, uh, have a problem.

(*Walking Noise*)

Harder than firing Hickel.

EHRLICHMAN: Oh, about the same.

PRESIDENT: Eleven?

HALDEMAN(?): Yes, sir.

[*Haldeman Leaves; Ehrlichman Dials Telephone*]

EHRLICHMAN: Call me? Oh, OK. Anything new? . . . Yeah, I'm . . . Our last conversation? . . . Can you give it to me now? . . . Well, okay. I, I'll see you in a little while. Alright.

PRESIDENT: Colson?

EHRLICHMAN: No, that was Dean.

PRESIDENT: What'd he say?

EHRLICHMAN: (*Unintelligible*)

PRESIDENT: I, I think there's, there are other reasons—

EHRLICHMAN: Well, you can, you can put—

PRESIDENT: He did not cover up, though, that's just what we, that's what (*Unintelligible*) that's what we—

EHRLICHMAN: (*Unintelligible*) to go testify. (*Unintelligible*)

PRESIDENT: My point is, my point is that as three of us talked here, I realize, that frankly—in Mitchell's case he's guilty. In Dean's case (*Tape Noise*) it's the question. And I do not consider him guilty. Now that's all there is to that.

EHRLICHMAN: Uh—

PRESIDENT: . . . Because if he's, if, if that's the case then hell, wouldn't you say, half the staff is guilty.

EHRLICHMAN: That's it. He's, he's guilty of really no more except in degree.

PRESIDENT: That's right.

EHRLICHMAN: Uh, and uh . . .

PRESIDENT: Then others.

EHRLICHMAN: . . . then, then a lot—

PRESIDENT: And frankly, than I have been since, uh, a week ago—

EHRLICHMAN: Well . . .

PRESIDENT: Two weeks ago,

EHRLICHMAN: . . . you see, that isn't—that kind of knowledge that we had was not action knowledge, like the kind of knowledge, that I put together last night. I hadn't known really what, what's been bothering me this week . . .

PRESIDENT: Yeah.

EHRLICHMAN: . . . But what's been bothering me is—

PRESIDENT: That with knowledge, we're still not doing anything.

EHRLICHMAN: That's right. That's exactly right.

PRESIDENT: The law and order—Goddamn it, that's the way I am. I, you know, it is a pain for me to do anything. The Mitchell thing is Goddamn painful.

(*Unintelligible With Noise*)

(*Haldeman Enters Room*)

PRESIDENT: Is he coming?

HALDEMAN: Yes, sir.

(*Noise*)

I said do you want to let us know what you're, what plane you're on so we can pick you up? And he said, no let me (*Unintelligible*) over his, uh—

PRESIDENT: Should you delay your meeting with Magruder until you see him?

EHRLICHMAN: I don't think it really matters. It's just, it comes under this whole heading of having knowledge and having to act on it.

PRESIDENT: Well, my point is that I think that you better see Magruder before you see him. No, no I guess you'll—

EHRLICHMAN: It doesn't matter, in my opinion.

PRESIDENT: You should see Magruder today. That's the main thing.

EHRLICHMAN: I think we ought to make a similar call to Magruder.

HALDEMAN: I think the way to do it then—I should call Jeb . . .

PRESIDENT: Yeah.

HALDEMAN: . . . and say that things have developed and all this and, and, uh—

PRESIDENT: Yeah.

HALDEMAN: (*Unintelligible*)

PRESIDENT: Yeah.

HALDEMAN: I didn't say that to Mitchell.

EHRLICHMAN: It doesn't matter.

PRESIDENT: Oh, Mitchell, he knows better. (*Tape Noise*) gotta say that to Jeb.

HALDEMAN: Well, I tell you, when I—the thing is when I say it to Jeb, it'll take probably thirty-seven seconds for him to turn up on your doorstep.

EHRLICHMAN: Well, that's alright.

PRESIDENT: That's alright.

EHRLICHMAN: It won't—

PRESIDENT: I think we should do it before you see Mitchell. Or you, do you feel uncomfortable about telling him?

EHRLICHMAN: No. As I say, I, I think it's almost immaterial as to which I see first. It's the fact of doing it rather than any particular sequence.

PRESIDENT: Well—

HALDEMAN: Mitchell won't be here, he can't be here 'til . . .

PRESIDENT: Yeah.

HALDEMAN: (*Unintelligible*)

PRESIDENT: I think, in my view, in my view, John, you can't wait to act. I think you should see Jeb Magruder and say now, Jeb, you're to testify. (*Unintelligible*)

EHRLICHMAN: I wouldn't quite say it that way. I'll say, I don't know if you know what I've been doing here, the last three weeks. I have been ranging over this whole subject matter trying to bring to the President something more than John Dean has charged.

PRESIDENT: Can you tell him as you talk to him that what he says is attorney-client or no? You can't tell him. Okay.

EHRLICHMAN: I, I, I'll simply say that, as, as you know, Dean did an investigation which determined whether or not the White House was involved. My responsibility was greater than that. It was to range over the whole thing and try and bring to the President a new (*Tape Noise*) of information on what actually happened, (*Tape Noise*) uh, uh, version of what transpired. And from what I have been able to put together, I have advised the President and he has—this morning—and he has directed me immediately to contact you (*Tape Noise*) uh, uh, having accepted a point of view in all of this (*Tape Noise*) people should not disclose what they know, because it somehow serves the President. (*Tape Noise*) apparently, considerable criminal jeopardy. (*Tape Noise*) what to do from your own standpoint. What I want you to have is the message from the President. (*Tape Noise*) in any way view it as serving his interests for you to remain silent. Decide what to do from your own personal standpoint and (*Unintelligible*) any right to interfere in that decision. If there ever was an impediment to your coming forward by reason of your impression of, uh, uh, assumed or otherwise, of what the President wanted you to do I think it's my job . . .

PRESIDENT: Right.

EHRLICHMAN: . . . to impart to you what is actually the case.

PRESIDENT: I would, also, though I'd put a couple of grace notes in and say, Jeb, let me just start here by telling you the President's own great affection for you and for your family—real affection—my mind was thinking last night of his poor little kids in school . . .

HALDEMAN: Yeah, beautiful kids.

PRESIDENT: . . . and his lovely wife and all the rest. And just, just put—it breaks your heart. And say this, this is a very painful message for me—for, for him too—I, I've been asked to give you, but, but, but I must do it and that's that. Let's put it right out that way. And also—I'd just put that in so that he knows that I have personal affection. That's the way to, that's the way the so-called clemency's got to be handled. Do you see, John?

EHRLICHMAN: I understand.

HALDEMAN: Do the same thing with Mitchell.

PRESIDENT: Yeah—oh, Mitchell? Well, you could say to Mitchell, I think you've got to say . . .

HALDEMAN: (*Unintelligible*)

PRESIDENT: . . . you're got to say that this is the toughest decision he's made. It's tougher than Cambodia, May 8th and December 18th put together. And that he, uh, just can't bring himself to talk to you about it. Just can't do it. And he's directed that I talk to you. Frankly, what I am doing, John, is putting you in the same position as President Eisenhower put me in with Adams (*Unintelligible*) But John Mitchell, let me say, will never go to prison. I agree with that assumption. I think what will happen is that he will put on the Goddamnedest defense that—the point, you have, your suggestion is gonna be he not put on a defense. You're suggesting he go in and say look I am responsible here. I had no knowledge but I am responsible. And uh, I uh, I, and nobody else had, and uh, that's it. I myself. That's it. And I want to plead, uh, this, this has got to stop—innocent people are being smeared in this thing.

EHRLICHMAN: He will understand . . .

PRESIDENT: (*Unintelligible*)

EHRLICHMAN: . . . that once you are possessed of a reasonable body of knowledge, (*Unintelligible*) you have an obligation to do something and, rather than simply to turn it over to the U.S. Attorney, the thing that you are doing, in the first instance is giving him an opportunity to come forward.

PRESIDENT: Or, rather than having a special prosecutor, say that he comes a special prosecutor. The President rejects that. Uh, the idea that, uh, we turn it over to the U.S. Attorney, call him in, which I could do, and uh, or call in the Attorney General which I could do, but I think it's—obligations to do, do this because I cannot have this. Now, of course, he's going to ask, well, now John what knowledge do you really have except hearsay. Answer.

EHRLICHMAN: I don't have any knowledge except hearsay, John, uh, but—

PRESIDENT: But I do know that Magruder—

EHRLICHMAN: . . . in other words, I don't have, I don't have documents and I . . .

PRESIDENT: (*Unintelligible*) Events are moving very speedily . . .

EHRLICHMAN: . . . but, but . . .

PRESIDENT: There is no question about what is going to happen.

EHRLICHMAN: . . . there can be—that's right. That's right. Tha-, tha-, that—

HALDEMAN: You won't have to appeal to him on that because he's made the point, you know, that if Dean testifies, it's going to unscramble the whole omelette.

PRESIDENT: Well, I'm sorry—I don't want to leave it at the point that Dean's or Magruder's testimony is essential to Mitchell (*Unintelligible*)

EHRLICHMAN: That's right. That's right.

PRESIDENT: You see that's the point of that. On the Dean thing, I, I wouldn't say that the President has stood, frankly, John, on, on the executive privilege thing, (*Unintelligible*) and so forth.

EHRLICHMAN: It, it, it isn't my purpose to prove to your satisfaction your guilt or that you're going to be indicted, but—

HALDEMAN: It's my purpose to say that the President now is in possession—

PRESIDENT: That I believe you should come—What are you going to suggest that he do, John?

EHRLICHMAN: Well, if he asks me, what do you want me to do? I am going to say I, if, if you would do what I ask you, what I would suggest, you would pick up the phone or you would allow me to pick it up and call Earl Silbert and make an appointment today, and go over, and talk with the U.S. Attorney about this case, with counsel.

PRESIDENT: "I'll see the President and tell him you're going to do it."

EHRLICHMAN: No.

PRESIDENT: Okay.

EHRLICHMAN: Uh, well you're asking me in effect to go down and enter a guilty plea. And I would say, look John, you're the only one who knows the basic (*Unintelligible*) and to decide whether there's any room between what you know and the ultimate action of the jury through which you might pass unpunished. I can't make that judgment for you and I don't have any right to make it for you. All I'm saying is that you're looking at this thing from the standpoint of the Presidency. Today is probably the last day that you can take that action, if you're ever going to take it. Uh, do the President a bit of good.

PRESIDENT: "Do you realize John, uh, that uh, that uh, that uh, uh, uh, (*Tape Noise*) on the White House? I mean Colson, maybe Haldeman, are going to get involved in this thing too."

EHRLICHMAN: Well, here again, we're looking at this thing not from the standpoint of any other individual. We're looking at it from the standpoint of the Presidency and that's the only way I think you and I can approach this.

PRESIDENT: And I'd, I'd go further and say the President has said let the chips fall where they may.

EHRLICHMAN: Yeah.

PRESIDENT: We are not gonna cover for anybody. I think you ought to say that.

EHRLICHMAN: That's right.

PRESIDENT: Don't you agree, Bob? That isn't it? We've a—

HALDEMAN: He may go, he may get Chuck. He may get you (*Unintelligible*) to ask him to do (*Unintelligible*)

PRESIDENT: (*Unintelligible*) on the whole House. Fine. But we on the other hand, have to do something else. Fine. I think he would take the latter. He thinks—

HALDEMAN: He thinks (*Unintelligible*) and that's the thing we've worried about all along, haven't we. That's uh, if somebody gets hit what will we do. But we can't worry about what we will do if he does anything. We'll have to deal with that. It's gonna expire.

EHRLICHMAN: And this is one that will permit him—and it might help the Presidency, rather than damage it.

PRESIDENT: Uh, Bob, do you think there's something to be said for having John wait to talk to Magruder until after he's seen Mitchell? (*Tape Noise*) something. Suppose you get stonewalled with Mitchell.

HALDEMAN: Well, I think John's in a stronger position if he's talked to Magruder than if he hasn't, but I, maybe, I—

EHRLICHMAN: I tell you, it is not what Mitchell says that matters today. It is the fact that you have acted on information today.

PRESIDENT: Yeah.

EHRLICHMAN: Now, let's suppose Mitchell turns us down cold, and says I'm going to preserve all my rights. I'm going to make, uh, fight every inch of turf and so on and so forth. Okay. That's that, alright. But at least you, having accumulated all this knowledge this week, have tried to get this thing out, so that sometime two months from now, three months from now, a year from now when there's an accounting, you can say, "On the 14th of April—

PRESIDENT: It's the 13th.

EHRLICHMAN: It's where? Uh, on the 14th day or the 14th?

PRESIDENT: This is the 14th, yeah.

EHRLICHMAN: Yeah, we had Friday the 13th yesterday.

PRESIDENT: (*Unintelligible*) the 13th.

EHRLICHMAN: On, on the 14th . . .

PRESIDENT: No, seriously (*Unintelligible*) as I have told both of you, the boil had to be pricked. That's—in a very different sense—that's what December 18th was about. We have to prick the Goddamn boil and take the heat. Now that's what we are doing here. We're going to prick this boil and take the heat. Am I, am I over-stating?

HALDEMAN: No.

PRESIDENT: (*Unintelligible*)

HALDEMAN: No, I think that's right. And uh, (*Unintelligible*)

EHRLICHMAN: The history of this—

HALDEMAN: . . . and this will prick the boil.

PRESIDENT: Yeah.

HALDEMAN: It may not.

EHRLICHMAN: The history of this thing has to be, though, that you did not tuck this under the rug . . .

PRESIDENT: Right.

EHRLICHMAN: . . . yesterday or today, and hope it would go away.

PRESIDENT: Now, uh, let me give the scenario—uh has Ehrlichman go out and tell people that I have done this.

EHRLICHMAN: I don't know. It depends on how it all turns out. If he does not go to the U.S. Attorney . . .

PRESIDENT: Yeah.

EHRLICHMAN: . . . if Magruder decides to stay clammed up . . .

PRESIDENT: Right.

HALDEMAN: Then what'd you do?

EHRLICHMAN: . . . then I'd take, uh—

PRESIDENT: Well, let's . . .

HALDEMAN: Would you do it again?

PRESIDENT: . . . let's suppose, let's suppose, let's suppose they still indict. You don't want them to indict and then have to say that on s-, on, on s-, on Saturday, the 14th of April, that you, John Ehrlichman—

HALDEMAN: Yeah, but you see yeah, but you see—

EHRLICHMAN: The problem there is . . .

HALDEMAN: . . . do you support the President—

EHRLICHMAN: . . . these things, at least you've got the record—

HALDEMAN: Yeah.

EHRLICHMAN: The problem is that if you were to go out on this kind of hearsay and say we know who did it, then you've prejudiced their rights, the, the, uh—

PRESIDENT: Then your, then your thought is to get out beforehand.

EHRLICHMAN: No, no, not at all.

PRESIDENT: Your thought is, just to make a record of the (*Unintelligible*)

EHRLICHMAN: When somebody comes to uh, uh (*Unintelligible*) indictments, what the hell was the White House doing all this time? Then you're in a position to say well, we began to investigate personally and, and the external circumstances and we came to some conclusions and we acted on those conclusions.

PRESIDENT: John Ehrlichman conducted an investigation for the President.

EHRLICHMAN: And we made un—

PRESIDENT: John Ehrlichman's—uh, now the 13th of—uh—

EHRLICHMAN: It may be that what should happen here is that if they both stonewall, I ought to sit down with Silbert and just say now I don't have a lot of evidence . . .

PRESIDENT: I agree with that. I agree with that.

EHRLICHMAN: . . . but I have an accumulation of hearsay

PRESIDENT: And the President wants you to go forward on this.

EHRLICHMAN: ... And I'll turn over to you that ...

PRESIDENT: (*Unintelligible*)

EHRLICHMAN: ... the report that I made for the President, for whatever it's worth. And I want to tell you that I had con-, uh, had contact with two of your targets to make clear to them nobody in the White House wanted them in any way to be reticent. Beyond that, I don't have anything to say to you.

PRESIDENT: (*Unintelligible*)

EHRLICHMAN: Well—

HALDEMAN: See what happens.

EHRLICHMAN: Let's, let's see what these guys go. But, uh, uh, I think maybe like tomorrow I ought to see Silbert.

PRESIDENT: I agree. I think the record should be made we have talked to him so that he knows that the President has moved on this (*Unintelligible*).

EHRLICHMAN: And that's, a, that, that, puts a th-, uh, uh—

PRESIDENT: And that we saw the U.S. Attorney and turned over our information to him. All the information we had.

EHRLICHMAN: I would like a record of my conversation with both Magruder and Mitchell. I personally think that maybe I ought to get my office geared up so that I can do that.

PRESIDENT: (*Unintelligible*) here, or do you remove that equipment?

EHRLICHMAN: Yeah.

PRESIDENT: (*Unintelligible*) my meetings with Henry, but I don't know.

EHRLICHMAN: I, I think it's better if I do it over there.

PRESIDENT: Why don't you just gear it up and, uh, you can, do you know, do you have a way to gear it up?

EHRLICHMAN: Yeah. I've done it before.

PRESIDENT: Well, go gear it.

EHRLICHMAN: (*Unintelligible*)

PRESIDENT: No, no, no, no, no, Well, wait a minute. No, I think that's too . . .

HALDEMAN: (*Unintelligible*)

PRESIDENT: . . . too little. I would just, I would just have it so that you'll know that, uh—what we've got here. I don't want to hear the record, let me say. (*Unintelligible*)

HALDEMAN: Raise a question and I don't know if it's a good idea or not but does it serve any purpose for me to sit in on the meeting?

EHRLICHMAN: I think you should come.

HALDEMAN: That's, maybe that's . . .

PRESIDENT: Or—

HALDEMAN: . . . it's—that would give you a witness, for one thing. If either of those people were questioned and you (*Tape Noise; Unintelligible*) anybody else in, you've got a problem.

PRESIDENT: And then when Mitchell says, Bob, you know, you were in this, too. What's Bob Haldeman say?

EHRLICHMAN: (*Unintelligible*) well he won't. He won't.

PRESIDENT: I think Bob should sit in . . .

EHRLICHMAN: That's good.

PRESIDENT: . . . because Haldeman is, uh—

EHRLICHMAN: (*Unintelligible*)

PRESIDENT: No, no. I think so. That gives you the witness. And also . . .

EHRLICHMAN: (*Unintelligible*)

PRESIDENT: Mitchell feels he's got a friend there. And he knows that you're not just doing this on your own, freewheeling it. Bob says we talked it all over. The President said we can't sit on information that's (*Unintelligible*) of this nature. (*Unintelligible*) information from the members of the White House staff, it's gonna be exactly the same procedure. I think we ought to move on the Jeb thing, Bob.

HALDEMAN: We'll get him in my office.

PRESIDENT: Of course, and give your report to me on, uh, as soon as you finish your conversation with Jeb . . .

UNIDENTIFIED: Okay.

PRESIDENT: . . . I'll be (*Unintelligible*)

HALDEMAN: (*Unintelligible*)

PRESIDENT: Incidentally—

List of Contributors

OLIVER STONE is the director, producer, and co-author of *Nixon*. He also directed *Platoon, Wall Street, Born on the Fourth of July, JFK, Natural Born Killers,* and other films.

ERIC HAMBURG is the co-producer of *Nixon*. He worked in the U.S. Congress as an aide to Rep. Lee Hamilton and to Sen. John Kerry.

STEPHEN J. RIVELE is the co-author of *Nixon*. He is the author of several books, including the forthcoming novel *A Booke of Days: A Journal of the Crusade,* to be published by Macmillan in 1996.

CHRISTOPHER WILKINSON is the co-author of *Nixon*. He wrote and directed several award-winning documentary films and was Second Unit Director of *The River, For the Boys,* and *Intersection*. His CD of original music, *Blues for Zontar,* was released in the fall of 1995.

JOHN DEAN was Counsel to President Nixon from 1970 to 1973. He is the author of *Blind Ambition* and *Lost Honor*.

DANIEL SCHORR is Senior News Analyst for National Public Radio. He won three Emmys for his coverage of Watergate for CBS News. He is the author of *Clearing the Air*.

E. HOWARD HUNT worked in the White House under President Nixon. He also worked for the CIA for many years. He is the author of more than 70 books, including *Undercover* and *Give Us This Day*.

JIM HOUGAN is an award-winning investigative reporter. He is the author of *Secret Agenda* and *Spooks*.

MICHAEL MANDELBAUM is Professor of American Foreign Policy at the Johns Hopkins School of Advanced International Studies. He also directs the East-West Project at the Council on Foreign Relations.

STANLEY KUTLER is Professor of American Institutions at the University of Wisconsin. He is the author of *The Wars of Watergate*.

ALEXANDER BUTTERFIELD served as Deputy Assistant to the President and Secretary to the Cabinet from 1969 to 1973. His testimony to the Senate Watergate Committee revealed the existence of President Nixon's taping system. He was a technical adviser to Oliver Stone on *Nixon*.

FRANK MANKIEWICZ was Campaign Manager for Democratic candidate George McGovern in 1972, as well as Press Secretary to Robert Kennedy in his 1968 Presidential campaign. He is the author of *Perfectly Clear: Nixon from Whittier to Watergate* and *The U.S. v. Richard M. Nixon.*

JOHN SEARS was a political adviser to Richard Nixon in his Presidential campaign of 1968. He also was Campaign Manager for Ronald Reagan in 1976 and 1980. He is an attorney in Washington.

EUGENIO MARTINEZ was arrested in the Watergate break-in. He worked for the CIA for many years and conducted over 350 missions to Cuba.

PAUL NITZE served in government under Presidents from Truman to Reagan. He was an Arms Control Negotiator and Foreign Policy Adviser to President Nixon. He is the author of *From Hiroshima to Glasnost.*

MICHAEL SINGER is the author of *The Making of Oliver Stone's Heaven and Earth* and *Film Directors: A Complete Guide.* He is writing *Etched in Stone,* a forthcoming book about Oliver Stone's film career.

Acknowledgments

The creation of a film requires the support of many people, and a "book of a film" involves almost as many. First and foremost, I would like to thank Oliver Stone for his vision, dedication, and courage in making this project possible. I would also like to give special thanks to Steve Rivele and Chris Wilkinson for their inspired writing. And of course, many thanks to Anthony Hopkins, James Woods, and all of our *Nixon* actors for their great performances.

Thanks are due also to Alexander Butterfield, John Dean, John Newman, Chris Scheer, and Robert Scheer for their assistance with research and consultation. Chris Wilkinson, Steve Rivele, and John Dean also provided invaluable assistance with the annotation and documentation of the script.

We are grateful to those friends, colleagues, associates, and observers of Richard Nixon who shared their thoughts with us, including Elliott Richardson, Alexander Haig, Paul Nitze, Howard Hunt, Rolando Martinez, Ron Ziegler, John Sears, Stephen Hess, Len Garment, Daniel Schorr, Frank Mankiewicz, Robert McNamara, John Kerry, Lee Hamilton, Leon Panetta, and others. And special thanks to all of the contributors of essays to this volume.

Thanks also to the staffs of Ixtlan, Illusion, Cinergi Productions, Hollywood Pictures, and Hyperion for making the film and the book possible. Thanks to Clayton Townsend, Bob Marshall, Steve Pines, Nanette Klein, Larry Kopeikin, Dan Halsted, Janet Yang, George Linardos, Naomi Despres, Richard Rutowski, Michael Singer, Sidney Baldwin, Annie Tien, Azita Zendel, and many others who helped. Thanks also to friends and colleagues who contributed thoughts and ideas, including Rick English, Anwyl McDonald, Doug Hofstadter, Dan Drell, Marsha Renwanz, Mark DeAntonio, and Jacklin Arastouzadeh.

And, on a personal note, this book and many other things would not have been possible without the support of my parents, David and Betty Hamburg, and my sister, Peggy. And I would like to remember with deep gratitude my grandfather, Sam C. Hamburg, for his belief and inspiration.